Addison-Wesley Mathematics

Robert E. Eicholz
Phares G. O'Daffer
Charles R. Fleenor

Randall I. Charles
Sharon Young
Carne S. Barnett

Addison-Wesley Publishing Company

Menlo Park, California • Reading, Massachusetts • Don Mills, Ontario • Wokingham, England
Amsterdam • Sydney • Singapore • Tokyo • Madrid • Bogotá • Santiago • San Juan

ILLUSTRATIONS

Kirk Caldwell 147-172, 196, 249, 252, 255, 256, 261, 263, 301-320

Maxie Chambliss 75-92, 99, 103, 197-226, 250, 251, 257

Masami Miyamoto 46, 107, 126, 235, 236, 258, 321, 322, 323, 324, 325, 326, 327, 328

Carol Nicklaus 93-112, 265-284

Bill Ogden 113-146, 249-264

Judy Sakaguchi 53-74, 227-248

Margaret Sanfilippo 33-52, 203, 209, 253, 259, 285-300

Sally Shimizu 333, 334, 335, 337, 338, 341, 342, 343, 344

Bari Weissman 1-32, 173-196

COVER PHOTOGRAPH
© Hope Alexander/Woodfin Camp and Associates

All line illustrations rendered by the Addison-Wesley Technical Graphics Department

Printed in the United States of America. Published simultaneously in Canada.

ISBN 0-201-26100-6

OPQRSTUV-WC-89210

Contents

CHAPTER 1 NUMBERS 0-12

CHAPTER 2 SUMS TO 5

CHAPTER 3 DIFFERENCES TO 5

CHAPTER 4 COUNTING ON TO ADD

CHAPTER 5 COUNTING BACK TO SUBTRACT

CHAPTER 6 PLACE VALUE AND COUNTING

CHAPTER 7 TIME AND MONEY

CHAPTER 8 SUMS TO 12

CHAPTER 9 DIFFERENCES TO 12

CHAPTER 10 GEOMETRY AND GRAPHING

CHAPTER 11 ADDITION AND SUBTRACTION: 2-DIGIT NUMBERS

CHAPTER 12 MEASUREMENT — METRIC UNITS

CHAPTER 13 SUMS AND DIFFERENCES TO 18

CHAPTER 14 FRACTIONS AND CUSTOMARY MEASUREMENTS

TECHNOLOGY RESOURCE BANK

APPENDIX

Name ___

NUMBERS 0-12

Name ___________

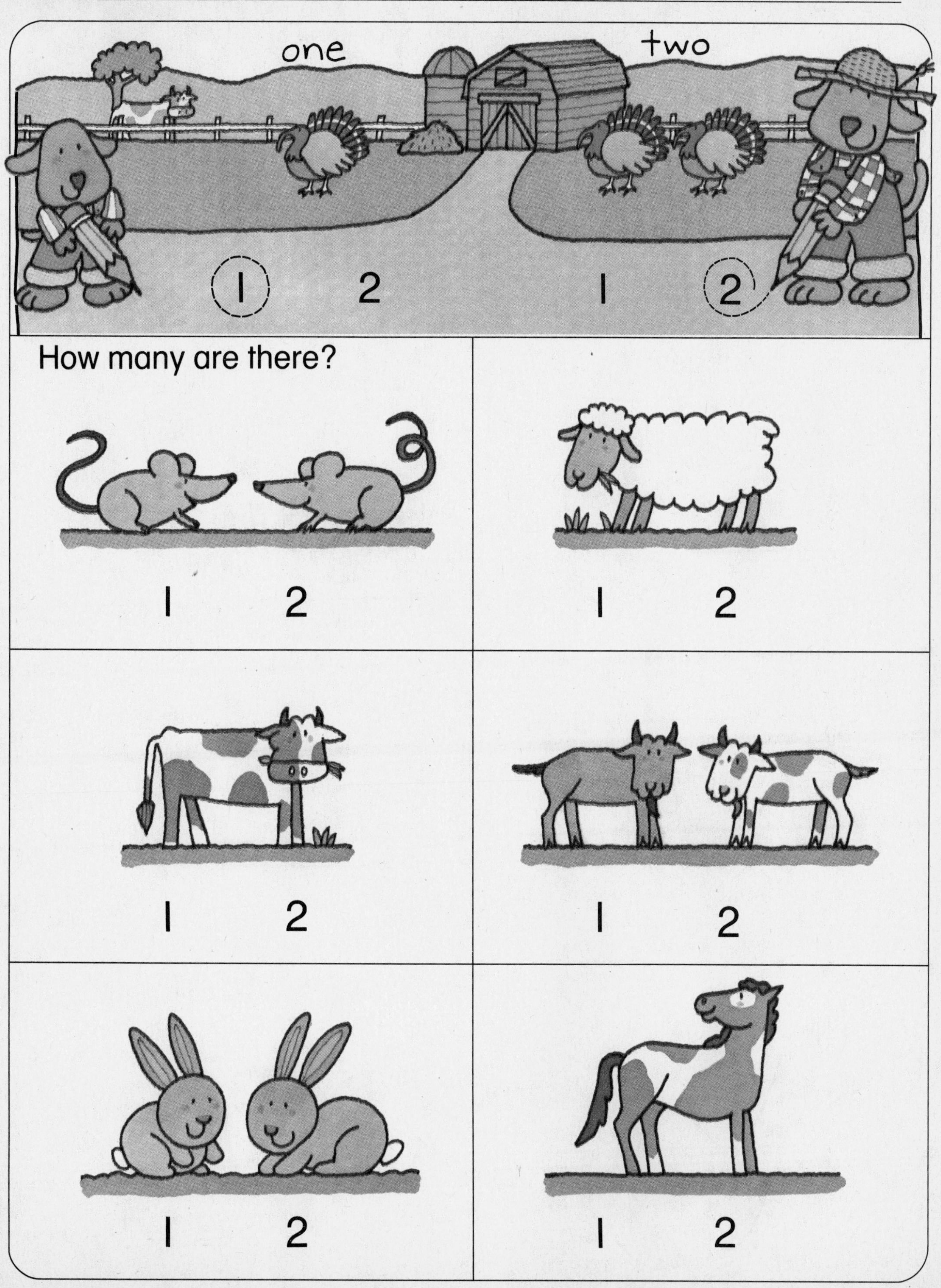
one
two
1 2
1 2
How many are there?
1 2
1 2
1 2
1 2
1 2
1 2

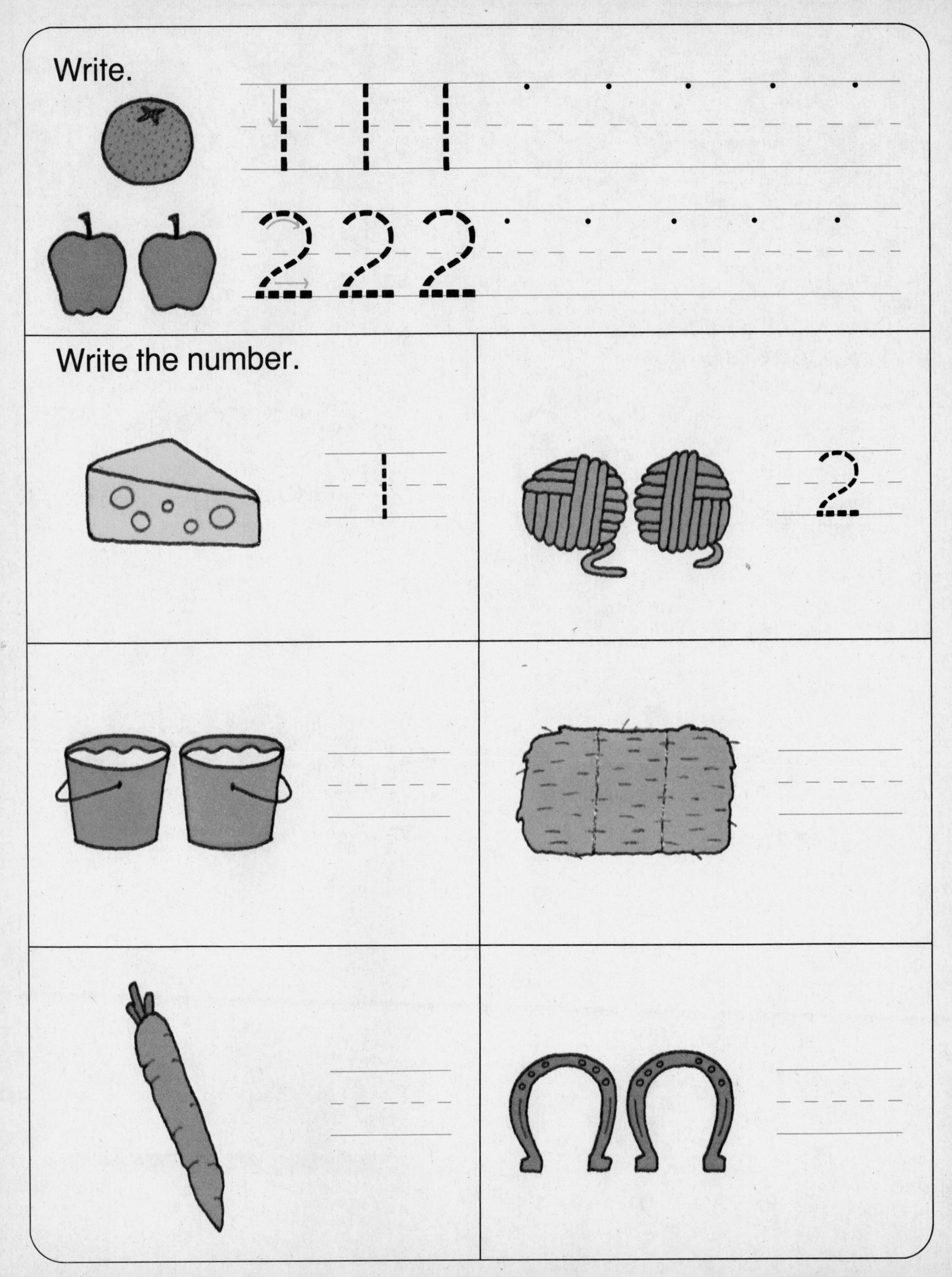
Write.
1 1 1
2 2 2
Write the number.
1
2

Name ___________________________

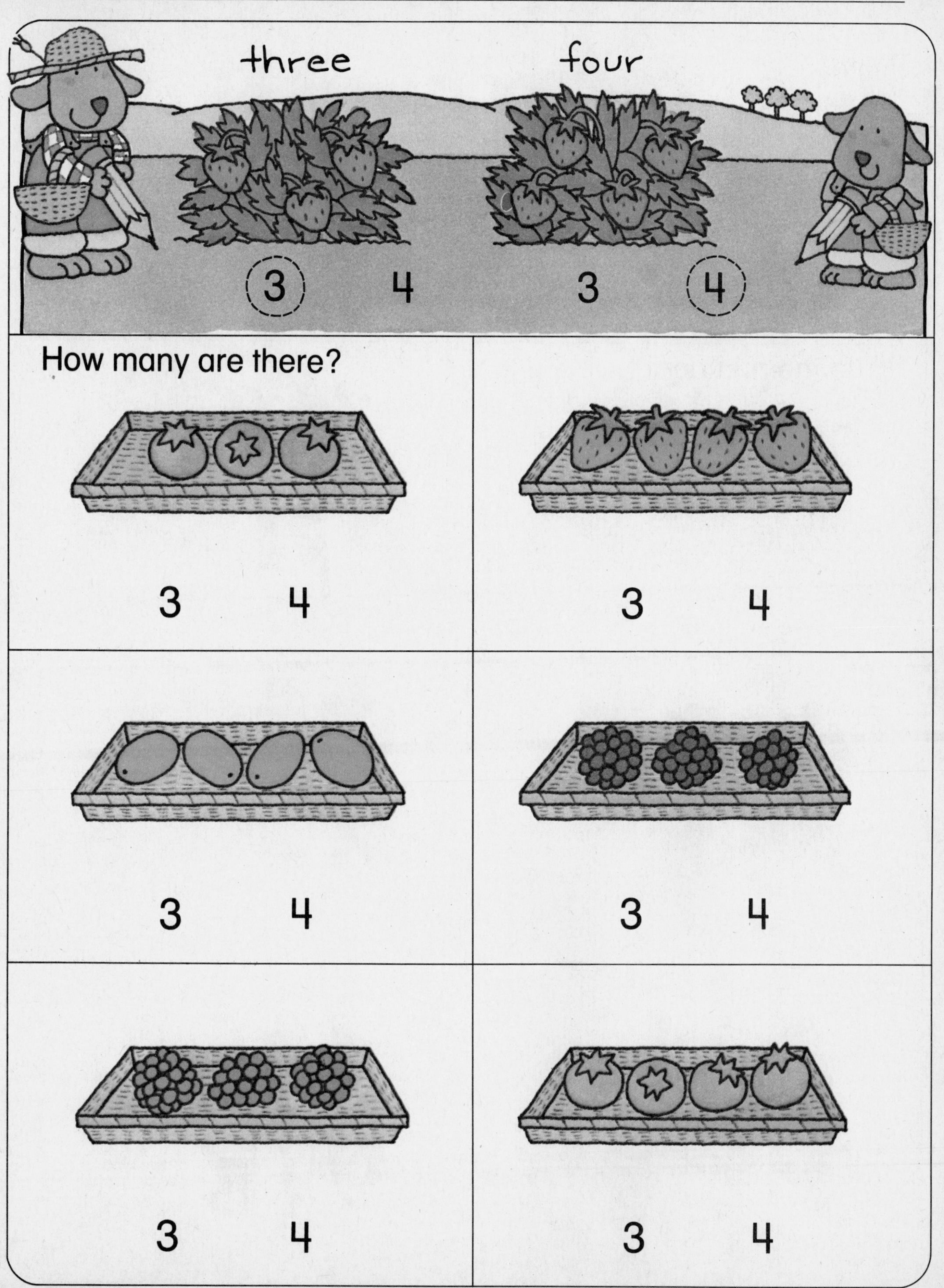

three four

(3) 4 3 (4)

How many are there?

3 4

3 4

3 4

3 4

3 4

3 4

Numbers 3 and 4 (five) 5

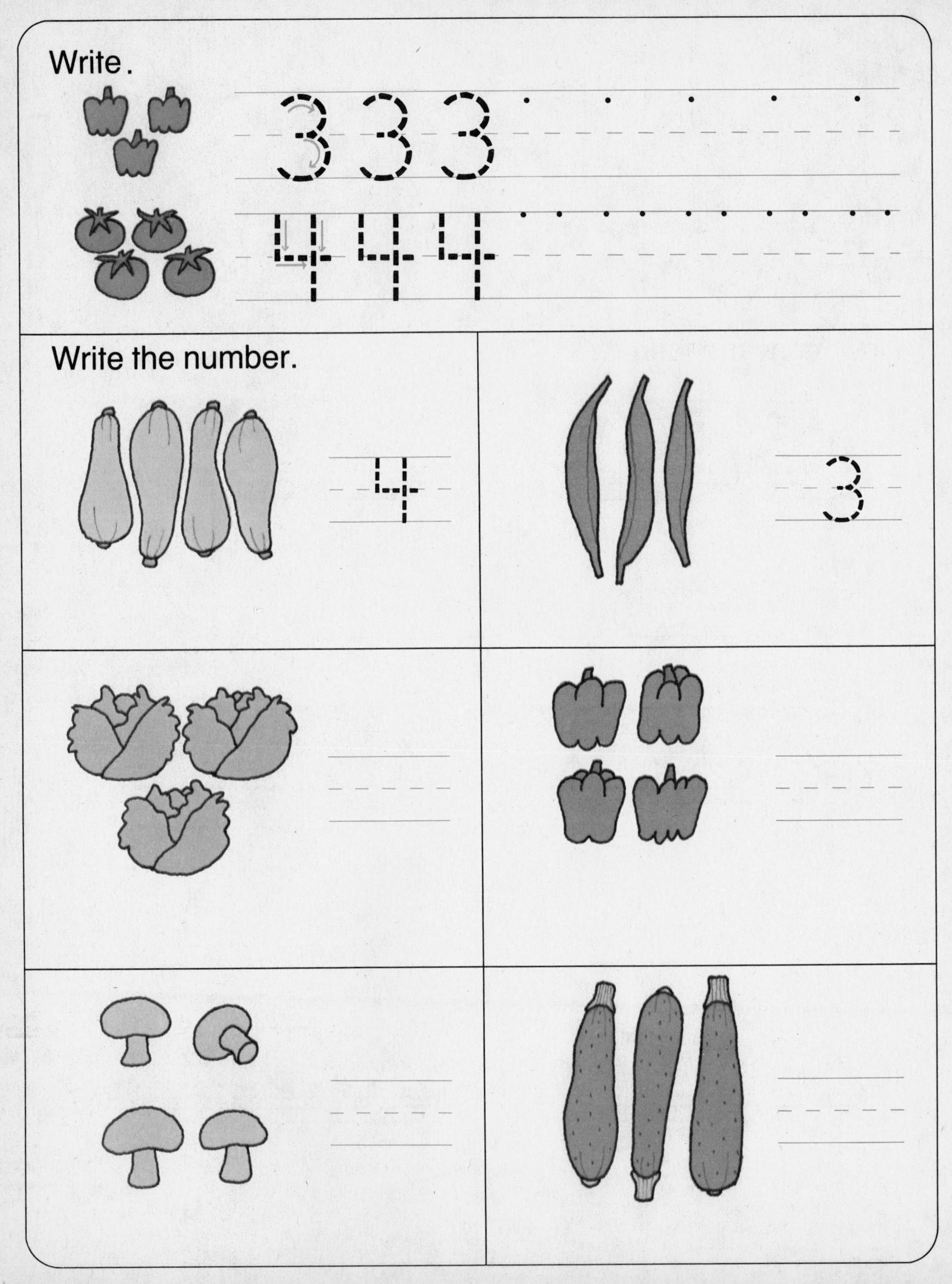
Write.
3 3 3
4 4 4
Write the number.
4
3

Name ______________________________

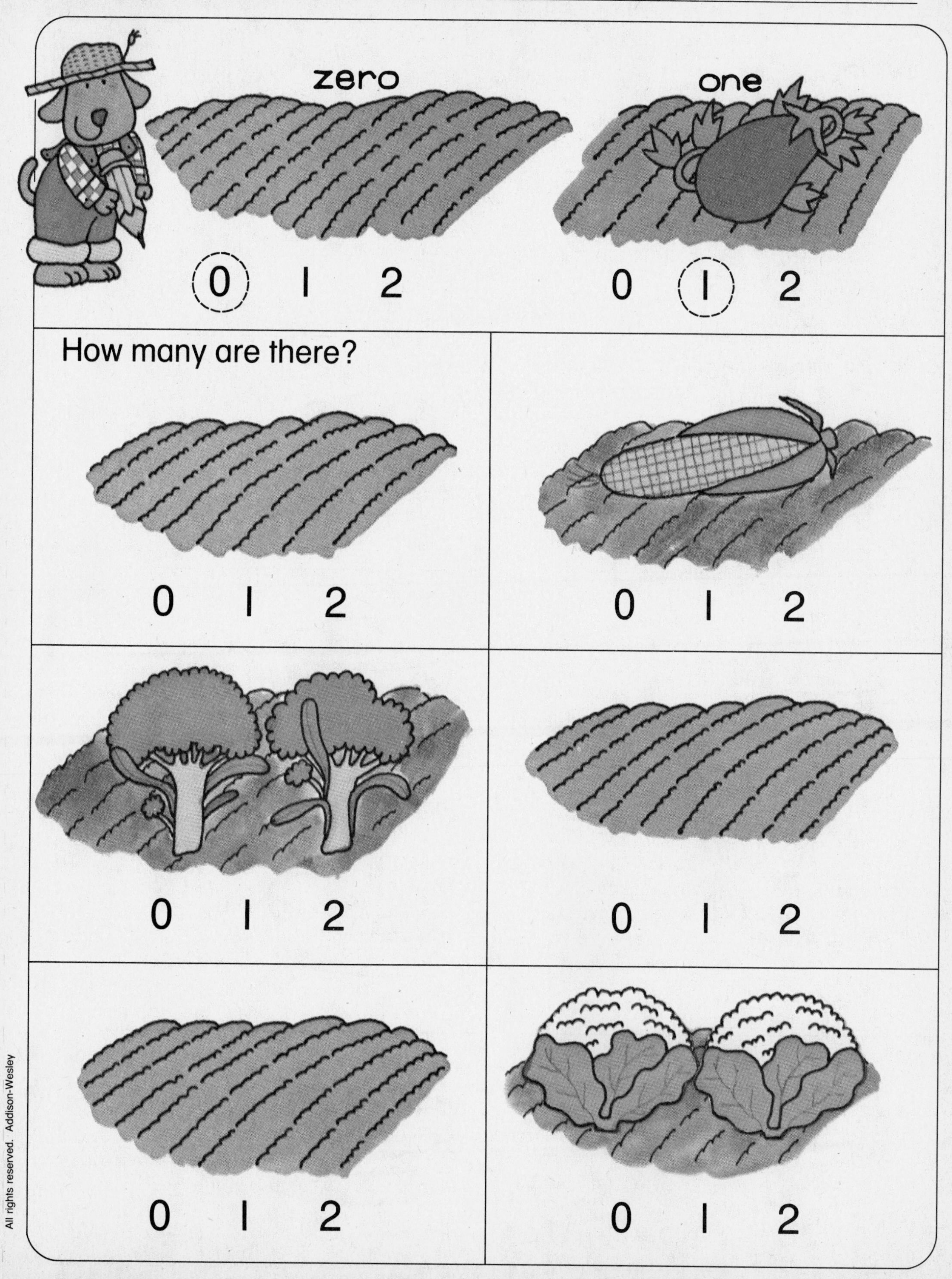

zero

one

0 1 2

0 1 2

How many are there?

0 1 2

0 1 2

0 1 2

0 1 2

0 1 2

0 1 2

Number 0

(seven) **7**

Write.
0 0 0
Write the number.
0

Name ______________________

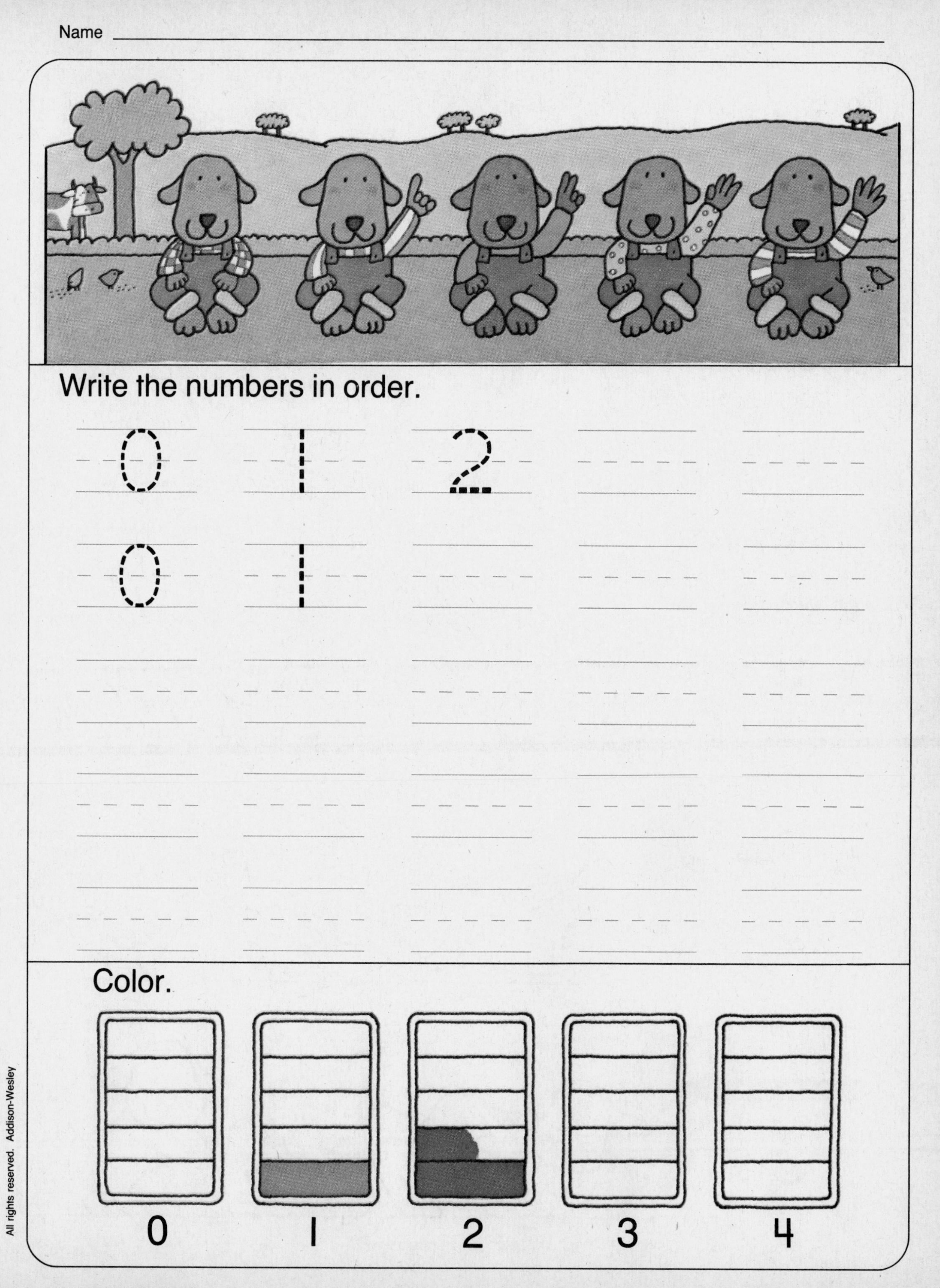

Write the numbers in order.
0 1 2
0 1
Color.
0 1 2 3 4

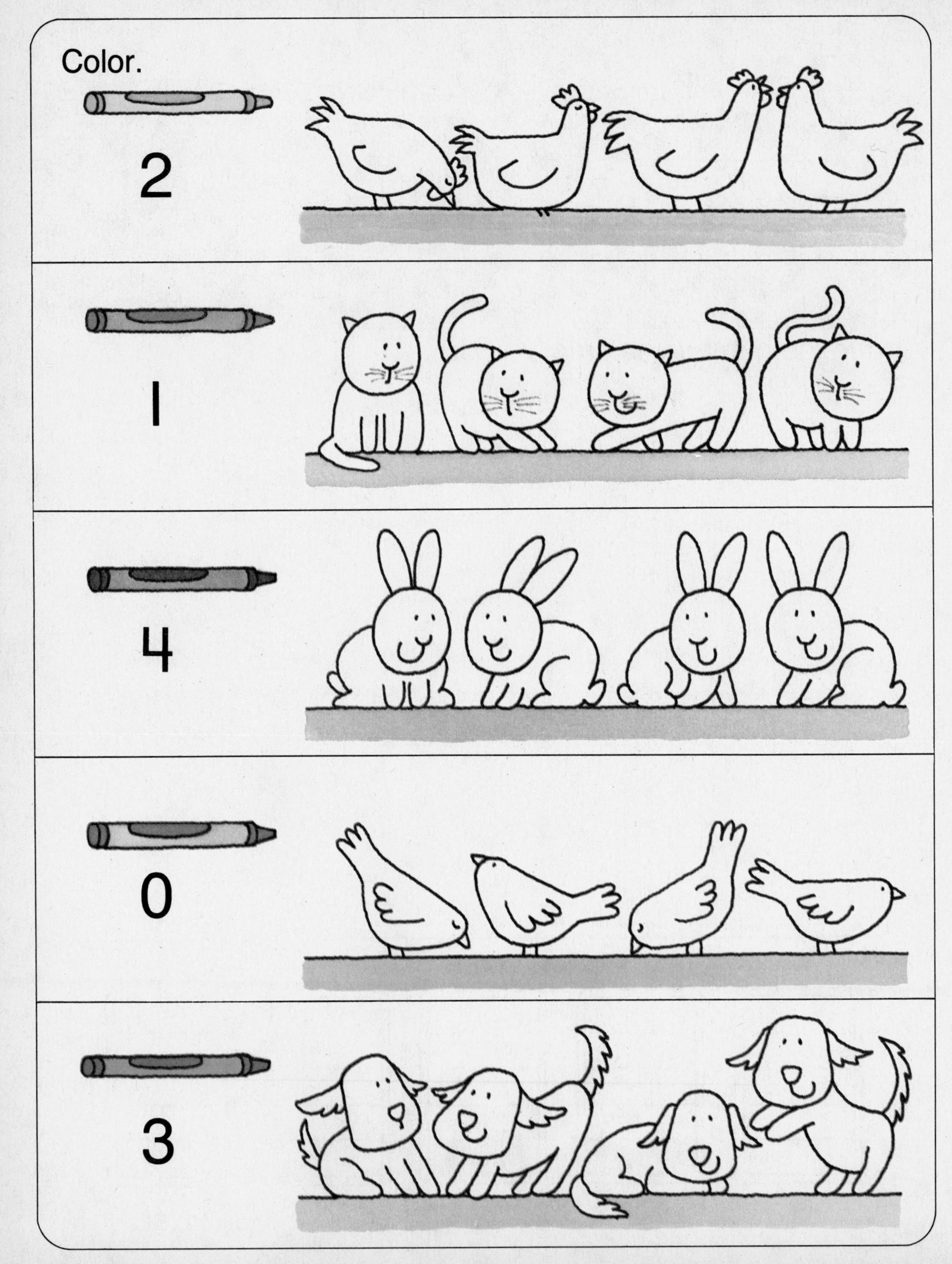
Color.
2
1
4
0
3

Name ____

1
2
3
4
5
five
5
Count.
1
2
3
4
5
6
six
6
How many are there?
5 6
5 6
5 6
5 6
5 6
5 6

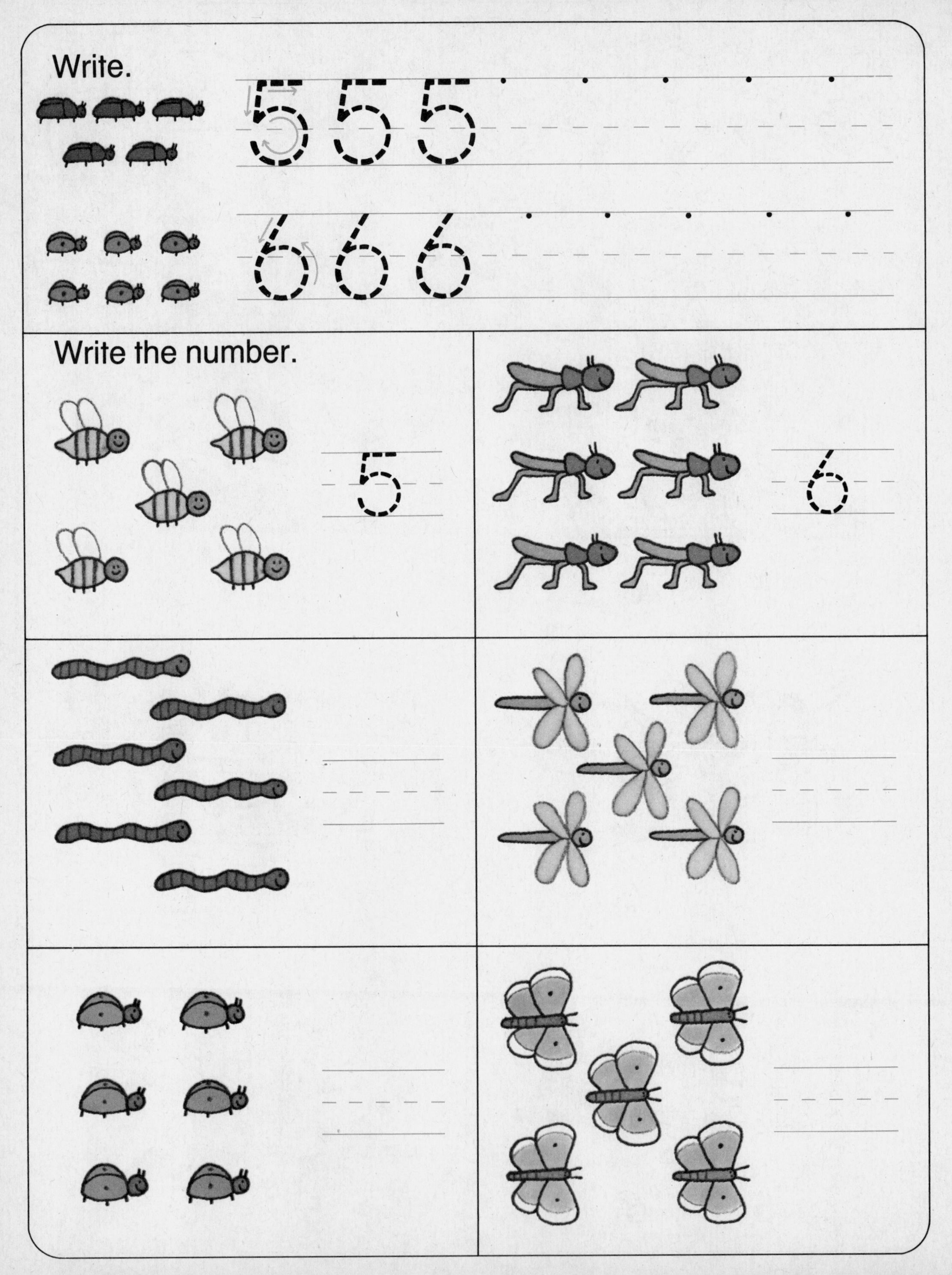
Write.
5 5 5
6 6 6
Write the number.
5
6

Name ______________________________

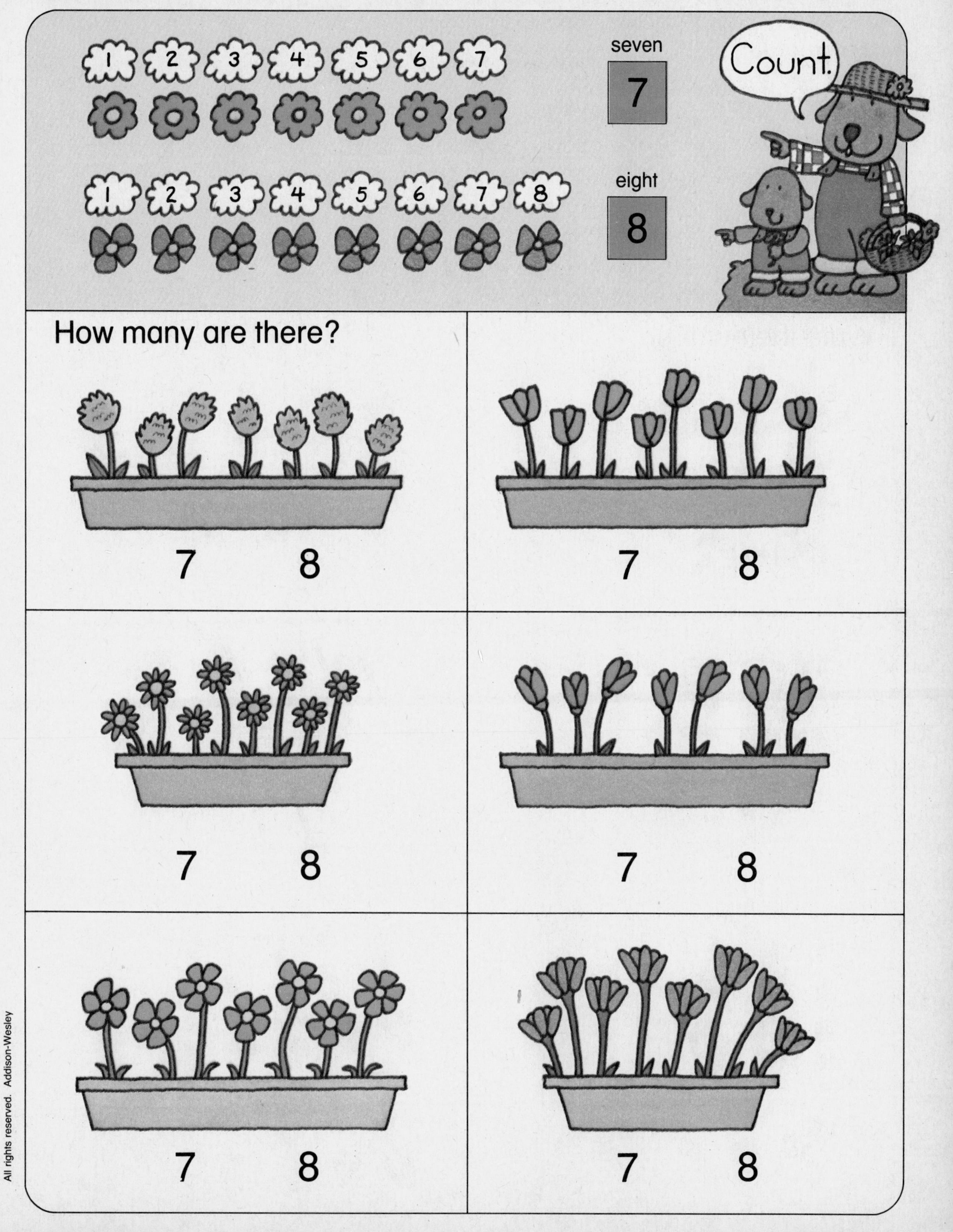
1
2
3
4
5
6
7
seven
7
Count.
1
2
3
4
5
6
7
8
eight
8
How many are there?
7 8
7 8
7 8
7 8
7 8
7 8

Write.

7 7 7

8 8 8

Write the number.

8

7

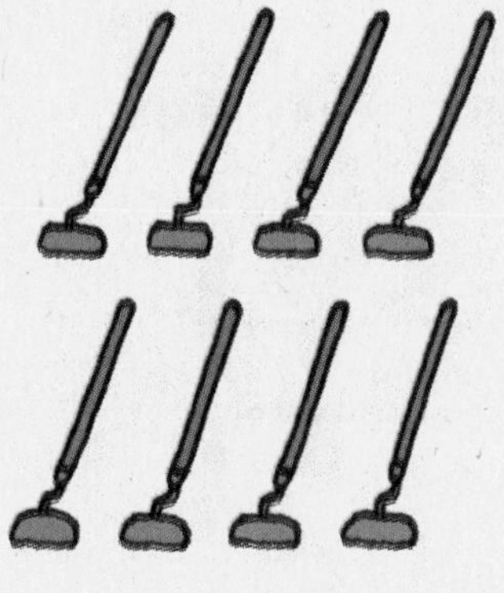

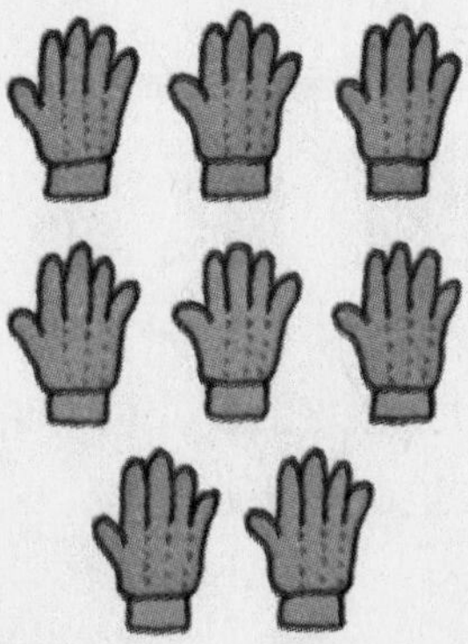

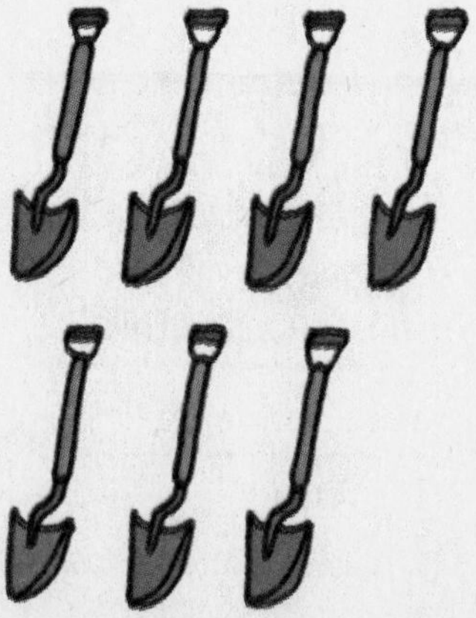

Name ___________________________

Write the numbers in order.

Color.

6

7

8

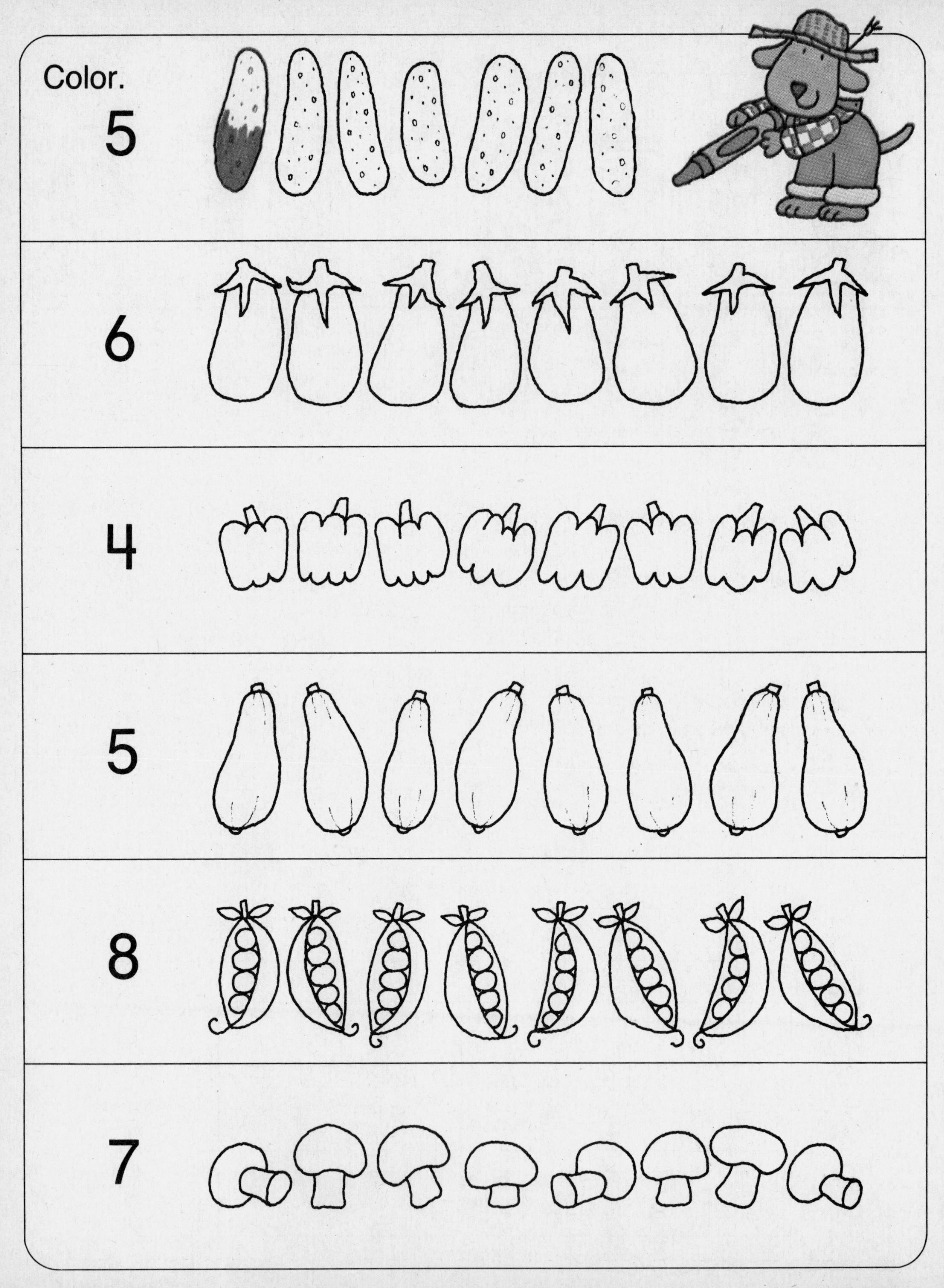
Color.
5
6
4
5
8
7

Name ______________________________

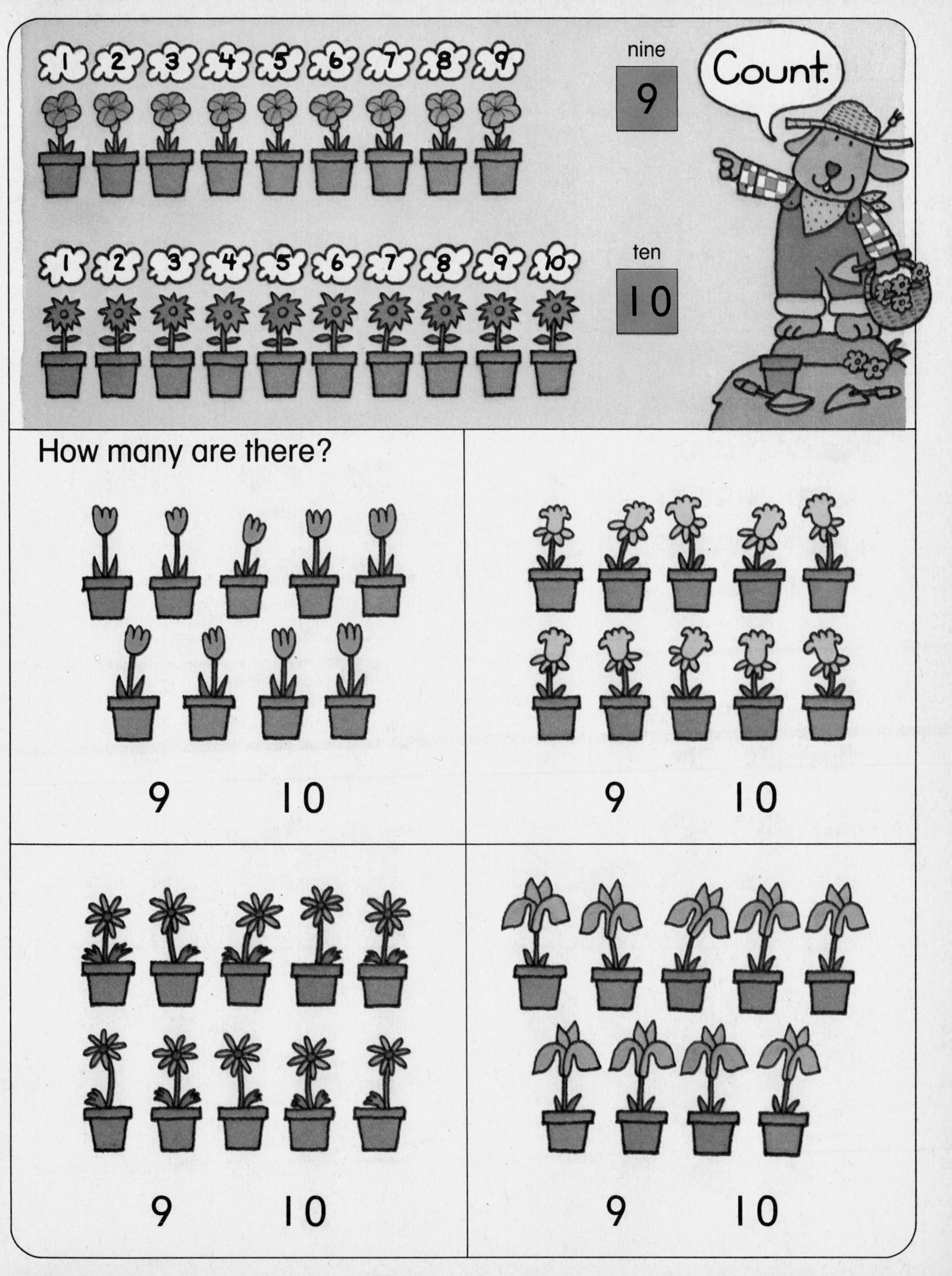

How many are there?

9 10

9 10

9 10

9 10

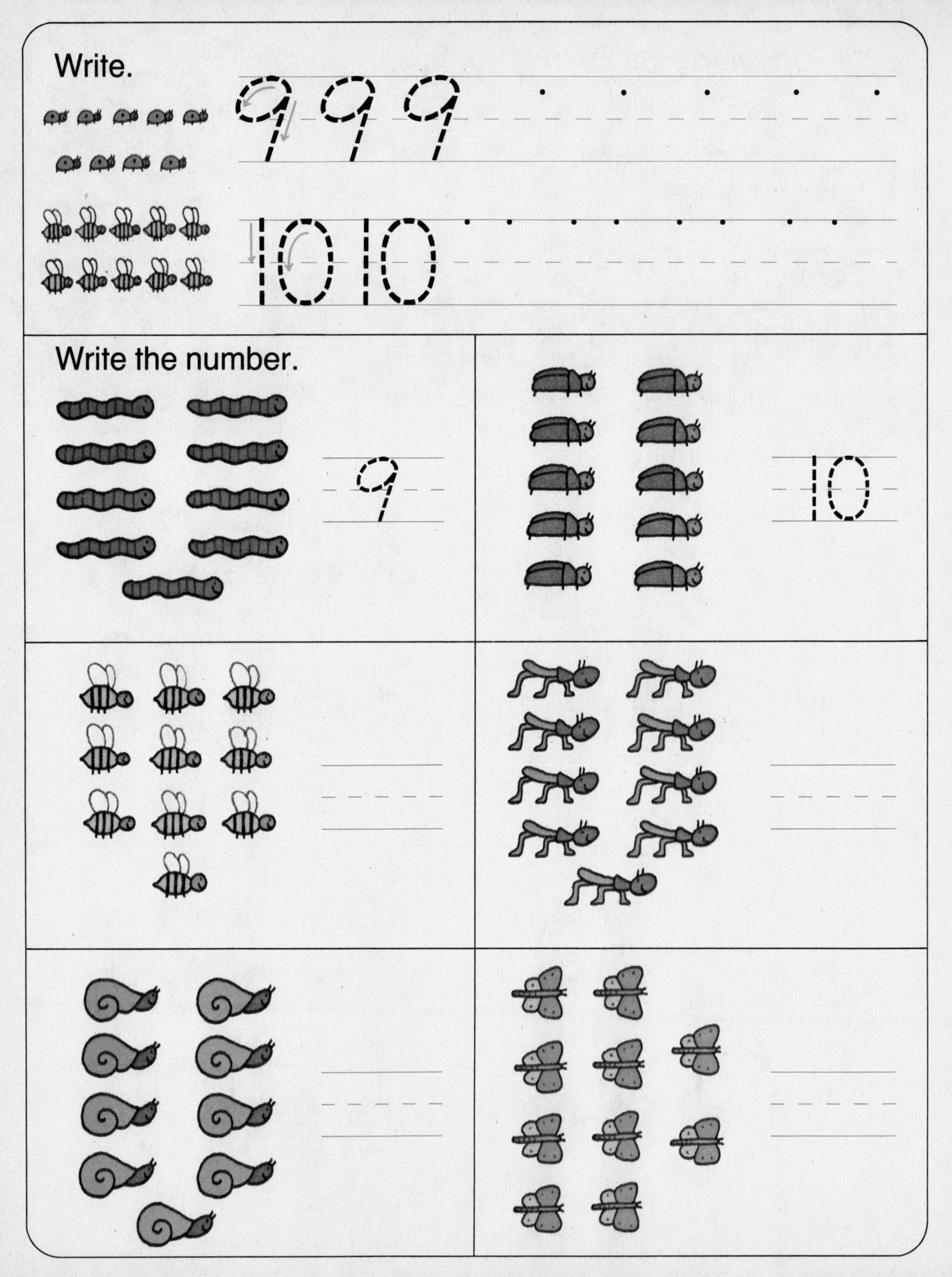
Write.
Write the number.

Name ______________________________

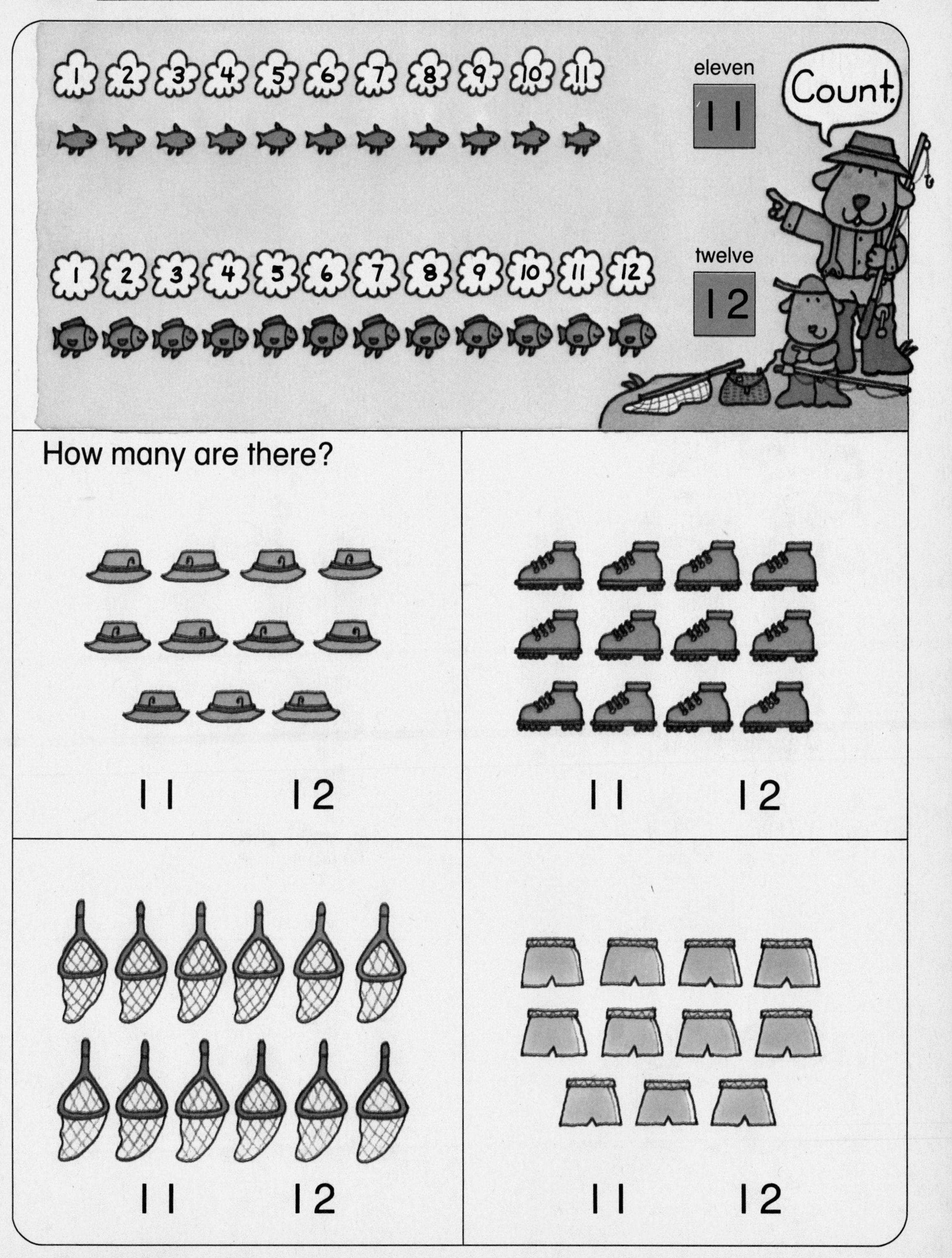

1 2 3 4 5 6 7 8 9 10 11
eleven
11
Count.
1 2 3 4 5 6 7 8 9 10 11 12
twelve
12
How many are there?
11 12
11 12
11 12
11 12

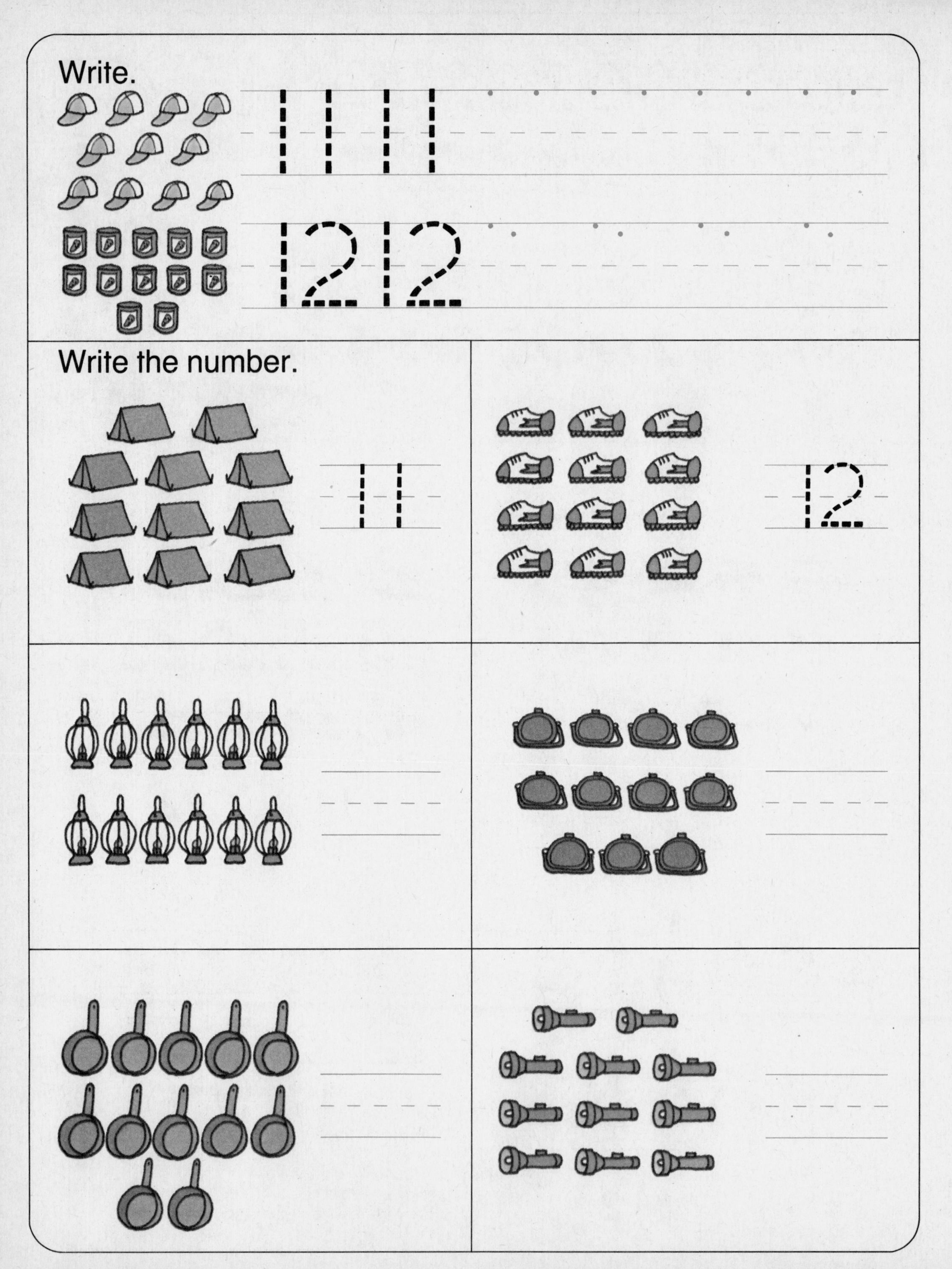
Write.
11
12
Write the number.
11
12

Name ____________________

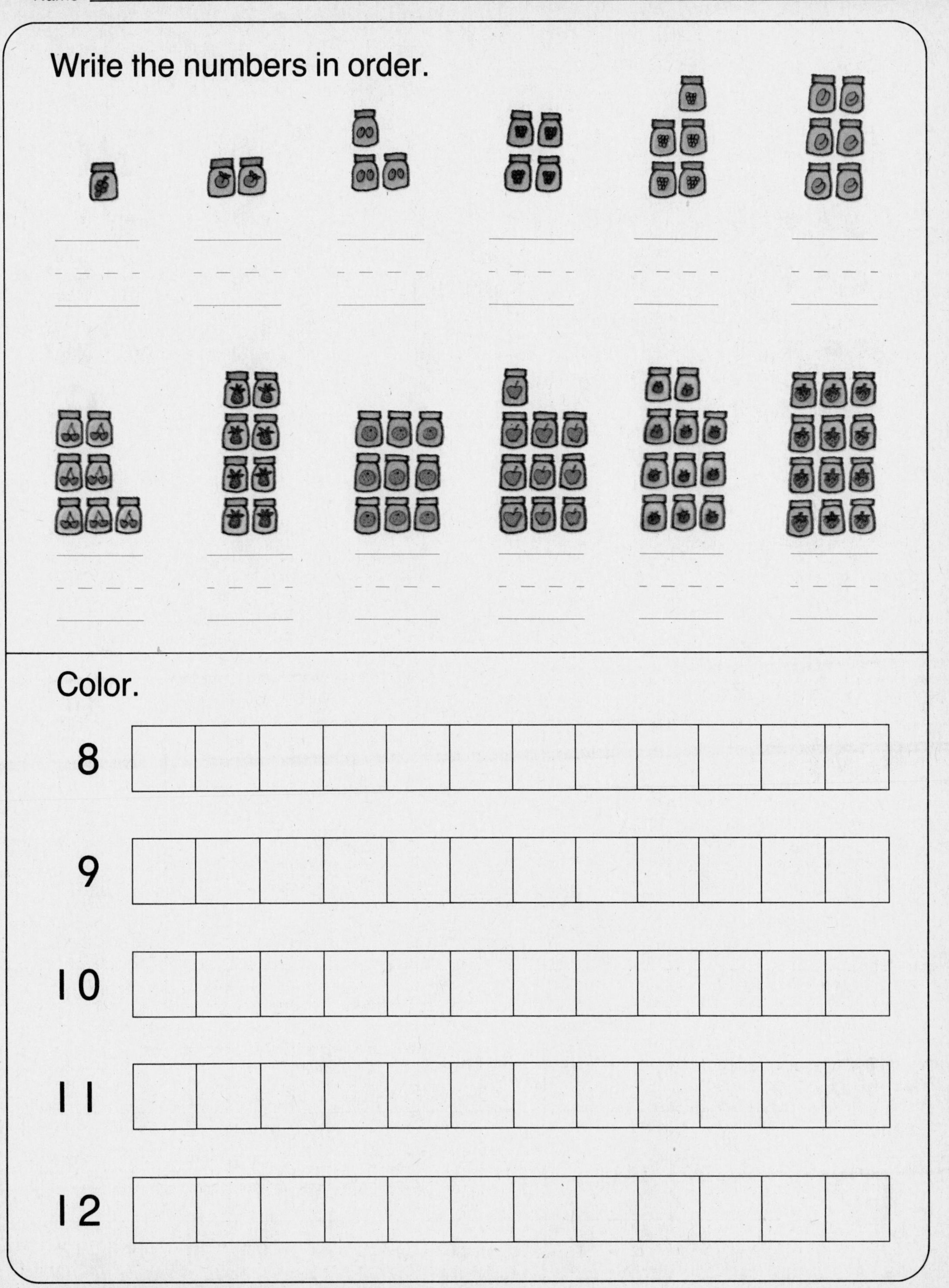
Write the numbers in order.
Color.
8
9
10
11
12

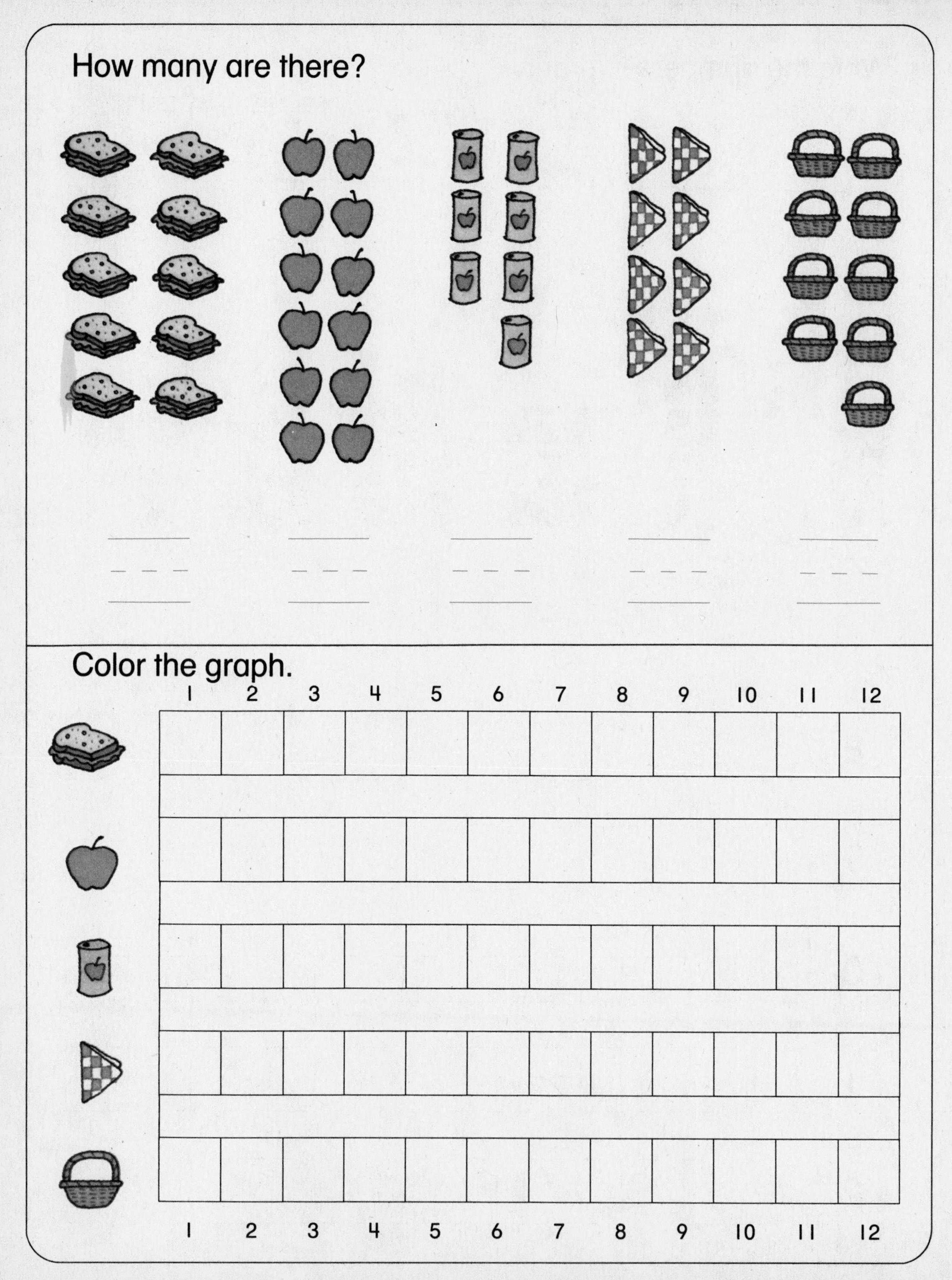
How many are there?
Color the graph.
1 2 3 4 5 6 7 8 9 10 11 12
1 2 3 4 5 6 7 8 9 10 11 12

Name

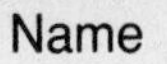

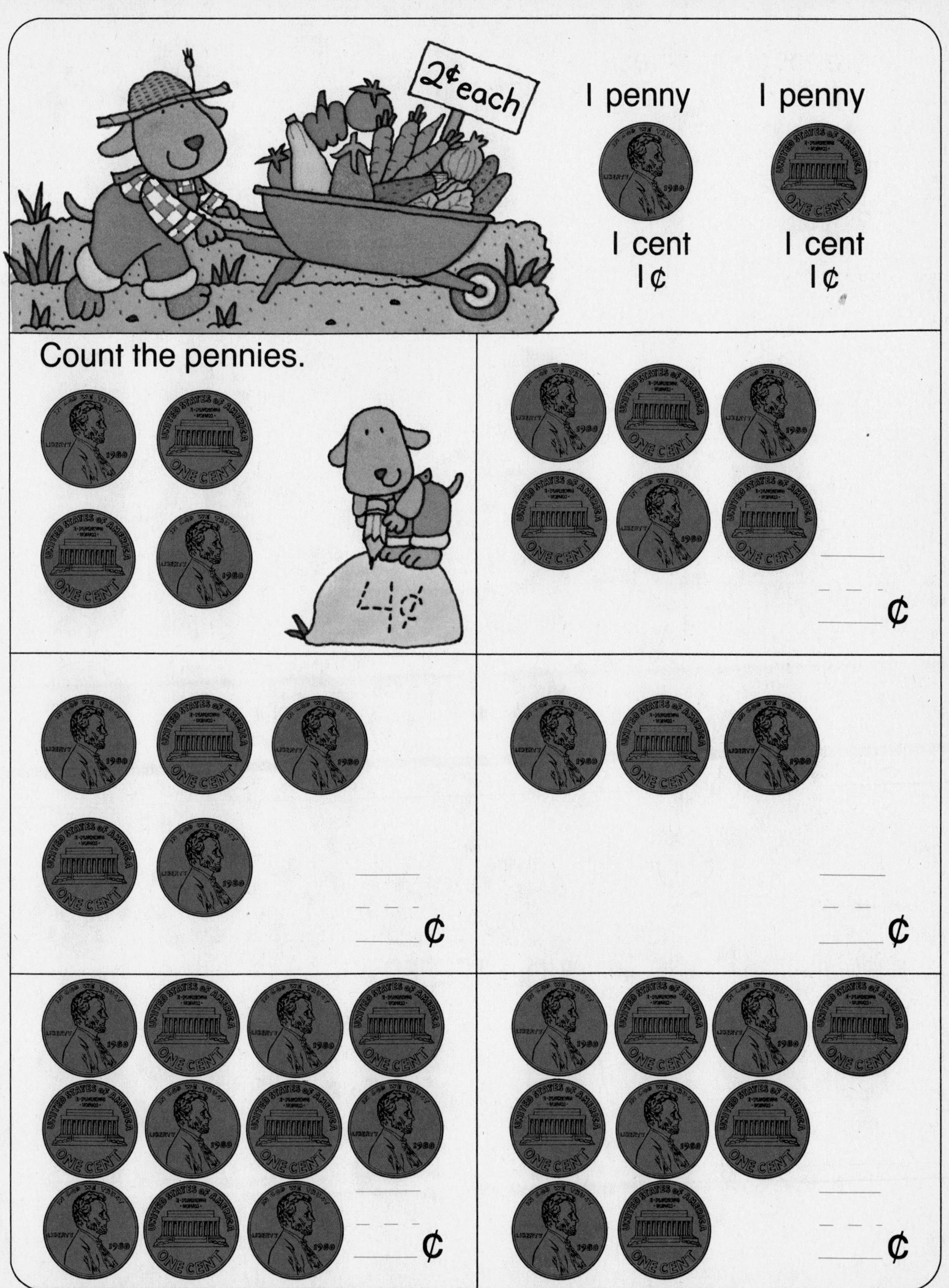

Ring enough pennies.

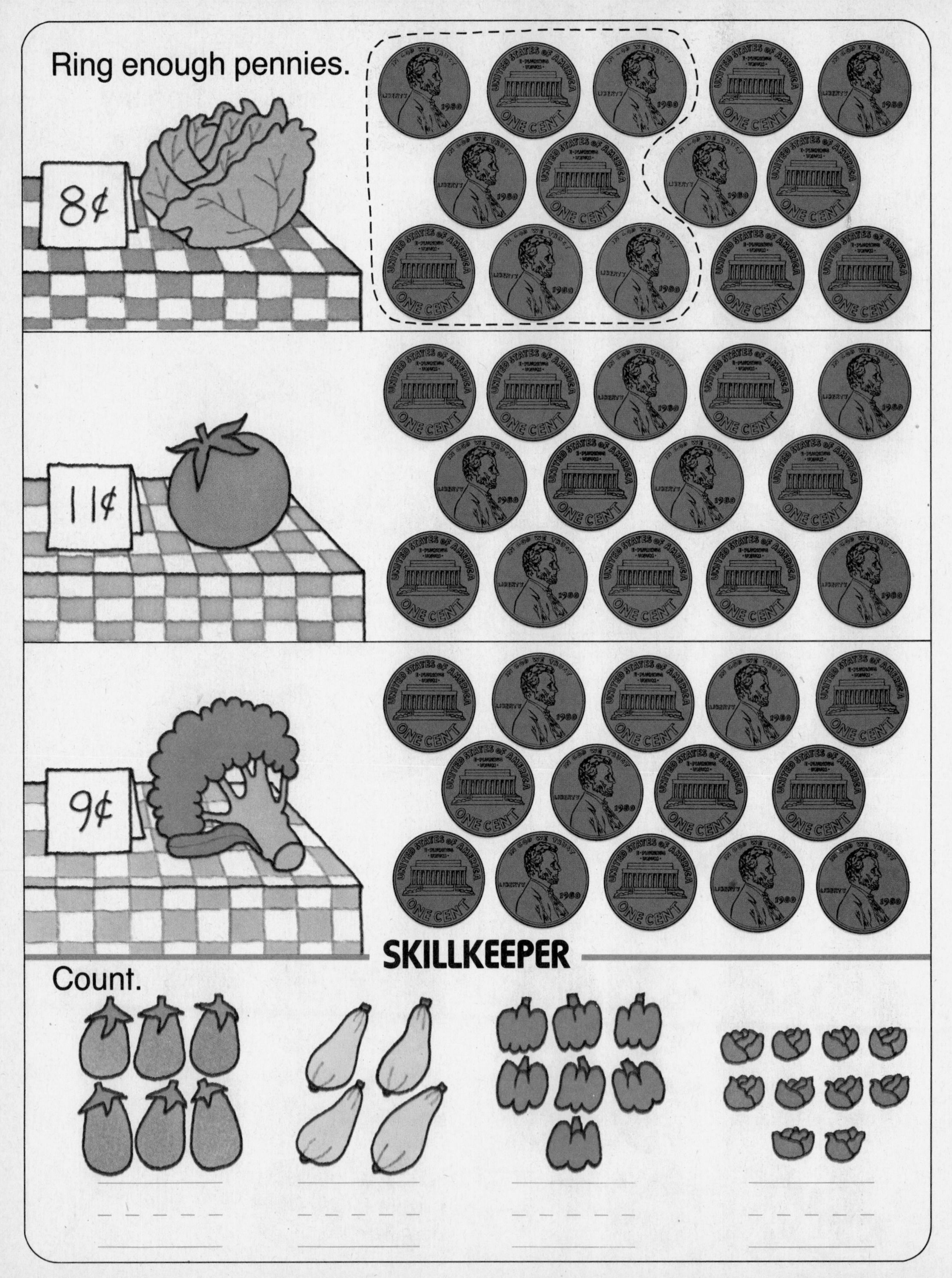

SKILLKEEPER

Count.

Name ______________________________

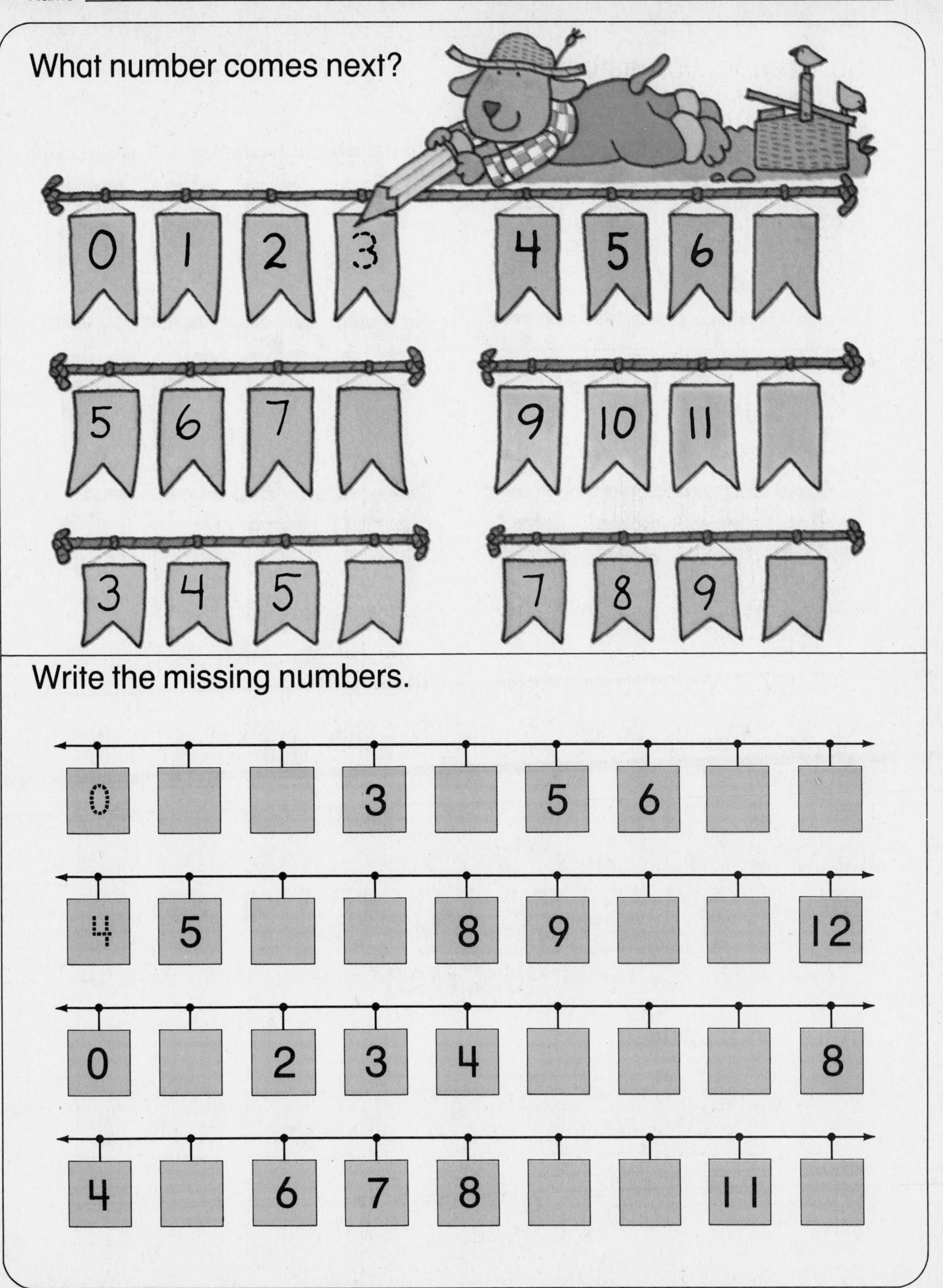
What number comes next?
0 1 2 3 4 5 6
5 6 7
9 10 11
3 4 5
7 8 9
Write the missing numbers.
0 3 5 6
4 5 8 9 12
0 2 3 4 8
4 6 7 8 11

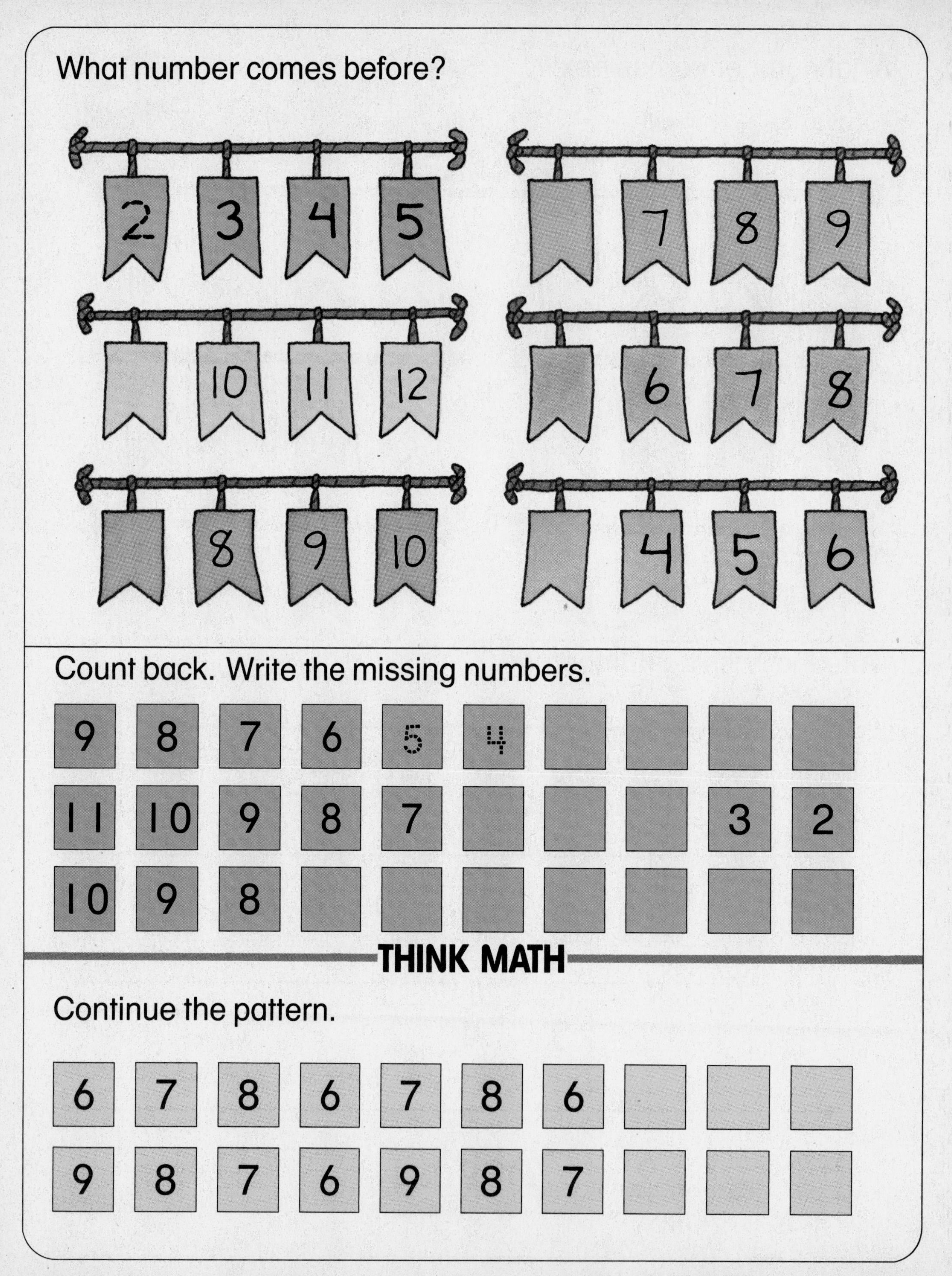
What number comes before?
2 3 4 5
7 8 9
10 11 12
6 7 8
8 9 10
4 5 6
Count back. Write the missing numbers.
9 8 7 6 5 4
11 10 9 8 7 3 2
10 9 8
THINK MATH
Continue the pattern.
6 7 8 6 7 8 6
9 8 7 6 9 8 7

Name ______________________________

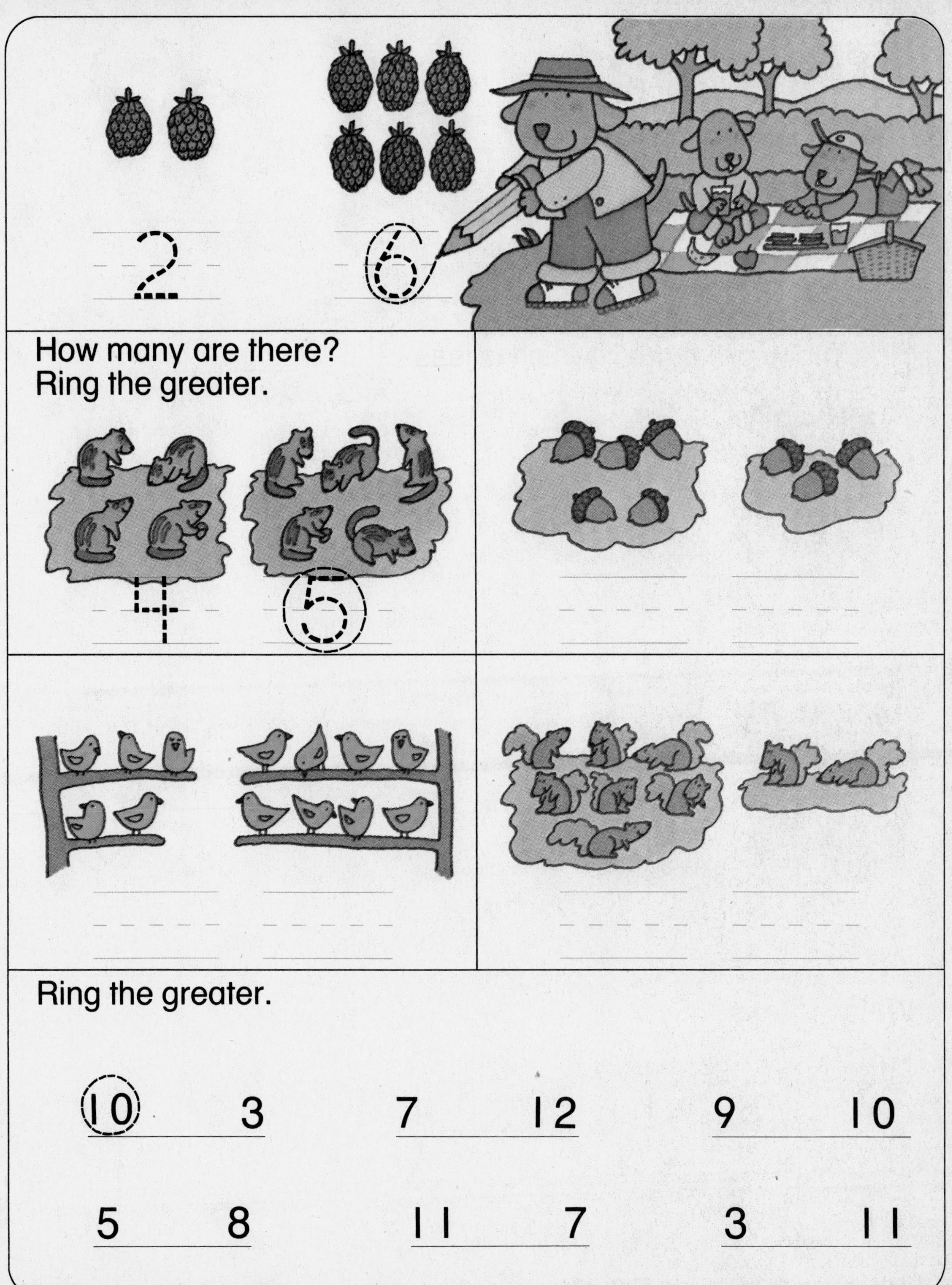

Ring the greater.

10	3	7	12	9	10
5	8	11	7	3	11

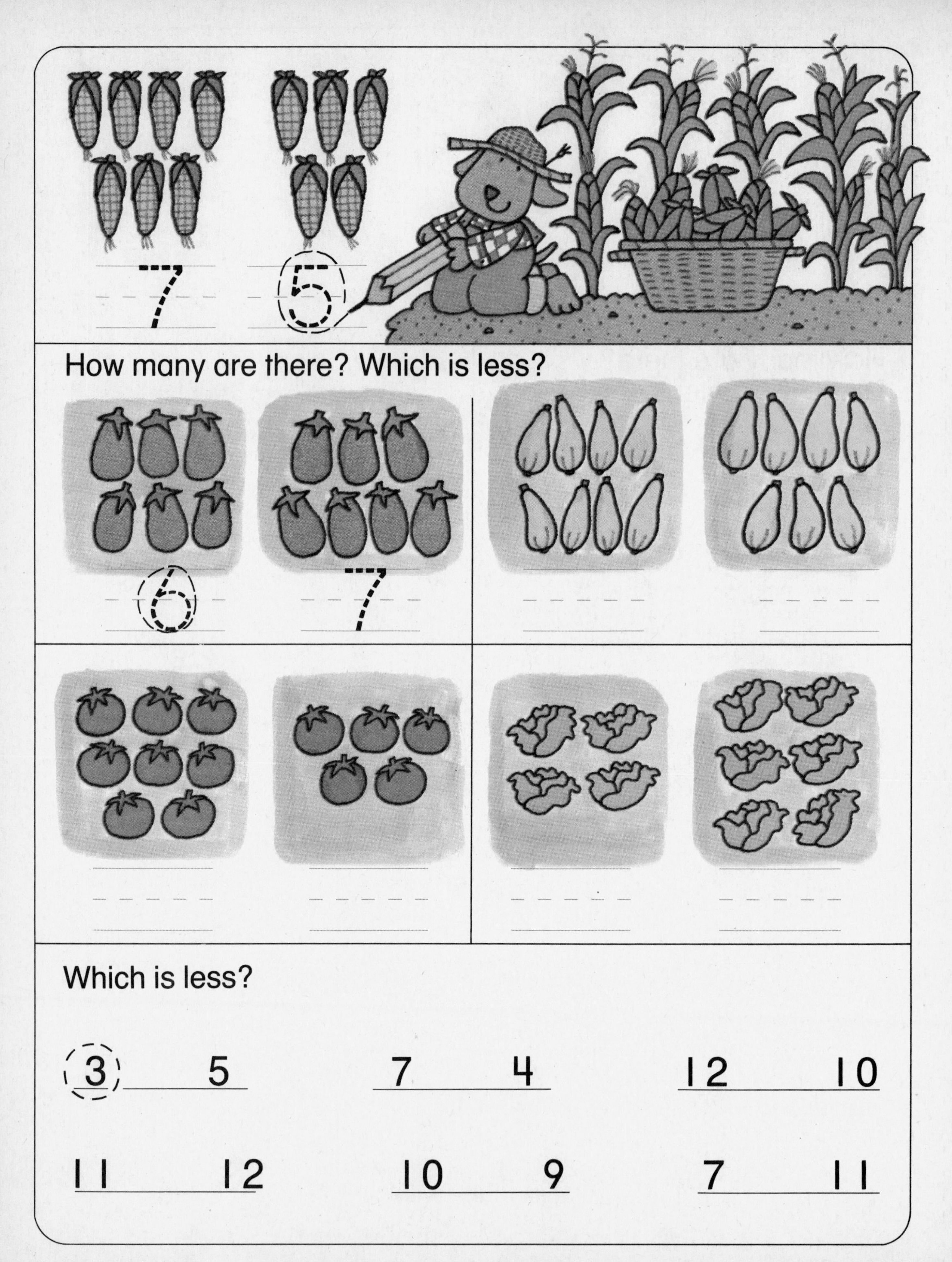
7
5
How many are there? Which is less?
6
7
Which is less?
3 5
7 4
12 10
11 12
10 9
7 11

Name ______________________

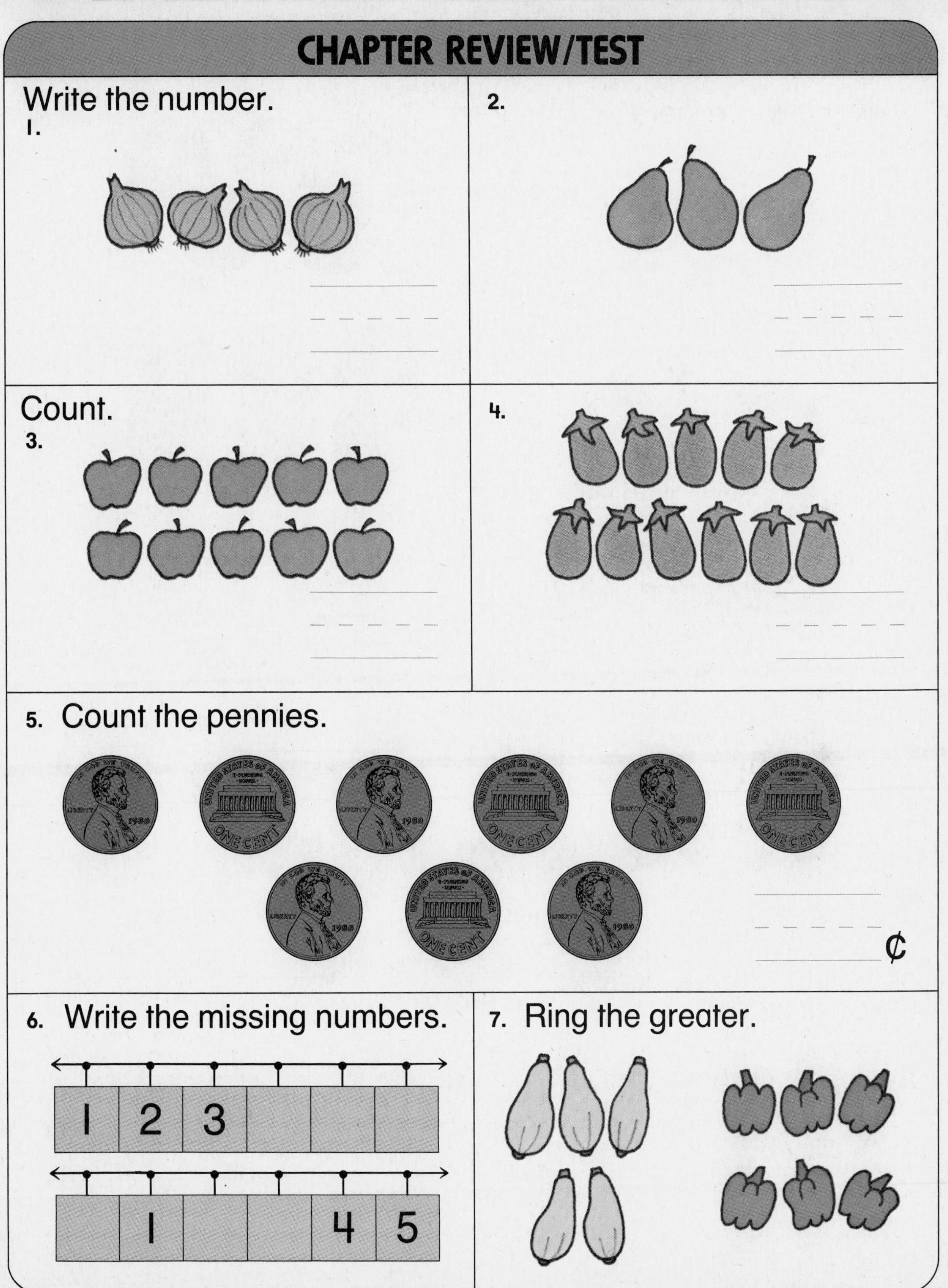

CHAPTER REVIEW/TEST

Write the number.

1.

2.

Count.

3.

4.

5. Count the pennies.

¢

6. Write the missing numbers.

1	2	3			

	1			4	5

7. Ring the greater.

Name ______________________________

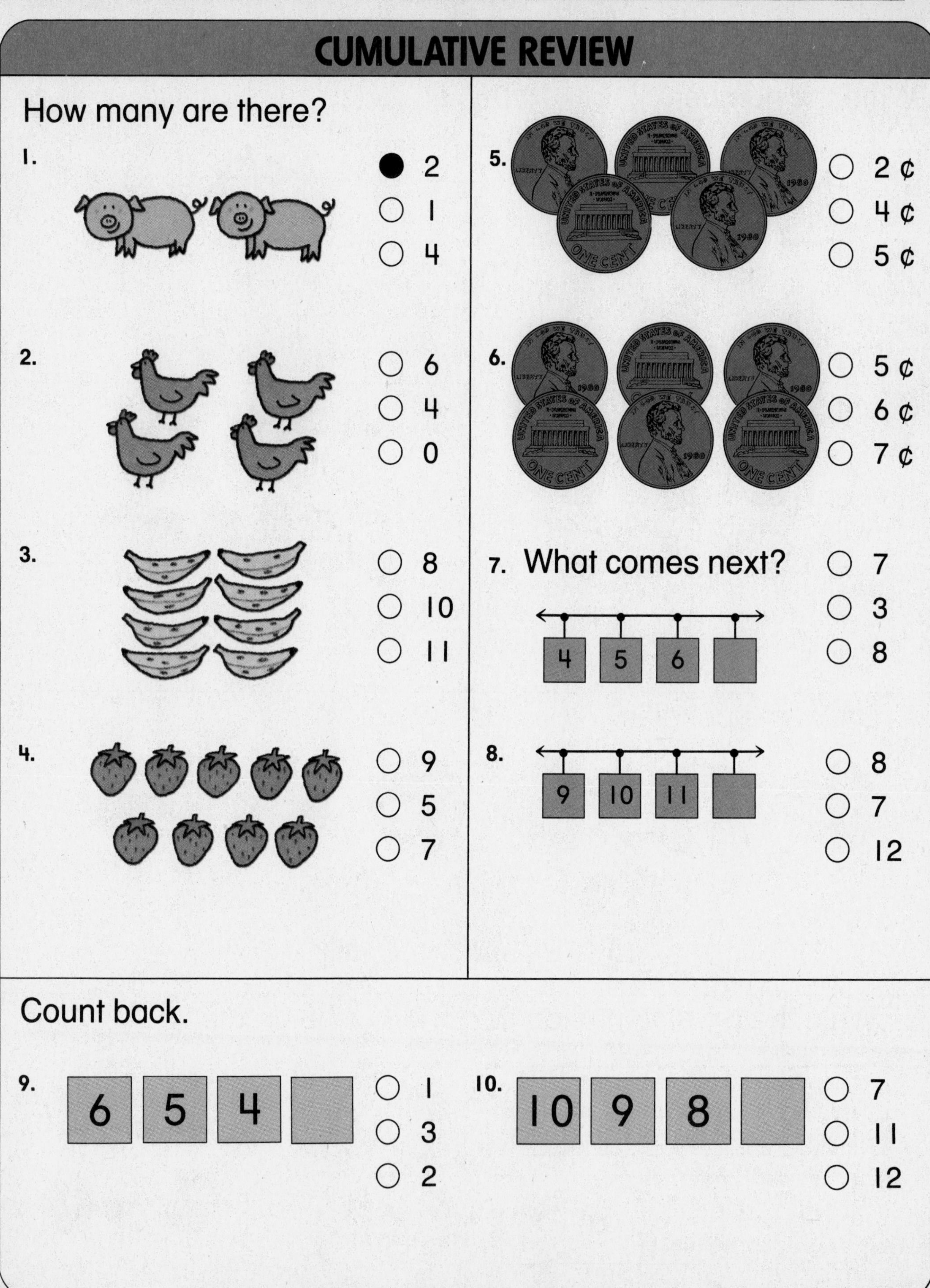

CUMULATIVE REVIEW

How many are there?

1. ● 2 ○ 1 ○ 4

2. ○ 6 ○ 4 ○ 0

3. ○ 8 ○ 10 ○ 11

4. ○ 9 ○ 5 ○ 7

5. ○ 2 ¢ ○ 4 ¢ ○ 5 ¢

6. ○ 5 ¢ ○ 6 ¢ ○ 7 ¢

7. What comes next?

4 5 6 ☐

○ 7 ○ 3 ○ 8

8. 9 10 11 ☐

○ 8 ○ 7 ○ 12

Count back.

9. 6 5 4 ☐

○ 1 ○ 3 ○ 2

10. 10 9 8 ☐

○ 7 ○ 11 ○ 12

Name ______________________________

ANOTHER LOOK

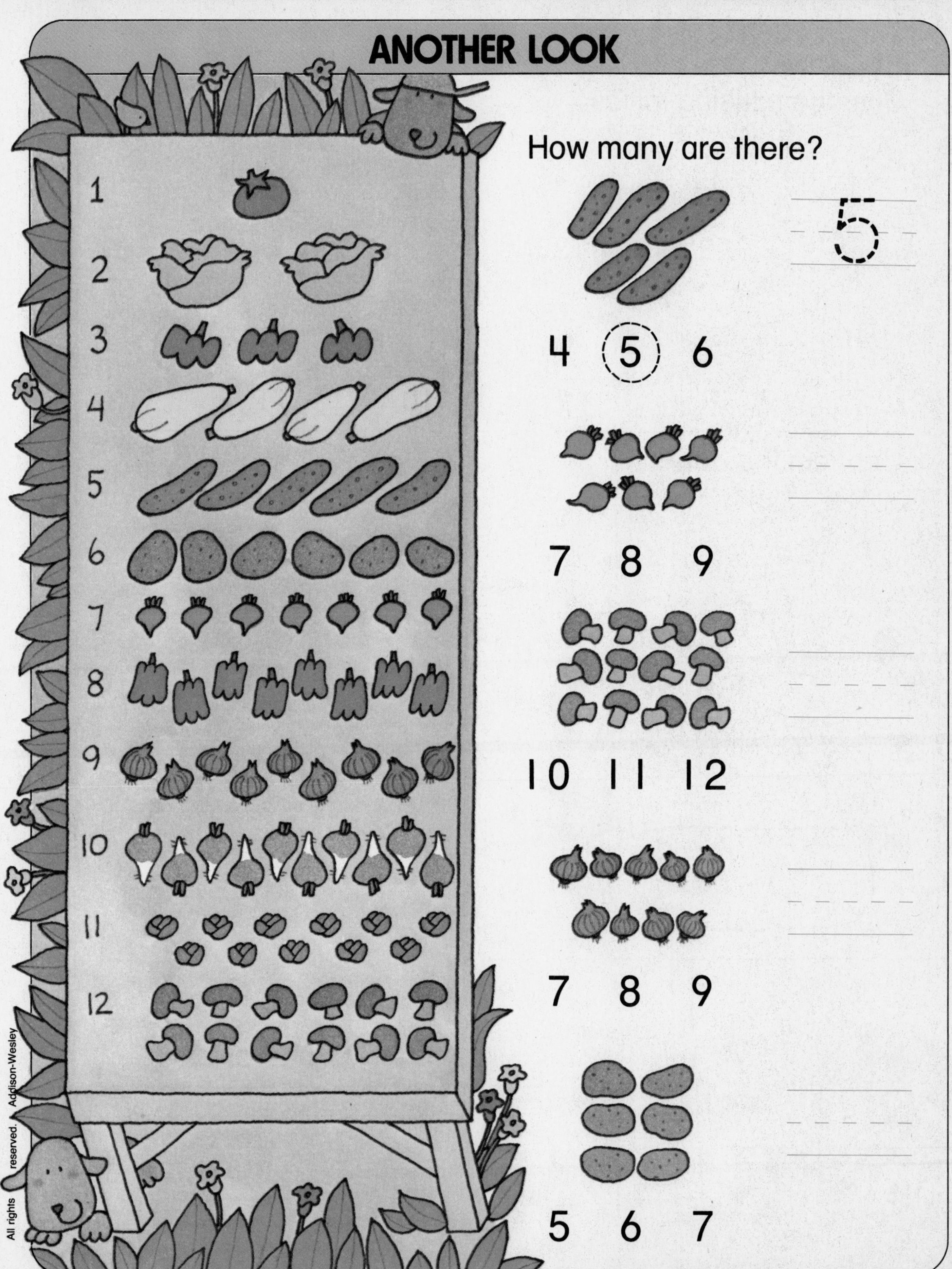

How many are there?

1
2
3
4
5
6
7
8
9
10
11
12

5

4 (5) 6

7 8 9

10 11 12

7 8 9

5 6 7

Name

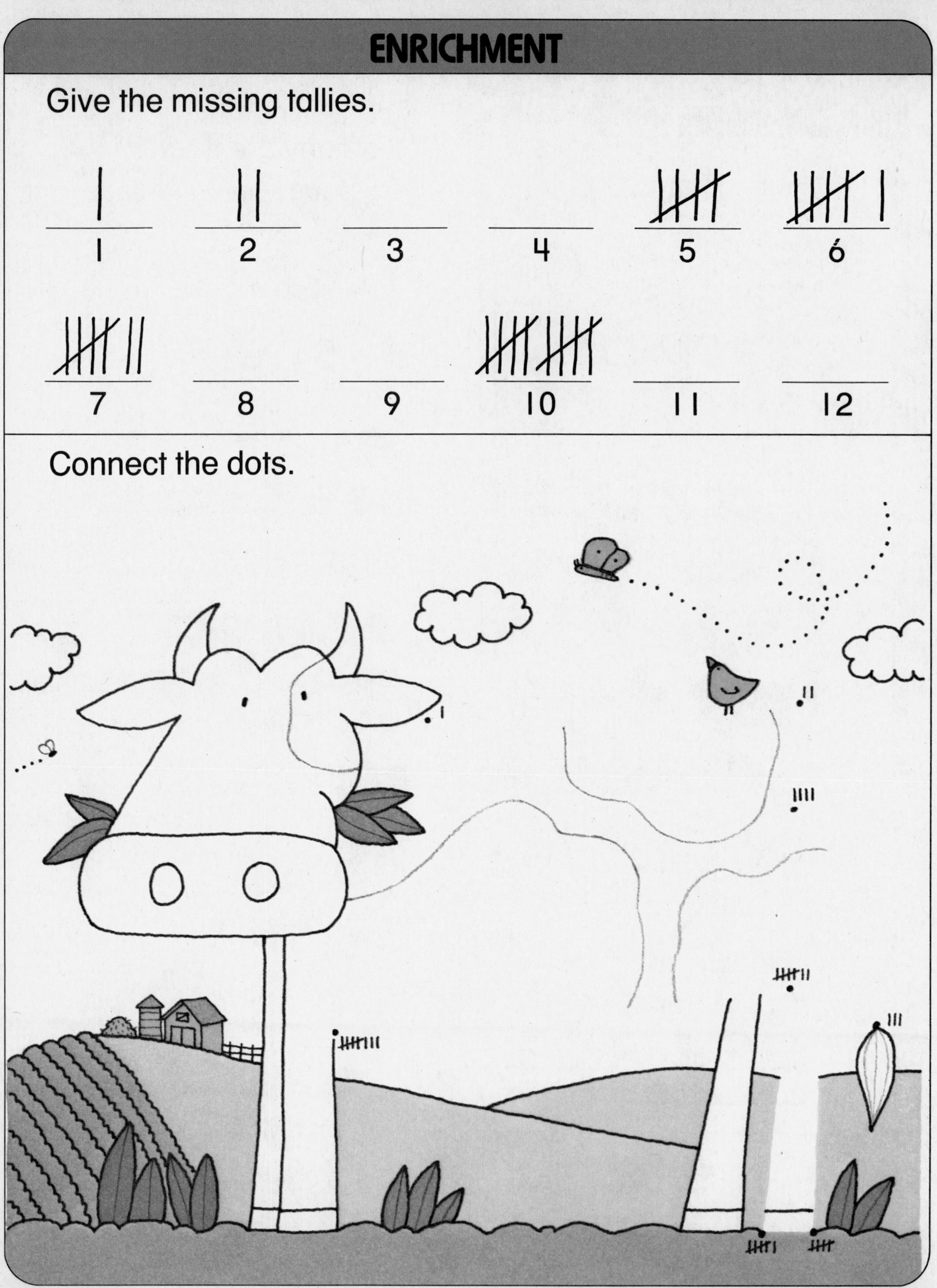
ENRICHMENT
Give the missing tallies.
1
2
3
4
5
6
7
8
9
10
11
12
Connect the dots.

Name ____________________

2 SUMS TO 5

Use counters.

1. Put in 1 Put in 3 4 in all

2. Put in 2 Put in 3 ____ in all

3. Put in 2 Put in 1 ____ in all

4. Put in 4 Put in 1 ____ in all

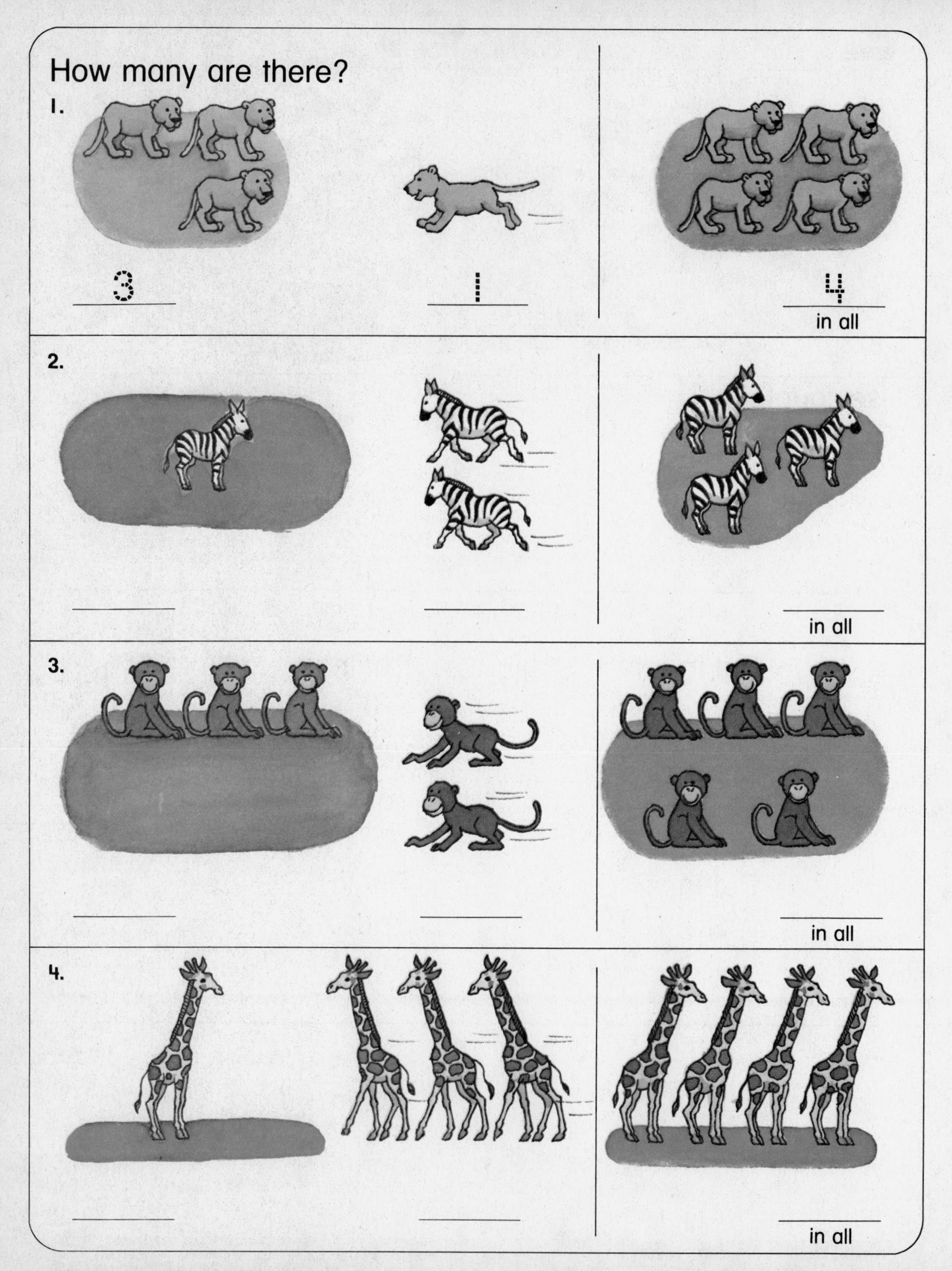
How many are there?
1.
3
1
4
in all
2.
in all
3.
in all
4.
in all

Name ______________________________

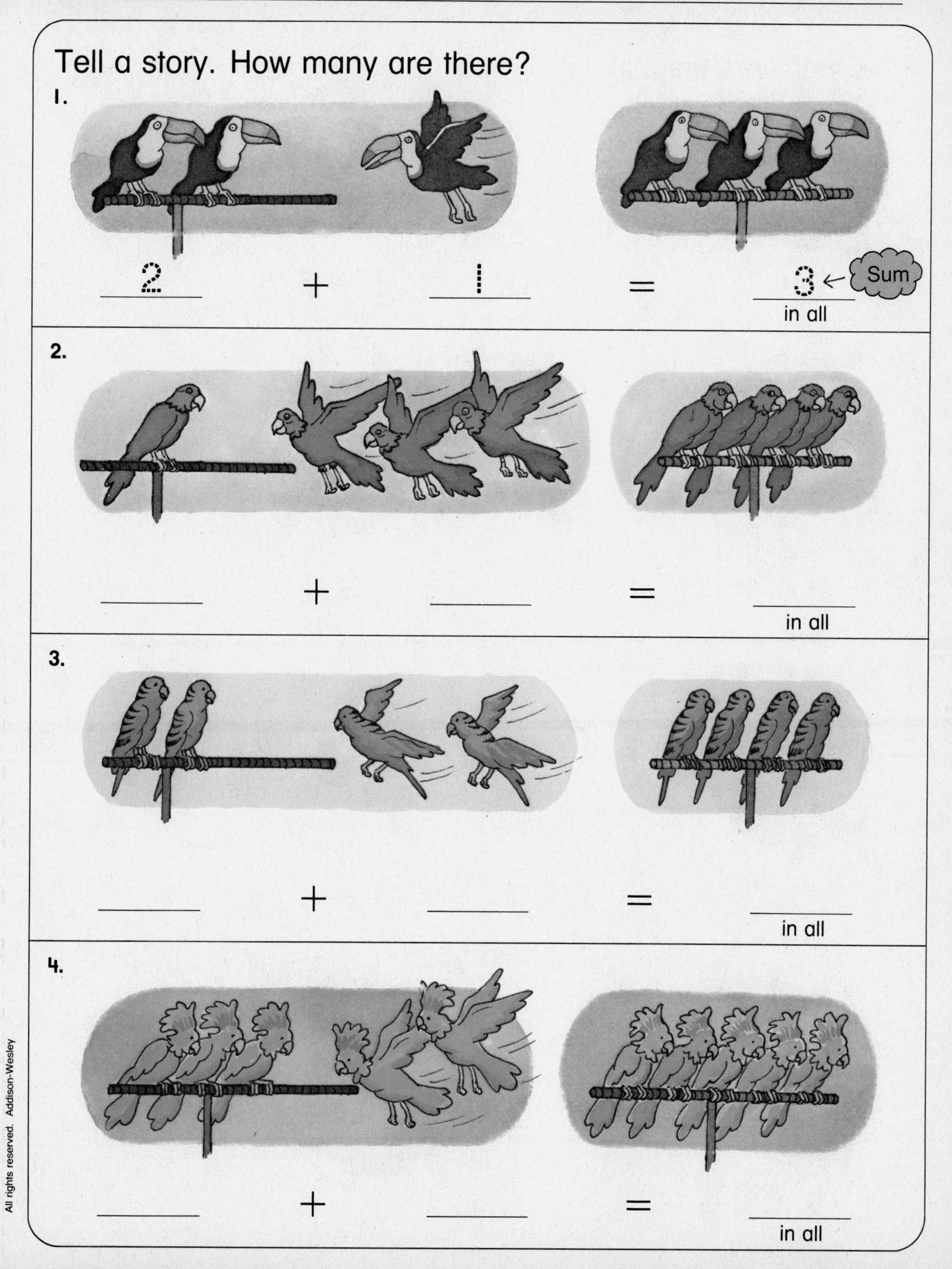
Tell a story. How many are there?
1.
2 + 1 = 3 in all
Sum
2.
+ =
in all
3.
+ =
in all
4.
+ =
in all

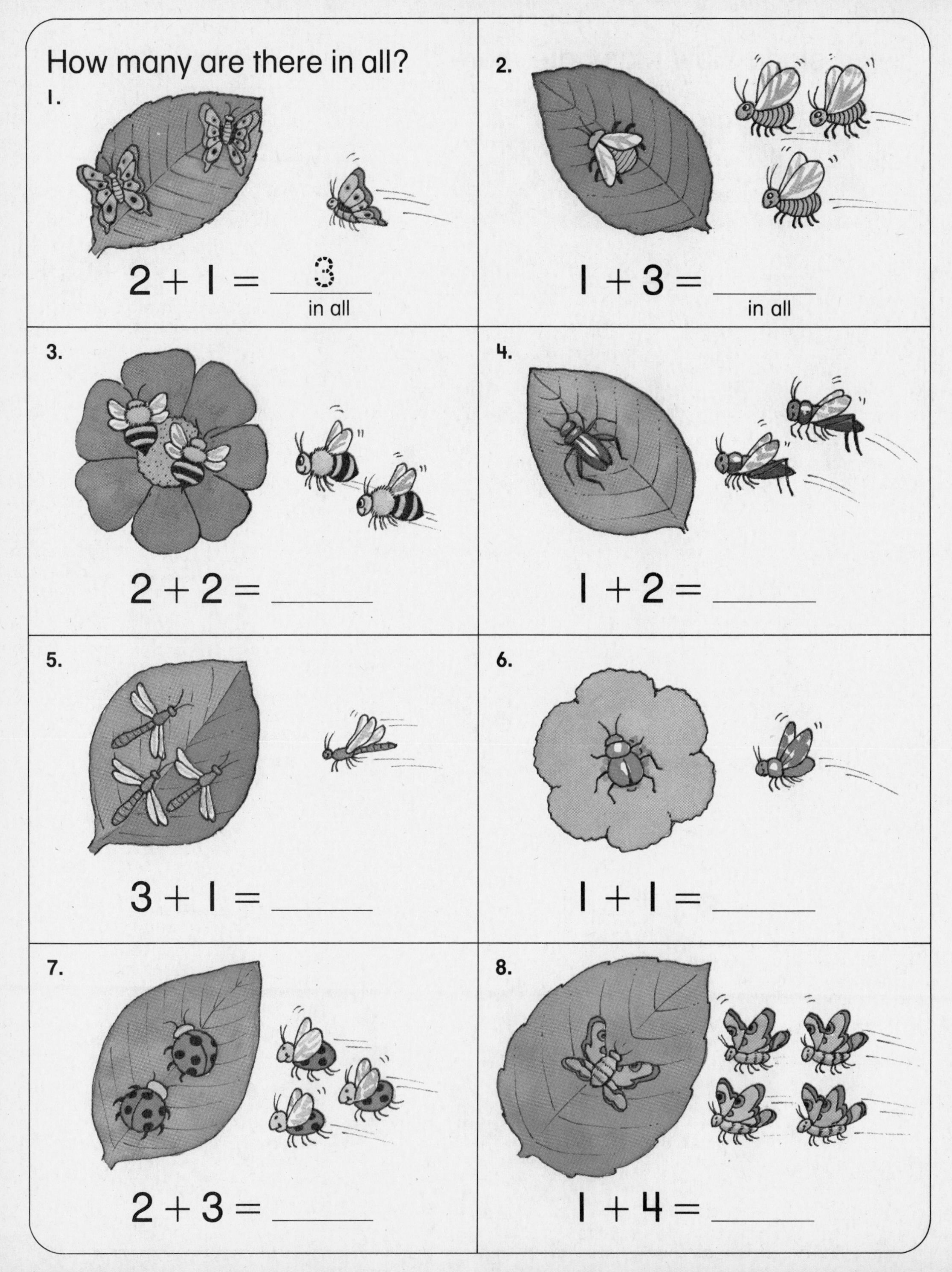
How many are there in all?
1.
2 + 1 = 3
in all
2.
1 + 3 = ____
in all
3.
2 + 2 = ____
4.
1 + 2 = ____
5.
3 + 1 = ____
6.
1 + 1 = ____
7.
2 + 3 = ____
8.
1 + 4 = ____

Name ______________________

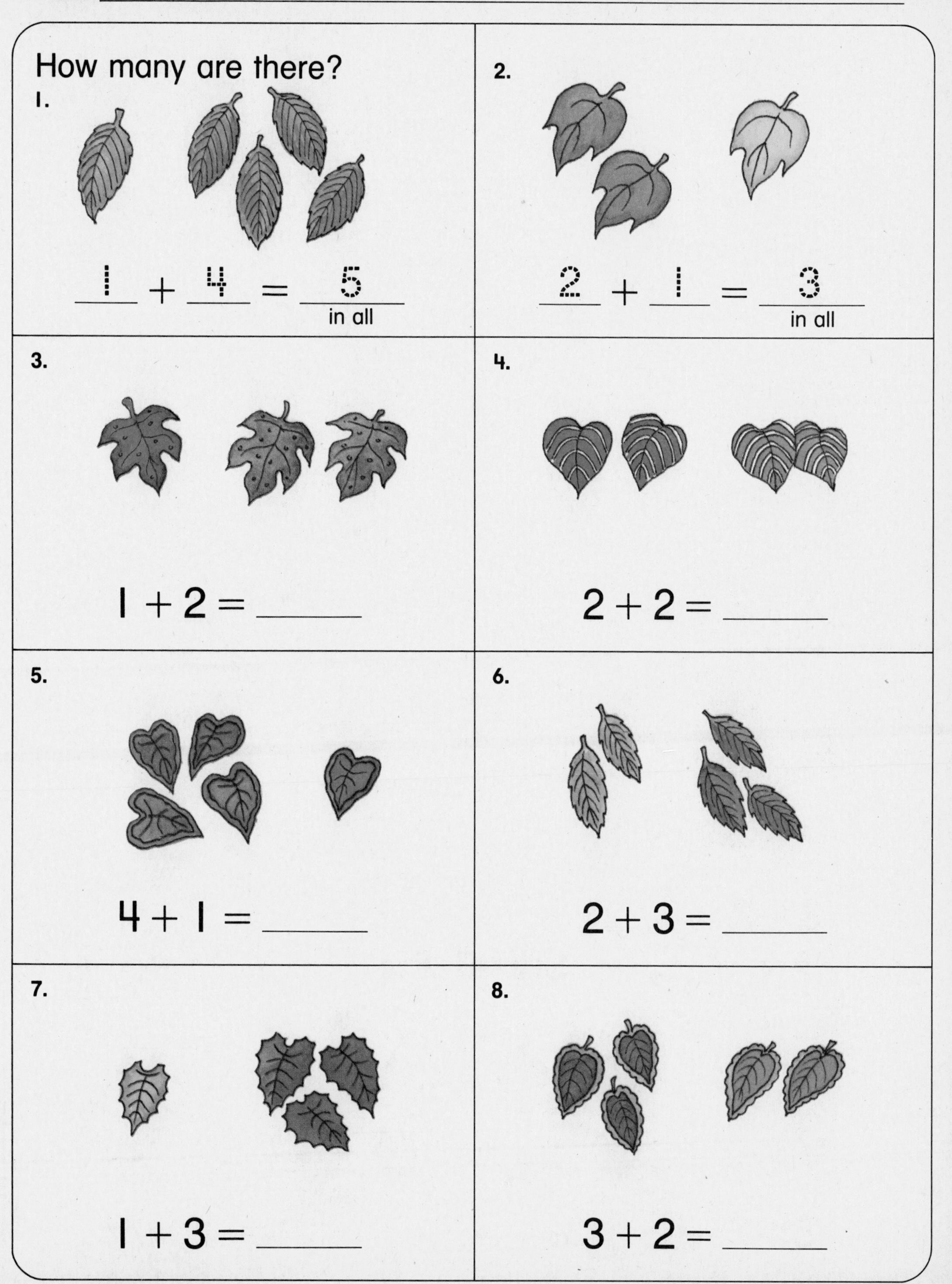

How many are there?

1. 1 + 4 = 5 in all

2. 2 + 1 = 3 in all

3. 1 + 2 = ______

4. 2 + 2 = ______

5. 4 + 1 = ______

6. 2 + 3 = ______

7. 1 + 3 = ______

8. 3 + 2 = ______

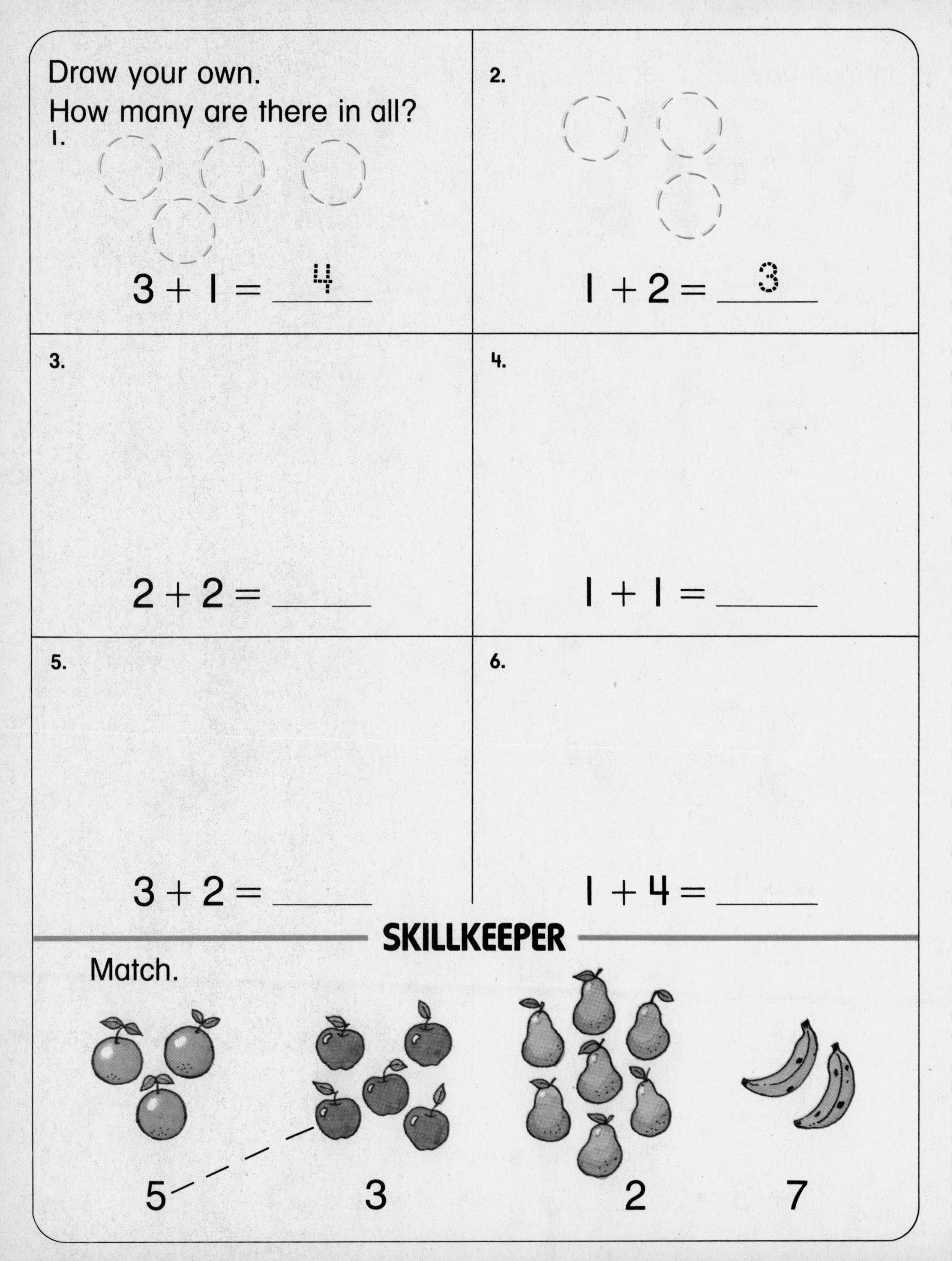

Draw your own.

How many are there in all?

1. $3 + 1 =$ 4

2. $1 + 2 =$ 3

3. $2 + 2 =$ ____

4. $1 + 1 =$ ____

5. $3 + 2 =$ ____

6. $1 + 4 =$ ____

SKILLKEEPER

Match.

5 3 2 7

Name ______________________________

These have the same sum.
2 + 1 = 3
1 + 2 = 3
Add.
1.
3 + 0 = 3
2.
0 + 3 = ____
3.
2 + 3 = ____
4.
3 + 2 = ____
5.
0 + 2 = ____
6.
2 + 0 = ____

Order and zero properties (thirty-nine) 39

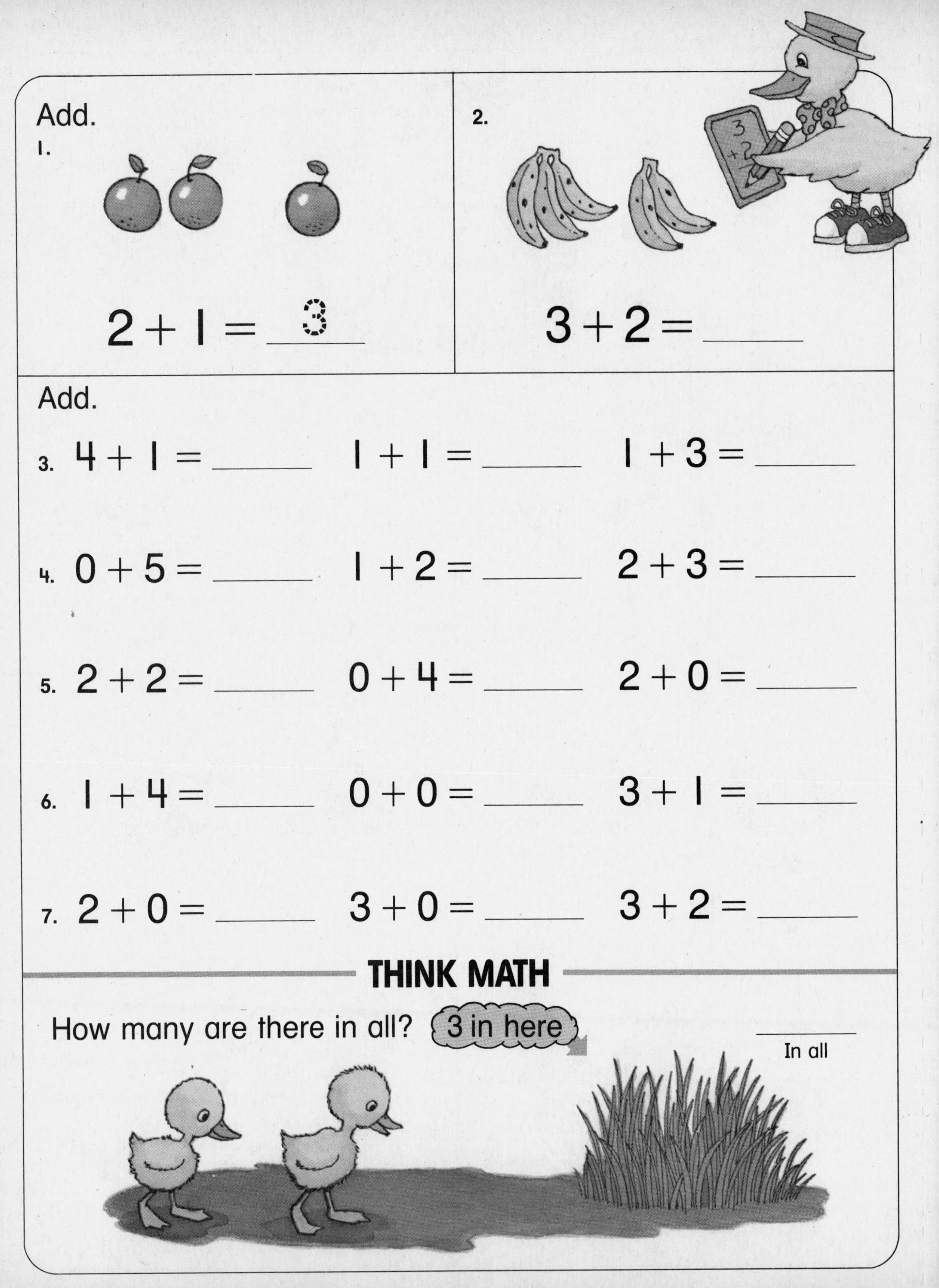

Add.

1. $2 + 1 = \underline{3}$

2. $3 + 2 = \underline{\quad}$

Add.

3. $4 + 1 = \underline{\quad}$ $1 + 1 = \underline{\quad}$ $1 + 3 = \underline{\quad}$

4. $0 + 5 = \underline{\quad}$ $1 + 2 = \underline{\quad}$ $2 + 3 = \underline{\quad}$

5. $2 + 2 = \underline{\quad}$ $0 + 4 = \underline{\quad}$ $2 + 0 = \underline{\quad}$

6. $1 + 4 = \underline{\quad}$ $0 + 0 = \underline{\quad}$ $3 + 1 = \underline{\quad}$

7. $2 + 0 = \underline{\quad}$ $3 + 0 = \underline{\quad}$ $3 + 2 = \underline{\quad}$

THINK MATH

How many are there in all? 3 in here

_____ In all

Name ______________________

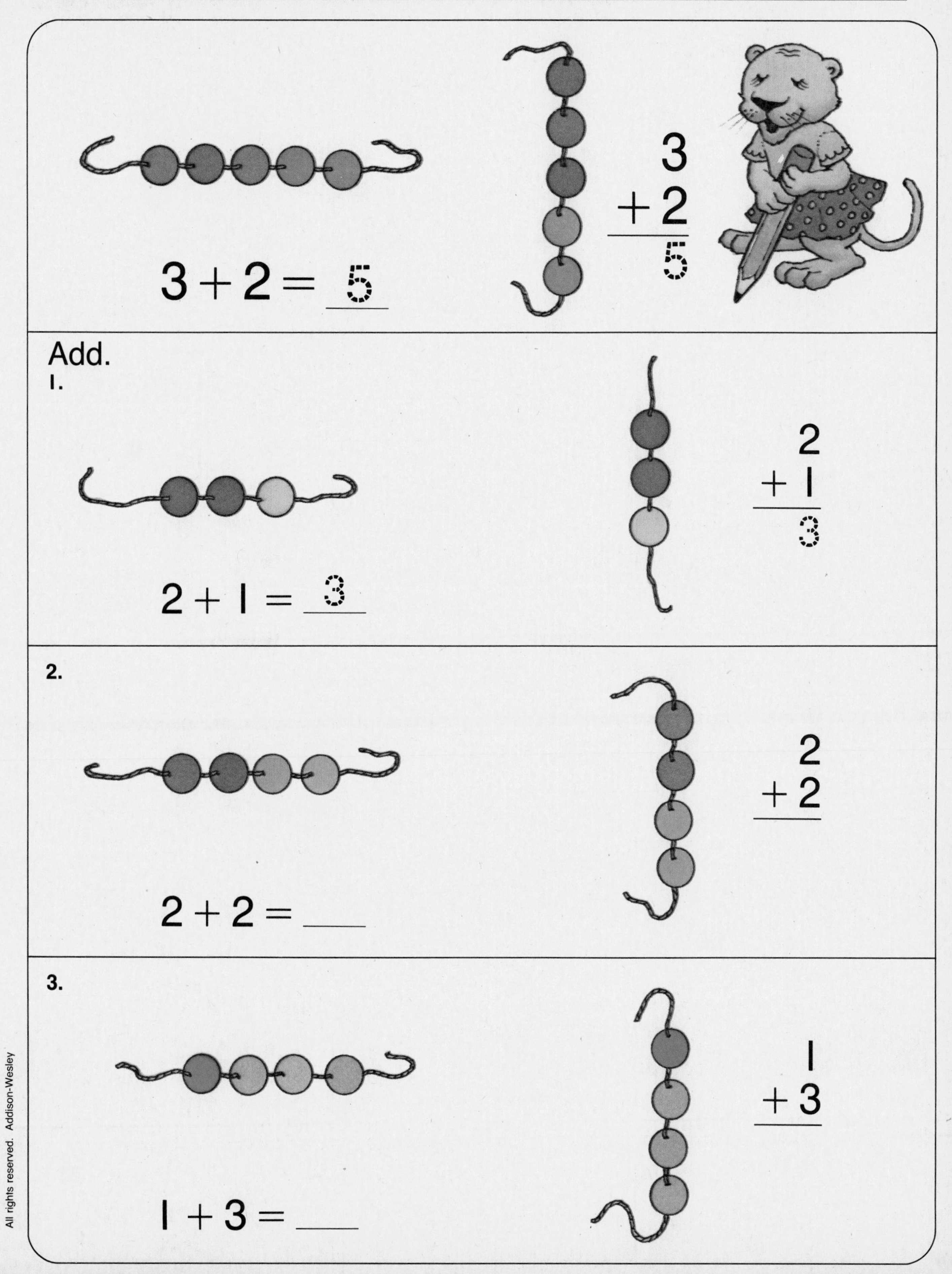

$3 + 2 = \underline{5}$

$$\begin{array}{r} 3 \\ +2 \\ \hline 5 \end{array}$$

Add.

1.

$2 + 1 = \underline{3}$

$$\begin{array}{r} 2 \\ +1 \\ \hline 3 \end{array}$$

2.

$2 + 2 = \underline{\quad}$

$$\begin{array}{r} 2 \\ +2 \\ \hline \end{array}$$

3.

$1 + 3 = \underline{\quad}$

$$\begin{array}{r} 1 \\ +3 \\ \hline \end{array}$$

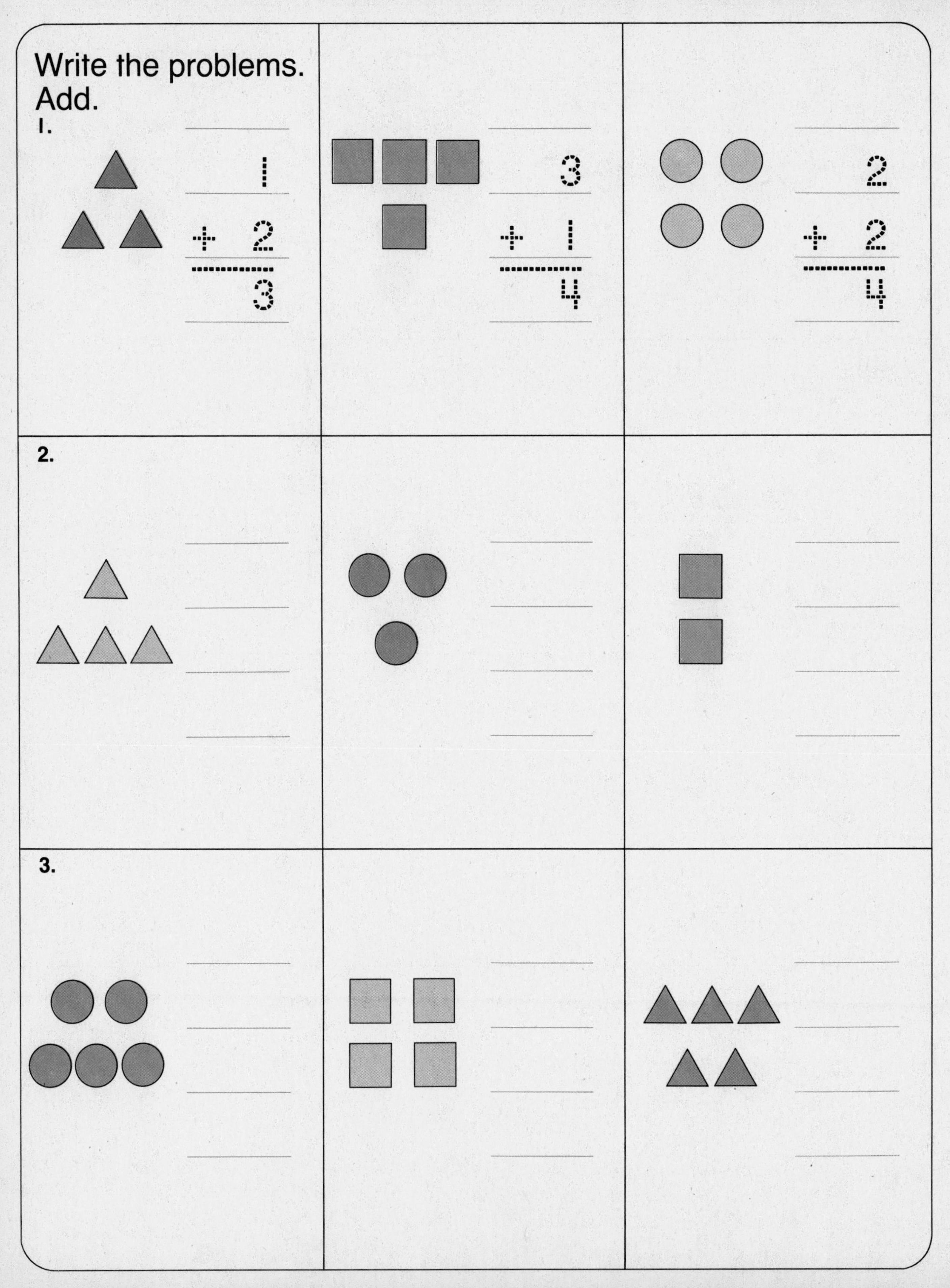
Write the problems.
Add.
1.
1
+ 2
3
3
+ 1
4
2
+ 2
4
2.
3.

Name ________________________________

Add. Color the balloons.
1 purple
2 yellow
3 green
4 red
5 blue
1 + 2
2 + 0
1 + 4
2 + 2
2 + 1
1 + 0
3 + 2
1 + 3
3 + 0
2 + 3
1 + 1
4 + 1
3 + 1

Add.

1. $\begin{array}{r} 1 \\ +4 \\ \hline \end{array}$ $\begin{array}{r} 3 \\ +0 \\ \hline \end{array}$ $\begin{array}{r} 1 \\ +3 \\ \hline \end{array}$ $\begin{array}{r} 2 \\ +2 \\ \hline \end{array}$ $\begin{array}{r} 0 \\ +2 \\ \hline \end{array}$

2. $\begin{array}{r} 2 \\ +1 \\ \hline \end{array}$ $\begin{array}{r} 0 \\ +4 \\ \hline \end{array}$ $\begin{array}{r} 2 \\ +3 \\ \hline \end{array}$ $\begin{array}{r} 3 \\ +1 \\ \hline \end{array}$ $\begin{array}{r} 1 \\ +2 \\ \hline \end{array}$ $\begin{array}{r} 1 \\ +0 \\ \hline \end{array}$

3. $\begin{array}{r} 4 \\ +1 \\ \hline \end{array}$ $\begin{array}{r} 0 \\ +1 \\ \hline \end{array}$ $\begin{array}{r} 4 \\ +0 \\ \hline \end{array}$ $\begin{array}{r} 3 \\ +2 \\ \hline \end{array}$ $\begin{array}{r} 5 \\ +0 \\ \hline \end{array}$ $\begin{array}{r} 2 \\ +1 \\ \hline \end{array}$

4. $\begin{array}{r} 0 \\ +3 \\ \hline \end{array}$ $\begin{array}{r} 2 \\ +3 \\ \hline \end{array}$ $\begin{array}{r} 2 \\ +0 \\ \hline \end{array}$ $\begin{array}{r} 2 \\ +2 \\ \hline \end{array}$ $\begin{array}{r} 3 \\ +1 \\ \hline \end{array}$ $\begin{array}{r} 1 \\ +1 \\ \hline \end{array}$

SKILLKEEPER

Write the missing numbers.

1, 2, ___, ___, ___, 6, 7, ___, ___, ___

3, 4, 5, ___, ___, ___, 9, 10, ___, ___

Name ______________________________

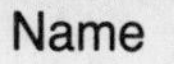

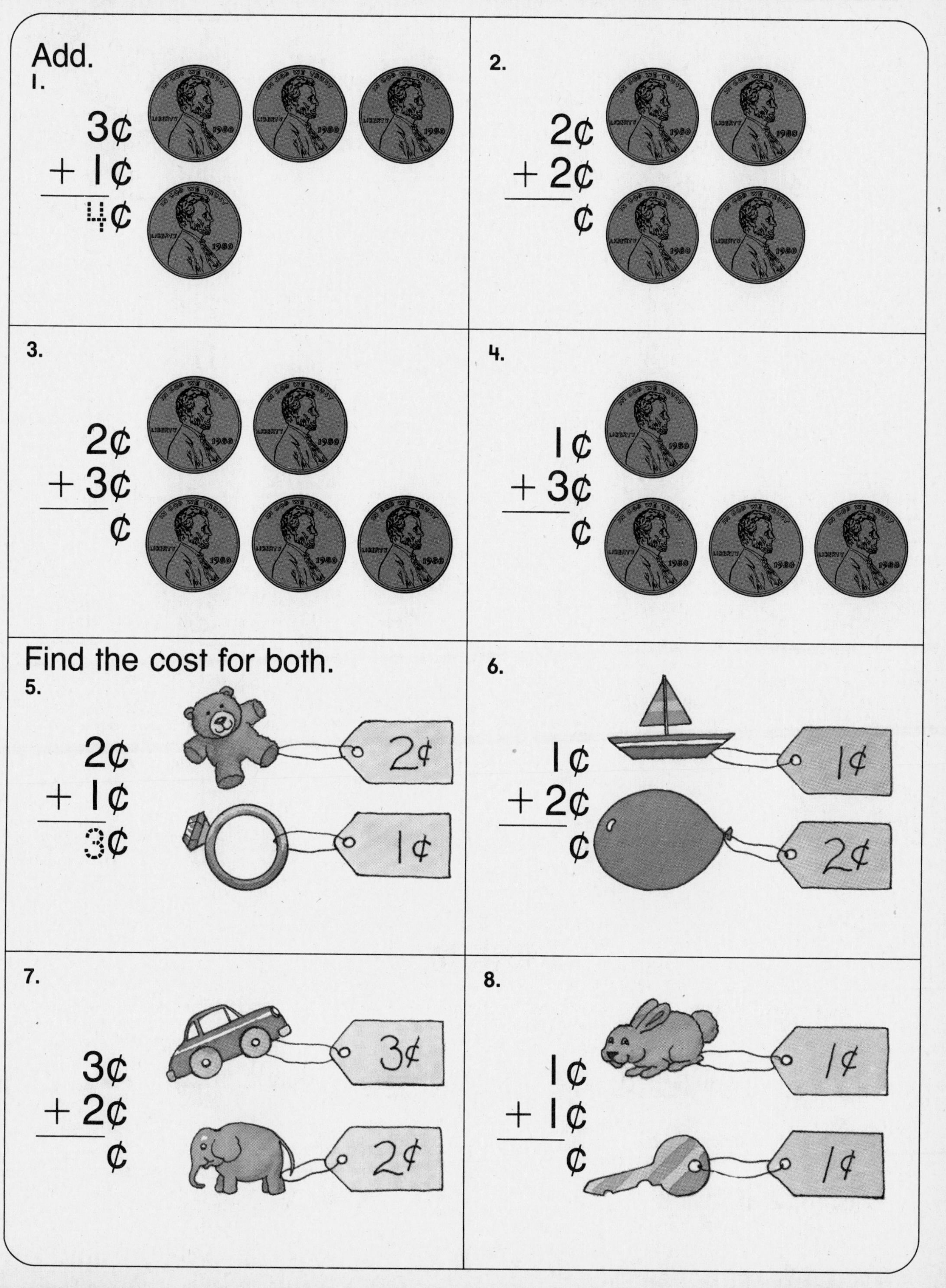

Add.

1. 3¢ + 1¢ = 4¢

2. 2¢ + 2¢ = ___¢

3. 2¢ + 3¢ = ___¢

4. 1¢ + 3¢ = ___¢

Find the cost for both.

5. 2¢ + 1¢ = 3¢

6. 1¢ + 2¢ = ___¢

7. 3¢ + 2¢ = ___¢

8. 1¢ + 1¢ = ___¢

1¢
1¢

Adding pennies

(forty-five) **45**

Add.

1. $\begin{array}{r} 2 \\ +2 \\ \hline \end{array}$ $\begin{array}{r} 3 \\ +2 \\ \hline \end{array}$ $\begin{array}{r} 1 \\ +0 \\ \hline \end{array}$ $\begin{array}{r} 0 \\ +4 \\ \hline \end{array}$ $\begin{array}{r} 3 \\ +1 \\ \hline \end{array}$

2. $\begin{array}{r} 1 \\ +4 \\ \hline \end{array}$ $\begin{array}{r} 3 \\ +0 \\ \hline \end{array}$ $\begin{array}{r} 2 \\ +3 \\ \hline \end{array}$ $\begin{array}{r} 4 \\ +1 \\ \hline \end{array}$ $\begin{array}{r} 0 \\ +0 \\ \hline \end{array}$ $\begin{array}{r} 2 \\ +1 \\ \hline \end{array}$

3. $\begin{array}{r} 4 \\ +0 \\ \hline \end{array}$ $\begin{array}{r} 0 \\ +1 \\ \hline \end{array}$ $\begin{array}{r} 3 \\ +1 \\ \hline \end{array}$ $\begin{array}{r} 1 \\ +3 \\ \hline \end{array}$ $\begin{array}{r} 2 \\ +2 \\ \hline \end{array}$ $\begin{array}{r} 0 \\ +5 \\ \hline \end{array}$

4. $\begin{array}{r} 2 \\ +0 \\ \hline \end{array}$ $\begin{array}{r} 1 \\ +2 \\ \hline \end{array}$ $\begin{array}{r} 4 \\ +1 \\ \hline \end{array}$ $\begin{array}{r} 3 \\ +2 \\ \hline \end{array}$ $\begin{array}{r} 1 \\ +1 \\ \hline \end{array}$ $\begin{array}{r} 2 \\ +3 \\ \hline \end{array}$

THINK MATH

Estimate. Which has more? Ring it.

Problem Solving

QUESTION
DATA
PLAN
ANSWER
CHECK

Name ____________________

Tell a story. Answer the question.

1. How many are there in all?

_____ in all

2. How many are there in all?

_____ in all

3. How many are there in all?

_____ in all

4. How many are there in all?

_____ in all

5. How many are there in all?

_____ in all

6. How many are there in all?

_____ in all

Problem-Solving Strategy

Cathy's Clothes

Color.

How many ways can you dress Cathy? _______ ways

Name ______________________________

CHAPTER REVIEW/TEST

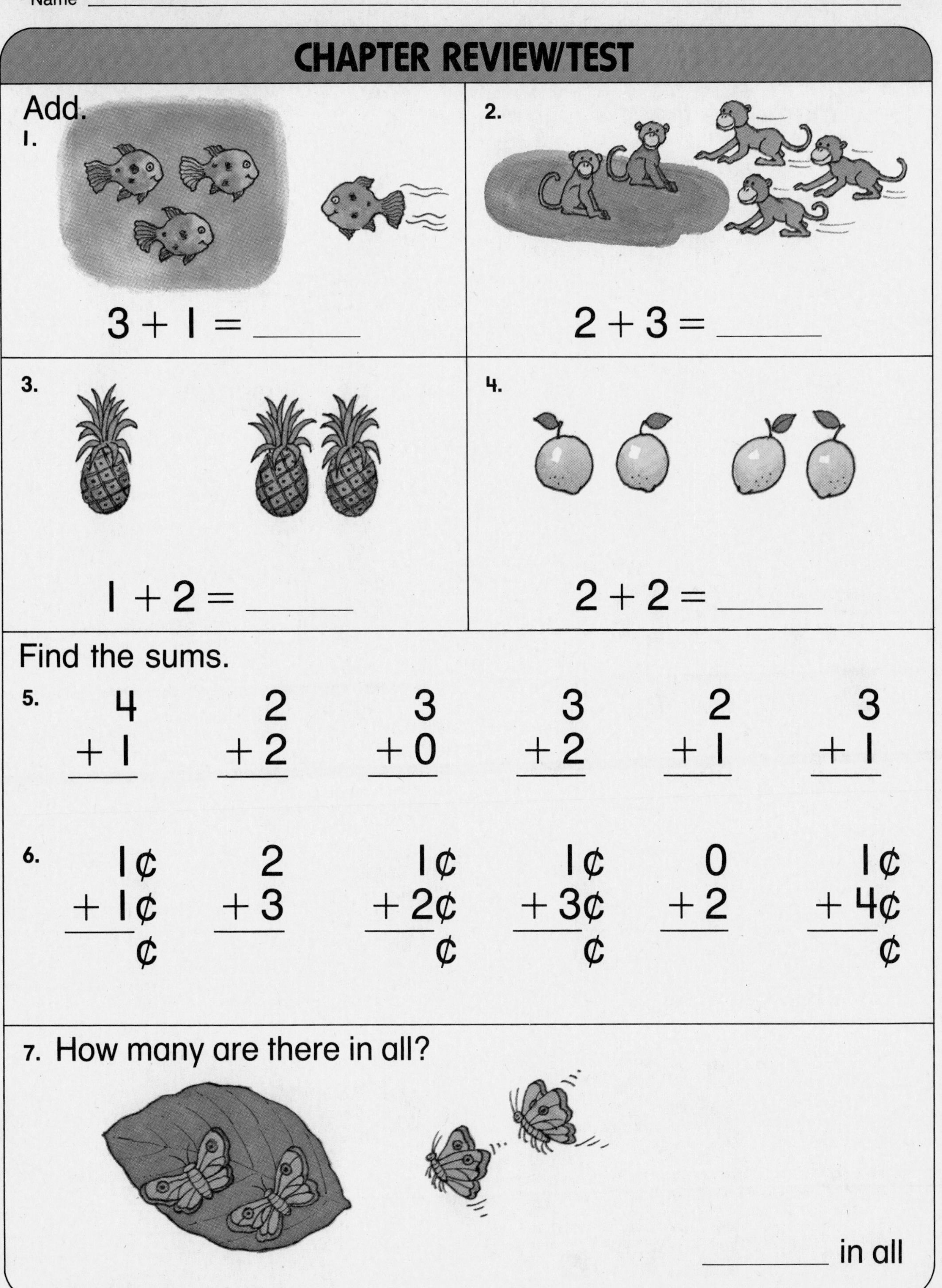

Add.

1. $3 + 1 =$ ______

2. $2 + 3 =$ ______

3. $1 + 2 =$ ______

4. $2 + 2 =$ ______

Find the sums.

5.

4	2	3	3	2	3
+ 1	+ 2	+ 0	+ 2	+ 1	+ 1

6.

1¢	2	1¢	1¢	0	1¢
+ 1¢	+ 3	+ 2¢	+ 3¢	+ 2	+ 4¢
¢		¢	¢		¢

7. How many are there in all?

______ in all

Name ______________________________

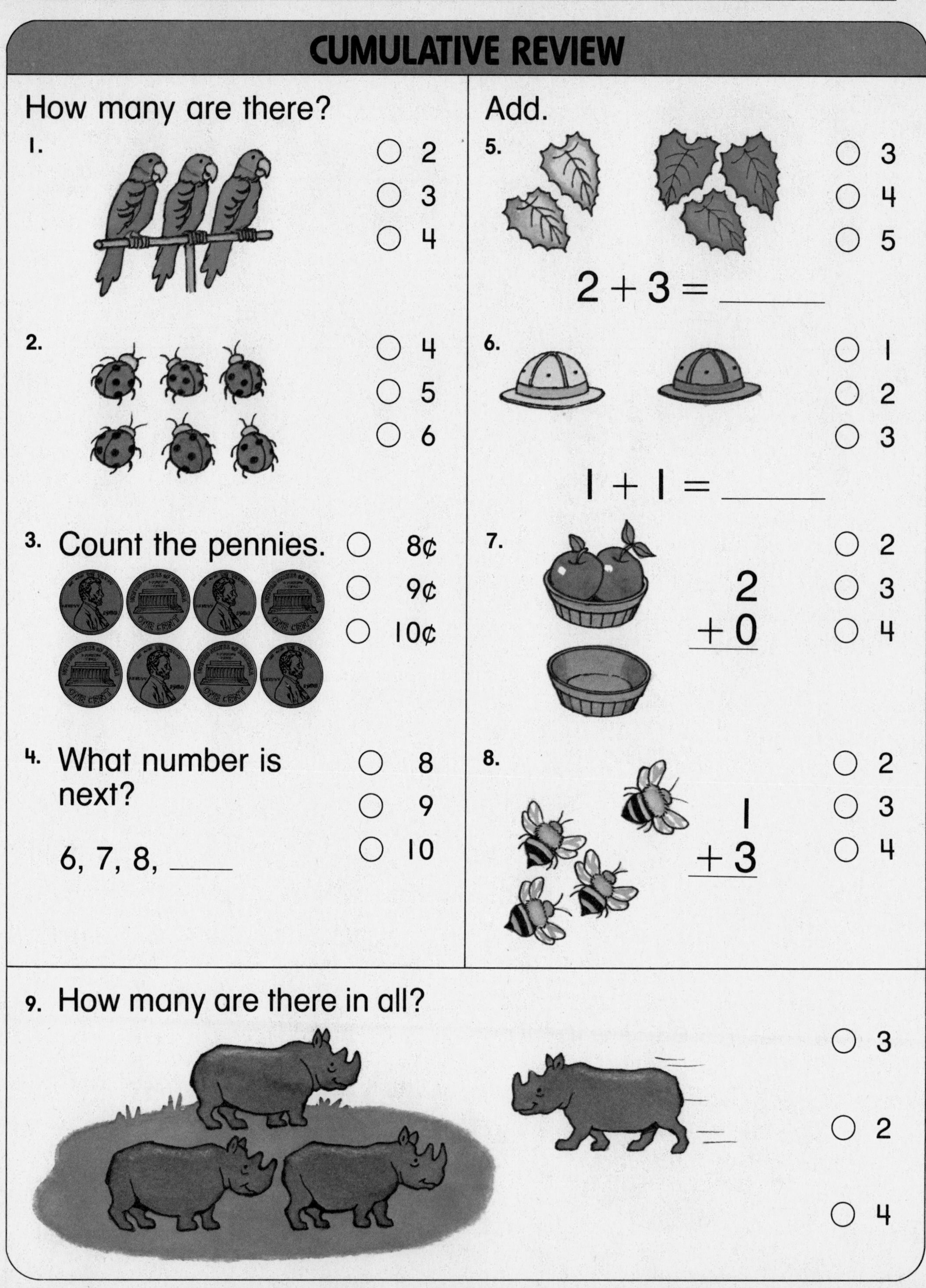

CUMULATIVE REVIEW

How many are there?

1\.
- ○ 2
- ○ 3
- ○ 4

2\.
- ○ 4
- ○ 5
- ○ 6

3\. Count the pennies.
- ○ 8¢
- ○ 9¢
- ○ 10¢

4\. What number is next?

6, 7, 8, ____
- ○ 8
- ○ 9
- ○ 10

Add.

5\. $2 + 3 =$ ______
- ○ 3
- ○ 4
- ○ 5

6\. $1 + 1 =$ ______
- ○ 1
- ○ 2
- ○ 3

7\. $\begin{array}{r} 2 \\ +0 \\ \hline \end{array}$
- ○ 2
- ○ 3
- ○ 4

8\. $\begin{array}{r} 1 \\ +3 \\ \hline \end{array}$
- ○ 2
- ○ 3
- ○ 4

9\. How many are there in all?
- ○ 3
- ○ 2
- ○ 4

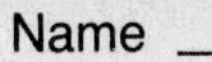

Name

ANOTHER LOOK

$$\begin{array}{r} 2 \\ +\ 1 \\ \hline 3 \end{array}$$ ← In all

$$\begin{array}{r} 3 \\ +\ 1 \\ \hline 4 \end{array}$$ ← In all

Add.

1.

$$\begin{array}{r} 1 \\ +\ 3 \\ \hline \end{array}$$ ← In all

$$\begin{array}{r} 2 \\ +\ 2 \\ \hline \end{array}$$ ← In all

2.

$$\begin{array}{r} 0 \\ +\ 3 \\ \hline \end{array}$$ ← In all

$$\begin{array}{r} 3 \\ +\ 2 \\ \hline \end{array}$$ ← In all

Draw your own pictures.
Find the sums.

3.

$$\begin{array}{r} 2 \\ +\ 2 \\ \hline \end{array}$$ ← In all

$$\begin{array}{r} 1 \\ +\ 2 \\ \hline \end{array}$$ ← In all

4.

$$\begin{array}{r} 2 \\ +\ 3 \\ \hline \end{array}$$ ← In all

$$\begin{array}{r} 1 \\ +\ 4 \\ \hline \end{array}$$ ← In all

Name ______________________________

ENRICHMENT

Write the sums in the table. Color.

+	0	1	2	3	4	5
0						5
1				4		
2						
3		4				
4						
5	5					

3 Name ______

DIFFERENCES TO 5

Use counters.

1\. Put in 4 Take out 1 — 3 are left

2\. Put in 3 Take out 2 — ___ is left

3\. Put in 5 Take out 3 — ___ are left

4\. Put in 3 Take out 1 — ___ are left

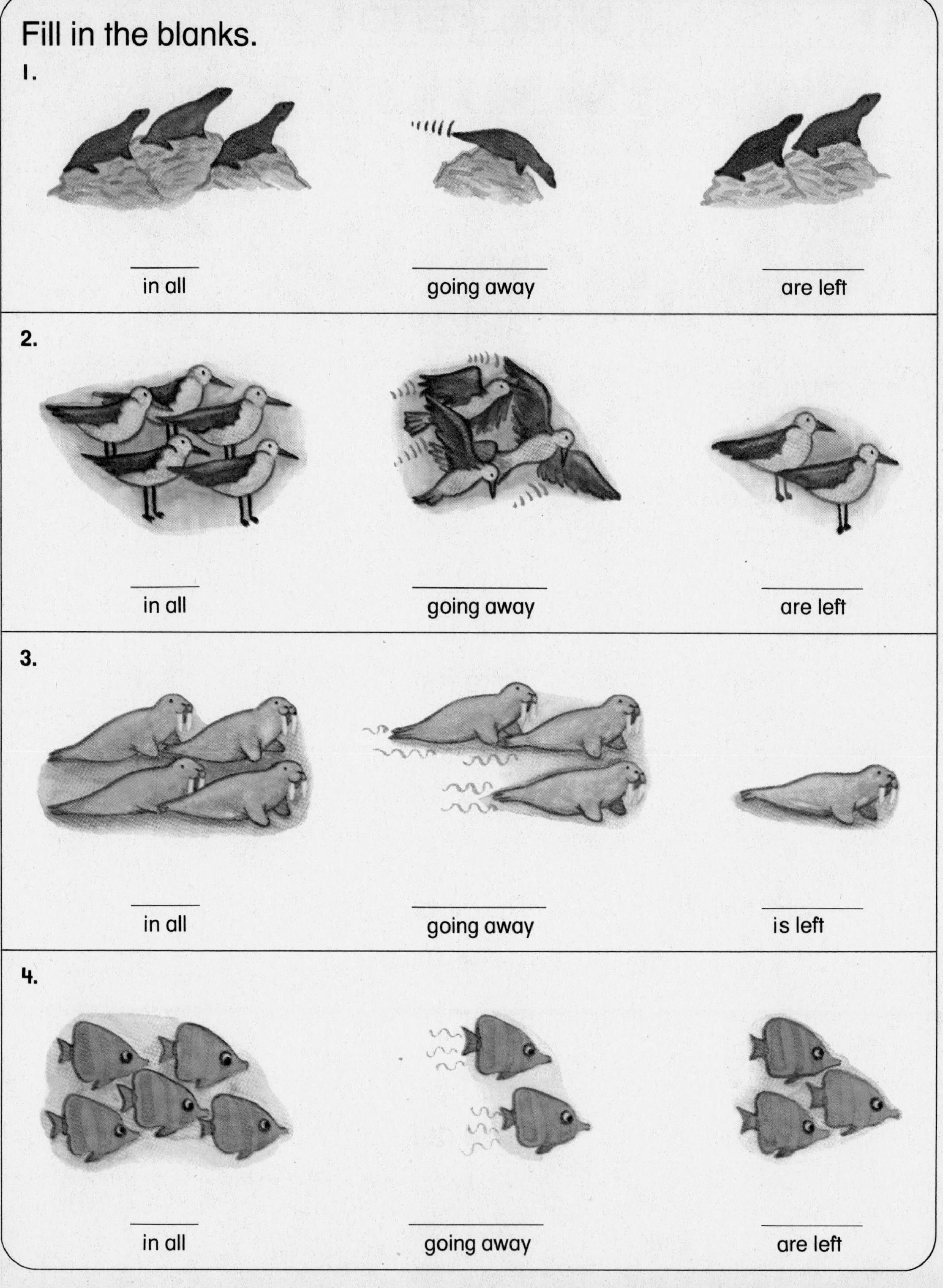

Fill in the blanks.

1.

_____ in all

_____ going away

_____ are left

2.

_____ in all

_____ going away

_____ are left

3.

_____ in all

_____ going away

_____ is left

4.

_____ in all

_____ going away

_____ are left

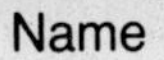

Name ____________________

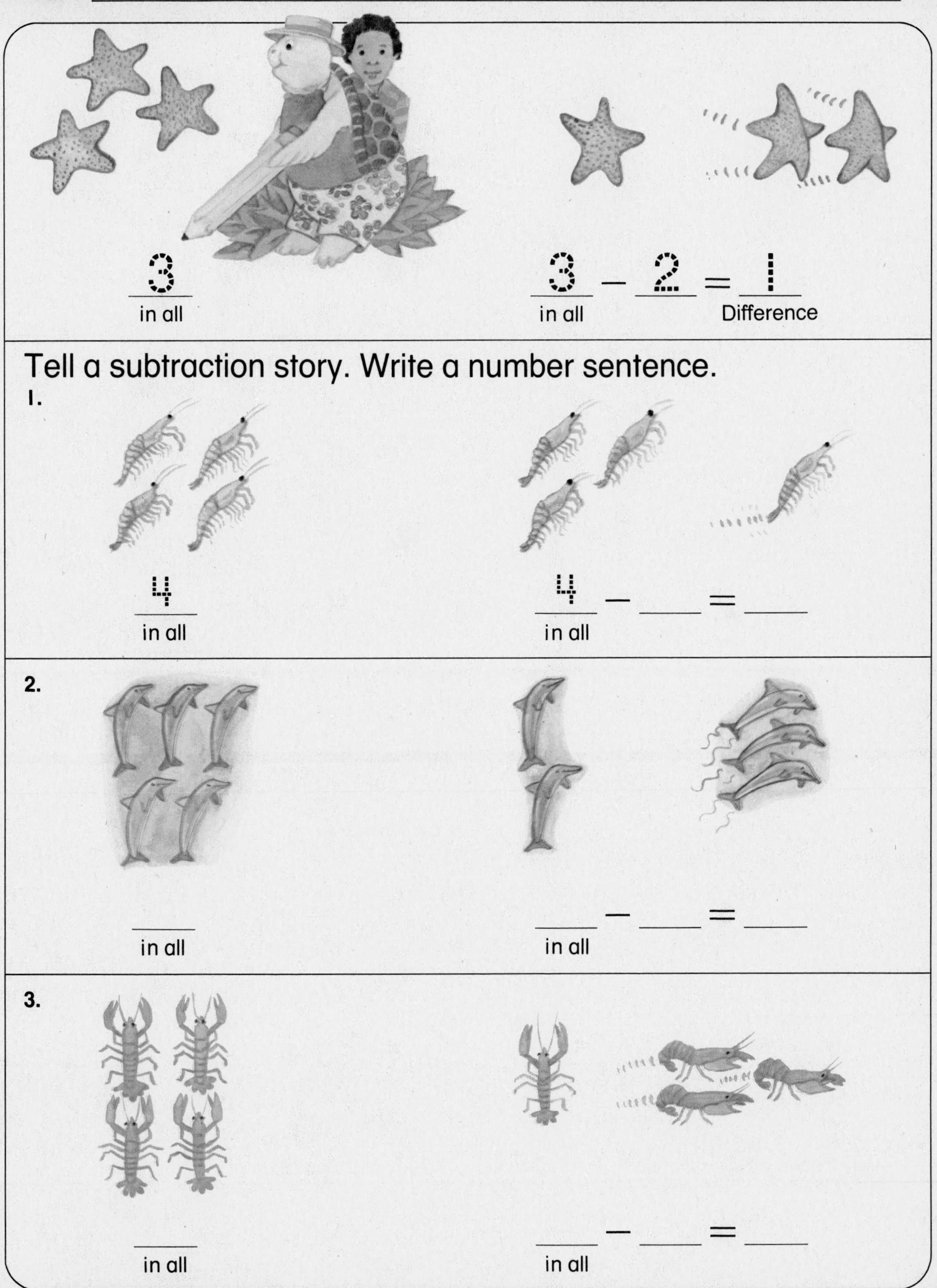

3 in all

3 − 2 = 1
in all　Difference

Tell a subtraction story. Write a number sentence.

1.

4 in all

4 − ___ = ___
in all

2.

___ in all

___ − ___ = ___
in all

3.

___ in all

___ − ___ = ___
in all

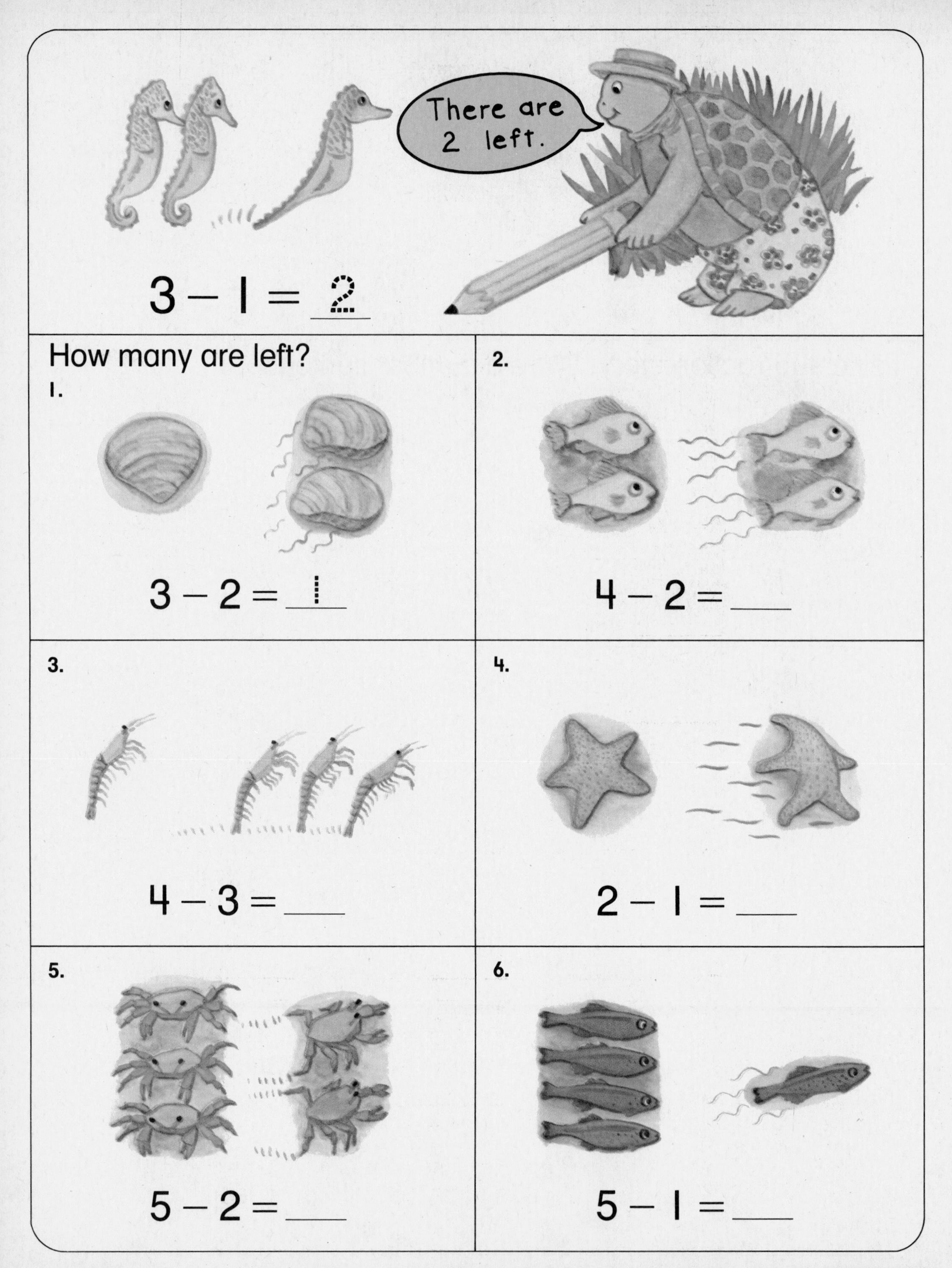
There are 2 left.
3 − 1 = 2
How many are left?
1.
3 − 2 = 1
2.
4 − 2 = ___
3.
4 − 3 = ___
4.
2 − 1 = ___
5.
5 − 2 = ___
6.
5 − 1 = ___

Name ___

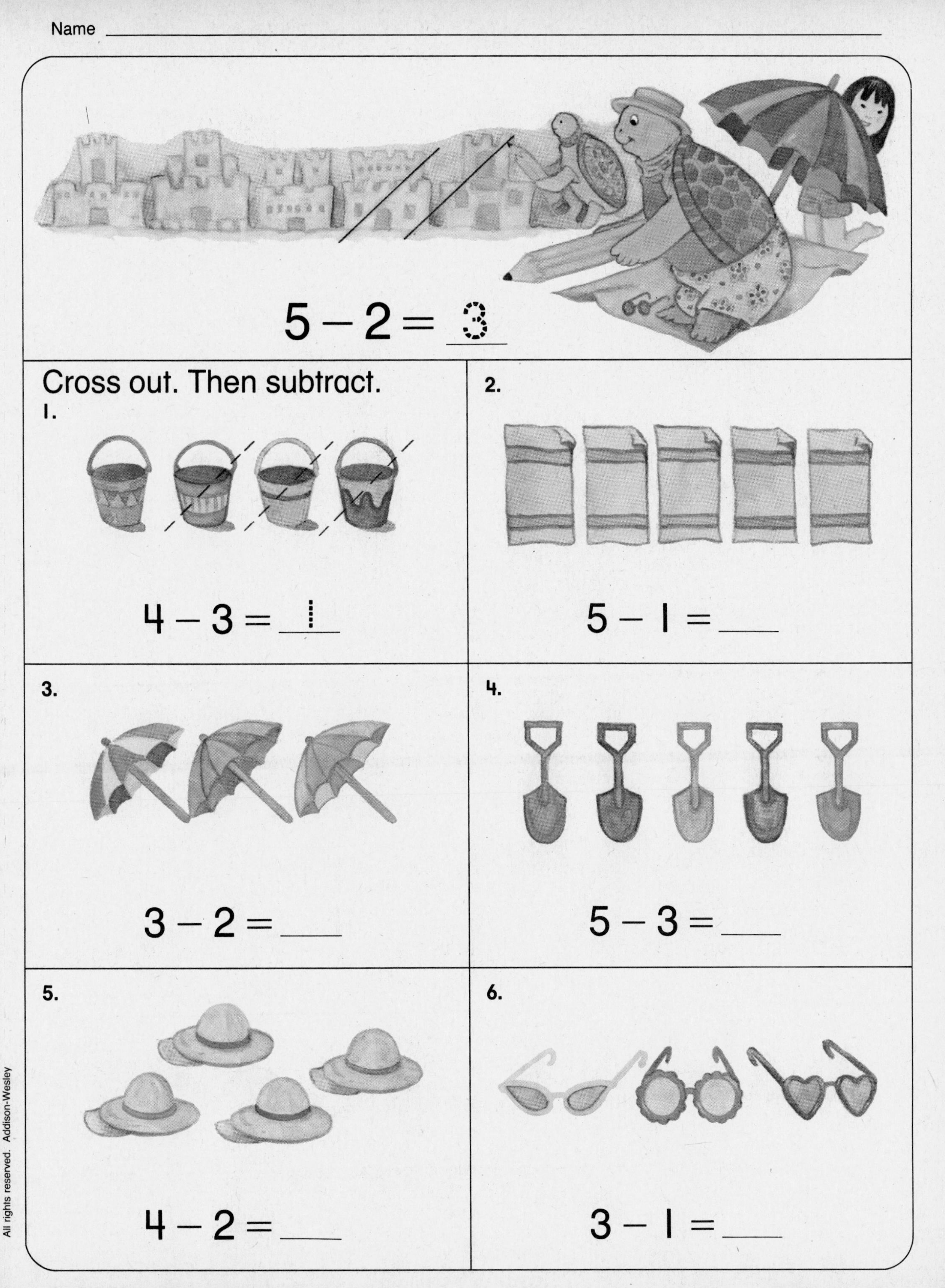

$5 - 2 =$ 3

Cross out. Then subtract.

1. $4 - 3 =$ 1

2. $5 - 1 =$ ___

3. $3 - 2 =$ ___

4. $5 - 3 =$ ___

5. $4 - 2 =$ ___

6. $3 - 1 =$ ___

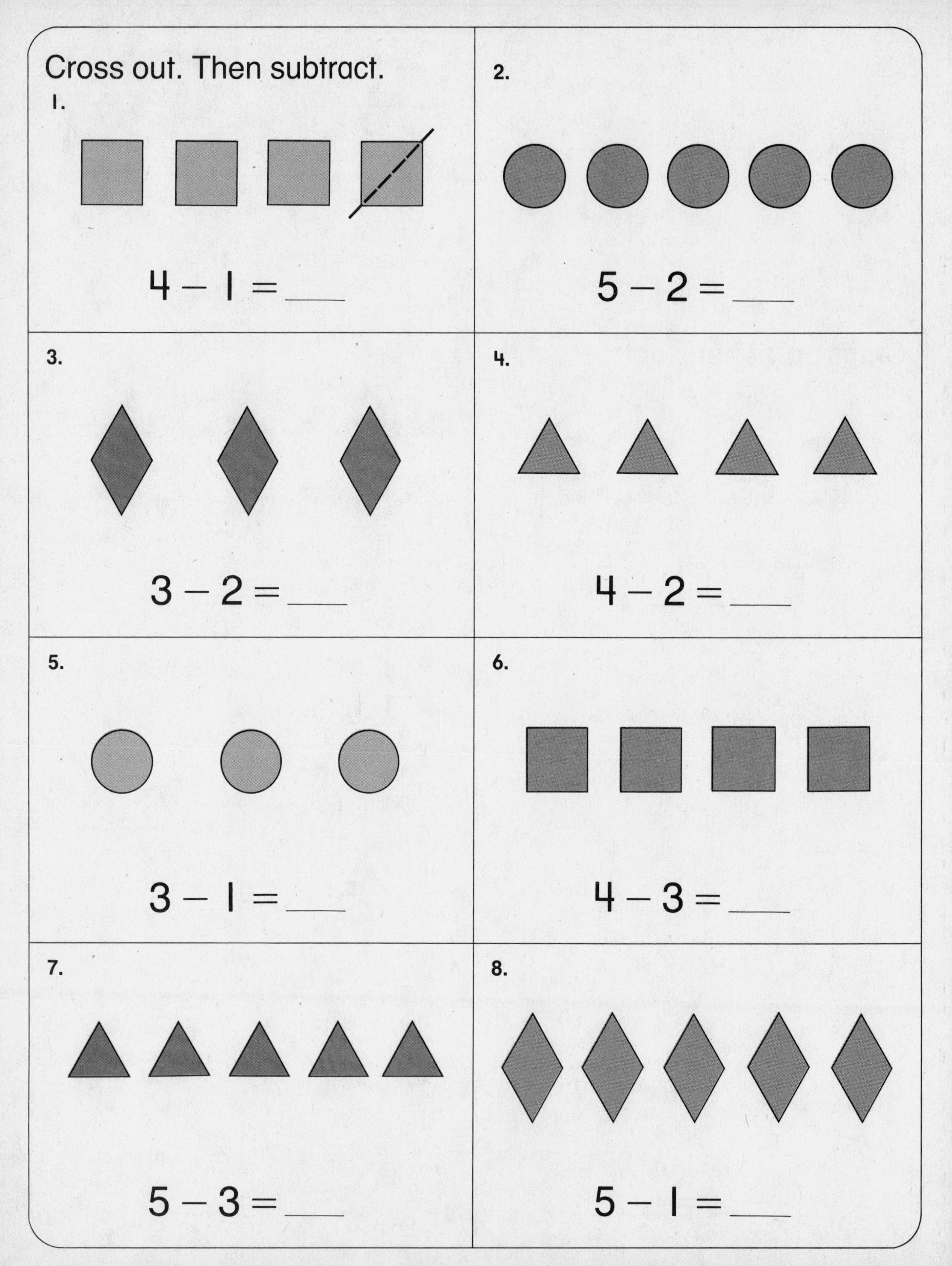
Cross out. Then subtract.
1.
4 − 1 = ___
2.
5 − 2 = ___
3.
3 − 2 = ___
4.
4 − 2 = ___
5.
3 − 1 = ___
6.
4 − 3 = ___
7.
5 − 3 = ___
8.
5 − 1 = ___

Name ______________________________

$2 - 2 =$ 0 $4 - 0 =$ 4

Subtract.

1. $3 - 3 =$ ____

2. $2 - 0 =$ ____

3. $5 - 0 =$ ____

4. $4 - 4 =$ ____

5. $3 - 0 =$ ____

6. $5 - 5 =$ ____

Subtract.

1. $4 - 1 =$ ___

2. $5 - 2 =$ ___

3. $2 - 1 =$ ___ $5 - 1 =$ ___ $4 - 2 =$ ___

4. $1 - 1 =$ ___ $4 - 4 =$ ___ $2 - 2 =$ ___

5. $5 - 3 =$ ___ $3 - 0 =$ ___ $3 - 2 =$ ___

6. $2 - 0 =$ ___ $5 - 0 =$ ___ $3 - 3 =$ ___

7. $4 - 1 =$ ___ $4 - 0 =$ ___ $5 - 4 =$ ___

THINK MATH

How many are hiding? ___

Name ____________________

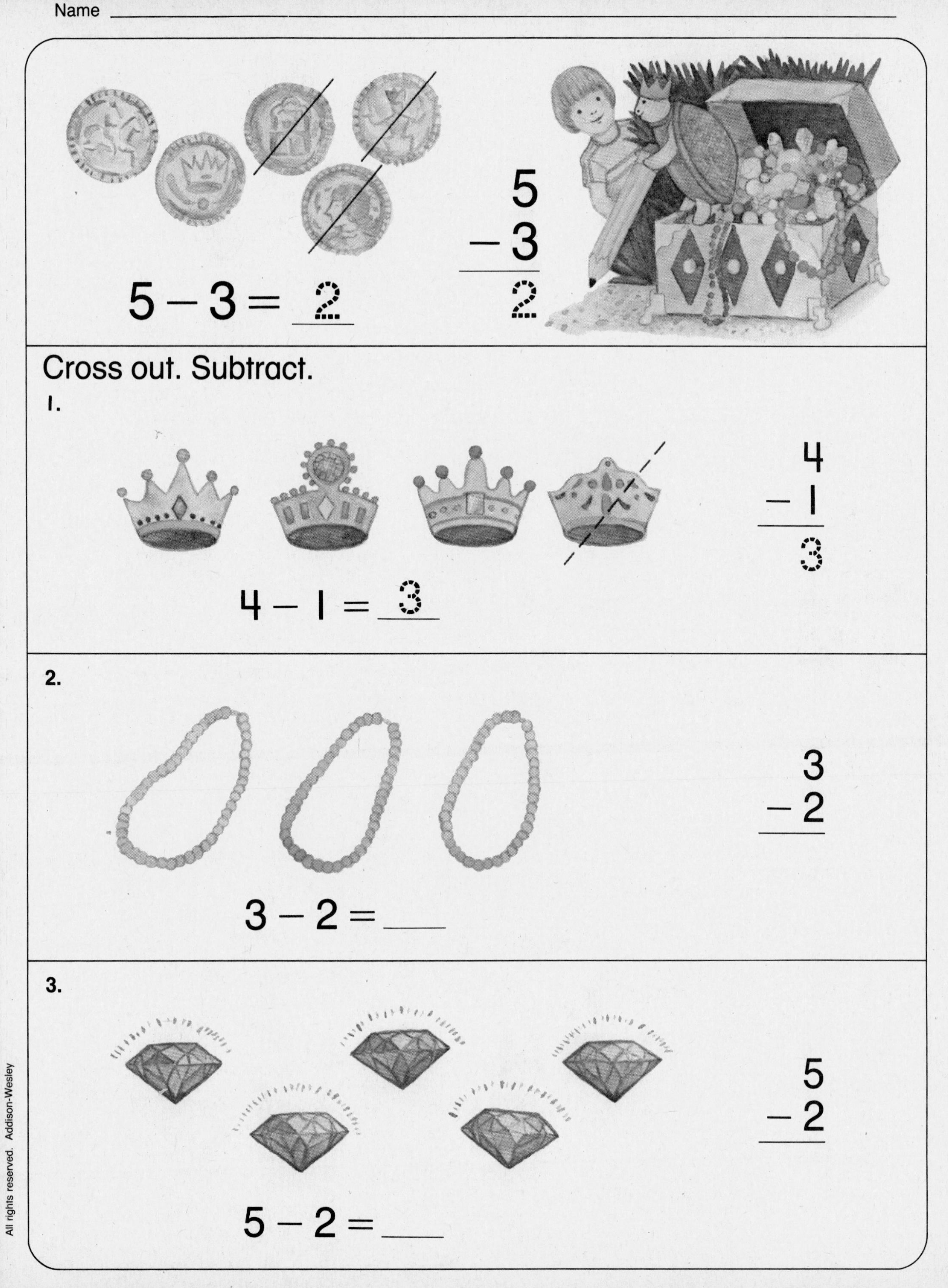

$5 - 3 = \underline{2}$

$$\begin{array}{r} 5 \\ -\ 3 \\ \hline 2 \end{array}$$

Cross out. Subtract.

1.

$4 - 1 = \underline{3}$

$$\begin{array}{r} 4 \\ -\ 1 \\ \hline 3 \end{array}$$

2.

$3 - 2 =$ ___

$$\begin{array}{r} 3 \\ -\ 2 \\ \hline \end{array}$$

3.

$5 - 2 =$ ___

$$\begin{array}{r} 5 \\ -\ 2 \\ \hline \end{array}$$

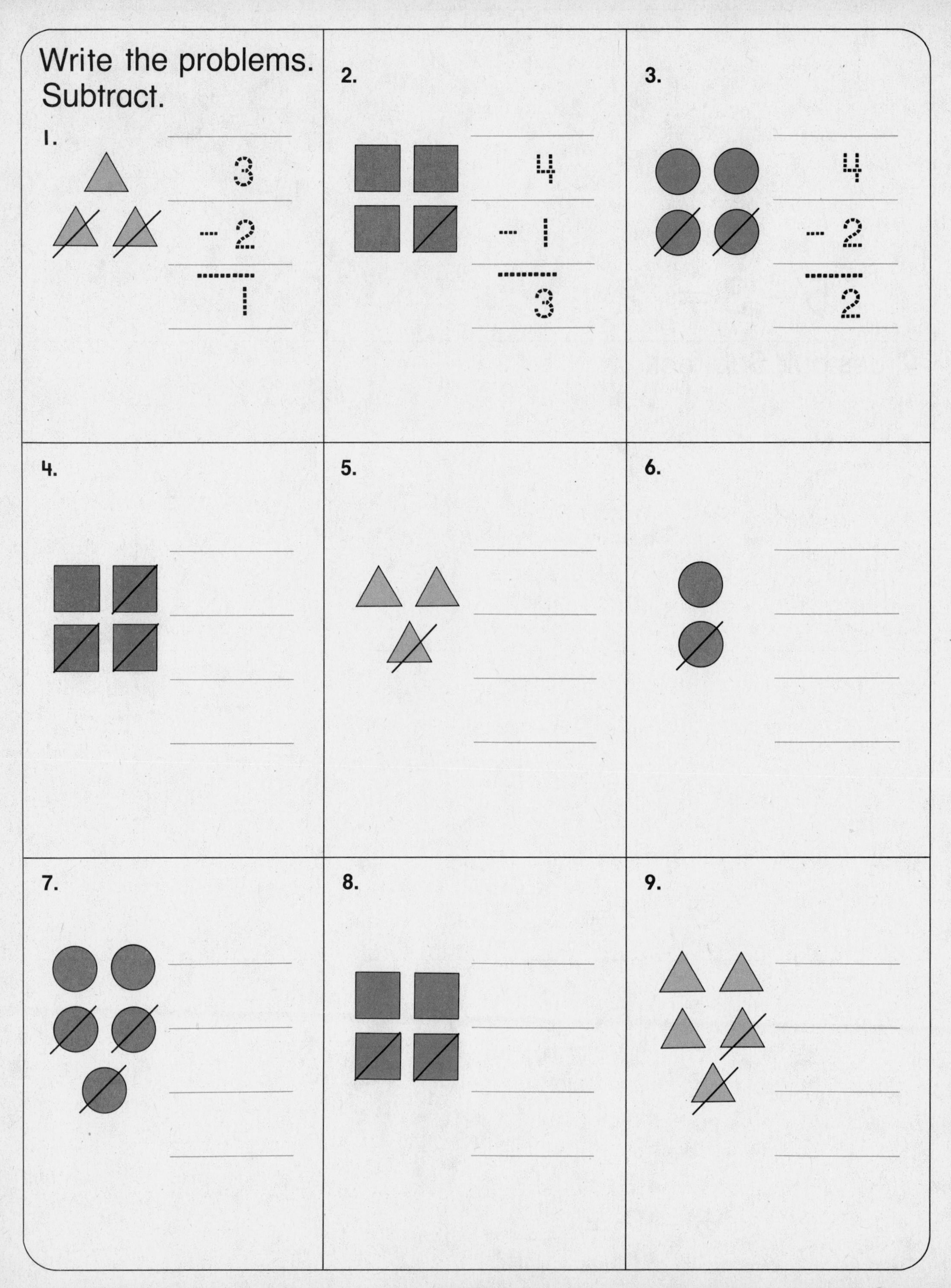

Write the problems.
Subtract.
1.
3
- 2
1
2.
4
- 1
3
3.
4
- 2
2
4.
5.
6.
7.
8.
9.

Name ______________________________

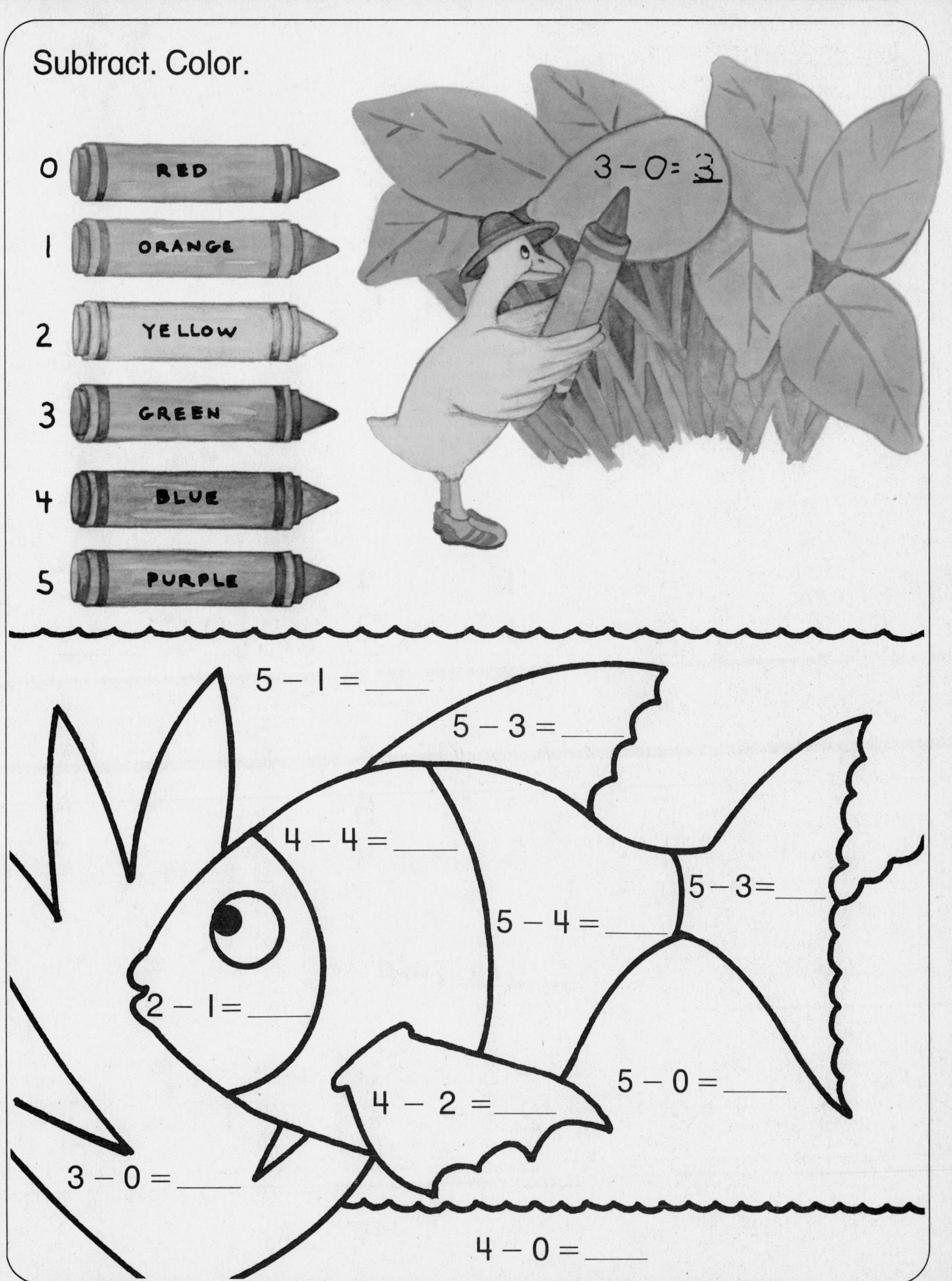

Subtract. Color.
0 RED
1 ORANGE
2 YELLOW
3 GREEN
4 BLUE
5 PURPLE
3 − 0 = 3
5 − 1 = ____
5 − 3 = ____
4 − 4 = ____
5 − 3 = ____
5 − 4 = ____
2 − 1 = ____
5 − 0 = ____
4 − 2 = ____
3 − 0 = ____
4 − 0 = ____

Subtract.

1. $2 - 0$ $3 - 1$ $1 - 0$ $5 - 3$ $2 - 1$

2. $5 - 3$ $4 - 1$ $5 - 1$ $3 - 2$ $4 - 0$ $5 - 5$

3. $1 - 1$ $5 - 2$ $4 - 3$ $4 - 2$ $3 - 0$ $5 - 0$

4. $2 - 1$ $5 - 1$ $3 - 3$ $5 - 4$ $4 - 4$ $5 - 2$

SKILLKEEPER

Add.

$3 + 1$ $2 + 3$ $2 + 2$ $4 + 1$ $1 + 2$ $3 + 2$

Name ______________________________

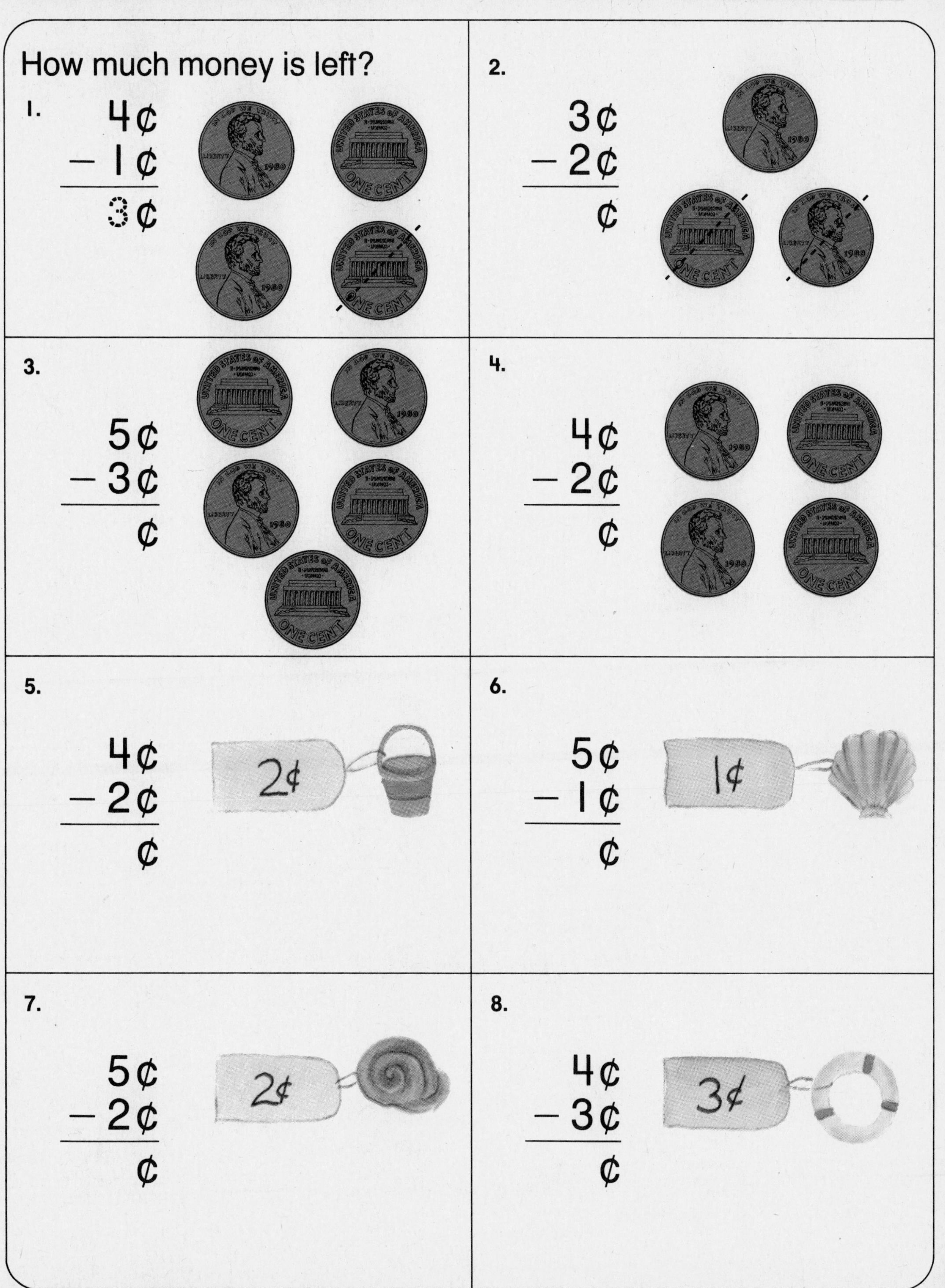
How much money is left?
1.
4¢
− 1¢
3¢
ONE CENT
LIBERTY
1980
2.
3¢
− 2¢
¢
3.
5¢
− 3¢
¢
4.
4¢
− 2¢
¢
5.
4¢
− 2¢
¢
2¢
6.
5¢
− 1¢
¢
1¢
7.
5¢
− 2¢
¢
2¢
8.
4¢
− 3¢
¢
3¢

Subtract.

1. $\begin{array}{r} 4 \\ -3 \\ \hline \end{array}$ $\begin{array}{r} 2 \\ -1 \\ \hline \end{array}$ $\begin{array}{r} 5 \\ -2 \\ \hline \end{array}$ $\begin{array}{r} 3 \\ -0 \\ \hline \end{array}$ $\begin{array}{r} 4 \\ -1 \\ \hline \end{array}$

2. $\begin{array}{r} 5 \\ -4 \\ \hline \end{array}$ $\begin{array}{r} 5 \\ -3 \\ \hline \end{array}$ $\begin{array}{r} 4 \\ -4 \\ \hline \end{array}$ $\begin{array}{r} 5 \\ -0 \\ \hline \end{array}$ $\begin{array}{r} 3 \\ -2 \\ \hline \end{array}$ $\begin{array}{r} 5 \\ -2 \\ \hline \end{array}$

3. $\begin{array}{r} 4 \\ -1 \\ \hline \end{array}$ $\begin{array}{r} 5 \\ -1 \\ \hline \end{array}$ $\begin{array}{r} 3 \\ -1 \\ \hline \end{array}$ $\begin{array}{r} 4 \\ -2 \\ \hline \end{array}$ $\begin{array}{r} 2 \\ -2 \\ \hline \end{array}$ $\begin{array}{r} 0 \\ -0 \\ \hline \end{array}$

4. $\begin{array}{r} 5 \\ -5 \\ \hline \end{array}$ $\begin{array}{r} 1 \\ -0 \\ \hline \end{array}$ $\begin{array}{r} 4 \\ -0 \\ \hline \end{array}$ $\begin{array}{r} 3 \\ -3 \\ \hline \end{array}$ $\begin{array}{r} 5 \\ -3 \\ \hline \end{array}$ $\begin{array}{r} 2 \\ -0 \\ \hline \end{array}$

THINK MATH

Write + or − in each ○.

$\begin{array}{r} 5 \\ \bigcirc 2 \\ \hline 3 \end{array}$ $\begin{array}{r} 2 \\ \bigcirc 2 \\ \hline 4 \end{array}$ $\begin{array}{r} 4 \\ \bigcirc 1 \\ \hline 3 \end{array}$ $\begin{array}{r} 3 \\ \bigcirc 2 \\ \hline 5 \end{array}$ $\begin{array}{r} 1 \\ \bigcirc 2 \\ \hline 3 \end{array}$ $\begin{array}{r} 5 \\ \bigcirc 3 \\ \hline 2 \end{array}$

Name ________________

Add or subtract.

1.

$\begin{array}{r} 4 \\ +1 \\ \hline \end{array}$	$\begin{array}{r} 3 \\ +2 \\ \hline \end{array}$	$\begin{array}{r} 0 \\ +0 \\ \hline \end{array}$	$\begin{array}{r} 1 \\ +3 \\ \hline \end{array}$	$\begin{array}{r} 2 \\ +1 \\ \hline \end{array}$

2.

$\begin{array}{r} 3 \\ -3 \\ \hline \end{array}$	$\begin{array}{r} 5 \\ -1 \\ \hline \end{array}$	$\begin{array}{r} 2 \\ -0 \\ \hline \end{array}$	$\begin{array}{r} 1 \\ -1 \\ \hline \end{array}$	$\begin{array}{r} 2 \\ -1 \\ \hline \end{array}$	$\begin{array}{r} 4 \\ -2 \\ \hline \end{array}$

3.

$\begin{array}{r} 1 \\ +1 \\ \hline \end{array}$	$\begin{array}{r} 2 \\ +2 \\ \hline \end{array}$	$\begin{array}{r} 1 \\ +2 \\ \hline \end{array}$	$\begin{array}{r} 4 \\ +0 \\ \hline \end{array}$	$\begin{array}{r} 2 \\ +3 \\ \hline \end{array}$	$\begin{array}{r} 2 \\ +1 \\ \hline \end{array}$

4.

$\begin{array}{r} 3 \\ -2 \\ \hline \end{array}$	$\begin{array}{r} 2 \\ -1 \\ \hline \end{array}$	$\begin{array}{r} 4 \\ -3 \\ \hline \end{array}$	$\begin{array}{r} 5 \\ -2 \\ \hline \end{array}$	$\begin{array}{r} 4 \\ -4 \\ \hline \end{array}$	$\begin{array}{r} 5 \\ -1 \\ \hline \end{array}$

5.

$\begin{array}{r} 4 \\ +1 \\ \hline \end{array}$	$\begin{array}{r} 3 \\ +2 \\ \hline \end{array}$	$\begin{array}{r} 1 \\ +3 \\ \hline \end{array}$	$\begin{array}{r} 1 \\ +1 \\ \hline \end{array}$	$\begin{array}{r} 1 \\ +3 \\ \hline \end{array}$	$\begin{array}{r} 3 \\ +0 \\ \hline \end{array}$

6.

$\begin{array}{r} 3 \\ -2 \\ \hline \end{array}$	$\begin{array}{r} 3 \\ -0 \\ \hline \end{array}$	$\begin{array}{r} 2 \\ -2 \\ \hline \end{array}$	$\begin{array}{r} 5 \\ -3 \\ \hline \end{array}$	$\begin{array}{r} 2 \\ +1 \\ \hline \end{array}$	$\begin{array}{r} 5 \\ +0 \\ \hline \end{array}$

Add or subtract.

1. $\begin{array}{r} 1 \\ +\,1 \\ \hline \end{array}$ $\begin{array}{r} 1 \\ +\,4 \\ \hline \end{array}$ $\begin{array}{r} 5 \\ -\,2 \\ \hline \end{array}$ $\begin{array}{r} 2 \\ +\,3 \\ \hline \end{array}$ $\begin{array}{r} 4 \\ -\,4 \\ \hline \end{array}$

2. $\begin{array}{r} 5 \\ +\,0 \\ \hline \end{array}$ $\begin{array}{r} 3 \\ -\,2 \\ \hline \end{array}$ $\begin{array}{r} 4 \\ -\,4 \\ \hline \end{array}$ $\begin{array}{r} 3 \\ -\,0 \\ \hline \end{array}$ $\begin{array}{r} 5 \\ -\,4 \\ \hline \end{array}$ $\begin{array}{r} 3 \\ +\,1 \\ \hline \end{array}$

3. $\begin{array}{r} 2 \\ +\,1 \\ \hline \end{array}$ $\begin{array}{r} 4 \\ -\,3 \\ \hline \end{array}$ $\begin{array}{r} 5 \\ -\,5 \\ \hline \end{array}$ $\begin{array}{r} 1 \\ +\,2 \\ \hline \end{array}$ $\begin{array}{r} 4 \\ +\,1 \\ \hline \end{array}$ $\begin{array}{r} 3 \\ -\,1 \\ \hline \end{array}$

4. $\begin{array}{r} 1 \\ +\,3 \\ \hline \end{array}$ $\begin{array}{r} 3 \\ +\,2 \\ \hline \end{array}$ $\begin{array}{r} 4 \\ -\,1 \\ \hline \end{array}$ $\begin{array}{r} 2 \\ +\,2 \\ \hline \end{array}$ $\begin{array}{r} 4 \\ -\,2 \\ \hline \end{array}$ $\begin{array}{r} 5 \\ -\,1 \\ \hline \end{array}$

SKILLKEEPER

Write the numbers.

1, 2, ____, 4   8, 9, ____, ____

5, ____, 7, ____   6, ____, ____, 9

Problem Solving

Name ____________________

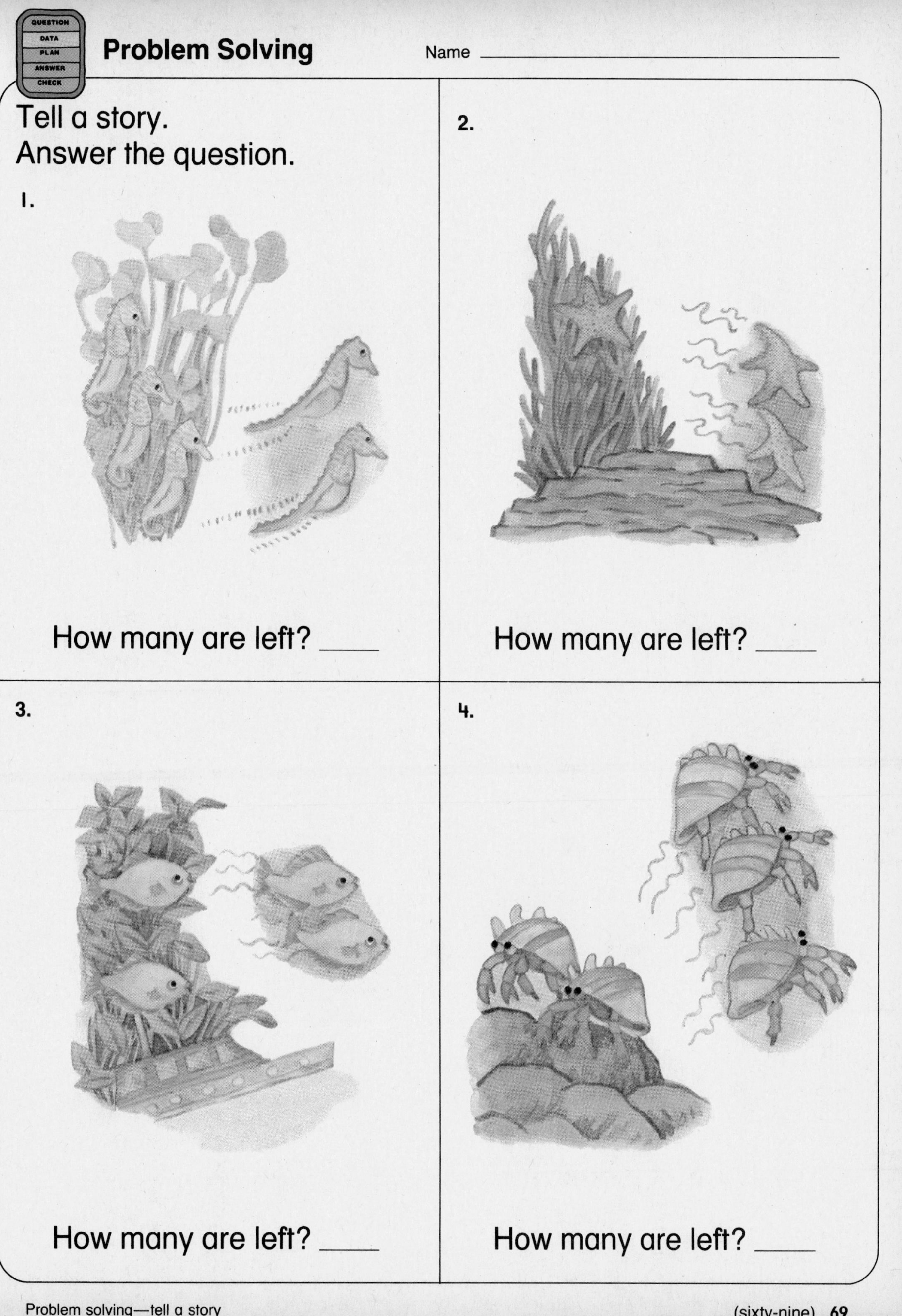

Tell a story.
Answer the question.

1.

How many are left? ____

2.

How many are left? ____

3.

How many are left? ____

4.

How many are left? ____

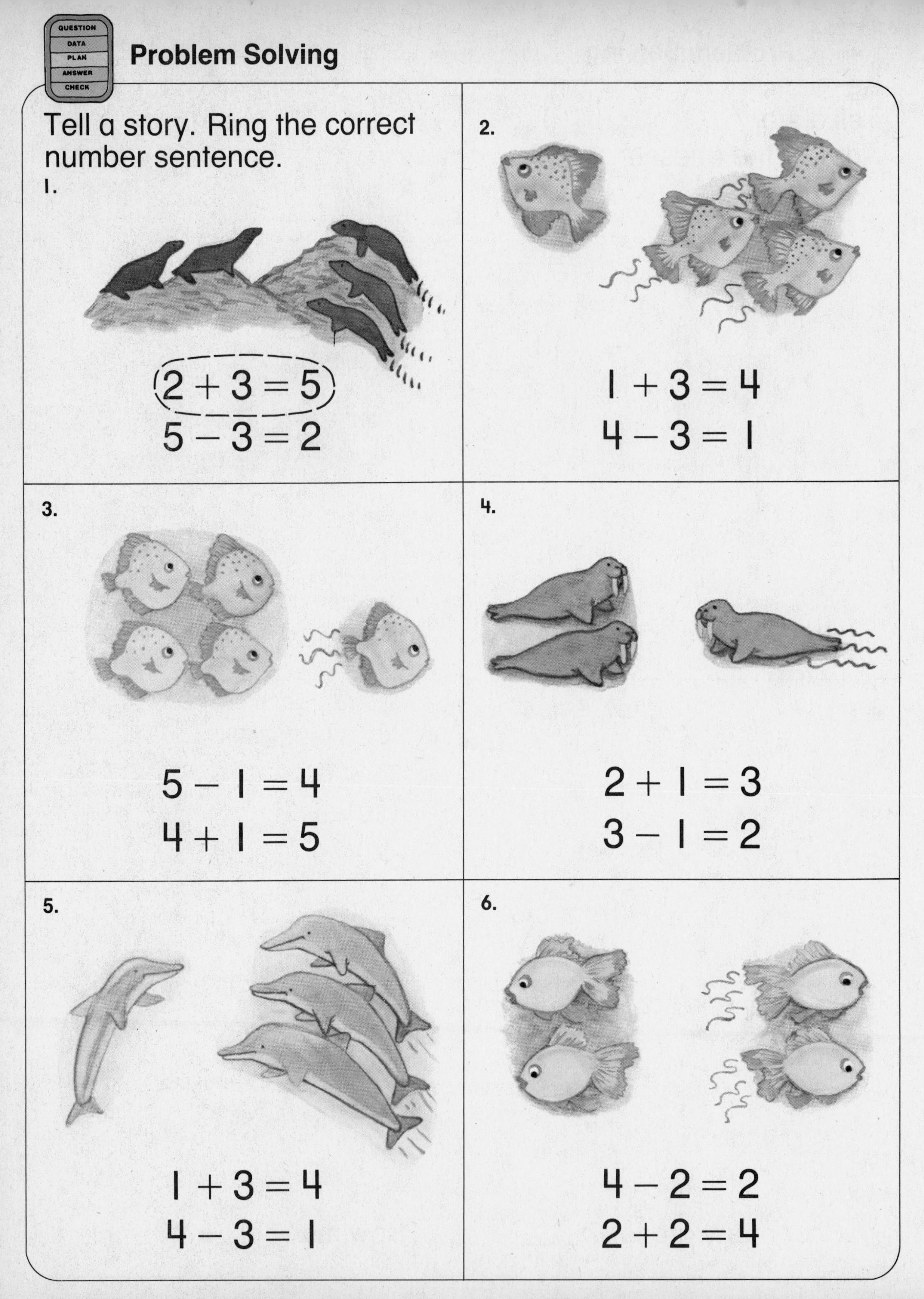
QUESTION
DATA
PLAN
ANSWER
CHECK
Problem Solving
Tell a story. Ring the correct number sentence.
1.
2 + 3 = 5
5 − 3 = 2
2.
1 + 3 = 4
4 − 3 = 1
3.
5 − 1 = 4
4 + 1 = 5
4.
2 + 1 = 3
3 − 1 = 2
5.
1 + 3 = 4
4 − 3 = 1
6.
4 − 2 = 2
2 + 2 = 4

Name ____________________

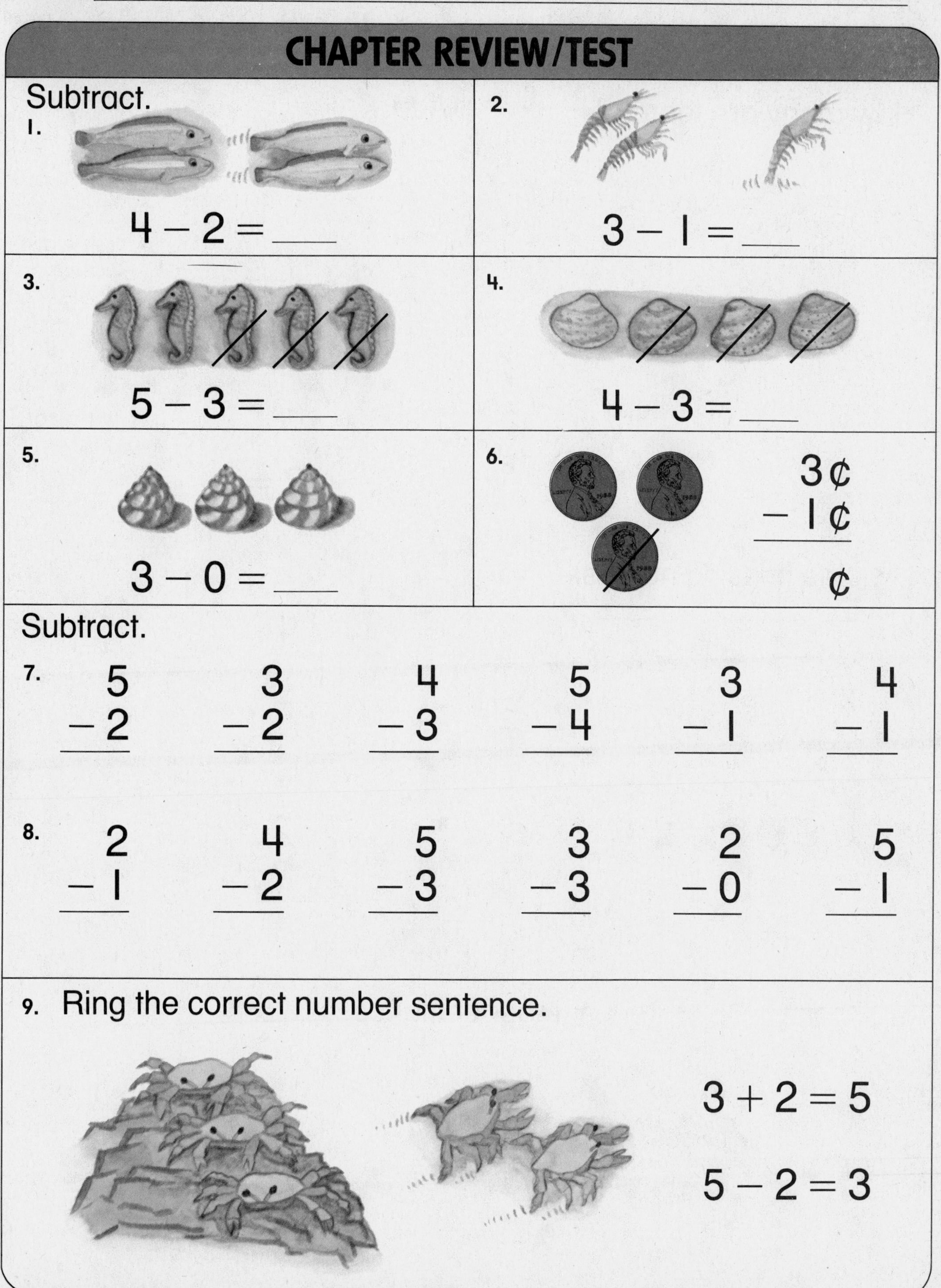

CHAPTER REVIEW/TEST

Subtract.

1. $4 - 2 = \_\_\_$

2. $3 - 1 = \_\_\_$

3. $5 - 3 = \_\_\_$

4. $4 - 3 = \_\_\_$

5. $3 - 0 = \_\_\_$

6. $3¢ - 1¢ = \_\_\_ ¢$

Subtract.

7. $5 - 2$ $3 - 2$ $4 - 3$ $5 - 4$ $3 - 1$ $4 - 1$

8. $2 - 1$ $4 - 2$ $5 - 3$ $3 - 3$ $2 - 0$ $5 - 1$

9. Ring the correct number sentence.

$3 + 2 = 5$

$5 - 2 = 3$

Name ____________________

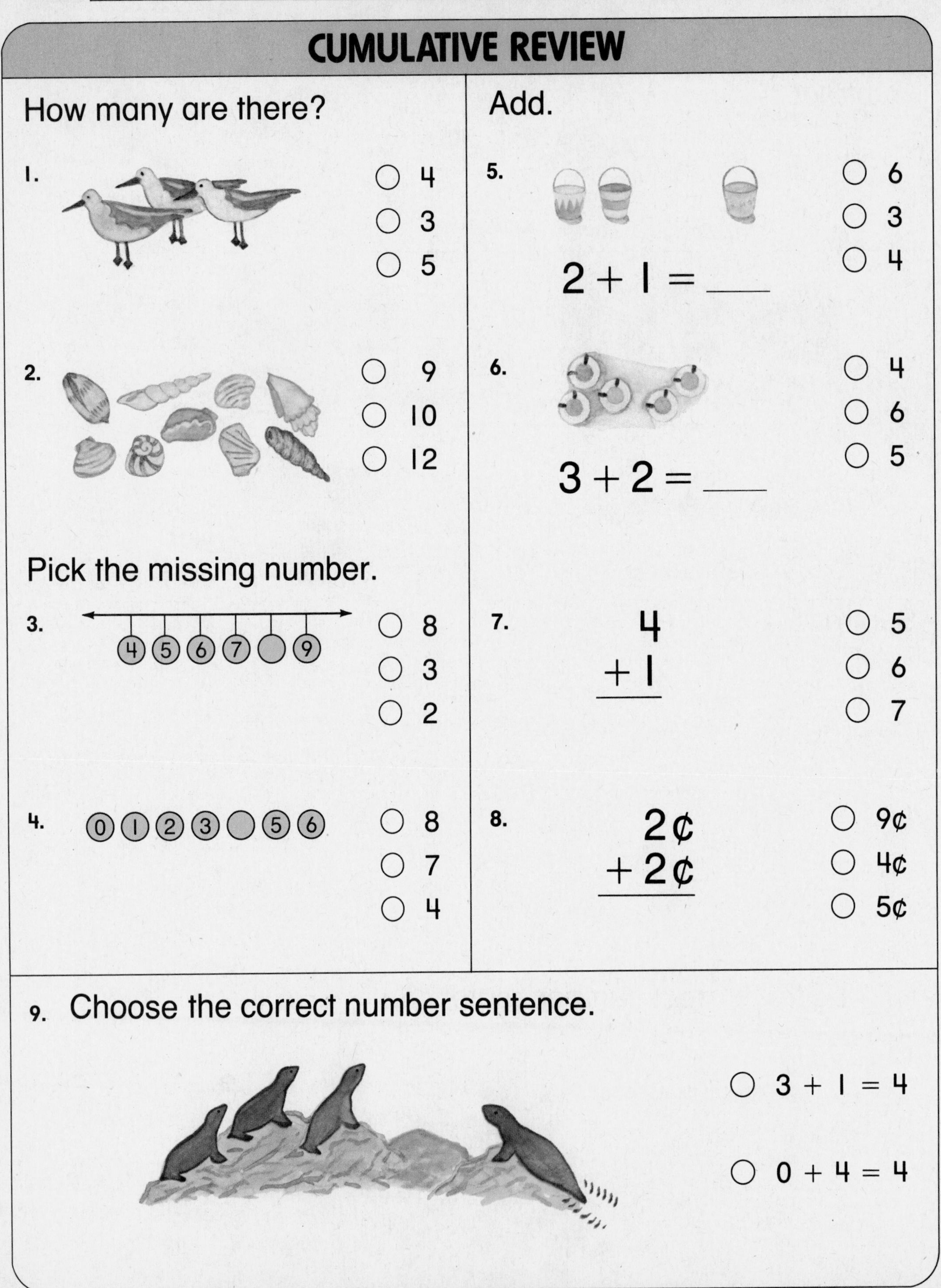

CUMULATIVE REVIEW

How many are there?

1.
- ○ 4
- ○ 3
- ○ 5

2.
- ○ 9
- ○ 10
- ○ 12

Pick the missing number.

3. 4 5 6 7 ◯ 9
- ○ 8
- ○ 3
- ○ 2

4. 0 1 2 3 ◯ 5 6
- ○ 8
- ○ 7
- ○ 4

Add.

5. $2 + 1 =$ ____
- ○ 6
- ○ 3
- ○ 4

6. $3 + 2 =$ ____
- ○ 4
- ○ 6
- ○ 5

7.

$$\begin{array}{r} 4 \\ +1 \\ \hline \end{array}$$

- ○ 5
- ○ 6
- ○ 7

8.

$$\begin{array}{r} 2¢ \\ +2¢ \\ \hline \end{array}$$

- ○ 9¢
- ○ 4¢
- ○ 5¢

9. Choose the correct number sentence.
- ○ $3 + 1 = 4$
- ○ $0 + 4 = 4$

Name ______________________________

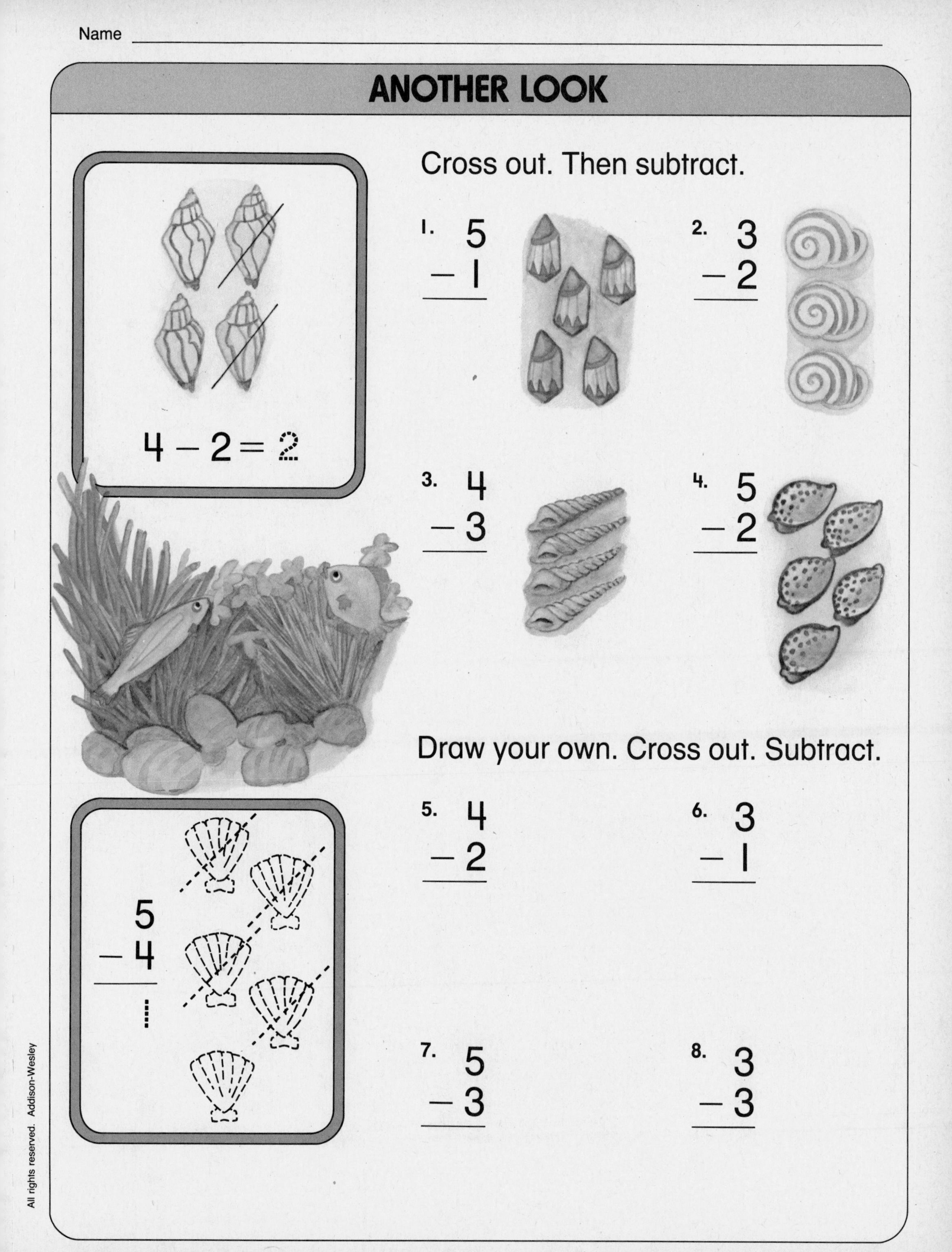

ANOTHER LOOK

$4 - 2 = 2$

$$\begin{array}{r} 5 \\ -\ 4 \\ \hline 1 \end{array}$$

Cross out. Then subtract.

1. $\begin{array}{r} 5 \\ -\ 1 \\ \hline \end{array}$

2. $\begin{array}{r} 3 \\ -\ 2 \\ \hline \end{array}$

3. $\begin{array}{r} 4 \\ -\ 3 \\ \hline \end{array}$

4. $\begin{array}{r} 5 \\ -\ 2 \\ \hline \end{array}$

Draw your own. Cross out. Subtract.

5. $\begin{array}{r} 4 \\ -\ 2 \\ \hline \end{array}$

6. $\begin{array}{r} 3 \\ -\ 1 \\ \hline \end{array}$

7. $\begin{array}{r} 5 \\ -\ 3 \\ \hline \end{array}$

8. $\begin{array}{r} 3 \\ -\ 3 \\ \hline \end{array}$

Name ____

ENRICHMENT

Follow the path.

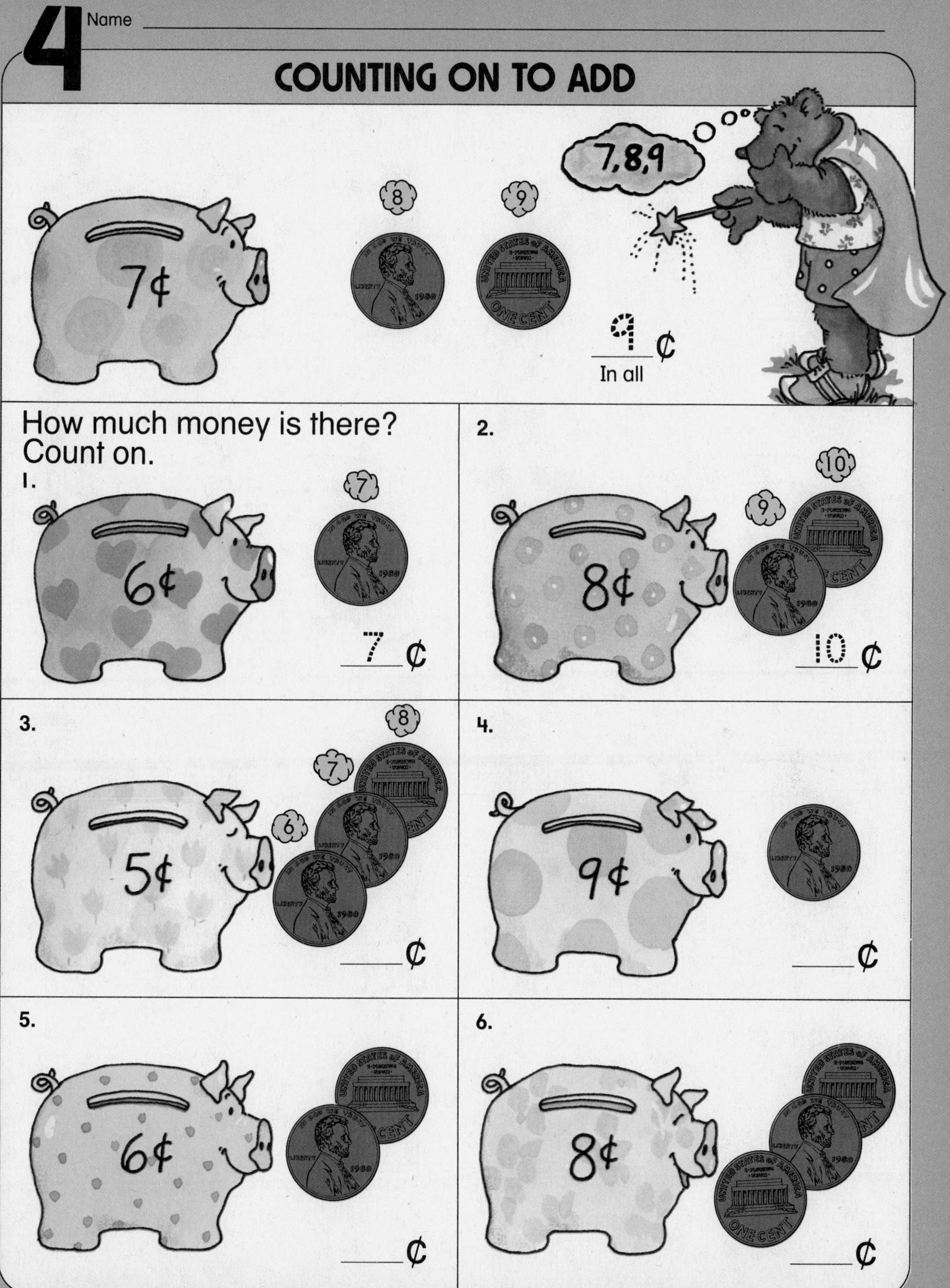
4
Name
COUNTING ON TO ADD
7,8,9
7¢
8
9
9 ¢
In all
How much money is there?
Count on.
1.
6¢
7
7 ¢
2.
8¢
9
10
10 ¢
3.
5¢
6
7
8
¢
4.
9¢
¢
5.
6¢
¢
6.
8¢
¢

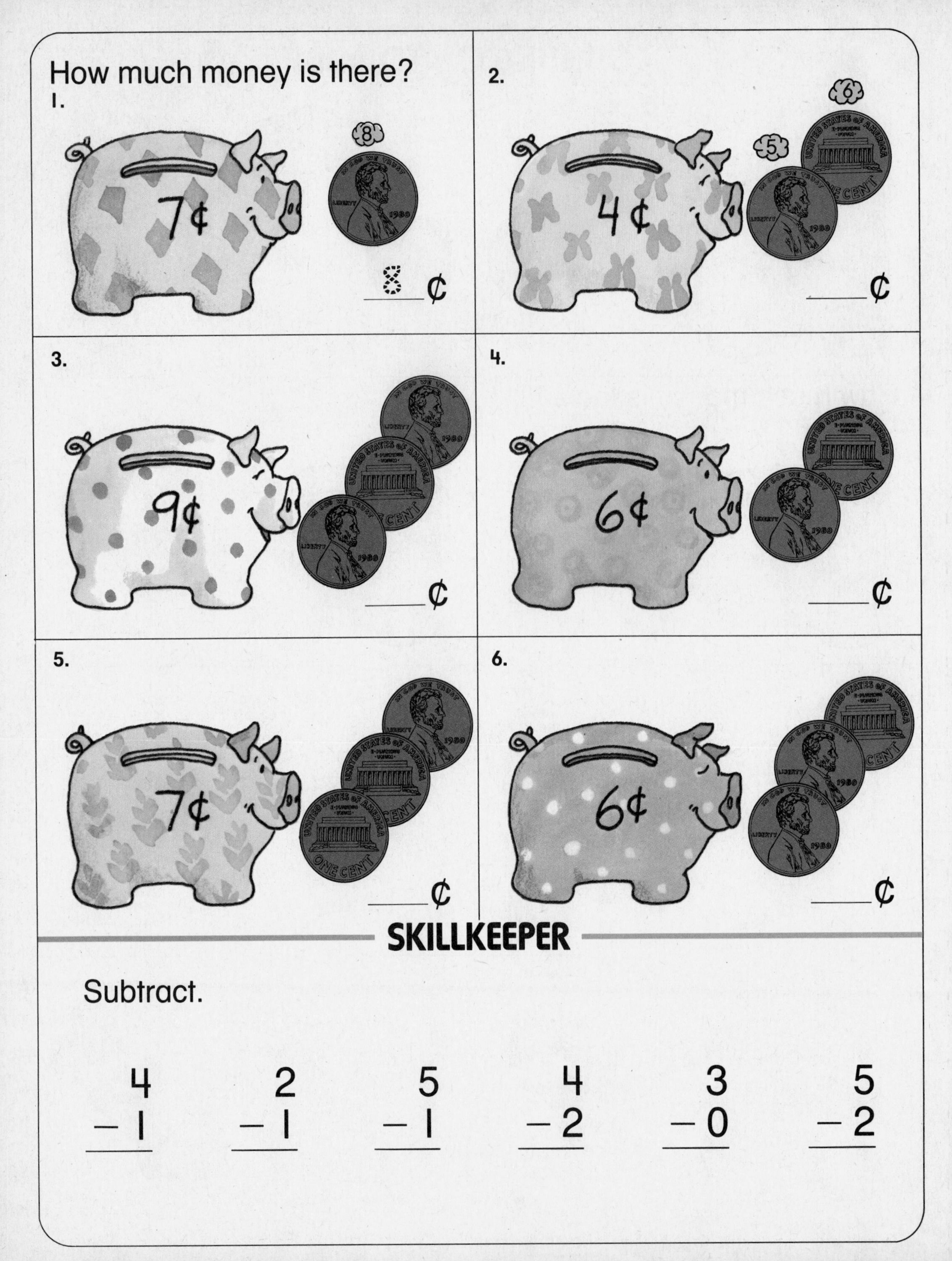
How much money is there?
1.
8
7¢
8 ¢
2.
6
5
4¢
¢
3.
9¢
¢
4.
6¢
¢
5.
7¢
¢
6.
6¢
¢
SKILLKEEPER
Subtract.
4 − 1
2 − 1
5 − 1
4 − 2
3 − 0
5 − 2

Name
6
6,7
6 + 1 = 7
Count on to add.
1.
5
5,6
5 + 1 = 6
2.
7
7,8
7 + 1 =
3.
8
8 + 1 =
4.
4
4 + 1 =
5.
9
9 + 1 =
6.
3
3 + 1 =

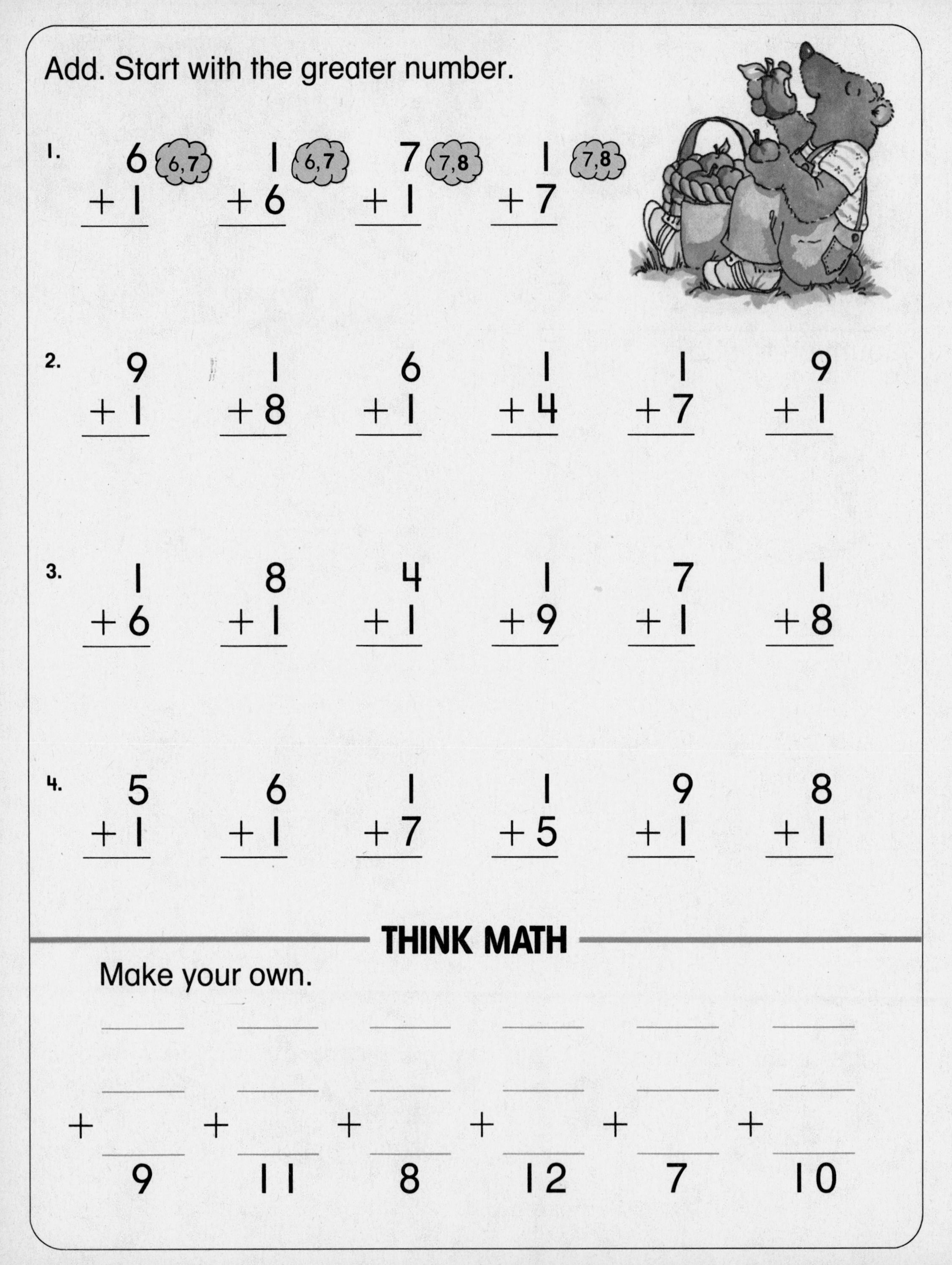

Add. Start with the greater number.

1.

6 (6,7)	1 (6,7)	7 (7,8)	1 (7,8)
$+1$	$+6$	$+1$	$+7$

2.

9	1	6	1	1	9
$+1$	$+8$	$+1$	$+4$	$+7$	$+1$

3.

1	8	4	1	7	1
$+6$	$+1$	$+1$	$+9$	$+1$	$+8$

4.

5	6	1	1	9	8
$+1$	$+1$	$+7$	$+5$	$+1$	$+1$

THINK MATH

Make your own.

___	___	___	___	___	___
+ ___	+ ___	+ ___	+ ___	+ ___	+ ___
9	11	8	12	7	10

Name ____________________

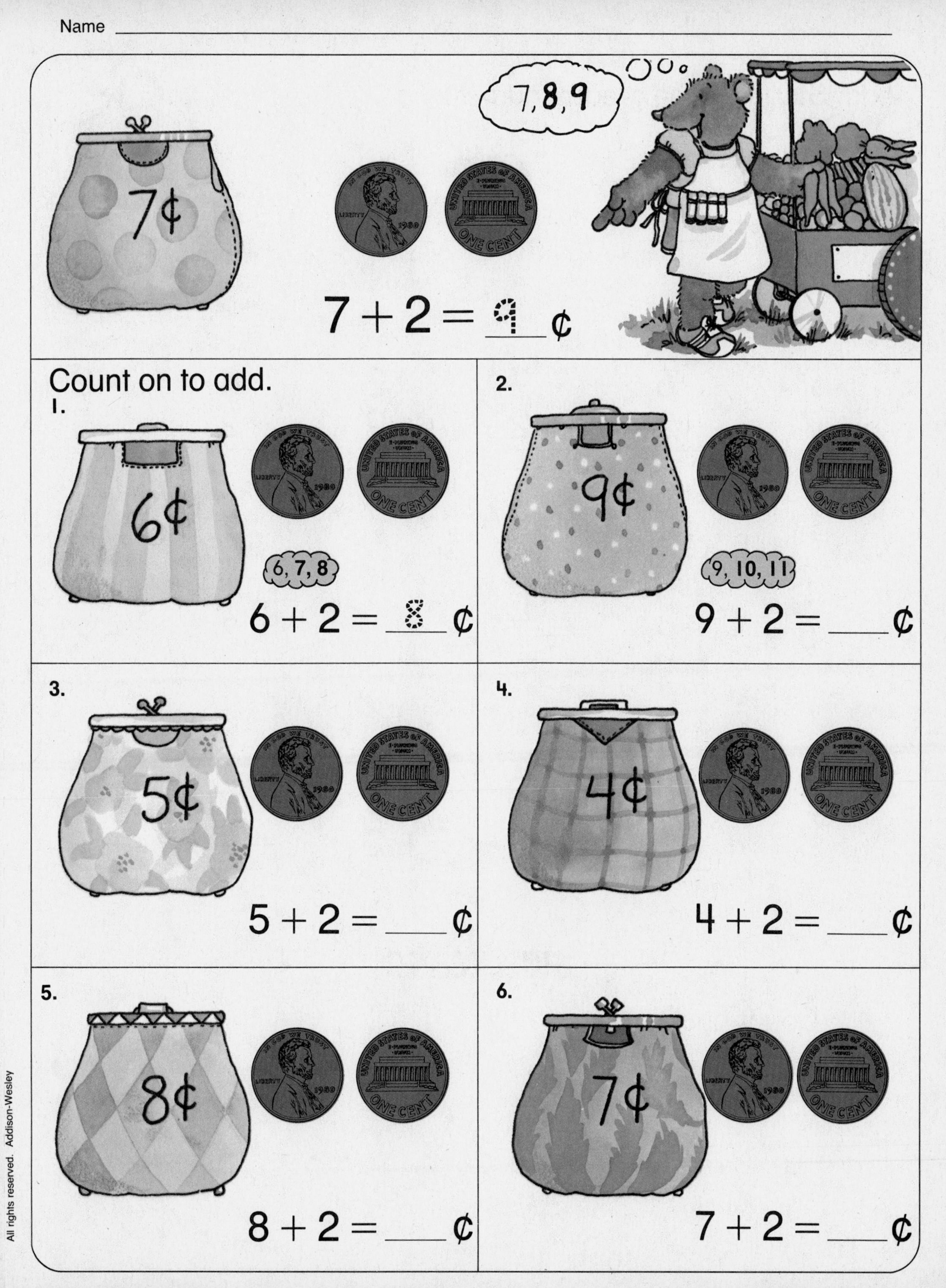

$7 + 2 = \underline{9}$ ¢

Count on to add.

1. 6¢ (6, 7, 8) $6 + 2 = \underline{8}$ ¢

2. 9¢ (9, 10, 11) $9 + 2 = \_\_\_$ ¢

3. 5¢ $5 + 2 = \_\_\_$ ¢

4. 4¢ $4 + 2 = \_\_\_$ ¢

5. 8¢ $8 + 2 = \_\_\_$ ¢

6. 7¢ $7 + 2 = \_\_\_$ ¢

Add. Start with the greater number.

1. $8 + 2$ (8, 9, 10) $2 + 7$ (7, 8, 9) $6 + 2$ (6, 7, 8) $2 + 9$ (9, 10, 11)

2. $2 + 7$ $6 + 2$ $4 + 2$ $2 + 9$ $8 + 2$ $2 + 5$

3. $1 + 6$ $5 + 2$ $2 + 7$ $4 + 1$ $1 + 7$ $8 + 2$

4. $2 + 4$ $9 + 1$ $1 + 5$ $6 + 2$ $2 + 9$ $8 + 1$

SKILLKEEPER

Count back.

10, 9, 8

8, 7, ___

4, ___, 2

9, ___, 7

Name ______________________________

0 1 2 3 4 5 6 7 8 9 10 11

6, 7, 8

$$\begin{array}{r} 2 \\ +6 \\ \hline 8 \end{array}$$

Add.

1. $\begin{array}{r} 2 \\ +9 \\ \hline \end{array}$ $\begin{array}{r} 2 \\ +3 \\ \hline \end{array}$ $\begin{array}{r} 7 \\ +1 \\ \hline \end{array}$ $\begin{array}{r} 7 \\ +2 \\ \hline \end{array}$

2. $\begin{array}{r} 5 \\ +2 \\ \hline \end{array}$ $\begin{array}{r} 3 \\ +1 \\ \hline \end{array}$ $\begin{array}{r} 1 \\ +8 \\ \hline \end{array}$ $\begin{array}{r} 0 \\ +4 \\ \hline \end{array}$ $\begin{array}{r} 2 \\ +4 \\ \hline \end{array}$ $\begin{array}{r} 9 \\ +1 \\ \hline \end{array}$

3. $\begin{array}{r} 1 \\ +3 \\ \hline \end{array}$ $\begin{array}{r} 6 \\ +2 \\ \hline \end{array}$ $\begin{array}{r} 3 \\ +2 \\ \hline \end{array}$ $\begin{array}{r} 9 \\ +2 \\ \hline \end{array}$ $\begin{array}{r} 8 \\ +2 \\ \hline \end{array}$ $\begin{array}{r} 2 \\ +2 \\ \hline \end{array}$

4. $\begin{array}{r} 1 \\ +9 \\ \hline \end{array}$ $\begin{array}{r} 0 \\ +2 \\ \hline \end{array}$ $\begin{array}{r} 6 \\ +1 \\ \hline \end{array}$ $\begin{array}{r} 8 \\ +1 \\ \hline \end{array}$ $\begin{array}{r} 4 \\ +1 \\ \hline \end{array}$ $\begin{array}{r} 2 \\ +7 \\ \hline \end{array}$

5. $\begin{array}{r} 2 \\ +5 \\ \hline \end{array}$ $\begin{array}{r} 2 \\ +8 \\ \hline \end{array}$ $\begin{array}{r} 1 \\ +4 \\ \hline \end{array}$ $\begin{array}{r} 2 \\ +6 \\ \hline \end{array}$ $\begin{array}{r} 3 \\ +0 \\ \hline \end{array}$ $\begin{array}{r} 1 \\ +6 \\ \hline \end{array}$

Add and color.

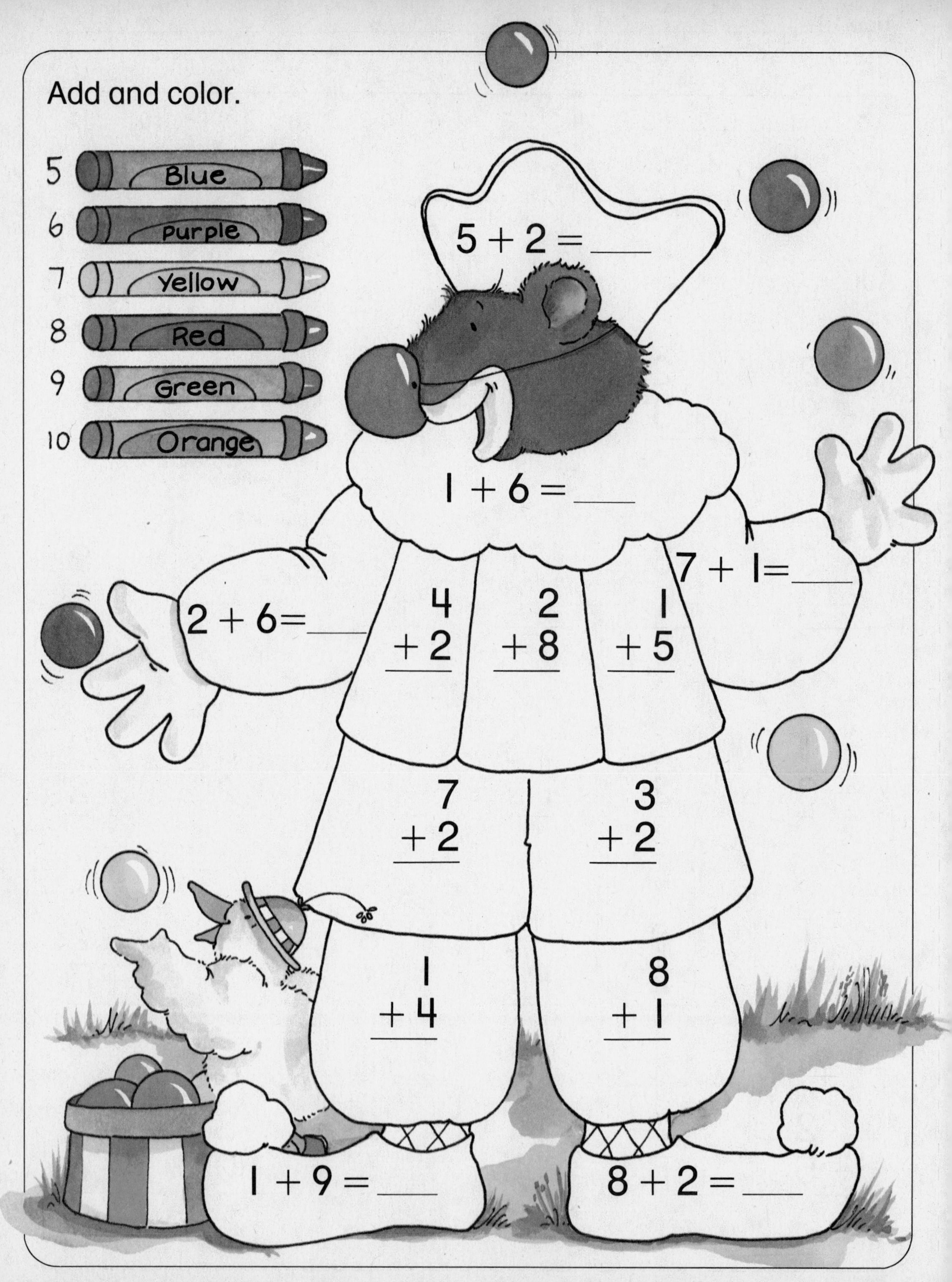

Name ____________________

6, 7, 8, 9
6
peaches
6 + 3 = 9
Count on to add.
1.
5
peaches
5, 6, 7, 8
5 + 3 = 8
2.
4
peaches
4, 5, 6, 7
4 + 3 = ___
3.
7
peaches
7 + 3 = ___
4.
8
peaches
8 + 3 = ___
5.
9
peaches
9 + 3 = ___
6.
3
peaches
3 + 3 = ___

Add.

1. $\begin{array}{r} 7 \\ +3 \\ \hline \end{array}$ (7,8,9,10) $\begin{array}{r} 3 \\ +8 \\ \hline \end{array}$ (8,9,10,11) $\begin{array}{r} 3 \\ +5 \\ \hline \end{array}$ (5,6,7,8) $\begin{array}{r} 9 \\ +3 \\ \hline \end{array}$ (9,10,11,12)

2. $\begin{array}{r} 3 \\ +5 \\ \hline \end{array}$ $\begin{array}{r} 3 \\ +3 \\ \hline \end{array}$ $\begin{array}{r} 3 \\ +8 \\ \hline \end{array}$ $\begin{array}{r} 3 \\ +6 \\ \hline \end{array}$ $\begin{array}{r} 4 \\ +3 \\ \hline \end{array}$ $\begin{array}{r} 7 \\ +3 \\ \hline \end{array}$

3. $\begin{array}{r} 2 \\ +7 \\ \hline \end{array}$ $\begin{array}{r} 6 \\ +1 \\ \hline \end{array}$ $\begin{array}{r} 3 \\ +9 \\ \hline \end{array}$ $\begin{array}{r} 1 \\ +9 \\ \hline \end{array}$ $\begin{array}{r} 8 \\ +2 \\ \hline \end{array}$ $\begin{array}{r} 3 \\ +7 \\ \hline \end{array}$

4. $\begin{array}{r} 2 \\ +9 \\ \hline \end{array}$ $\begin{array}{r} 6 \\ +3 \\ \hline \end{array}$ $\begin{array}{r} 1 \\ +8 \\ \hline \end{array}$ $\begin{array}{r} 3 \\ +8 \\ \hline \end{array}$ $\begin{array}{r} 7 \\ +1 \\ \hline \end{array}$ $\begin{array}{r} 2 \\ +6 \\ \hline \end{array}$

THINK MATH

7 in all.
How many are hiding? ____ more

Name ______________________________

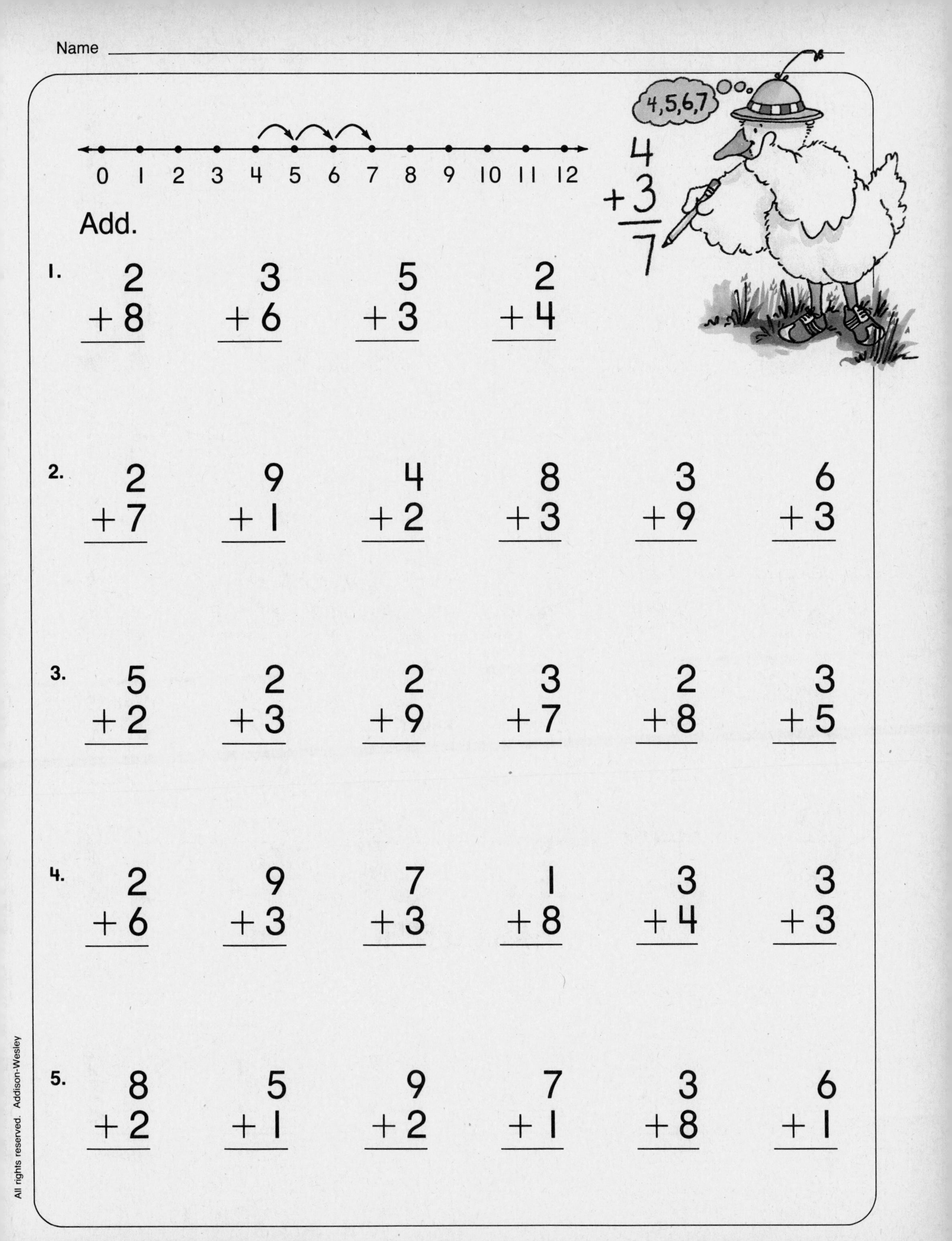

Add.

1. $\begin{array}{r} 2 \\ +8 \\ \hline \end{array}$ $\begin{array}{r} 3 \\ +6 \\ \hline \end{array}$ $\begin{array}{r} 5 \\ +3 \\ \hline \end{array}$ $\begin{array}{r} 2 \\ +4 \\ \hline \end{array}$

2. $\begin{array}{r} 2 \\ +7 \\ \hline \end{array}$ $\begin{array}{r} 9 \\ +1 \\ \hline \end{array}$ $\begin{array}{r} 4 \\ +2 \\ \hline \end{array}$ $\begin{array}{r} 8 \\ +3 \\ \hline \end{array}$ $\begin{array}{r} 3 \\ +9 \\ \hline \end{array}$ $\begin{array}{r} 6 \\ +3 \\ \hline \end{array}$

3. $\begin{array}{r} 5 \\ +2 \\ \hline \end{array}$ $\begin{array}{r} 2 \\ +3 \\ \hline \end{array}$ $\begin{array}{r} 2 \\ +9 \\ \hline \end{array}$ $\begin{array}{r} 3 \\ +7 \\ \hline \end{array}$ $\begin{array}{r} 2 \\ +8 \\ \hline \end{array}$ $\begin{array}{r} 3 \\ +5 \\ \hline \end{array}$

4. $\begin{array}{r} 2 \\ +6 \\ \hline \end{array}$ $\begin{array}{r} 9 \\ +3 \\ \hline \end{array}$ $\begin{array}{r} 7 \\ +3 \\ \hline \end{array}$ $\begin{array}{r} 1 \\ +8 \\ \hline \end{array}$ $\begin{array}{r} 3 \\ +4 \\ \hline \end{array}$ $\begin{array}{r} 3 \\ +3 \\ \hline \end{array}$

5. $\begin{array}{r} 8 \\ +2 \\ \hline \end{array}$ $\begin{array}{r} 5 \\ +1 \\ \hline \end{array}$ $\begin{array}{r} 9 \\ +2 \\ \hline \end{array}$ $\begin{array}{r} 7 \\ +1 \\ \hline \end{array}$ $\begin{array}{r} 3 \\ +8 \\ \hline \end{array}$ $\begin{array}{r} 6 \\ +1 \\ \hline \end{array}$

5 + 2
Add 2
4 6
5 7
Finish each table.
1.
Add 2
7 9
5 7
8
Add 1
6
5
8
2.
Add 3
6
9
8
Add 0
9
6
8
Add 2
6
9
4
3.
Add 3
4
2
7
Add 1
7
9
4
Add 3
8
3
5
SKILLKEEPER
Add or subtract.
4 + 1
3 − 2
1 + 3
5 − 1
0 + 4
2 − 2

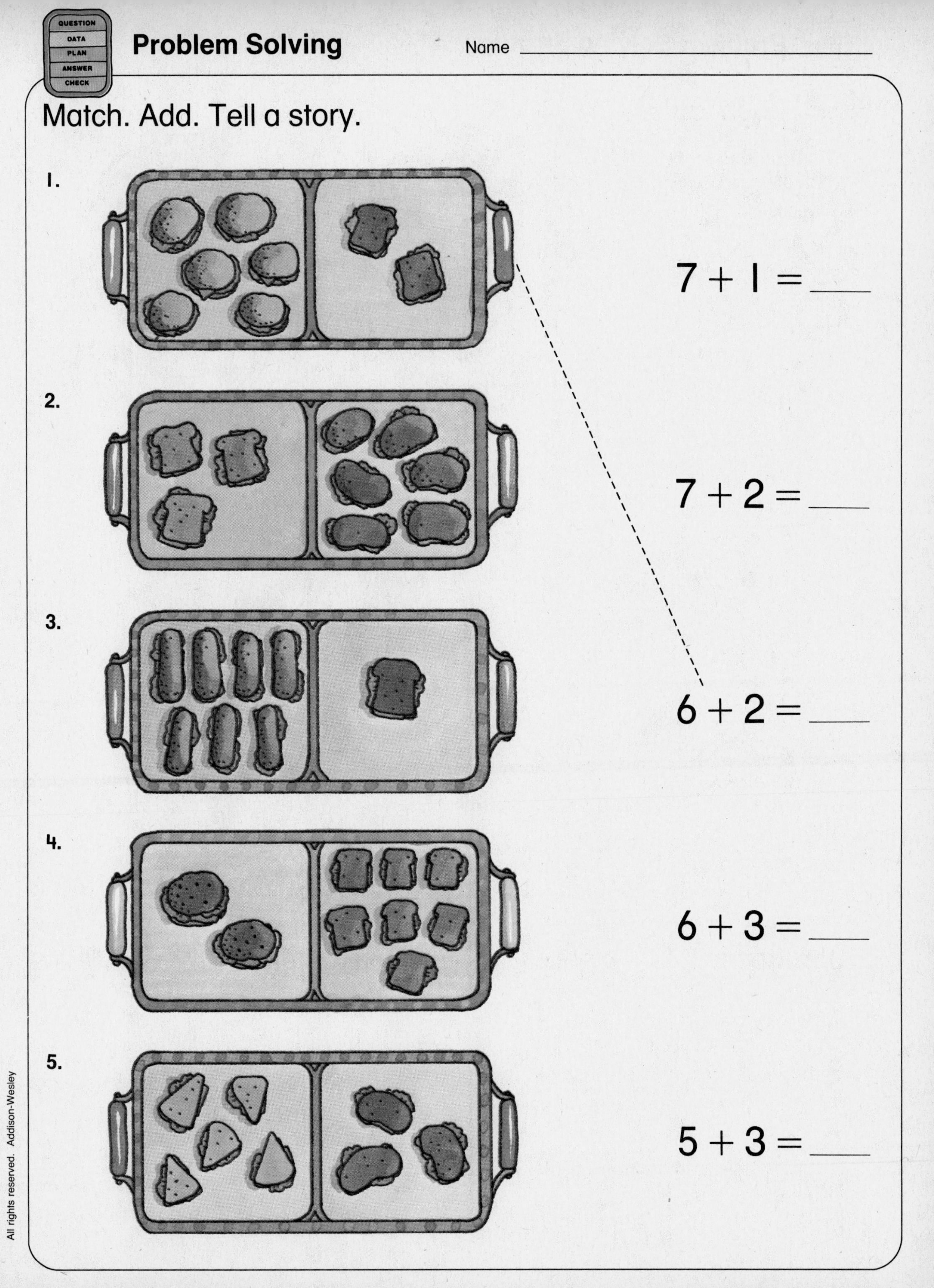

Problem Solving

Name ____________________

Match. Add. Tell a story.

1.

2.

3.

4.

5.

7 + 1 = ____

7 + 2 = ____

6 + 2 = ____

6 + 3 = ____

5 + 3 = ____

Problem-Solving Strategy

QUESTION
DATA
PLAN
ANSWER
CHECK
B
Jan has a .
Jim has a .
Sue has .
Draw a ring
around Lyn!
Lyn gave Ed a .

Name ______________________________

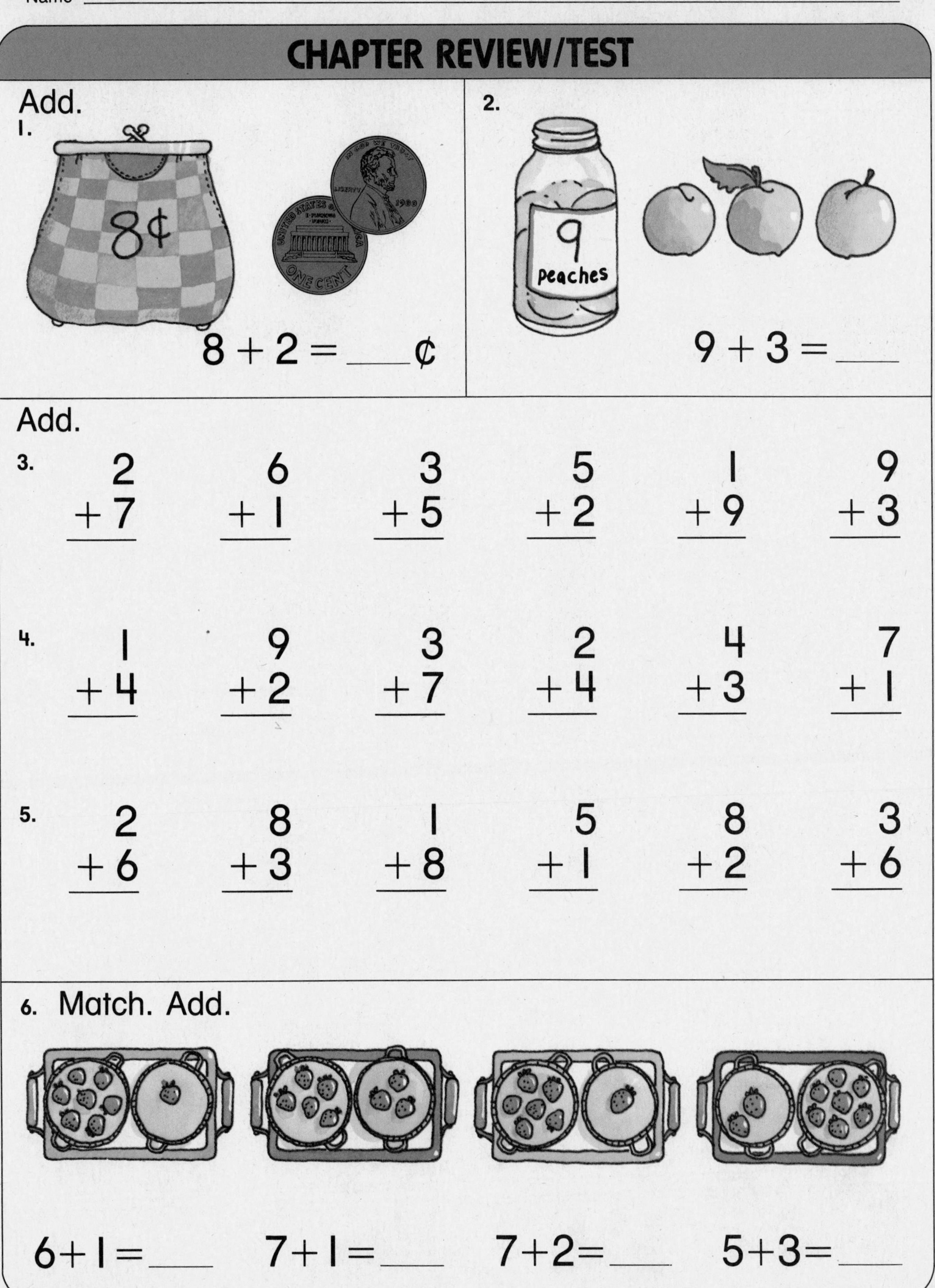
CHAPTER REVIEW/TEST
Add.
1.
8¢
8 + 2 = ___ ¢
2.
9
peaches
9 + 3 = ___
Add.
3. 2 + 7   6 + 1   3 + 5   5 + 2   1 + 9   9 + 3
4. 1 + 4   9 + 2   3 + 7   2 + 4   4 + 3   7 + 1
5. 2 + 6   8 + 3   1 + 8   5 + 1   8 + 2   3 + 6
6. Match. Add.
6+1= ___   7+1= ___   7+2= ___   5+3= ___

Name ____________________

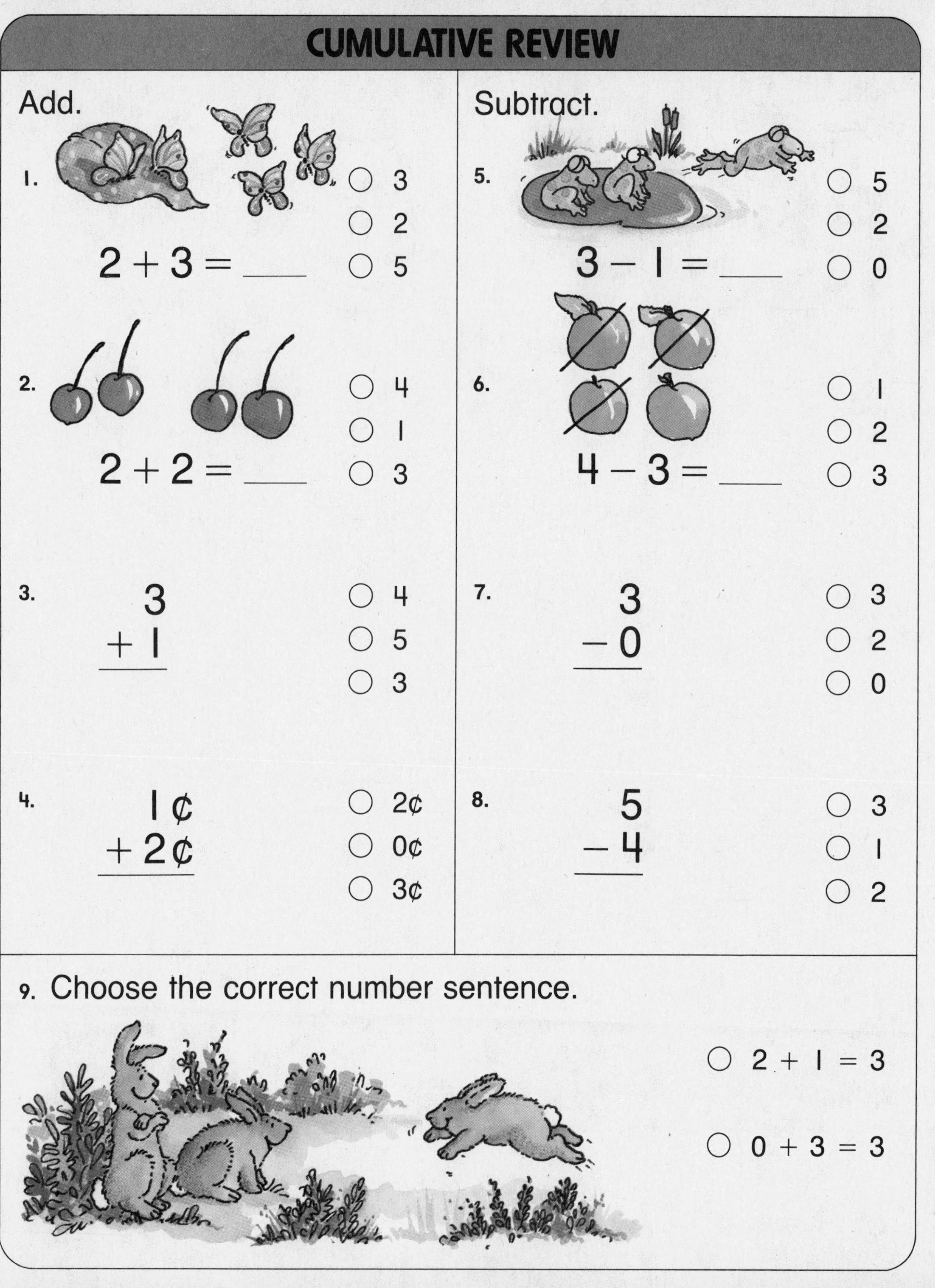

CUMULATIVE REVIEW

Add.

1. $2 + 3 = \_\_\_$

○ 3
○ 2
○ 5

2. $2 + 2 = \_\_\_$

○ 4
○ 1
○ 3

3. $\begin{array}{r} 3 \\ +\ 1 \\ \hline \end{array}$

○ 4
○ 5
○ 3

4. $\begin{array}{r} 1¢ \\ +\ 2¢ \\ \hline \end{array}$

○ 2¢
○ 0¢
○ 3¢

Subtract.

5. $3 - 1 = \_\_\_$

○ 5
○ 2
○ 0

6. $4 - 3 = \_\_\_$

○ 1
○ 2
○ 3

7. $\begin{array}{r} 3 \\ -\ 0 \\ \hline \end{array}$

○ 3
○ 2
○ 0

8. $\begin{array}{r} 5 \\ -\ 4 \\ \hline \end{array}$

○ 3
○ 1
○ 2

9. Choose the correct number sentence.

○ $2 + 1 = 3$

○ $0 + 3 = 3$

Name ______________________________

ANOTHER LOOK
8
8
+ 1
8,9,
9
9
9
+ 2
9,10,11,
11
7
7
+ 3
7,8,9,10
10
Add.
1. 7 + 1 (7,8)   1 + 6 (6,7)   9 + 1 (9,10)
2. 1 + 8   1 + 5   3 + 1
3. 5 + 2 (5,6,7)   2 + 8 (8,9,10)   6 + 2 (6,7,8)
4. 2 + 3   4 + 2   2 + 7
5. 3 + 6 (6,7,8,9)   9 + 3 (9,10,11,12)
6. 7 + 3   3 + 4   5 + 3

Name ____________________

ENRICHMENT
1.
5 birds in all.
How many are hiding? ____
2.
4 cats in all.
How many are hiding? ____
3.
7 fish in all.
How many are hiding? ____
4.
6 dogs in all.
How many are hiding? ____

5 Name ______ ______

COUNTING BACK TO SUBTRACT

8, 7, 6

8¢

6 ¢

1. **How much money is left? Count back.**

7, 6

7¢

6 ¢

2.

9, 8, 7

9¢

___ ¢

3.

7, 6, 5, 4

7¢

___ ¢

4.

8¢

___ ¢

5.

10¢

___ ¢

6.

12¢

___ ¢

Counting back

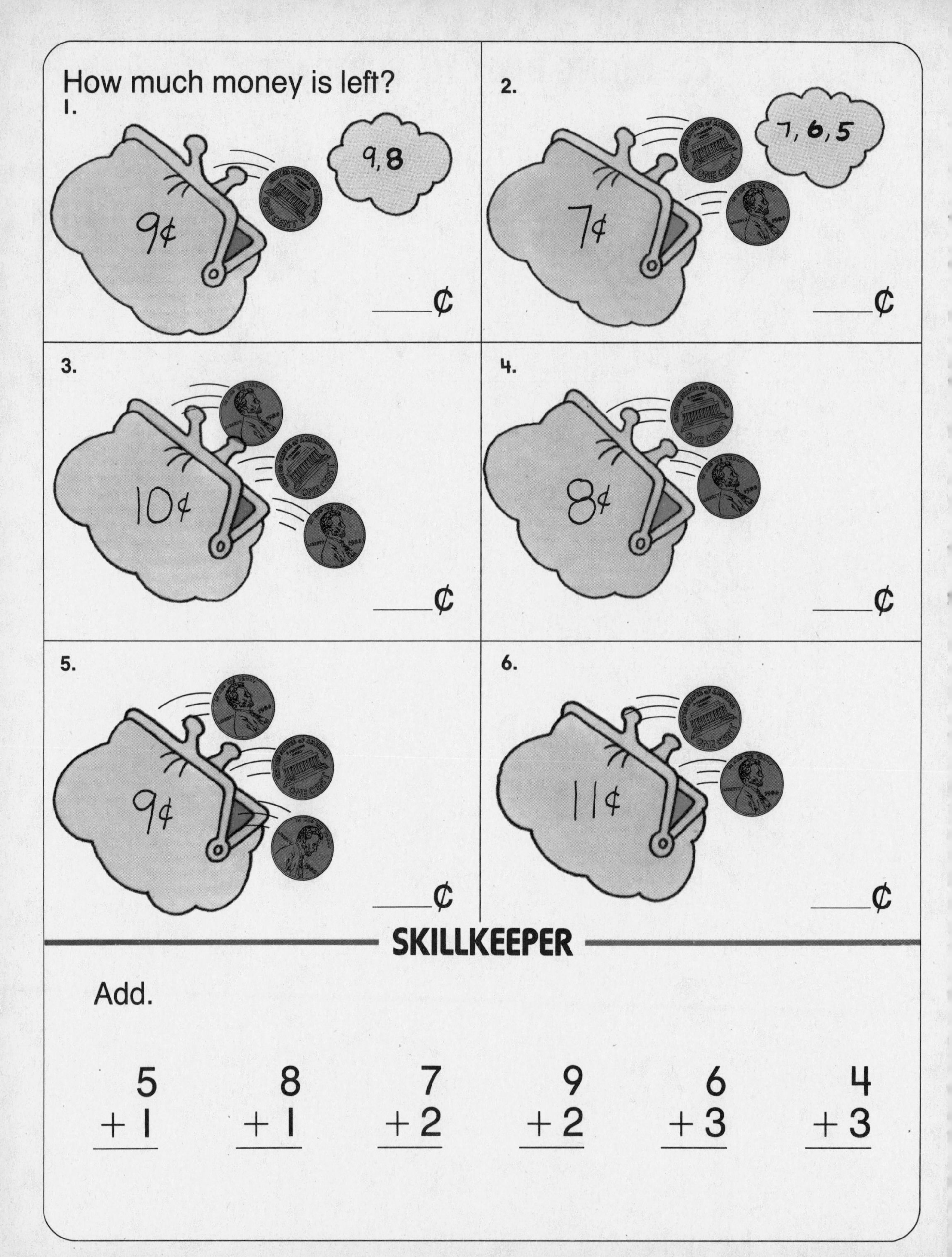
How much money is left?
1.
9, 8
9¢
ONE CENT
¢
2.
7, 6, 5
7¢
ONE CENT
¢
3.
10¢
ONE CENT
¢
4.
8¢
ONE CENT
¢
5.
9¢
ONE CENT
¢
6.
11¢
ONE CENT
¢
SKILLKEEPER
Add.
5 + 1
8 + 1
7 + 2
9 + 2
6 + 3
4 + 3

Name ______________________________

6
6, 5
6 − 1 = 5
Count back to subtract.
1.
5
5, 4
5 − 1 = 4
2.
7
7, 6
7 − 1 = ___
3.
8
8 − 1 = ___
4.
4
4 − 1 = ___
5.
10
10 − 1 = ___
6.
9
9 − 1 = ___

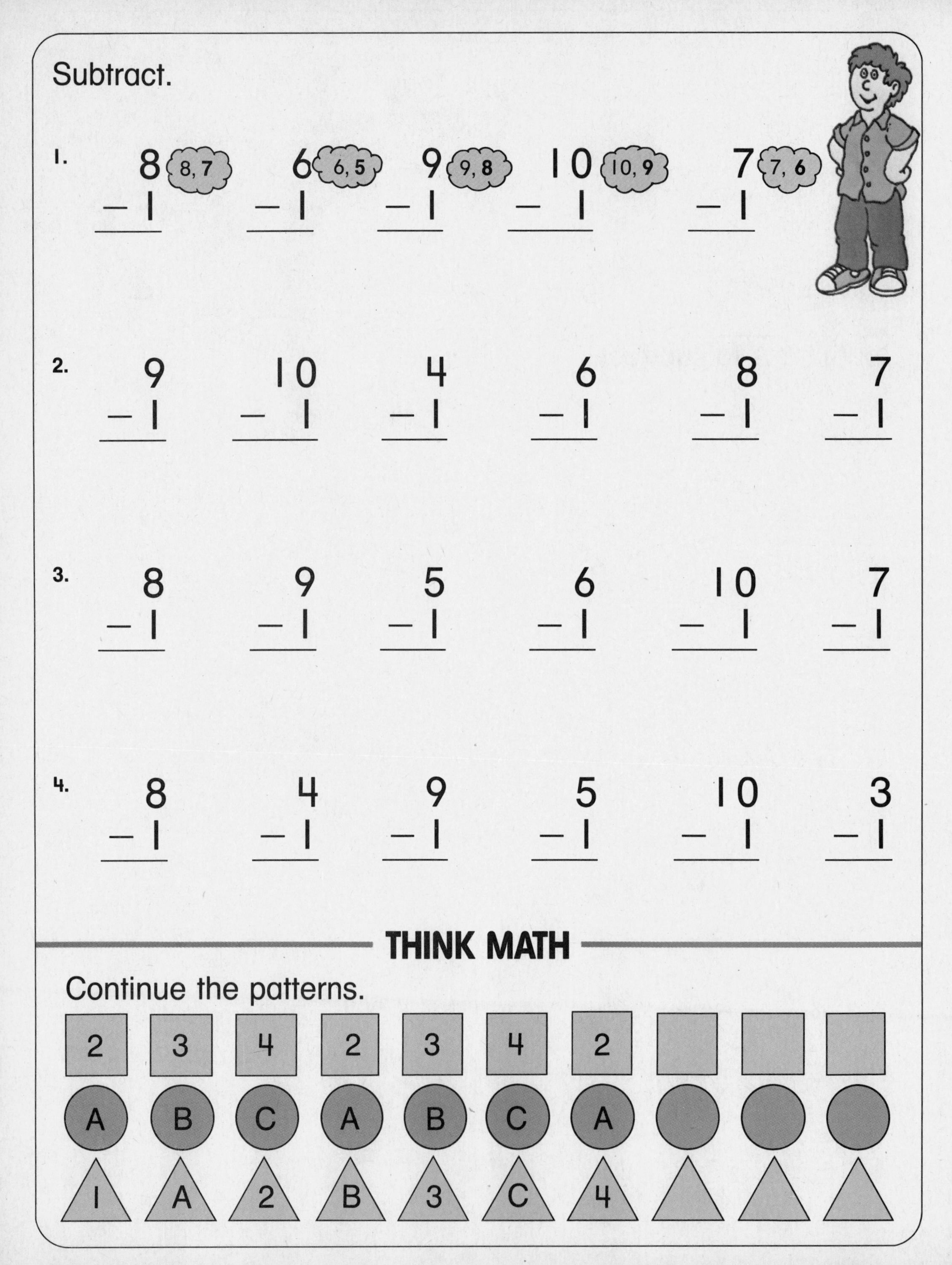

Subtract.

1. $8 - 1$ (8, 7)　　$6 - 1$ (6, 5)　　$9 - 1$ (9, 8)　　$10 - 1$ (10, 9)　　$7 - 1$ (7, 6)

2. $9 - 1$　　$10 - 1$　　$4 - 1$　　$6 - 1$　　$8 - 1$　　$7 - 1$

3. $8 - 1$　　$9 - 1$　　$5 - 1$　　$6 - 1$　　$10 - 1$　　$7 - 1$

4. $8 - 1$　　$4 - 1$　　$9 - 1$　　$5 - 1$　　$10 - 1$　　$3 - 1$

THINK MATH

Continue the patterns.

2	3	4	2	3	4	2			
A	B	C	A	B	C	A			
1	A	2	B	3	C	4			

Name ______

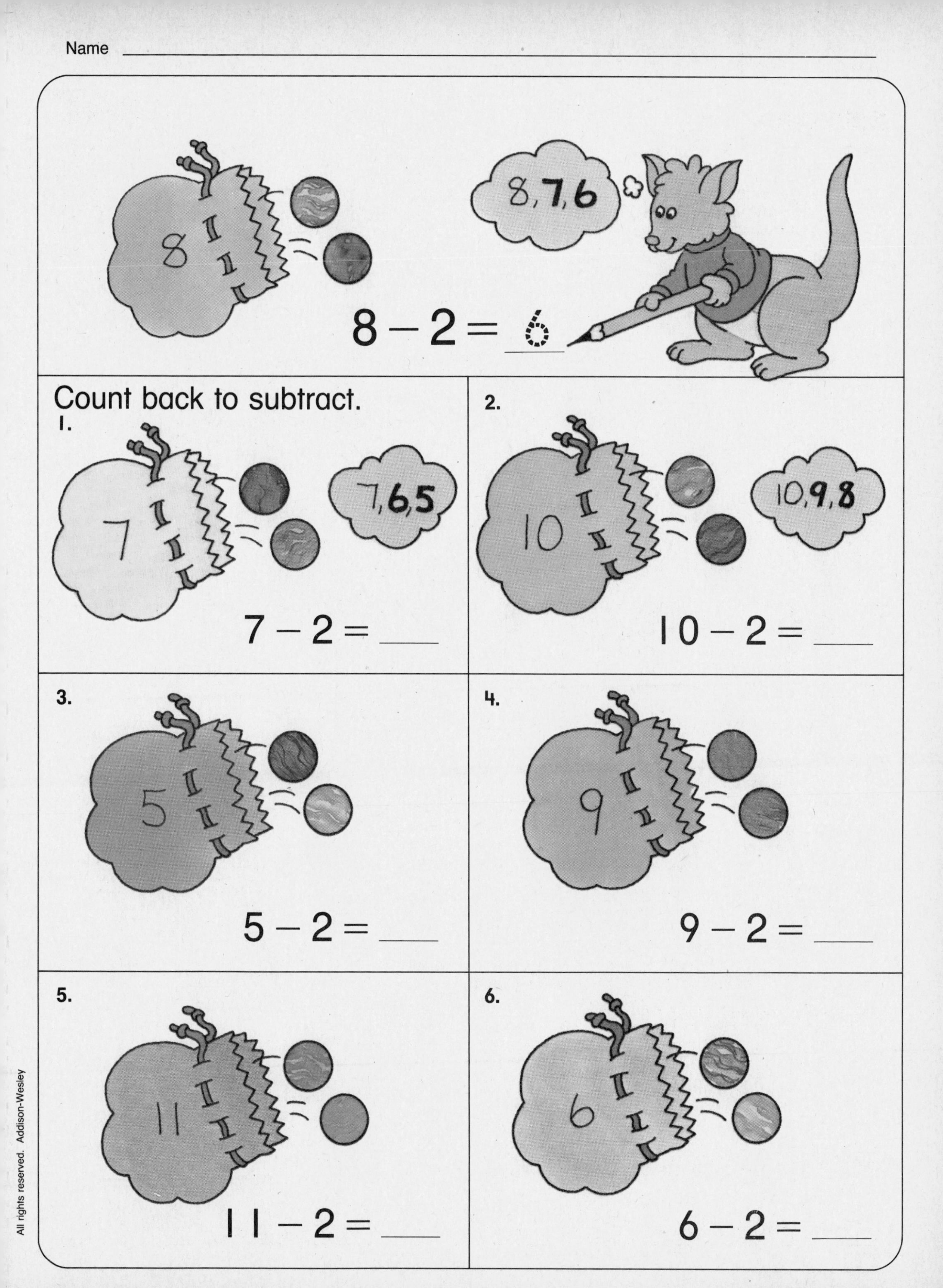
8
8, 7, 6
8 − 2 = 6
Count back to subtract.
1.
7
7, 6, 5
7 − 2 = ___
2.
10
10, 9, 8
10 − 2 = ___
3.
5
5 − 2 = ___
4.
9
9 − 2 = ___
5.
11
11 − 2 = ___
6.
6
6 − 2 = ___

Subtract.

8, 7, 6

1.

9 (9, 8, 7)	10 (10, 9, 8)	7 (7, 6, 5)	11 (11, 10, 9)	8
− 2	− 2	− 2	− 2	− 2

2.

8	11	9	10	5	7
− 2	− 2	− 1	− 2	− 2	− 1

3.

9	2	6	11	5	10
− 2	− 2	− 2	− 2	− 0	− 1

4.

6	7	11	1	10	9
− 2	− 1	− 2	− 1	− 2	− 1

SKILLKEEPER

Add.

1	2	7	9	6	3
+ 9	+ 8	+ 3	+ 2	+ 1	+ 4

Name ____________________

0 1 2 3 4 5 6 7 8 9 10 11 12

Subtract.

$$\begin{array}{r} 9 \\ -\,2 \\ \hline 7 \end{array}$$

1. $7 - 1$ $\quad 10 - 2$ $\quad 8 - 1$ $\quad 9 - 1$

2. $2 - 2$ $\quad 5 - 1$ $\quad 7 - 1$ $\quad 6 - 2$ $\quad 4 - 1$ $\quad 5 - 2$

3. $6 - 2$ $\quad 1 - 1$ $\quad 10 - 2$ $\quad 3 - 2$ $\quad 10 - 1$ $\quad 4 - 2$

4. $4 - 1$ $\quad 9 - 2$ $\quad 9 - 1$ $\quad 3 - 1$ $\quad 11 - 2$ $\quad 2 - 1$

5. $7 - 2$ $\quad 8 - 1$ $\quad 9 - 2$ $\quad 10 - 1$ $\quad 6 - 1$ $\quad 5 - 2$

Practice the facts—using the number line

Some birds are in the wrong nests.
Mark them.

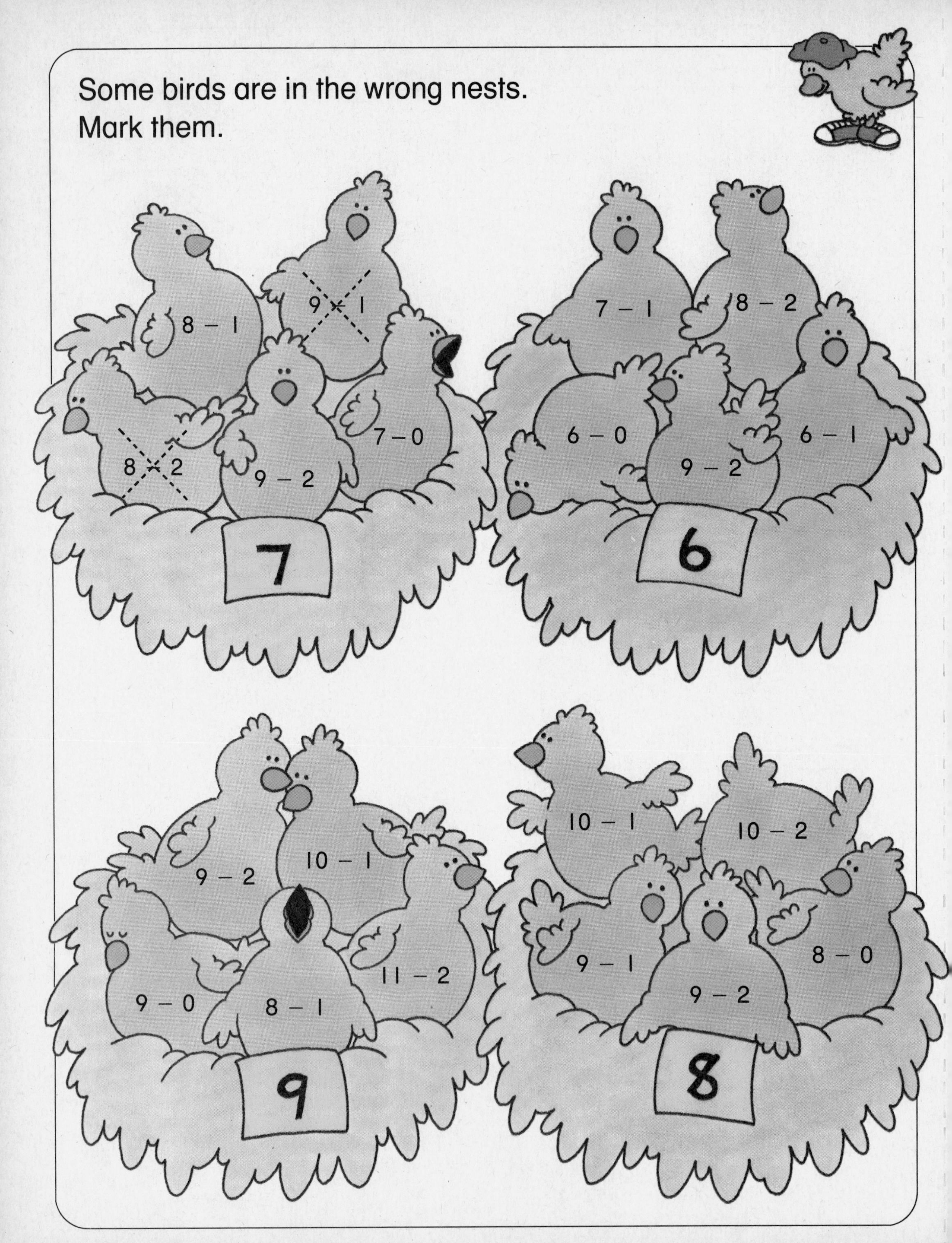

 Practice the facts

Name ____________________

7
7,6,5,4
7 − 3 = 4
Count back to subtract.
1.
9
9,8,7,6
9 − 3 = 6
2.
6
6,5,4,3
6 − 3 = ____
3.
11
11,10,9,8
11 − 3 = ____
4.
8
8,7,6,5
8 − 3 = ____
5.
12
12,11,10,9
12 − 3 = ____
6.
10
10,9,8,7
10 − 3 = ____

Subtract.

1. $\begin{array}{r} 8 \\ -3 \\ \hline \end{array}$ (8,7,6,5) $\begin{array}{r} 10 \\ -3 \\ \hline \end{array}$ (10,9,8,7) $\begin{array}{r} 12 \\ -3 \\ \hline \end{array}$ (12,11,10,9) $\begin{array}{r} 9 \\ -3 \\ \hline \end{array}$ (9,8,7,6) $\begin{array}{r} 7 \\ -3 \\ \hline \end{array}$ (7,6,5,4)

2. $\begin{array}{r} 6 \\ -3 \\ \hline \end{array}$ $\begin{array}{r} 12 \\ -3 \\ \hline \end{array}$ $\begin{array}{r} 8 \\ -2 \\ \hline \end{array}$ $\begin{array}{r} 11 \\ -3 \\ \hline \end{array}$ $\begin{array}{r} 9 \\ -2 \\ \hline \end{array}$ $\begin{array}{r} 10 \\ -3 \\ \hline \end{array}$

3. $\begin{array}{r} 7 \\ -1 \\ \hline \end{array}$ $\begin{array}{r} 11 \\ -2 \\ \hline \end{array}$ $\begin{array}{r} 6 \\ -1 \\ \hline \end{array}$ $\begin{array}{r} 9 \\ -3 \\ \hline \end{array}$ $\begin{array}{r} 12 \\ -3 \\ \hline \end{array}$ $\begin{array}{r} 8 \\ -3 \\ \hline \end{array}$

4. $\begin{array}{r} 7 \\ -2 \\ \hline \end{array}$ $\begin{array}{r} 10 \\ -3 \\ \hline \end{array}$ $\begin{array}{r} 8 \\ -1 \\ \hline \end{array}$ $\begin{array}{r} 12 \\ -3 \\ \hline \end{array}$ $\begin{array}{r} 9 \\ -3 \\ \hline \end{array}$ $\begin{array}{r} 11 \\ -3 \\ \hline \end{array}$

THINK MATH

Ted lost 3 of his pencils. How many does he have left?

8 pencils

____ pencils

Name ______________________

8,7,6,5

0 1 2 3 4 5 6 7 8 9 10 11 12

$$\begin{array}{r} 8 \\ -3 \\ \hline 5 \end{array}$$

Subtract.

1. $\begin{array}{r} 8 \\ -1 \\ \hline \end{array}$ $\begin{array}{r} 3 \\ -1 \\ \hline \end{array}$ $\begin{array}{r} 8 \\ -3 \\ \hline \end{array}$ $\begin{array}{r} 9 \\ -1 \\ \hline \end{array}$ $\begin{array}{r} 11 \\ -2 \\ \hline \end{array}$ $\begin{array}{r} 6 \\ -2 \\ \hline \end{array}$

2. $\begin{array}{r} 9 \\ -2 \\ \hline \end{array}$ $\begin{array}{r} 7 \\ -1 \\ \hline \end{array}$ $\begin{array}{r} 9 \\ -3 \\ \hline \end{array}$ $\begin{array}{r} 3 \\ -3 \\ \hline \end{array}$ $\begin{array}{r} 7 \\ -2 \\ \hline \end{array}$ $\begin{array}{r} 11 \\ -3 \\ \hline \end{array}$

3. $\begin{array}{r} 7 \\ -3 \\ \hline \end{array}$ $\begin{array}{r} 5 \\ -2 \\ \hline \end{array}$ $\begin{array}{r} 3 \\ -3 \\ \hline \end{array}$ $\begin{array}{r} 11 \\ -2 \\ \hline \end{array}$ $\begin{array}{r} 6 \\ -3 \\ \hline \end{array}$ $\begin{array}{r} 5 \\ -1 \\ \hline \end{array}$

4. $\begin{array}{r} 6 \\ -1 \\ \hline \end{array}$ $\begin{array}{r} 8 \\ -0 \\ \hline \end{array}$ $\begin{array}{r} 6 \\ -2 \\ \hline \end{array}$ $\begin{array}{r} 5 \\ -3 \\ \hline \end{array}$ $\begin{array}{r} 10 \\ -1 \\ \hline \end{array}$ $\begin{array}{r} 4 \\ -2 \\ \hline \end{array}$

5. $\begin{array}{r} 10 \\ -2 \\ \hline \end{array}$ $\begin{array}{r} 10 \\ -3 \\ \hline \end{array}$ $\begin{array}{r} 0 \\ -0 \\ \hline \end{array}$ $\begin{array}{r} 8 \\ -2 \\ \hline \end{array}$ $\begin{array}{r} 12 \\ -3 \\ \hline \end{array}$ $\begin{array}{r} 4 \\ -1 \\ \hline \end{array}$

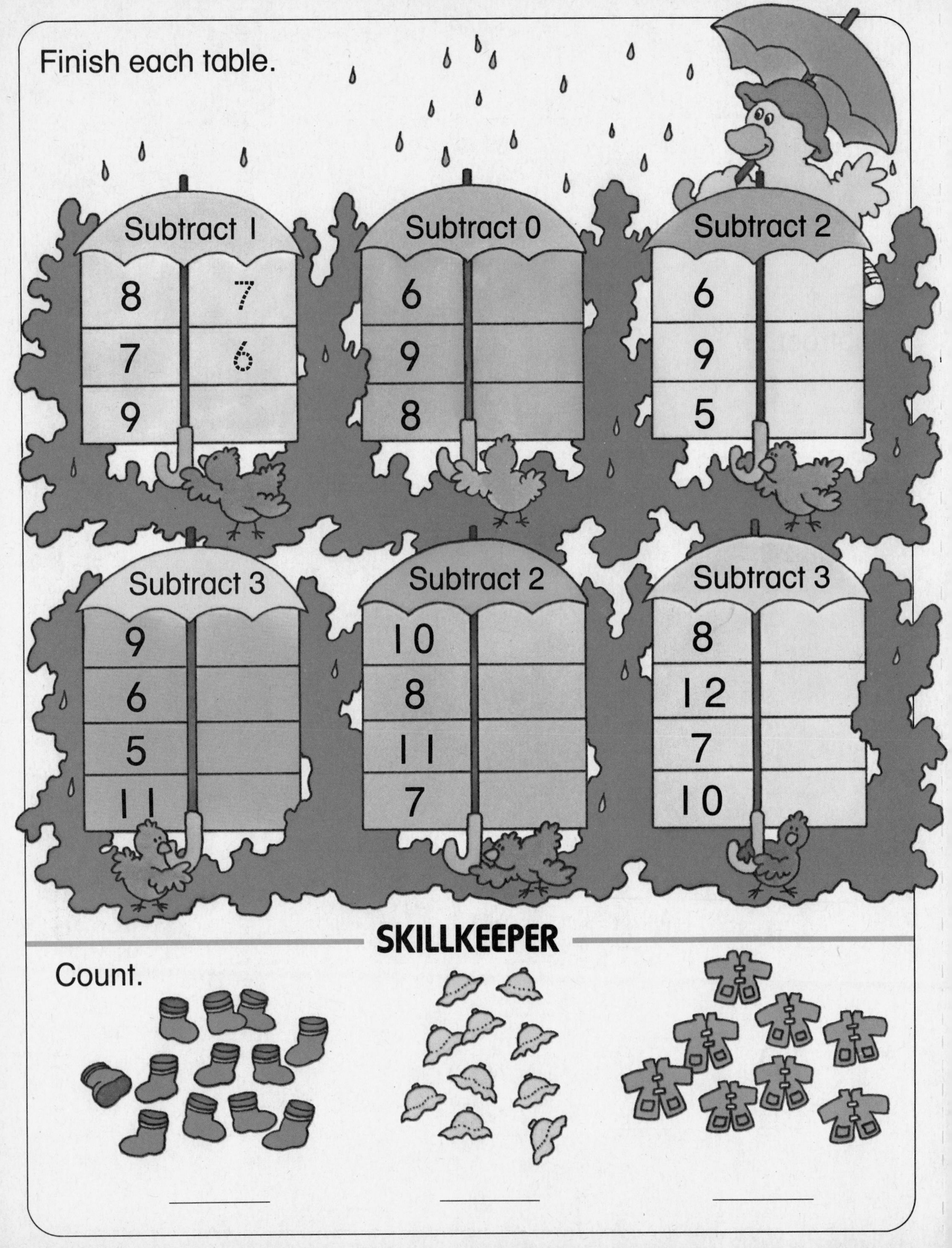
Finish each table.
Subtract 1
8 7
7 6
9
Subtract 0
6
9
8
Subtract 2
6
9
5
Subtract 3
9
6
5
11
Subtract 2
10
8
11
7
Subtract 3
8
12
7
10
SKILLKEEPER
Count.

Name ______________________________

Add or subtract.

1. $\begin{array}{r} 9 \\ -\ 1 \\ \hline \end{array}$ $\begin{array}{r} 7 \\ +\ 2 \\ \hline \end{array}$

2. $\begin{array}{r} 8 \\ +\ 1 \\ \hline \end{array}$ $\begin{array}{r} 10 \\ -\ \ 2 \\ \hline \end{array}$

3. $\begin{array}{r} 7 \\ -\ 2 \\ \hline \end{array}$ $\begin{array}{r} 6 \\ +\ 3 \\ \hline \end{array}$

4. $\begin{array}{r} 11 \\ -\ \ 3 \\ \hline \end{array}$ $\begin{array}{r} 6 \\ +\ 0 \\ \hline \end{array}$ $\begin{array}{r} 6 \\ +\ 2 \\ \hline \end{array}$ $\begin{array}{r} 10 \\ -\ \ 1 \\ \hline \end{array}$ $\begin{array}{r} 9 \\ +\ 1 \\ \hline \end{array}$ $\begin{array}{r} 8 \\ -\ 2 \\ \hline \end{array}$

5. $\begin{array}{r} 7 \\ +\ 1 \\ \hline \end{array}$ $\begin{array}{r} 9 \\ -\ 3 \\ \hline \end{array}$ $\begin{array}{r} 9 \\ +\ 3 \\ \hline \end{array}$ $\begin{array}{r} 11 \\ -\ \ 2 \\ \hline \end{array}$ $\begin{array}{r} 8 \\ -\ 8 \\ \hline \end{array}$ $\begin{array}{r} 5 \\ +\ 2 \\ \hline \end{array}$

6. $\begin{array}{r} 8 \\ -\ 3 \\ \hline \end{array}$ $\begin{array}{r} 7 \\ +\ 3 \\ \hline \end{array}$ $\begin{array}{r} 9 \\ -\ 2 \\ \hline \end{array}$ $\begin{array}{r} 9 \\ +\ 2 \\ \hline \end{array}$ $\begin{array}{r} 12 \\ -\ \ 3 \\ \hline \end{array}$ $\begin{array}{r} 5 \\ +\ 3 \\ \hline \end{array}$

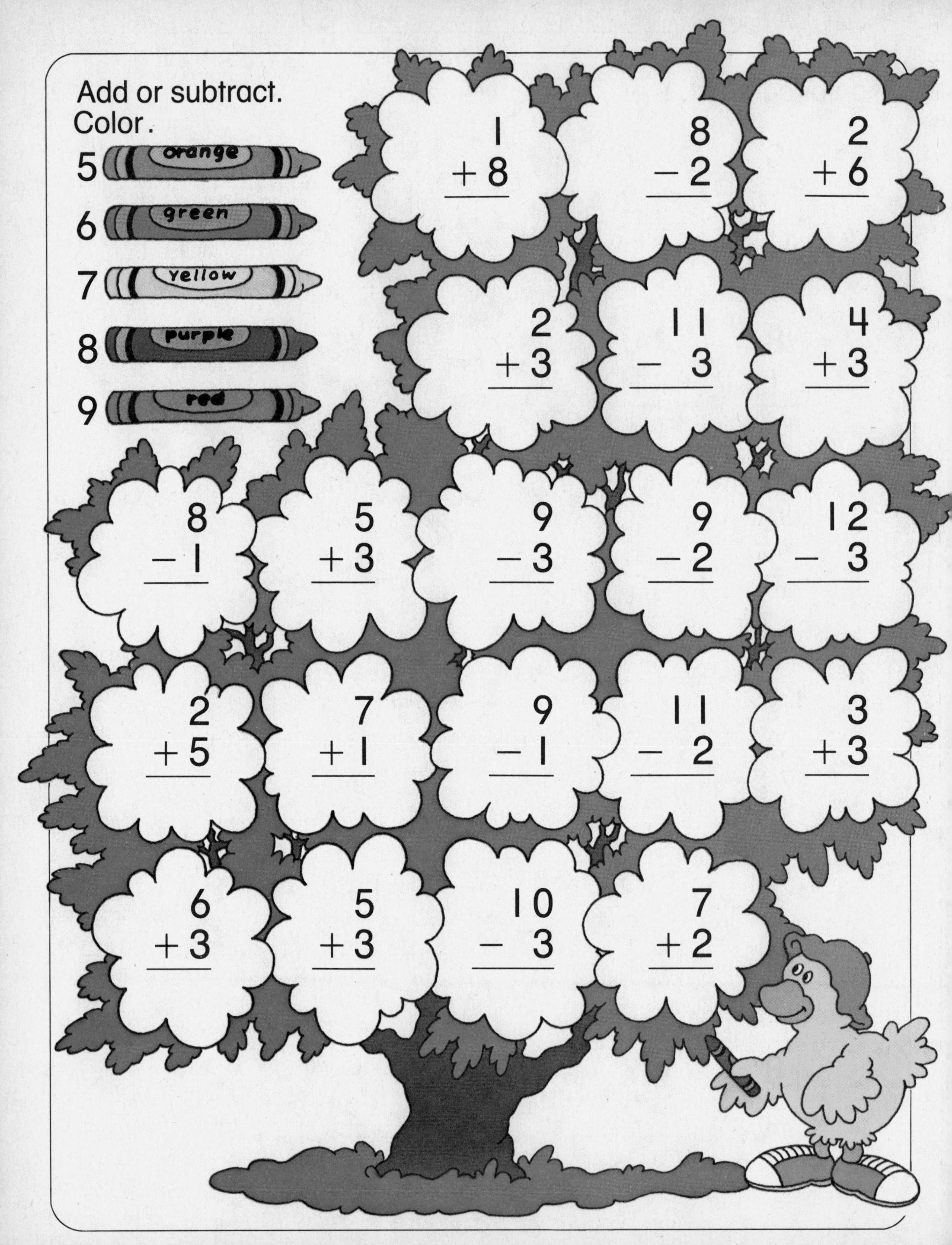
Add or subtract.
Color.
5 orange
6 green
7 yellow
8 purple
9 red
1 + 8
8 − 2
2 + 6
2 + 3
11 − 3
4 + 3
8 − 1
5 + 3
9 − 3
9 − 2
12 − 3
2 + 5
7 + 1
9 − 1
11 − 2
3 + 3
6 + 3
5 + 3
10 − 3
7 + 2

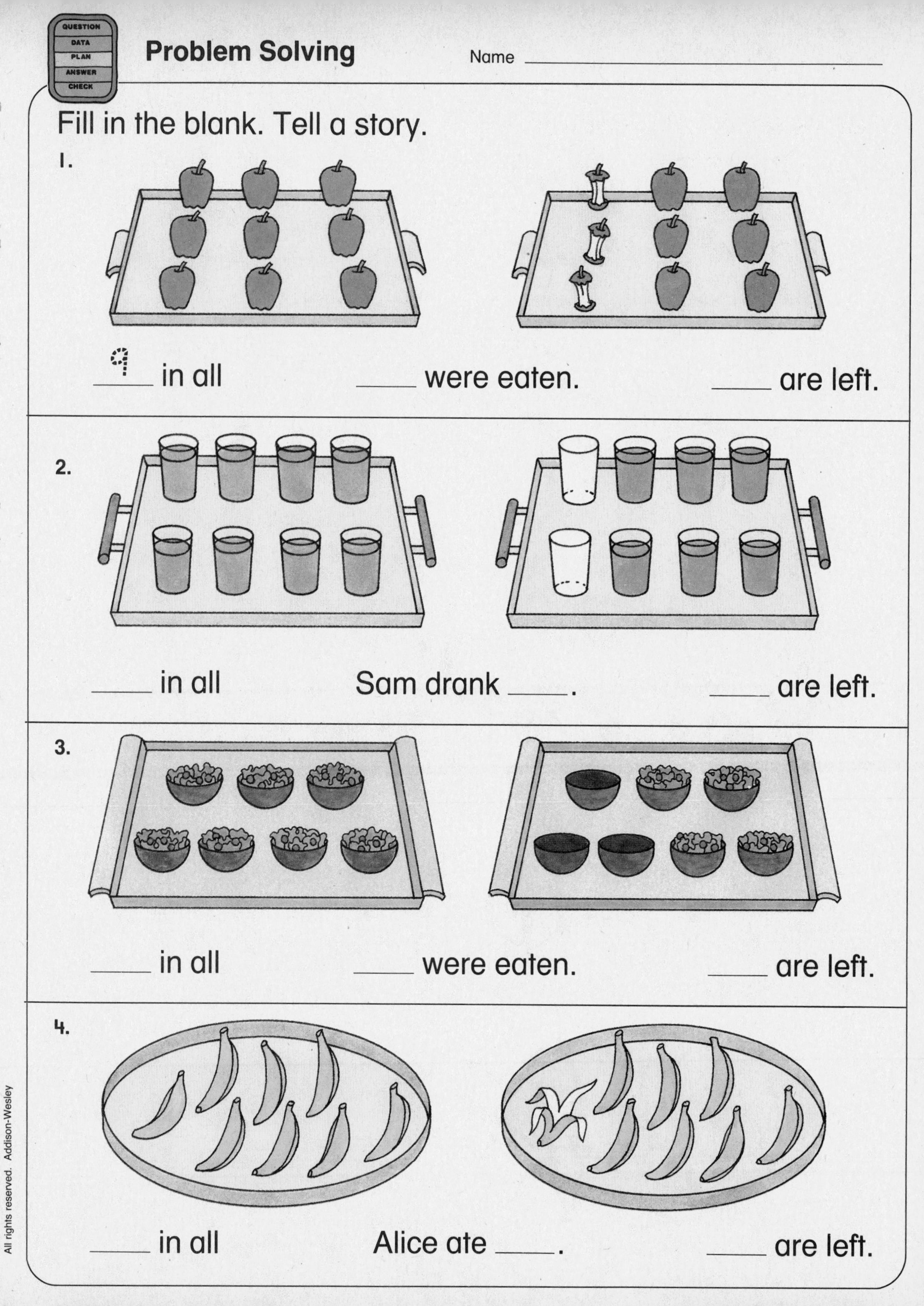

Problem Solving

Name ______________________________

Fill in the blank. Tell a story.

1\.

9 in all ____ were eaten. ____ are left.

2\.

____ in all Sam drank ____. ____ are left.

3\.

____ in all ____ were eaten. ____ are left.

4\.

____ in all Alice ate ____. ____ are left.

Problem Solving

Tell a story. Match. Subtract.

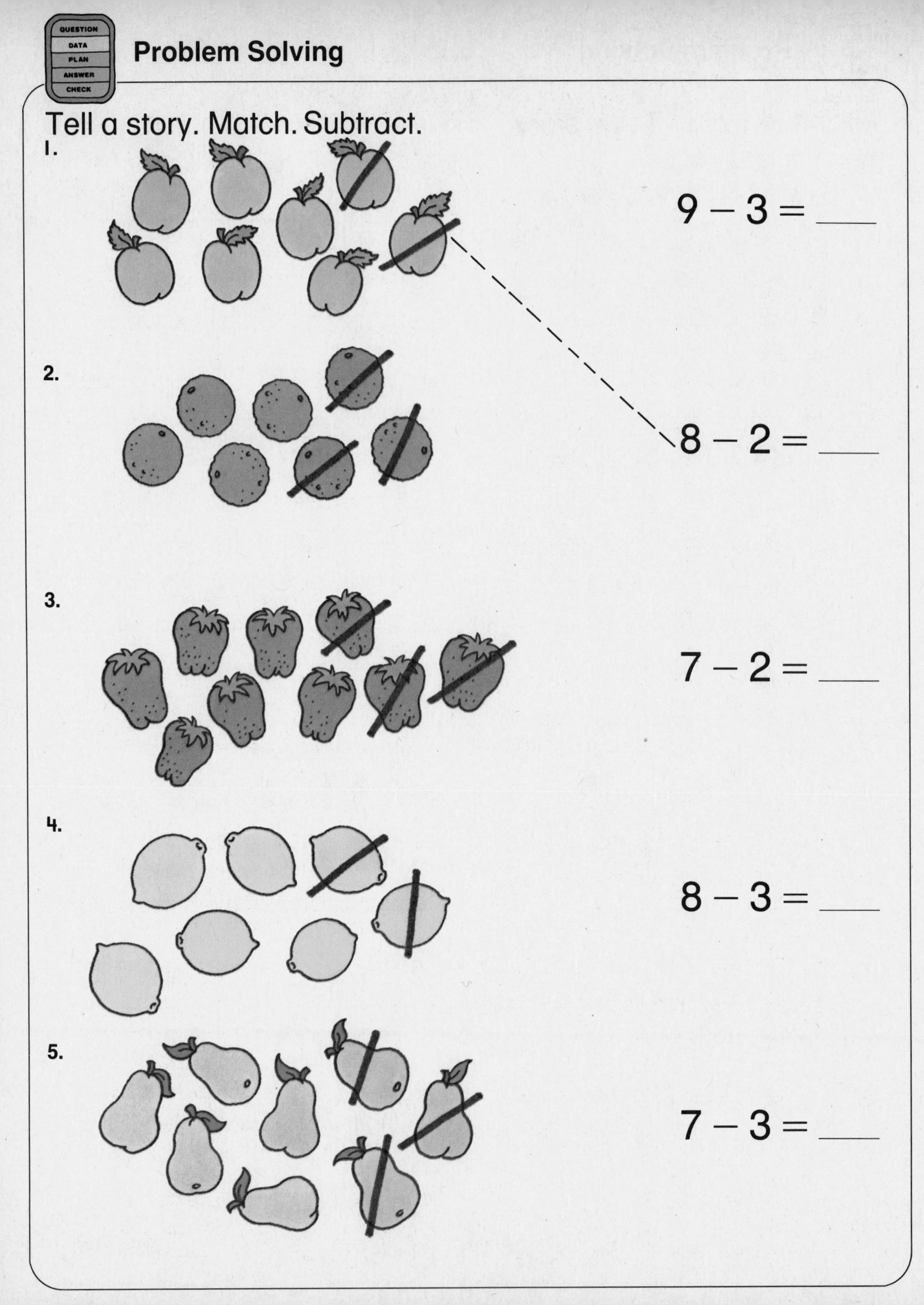

1\.

2\.

3\.

4\.

5\.

$9 - 3 =$ ____

$8 - 2 =$ ____

$7 - 2 =$ ____

$8 - 3 =$ ____

$7 - 3 =$ ____

Name ______________________________

CHAPTER REVIEW/TEST

1.

2

$2 - 1 =$ ____

2.

9

$9 - 2 =$ ____

Subtract.

3.

10	9	7	2	10	8
− 2	− 1	− 1	− 1	− 1	− 1

4.

6	4	5	7	6	9
− 1	− 1	− 1	− 3	− 2	− 3

5.

11	8	5	10	12	3
− 3	− 2	− 2	− 3	− 3	− 2

Ring the correct card. Subtract.

6.

$9 - 2 =$ $8 - 2 =$

7.

$8 - 3 =$ $8 - 2 =$

Name ____________________

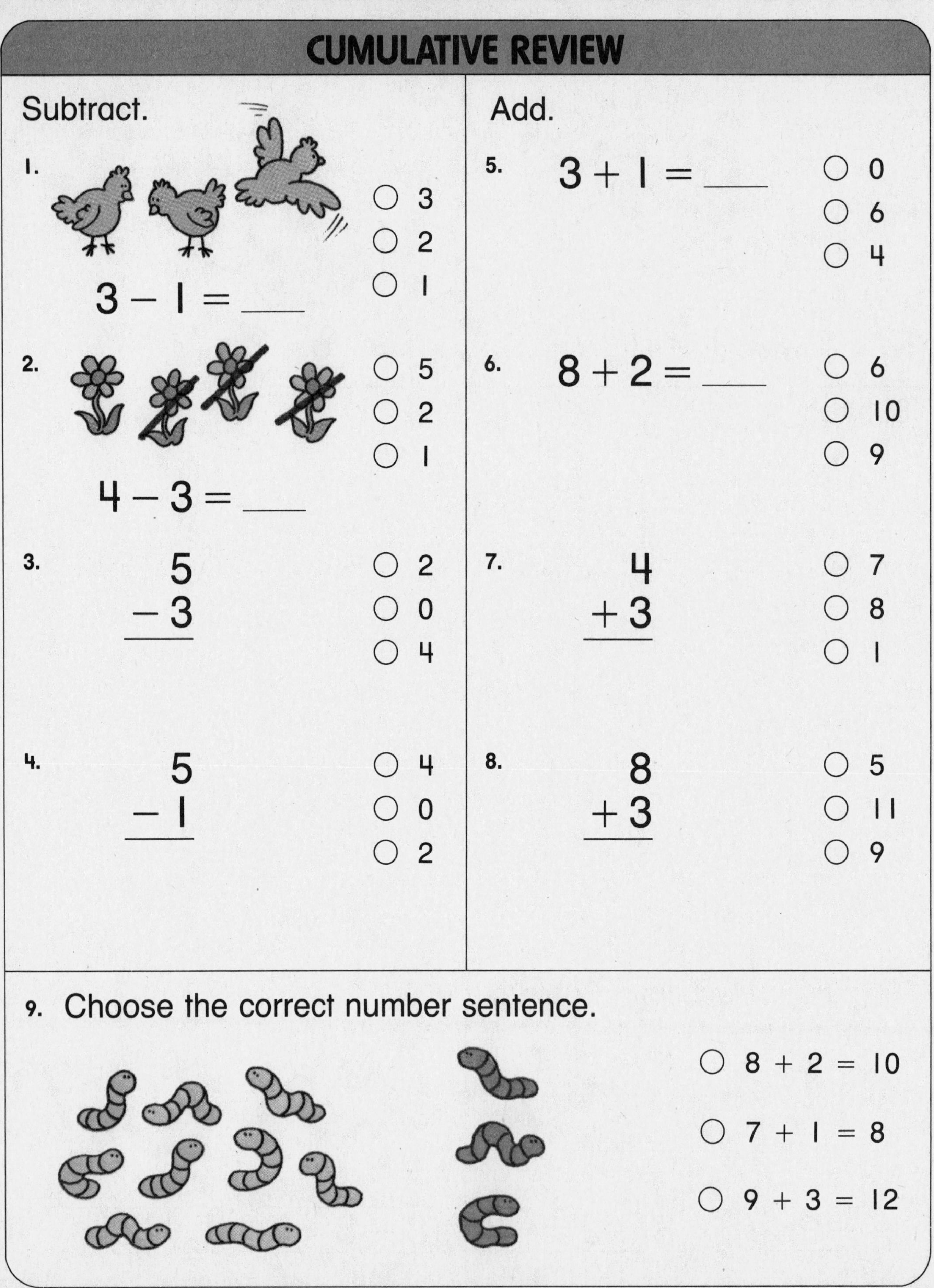

CUMULATIVE REVIEW

Subtract.

1. $3 - 1 = $ ____
   ○ 3
   ○ 2
   ○ 1

2. $4 - 3 = $ ____
   ○ 5
   ○ 2
   ○ 1

3. $\begin{array}{r} 5 \\ -\ 3 \\ \hline \end{array}$
   ○ 2
   ○ 0
   ○ 4

4. $\begin{array}{r} 5 \\ -\ 1 \\ \hline \end{array}$
   ○ 4
   ○ 0
   ○ 2

Add.

5. $3 + 1 = $ ____
   ○ 0
   ○ 6
   ○ 4

6. $8 + 2 = $ ____
   ○ 6
   ○ 10
   ○ 9

7. $\begin{array}{r} 4 \\ +\ 3 \\ \hline \end{array}$
   ○ 7
   ○ 8
   ○ 1

8. $\begin{array}{r} 8 \\ +\ 3 \\ \hline \end{array}$
   ○ 5
   ○ 11
   ○ 9

9. Choose the correct number sentence.
   ○ $8 + 2 = 10$
   ○ $7 + 1 = 8$
   ○ $9 + 3 = 12$

Name ______________________________

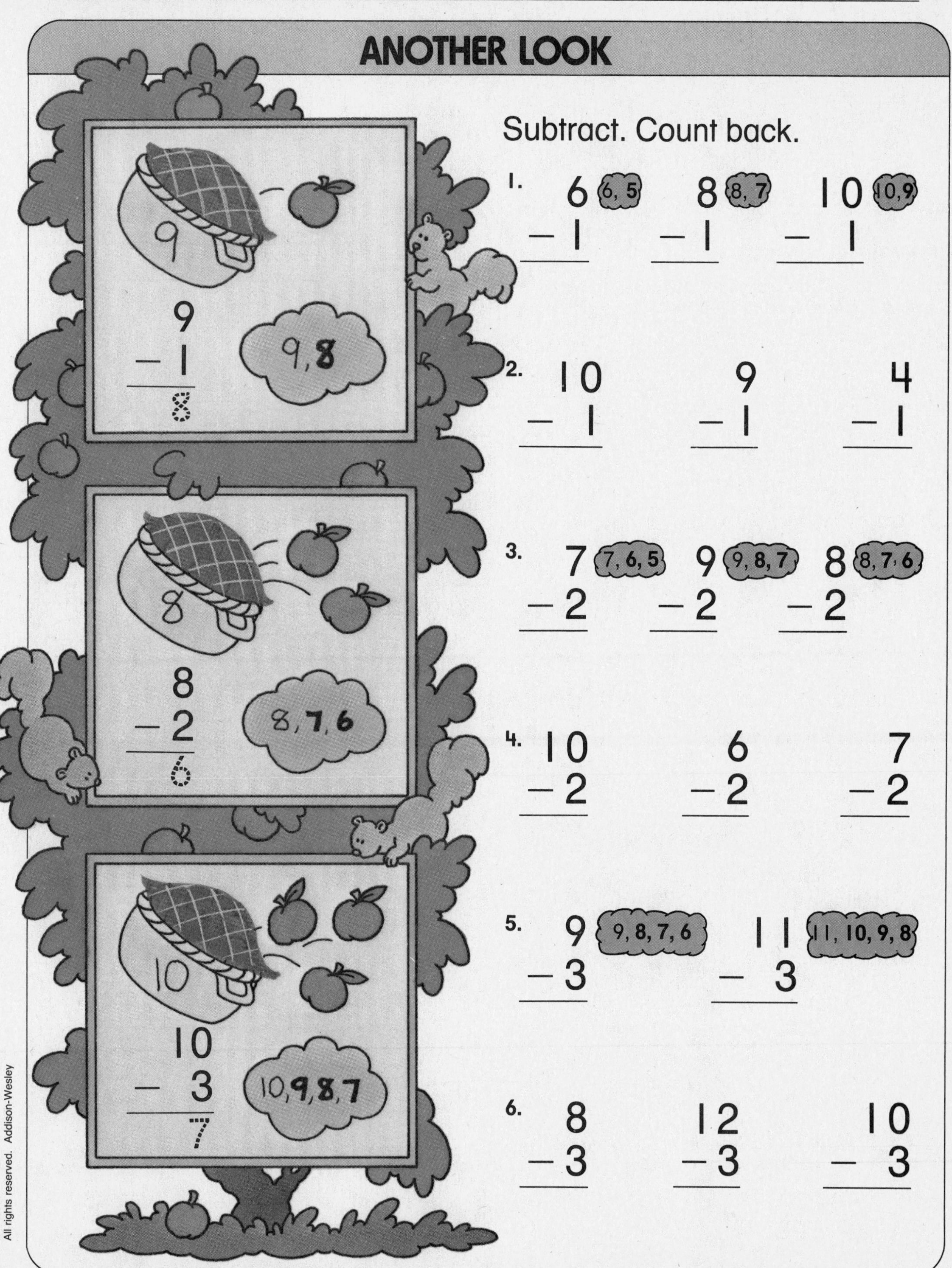

ANOTHER LOOK

Subtract. Count back.

1. $6 - 1$ (6, 5) $8 - 1$ (8, 7) $10 - 1$ (10, 9)

2. $10 - 1$ $9 - 1$ $4 - 1$

3. $7 - 2$ (7, 6, 5) $9 - 2$ (9, 8, 7) $8 - 2$ (8, 7, 6)

4. $10 - 2$ $6 - 2$ $7 - 2$

5. $9 - 3$ (9, 8, 7, 6) $11 - 3$ (11, 10, 9, 8)

6. $8 - 3$ $12 - 3$ $10 - 3$

Name ______________________________

ENRICHMENT

Ring the mystery number.
It is in the picture only one time.

6 Name ____________________

PLACE VALUE AND COUNTING

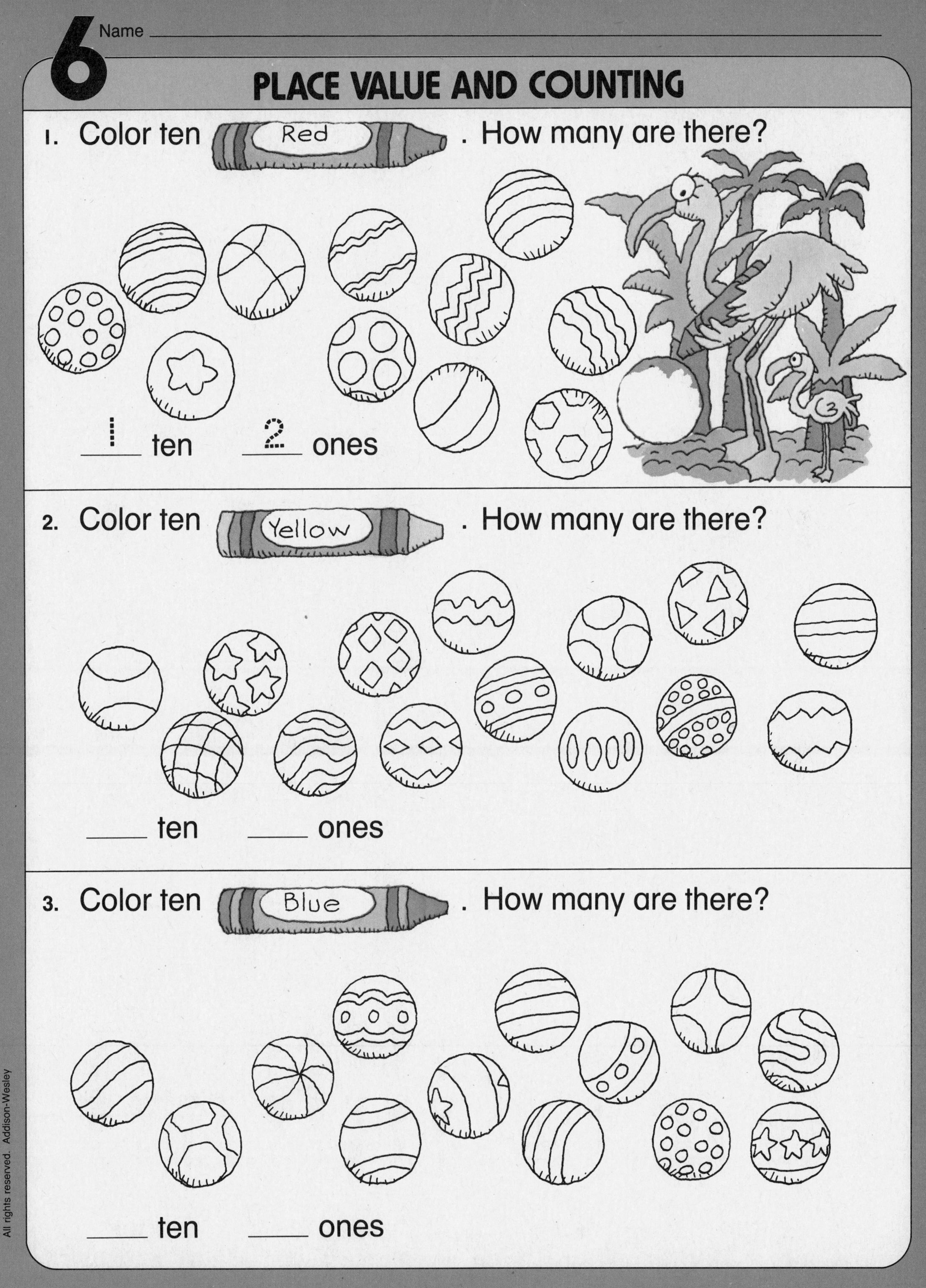

1. Color ten Red . How many are there?
1 ten 2 ones
2. Color ten Yellow . How many are there?
____ ten ____ ones
3. Color ten Blue . How many are there?
____ ten ____ ones

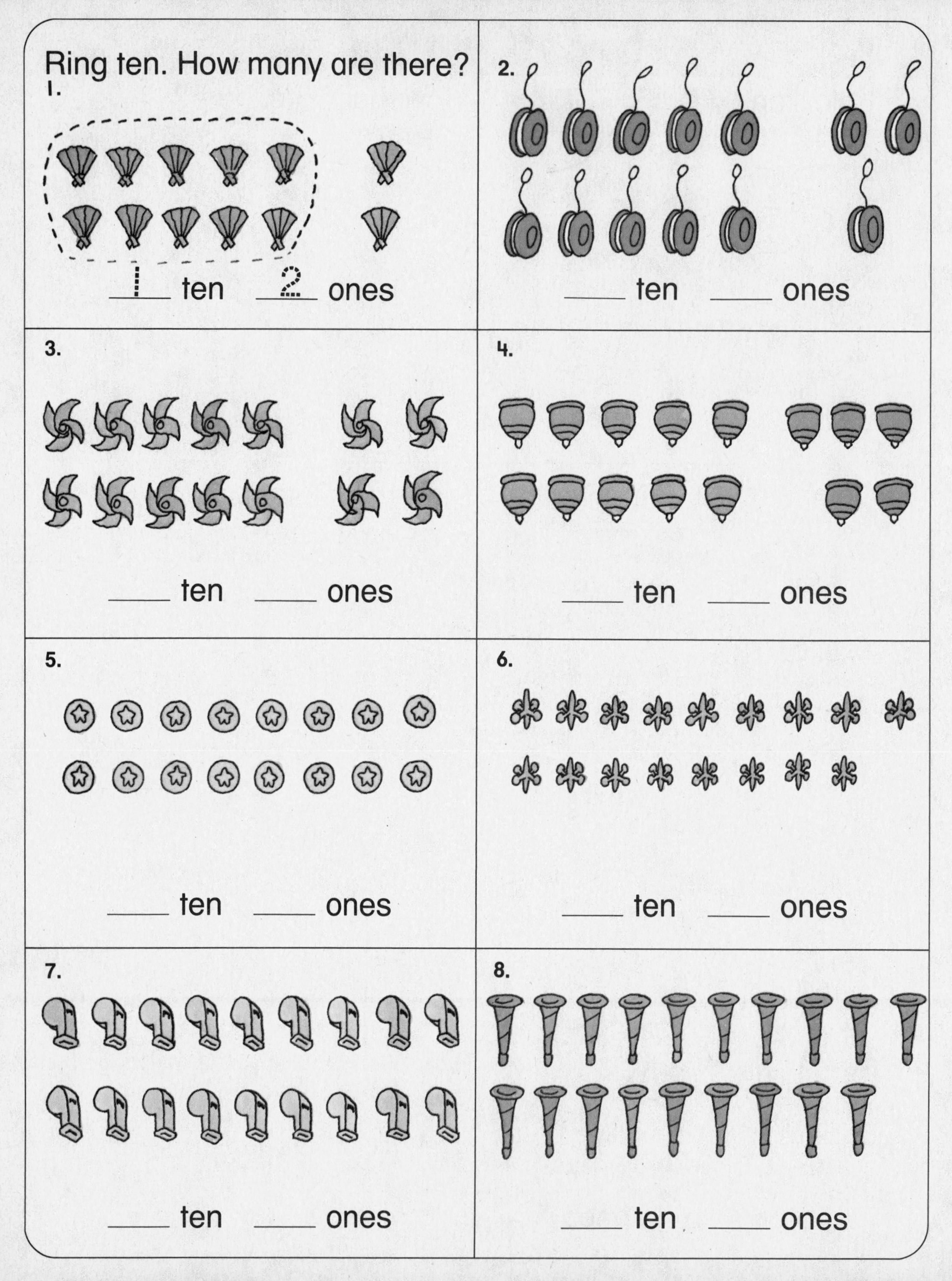
Ring ten. How many are there?
1.
1 ten 2 ones
2.
ten ones
3.
ten ones
4.
ten ones
5.
ten ones
6.
ten ones
7.
ten ones
8.
ten ones

Name ______________________________

___1___ ten ___0___ ones ___10___
ten

___1___ ten ___1___ one ___11___
eleven

How many are there?

1.	____ ten ____ ones ____ twelve
2.	____ ten ____ ones ____ thirteen
3.	____ ten ____ ones ____ fourteen
4.	____ ten ____ ones ____ fifteen
5.	____ ten ____ ones ____ sixteen
6.	____ ten ____ ones ____ seventeen
7.	____ ten ____ ones ____ eighteen
8.	____ ten ____ ones ____ nineteen

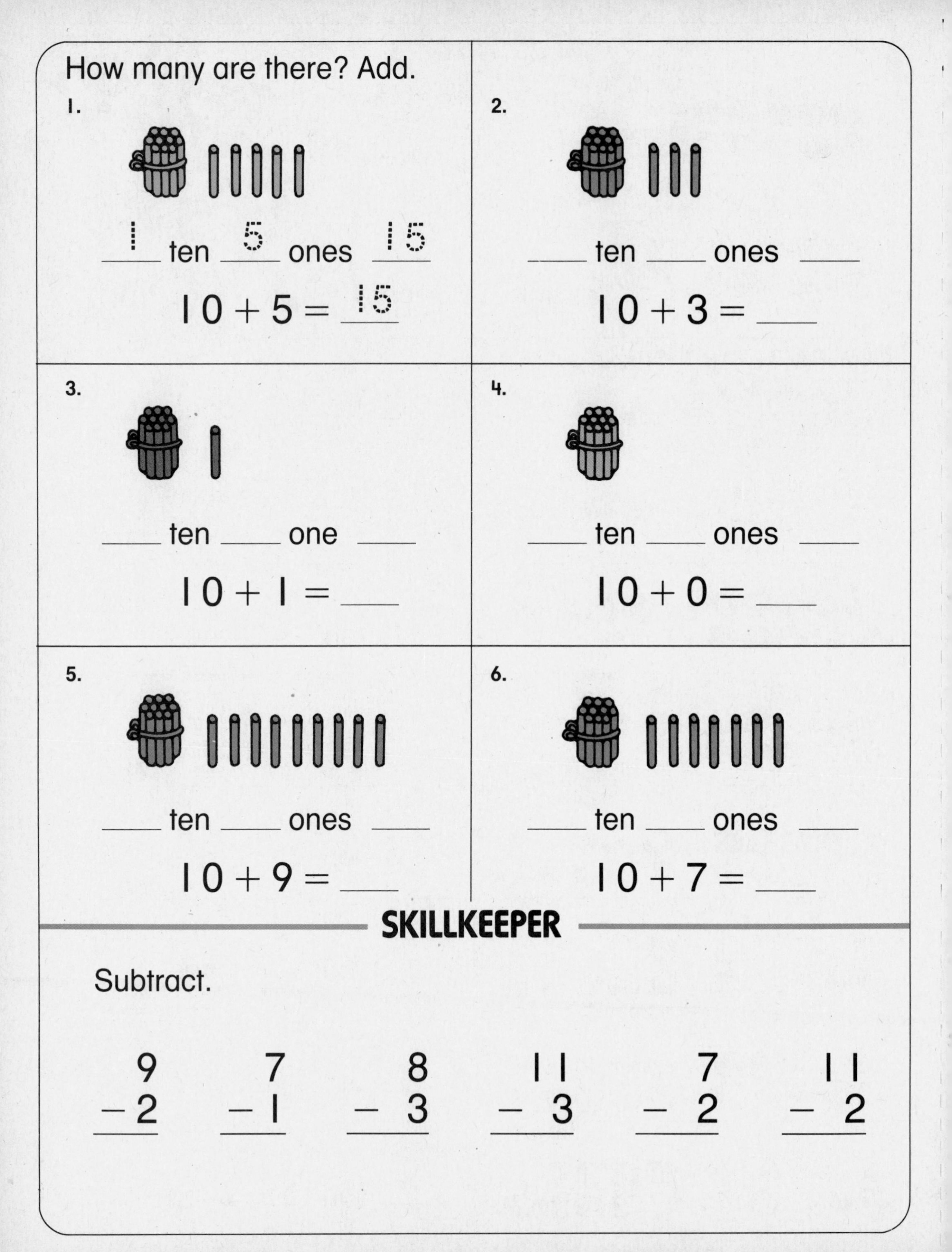

How many are there? Add.

1.

1 ten 5 ones 15

10 + 5 = 15

2.

____ ten ____ ones ____

10 + 3 = ____

3.

____ ten ____ one ____

10 + 1 = ____

4.

____ ten ____ ones ____

10 + 0 = ____

5.

____ ten ____ ones ____

10 + 9 = ____

6.

____ ten ____ ones ____

10 + 7 = ____

SKILLKEEPER

Subtract.

$$\begin{array}{r} 9 \\ -\ 2 \\ \hline \end{array} \quad \begin{array}{r} 7 \\ -\ 1 \\ \hline \end{array} \quad \begin{array}{r} 8 \\ -\ 3 \\ \hline \end{array} \quad \begin{array}{r} 11 \\ -\ 3 \\ \hline \end{array} \quad \begin{array}{r} 7 \\ -\ 2 \\ \hline \end{array} \quad \begin{array}{r} 11 \\ -\ 2 \\ \hline \end{array}$$

Name
2 tens 4 ones
How many are there?
1.
3 tens 2 ones
2.
tens ones
3.
tens ones
4.
tens ones
5.
tens ones
6.
tens ones

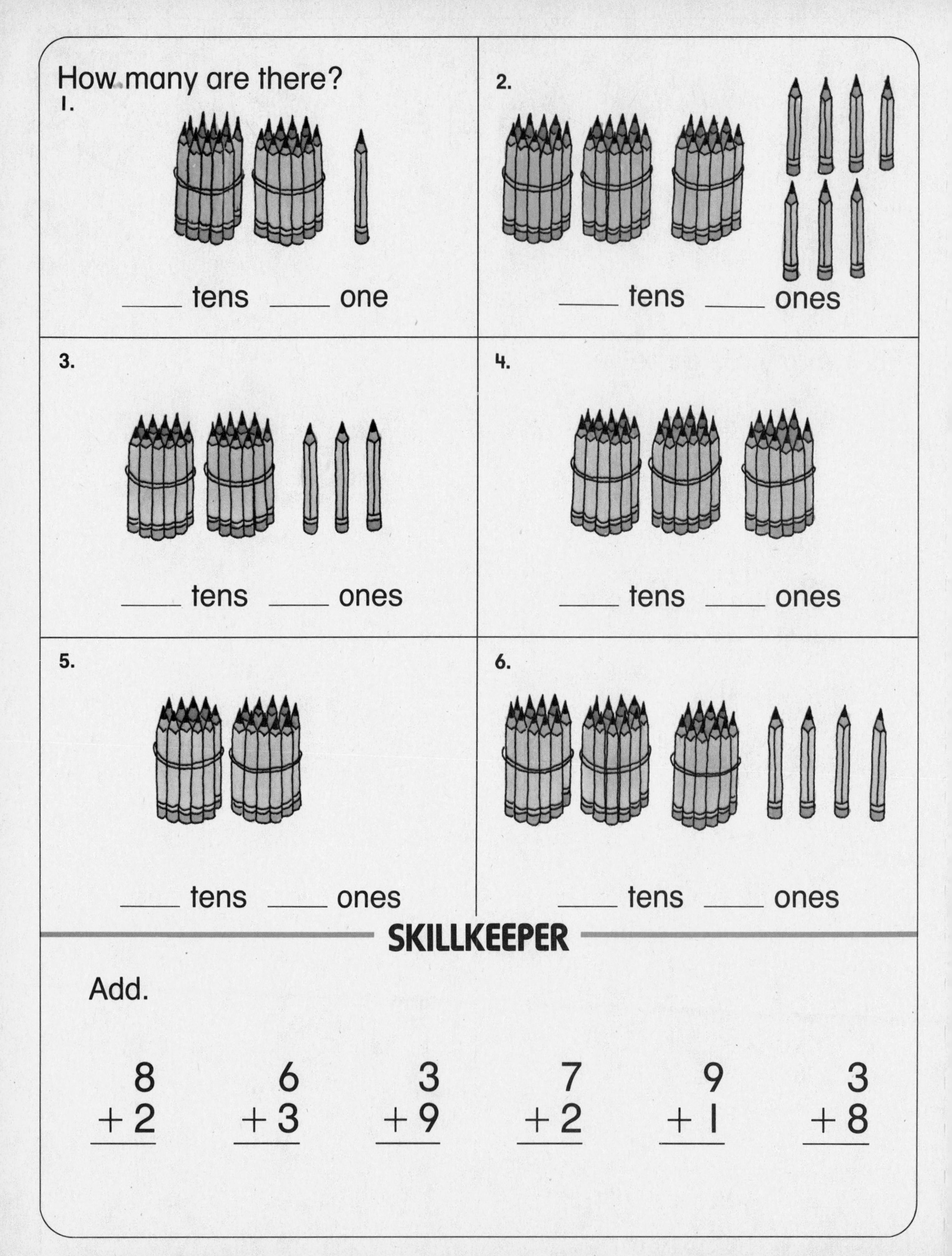

How many are there?

1.

____ tens ____ one

2.

____ tens ____ ones

3.

____ tens ____ ones

4.

____ tens ____ ones

5.

____ tens ____ ones

6.

____ tens ____ ones

SKILLKEEPER

Add.

$$\begin{array}{r} 8 \\ +2 \\ \hline \end{array} \quad \begin{array}{r} 6 \\ +3 \\ \hline \end{array} \quad \begin{array}{r} 3 \\ +9 \\ \hline \end{array} \quad \begin{array}{r} 7 \\ +2 \\ \hline \end{array} \quad \begin{array}{r} 9 \\ +1 \\ \hline \end{array} \quad \begin{array}{r} 3 \\ +8 \\ \hline \end{array}$$

Name ___

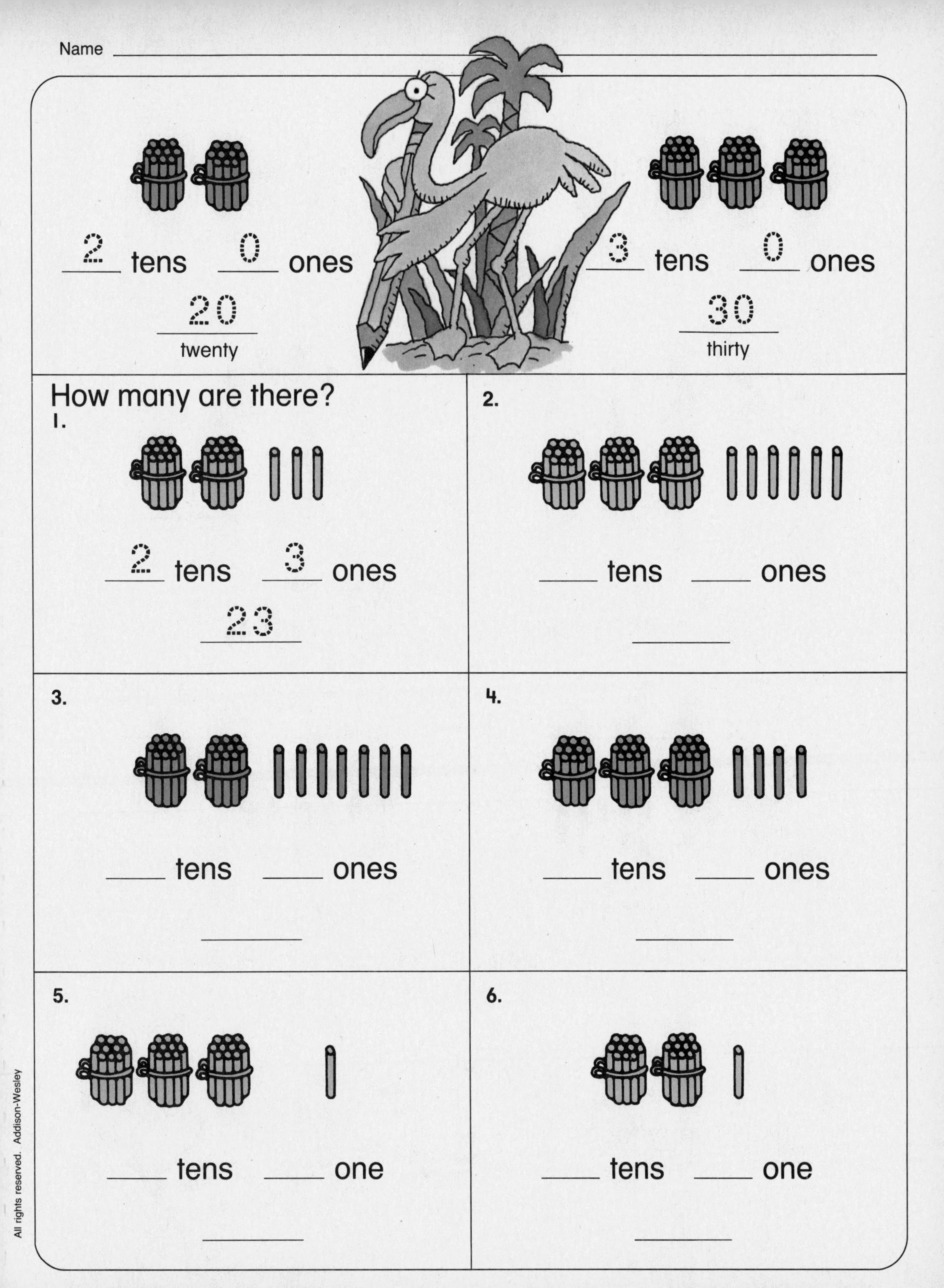
2 tens 0 ones
20
twenty
3 tens 0 ones
30
thirty
How many are there?
1.
2 tens 3 ones
23
2.
tens ones
3.
tens ones
4.
tens ones
5.
tens one
6.
tens one

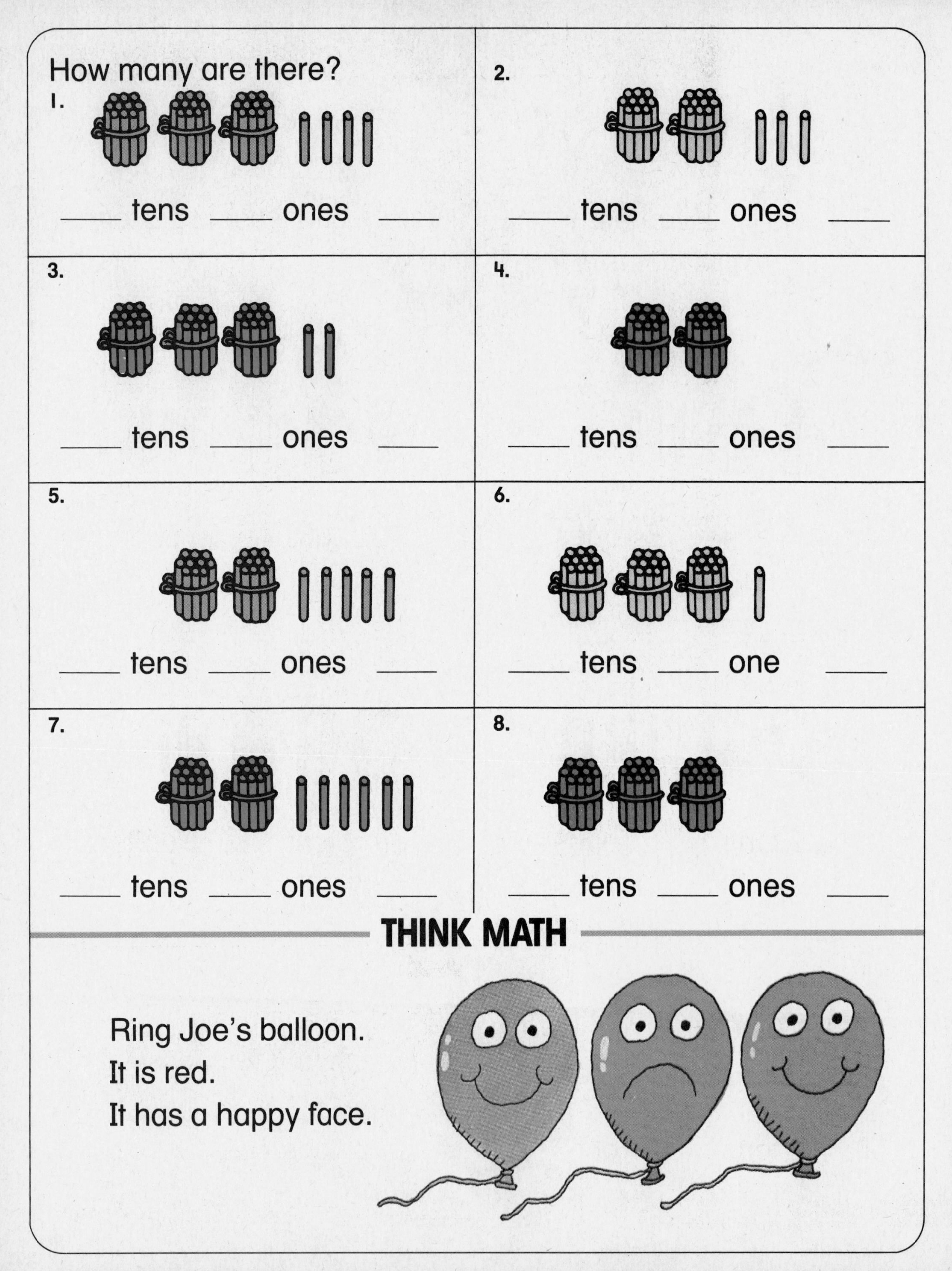
How many are there?
1.
____ tens ____ ones ____
2.
____ tens ____ ones ____
3.
____ tens ____ ones ____
4.
____ tens ____ ones ____
5.
____ tens ____ ones ____
6.
____ tens ____ one ____
7.
____ tens ____ ones ____
8.
____ tens ____ ones ____
THINK MATH
Ring Joe's balloon.
It is red.
It has a happy face.

Name ______________________________

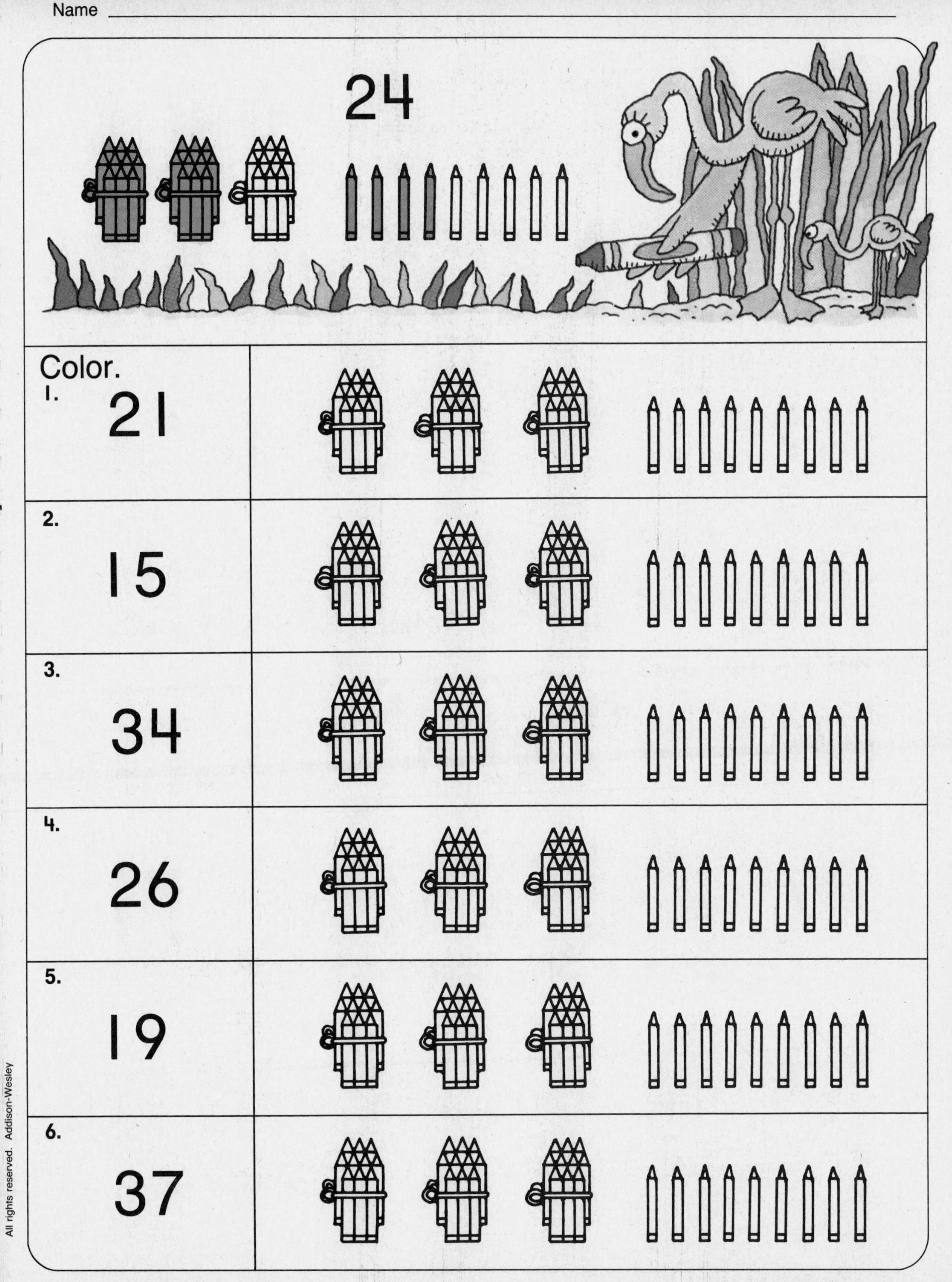

24
Color.
1.
21
2.
15
3.
34
4.
26
5.
19
6.
37

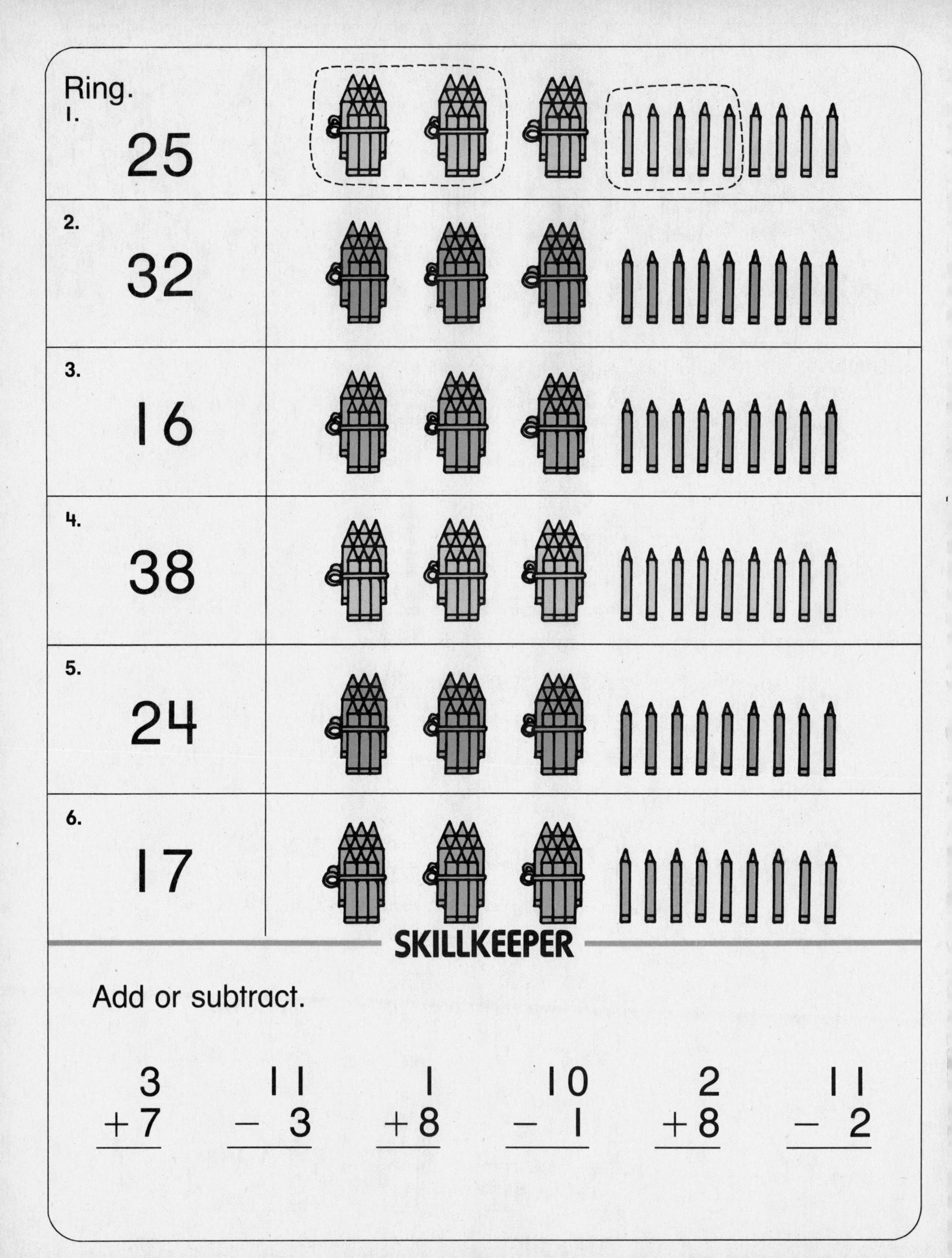
Ring.
1.
25
2.
32
3.
16
4.
38
5.
24
6.
17
SKILLKEEPER
Add or subtract.
3
+ 7
11
− 3
1
+ 8
10
− 1
2
+ 8
11
− 2

Name ______________________________

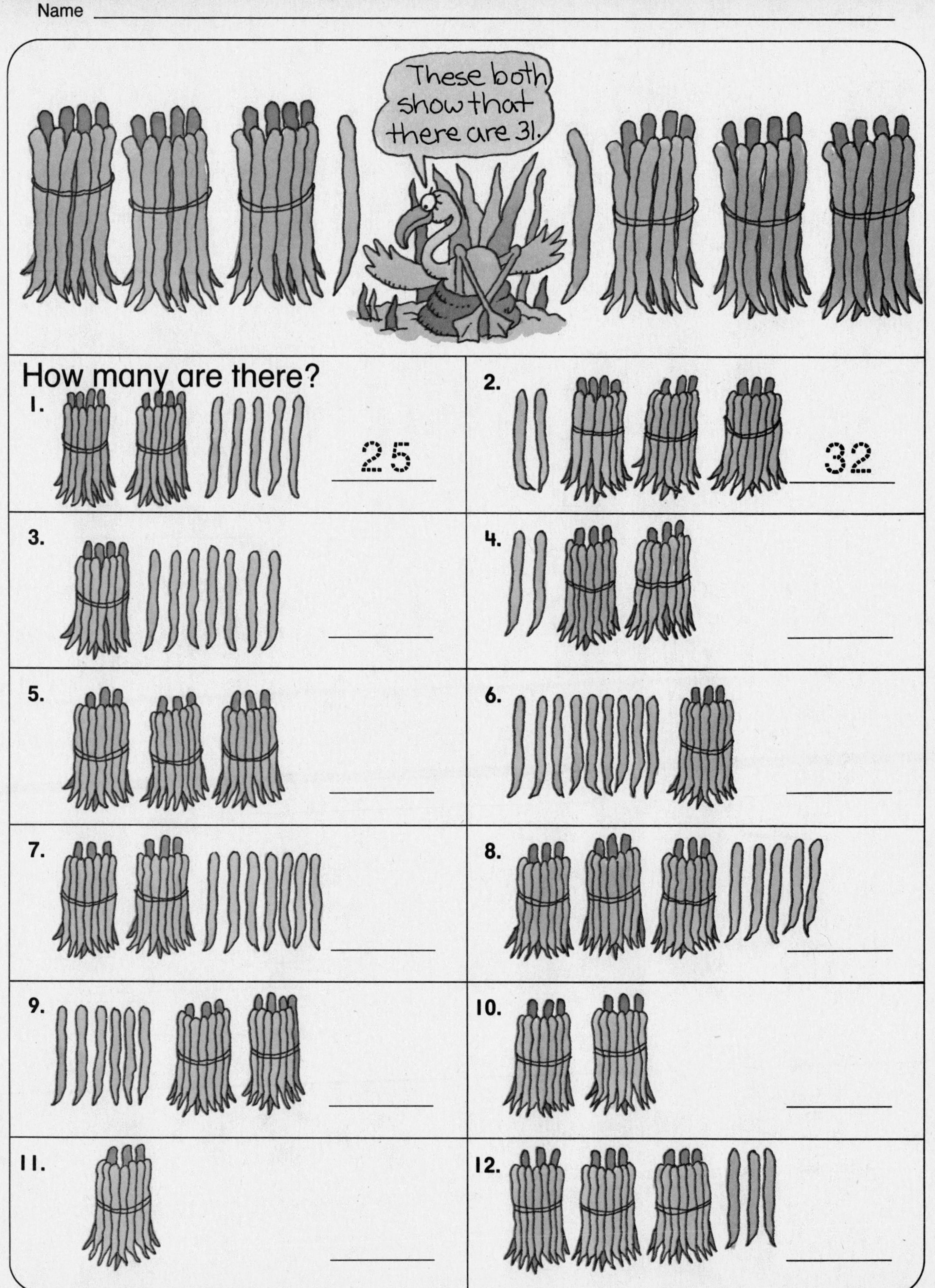
These both show that there are 31.
How many are there?
1.
25
2.
32
3.
4.
5.
6.
7.
8.
9.
10.
11.
12.

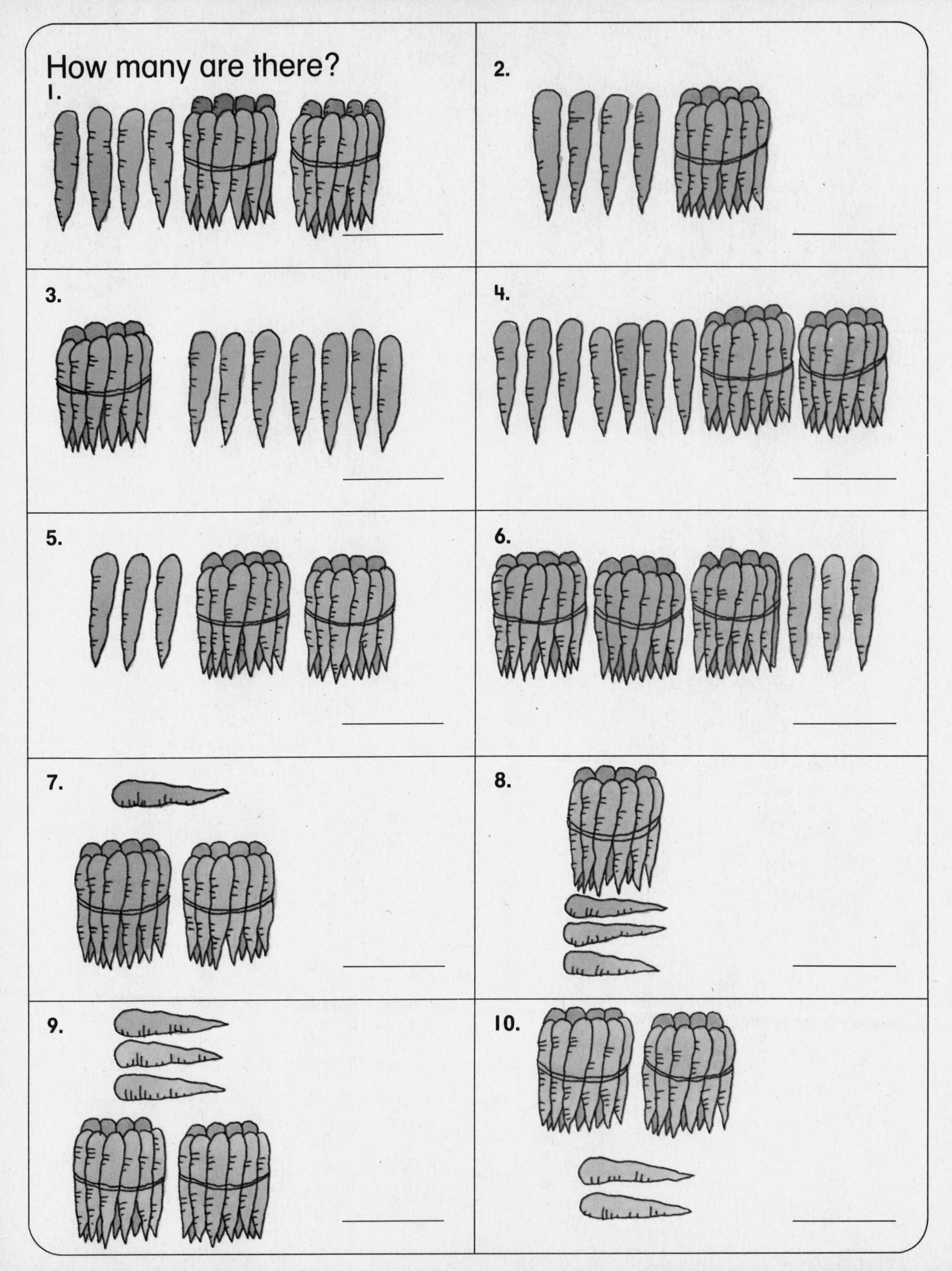
How many are there?
1.
2.
3.
4.
5.
6.
7.
8.
9.
10.

Name ______________________________

This means that there are 3 tens.
36
3 tens
3 ones
Color the card for the red digit.
1.
17
1 ten
1 one
2.
35
3 tens
3 ones
3.
26
6 tens
6 ones
4.
22
2 tens
2 ones
5.
32
2 tens
2 ones
6.
19
1 ten
1 one

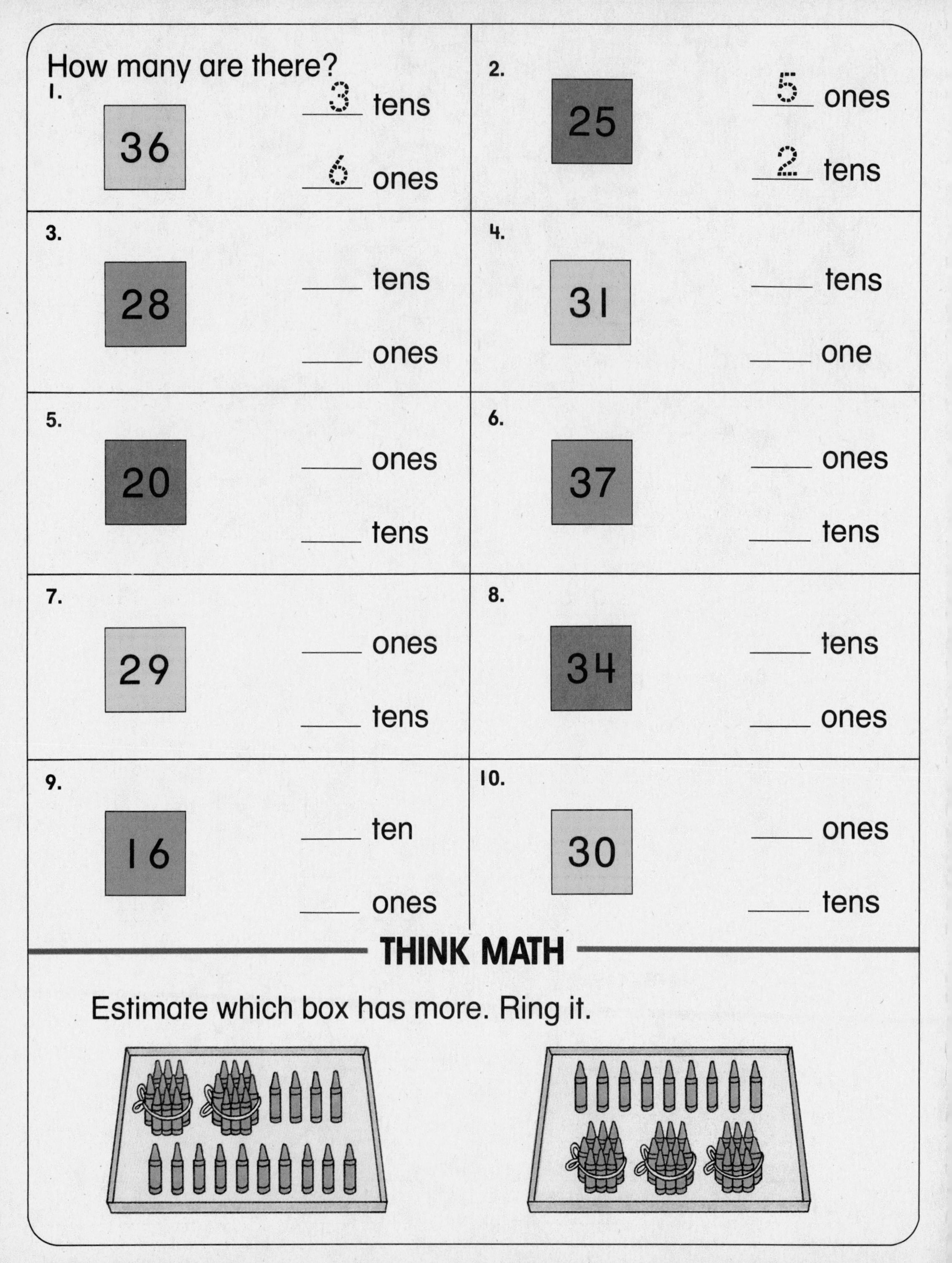

How many are there?

1. 36 — 3 tens, 6 ones

2. 25 — 5 ones, 2 tens

3. 28 — ____ tens, ____ ones

4. 31 — ____ tens, ____ one

5. 20 — ____ ones, ____ tens

6. 37 — ____ ones, ____ tens

7. 29 — ____ ones, ____ tens

8. 34 — ____ tens, ____ ones

9. 16 — ____ ten, ____ ones

10. 30 — ____ ones, ____ tens

THINK MATH

Estimate which box has more. Ring it.

Name ____________________

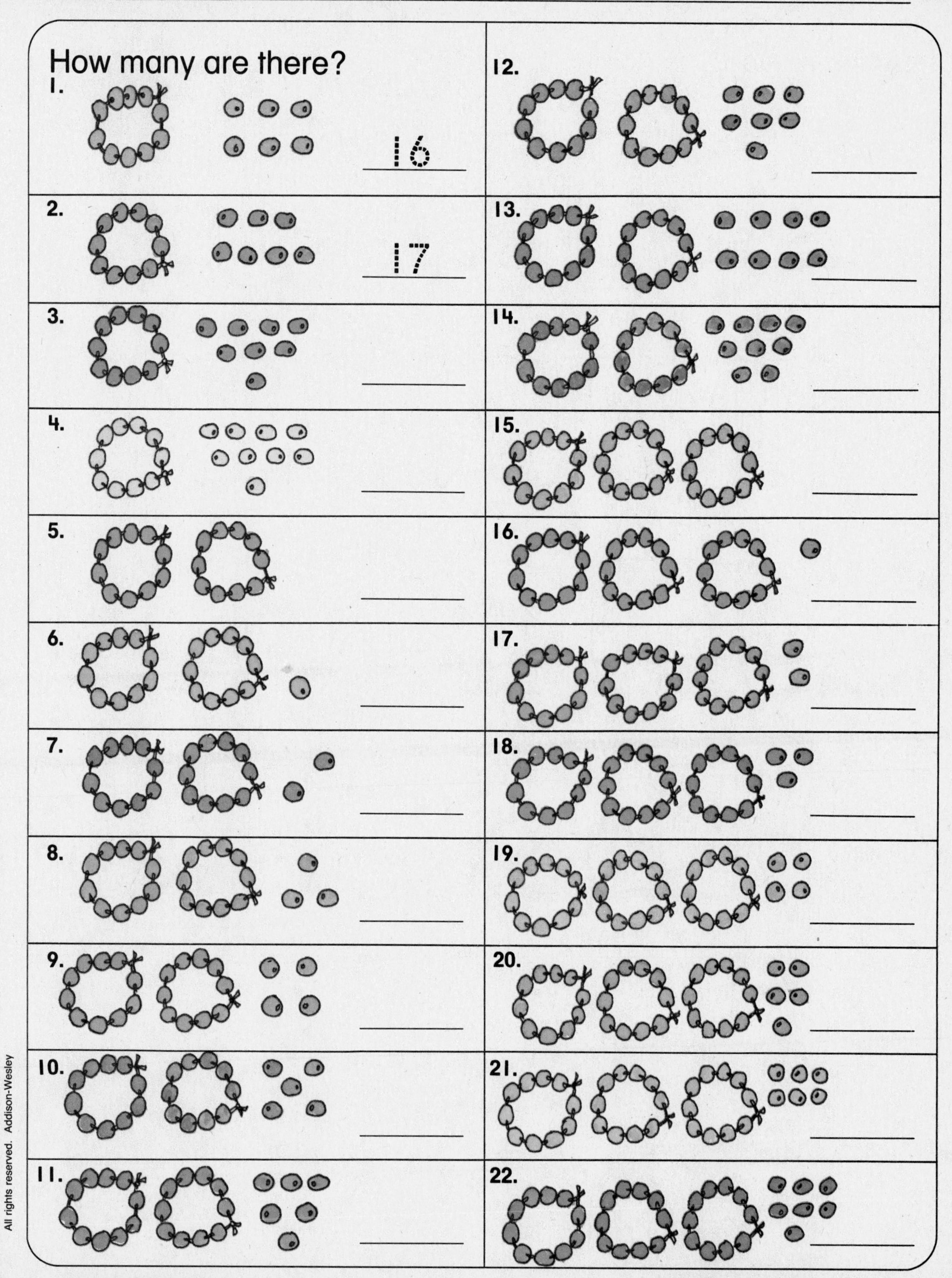
How many are there?
1.
16
2.
17
3.
4.
5.
6.
7.
8.
9.
10.
11.
12.
13.
14.
15.
16.
17.
18.
19.
20.
21.
22.

Finish each row.

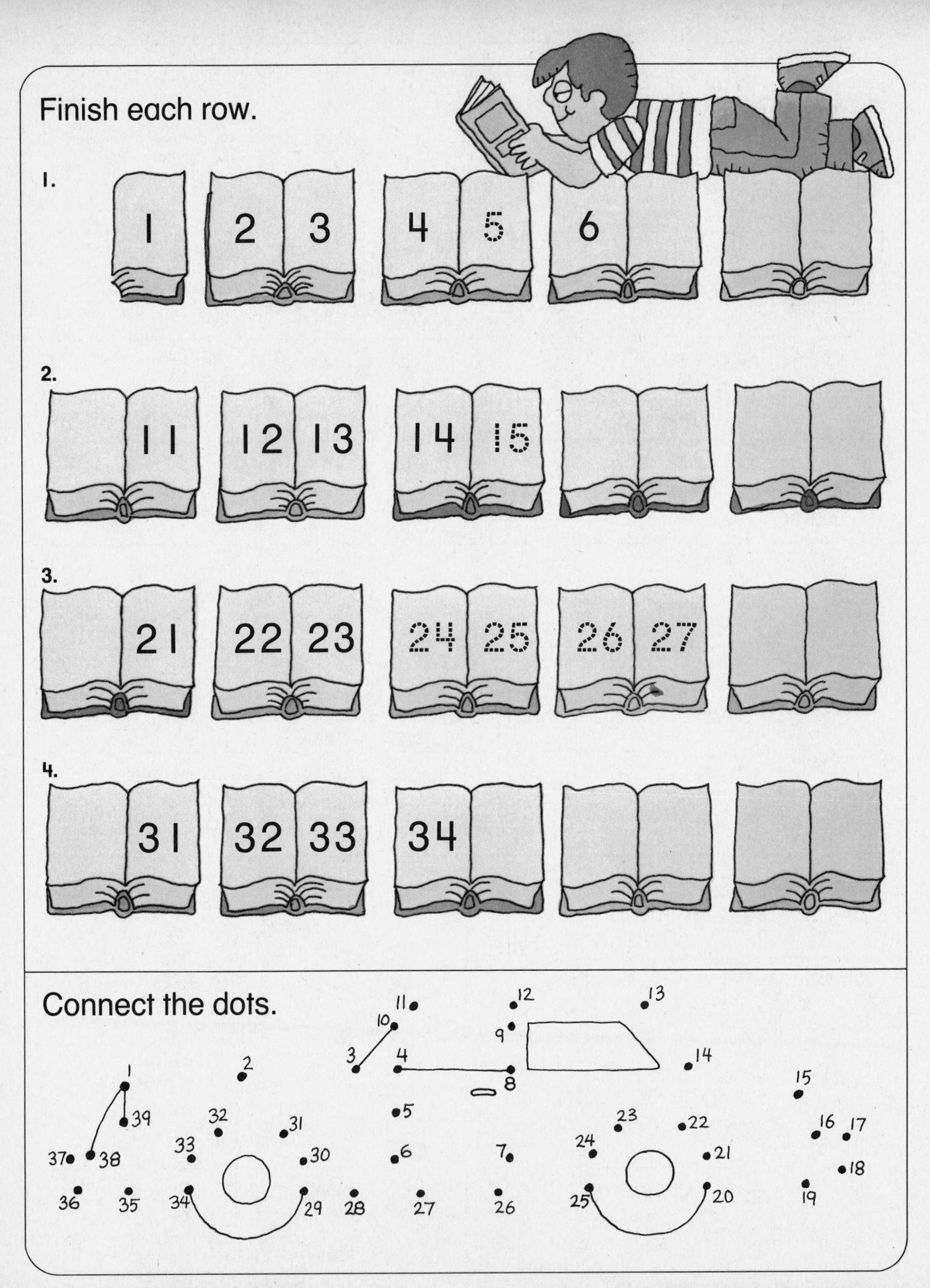

Connect the dots.

Name ___

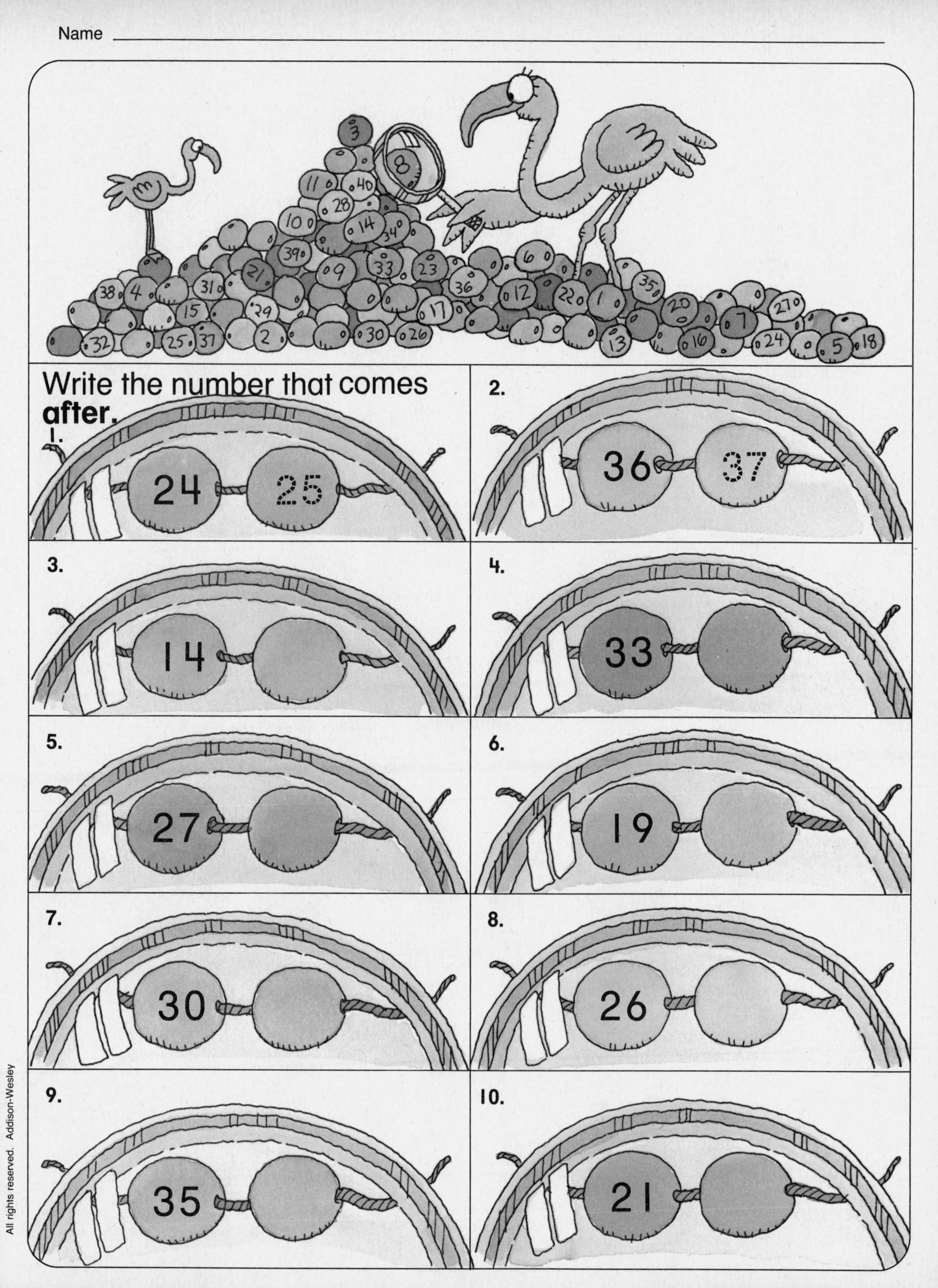

3
8
11
40
28
10
14
34
39
21
33
23
9
38
4
31
15
29
36
6
12
22
1
35
20
27
17
7
16
24
5
18
13
32
25
37
2
30
26
Write the number that comes **after.**
1.
24
25
2.
36
37
3.
14
4.
33
5.
27
6.
19
7.
30
8.
26
9.
35
10.
21

Write the number that comes **before.**

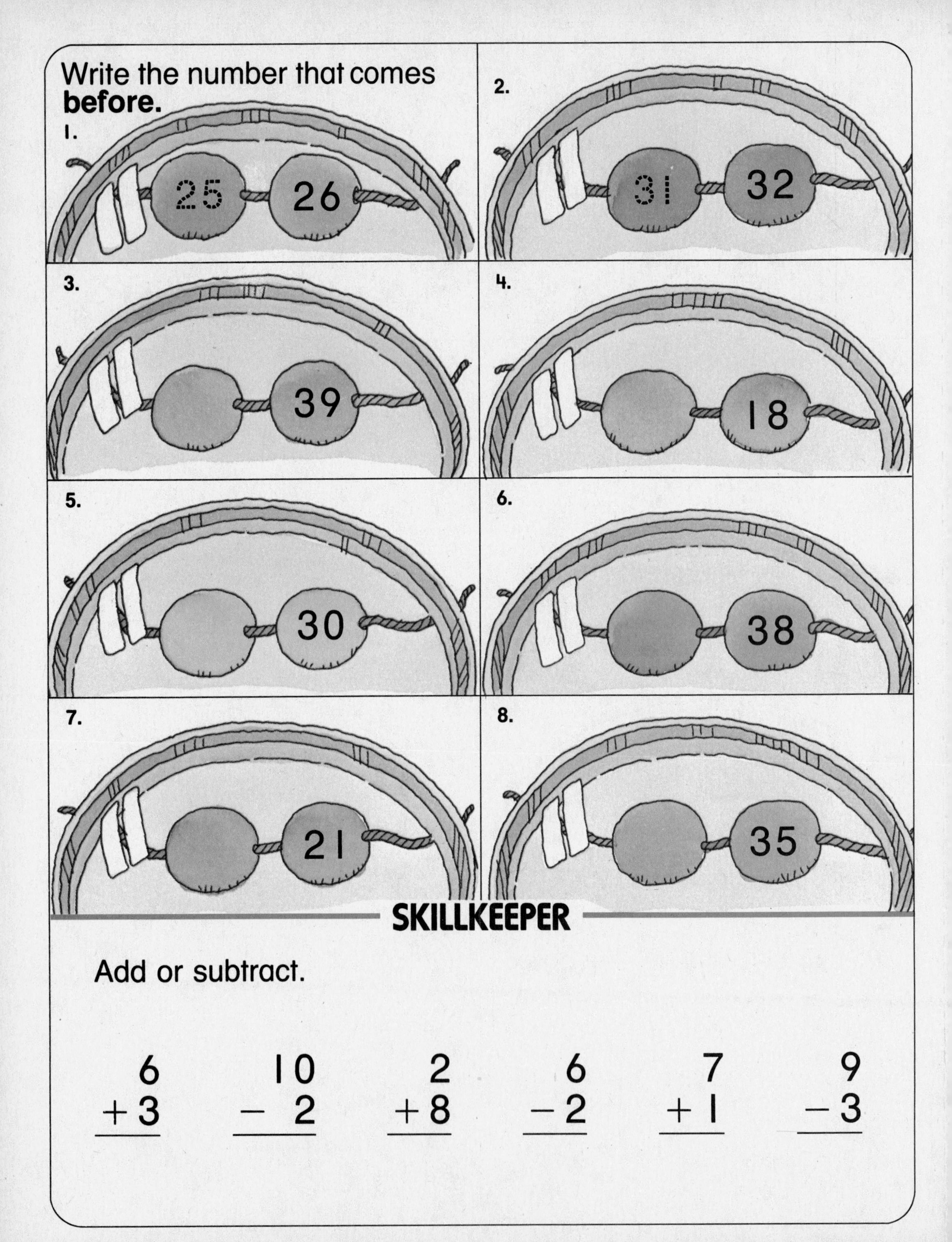

SKILLKEEPER

Add or subtract.

$\begin{array}{r} 6 \\ +3 \\ \hline \end{array}$ $\begin{array}{r} 10 \\ -\ 2 \\ \hline \end{array}$ $\begin{array}{r} 2 \\ +8 \\ \hline \end{array}$ $\begin{array}{r} 6 \\ -2 \\ \hline \end{array}$ $\begin{array}{r} 7 \\ +1 \\ \hline \end{array}$ $\begin{array}{r} 9 \\ -3 \\ \hline \end{array}$

Name ______________________________

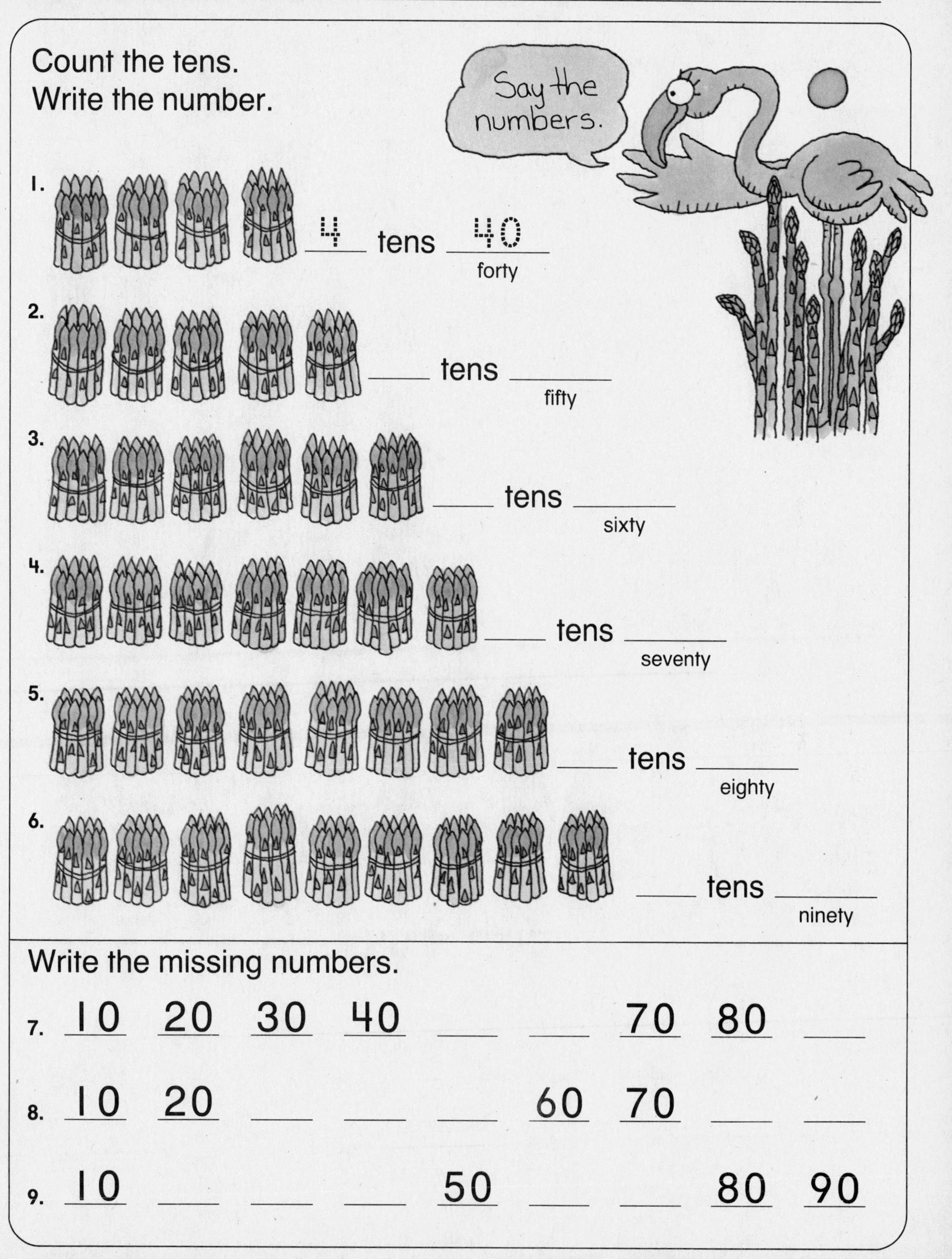

Count the tens.
Write the number.

1. 4 tens 40
forty

2. ____ tens ______
fifty

3. ____ tens ______
sixty

4. ____ tens ______
seventy

5. ____ tens ______
eighty

6. ____ tens ______
ninety

Write the missing numbers.

7. 10 20 30 40 ____ ____ 70 80 ____

8. 10 20 ____ ____ ____ 60 70 ____ ____

9. 10 ____ ____ ____ 50 ____ ____ 80 90

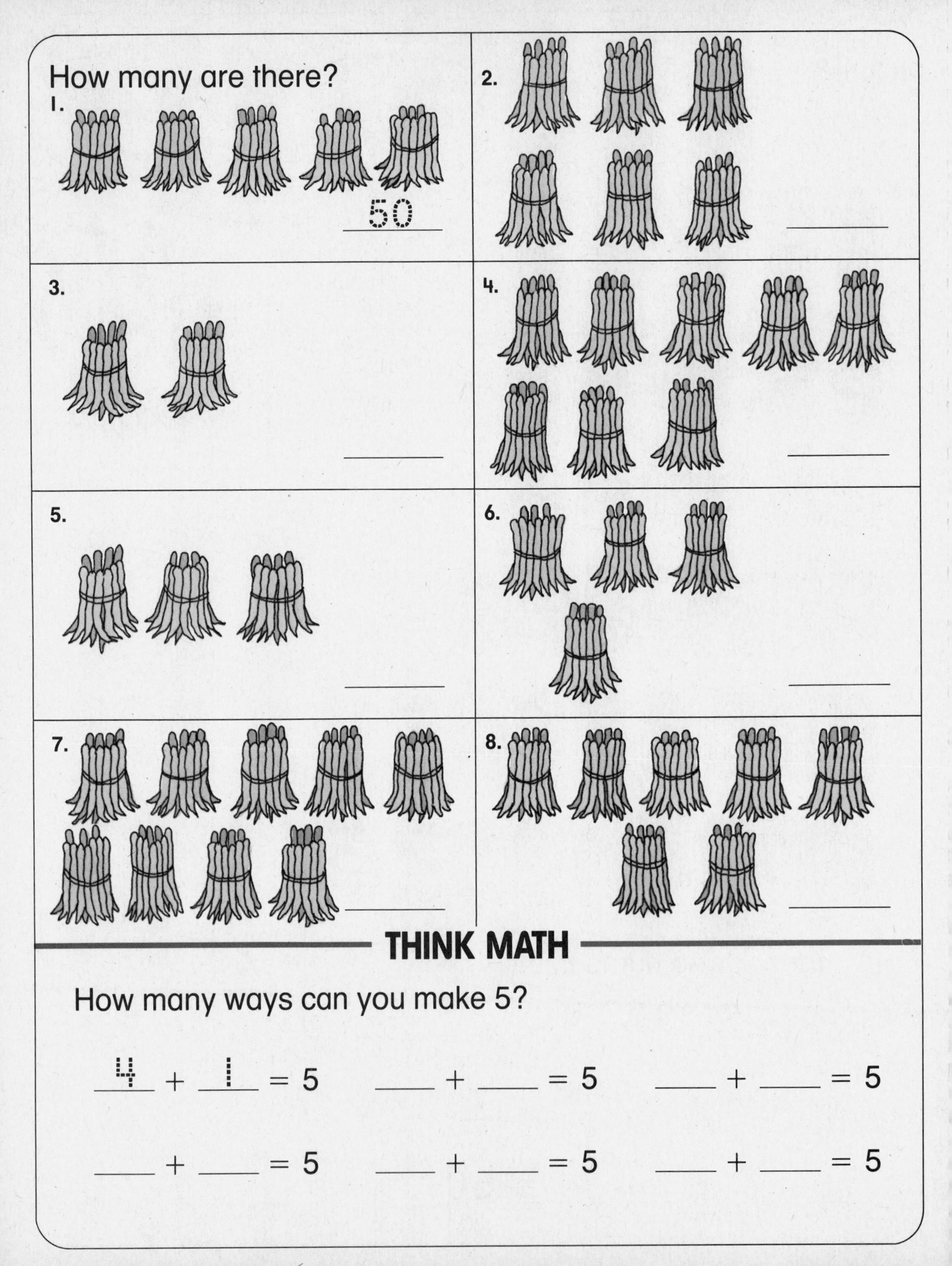
How many are there?
1.
50
2.
3.
4.
5.
6.
7.
8.
THINK MATH
How many ways can you make 5?
4 + 1 = 5
___ + ___ = 5
___ + ___ = 5
___ + ___ = 5
___ + ___ = 5
___ + ___ = 5

Name

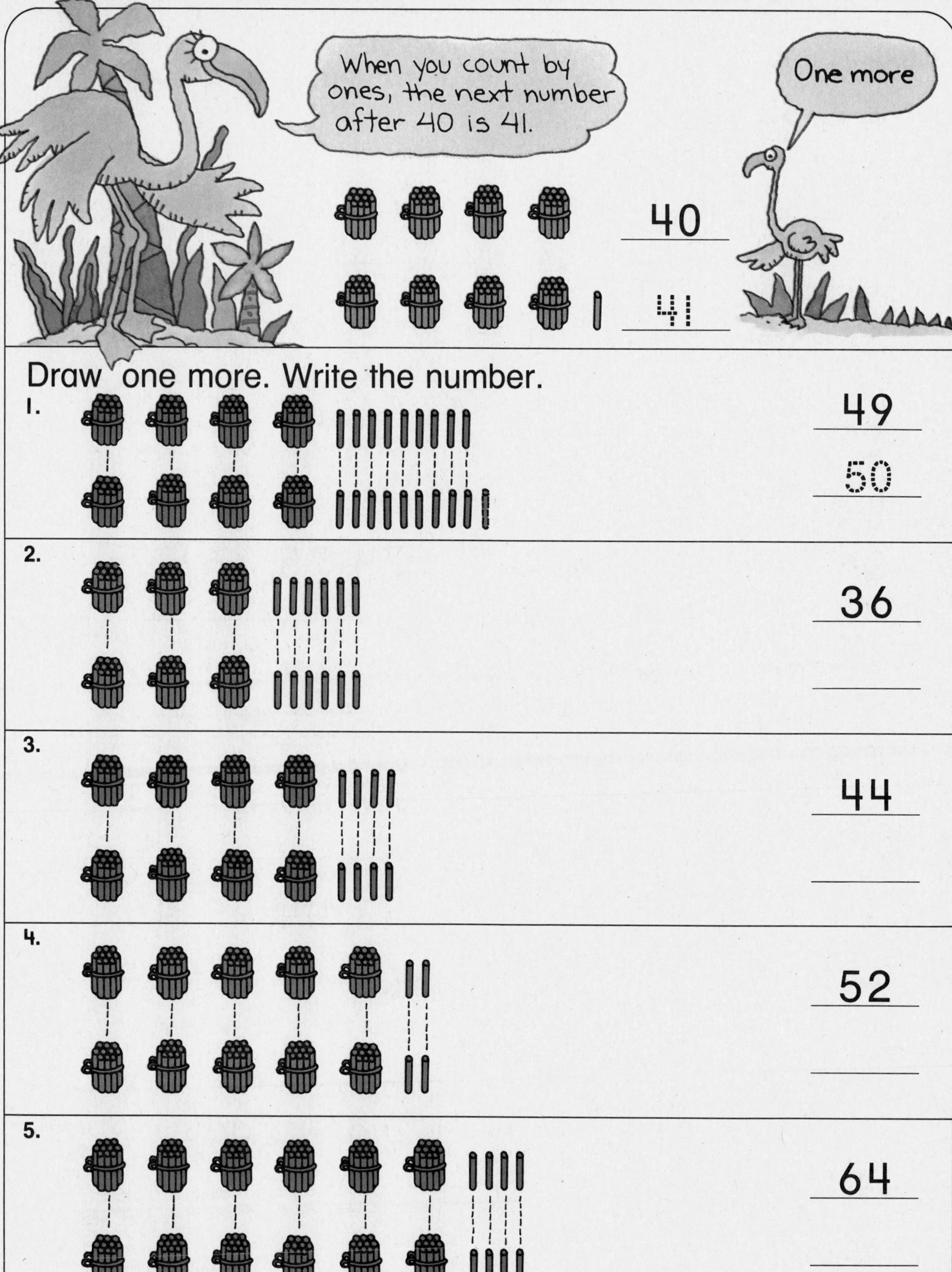

When you count by ones, the next number after 40 is 41.
One more
40
41
Draw one more. Write the number.
1.
49
50
2.
36
3.
44
4.
52
5.
64

Write the number that is next.

1. 31, 32, 33, 34, ___	2. 26, 27, 28, 29, ___
3. 51, 52, 53, 54, ___	4. 72, 73, 74, 75, ___
5. 61, 62, 63, 64, ___	6. 16, 17, 18, 19, ___
7. 37, 38, 39, 40, ___	8. 89, 90, 91, 92, ___
9. 36, 37, 38, 39, ___	10. 74, 75, 76, 77, ___
11. 77, 78, 79, 80, ___	12. 66, 67, 68, 69, ___
13. 15, 16, 17, 18, ___	14. 79, 80, 81, 82, ___
15. 86, 87, 88, 89, ___	16. 43, 44, 45, 46, ___

SKILLKEEPER

Add or subtract.

$\begin{array}{r} 8 \\ +3 \\ \hline \end{array}$ $\begin{array}{r} 11 \\ -\ 2 \\ \hline \end{array}$ $\begin{array}{r} 2 \\ +7 \\ \hline \end{array}$ $\begin{array}{r} 10 \\ -\ 3 \\ \hline \end{array}$ $\begin{array}{r} 9 \\ -2 \\ \hline \end{array}$ $\begin{array}{r} 3 \\ +8 \\ \hline \end{array}$

Name ______________________________

Finish each row.

1.	40	41	42	43	44	45	46			
2.	50	51	52	53	54					
3.	60	61	62	63						
4.	70	71	72							
5.	80	81								
6.	90									

Join the dots. Start at 55.

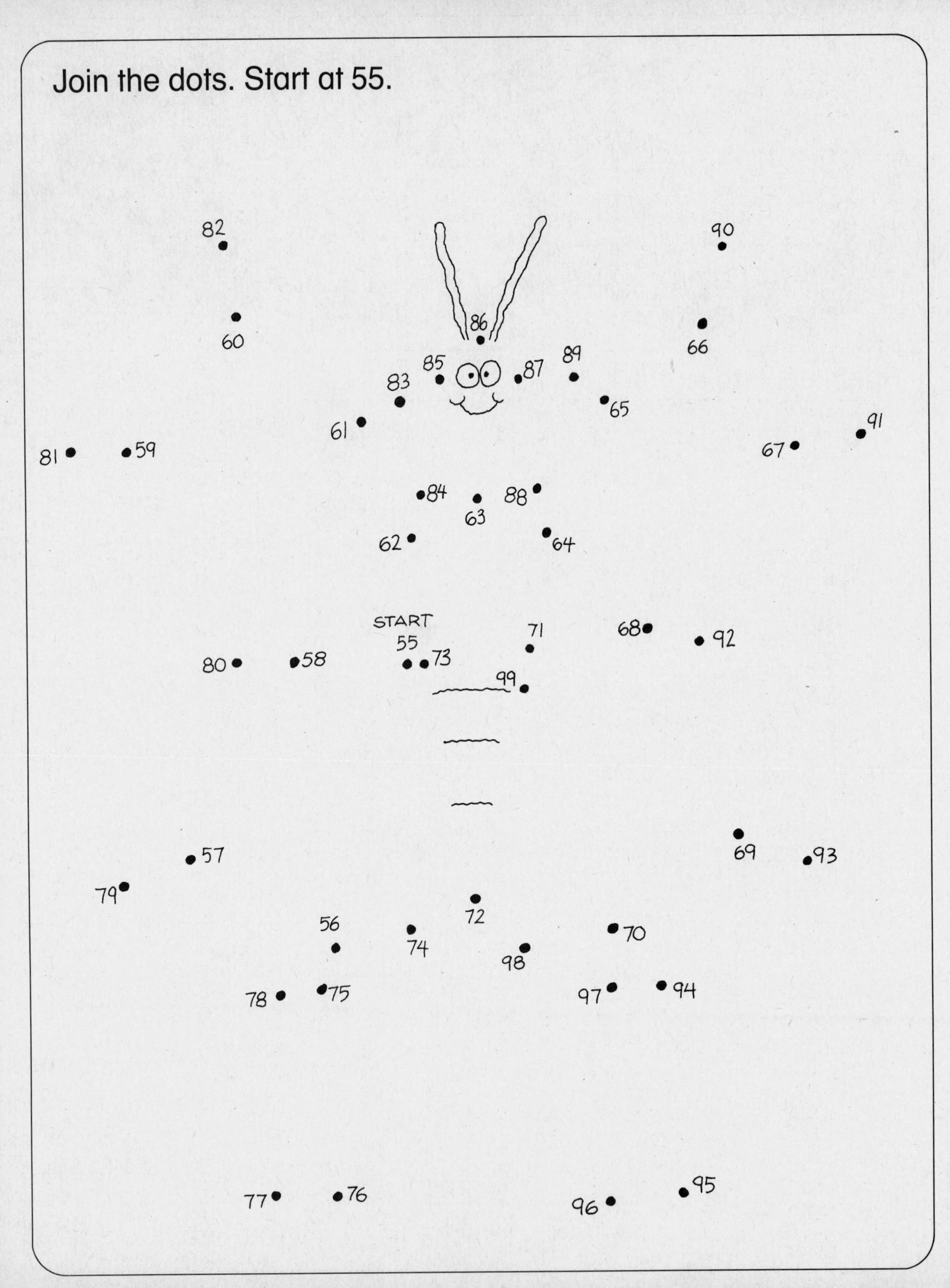

Name ____________________

32

25

32 is greater than 25.

Ring the greater number.

1\. 34 24

2\. 26 29

3\. 17 22

4\. 32 28

5.	6.	7.	8.	9.	10.
24	56	35	67	28	90
27	46	53	71	31	88

34

24

24 is less than 34.

Ring the number that is less.

1.

26

23

2.

32

22

3.

27

31

4.

40

34

5.	6.	7.	8.	9.	10.
75	46	76	30	90	87
85	43	81	27	92	78

Name ______________________________

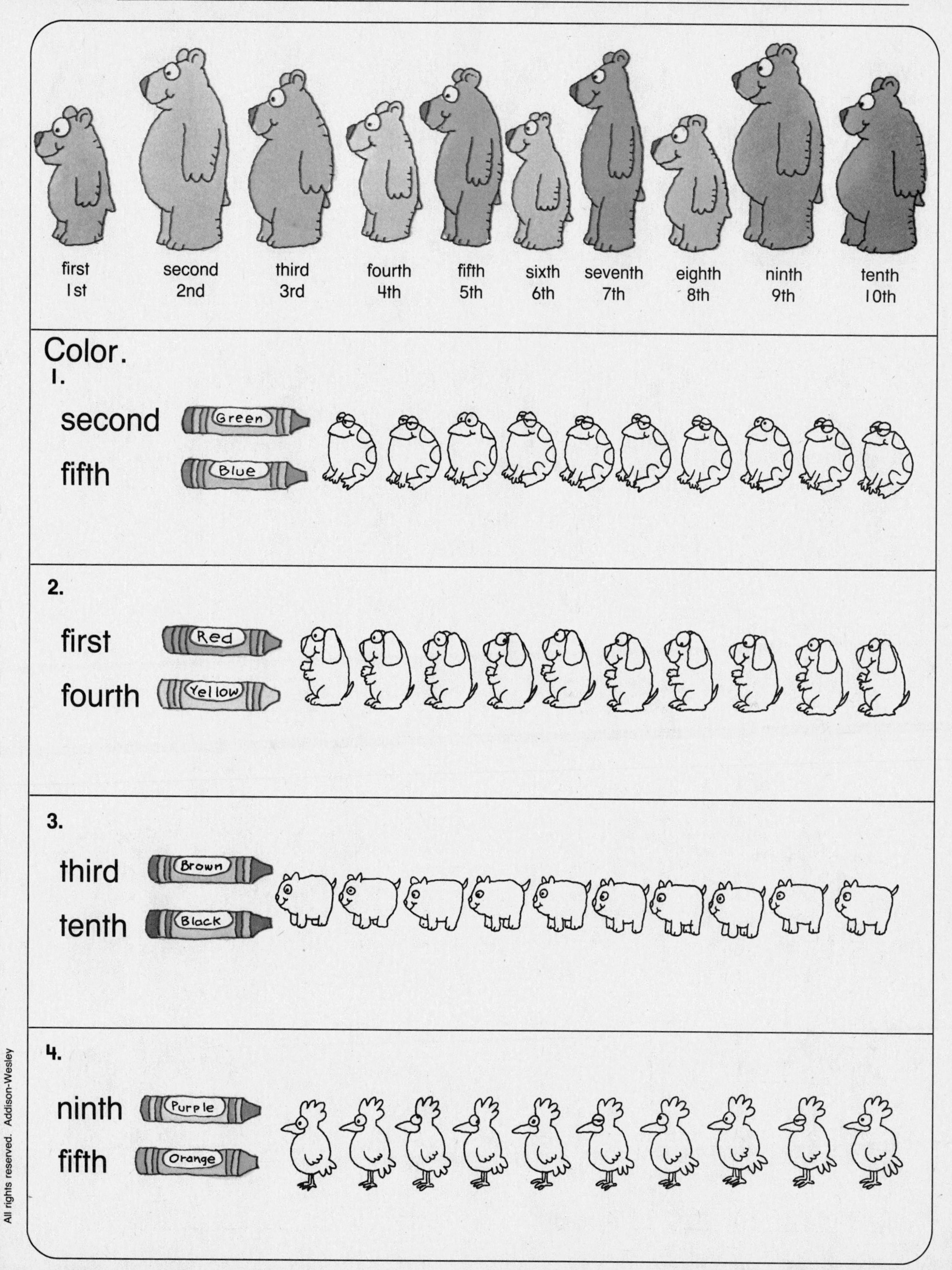
first
1st
second
2nd
third
3rd
fourth
4th
fifth
5th
sixth
6th
seventh
7th
eighth
8th
ninth
9th
tenth
10th
Color.
1.
second
Green
fifth
Blue
2.
first
Red
fourth
Yellow
3.
third
Brown
tenth
Black
4.
ninth
Purple
fifth
Orange

Match.
1.
first
fourth
seventh
third
2.
TICKETS
fifth
sixth
second
first
3.
first
third
fourth
second
third
second
fourth
first

Name ______________________________

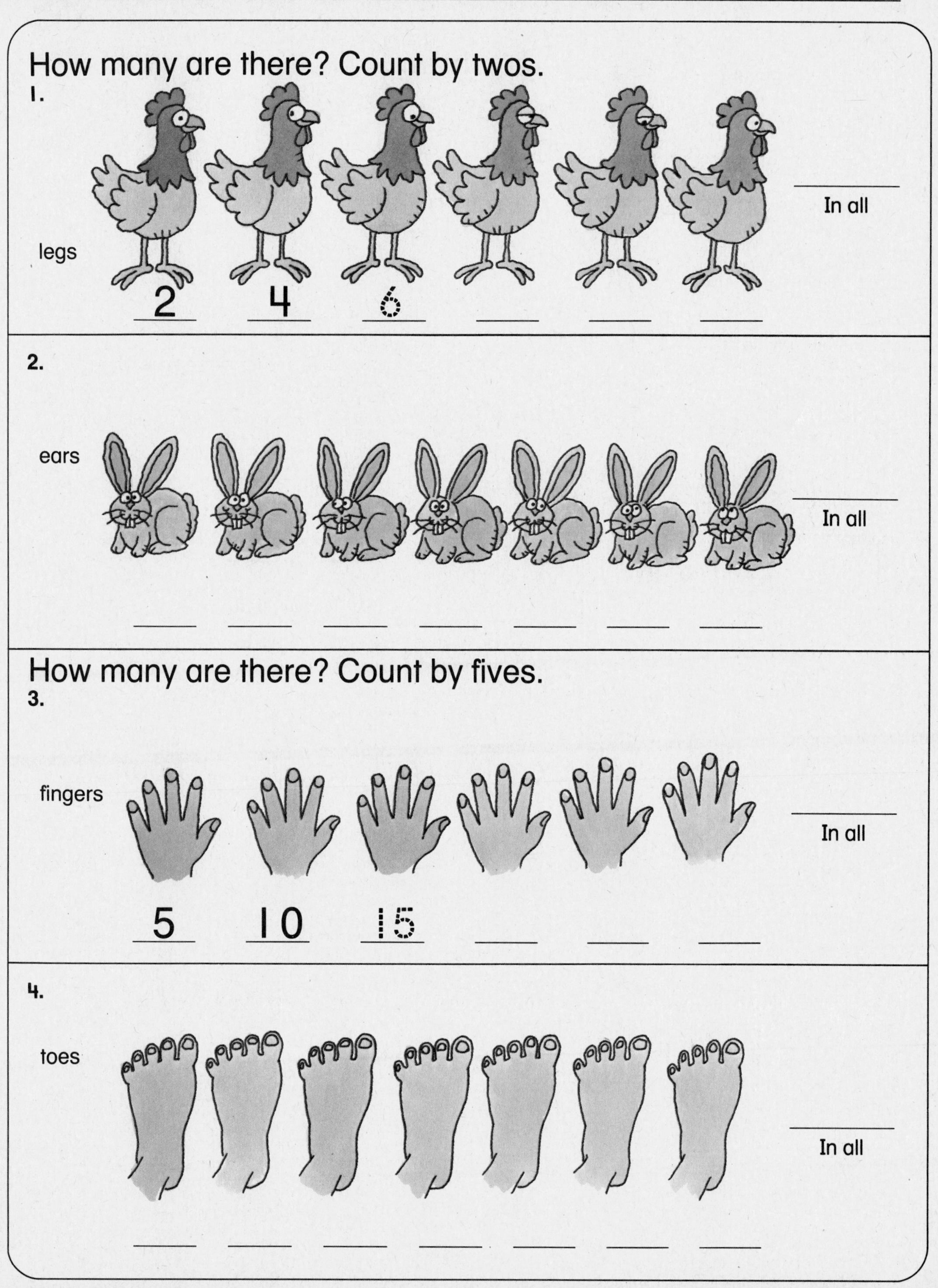
How many are there? Count by twos.
1.
legs
2
4
6
In all
2.
ears
In all
How many are there? Count by fives.
3.
fingers
5
10
15
In all
4.
toes
In all

QUESTION
DATA
PLAN
ANSWER
CHECK

Problem-Solving Strategy

Finish the picture. Solve the problem.

1. 7 apples are on the table.
   4 apples are in the box.
   How many apples are there in all? ______ apples

2. 4 boats are in the grass.
   4 boats are in the water.
   How many boats are there in all? ______ boats

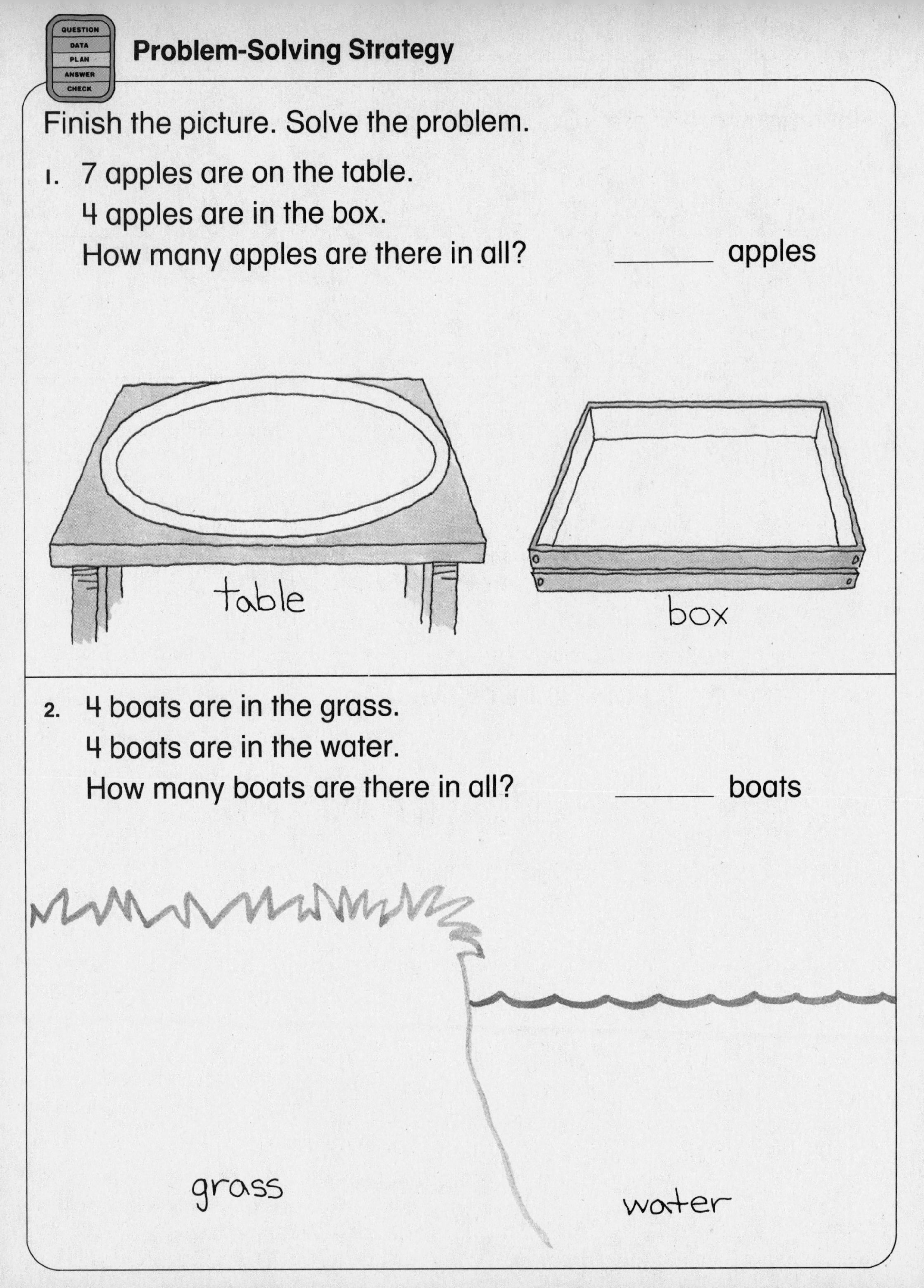

Name ______________________________

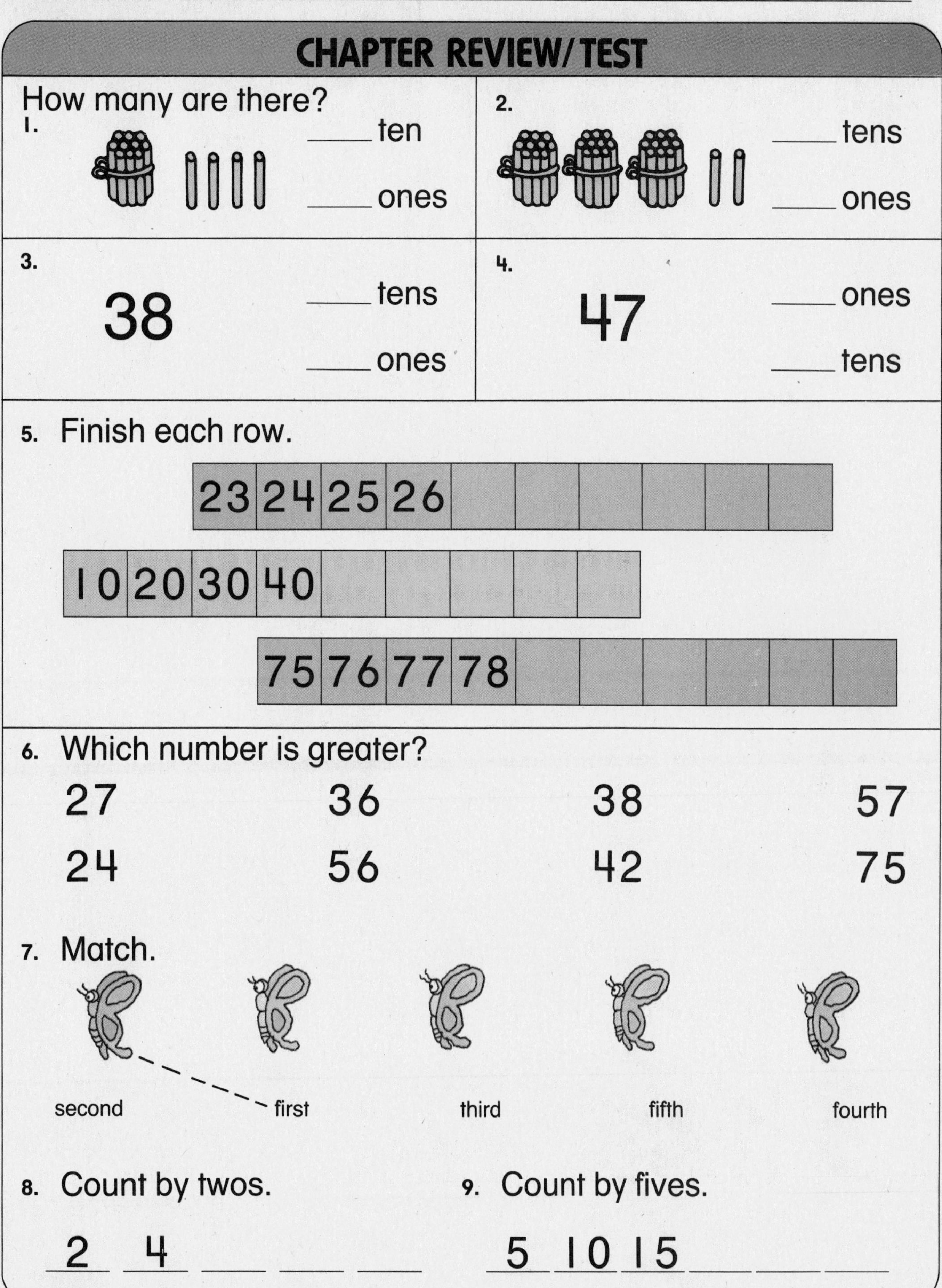

CHAPTER REVIEW/TEST

How many are there?

1. ____ ten ____ ones

2. ____ tens ____ ones

3. 38 ____ tens ____ ones

4. 47 ____ ones ____ tens

5. Finish each row.

23	24	25	26						

10	20	30	40					

75	76	77	78						

6. Which number is greater?

27	36	38	57
24	56	42	75

7. Match.

second first third fifth fourth

8. Count by twos.

2 4 ____ ____ ____

9. Count by fives.

5 10 15 ____ ____ ____

Name ______________________________

CUMULATIVE REVIEW

Add.

1. $7 + 1 =$ ____

○ 8
○ 9
○ 6

2. $5 + 2 =$ ____

○ 4
○ 7
○ 5

3. $1 + 4$

○ 3
○ 5
○ 7

4. $8 + 2$

○ 6
○ 12
○ 10

Subtract.

5. $6 - 1 =$ ____

○ 4
○ 5
○ 7

6. $9 - 2 =$ ____

○ 7
○ 11
○ 10

7. $12 - 3$

○ 11
○ 12
○ 9

8. $11 - 2$

○ 7
○ 6
○ 9

9. Choose the correct one.

○ $9 + 2 = \underline{11}$
○ $8 + 1 = \underline{9}$
○ $11 + 1 = \underline{12}$

Name ______________________________

ANOTHER LOOK

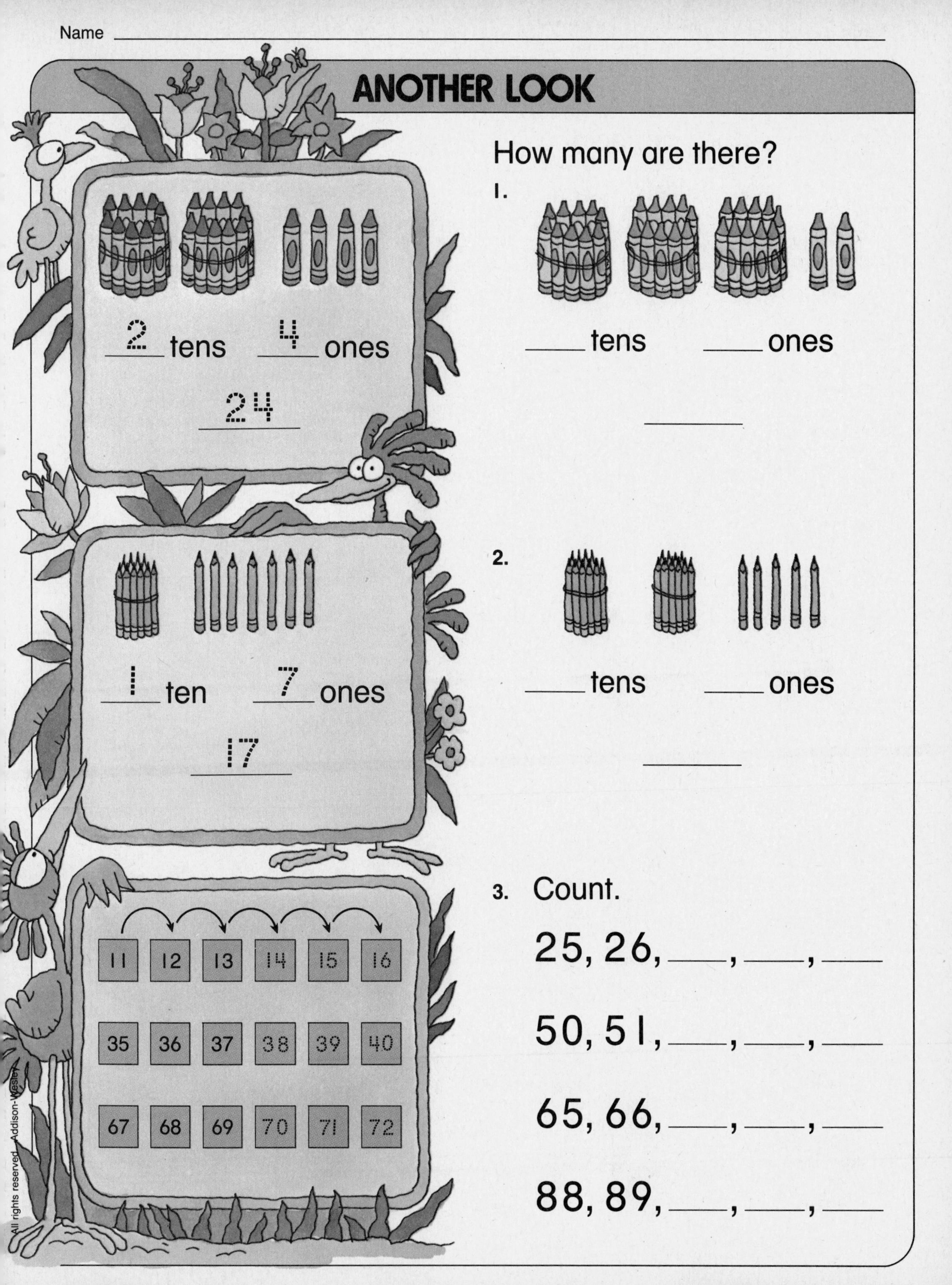

How many are there?

1.

____ tens ____ ones

______

2.

____ tens ____ ones

______

3. Count.

25, 26, ____, ____, ____

50, 51, ____, ____, ____

65, 66, ____, ____, ____

88, 89, ____, ____, ____

Name ____________________

ENRICHMENT
Which one does not belong?
1.
2.
3.
4.
5.

146 (one hundred forty-six)

Enrichment—classification

7 Name

TIME AND MONEY

Write the numbers. Color the long hand Blue.

Color the short hand Red.

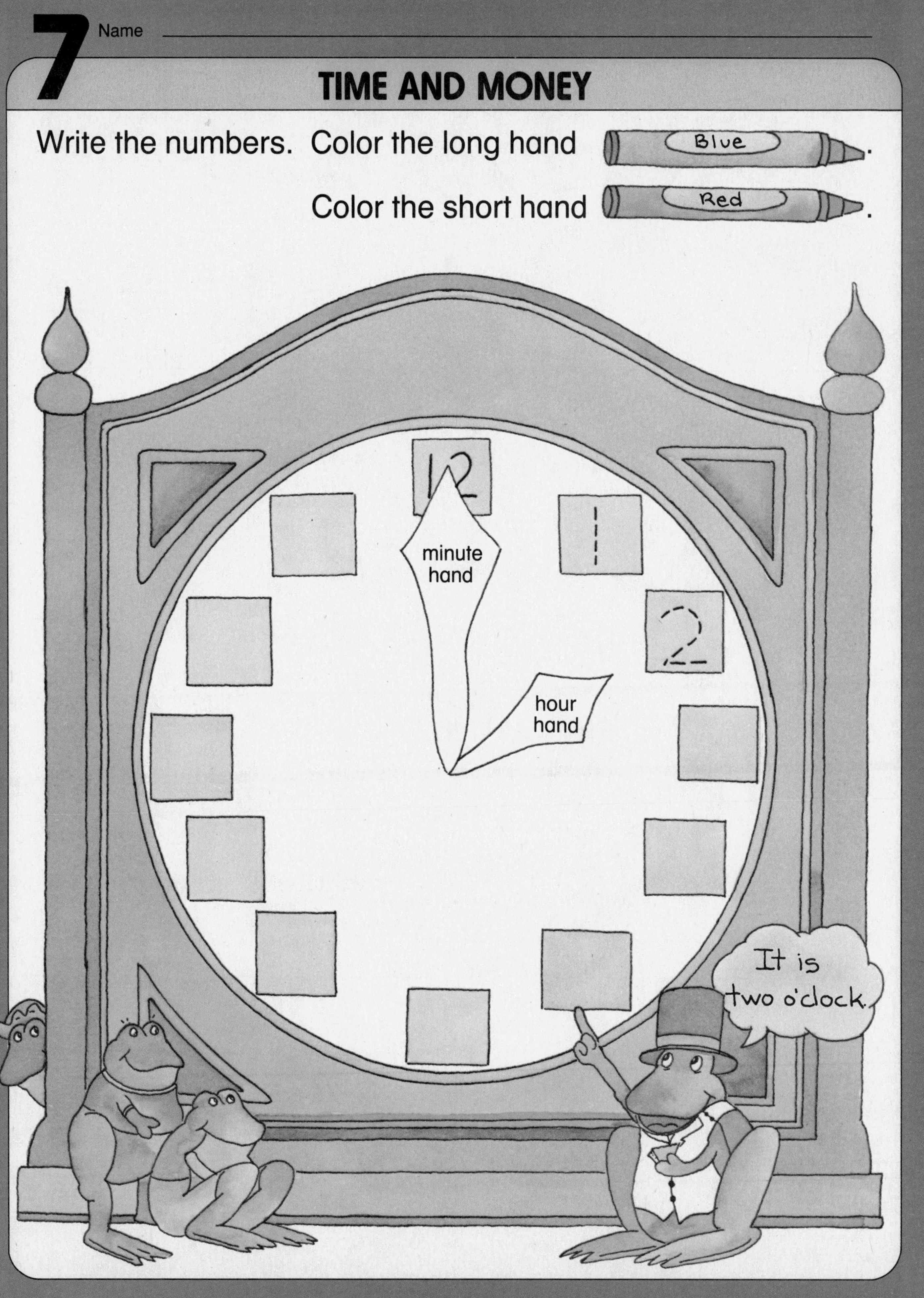

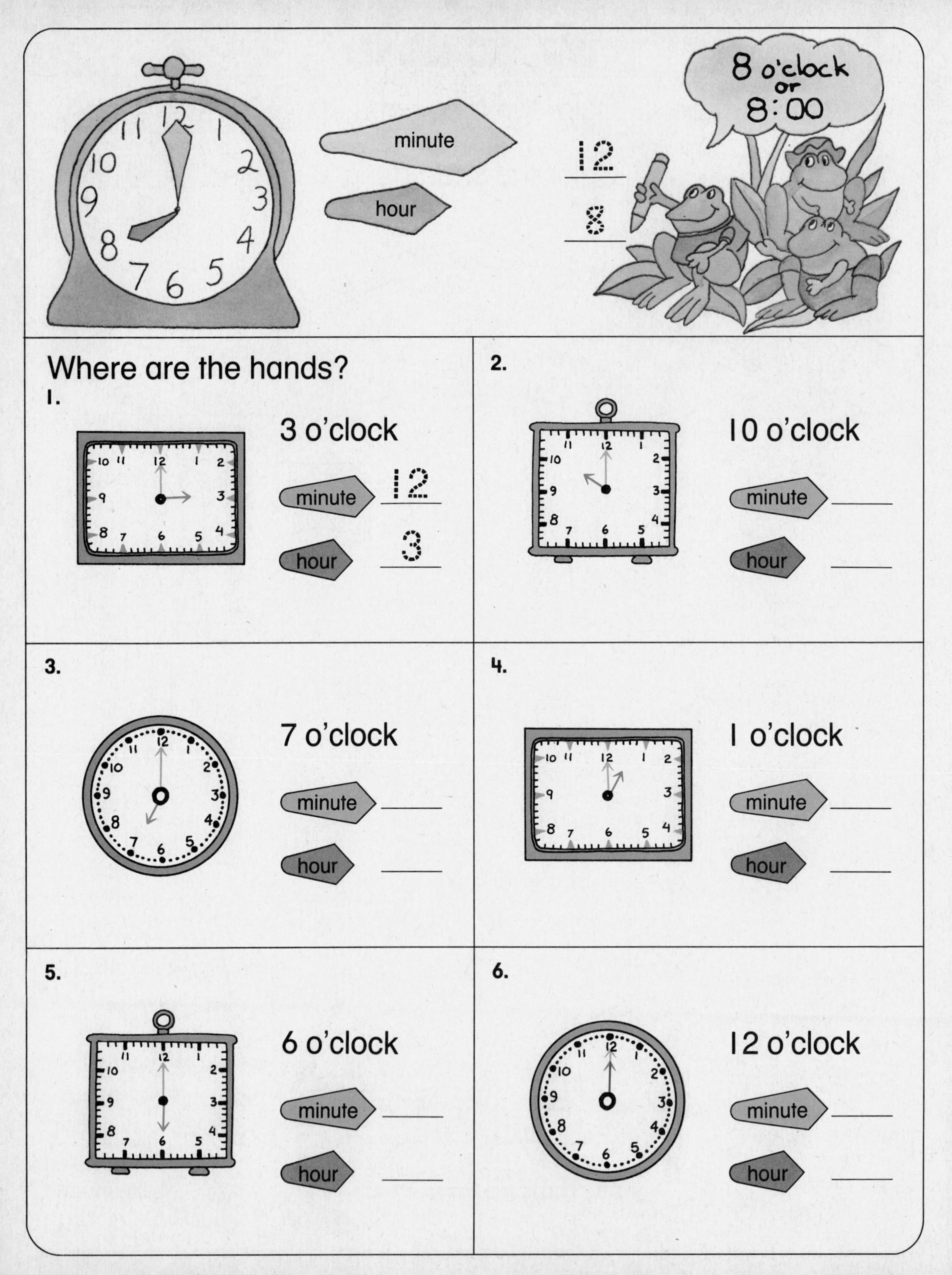

minute
hour
12
8
8 o'clock
or
8:00
Where are the hands?
1.
3 o'clock
minute
12
hour
3
2.
10 o'clock
minute
hour
3.
7 o'clock
minute
hour
4.
1 o'clock
minute
hour
5.
6 o'clock
minute
hour
6.
12 o'clock
minute
hour

Name ______________________________

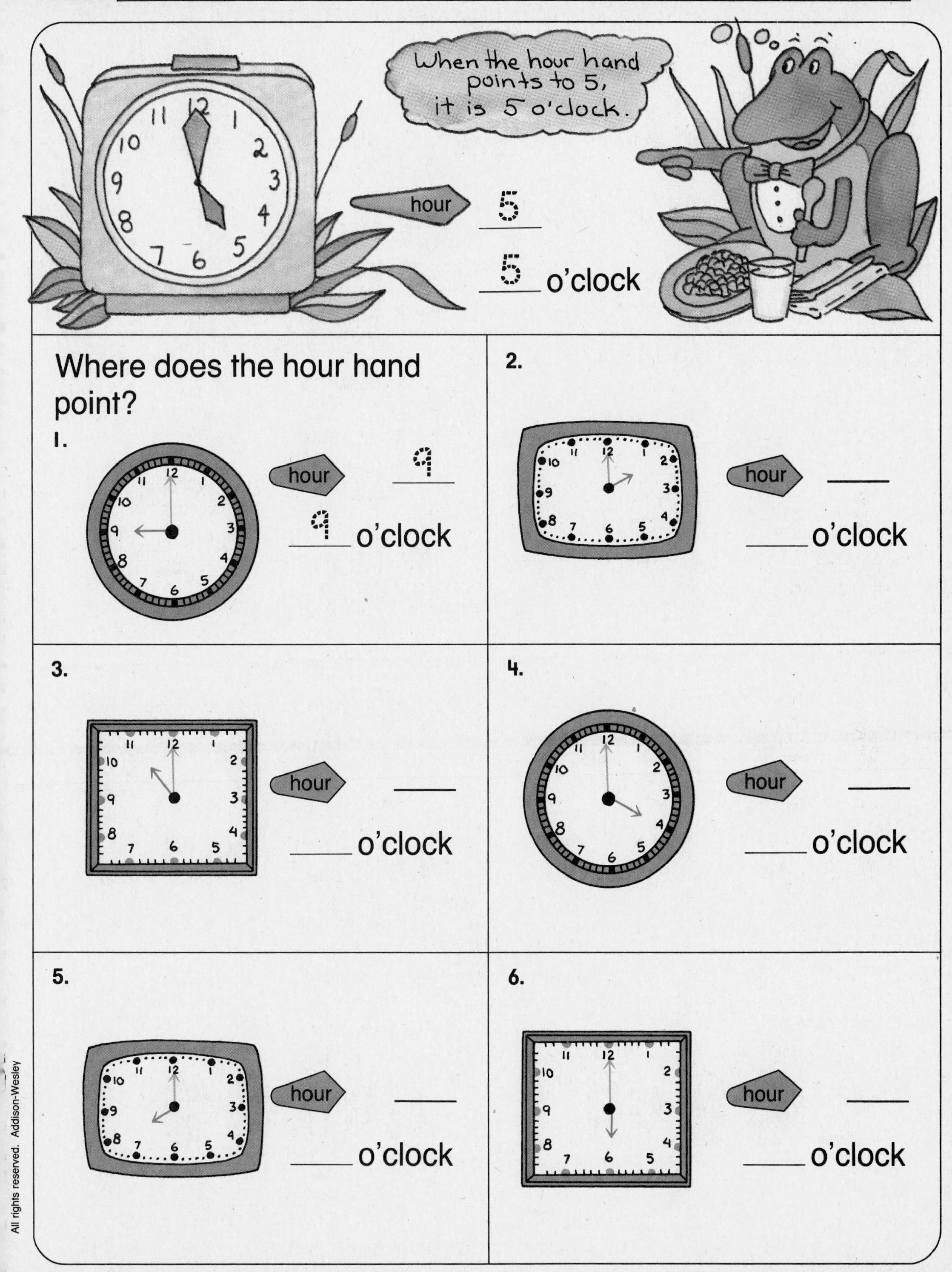
When the hour hand points to 5, it is 5 o'clock.
hour 5
5 o'clock
Where does the hour hand point?
1.
hour 9
9 o'clock
2.
hour ____
____ o'clock
3.
hour ____
____ o'clock
4.
hour ____
____ o'clock
5.
hour ____
____ o'clock
6.
hour ____
____ o'clock

Draw the hour hands on the clocks.

1.

2.

3.

4.

SKILLKEEPER

How many are there?

_______ _______

Name 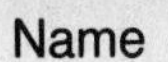 ______________________________

1 o'clock

1:00

Write the time two ways.

1. ____ o'clock

____ : ____

2. ____ o'clock

____ : ____

3. ____ o'clock

____ : ____

4. ____ o'clock

____ : ____

5. ____ o'clock

____ : ____

6. ____ o'clock

____ : ____

Match the clocks.

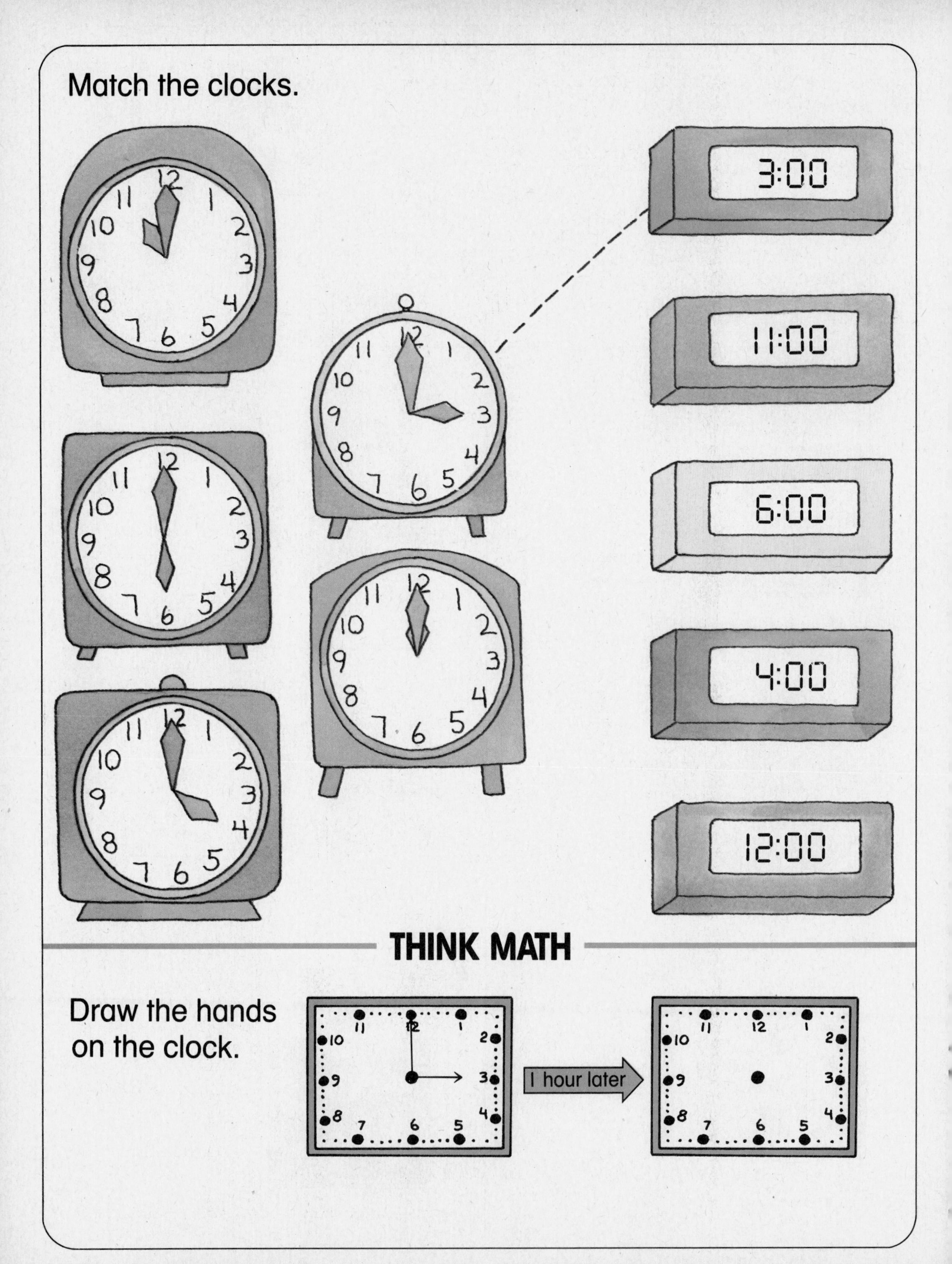

3:00
11:00
6:00
4:00
12:00
THINK MATH
Draw the hands on the clock.
1 hour later

152 (one hundred fifty-two)

Matching clock faces with digital clocks

Name ____

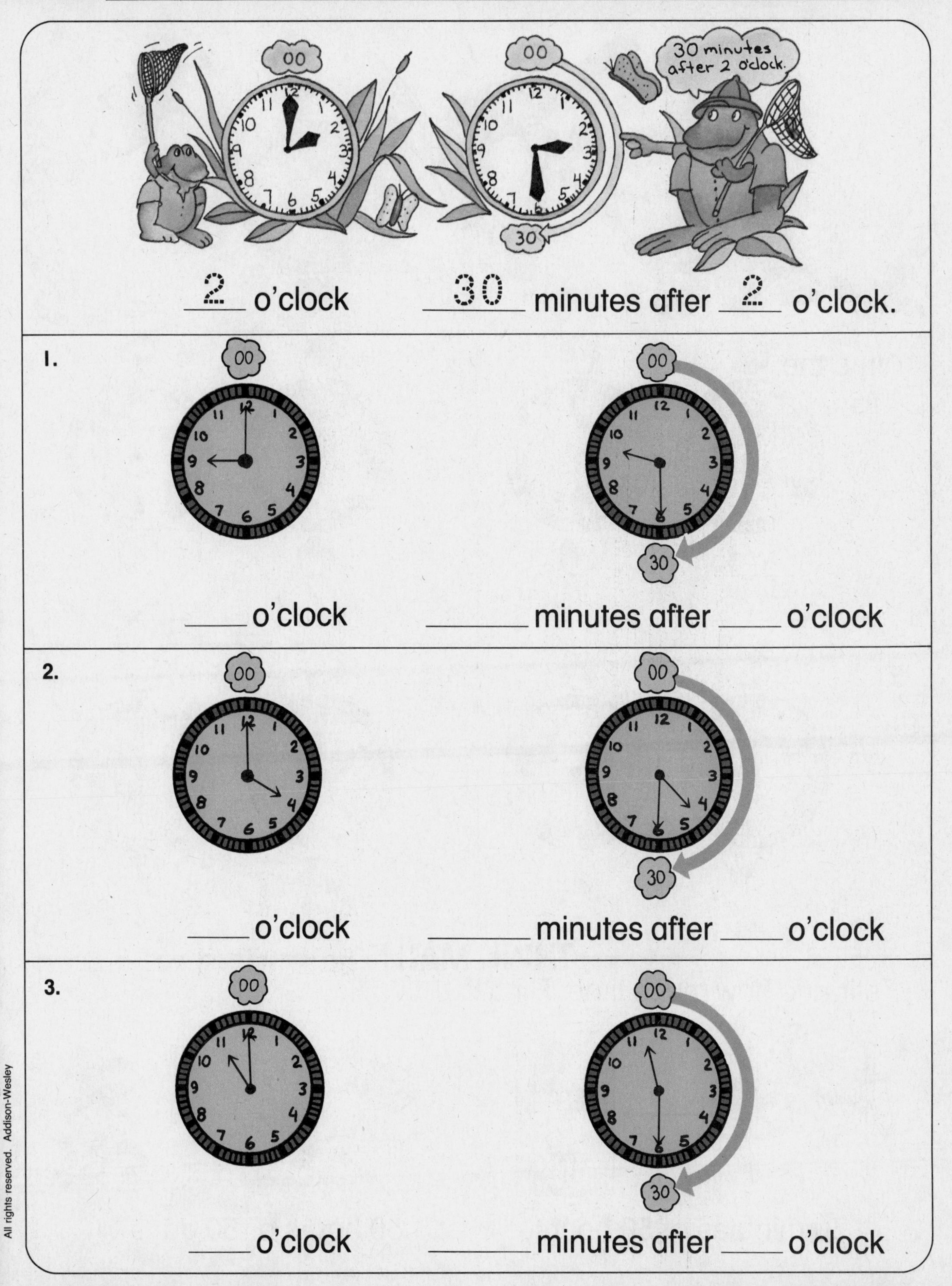

00
30 minutes after 2 o'clock.
30
2 o'clock
30 minutes after 2 o'clock.
1.
____ o'clock
______ minutes after ____ o'clock
2.
____ o'clock
______ minutes after ____ o'clock
3.
____ o'clock
______ minutes after ____ o'clock

Write the times.

1. ___:___ ___:___

2. ___:___ ___:___

3. ___:___ ___:___

4. ___:___ ___:___

THINK MATH

Estimate how much time. Ring it.

50 minutes or 50 hours

50 hours or 50 days

Name ____________________

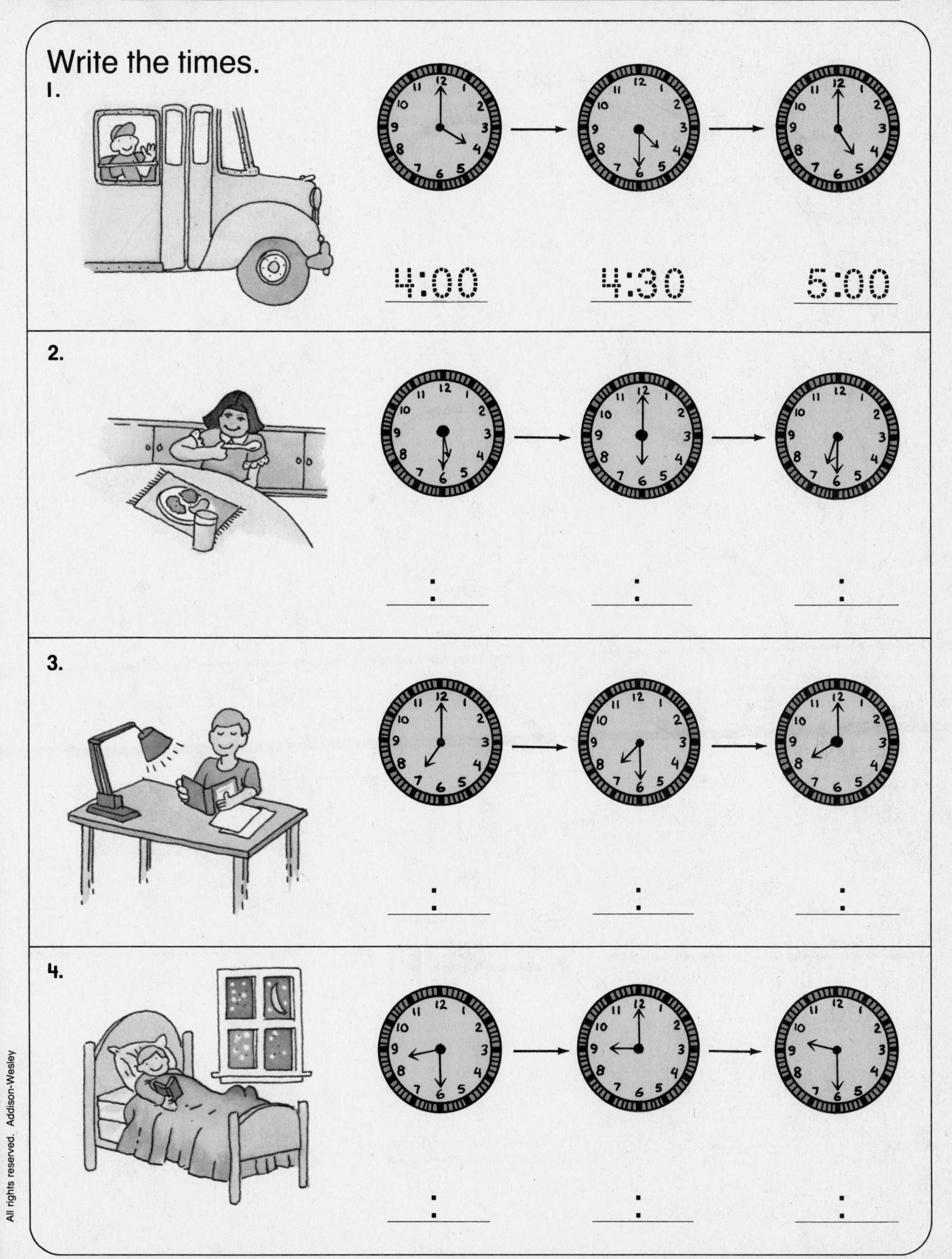
Write the times.
1.
4:00
4:30
5:00
2.
3.
4.

Hour and half-hour sequence (one hundred fifty-five) 155

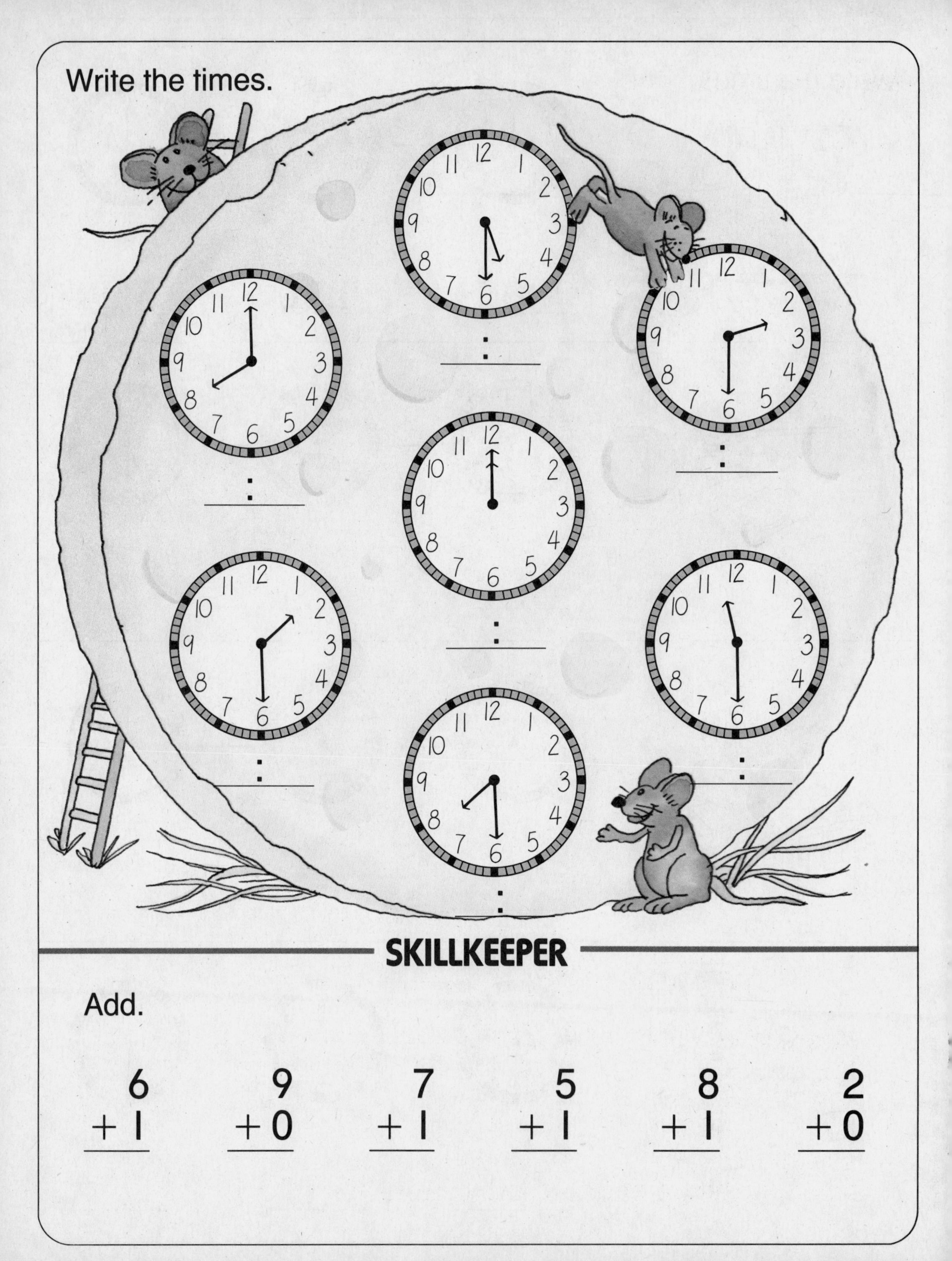
Write the times.
SKILLKEEPER
Add.
6 + 1
9 + 0
7 + 1
5 + 1
8 + 1
2 + 0

Practice reading and writing time

Name ______________________________

Make a calendar.

Month ______________________

Sunday	Monday	Tuesday	Wednesday	Thursday	Friday	Saturday

1. How many days are in a week? ____
2. How many school days are in a week? ____
3. How many days are in this month? ____
4. How many school days are in this month? ____

MAY

Sunday	Monday	Tuesday	Wednesday	Thursday	Friday	Saturday
			1	2	3	4
5	6	7	8	9	10	11
12	13	14	15	16	17	18
19	20	21	22	23	24	25
26	27	28	29	30	31	

Ring the day or write the date.

1. Mother's Day — Wednesday — Saturday — Sunday
2. Memorial Day — Thursday — Friday — Saturday
3. May 1 — Sunday — Wednesday — Thursday
4. May 16 — Tuesday — Wednesday — Thursday
5. May 5 — Saturday — Sunday — Monday
6. first Saturday May 4
7. second Monday ________
8. **DATA BANK** first Friday in May of year 2000 ________
(See page 325.)

Name ______________________________

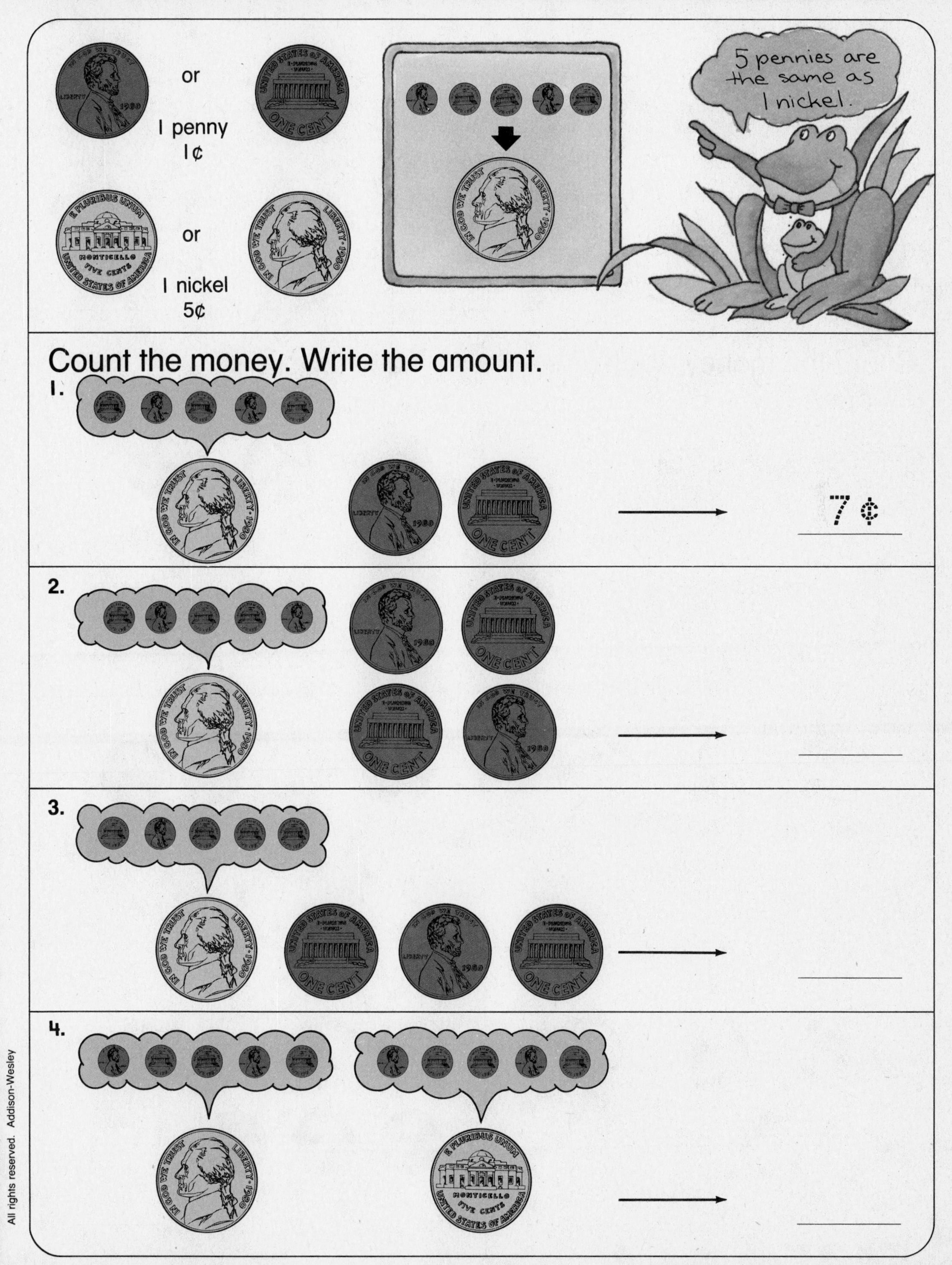
or
1 penny
1¢
or
1 nickel
5¢
5 pennies are the same as 1 nickel.
Count the money. Write the amount.
1.
7 ¢
2.
3.
4.

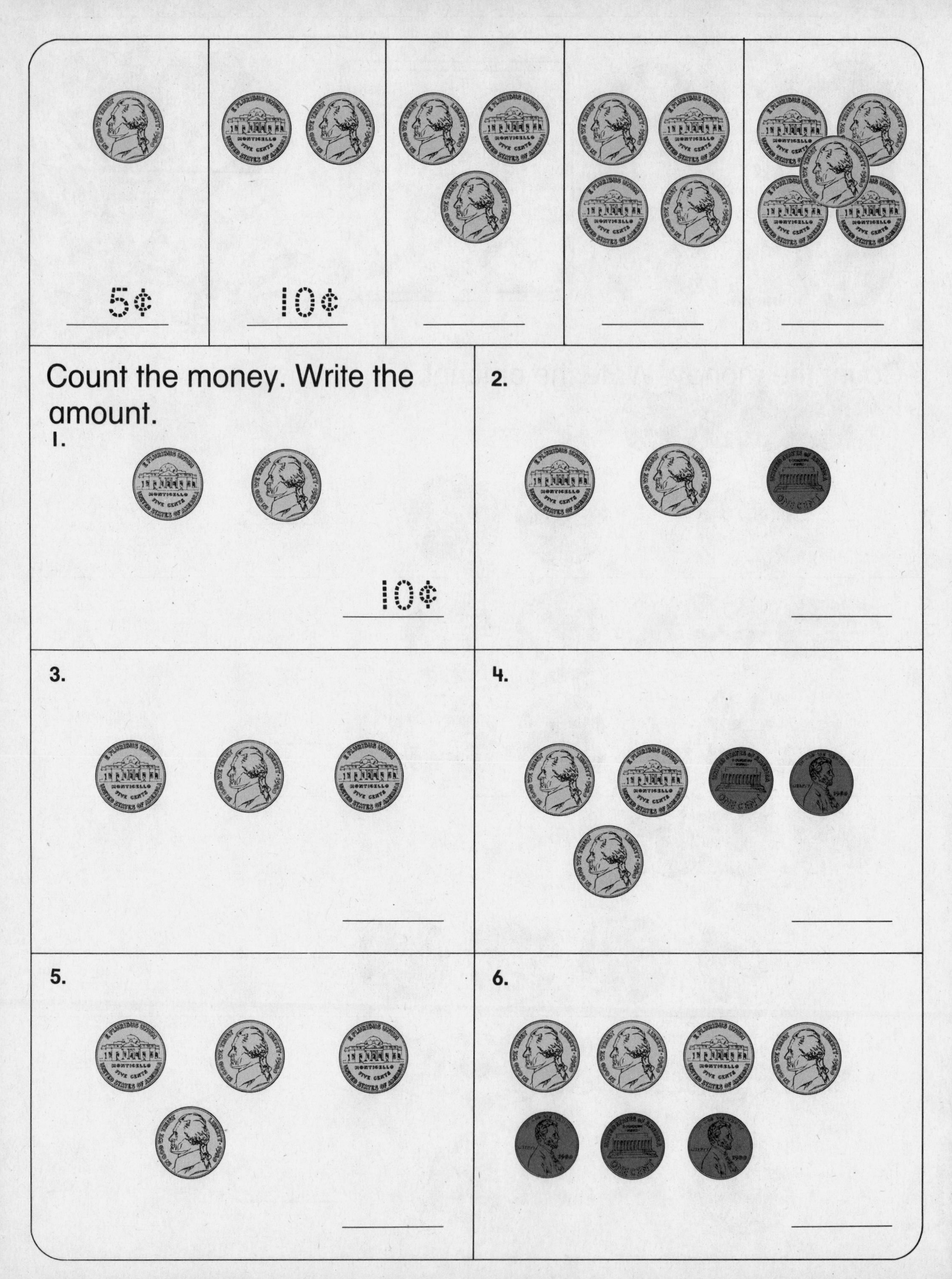

Count the money. Write the amount.

1.

10¢

2.

3.

4.

5.

6.

Name ______________________________

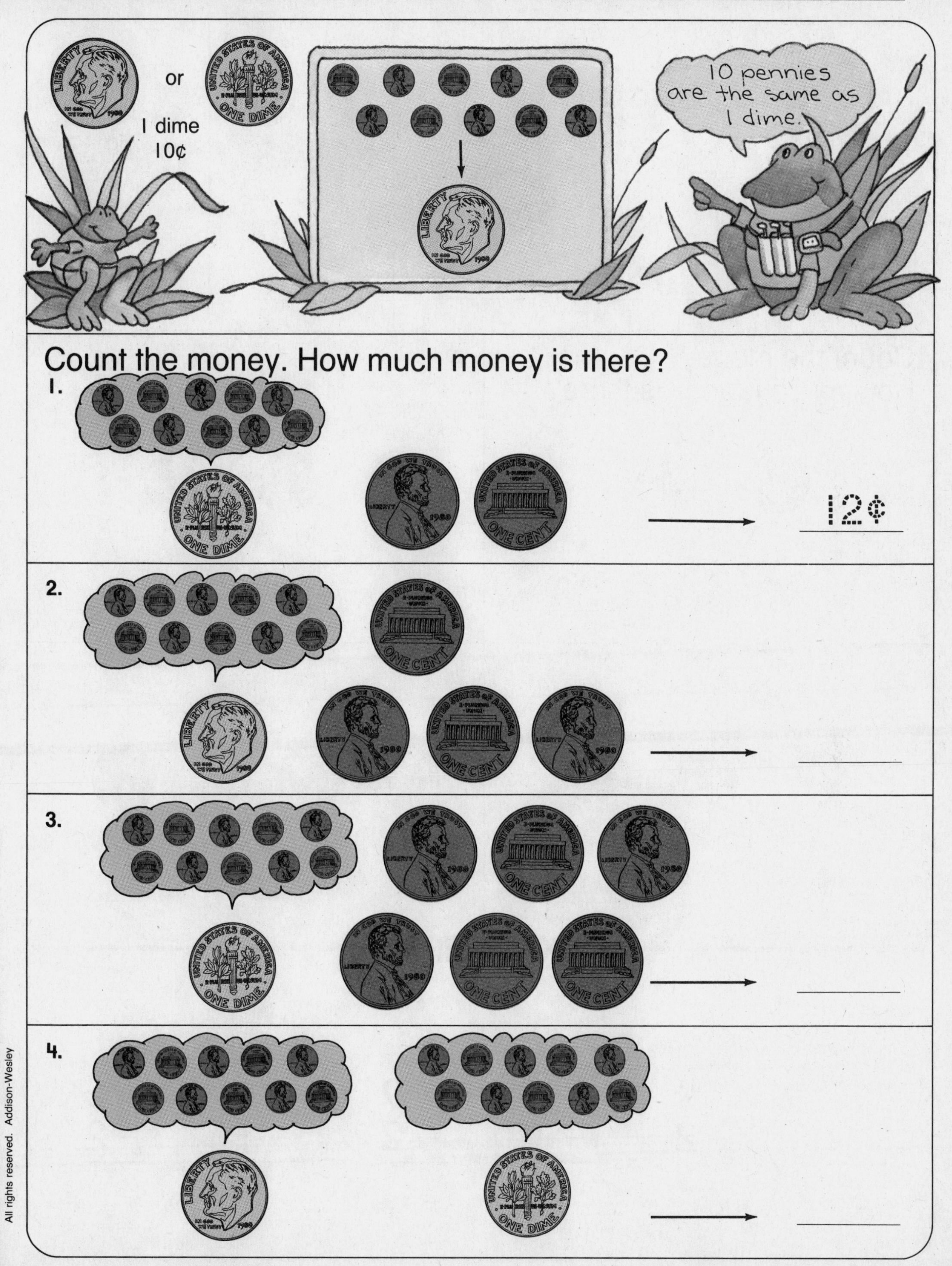

Count the money. How much money is there?

I. → 12¢

2. → ______

3. → ______

4. → ______

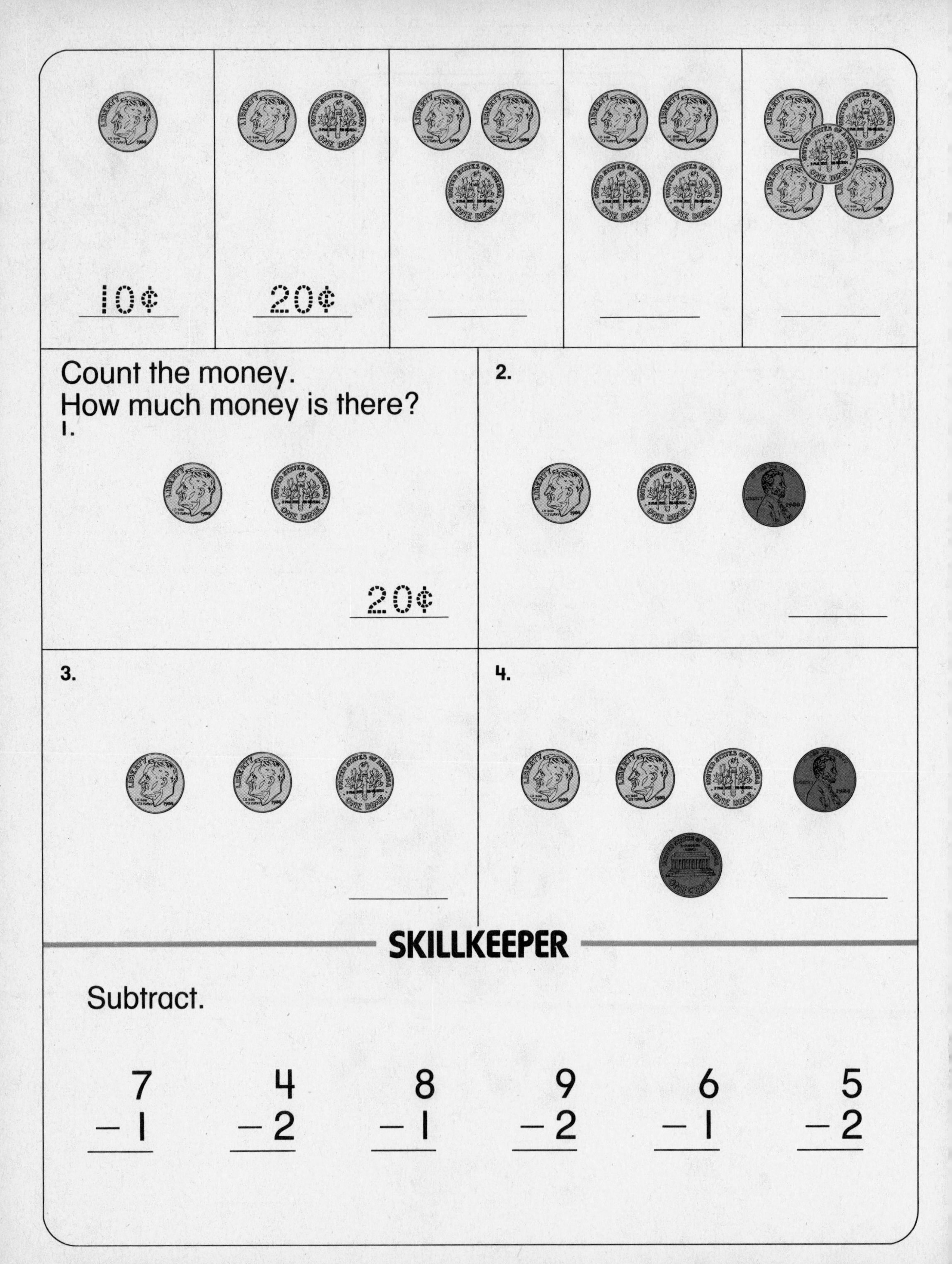
10¢
20¢
Count the money.
How much money is there?
1.
20¢
2.
3.
4.
SKILLKEEPER
Subtract.
7 − 1
4 − 2
8 − 1
9 − 2
6 − 1
5 − 2

Name ________________________________

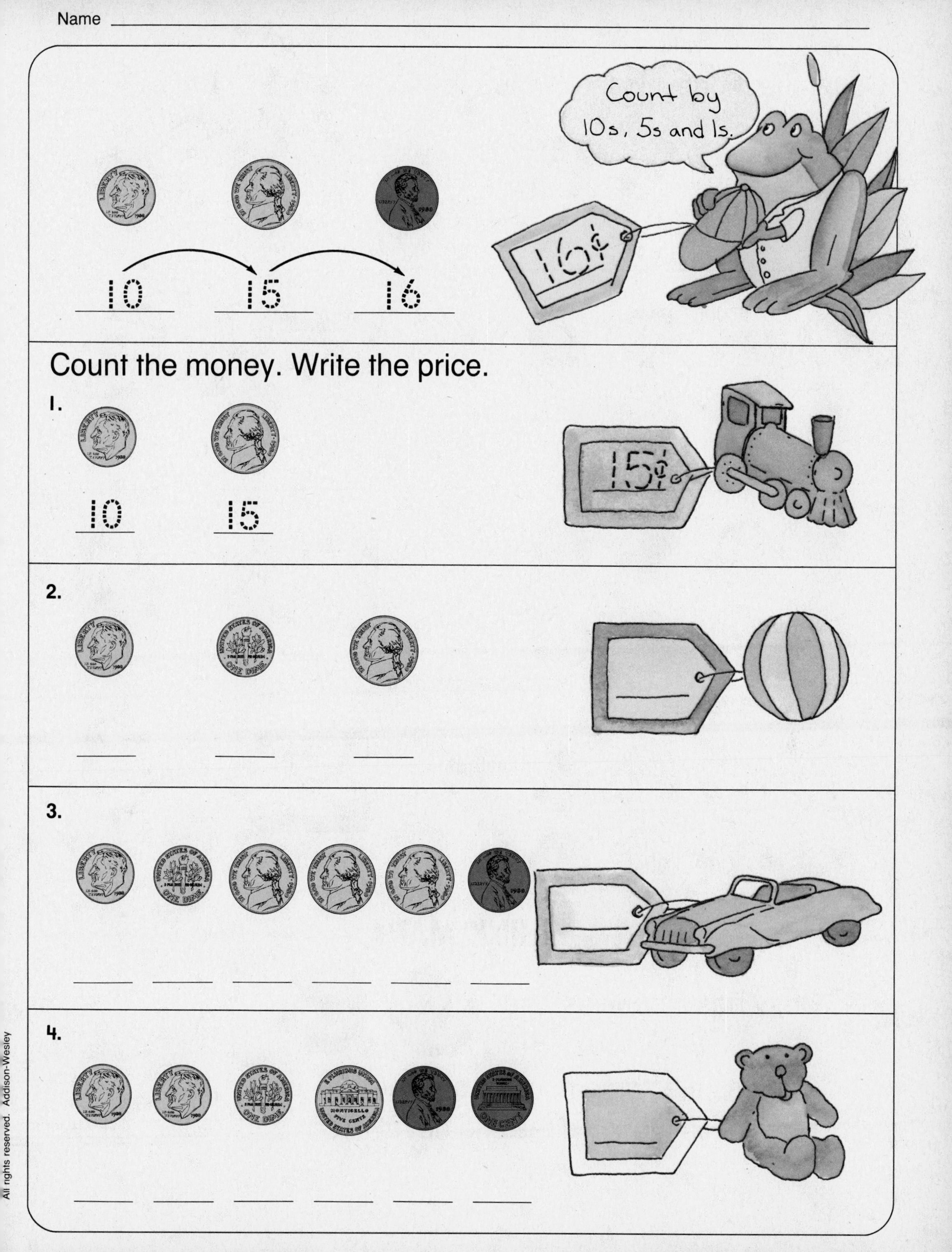
Count by
10s, 5s and 1s.
16¢
10
15
16
Count the money. Write the price.
1.
10
15
15¢
2.
3.
4.

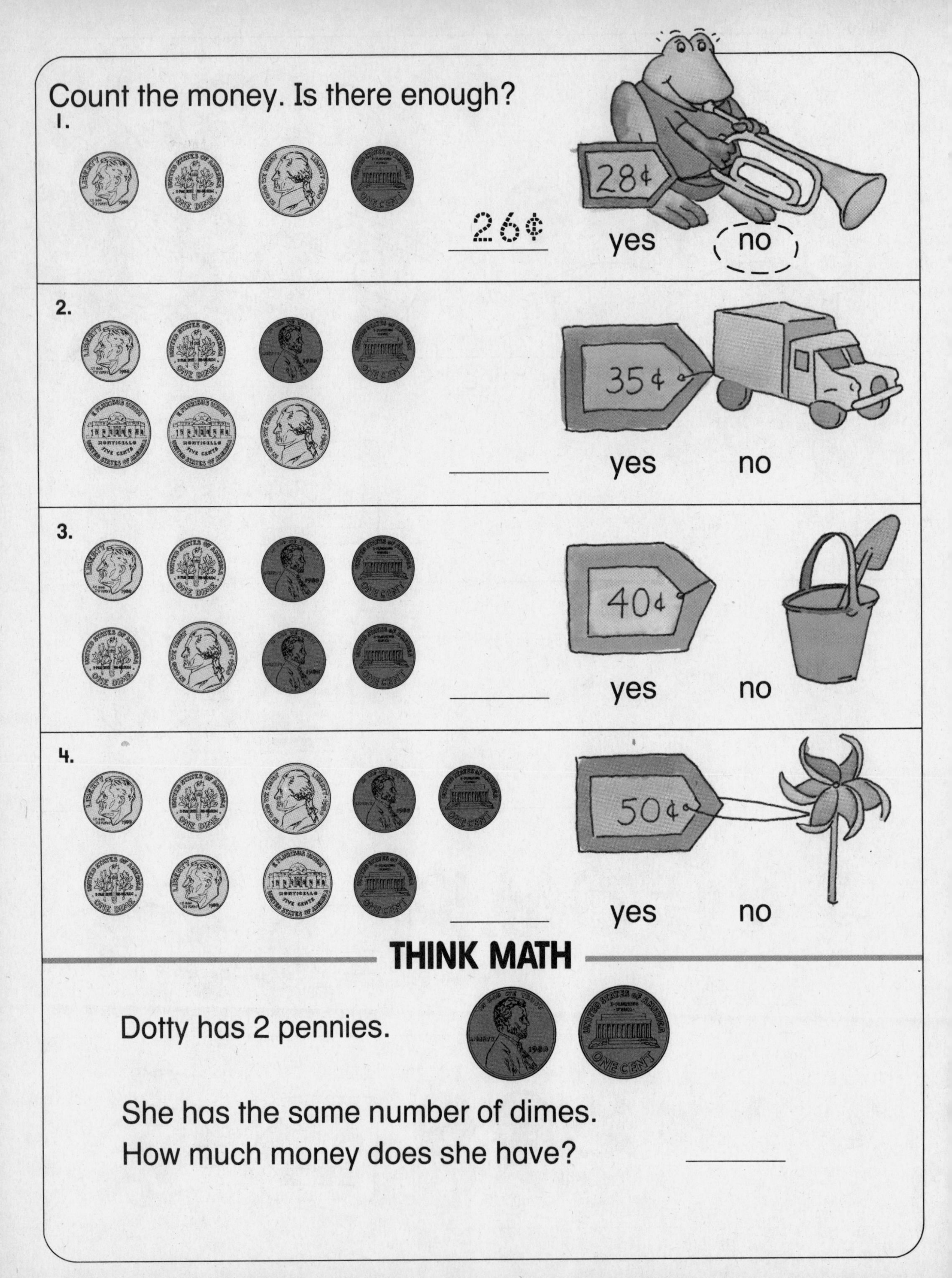
Count the money. Is there enough?
1.
28¢
26¢
yes no
2.
35¢
yes no
3.
40¢
yes no
4.
50¢
yes no
THINK MATH
Dotty has 2 pennies.
She has the same number of dimes.
How much money does she have?

Name ______________________________

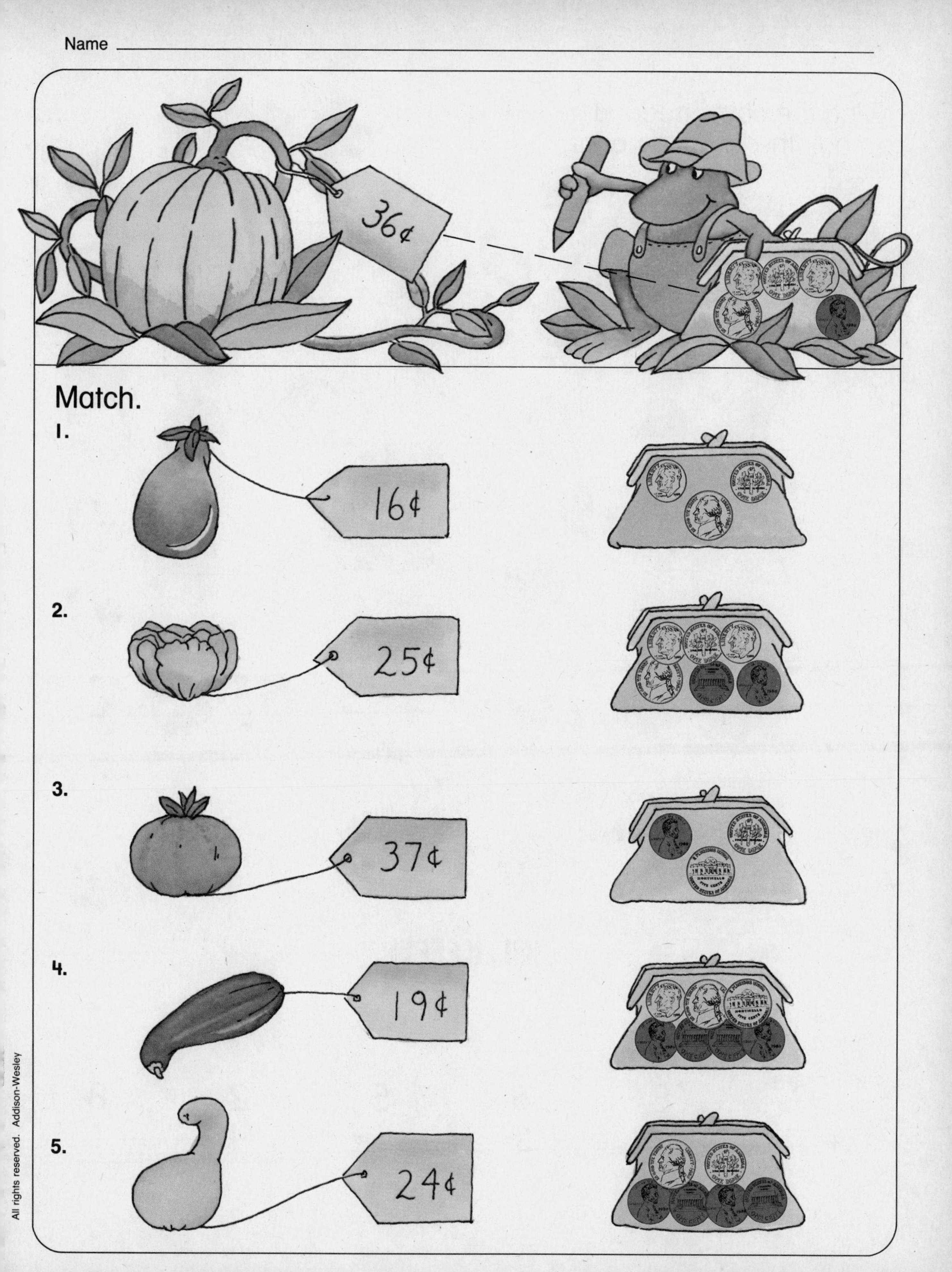

36¢
Match.
1.
16¢
2.
25¢
3.
37¢
4.
19¢
5.
24¢

Matching coins and prices (one hundred sixty-five) 165

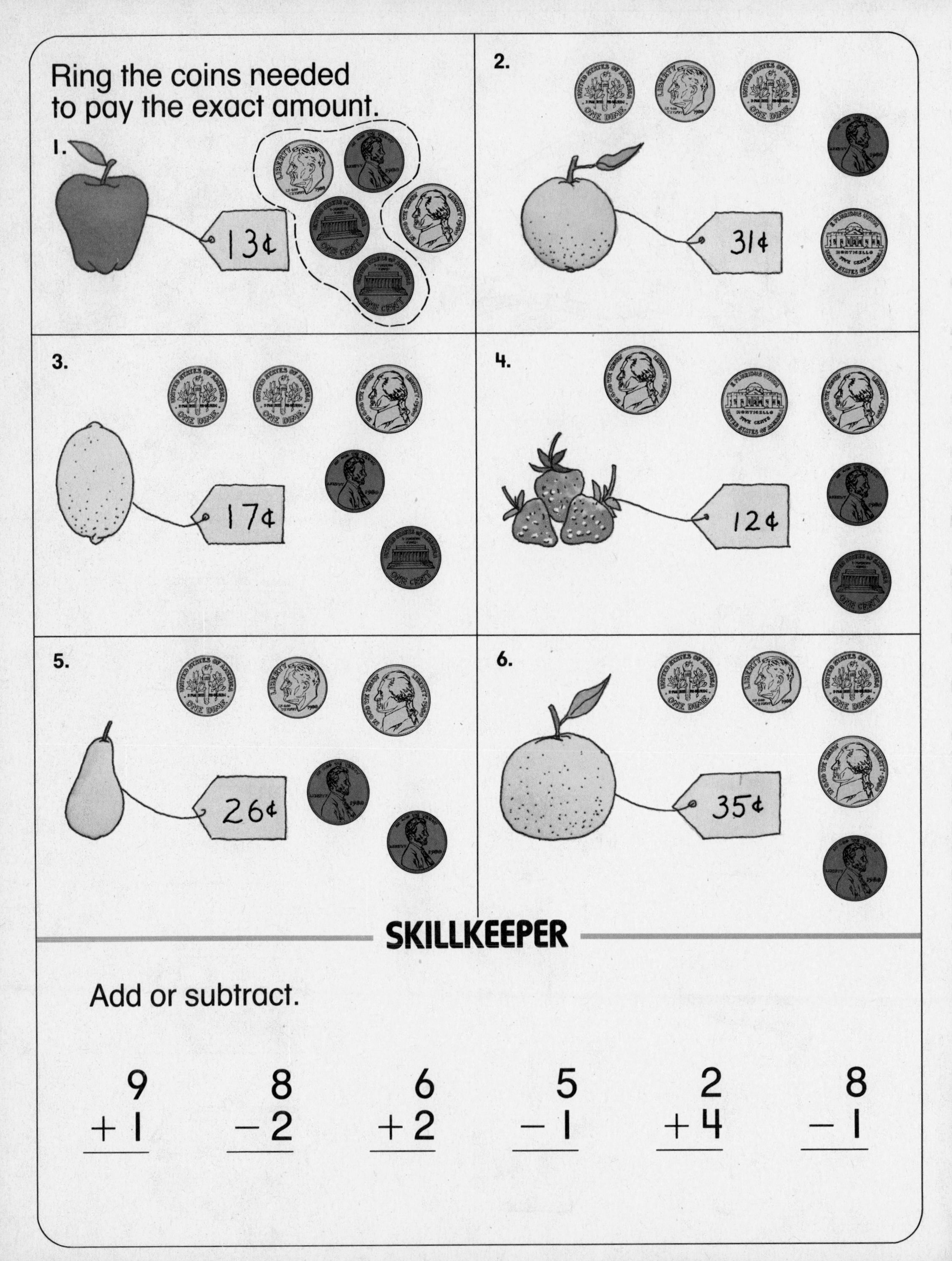

Ring the coins needed to pay the exact amount.
1.
13¢
2.
31¢
3.
17¢
4.
12¢
5.
26¢
6.
35¢
SKILLKEEPER
Add or subtract.
9 + 1
8 − 2
6 + 2
5 − 1
2 + 4
8 − 1

Counting and matching amounts of money

Name ______________________

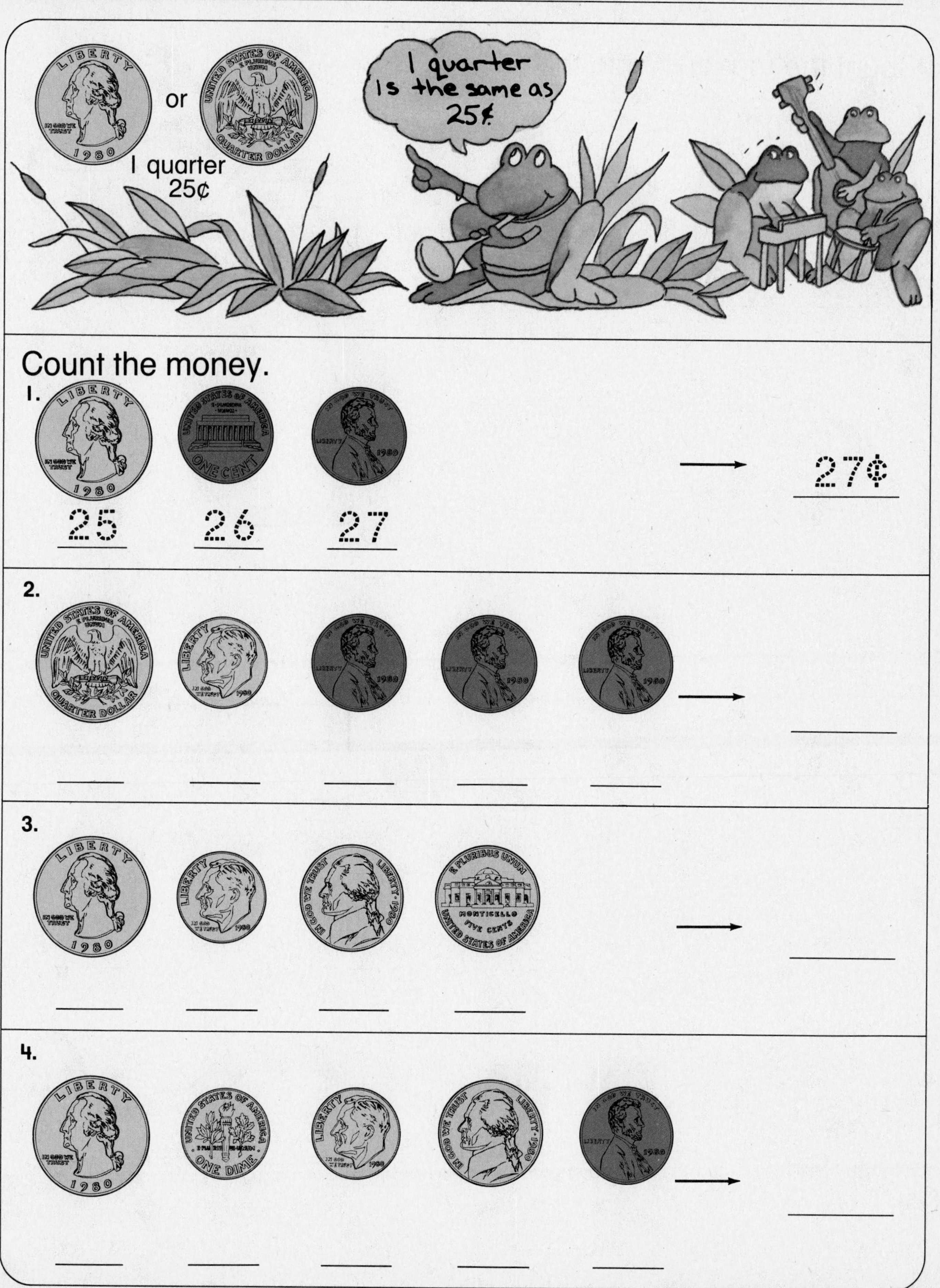
or
1 quarter
25¢
I quarter
is the same as
25¢
Count the money.
1.
25
26
27
27¢
2.
3.
4.

Count the money. Write the price.

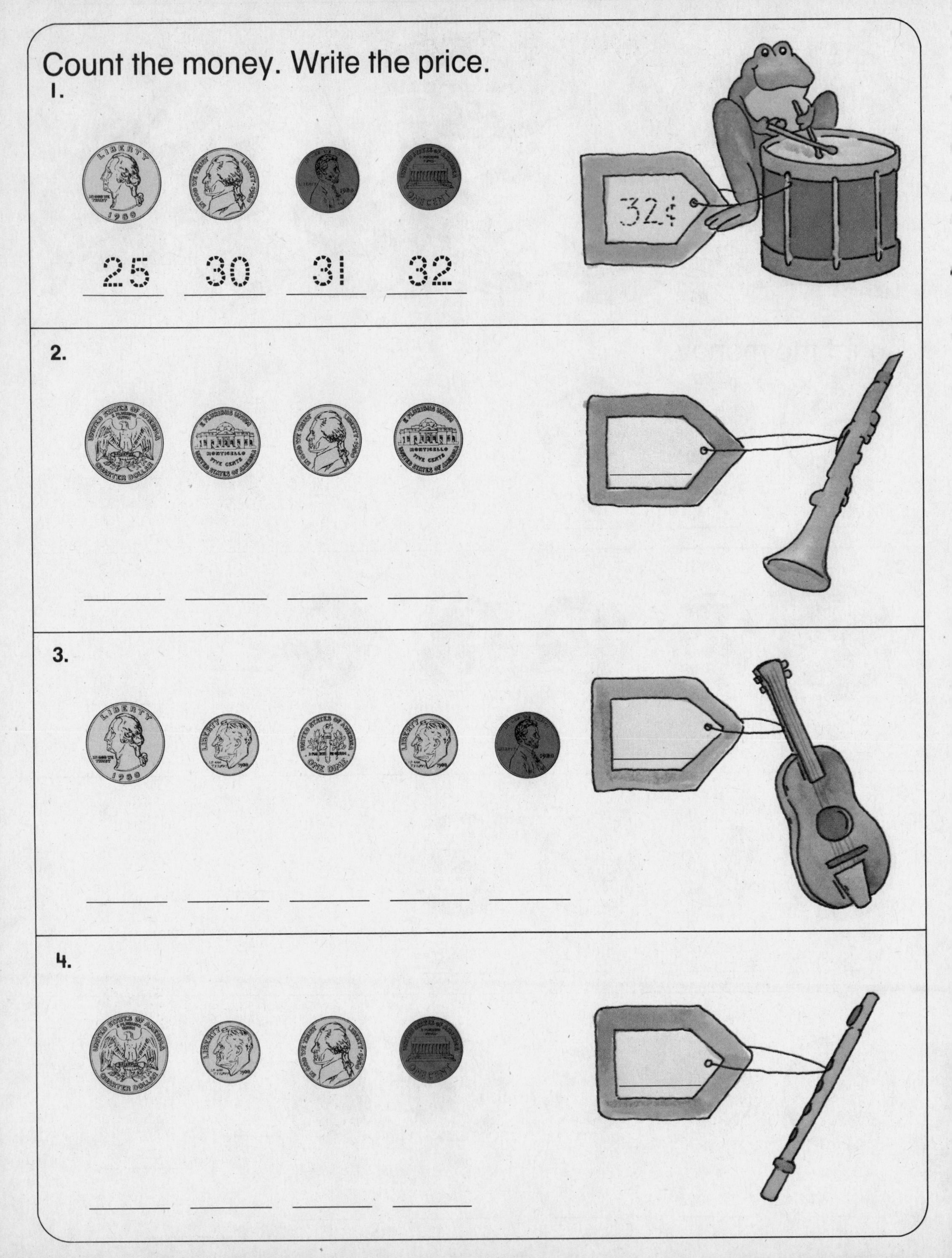

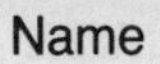
Name

CHAPTER REVIEW/TEST

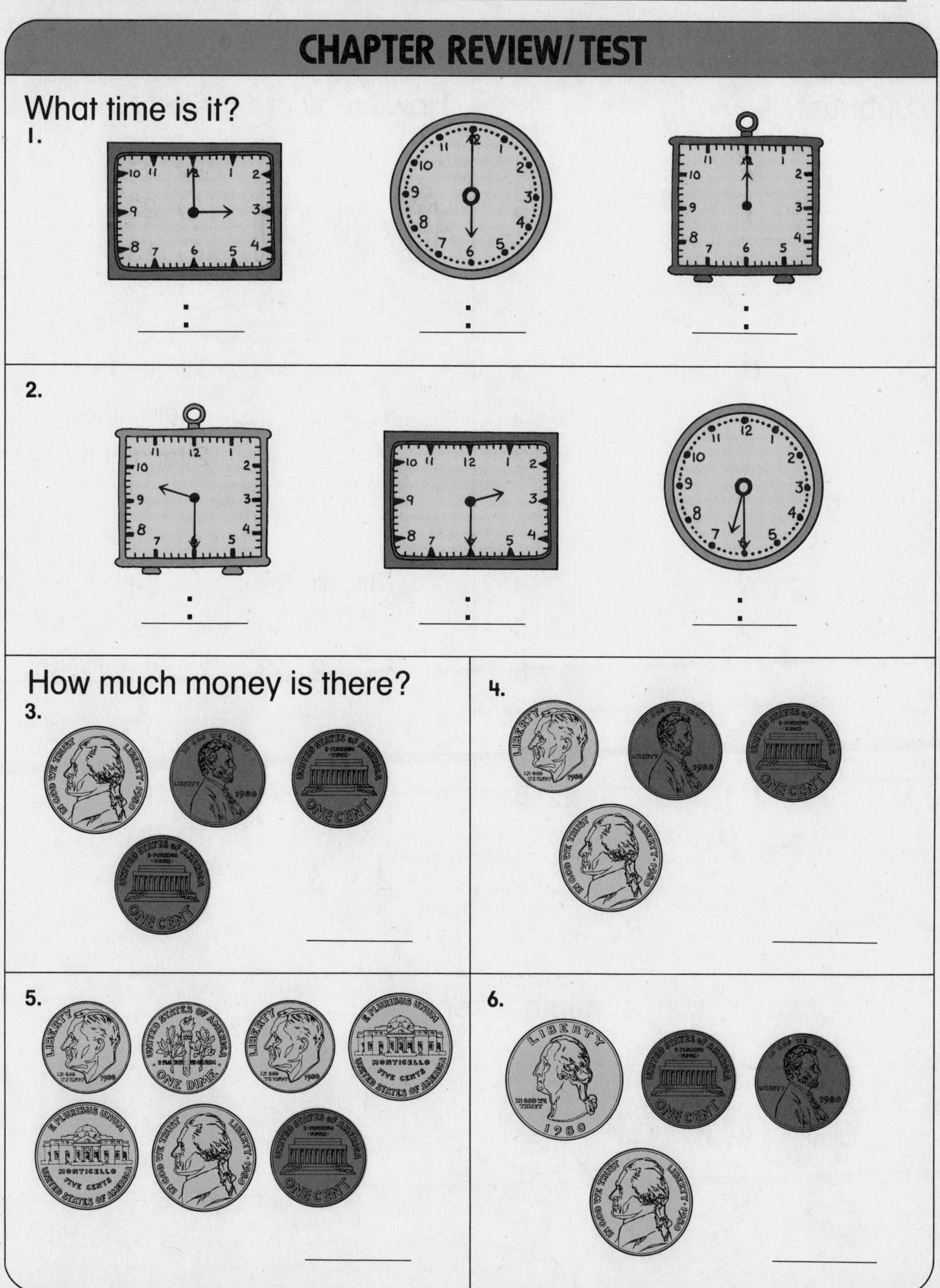

What time is it?
1.
:
:
:
2.
:
:
:
How much money is there?
3.
4.
5.
6.

Name ______________________________

CUMULATIVE REVIEW

Subtract.

1. 7 − 1

○ 3
○ 5
○ 6

2. 4 − 1

○ 3
○ 5
○ 2

3. 6 − 2

○ 4
○ 5
○ 8

4. 11 − 2

○ 8
○ 12
○ 9

How many are there?

5.

○ 33
○ 23
○ 13

6. 42

○ 3 tens 1 one
○ 4 tens 2 ones
○ 2 tens 4 ones

7. Finish the row.

51, 52, 53

○ 54, 55, 56
○ 55, 56, 57
○ 48, 49, 50

8. Count by twos.

2, 4, 6

○ 12
○ 10
○ 8

9. Choose the correct number sentence.

○ 8 − 2 = 6
○ 7 − 2 = 5
○ 5 − 1 = 4

Name ______________________________

ANOTHER LOOK

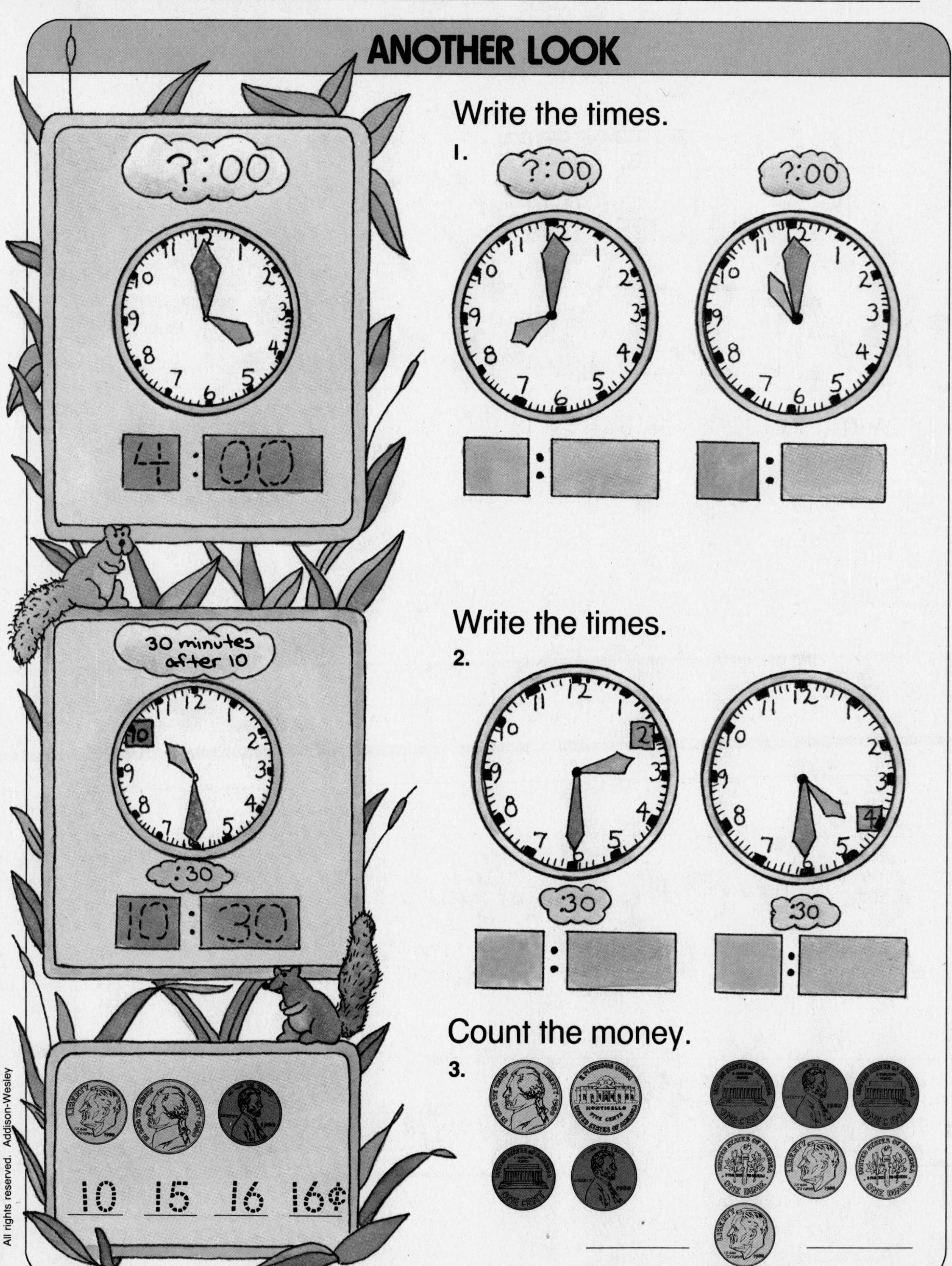

Write the times.

1.

?:00 ___ : ___

?:00 ___ : ___

Write the times.

2.

:30 ___ : ___

:30 ___ : ___

Count the money.

3.

____

____

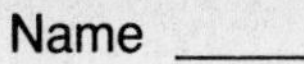

Name ___________________________

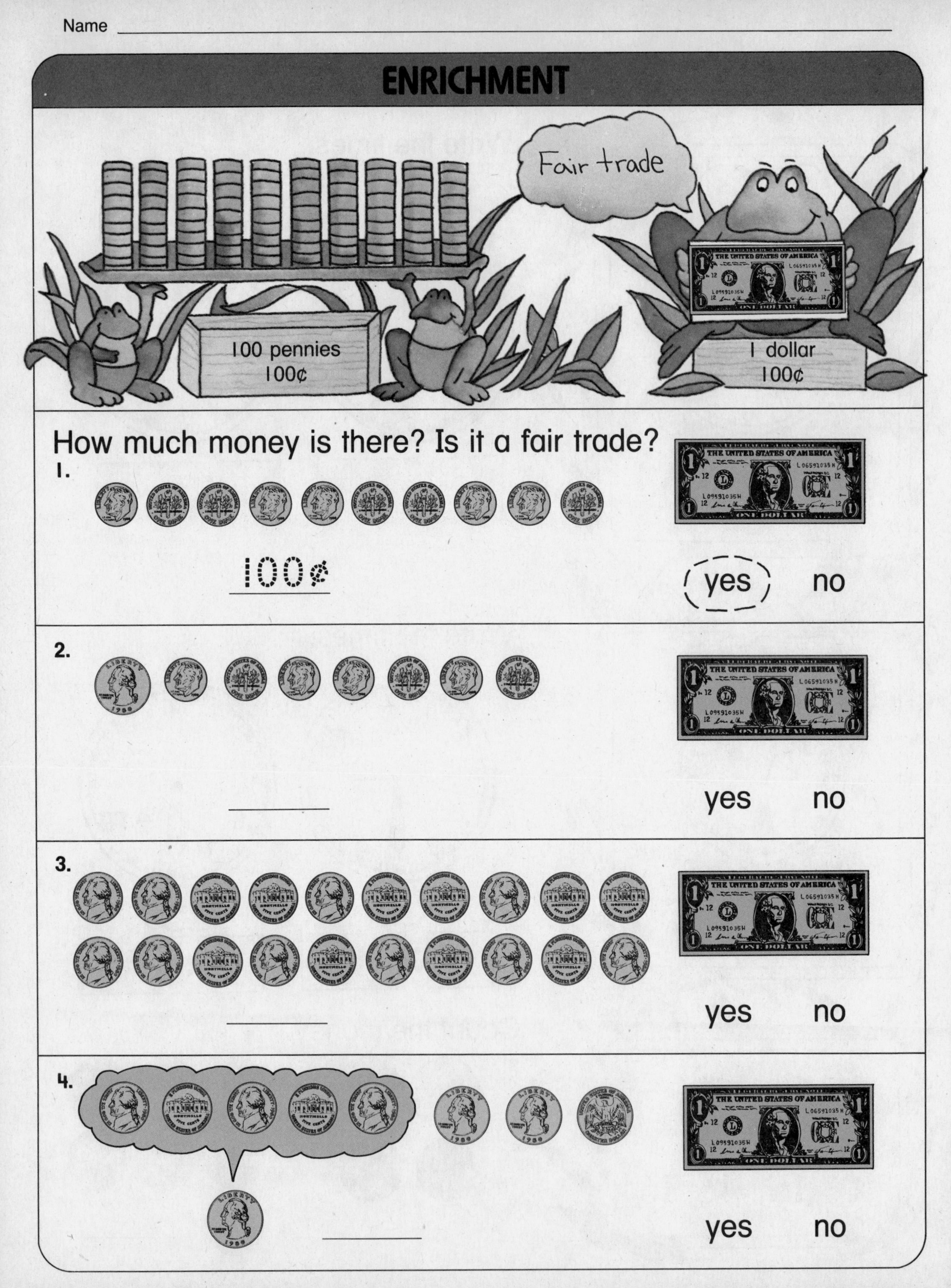
ENRICHMENT
Fair trade
100 pennies
100¢
1 dollar
100¢
How much money is there? Is it a fair trade?
1.
100¢
yes no
2.
yes no
3.
yes no
4.
yes no

8 Name ______________________

SUMS TO 12

Add.

1.

$4 + 1$	$0 + 5$	$2 + 1$	$3 + 2$

2.

$1 + 1$	$2 + 3$	$1 + 2$	$3 + 1$	$2 + 2$	$1 + 4$

3.

$8 + 1$	$1 + 6$	$9 + 1$	$5 + 1$	$1 + 7$	$1 + 4$

4.

$2 + 5$	$8 + 2$	$4 + 2$	$7 + 2$	$2 + 9$	$6 + 2$

5.

$7 + 3$	$3 + 5$	$3 + 8$	$6 + 3$	$3 + 4$	$9 + 3$

Add.

1.	$3 + 6$	$7 + 1$	$1 + 4$	$6 + 0$	$2 + 7$	
2.	$2 + 1$	$8 + 3$	$0 + 7$	$5 + 2$	$1 + 8$	$0 + 1$
3.	$3 + 3$	$9 + 1$	$2 + 8$	$3 + 7$	$1 + 1$	$4 + 2$
4.	$2 + 2$	$5 + 3$	$5 + 1$	$9 + 0$	$6 + 2$	$3 + 9$
5.	$3 + 1$	$0 + 8$	$2 + 9$	$1 + 6$	$3 + 4$	$4 + 0$

THINK MATH

How many acorns are there in all?

5 acorns 5 acorns 5 acorns 5 acorns

_____ acorns

Name ______________________________

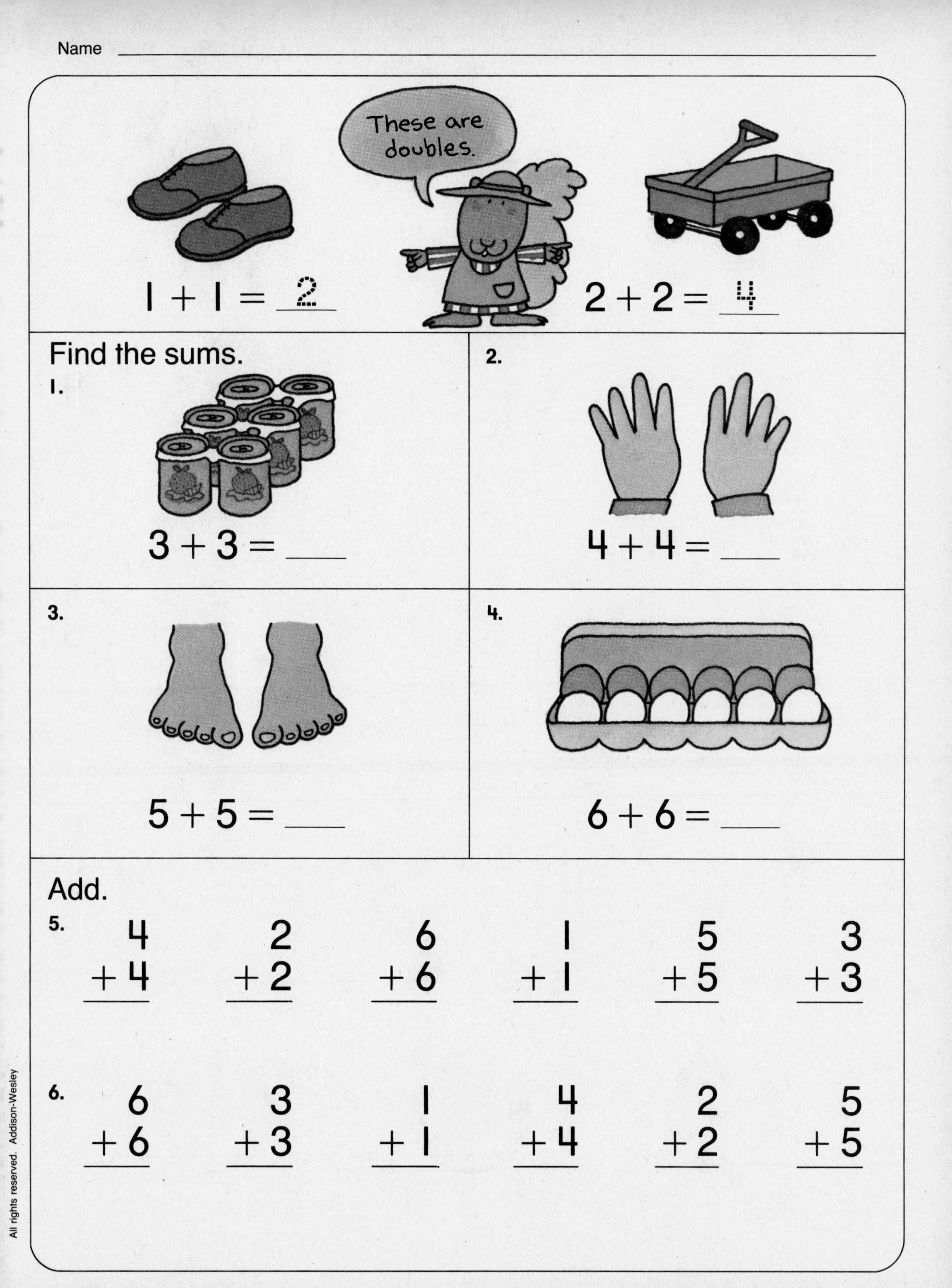

$1 + 1 = \underline{2}$

$2 + 2 = \underline{4}$

Find the sums.

1. $3 + 3 =$ ____

2. $4 + 4 =$ ____

3. $5 + 5 =$ ____

4. $6 + 6 =$ ____

Add.

5. $4 + 4$ ____ $2 + 2$ ____ $6 + 6$ ____ $1 + 1$ ____ $5 + 5$ ____ $3 + 3$ ____

6. $6 + 6$ ____ $3 + 3$ ____ $1 + 1$ ____ $4 + 4$ ____ $2 + 2$ ____ $5 + 5$ ____

Add.

1. $2 + 2 =$ ___ $3 + 3 =$ ___

2. $4 + 4 =$ ___ $5 + 5 =$ ___ $6 + 6 =$ ___

3. $\begin{array}{r} 2 \\ +2 \\ \hline \end{array}$ $\begin{array}{r} 3 \\ +3 \\ \hline \end{array}$ $\begin{array}{r} 5 \\ +5 \\ \hline \end{array}$ $\begin{array}{r} 6 \\ +6 \\ \hline \end{array}$ $\begin{array}{r} 1 \\ +1 \\ \hline \end{array}$ $\begin{array}{r} 4 \\ +4 \\ \hline \end{array}$

4. $\begin{array}{r} 3 \\ +3 \\ \hline \end{array}$ $\begin{array}{r} 5 \\ +5 \\ \hline \end{array}$ $\begin{array}{r} 1 \\ +1 \\ \hline \end{array}$ $\begin{array}{r} 4 \\ +4 \\ \hline \end{array}$ $\begin{array}{r} 2 \\ +2 \\ \hline \end{array}$ $\begin{array}{r} 6 \\ +6 \\ \hline \end{array}$

5. $\begin{array}{r} 5 \\ +5 \\ \hline \end{array}$ $\begin{array}{r} 2 \\ +2 \\ \hline \end{array}$ $\begin{array}{r} 4 \\ +4 \\ \hline \end{array}$ $\begin{array}{r} 1 \\ +1 \\ \hline \end{array}$ $\begin{array}{r} 3 \\ +3 \\ \hline \end{array}$ $\begin{array}{r} 6 \\ +6 \\ \hline \end{array}$

SKILLKEEPER

Write the times.

___:___ ___:___ ___:___

Name ______________________

$3 + 3 = 6$ $3 + 4 = 7$

Add.

1. $\begin{array}{r} 2 \\ +2 \\ \hline 4 \end{array}$ $\begin{array}{r} 3 \\ +2 \\ \hline 5 \end{array}$

2. $\begin{array}{r} 3 \\ +3 \\ \hline \end{array}$ $\begin{array}{r} 3 \\ +4 \\ \hline \end{array}$

3. $\begin{array}{r} 4 \\ +4 \\ \hline \end{array}$ $\begin{array}{r} 4 \\ +5 \\ \hline \end{array}$

4. $\begin{array}{r} 5 \\ +5 \\ \hline \end{array}$ $\begin{array}{r} 6 \\ +5 \\ \hline \end{array}$

Add.

5. $\begin{array}{r} 4 \\ +4 \\ \hline \end{array}$ $\begin{array}{r} 5 \\ +4 \\ \hline \end{array}$ $\begin{array}{r} 5 \\ +5 \\ \hline \end{array}$ $\begin{array}{r} 5 \\ +6 \\ \hline \end{array}$ $\begin{array}{r} 2 \\ +2 \\ \hline \end{array}$ $\begin{array}{r} 2 \\ +3 \\ \hline \end{array}$

6. $\begin{array}{r} 3 \\ +3 \\ \hline \end{array}$ $\begin{array}{r} 4 \\ +3 \\ \hline \end{array}$ $\begin{array}{r} 1 \\ +1 \\ \hline \end{array}$ $\begin{array}{r} 2 \\ +1 \\ \hline \end{array}$ $\begin{array}{r} 5 \\ +5 \\ \hline \end{array}$ $\begin{array}{r} 6 \\ +5 \\ \hline \end{array}$

Add.

1.

$\begin{array}{r} 4 \\ +5 \\ \hline \end{array}$	$\begin{array}{r} 6 \\ +6 \\ \hline \end{array}$	$\begin{array}{r} 7 \\ +2 \\ \hline \end{array}$	$\begin{array}{r} 4 \\ +4 \\ \hline \end{array}$	$\begin{array}{r} 3 \\ +8 \\ \hline \end{array}$

2.

$\begin{array}{r} 2 \\ +6 \\ \hline \end{array}$	$\begin{array}{r} 6 \\ +5 \\ \hline \end{array}$	$\begin{array}{r} 5 \\ +1 \\ \hline \end{array}$	$\begin{array}{r} 5 \\ +4 \\ \hline \end{array}$	$\begin{array}{r} 2 \\ +7 \\ \hline \end{array}$	$\begin{array}{r} 5 \\ +5 \\ \hline \end{array}$

3.

$\begin{array}{r} 6 \\ +3 \\ \hline \end{array}$	$\begin{array}{r} 4 \\ +5 \\ \hline \end{array}$	$\begin{array}{r} 4 \\ +3 \\ \hline \end{array}$	$\begin{array}{r} 5 \\ +6 \\ \hline \end{array}$	$\begin{array}{r} 3 \\ +3 \\ \hline \end{array}$	$\begin{array}{r} 9 \\ +1 \\ \hline \end{array}$

4.

$\begin{array}{r} 3 \\ +9 \\ \hline \end{array}$	$\begin{array}{r} 2 \\ +2 \\ \hline \end{array}$	$\begin{array}{r} 6 \\ +5 \\ \hline \end{array}$	$\begin{array}{r} 8 \\ +1 \\ \hline \end{array}$	$\begin{array}{r} 5 \\ +4 \\ \hline \end{array}$	$\begin{array}{r} 2 \\ +3 \\ \hline \end{array}$

SKILLKEEPER

Count the money.

____

____

Name ____________________

Add.

1. $4 + 5$ $9 + 1$ $3 + 3$ $2 + 7$ $6 + 5$

2. $3 + 8$ $5 + 5$ $5 + 6$ $5 + 4$ $3 + 4$ $9 + 2$

3. $2 + 8$ $4 + 5$ $3 + 9$ $2 + 2$ $6 + 5$ $3 + 5$

4. $4 + 3$ $6 + 6$ $5 + 6$ $3 + 7$ $5 + 4$ $6 + 2$

5.

Add 3	
6	9
8	
9	
7	

Add 4	
2	
4	
5	
3	

Add 5	
4	
6	
3	
5	

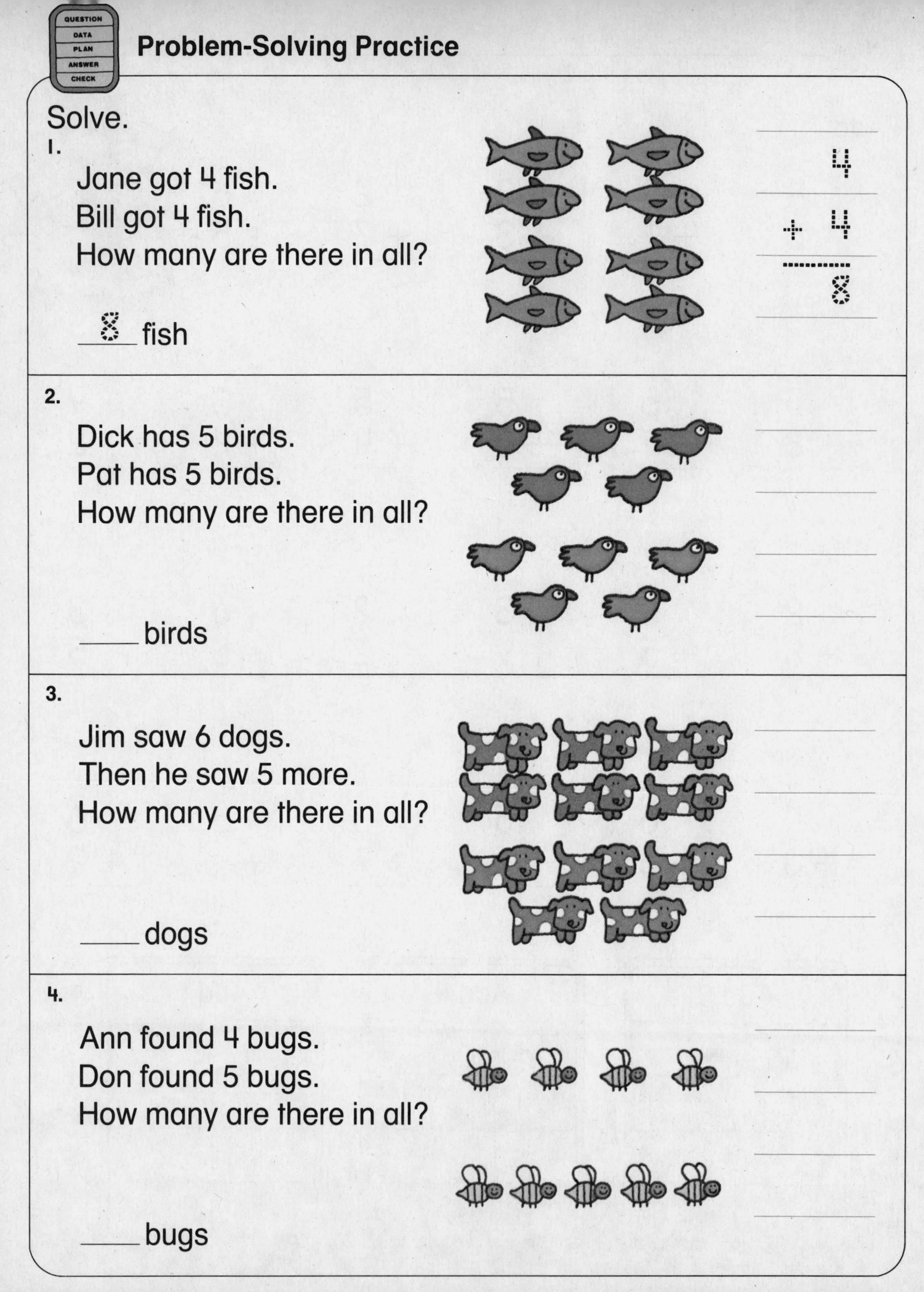

Problem-Solving Practice

Solve.

1.

Jane got 4 fish.
Bill got 4 fish.
How many are there in all?

8 fish

$$\begin{array}{r} 4 \\ + \ 4 \\ \hline 8 \end{array}$$

2.

Dick has 5 birds.
Pat has 5 birds.
How many are there in all?

____ birds

3.

Jim saw 6 dogs.
Then he saw 5 more.
How many are there in all?

____ dogs

4.

Ann found 4 bugs.
Don found 5 bugs.
How many are there in all?

____ bugs

Name ____________________

$\begin{array}{r} 4 \\ +4 \\ \hline \end{array}$ $\begin{array}{r} 4 \\ +5 \\ \hline \end{array}$ $\begin{array}{r} 4 \\ +6 \\ \hline 10 \end{array}$ $\begin{array}{r} 4 \\ +7 \\ \hline 11 \end{array}$

These are new facts.

$\begin{array}{r} 6 \\ +4 \\ \hline 10 \end{array}$ Same as $\begin{array}{r} 4 \\ +6 \\ \hline \end{array}$

$\begin{array}{r} 7 \\ +4 \\ \hline 11 \end{array}$ Same as $\begin{array}{r} 4 \\ +7 \\ \hline \end{array}$

Add.

1. $\begin{array}{r} 6 \\ +4 \\ \hline \end{array}$ $\begin{array}{r} 5 \\ +5 \\ \hline \end{array}$ $\begin{array}{r} 4 \\ +6 \\ \hline \end{array}$ $\begin{array}{r} 7 \\ +2 \\ \hline \end{array}$ $\begin{array}{r} 7 \\ +4 \\ \hline \end{array}$ $\begin{array}{r} 5 \\ +4 \\ \hline \end{array}$

2. $\begin{array}{r} 6 \\ +5 \\ \hline \end{array}$ $\begin{array}{r} 3 \\ +8 \\ \hline \end{array}$ $\begin{array}{r} 4 \\ +7 \\ \hline \end{array}$ $\begin{array}{r} 3 \\ +3 \\ \hline \end{array}$ $\begin{array}{r} 6 \\ +4 \\ \hline \end{array}$ $\begin{array}{r} 7 \\ +4 \\ \hline \end{array}$

3. $\begin{array}{r} 4 \\ +3 \\ \hline \end{array}$ $\begin{array}{r} 4 \\ +6 \\ \hline \end{array}$ $\begin{array}{r} 6 \\ +6 \\ \hline \end{array}$ $\begin{array}{r} 6 \\ +4 \\ \hline \end{array}$ $\begin{array}{r} 7 \\ +4 \\ \hline \end{array}$ $\begin{array}{r} 3 \\ +2 \\ \hline \end{array}$

4. $\begin{array}{r} 4 \\ +7 \\ \hline \end{array}$ $\begin{array}{r} 9 \\ +2 \\ \hline \end{array}$ $\begin{array}{r} 4 \\ +4 \\ \hline \end{array}$ $\begin{array}{r} 6 \\ +4 \\ \hline \end{array}$ $\begin{array}{r} 4 \\ +7 \\ \hline \end{array}$ $\begin{array}{r} 9 \\ +3 \\ \hline \end{array}$

Add.

1. $7 + 4$ | $2 + 9$ | $6 + 3$ | $4 + 6$ | $6 + 6$ | $2 + 8$

2. $7 + 2$ | $6 + 4$ | $5 + 5$ | $4 + 7$ | $5 + 4$ | $6 + 4$

3. $3 + 4$ | $7 + 4$ | $7 + 3$ | $9 + 1$ | $4 + 6$ | $4 + 7$

4. $7 + 4$ | $4 + 6$ | $5 + 6$ | $4 + 7$ | $5 + 3$ | $6 + 4$

THINK MATH

Write the numbers in order.

6 4 5 8 7

11 10 12 9 13

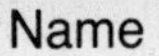
Name ____________________

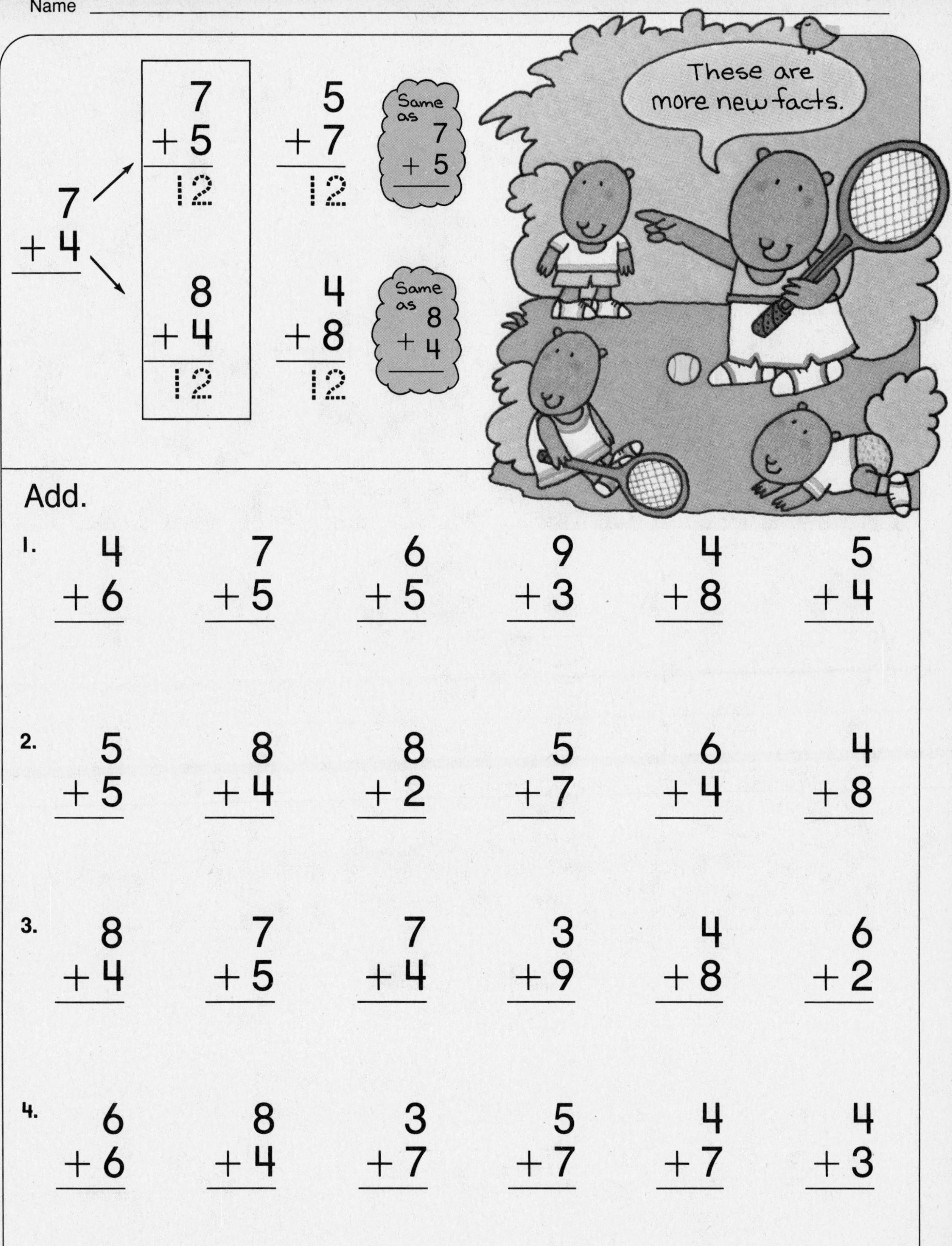

These are more new facts.
Same as 7 + 5
Same as 8 + 4

$$\begin{array}{r} 7 \\ +\,4 \\ \hline \end{array} \rightarrow \begin{array}{r} 7 \\ +\,5 \\ \hline 12 \end{array} \quad \begin{array}{r} 5 \\ +\,7 \\ \hline 12 \end{array}$$

$$\begin{array}{r} 7 \\ +\,4 \\ \hline \end{array} \rightarrow \begin{array}{r} 8 \\ +\,4 \\ \hline 12 \end{array} \quad \begin{array}{r} 4 \\ +\,8 \\ \hline 12 \end{array}$$

Add.

1. $\begin{array}{r} 4 \\ +\,6 \\ \hline \end{array}$ $\begin{array}{r} 7 \\ +\,5 \\ \hline \end{array}$ $\begin{array}{r} 6 \\ +\,5 \\ \hline \end{array}$ $\begin{array}{r} 9 \\ +\,3 \\ \hline \end{array}$ $\begin{array}{r} 4 \\ +\,8 \\ \hline \end{array}$ $\begin{array}{r} 5 \\ +\,4 \\ \hline \end{array}$

2. $\begin{array}{r} 5 \\ +\,5 \\ \hline \end{array}$ $\begin{array}{r} 8 \\ +\,4 \\ \hline \end{array}$ $\begin{array}{r} 8 \\ +\,2 \\ \hline \end{array}$ $\begin{array}{r} 5 \\ +\,7 \\ \hline \end{array}$ $\begin{array}{r} 6 \\ +\,4 \\ \hline \end{array}$ $\begin{array}{r} 4 \\ +\,8 \\ \hline \end{array}$

3. $\begin{array}{r} 8 \\ +\,4 \\ \hline \end{array}$ $\begin{array}{r} 7 \\ +\,5 \\ \hline \end{array}$ $\begin{array}{r} 7 \\ +\,4 \\ \hline \end{array}$ $\begin{array}{r} 3 \\ +\,9 \\ \hline \end{array}$ $\begin{array}{r} 4 \\ +\,8 \\ \hline \end{array}$ $\begin{array}{r} 6 \\ +\,2 \\ \hline \end{array}$

4. $\begin{array}{r} 6 \\ +\,6 \\ \hline \end{array}$ $\begin{array}{r} 8 \\ +\,4 \\ \hline \end{array}$ $\begin{array}{r} 3 \\ +\,7 \\ \hline \end{array}$ $\begin{array}{r} 5 \\ +\,7 \\ \hline \end{array}$ $\begin{array}{r} 4 \\ +\,7 \\ \hline \end{array}$ $\begin{array}{r} 4 \\ +\,3 \\ \hline \end{array}$

Finish each table.

1.

Add 7	
3	
5	
2	
4	

Add 5	
7	
5	
4	
6	

2.

Add 6	
6	
4	
3	
5	

Add 3	
6	
2	
9	
4	

Add 4	
7	
5	
8	
6	

SKILLKEEPER

Subtract.

$\begin{array}{r} 10 \\ -\ 3 \\ \hline \end{array}$ $\begin{array}{r} 6 \\ -2 \\ \hline \end{array}$ $\begin{array}{r} 9 \\ -1 \\ \hline \end{array}$ $\begin{array}{r} 8 \\ -3 \\ \hline \end{array}$ $\begin{array}{r} 4 \\ -2 \\ \hline \end{array}$ $\begin{array}{r} 5 \\ -1 \\ \hline \end{array}$

Name ____________________

Add.

1. $4 + 5$ $\quad 7 + 4$ $\quad 4 + 6$ $\quad 4 + 8$ $\quad 5 + 3$ $\quad 3 + 3$

2. $6 + 3$ $\quad 6 + 2$ $\quad 3 + 8$ $\quad 5 + 2$ $\quad 5 + 5$ $\quad 6 + 6$

3. $2 + 7$ $\quad 4 + 2$ $\quad 7 + 5$ $\quad 4 + 4$ $\quad 2 + 8$ $\quad 9 + 2$

4. $3 + 4$ $\quad 9 + 3$ $\quad 2 + 6$ $\quad 3 + 2$ $\quad 5 + 6$ $\quad 8 + 1$

Add. Color.
7
9
11
8
10
12
3 + 8
4 + 3
4 + 4
4 + 6
5 + 4
3 + 9
7 + 5
6 + 6
7 + 4
6 + 3
8 + 2
7 + 3 = ___
6 + 5 = ___
5 + 5 = ___
9 + 2 = ___

Name ______________________________

Add.

1.

8	5	6
+ 3	+ 7	+ 5

2.

9	4	2
+ 2	+ 7	+ 8

3.

3	9	4	2	7	5
+ 4	+ 3	+ 5	+ 9	+ 5	+ 3

4.

5	8	3	8	3	6
+ 6	+ 4	+ 6	+ 3	+ 9	+ 4

5.

9	5	6	5	4	6
+ 1	+ 4	+ 5	+ 7	+ 4	+ 3

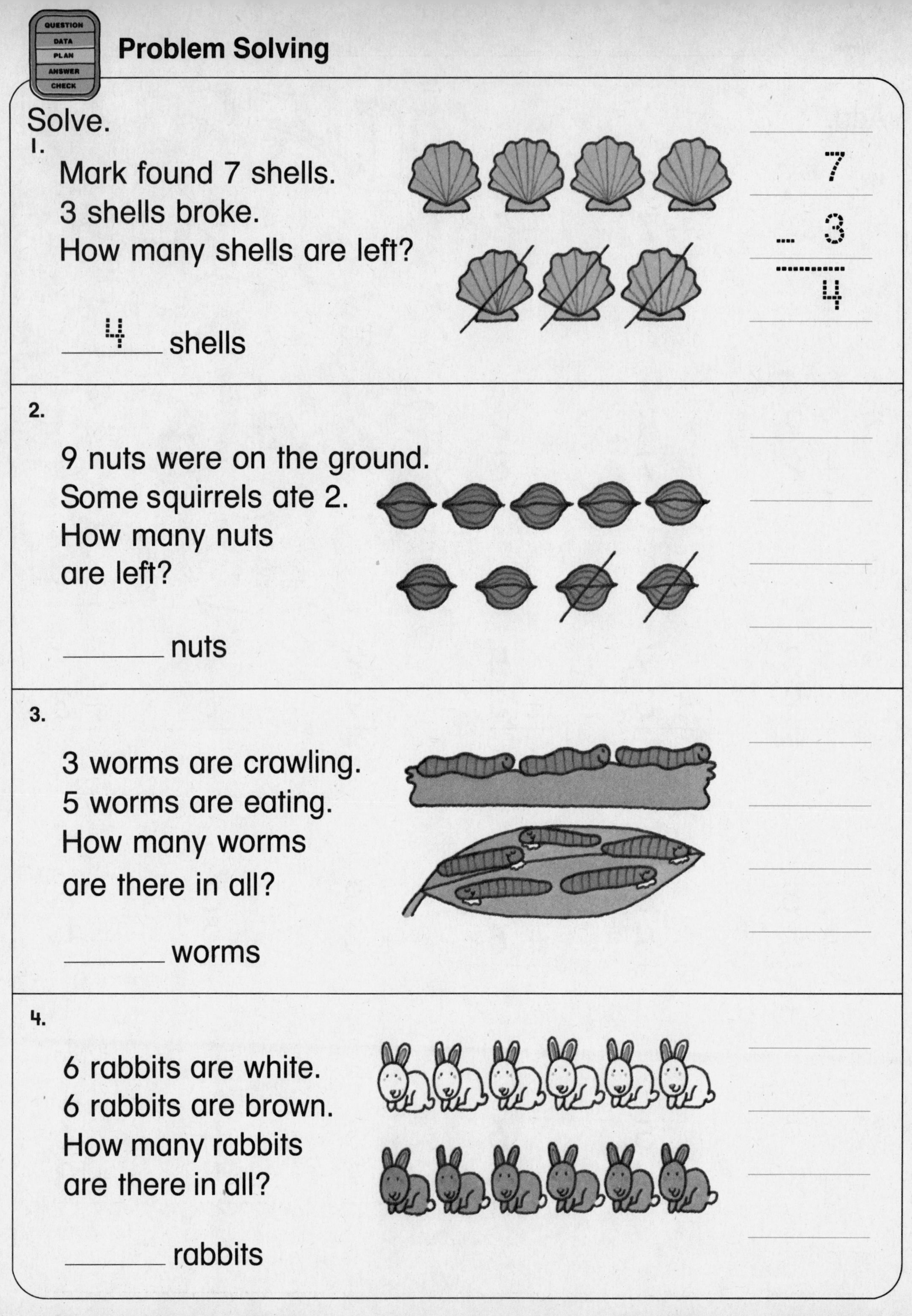

Problem Solving

Solve.

1. Mark found 7 shells.
3 shells broke.
How many shells are left?

4 shells

$$\begin{array}{r} 7 \\ -\ 3 \\ \hline 4 \end{array}$$

2. 9 nuts were on the ground.
Some squirrels ate 2.
How many nuts
are left?

_______ nuts

3. 3 worms are crawling.
5 worms are eating.
How many worms
are there in all?

_______ worms

4. 6 rabbits are white.
6 rabbits are brown.
How many rabbits
are there in all?

_______ rabbits

Name ______________________________

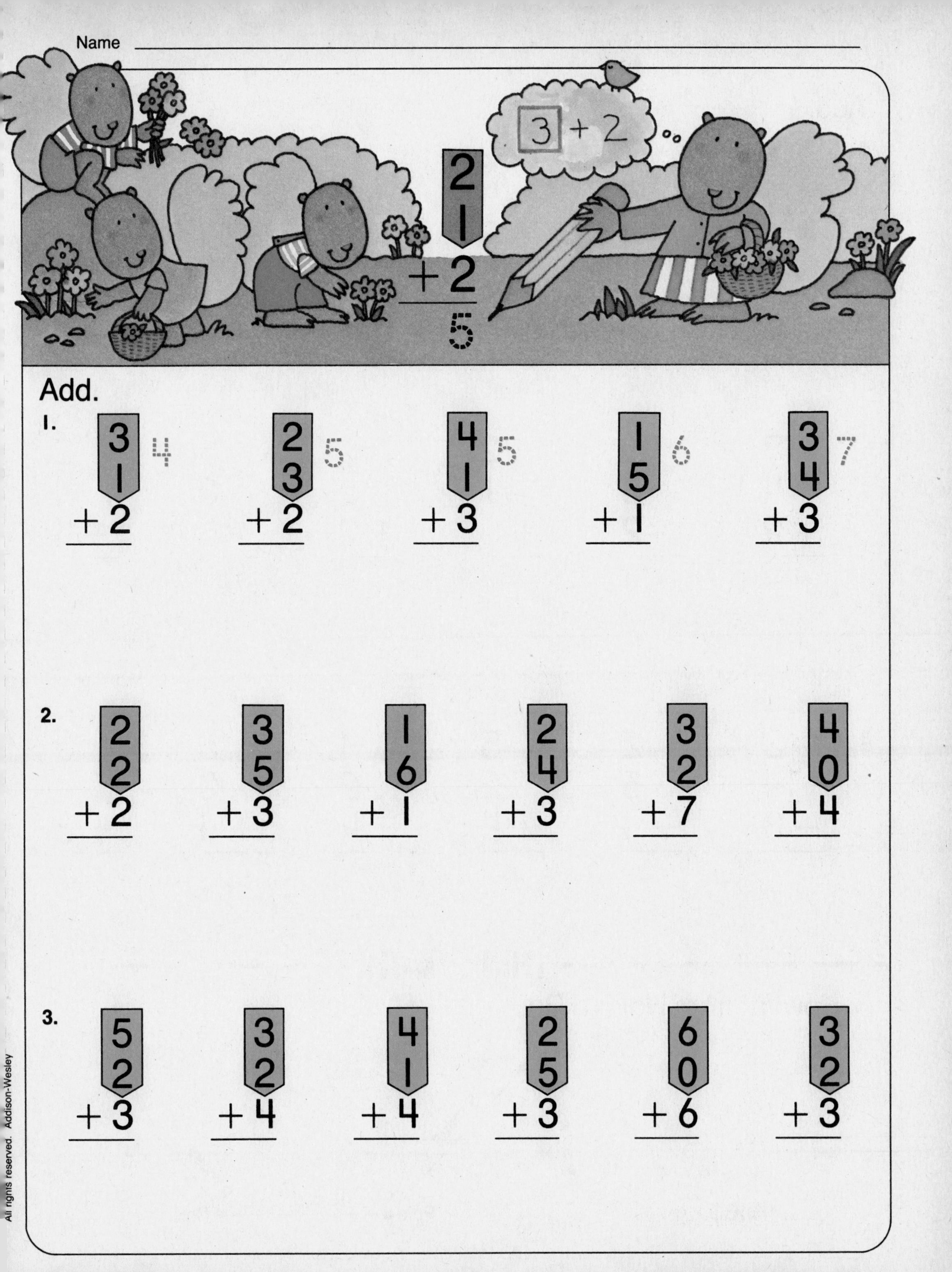

Add.

1.

3	2	4	1	3
1 (4)	3 (5)	1 (5)	5 (6)	4 (7)
+ 2	+ 2	+ 3	+ 1	+ 3

2.

2	3	1	2	3	4
2	5	6	4	2	0
+ 2	+ 3	+ 1	+ 3	+ 7	+ 4

3.

5	3	4	2	6	3
2	2	1	5	0	2
+ 3	+ 4	+ 4	+ 3	+ 6	+ 3

Add.

1.

2	1	2	1	2
1	2	4	2	2
+ 1	+ 3	+ 3	+ 5	+ 3

2.

3	6	2	5	2	2
4	3	1	2	3	4
+ 2	+ 2	+ 5	+ 2	+ 5	+ 4

3.

3	2	5	4	5	3
4	5	2	2	3	2
+ 3	+ 4	+ 4	+ 4	+ 4	+ 3

THINK MATH

How far from Nale to Rale?

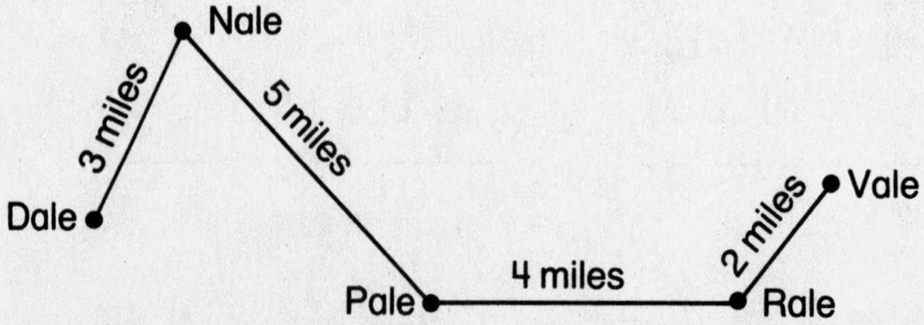

Nale
3 miles
5 miles
Dale
2 miles
Vale
4 miles
Pale
Rale

____ miles

Problem Solving

Name ______________________

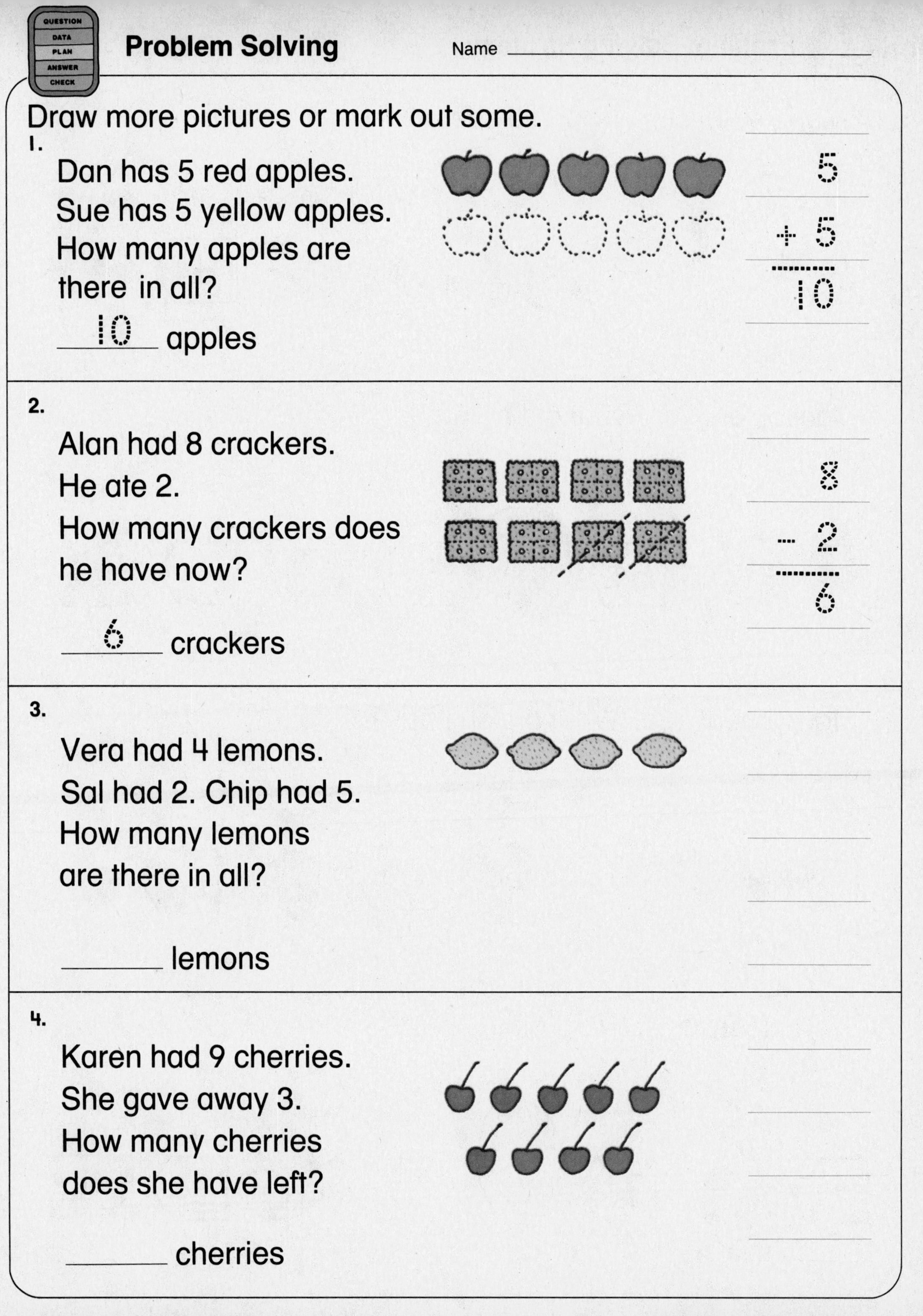

Draw more pictures or mark out some.

1. Dan has 5 red apples.
   Sue has 5 yellow apples.
   How many apples are there in all?

   10 apples

$$\begin{array}{r} 5 \\ +\ 5 \\ \hline 10 \end{array}$$

2. Alan had 8 crackers.
   He ate 2.
   How many crackers does he have now?

   6 crackers

$$\begin{array}{r} 8 \\ -\ 2 \\ \hline 6 \end{array}$$

3. Vera had 4 lemons.
   Sal had 2. Chip had 5.
   How many lemons are there in all?

   ______ lemons

4. Karen had 9 cherries.
   She gave away 3.
   How many cherries does she have left?

   ______ cherries

Problem-Solving Strategy

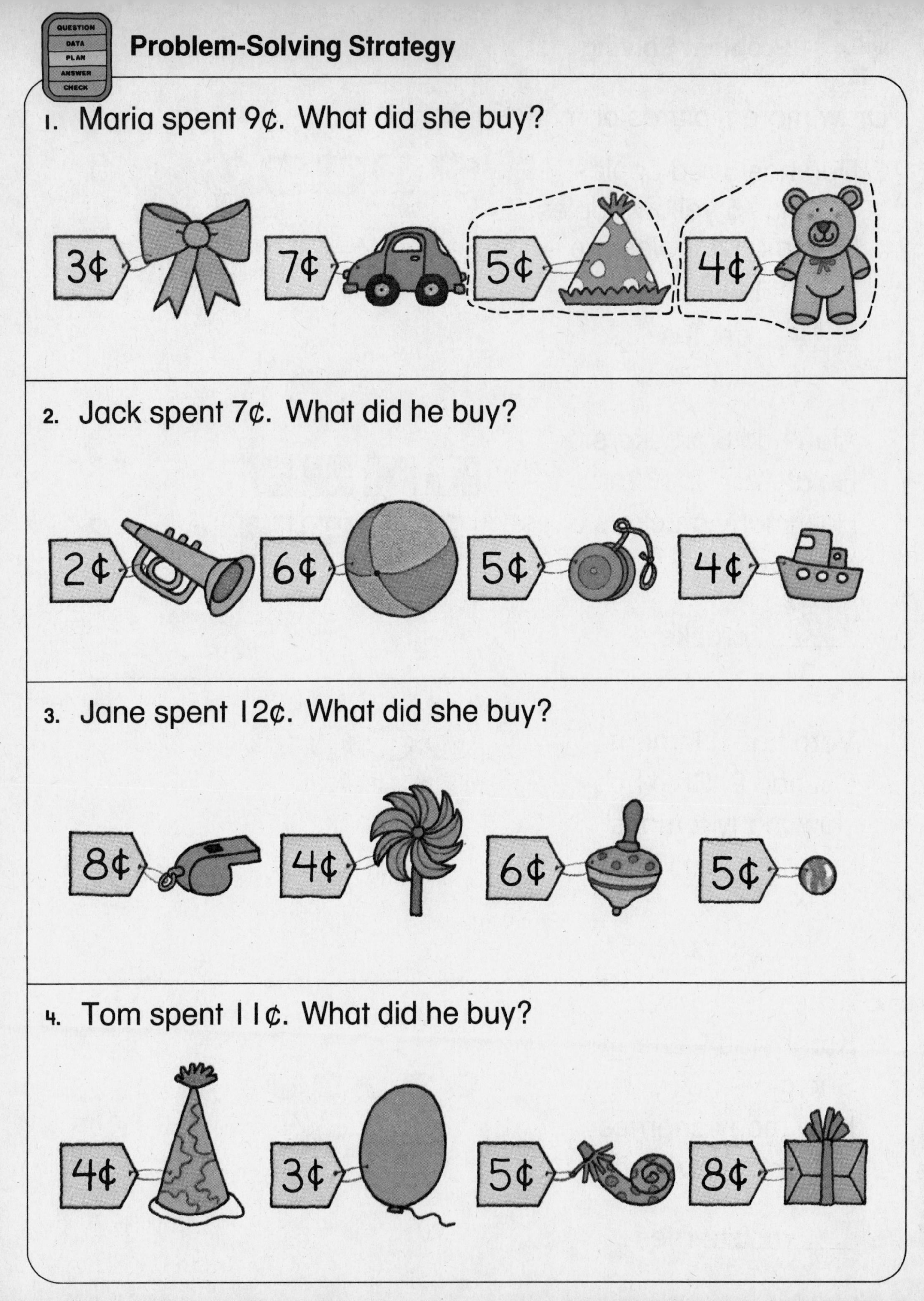

1. Maria spent 9¢. What did she buy?

2. Jack spent 7¢. What did he buy?

3. Jane spent 12¢. What did she buy?

4. Tom spent 11¢. What did he buy?

Name ______________________________

CHAPTER REVIEW/TEST

Add.

1.

0	2	1	4	9	7
+ 5	+ 1	+ 3	+ 0	+ 1	+ 2

2.

5	4	1	3	6	2
+ 5	+ 4	+ 1	+ 3	+ 6	+ 2

3.

6	3	4	3	1	6
+ 5	+ 2	+ 5	+ 4	+ 2	+ 5

4.

2	2	4	3	2	3
5	4	3	4	1	2
+ 4	+ 4	+ 5	+ 2	+ 3	+ 4

5. Solve.

Ellen saw 5 rabbits.
2 ran away.
How many rabbits were left?

____ rabbits

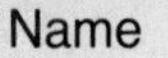

Name ______________________________

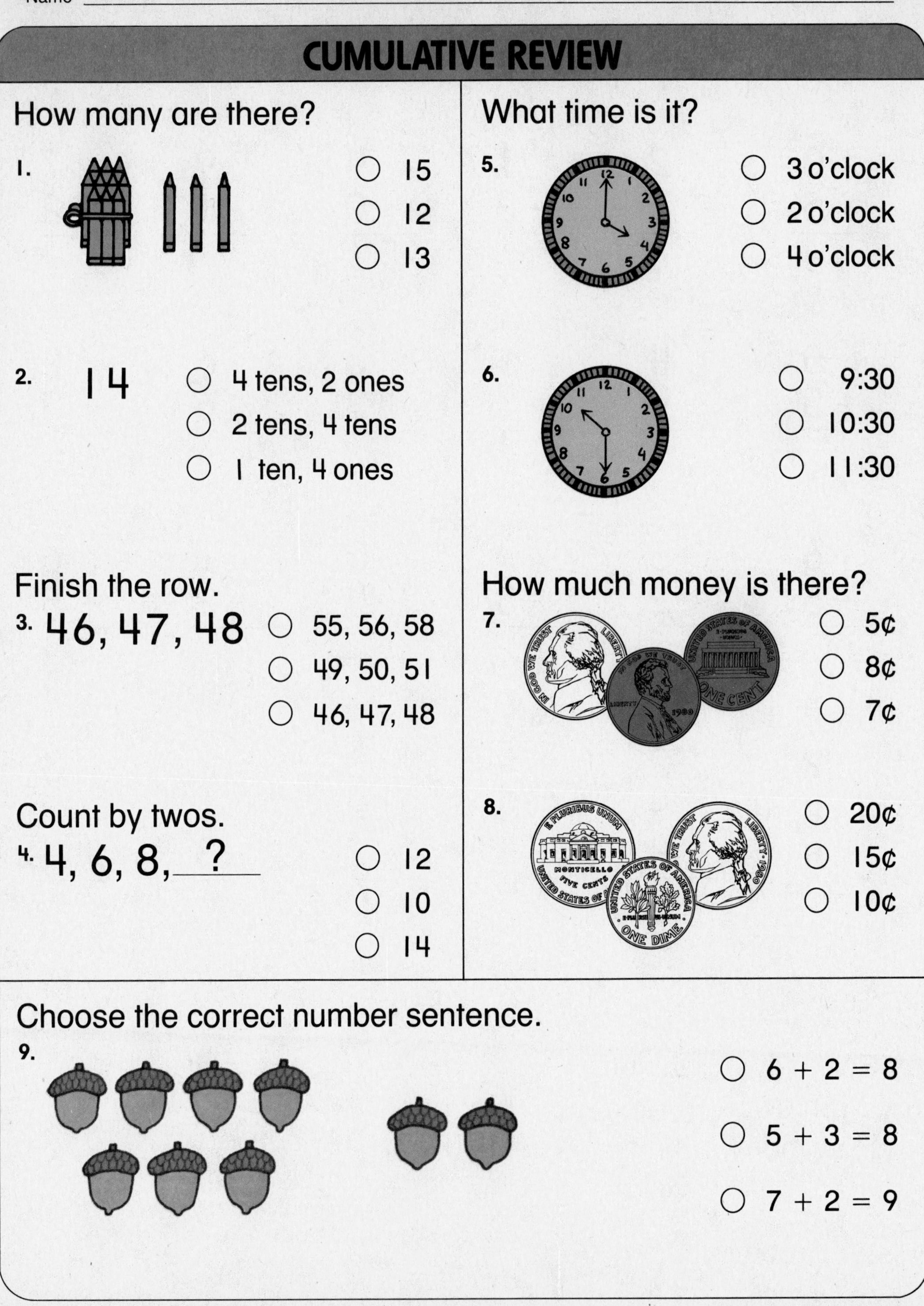

CUMULATIVE REVIEW

How many are there?

1.
- ○ 15
- ○ 12
- ○ 13

2. 14
- ○ 4 tens, 2 ones
- ○ 2 tens, 4 tens
- ○ 1 ten, 4 ones

Finish the row.

3. 46, 47, 48
- ○ 55, 56, 58
- ○ 49, 50, 51
- ○ 46, 47, 48

Count by twos.

4. 4, 6, 8, __?__
- ○ 12
- ○ 10
- ○ 14

What time is it?

5.
- ○ 3 o'clock
- ○ 2 o'clock
- ○ 4 o'clock

6.
- ○ 9:30
- ○ 10:30
- ○ 11:30

How much money is there?

7.
- ○ 5¢
- ○ 8¢
- ○ 7¢

8.
- ○ 20¢
- ○ 15¢
- ○ 10¢

Choose the correct number sentence.

9.
- ○ 6 + 2 = 8
- ○ 5 + 3 = 8
- ○ 7 + 2 = 9

Name ______________________

ANOTHER LOOK

These are doubles facts.

$1 + 1 = 2$ $2 + 2 = 4$ $3 + 3 = 6$

$4 + 4 = 8$ $5 + 5 = 10$ $6 + 6 = 12$

The doubles help with these.

$3 + 3 = 6$ (one more) $4 + 3 = 7$

$4 + 4 = 8$ (one more) $5 + 4 = 9$

$5 + 5 = 10$ (one more) $6 + 5 = 11$

$6 + 4 = 10$ $7 + 4 = 11$ $7 + 5 = 12$ $8 + 4 = 12$

Add.

1. $2 + 2$ $5 + 5$
2. $4 + 5$ $3 + 4$
3. $6 + 4$ $7 + 5$
4. $6 + 6$ $4 + 8$
5. $4 + 7$ $3 + 3$
6. $4 + 4$ $5 + 7$

Name ____________________

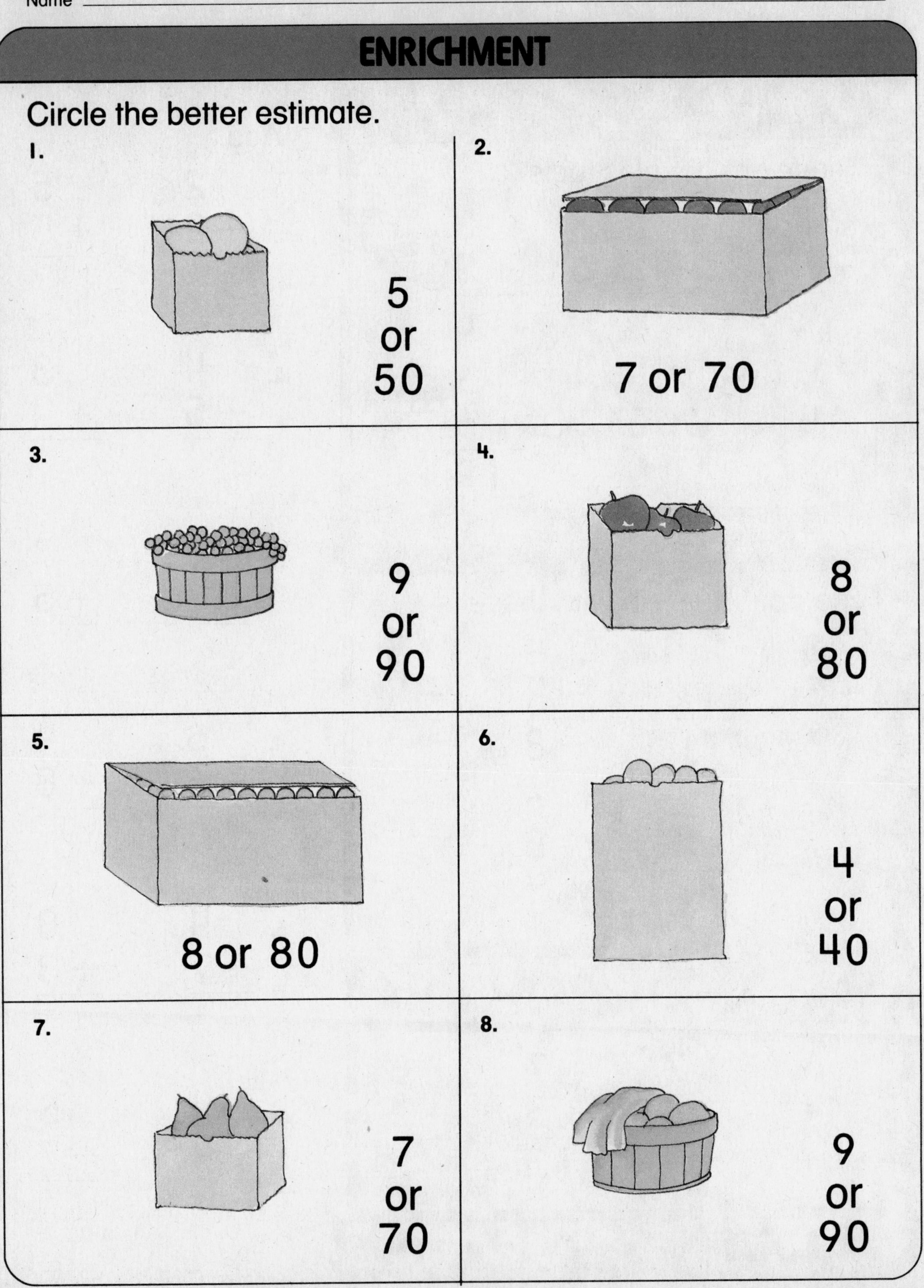

ENRICHMENT

Circle the better estimate.

1. 5 or 50

2. 7 or 70

3. 9 or 90

4. 8 or 80

5. 8 or 80

6. 4 or 40

7. 7 or 70

8. 9 or 90

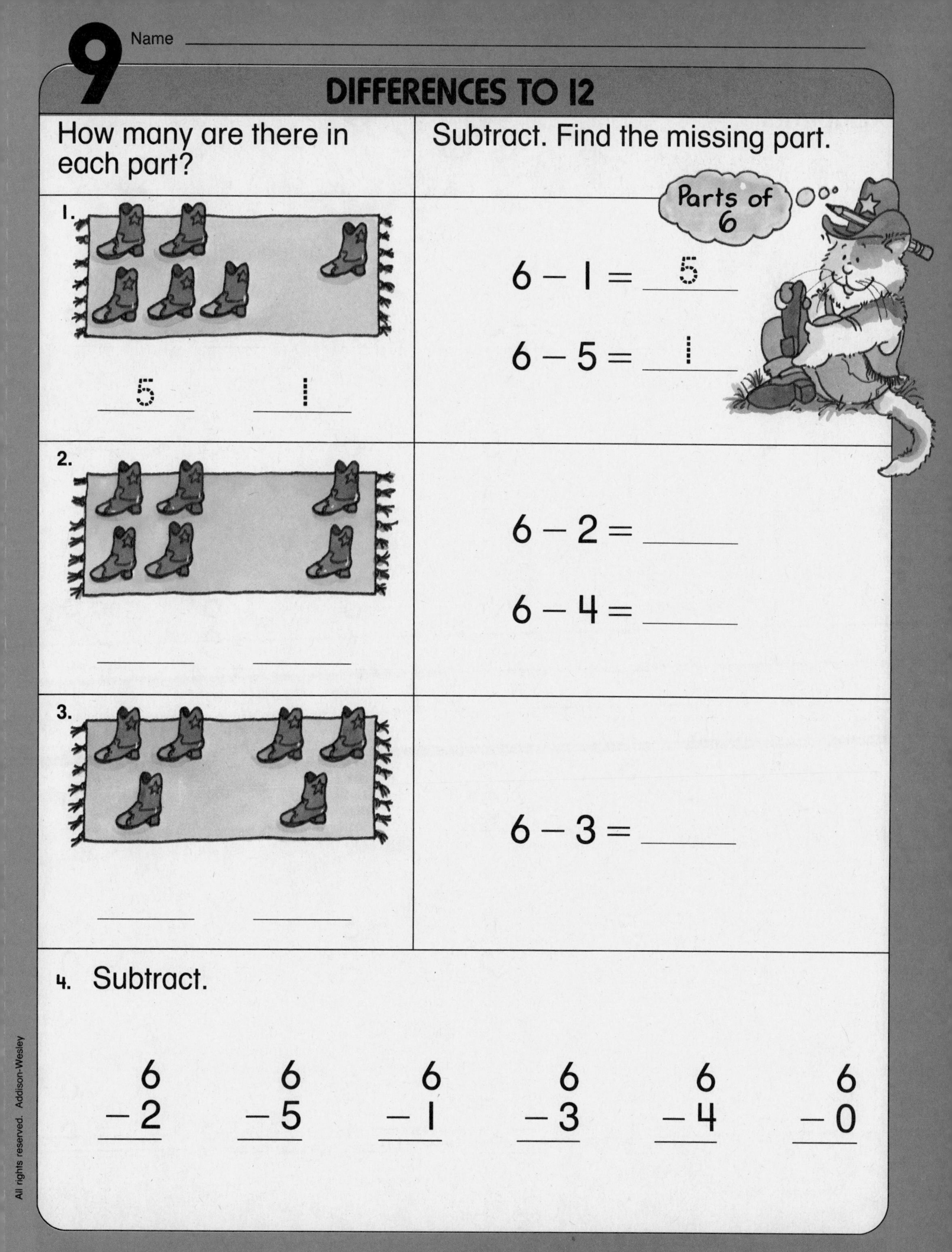

9 Name ____________________

DIFFERENCES TO 12

How many are there in each part?

Subtract. Find the missing part.

1. 5 ____ 1 ____

$6 - 1 =$ 5

$6 - 5 =$ 1

2. ____ ____

$6 - 2 =$ ____

$6 - 4 =$ ____

3. ____ ____

$6 - 3 =$ ____

4. Subtract.

$6 - 2$	$6 - 5$	$6 - 1$	$6 - 3$	$6 - 4$	$6 - 0$
____	____	____	____	____	____

Subtract.

1. $6 - 4$ $\quad 4 - 2$ $\quad 6 - 3$ $\quad 5 - 2$ $\quad 3 - 2$ $\quad 6 - 2$

2. $4 - 3$ $\quad 6 - 1$ $\quad 5 - 4$ $\quad 6 - 6$ $\quad 6 - 5$ $\quad 2 - 1$

3. $6 - 2$ $\quad 5 - 5$ $\quad 6 - 5$ $\quad 3 - 1$ $\quad 6 - 0$ $\quad 5 - 1$

4. $4 - 1$ $\quad 6 - 0$ $\quad 5 - 3$ $\quad 6 - 4$ $\quad 6 - 3$ $\quad 3 - 0$

5. $6 - 1$ $\quad 5 - 4$ $\quad 4 - 2$ $\quad 6 - 4$ $\quad 6 - 5$ $\quad 5 - 0$

6. $5 - 3$ $\quad 6 - 0$ $\quad 6 - 3$ $\quad 3 - 1$ $\quad 5 - 3$ $\quad 6 - 6$

Name ______________________

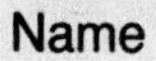

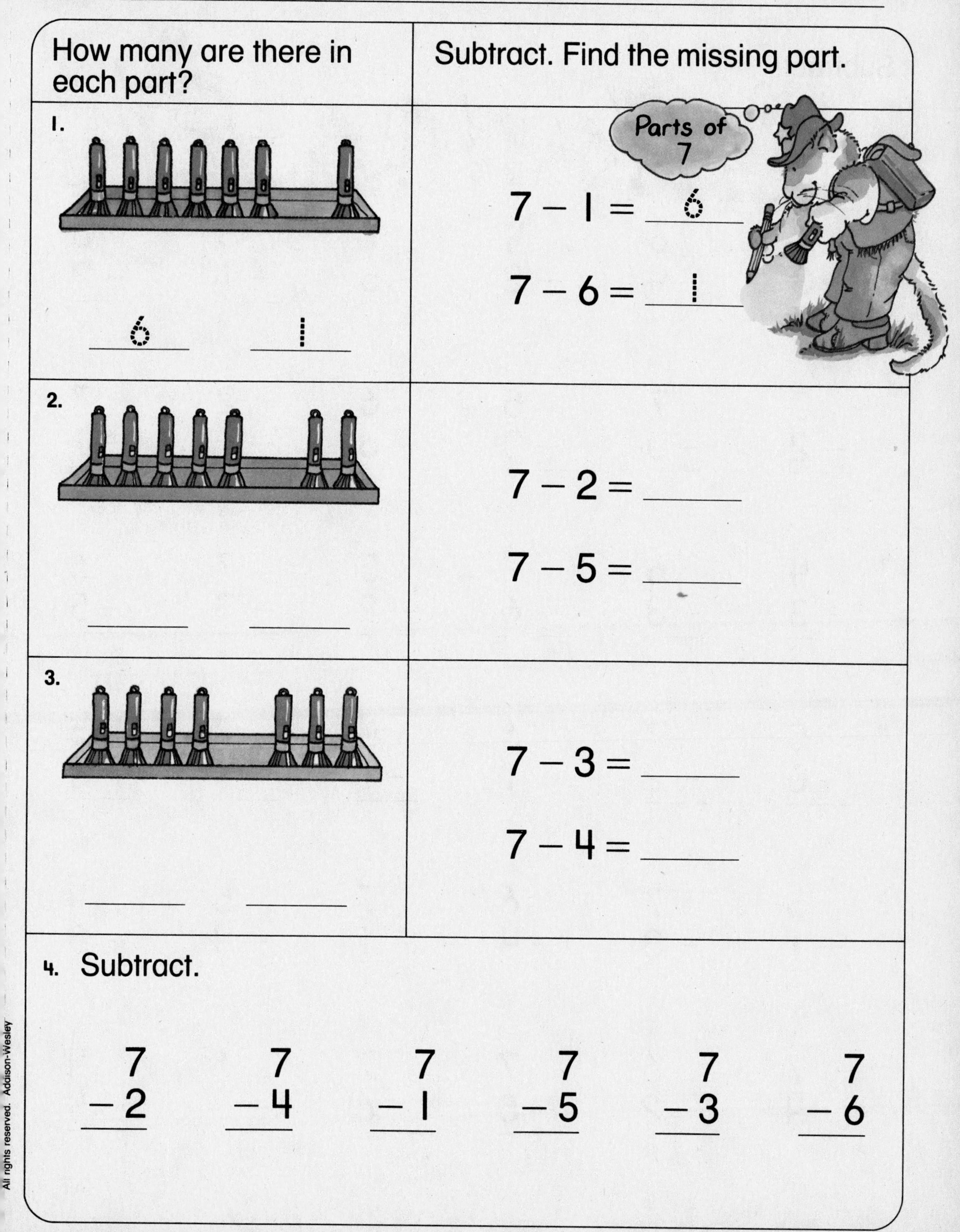

How many are there in each part?	Subtract. Find the missing part.
1. 6 ___ 1 ___	$7 - 1 =$ 6 $7 - 6 =$ 1
2. ___ ___	$7 - 2 =$ ___ $7 - 5 =$ ___
3. ___ ___	$7 - 3 =$ ___ $7 - 4 =$ ___

4. Subtract.

$\begin{array}{r} 7 \\ -2 \\ \hline \end{array}$ $\begin{array}{r} 7 \\ -4 \\ \hline \end{array}$ $\begin{array}{r} 7 \\ -1 \\ \hline \end{array}$ $\begin{array}{r} 7 \\ -5 \\ \hline \end{array}$ $\begin{array}{r} 7 \\ -3 \\ \hline \end{array}$ $\begin{array}{r} 7 \\ -6 \\ \hline \end{array}$

Subtract.

1. $7 - 3 =$ ___ $6 - 4 =$ ___ $4 - 2 =$ ___ $7 - 5 =$ ___ $5 - 1 =$ ___ $6 - 2 =$ ___

2. $3 - 2 =$ ___ $7 - 0 =$ ___ $5 - 3 =$ ___ $6 - 6 =$ ___ $2 - 1 =$ ___ $7 - 1 =$ ___

3. $4 - 3 =$ ___ $6 - 3 =$ ___ $7 - 6 =$ ___ $5 - 2 =$ ___ $7 - 7 =$ ___ $6 - 5 =$ ___

4. $5 - 0 =$ ___ $7 - 2 =$ ___ $6 - 1 =$ ___ $4 - 1 =$ ___ $7 - 4 =$ ___ $5 - 4 =$ ___

5. $5 - 1 =$ ___ $7 - 3 =$ ___ $6 - 4 =$ ___ $7 - 1 =$ ___ $5 - 4 =$ ___ $4 - 3 =$ ___

6. $7 - 4 =$ ___ $6 - 2 =$ ___ $7 - 5 =$ ___ $7 - 6 =$ ___ $6 - 3 =$ ___ $4 - 4 =$ ___

Subtract.

1.

$$\begin{array}{r} 7 \\ -3 \\ \hline \end{array}\qquad \begin{array}{r} 6 \\ -4 \\ \hline \end{array}\qquad \begin{array}{r} 4 \\ -2 \\ \hline \end{array}\qquad \begin{array}{r} 7 \\ -5 \\ \hline \end{array}\qquad \begin{array}{r} 5 \\ -1 \\ \hline \end{array}\qquad \begin{array}{r} 6 \\ -2 \\ \hline \end{array}$$

2.

$$\begin{array}{r} 3 \\ -2 \\ \hline \end{array}\qquad \begin{array}{r} 7 \\ -0 \\ \hline \end{array}\qquad \begin{array}{r} 5 \\ -3 \\ \hline \end{array}\qquad \begin{array}{r} 6 \\ -6 \\ \hline \end{array}\qquad \begin{array}{r} 2 \\ -1 \\ \hline \end{array}\qquad \begin{array}{r} 7 \\ -1 \\ \hline \end{array}$$

3.

$$\begin{array}{r} 4 \\ -3 \\ \hline \end{array}\qquad \begin{array}{r} 6 \\ -3 \\ \hline \end{array}\qquad \begin{array}{r} 7 \\ -6 \\ \hline \end{array}\qquad \begin{array}{r} 5 \\ -2 \\ \hline \end{array}\qquad \begin{array}{r} 7 \\ -7 \\ \hline \end{array}\qquad \begin{array}{r} 6 \\ -5 \\ \hline \end{array}$$

4.

$$\begin{array}{r} 5 \\ -0 \\ \hline \end{array}\qquad \begin{array}{r} 7 \\ -2 \\ \hline \end{array}\qquad \begin{array}{r} 6 \\ -1 \\ \hline \end{array}\qquad \begin{array}{r} 4 \\ -1 \\ \hline \end{array}\qquad \begin{array}{r} 7 \\ -4 \\ \hline \end{array}\qquad \begin{array}{r} 5 \\ -4 \\ \hline \end{array}$$

5.

$$\begin{array}{r} 5 \\ -1 \\ \hline \end{array}\qquad \begin{array}{r} 7 \\ -3 \\ \hline \end{array}\qquad \begin{array}{r} 6 \\ -4 \\ \hline \end{array}\qquad \begin{array}{r} 7 \\ -1 \\ \hline \end{array}\qquad \begin{array}{r} 5 \\ -4 \\ \hline \end{array}\qquad \begin{array}{r} 4 \\ -3 \\ \hline \end{array}$$

6.

$$\begin{array}{r} 7 \\ -4 \\ \hline \end{array}\qquad \begin{array}{r} 6 \\ -2 \\ \hline \end{array}\qquad \begin{array}{r} 7 \\ -5 \\ \hline \end{array}\qquad \begin{array}{r} 7 \\ -6 \\ \hline \end{array}\qquad \begin{array}{r} 6 \\ -3 \\ \hline \end{array}\qquad \begin{array}{r} 4 \\ -4 \\ \hline \end{array}$$

Subtracting from 7

Name ______________________

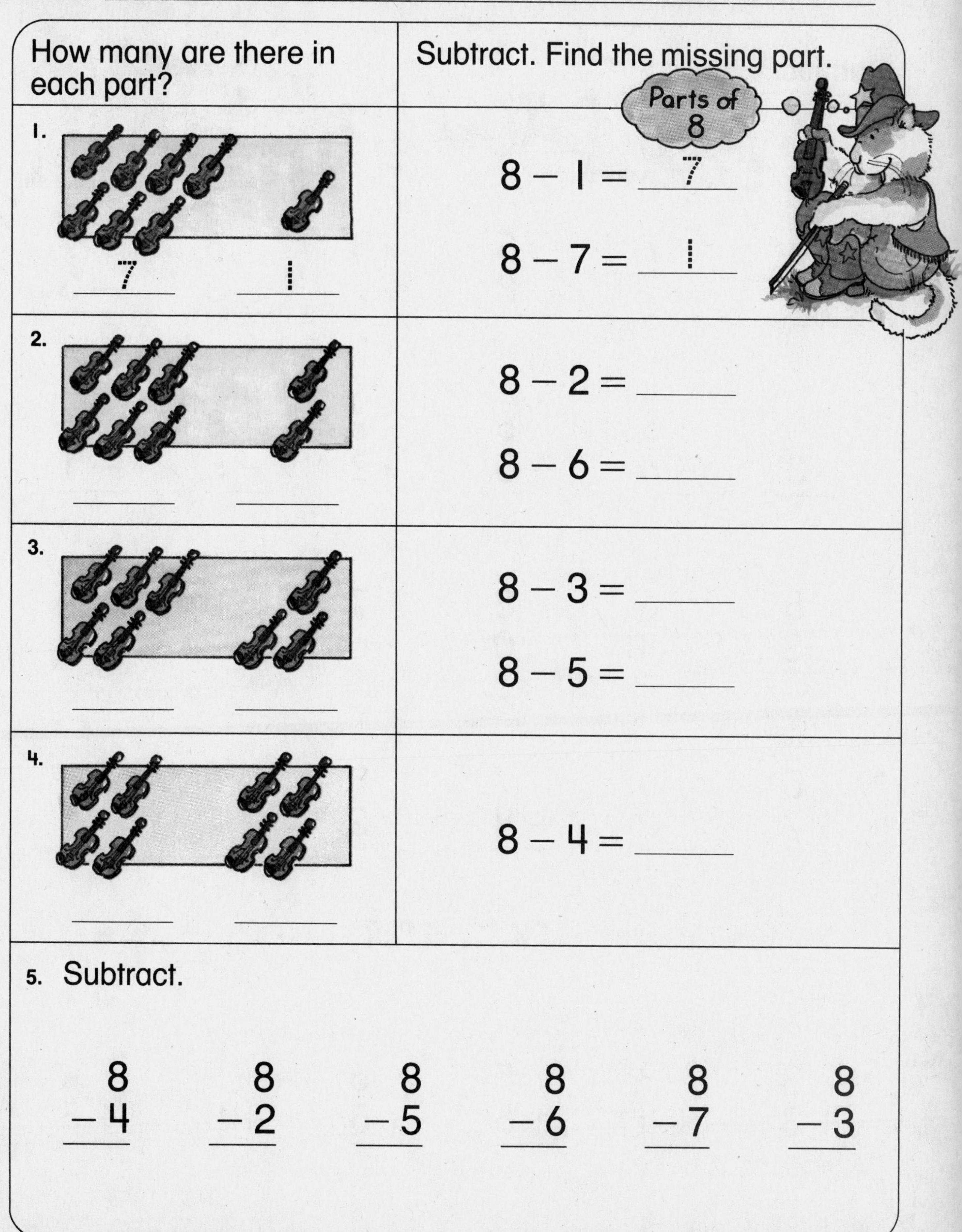

How many are there in each part?

Subtract. Find the missing part.

1. 7 ____ 1 ____

$8 - 1 =$ 7

$8 - 7 =$ 1

2. ____ ____

$8 - 2 =$ ____

$8 - 6 =$ ____

3. ____ ____

$8 - 3 =$ ____

$8 - 5 =$ ____

4. ____ ____

$8 - 4 =$ ____

5. Subtract.

8	8	8	8	8	8
− 4	− 2	− 5	− 6	− 7	− 3
____	____	____	____	____	____

Subtract.

1. $\begin{array}{r} 8 \\ -3 \\ \hline \end{array}$ $\begin{array}{r} 7 \\ -5 \\ \hline \end{array}$ $\begin{array}{r} 5 \\ -3 \\ \hline \end{array}$ $\begin{array}{r} 8 \\ -1 \\ \hline \end{array}$ $\begin{array}{r} 6 \\ -3 \\ \hline \end{array}$ $\begin{array}{r} 7 \\ -3 \\ \hline \end{array}$

2. $\begin{array}{r} 4 \\ -3 \\ \hline \end{array}$ $\begin{array}{r} 8 \\ -6 \\ \hline \end{array}$ $\begin{array}{r} 6 \\ -5 \\ \hline \end{array}$ $\begin{array}{r} 7 \\ -2 \\ \hline \end{array}$ $\begin{array}{r} 8 \\ -5 \\ \hline \end{array}$ $\begin{array}{r} 6 \\ -1 \\ \hline \end{array}$

3. $\begin{array}{r} 8 \\ -8 \\ \hline \end{array}$ $\begin{array}{r} 6 \\ -4 \\ \hline \end{array}$ $\begin{array}{r} 8 \\ -0 \\ \hline \end{array}$ $\begin{array}{r} 7 \\ -6 \\ \hline \end{array}$ $\begin{array}{r} 5 \\ -2 \\ \hline \end{array}$ $\begin{array}{r} 8 \\ -4 \\ \hline \end{array}$

4. $\begin{array}{r} 8 \\ -7 \\ \hline \end{array}$ $\begin{array}{r} 6 \\ -2 \\ \hline \end{array}$ $\begin{array}{r} 7 \\ -4 \\ \hline \end{array}$ $\begin{array}{r} 8 \\ -2 \\ \hline \end{array}$ $\begin{array}{r} 4 \\ -2 \\ \hline \end{array}$ $\begin{array}{r} 7 \\ -1 \\ \hline \end{array}$

SKILLKEEPER

Add.

$\begin{array}{r} 3 \\ +3 \\ \hline \end{array}$ $\begin{array}{r} 3 \\ +4 \\ \hline \end{array}$ $\begin{array}{r} 5 \\ +5 \\ \hline \end{array}$ $\begin{array}{r} 6 \\ +5 \\ \hline \end{array}$ $\begin{array}{r} 4 \\ +4 \\ \hline \end{array}$ $\begin{array}{r} 4 \\ +5 \\ \hline \end{array}$

Name ____________________

5, 6, 7 (2)

$$\begin{array}{r} 7 \\ -5 \\ \hline 2 \end{array}$$

5, 6, 7, 8 (3)

$$\begin{array}{r} 8 \\ -5 \\ \hline 3 \end{array}$$

Subtract.

4, 5, 6 (2) | 4, 5, 6, 7 (3) | 6, 7, 8 (2) | 5, 6 (1) | 5, 6, 7 (2)

1. $\begin{array}{r} 6 \\ -4 \\ \hline 2 \end{array}$ $\begin{array}{r} 7 \\ -4 \\ \hline \end{array}$ $\begin{array}{r} 8 \\ -6 \\ \hline \end{array}$ $\begin{array}{r} 6 \\ -5 \\ \hline \end{array}$ $\begin{array}{r} 7 \\ -5 \\ \hline \end{array}$

2. $\begin{array}{r} 8 \\ -5 \\ \hline \end{array}$ $\begin{array}{r} 5 \\ -3 \\ \hline \end{array}$ $\begin{array}{r} 6 \\ -2 \\ \hline \end{array}$ $\begin{array}{r} 4 \\ -1 \\ \hline \end{array}$ $\begin{array}{r} 7 \\ -6 \\ \hline \end{array}$ $\begin{array}{r} 3 \\ -2 \\ \hline \end{array}$

3. $\begin{array}{r} 5 \\ -1 \\ \hline \end{array}$ $\begin{array}{r} 7 \\ -4 \\ \hline \end{array}$ $\begin{array}{r} 8 \\ -6 \\ \hline \end{array}$ $\begin{array}{r} 6 \\ -0 \\ \hline \end{array}$ $\begin{array}{r} 4 \\ -2 \\ \hline \end{array}$ $\begin{array}{r} 3 \\ -3 \\ \hline \end{array}$

4. $\begin{array}{r} 7 \\ -3 \\ \hline \end{array}$ $\begin{array}{r} 6 \\ -3 \\ \hline \end{array}$ $\begin{array}{r} 8 \\ -7 \\ \hline \end{array}$ $\begin{array}{r} 5 \\ -2 \\ \hline \end{array}$ $\begin{array}{r} 6 \\ -4 \\ \hline \end{array}$ $\begin{array}{r} 8 \\ -5 \\ \hline \end{array}$

Finish each table.

Subtract 4	
6	2
8	
5	
7	

Subtract 3	
7	
8	
10	
9	

Subtract 5	
6	
8	
5	
7	

Subtract 1	
9	
7	
10	
8	

Subtract 3	
6	
11	
12	
5	

Subtract 2	
9	
10	
8	
11	

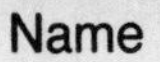

Name ______________________________

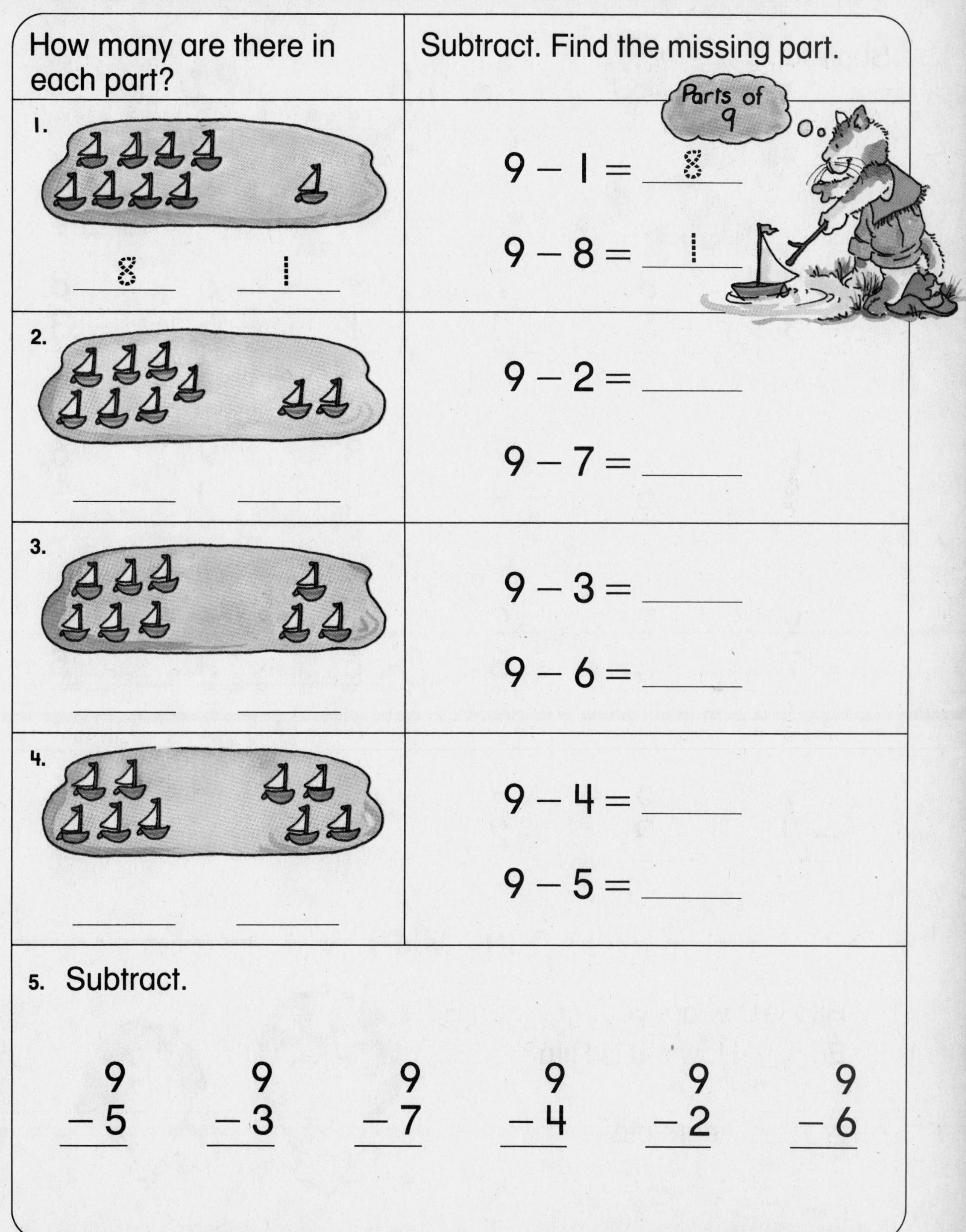

How many are there in each part?	Subtract. Find the missing part.
1. 8 ____ 1 ____	$9 - 1 =$ 8 ____ $9 - 8 =$ 1 ____
2. ____ ____	$9 - 2 =$ ____ $9 - 7 =$ ____
3. ____ ____	$9 - 3 =$ ____ $9 - 6 =$ ____
4. ____ ____	$9 - 4 =$ ____ $9 - 5 =$ ____

5. Subtract.

$$\begin{array}{r} 9 \\ -5 \\ \hline \end{array} \quad \begin{array}{r} 9 \\ -3 \\ \hline \end{array} \quad \begin{array}{r} 9 \\ -7 \\ \hline \end{array} \quad \begin{array}{r} 9 \\ -4 \\ \hline \end{array} \quad \begin{array}{r} 9 \\ -2 \\ \hline \end{array} \quad \begin{array}{r} 9 \\ -6 \\ \hline \end{array}$$

Subtract.

1.	$9 - 3$	$8 - 5$	$7 - 5$	$9 - 1$	$6 - 5$	$8 - 3$
2.	$5 - 3$	$9 - 6$	$7 - 4$	$8 - 4$	$9 - 0$	$6 - 3$
3.	$9 - 7$	$7 - 3$	$9 - 8$	$8 - 6$	$6 - 4$	$9 - 5$
4.	$9 - 4$	$8 - 2$	$9 - 2$	$7 - 2$	$9 - 9$	$6 - 2$

THINK MATH

Rita is 2 years younger than Ed.
Ed is 9. How old is Rita?

______ years old

Name ___

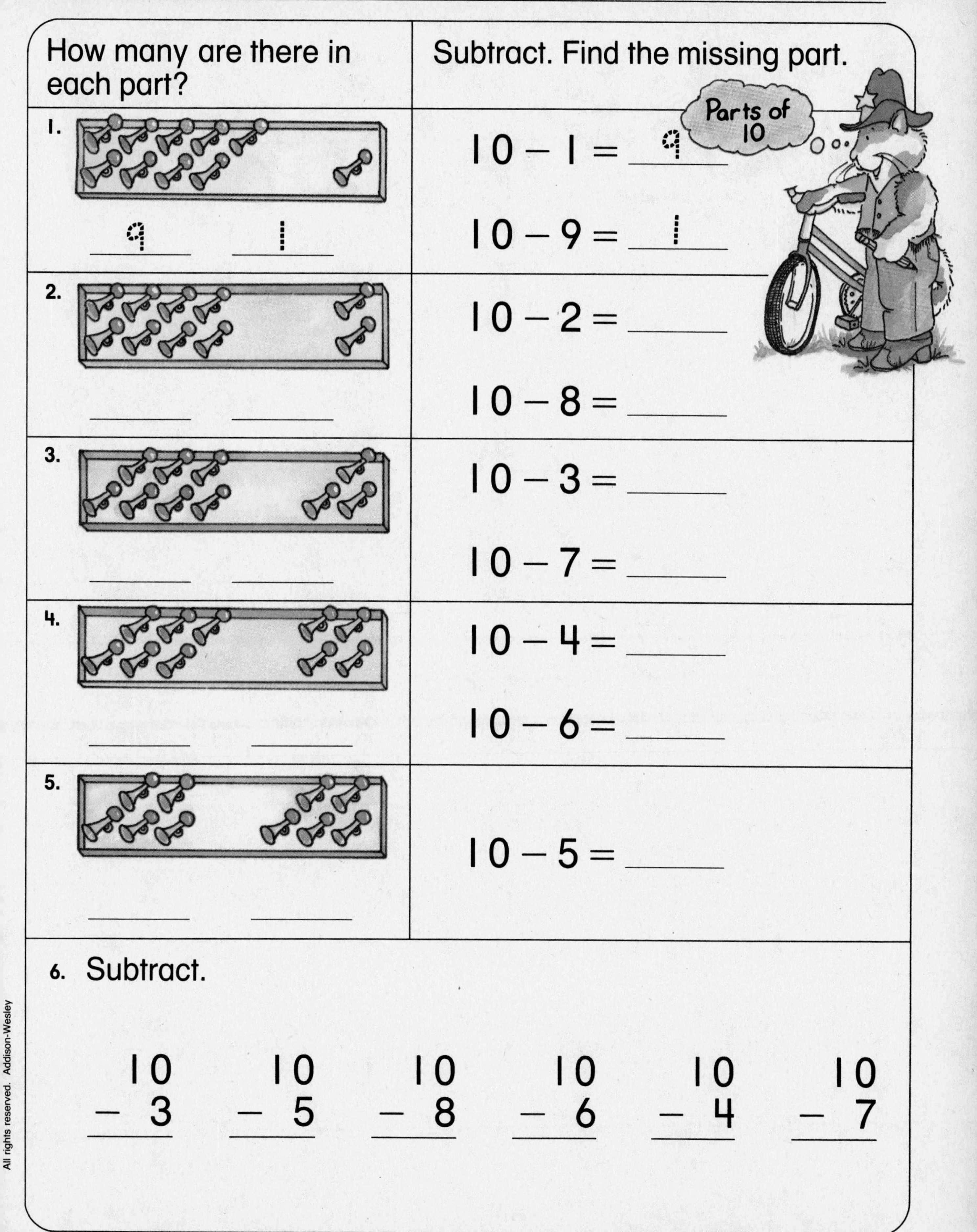

How many are there in each part?

Subtract. Find the missing part.

1. 9 1

$10 - 1 = 9$

$10 - 9 = 1$

2. ___ ___

$10 - 2 =$ ___

$10 - 8 =$ ___

3. ___ ___

$10 - 3 =$ ___

$10 - 7 =$ ___

4. ___ ___

$10 - 4 =$ ___

$10 - 6 =$ ___

5. ___ ___

$10 - 5 =$ ___

6. Subtract.

10	10	10	10	10	10
− 3	− 5	− 8	− 6	− 4	− 7
___	___	___	___	___	___

Subtract.

1. $10 - 3$ $8 - 5$ $10 - 7$ $9 - 4$ $10 - 4$ $7 - 4$

2. $9 - 7$ $10 - 6$ $6 - 5$ $9 - 2$ $10 - 1$ $8 - 6$

3. $10 - 8$ $7 - 6$ $9 - 3$ $7 - 5$ $8 - 4$ $10 - 9$

4. $9 - 6$ $6 - 4$ $10 - 2$ $8 - 7$ $10 - 5$ $9 - 8$

5. $10 - 4$ $7 - 3$ $8 - 4$ $10 - 6$ $7 - 5$ $9 - 3$

6. $8 - 2$ $10 - 7$ $9 - 4$ $10 - 4$ $8 - 5$ $8 - 1$

Name ____________________

Subtract.

1. $\begin{array}{r} 9 \\ -7 \\ \hline 2 \end{array}$ $\begin{array}{r} 10 \\ -7 \\ \hline \end{array}$ $\begin{array}{r} 9 \\ -8 \\ \hline \end{array}$ $\begin{array}{r} 8 \\ -6 \\ \hline \end{array}$ $\begin{array}{r} 10 \\ -9 \\ \hline \end{array}$

2. $\begin{array}{r} 9 \\ -4 \\ \hline \end{array}$ $\begin{array}{r} 10 \\ -8 \\ \hline \end{array}$ $\begin{array}{r} 8 \\ -5 \\ \hline \end{array}$ $\begin{array}{r} 10 \\ -3 \\ \hline \end{array}$ $\begin{array}{r} 9 \\ -5 \\ \hline \end{array}$ $\begin{array}{r} 10 \\ -6 \\ \hline \end{array}$

3. $\begin{array}{r} 7 \\ -5 \\ \hline \end{array}$ $\begin{array}{r} 9 \\ -6 \\ \hline \end{array}$ $\begin{array}{r} 6 \\ -4 \\ \hline \end{array}$ $\begin{array}{r} 10 \\ -2 \\ \hline \end{array}$ $\begin{array}{r} 8 \\ -7 \\ \hline \end{array}$ $\begin{array}{r} 9 \\ -3 \\ \hline \end{array}$

4. $\begin{array}{r} 10 \\ -4 \\ \hline \end{array}$ $\begin{array}{r} 6 \\ -3 \\ \hline \end{array}$ $\begin{array}{r} 9 \\ -7 \\ \hline \end{array}$ $\begin{array}{r} 10 \\ -5 \\ \hline \end{array}$ $\begin{array}{r} 5 \\ -3 \\ \hline \end{array}$ $\begin{array}{r} 10 \\ -9 \\ \hline \end{array}$

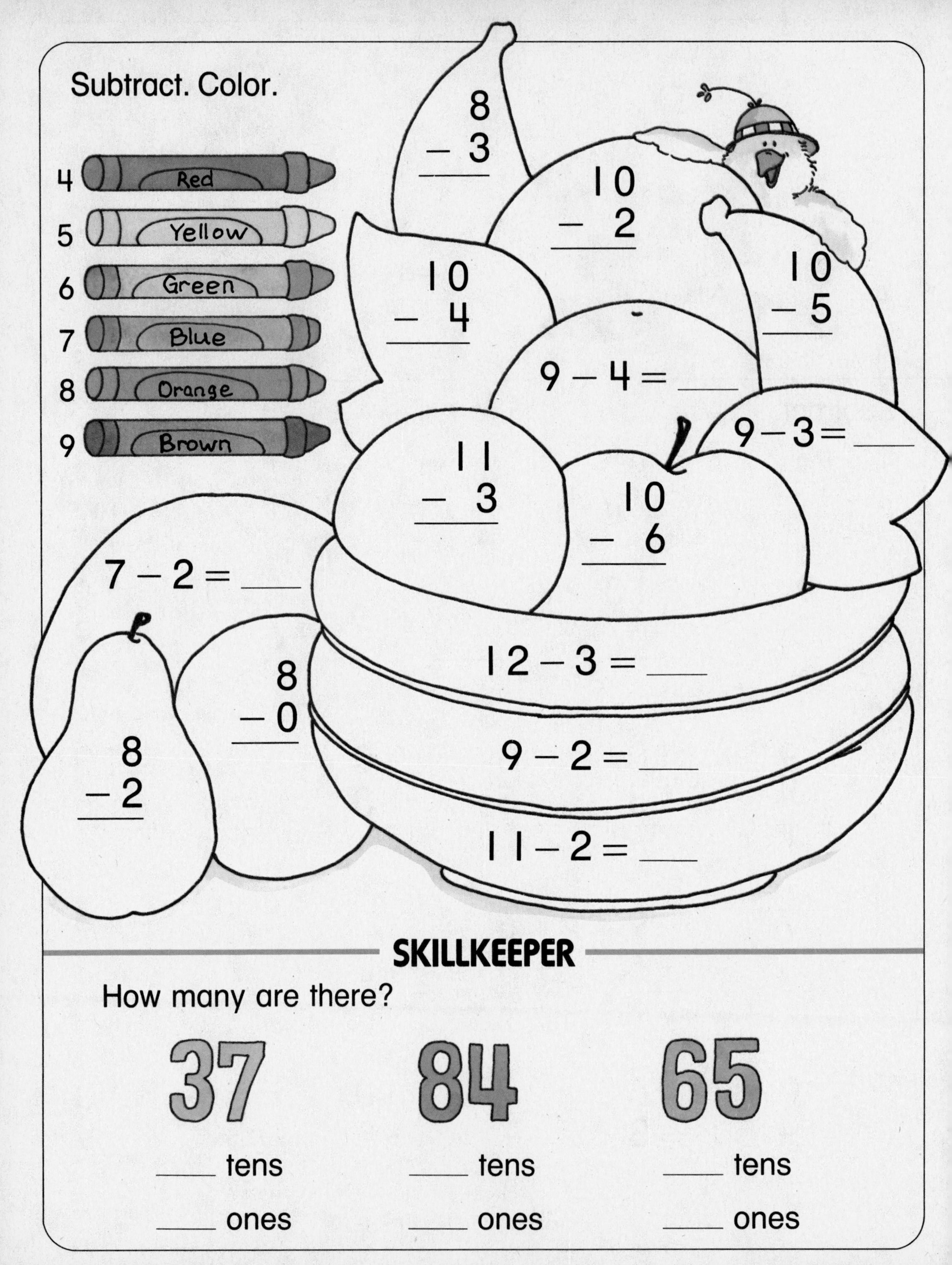
Subtract. Color.
4 Red
5 Yellow
6 Green
7 Blue
8 Orange
9 Brown
8 − 3
10 − 2
10 − 4
10 − 5
9 − 4 = ___
9 − 3 = ___
11 − 3
10 − 6
7 − 2 = ___
12 − 3 = ___
8 − 0
8 − 2
9 − 2 = ___
11 − 2 = ___
SKILLKEEPER
How many are there?
37
84
65
___ tens
___ ones
___ tens
___ ones
___ tens
___ ones

Name ____________________

Subtract.

1.

$$\begin{array}{r} 9 \\ -6 \\ \hline \end{array} \quad \begin{array}{r} 7 \\ -4 \\ \hline \end{array} \quad \begin{array}{r} 10 \\ -8 \\ \hline \end{array} \quad \begin{array}{r} 8 \\ -6 \\ \hline \end{array}$$

2.

$$\begin{array}{r} 8 \\ -7 \\ \hline \end{array} \quad \begin{array}{r} 10 \\ -5 \\ \hline \end{array} \quad \begin{array}{r} 7 \\ -5 \\ \hline \end{array} \quad \begin{array}{r} 9 \\ -4 \\ \hline \end{array} \quad \begin{array}{r} 10 \\ -3 \\ \hline \end{array} \quad \begin{array}{r} 8 \\ -4 \\ \hline \end{array}$$

3.

$$\begin{array}{r} 10 \\ -6 \\ \hline \end{array} \quad \begin{array}{r} 8 \\ -3 \\ \hline \end{array} \quad \begin{array}{r} 9 \\ -5 \\ \hline \end{array} \quad \begin{array}{r} 10 \\ -9 \\ \hline \end{array} \quad \begin{array}{r} 6 \\ -4 \\ \hline \end{array} \quad \begin{array}{r} 7 \\ -3 \\ \hline \end{array}$$

4.

$$\begin{array}{r} 8 \\ -5 \\ \hline \end{array} \quad \begin{array}{r} 10 \\ -7 \\ \hline \end{array} \quad \begin{array}{r} 7 \\ -6 \\ \hline \end{array} \quad \begin{array}{r} 9 \\ -8 \\ \hline \end{array} \quad \begin{array}{r} 10 \\ -4 \\ \hline \end{array} \quad \begin{array}{r} 6 \\ -3 \\ \hline \end{array}$$

5.

Subtract 5	
8	
10	
7	
9	

Subtract 3	
9	
12	
8	
10	

Subtract 4	
9	
7	
10	
8	

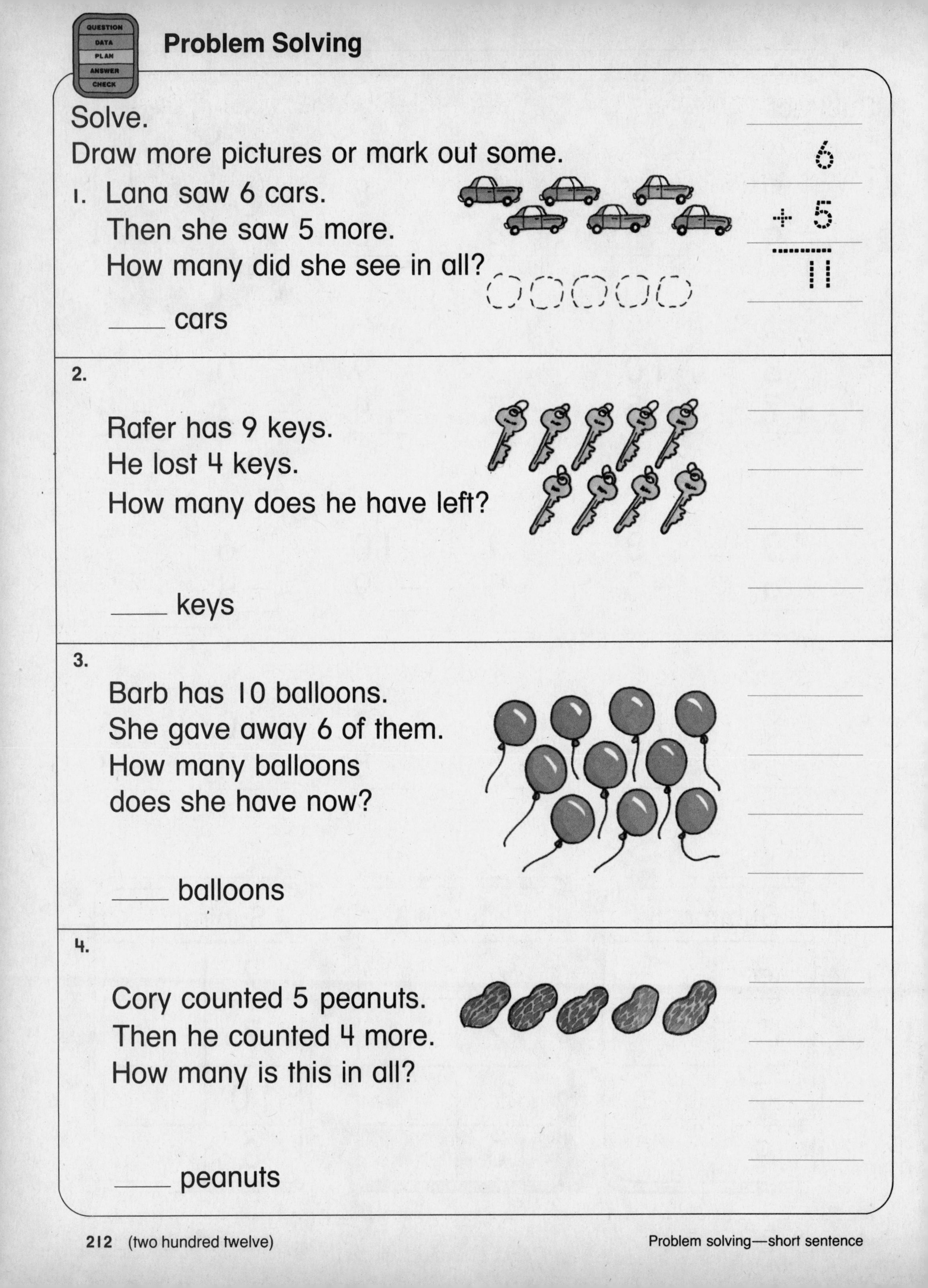

Problem Solving

Solve.

Draw more pictures or mark out some.

1. Lana saw 6 cars.
   Then she saw 5 more.
   How many did she see in all?

   ____ cars

   $6 + 5 = 11$

2. Rafer has 9 keys.
   He lost 4 keys.
   How many does he have left?

   ____ keys

3. Barb has 10 balloons.
   She gave away 6 of them.
   How many balloons does she have now?

   ____ balloons

4. Cory counted 5 peanuts.
   Then he counted 4 more.
   How many is this in all?

   ____ peanuts

Name ______

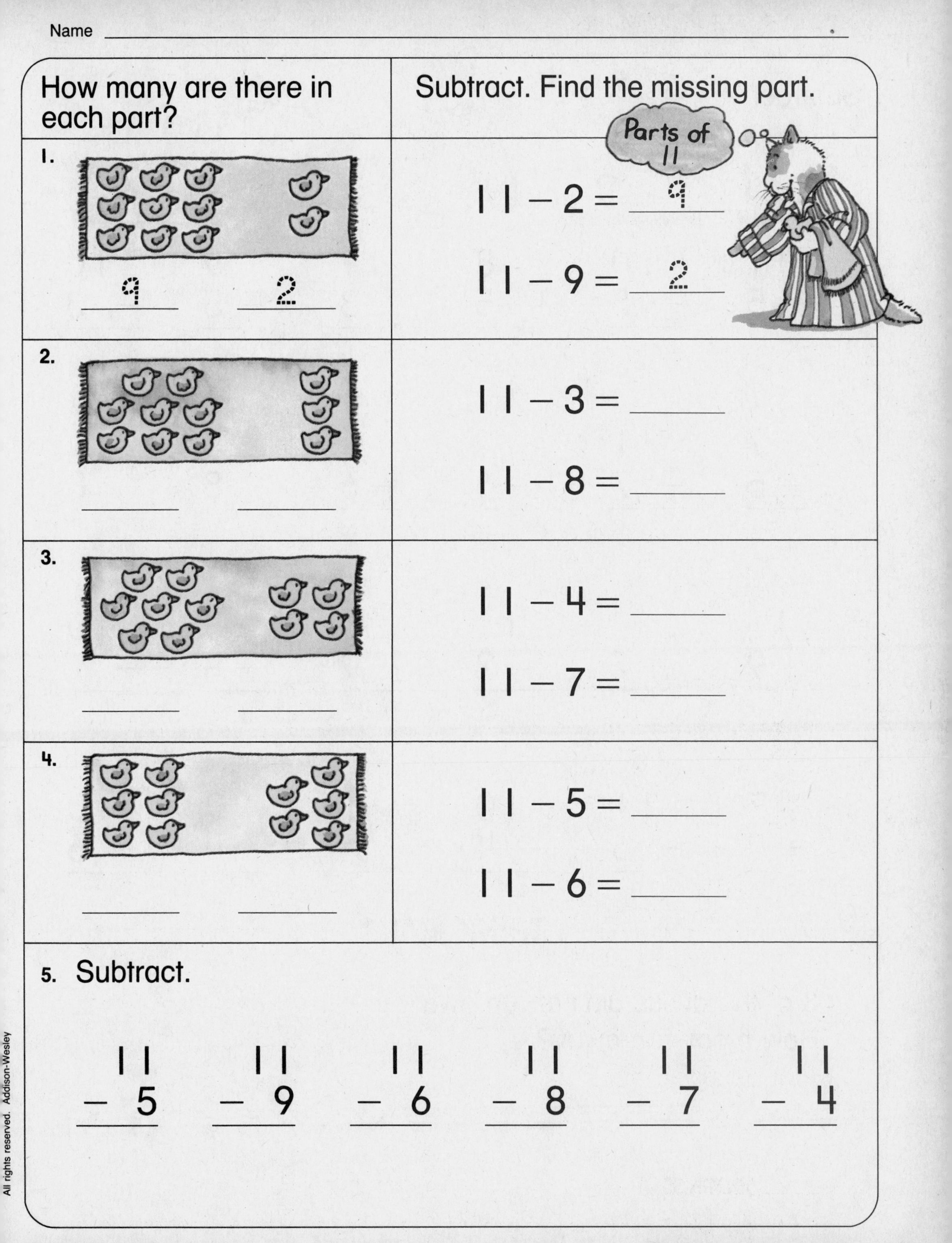

How many are there in each part?
Subtract. Find the missing part.
Parts of 11
1.
9
2
11 − 2 = 9
11 − 9 = 2
2.
11 − 3 = ______
11 − 8 = ______
3.
11 − 4 = ______
11 − 7 = ______
4.
11 − 5 = ______
11 − 6 = ______
5. Subtract.
11 − 5
11 − 9
11 − 6
11 − 8
11 − 7
11 − 4

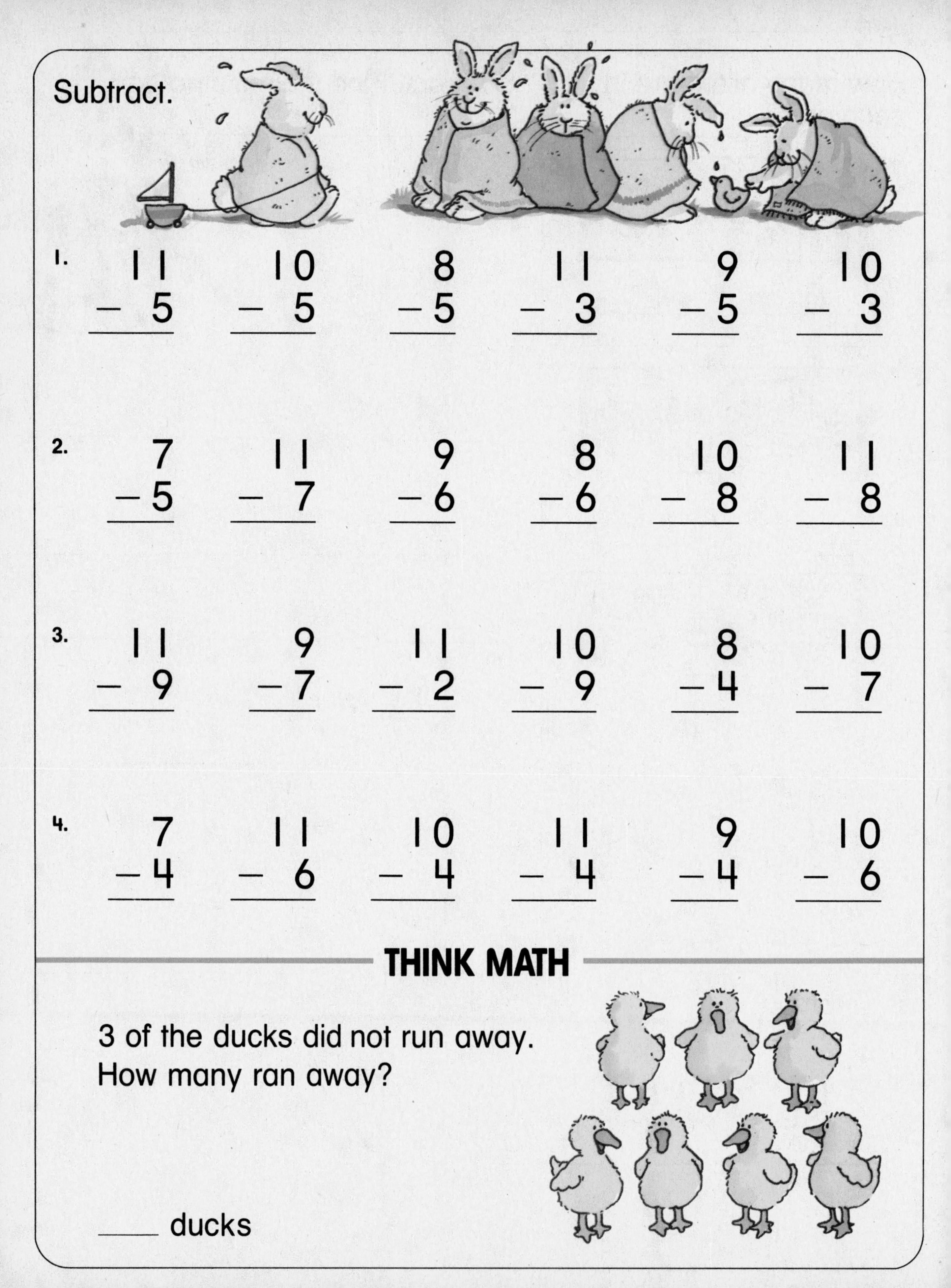

Subtract.

1. $\begin{array}{r} 11 \\ -\ 5 \\ \hline \end{array}$ $\begin{array}{r} 10 \\ -\ 5 \\ \hline \end{array}$ $\begin{array}{r} 8 \\ -5 \\ \hline \end{array}$ $\begin{array}{r} 11 \\ -\ 3 \\ \hline \end{array}$ $\begin{array}{r} 9 \\ -5 \\ \hline \end{array}$ $\begin{array}{r} 10 \\ -\ 3 \\ \hline \end{array}$

2. $\begin{array}{r} 7 \\ -5 \\ \hline \end{array}$ $\begin{array}{r} 11 \\ -\ 7 \\ \hline \end{array}$ $\begin{array}{r} 9 \\ -6 \\ \hline \end{array}$ $\begin{array}{r} 8 \\ -6 \\ \hline \end{array}$ $\begin{array}{r} 10 \\ -\ 8 \\ \hline \end{array}$ $\begin{array}{r} 11 \\ -\ 8 \\ \hline \end{array}$

3. $\begin{array}{r} 11 \\ -\ 9 \\ \hline \end{array}$ $\begin{array}{r} 9 \\ -7 \\ \hline \end{array}$ $\begin{array}{r} 11 \\ -\ 2 \\ \hline \end{array}$ $\begin{array}{r} 10 \\ -\ 9 \\ \hline \end{array}$ $\begin{array}{r} 8 \\ -4 \\ \hline \end{array}$ $\begin{array}{r} 10 \\ -\ 7 \\ \hline \end{array}$

4. $\begin{array}{r} 7 \\ -4 \\ \hline \end{array}$ $\begin{array}{r} 11 \\ -\ 6 \\ \hline \end{array}$ $\begin{array}{r} 10 \\ -\ 4 \\ \hline \end{array}$ $\begin{array}{r} 11 \\ -\ 4 \\ \hline \end{array}$ $\begin{array}{r} 9 \\ -4 \\ \hline \end{array}$ $\begin{array}{r} 10 \\ -\ 6 \\ \hline \end{array}$

THINK MATH

3 of the ducks did not run away.
How many ran away?

____ ducks

Name ______

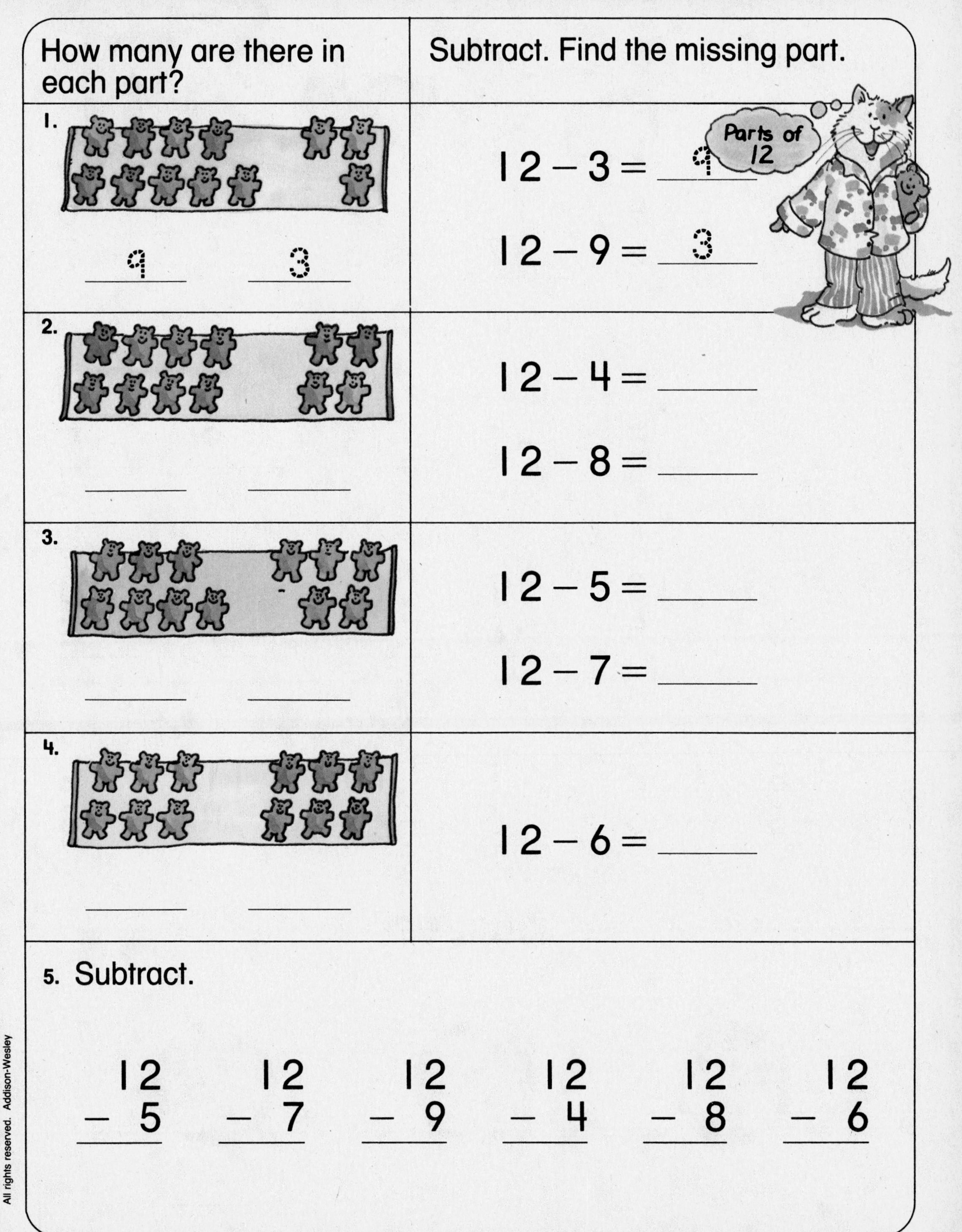

How many are there in each part?

Subtract. Find the missing part.

1. 9 3

$12 - 3 =$ 9

$12 - 9 =$ 3

2. ____ ____

$12 - 4 =$ ____

$12 - 8 =$ ____

3. ____ ____

$12 - 5 =$ ____

$12 - 7 =$ ____

4. ____ ____

$12 - 6 =$ ____

5. Subtract.

$\begin{array}{r} 12 \\ -\ 5 \\ \hline \end{array}$ $\begin{array}{r} 12 \\ -\ 7 \\ \hline \end{array}$ $\begin{array}{r} 12 \\ -\ 9 \\ \hline \end{array}$ $\begin{array}{r} 12 \\ -\ 4 \\ \hline \end{array}$ $\begin{array}{r} 12 \\ -\ 8 \\ \hline \end{array}$ $\begin{array}{r} 12 \\ -\ 6 \\ \hline \end{array}$

Subtract.

1. $\begin{array}{r} 12 \\ -\ 7 \\ \hline \end{array}$ $\begin{array}{r} 9 \\ -6 \\ \hline \end{array}$ $\begin{array}{r} 11 \\ -\ 7 \\ \hline \end{array}$ $\begin{array}{r} 12 \\ -\ 5 \\ \hline \end{array}$ $\begin{array}{r} 8 \\ -5 \\ \hline \end{array}$ $\begin{array}{r} 10 \\ -\ 7 \\ \hline \end{array}$

2. $\begin{array}{r} 7 \\ -5 \\ \hline \end{array}$ $\begin{array}{r} 11 \\ -\ 5 \\ \hline \end{array}$ $\begin{array}{r} 9 \\ -5 \\ \hline \end{array}$ $\begin{array}{r} 10 \\ -\ 6 \\ \hline \end{array}$ $\begin{array}{r} 12 \\ -\ 9 \\ \hline \end{array}$ $\begin{array}{r} 11 \\ -\ 9 \\ \hline \end{array}$

3. $\begin{array}{r} 12 \\ -\ 3 \\ \hline \end{array}$ $\begin{array}{r} 10 \\ -\ 5 \\ \hline \end{array}$ $\begin{array}{r} 11 \\ -\ 8 \\ \hline \end{array}$ $\begin{array}{r} 12 \\ -\ 4 \\ \hline \end{array}$ $\begin{array}{r} 9 \\ -7 \\ \hline \end{array}$ $\begin{array}{r} 10 \\ -\ 4 \\ \hline \end{array}$

4. $\begin{array}{r} 8 \\ -6 \\ \hline \end{array}$ $\begin{array}{r} 12 \\ -\ 6 \\ \hline \end{array}$ $\begin{array}{r} 11 \\ -\ 6 \\ \hline \end{array}$ $\begin{array}{r} 10 \\ -\ 8 \\ \hline \end{array}$ $\begin{array}{r} 11 \\ -\ 4 \\ \hline \end{array}$ $\begin{array}{r} 12 \\ -\ 8 \\ \hline \end{array}$

SKILLKEEPER

Write the times.

____ : ____ ____ : ____ ____ : ____

Name ______________________________

Subtract.

2: 9, 10, 11 | 2: 8, 9, 10 | 3: 9, 10, 11, 12

1.

11 − 9	10 − 8	12 − 9

2.

11 − 6	7 − 4	10 − 5	12 − 7	9 − 6	11 − 4

3.

10 − 6	12 − 6	8 − 6	11 − 9	12 − 4	7 − 5

4.

11 − 8	9 − 7	12 − 9	10 − 8	6 − 4	11 − 5

5.

Subtract 7	
11	
9	
12	
10	

Subtract 6	
10	
11	
9	
12	

Subtract 8	
12	
9	
10	
11	

Name

Subtract. Color.

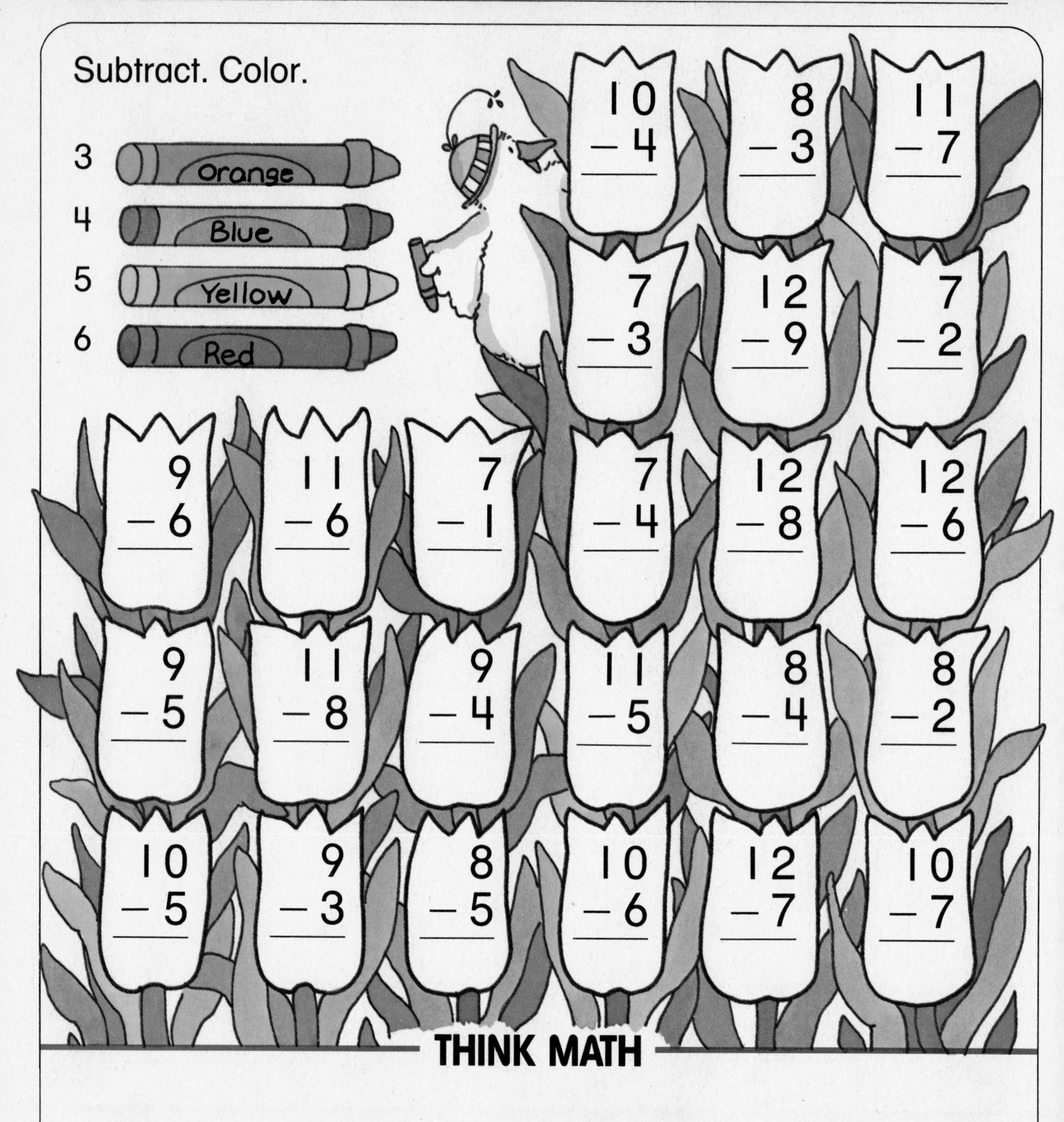

THINK MATH

Jenny bought 5 toy cars.
Ring what she bought.

Name ______________________________

Add or subtract.

1.	$\begin{array}{r} 7 \\ +4 \\ \hline \end{array}$	$\begin{array}{r} 5 \\ +4 \\ \hline \end{array}$	$\begin{array}{r} 8 \\ +4 \\ \hline \end{array}$	$\begin{array}{r} 3 \\ +4 \\ \hline \end{array}$	$\begin{array}{r} 3 \\ +7 \\ \hline \end{array}$	$\begin{array}{r} 3 \\ +5 \\ \hline \end{array}$
2.	$\begin{array}{r} 10 \\ -\ 8 \\ \hline \end{array}$	$\begin{array}{r} 12 \\ -\ 6 \\ \hline \end{array}$	$\begin{array}{r} 8 \\ -2 \\ \hline \end{array}$	$\begin{array}{r} 9 \\ -4 \\ \hline \end{array}$	$\begin{array}{r} 11 \\ -\ 4 \\ \hline \end{array}$	$\begin{array}{r} 7 \\ -3 \\ \hline \end{array}$
3.	$\begin{array}{r} 6 \\ +2 \\ \hline \end{array}$	$\begin{array}{r} 7 \\ -5 \\ \hline \end{array}$	$\begin{array}{r} 5 \\ +7 \\ \hline \end{array}$	$\begin{array}{r} 12 \\ -\ 8 \\ \hline \end{array}$	$\begin{array}{r} 10 \\ -\ 5 \\ \hline \end{array}$	$\begin{array}{r} 8 \\ +2 \\ \hline \end{array}$
4.	$\begin{array}{r} 9 \\ -6 \\ \hline \end{array}$	$\begin{array}{r} 7 \\ +2 \\ \hline \end{array}$	$\begin{array}{r} 11 \\ -\ 6 \\ \hline \end{array}$	$\begin{array}{r} 2 \\ +5 \\ \hline \end{array}$	$\begin{array}{r} 3 \\ +8 \\ \hline \end{array}$	$\begin{array}{r} 8 \\ -5 \\ \hline \end{array}$
5.	$\begin{array}{r} 10 \\ -\ 2 \\ \hline \end{array}$	$\begin{array}{r} 8 \\ -4 \\ \hline \end{array}$	$\begin{array}{r} 9 \\ -9 \\ \hline \end{array}$	$\begin{array}{r} 12 \\ -\ 7 \\ \hline \end{array}$	$\begin{array}{r} 10 \\ -\ 6 \\ \hline \end{array}$	$\begin{array}{r} 6 \\ -2 \\ \hline \end{array}$
6.	$\begin{array}{r} 7 \\ -0 \\ \hline \end{array}$	$\begin{array}{r} 5 \\ -3 \\ \hline \end{array}$	$\begin{array}{r} 12 \\ -\ 9 \\ \hline \end{array}$	$\begin{array}{r} 11 \\ -\ 4 \\ \hline \end{array}$	$\begin{array}{r} 9 \\ -5 \\ \hline \end{array}$	$\begin{array}{r} 8 \\ -3 \\ \hline \end{array}$

QUESTION
DATA
PLAN
ANSWER
CHECK

Problem Solving

Solve.

1. Mary had 11¢.
   She bought a [stickers].
   How much does she have left?
   7¢

   11¢
   − 4¢
   7¢

2. Jim bought an [elephant] and a [ring].
   How much did he spend?

3. Pam bought a [balloon] and a [whistle].
   How much did she spend?

4. Ann had 10¢.
   She bought a [whistle].
   How much does she have left?

5. Ted bought a [whistle] and an [elephant].
   How much did he spend?

6. **DATA BANK**
   Joe had 12¢.
   He bought a [ball].
   How much does he have left? (See page 325.)

Name ______________________

Ring names for the number.

1.	7	(3 + 4)	5 + 3	(2 + 5)	3 + 3
2.	9	4 + 4	5 + 4	2 + 7	6 + 2	3 + 6
3.	6	10 − 4	9 − 3	11 − 2	10 − 5	12 − 6
4.	11	5 + 5	7 + 5	8 + 3	4 + 7	5 + 6
5.	5	12 − 7	11 − 4	10 − 5	9 − 4	11 − 7
6.	12	6 + 4	4 + 8	3 + 9	2 + 7	7 + 5
7.	8	4 + 4	1 + 9	3 + 5	6 + 2	2 + 9
8.	10	8 + 2	3 + 7	6 + 3	5 + 5	7 + 2

Problem Solving

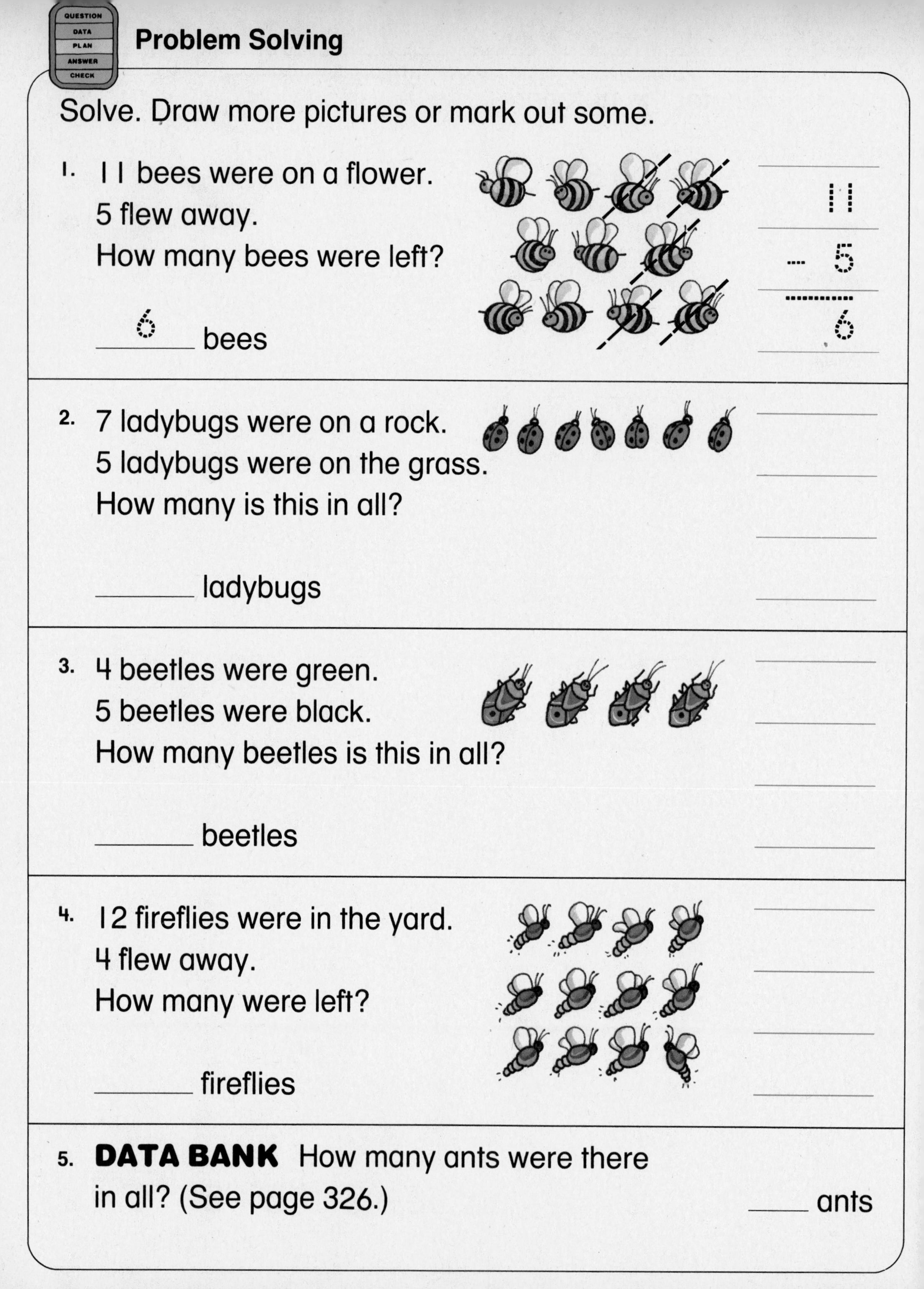

Solve. Draw more pictures or mark out some.

1. 11 bees were on a flower.
   5 flew away.
   How many bees were left?

   6 bees

   $$\begin{array}{r} 11 \\ -\ 5 \\ \hline 6 \end{array}$$

2. 7 ladybugs were on a rock.
   5 ladybugs were on the grass.
   How many is this in all?

   ______ ladybugs

3. 4 beetles were green.
   5 beetles were black.
   How many beetles is this in all?

   ______ beetles

4. 12 fireflies were in the yard.
   4 flew away.
   How many were left?

   ______ fireflies

5. **DATA BANK** How many ants were there in all? (See page 326.)

   ______ ants

Name ______________________________

CHAPTER REVIEW/TEST

Subtract.

1.

9	12	10	11	7	8
− 5	− 7	− 8	− 5	− 4	− 5

2.

10	6	12	8	9	11
− 5	− 4	− 8	− 6	− 6	− 7

3.

12	7	10	9	11	10
− 5	− 5	− 7	− 4	− 4	− 6

4.

9	12	10	11	8	12
− 7	− 9	− 4	− 6	− 4	− 6

5. Solve. Draw more pictures or mark out some.

11 birds were on a rock.
5 flew away.
How many birds were left?

_______ birds

Name ____________________

CUMULATIVE REVIEW

Give the times.

1. 

○ 3:00
○ 4:00
○ 5:00

2. 

○ 2:30
○ 6:30
○ 1:30

Count the money.

3. 

○ 12¢
○ 14¢
○ 16¢

4. 

○ 40¢
○ 35¢
○ 31¢

Add.

5. $5 + 4$

○ 7
○ 8
○ 9

6. $6 + 6$

○ 10
○ 12
○ 14

7. $8 + 4$

○ 11
○ 12
○ 13

8. $5 + 2 + 3$

○ 10
○ 8
○ 9

9. Draw or mark out to solve.

Vince saw 5 butterflies.
Then he saw 6 more.
How many butterflies
did Vince see?

○ 9
○ 10
○ 11

Name ______________________________

ANOTHER LOOK

6	7
3 + 3	4 + 3
4 + 2	5 + 2
5 + 1	6 + 1

8	9
4 + 4	5 + 4
5 + 3	6 + 3
6 + 2	7 + 2
7 + 1	8 + 1

10	11
5 + 5	6 + 5
6 + 4	7 + 4
7 + 3	8 + 3
8 + 2	9 + 2
9 + 1	

12
6 + 6
7 + 5
8 + 4
9 + 3

Subtract.

1. $9 - 6$ $11 - 6$ $10 - 2$

2. $7 - 5$ $12 - 6$ $8 - 4$

3. $11 - 4$ $9 - 4$ $10 - 4$

4. $12 - 5$ $8 - 1$ $9 - 8$

5. $6 - 2$ $10 - 9$ $11 - 2$

6. $10 - 5$ $8 - 6$ $12 - 8$

7. $7 - 0$ $11 - 8$ $10 - 7$

Name 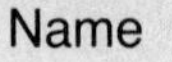 ______________________________

ENRICHMENT

Each [envelope] means 2 letters.

How many letters were mailed?

1. Monday 6
2. Tuesday ______
3. Wednesday ______
4. Thursday ______
5. Friday ______

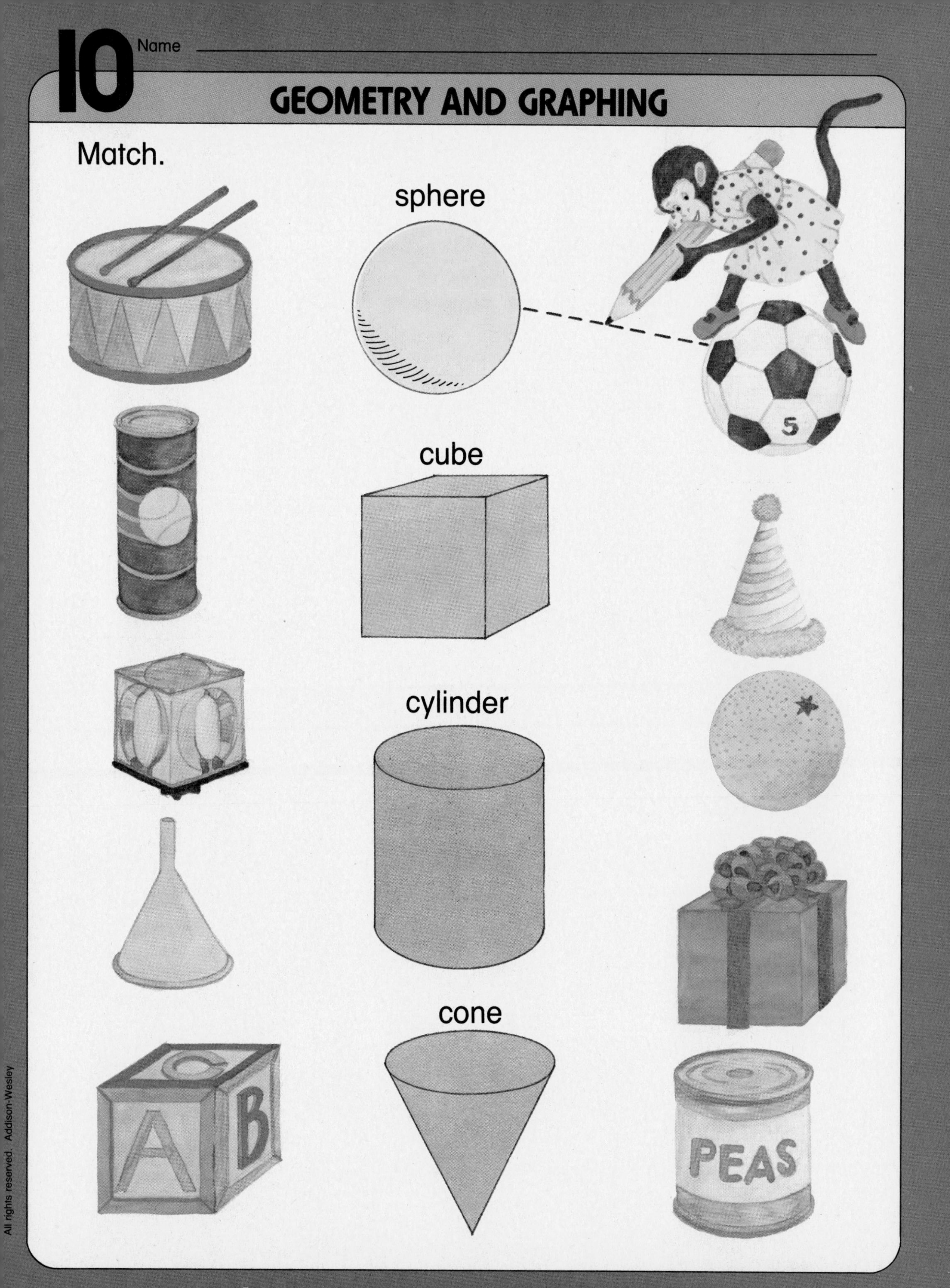
10
Name
GEOMETRY AND GRAPHING
Match.
sphere
cube
cylinder
cone
5
C
A
B
PEAS
All rights reserved. Addison-Wesley

OFFICIAL
X600
Ring the shape that does not belong.
1.
2.
3.
THINK MATH
Ring Jo's dog.
She is standing.
She has spots.

Name ____________________

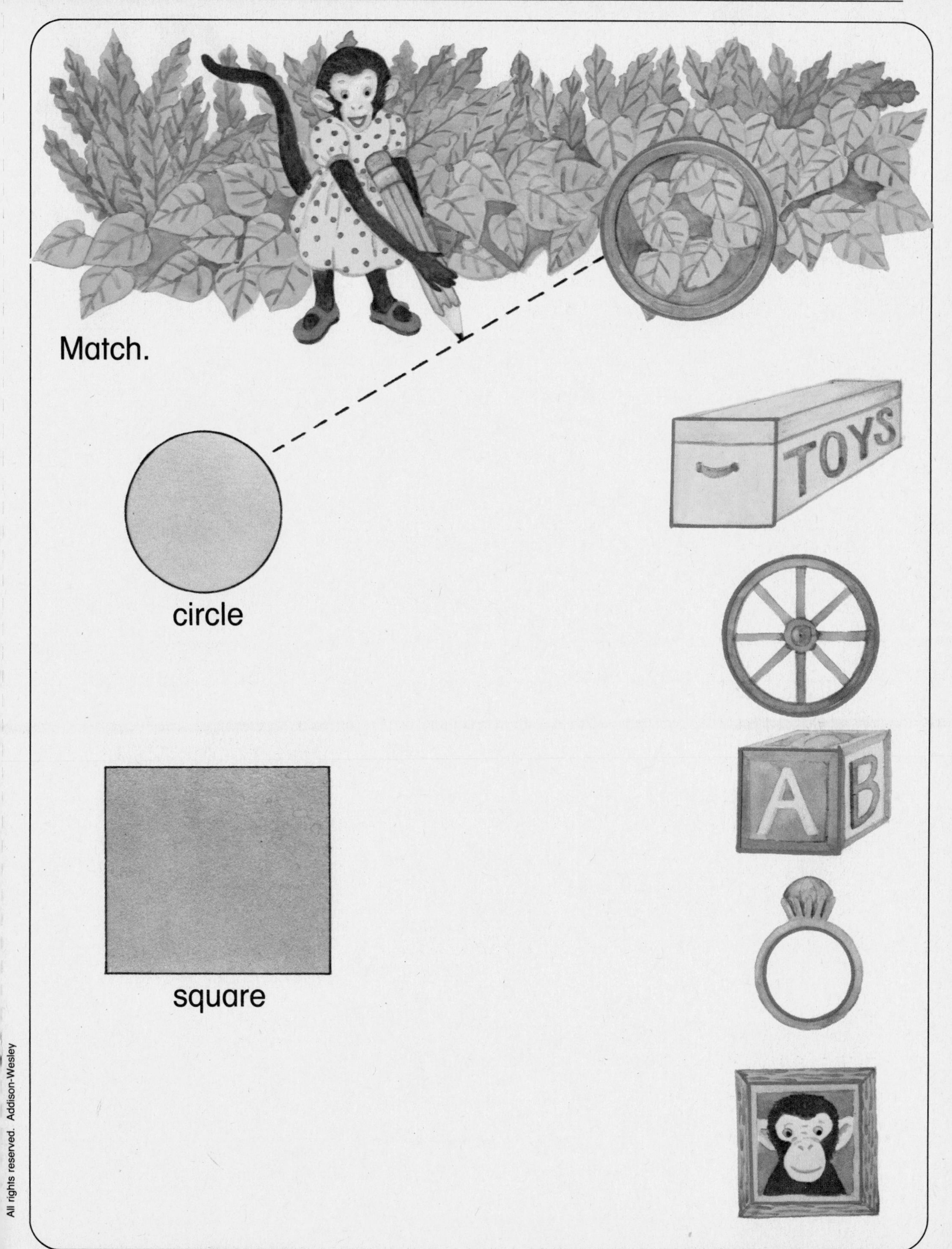

Match.
circle
square
TOYS
A
B

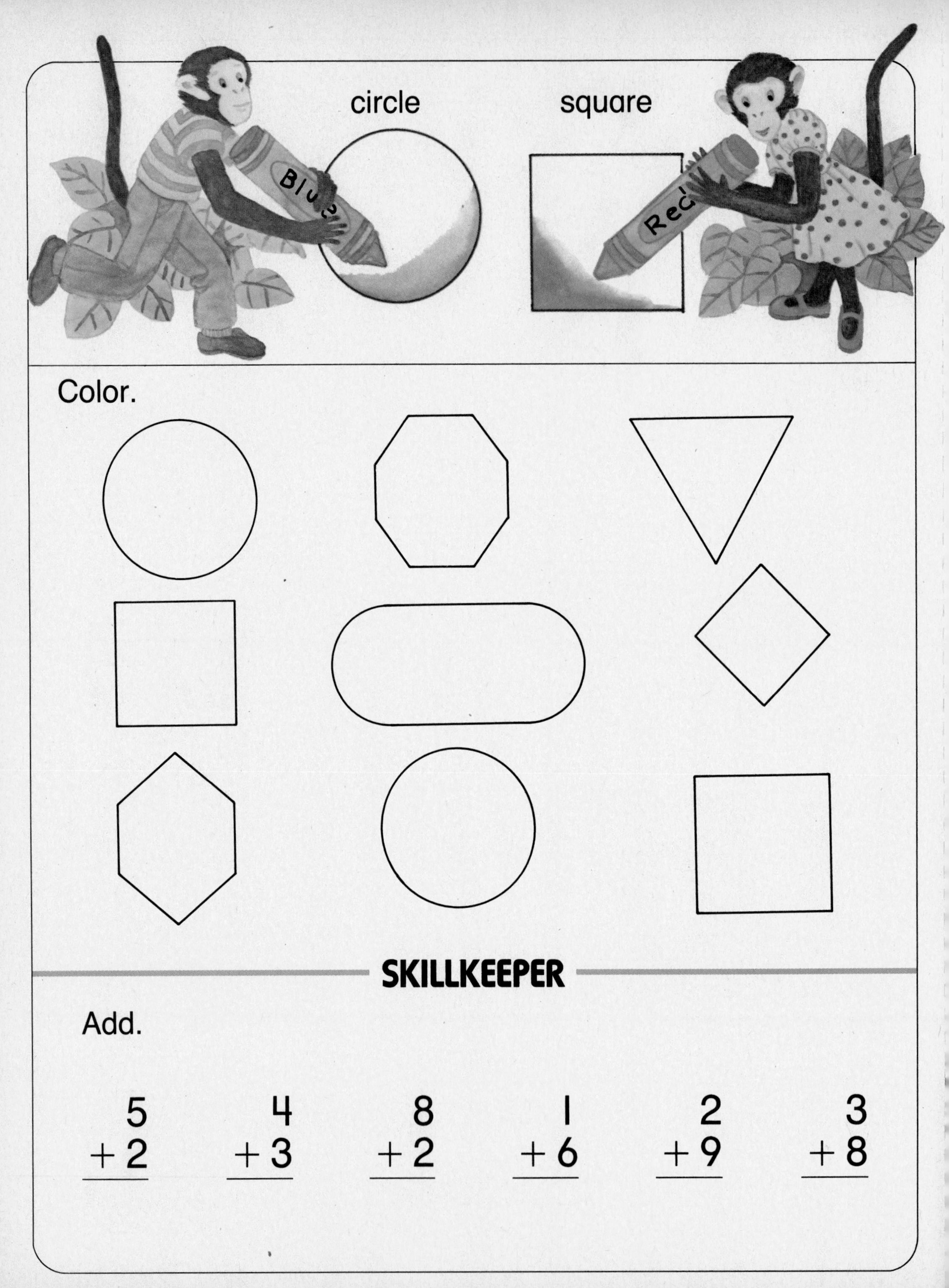

Color.

SKILLKEEPER

Add.

$$\begin{array}{r} 5 \\ +\,2 \\ \hline \end{array} \qquad \begin{array}{r} 4 \\ +\,3 \\ \hline \end{array} \qquad \begin{array}{r} 8 \\ +\,2 \\ \hline \end{array} \qquad \begin{array}{r} 1 \\ +\,6 \\ \hline \end{array} \qquad \begin{array}{r} 2 \\ +\,9 \\ \hline \end{array} \qquad \begin{array}{r} 3 \\ +\,8 \\ \hline \end{array}$$

Name ____________________

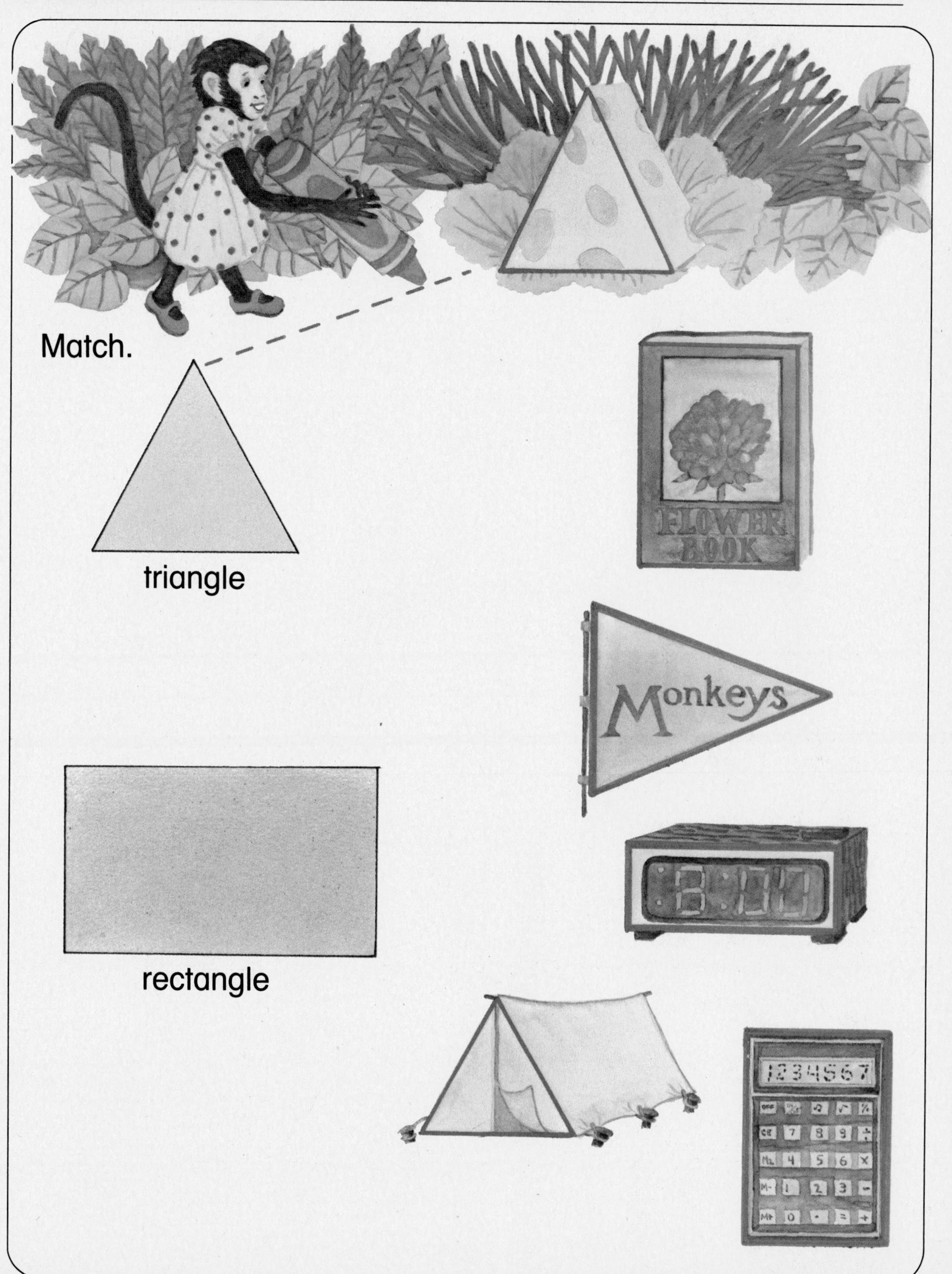

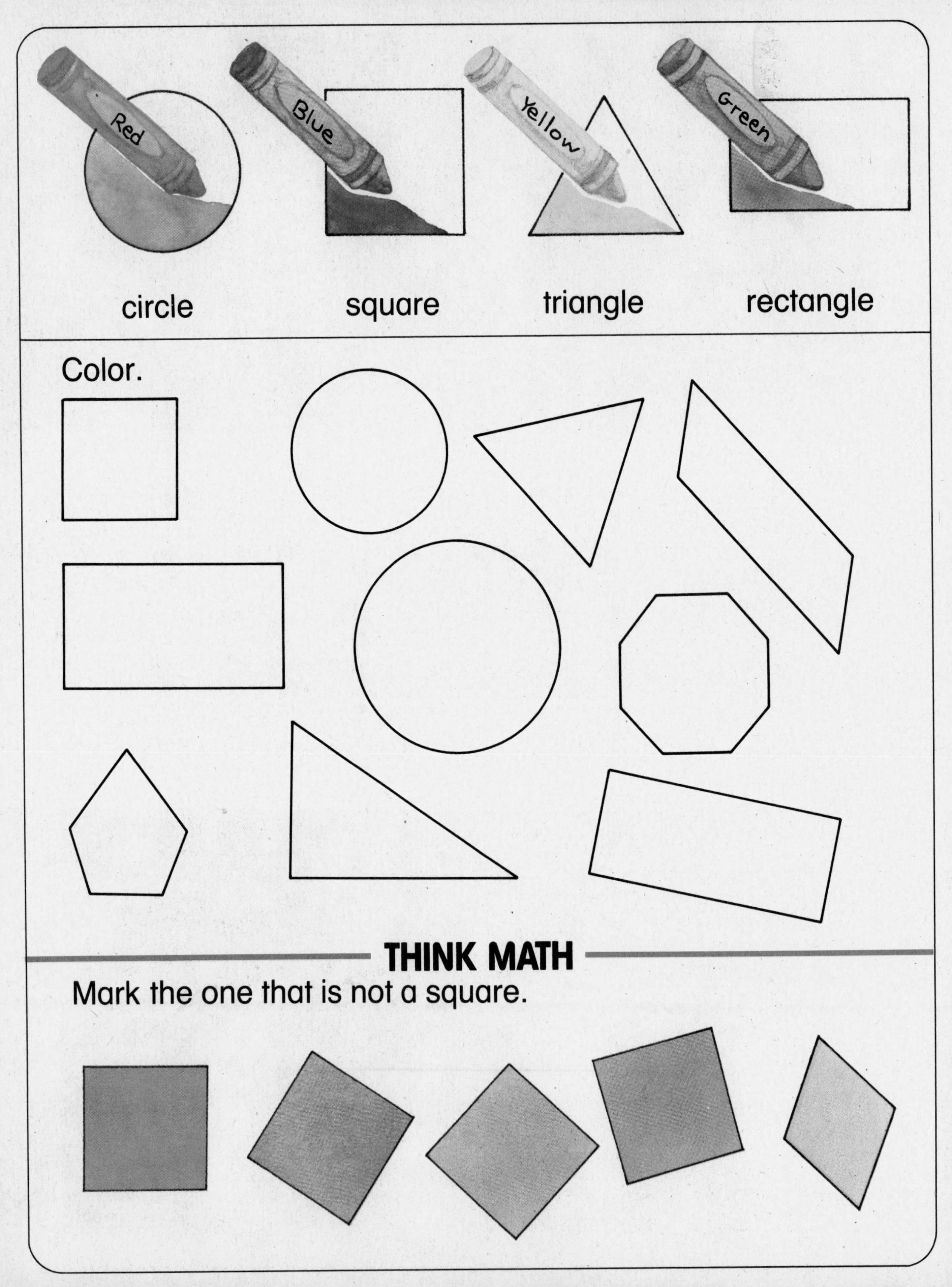
Red
Blue
Yellow
Green
circle
square
triangle
rectangle
Color.
THINK MATH
Mark the one that is not a square.

Name ____________________

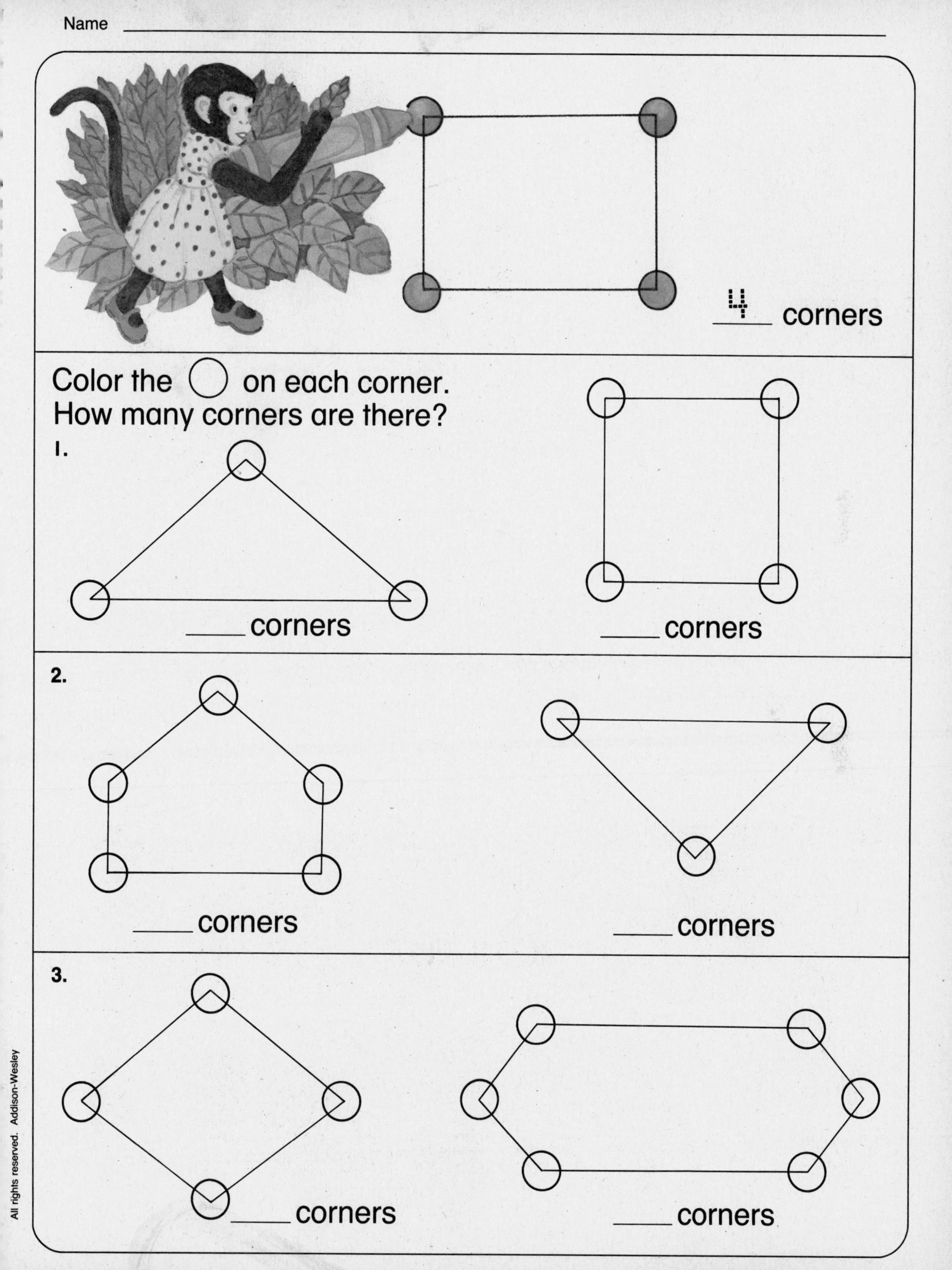

4 corners

Color the ◯ on each corner.
How many corners are there?

1.

____ corners

____ corners

2.

____ corners

____ corners

3.

____ corners

____ corners

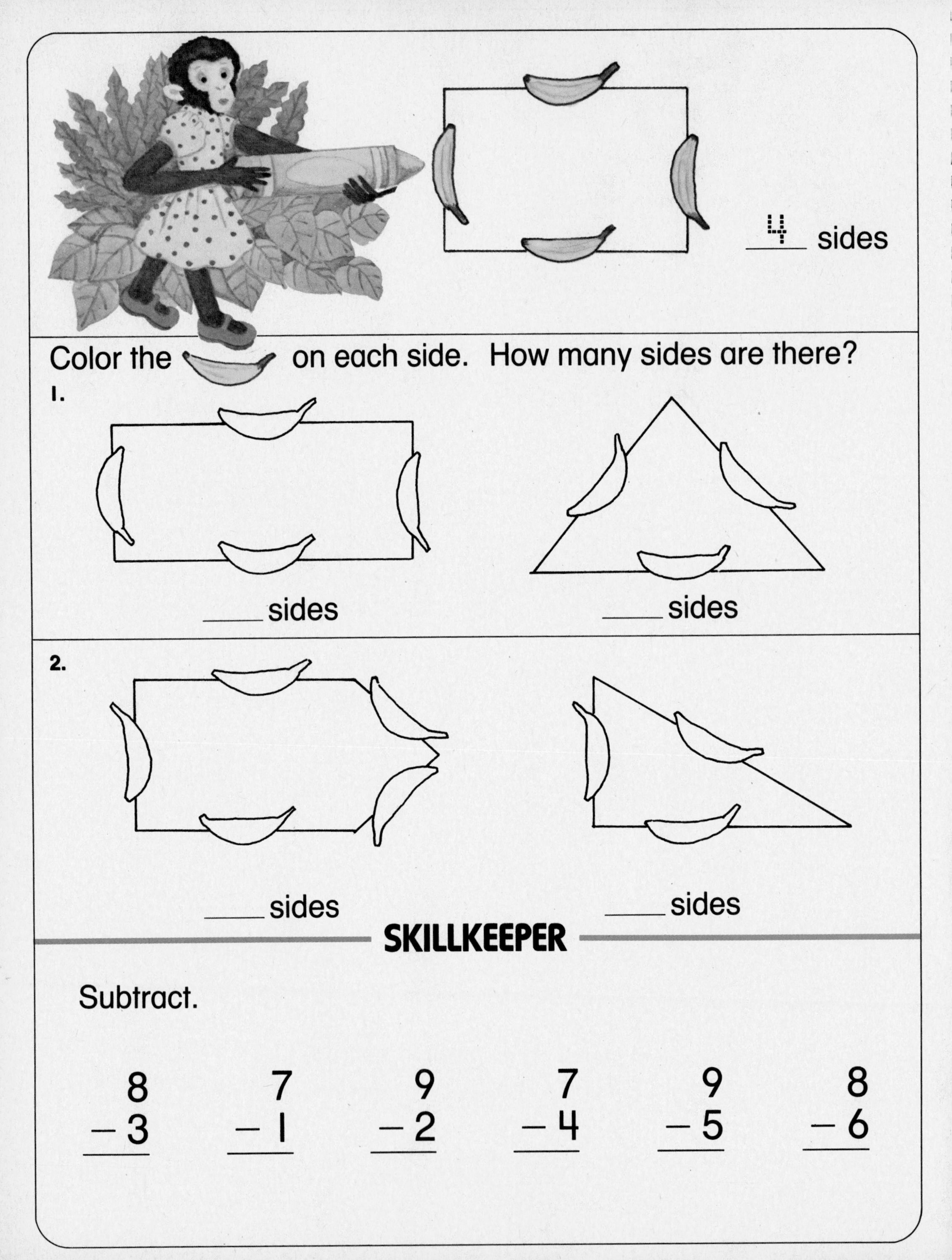

4 sides

Color the banana on each side. How many sides are there?

1.

____ sides

____ sides

2.

____ sides

____ sides

SKILLKEEPER

Subtract.

8	7	9	7	9	8
− 3	− 1	− 2	− 4	− 5	− 6

Name ______________________________

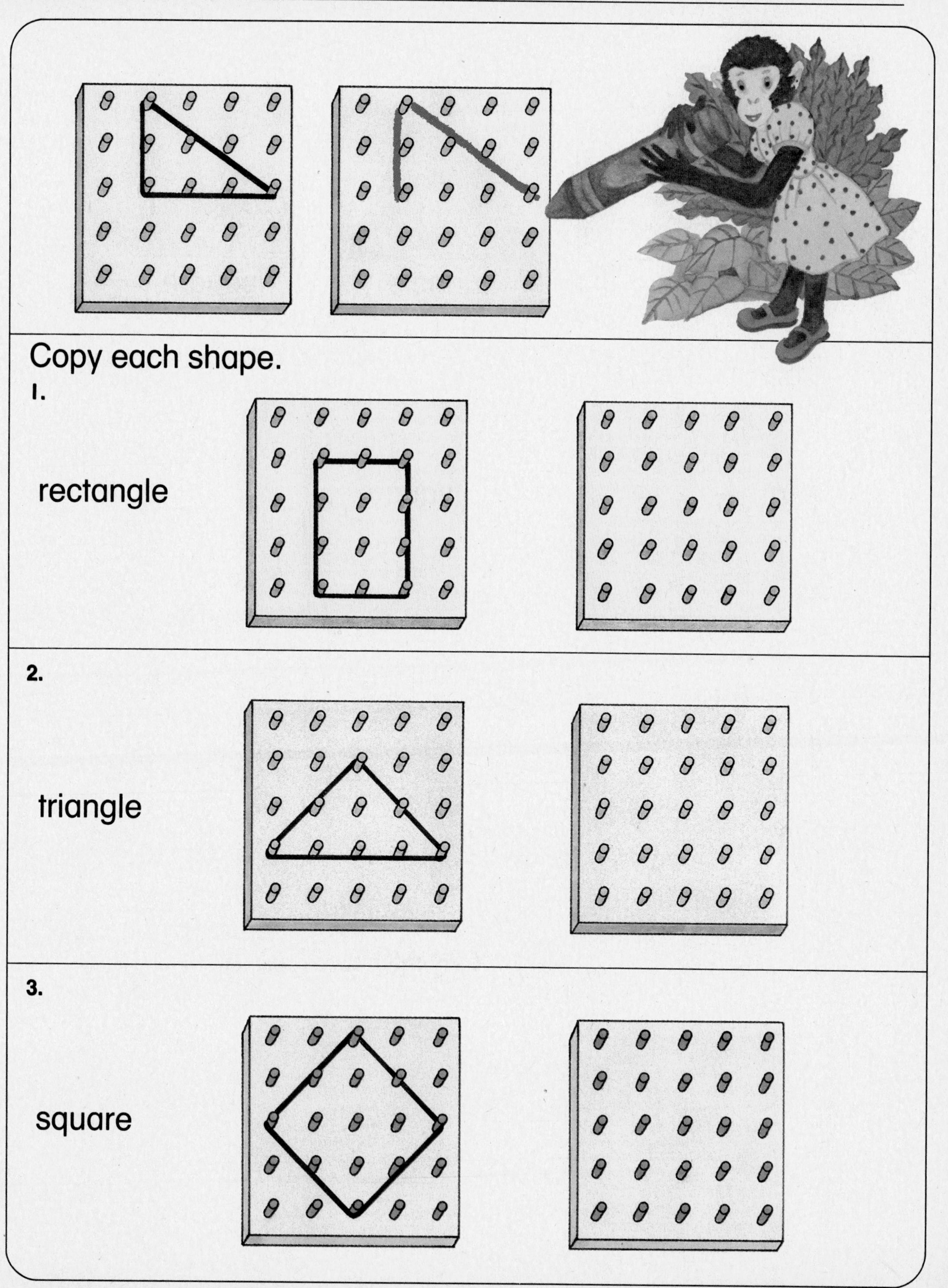

Copy each shape.
1.
rectangle
2.
triangle
3.
square

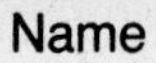

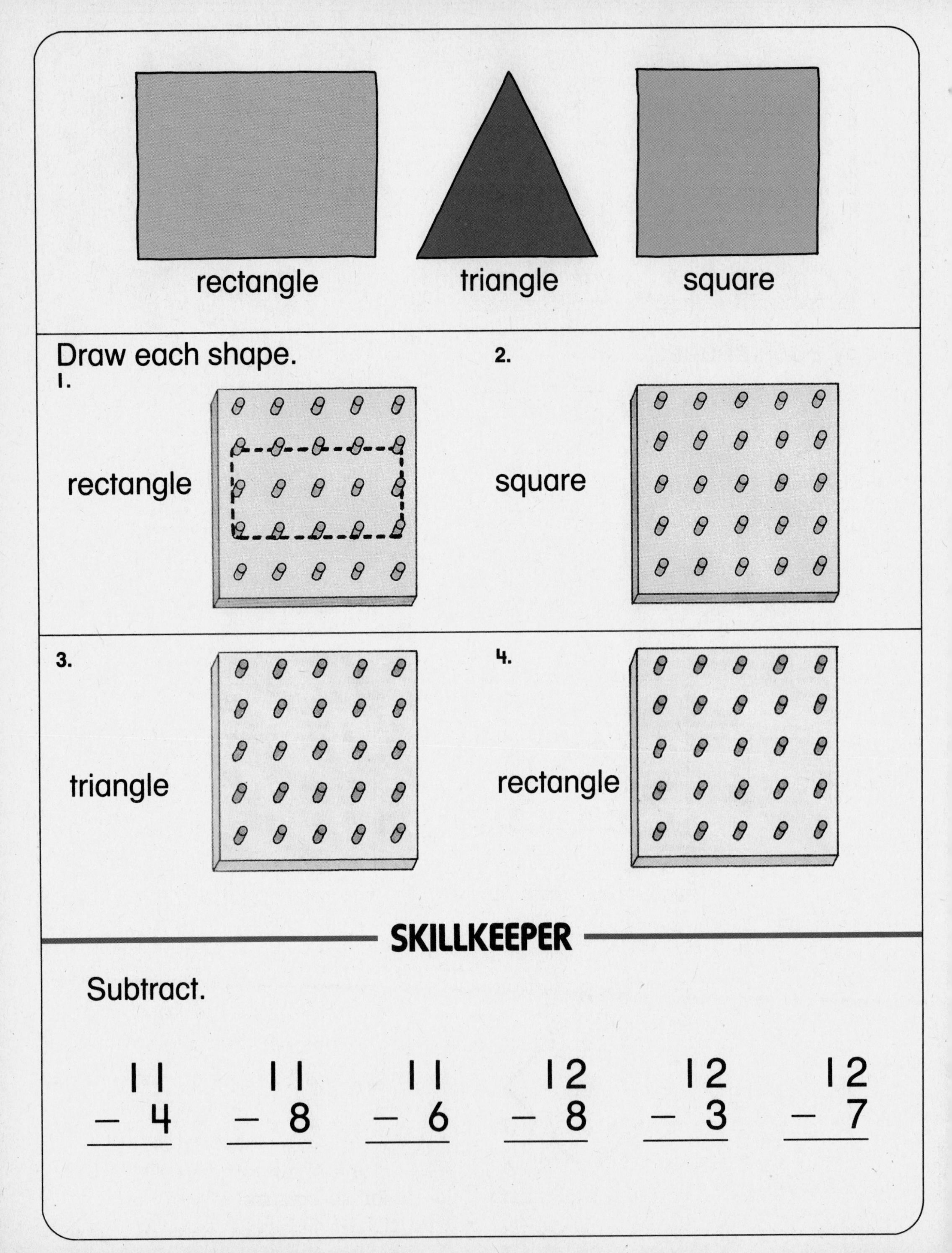

Draw each shape.

1. rectangle

2. square

3. triangle

4. rectangle

SKILLKEEPER

Subtract.

11	11	11	12	12	12
− 4	− 8	− 6	− 8	− 3	− 7

Name

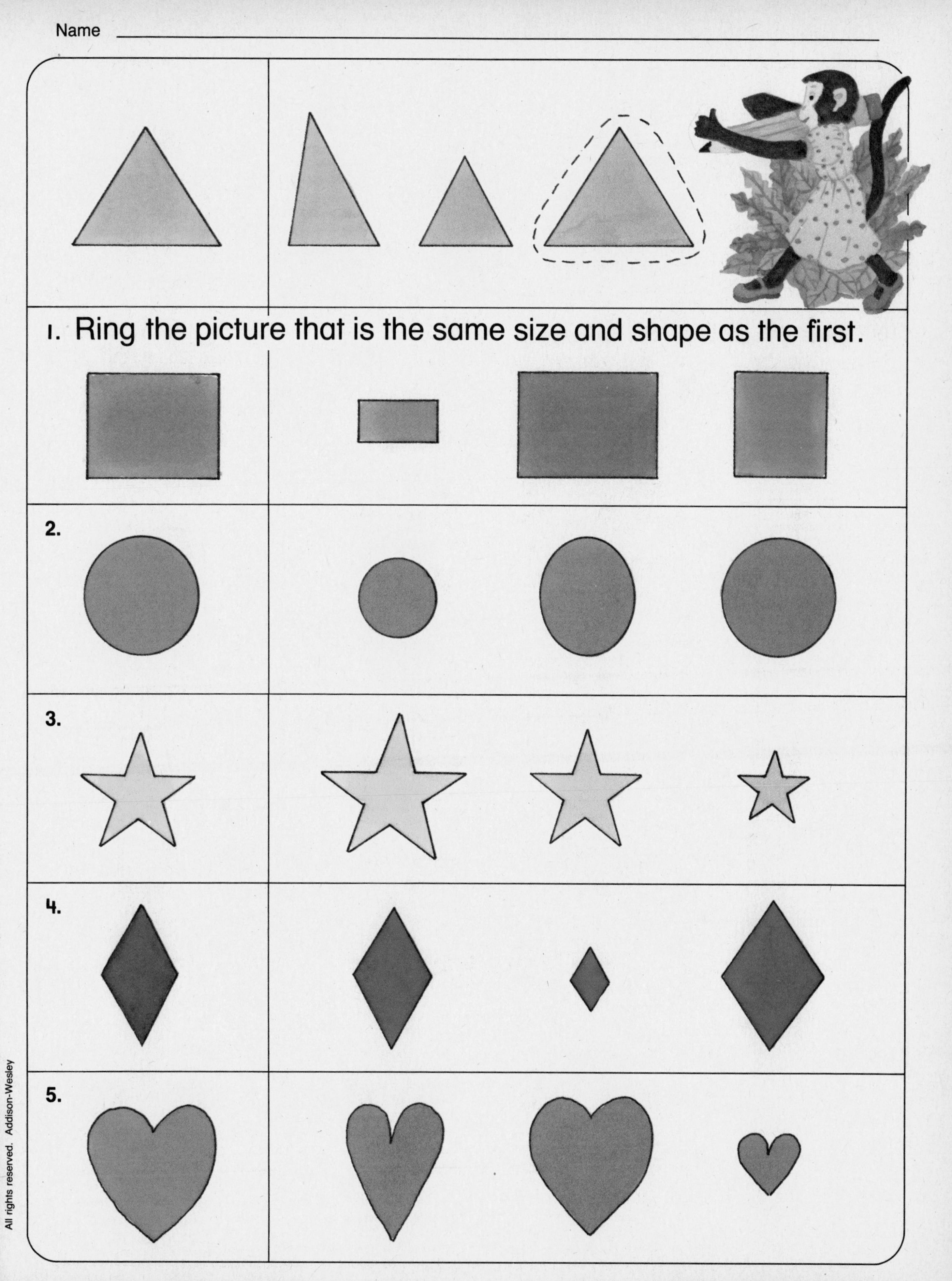

1. Ring the picture that is the same size and shape as the first.
2.
3.
4.
5.

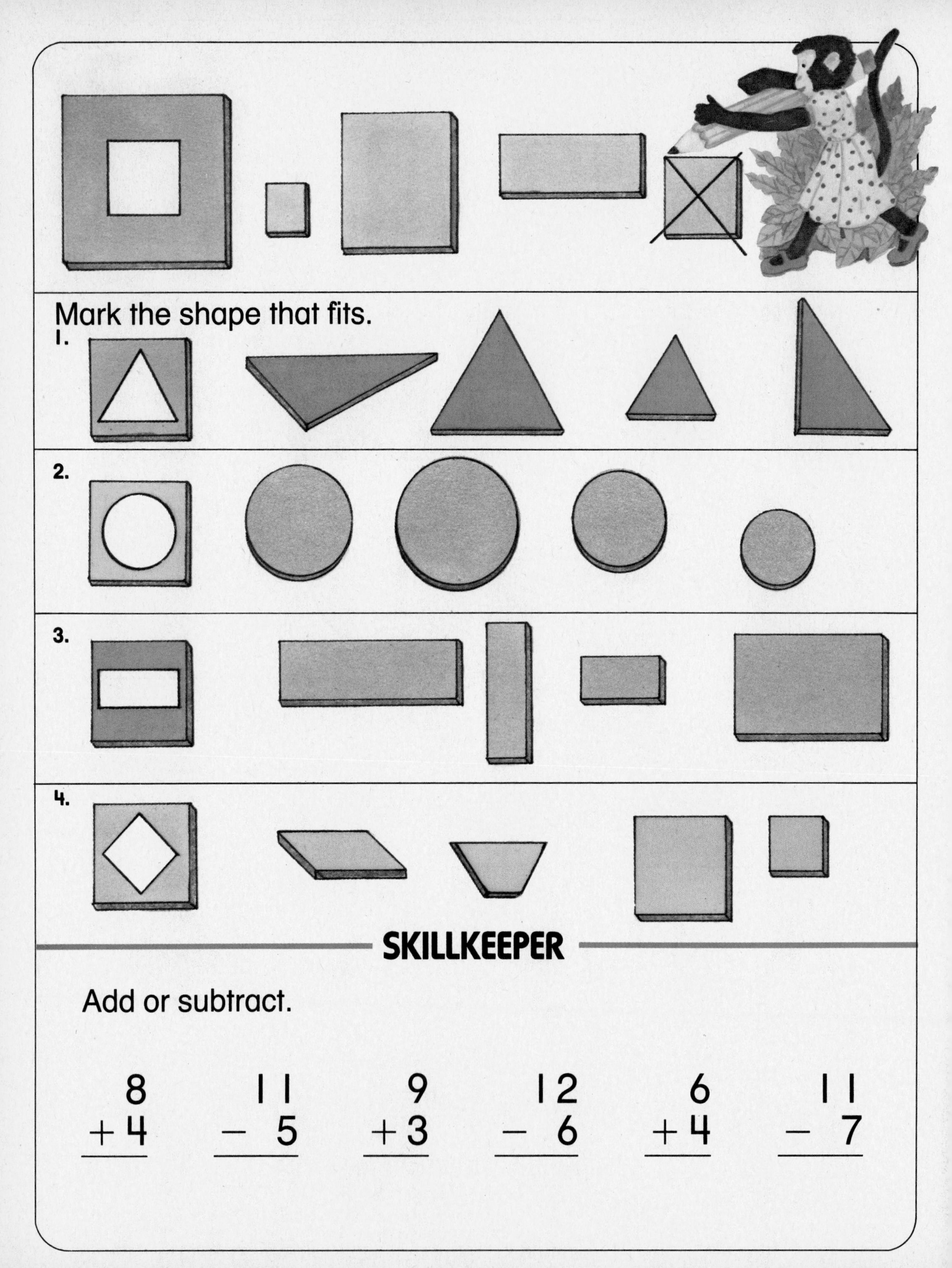

Mark the shape that fits.

1.

2.

3.

4.

Add or subtract.

$$\begin{array}{r} 8 \\ +4 \\ \hline \end{array} \qquad \begin{array}{r} 11 \\ -5 \\ \hline \end{array} \qquad \begin{array}{r} 9 \\ +3 \\ \hline \end{array} \qquad \begin{array}{r} 12 \\ -6 \\ \hline \end{array} \qquad \begin{array}{r} 6 \\ +4 \\ \hline \end{array} \qquad \begin{array}{r} 11 \\ -7 \\ \hline \end{array}$$

Congruence—same size and shape

Name ____

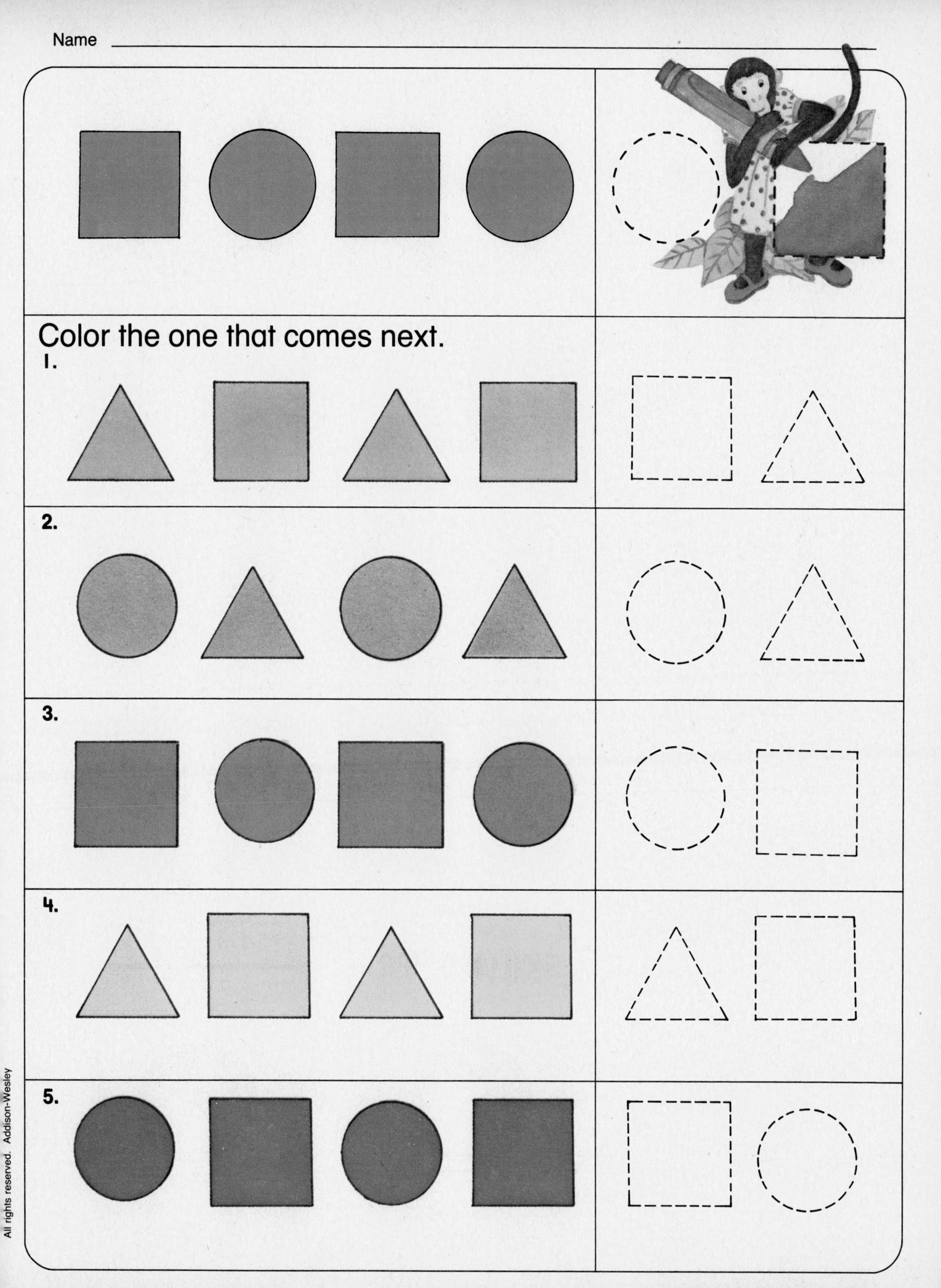

Color the one that comes next.
1.
2.
3.
4.
5.

Shape patterns (two hundred thirty-nine) 239

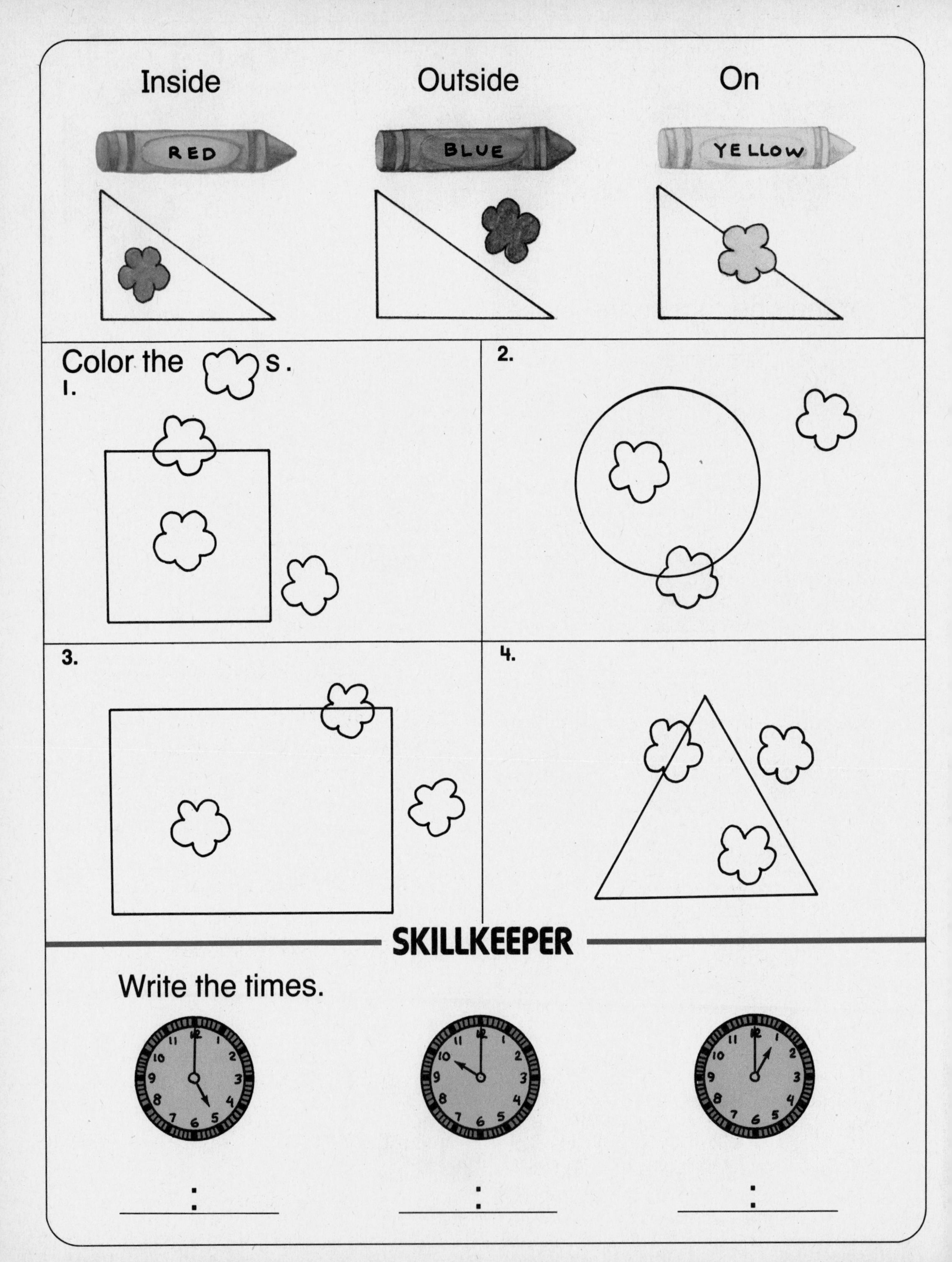
Inside
Outside
On
RED
BLUE
YELLOW
Color the s.
1.
2.
3.
4.
SKILLKEEPER
Write the times.
:
:
:

Name ______________________________

Color a ☐ for each tally mark.

1. How many visited on Monday? ____

2. How many visited on Wednesday? ____

3. Ring the day with the most visitors.

Monday Tuesday Wednesday

Thursday Friday

Color a ☐ for each coin.
Mark each coin as you color.

How many coins are there in all? ______

Name ______________________________

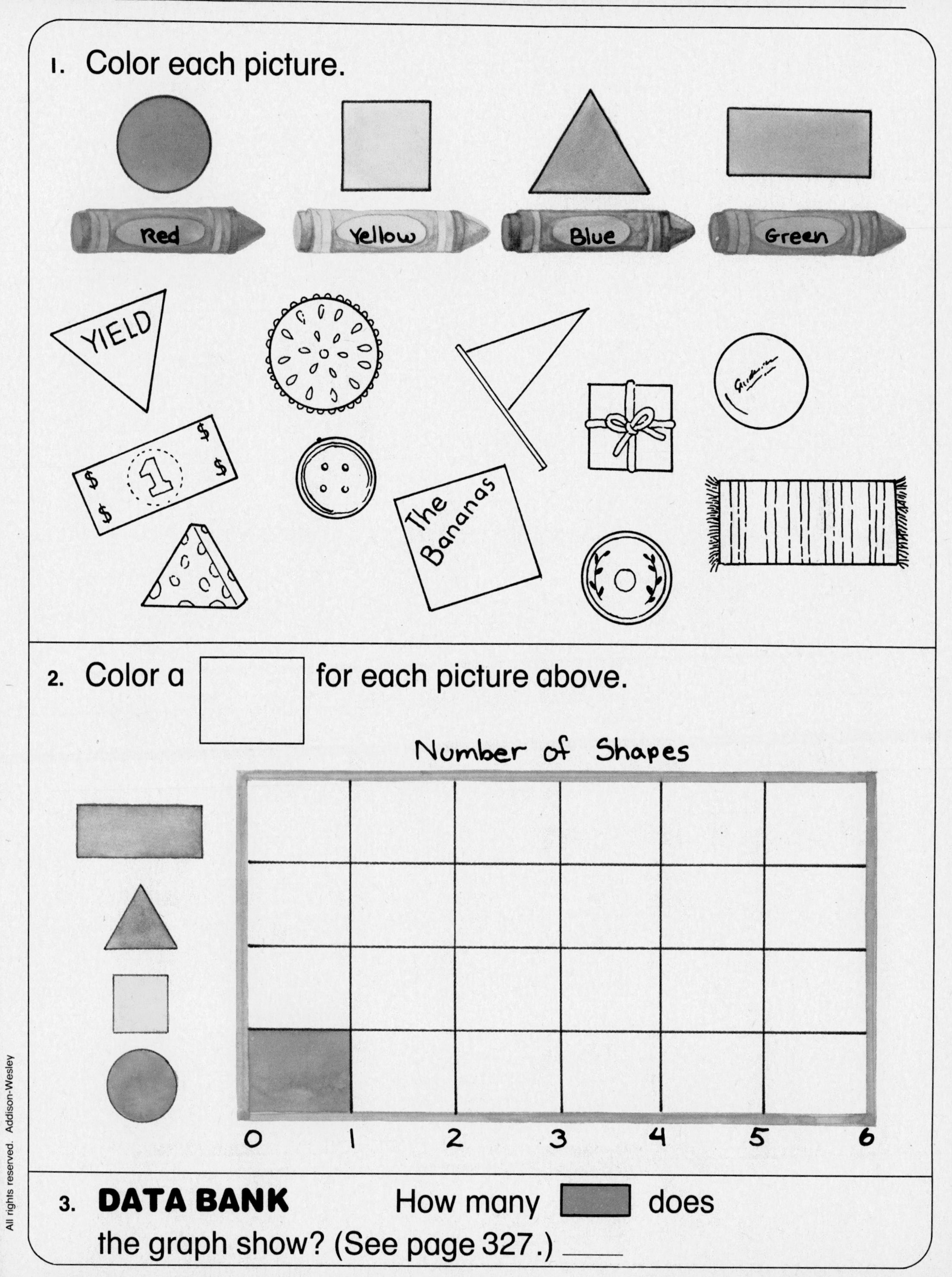

1. Color each picture.
Red
Yellow
Blue
Green
YIELD
$
1
The Bananas
2. Color a for each picture above.
Number of Shapes
0
1
2
3
4
5
6
3. DATA BANK How many does the graph show? (See page 327.) ____

QUESTION
DATA
PLAN
ANSWER
CHECK

Problem-Solving Strategy

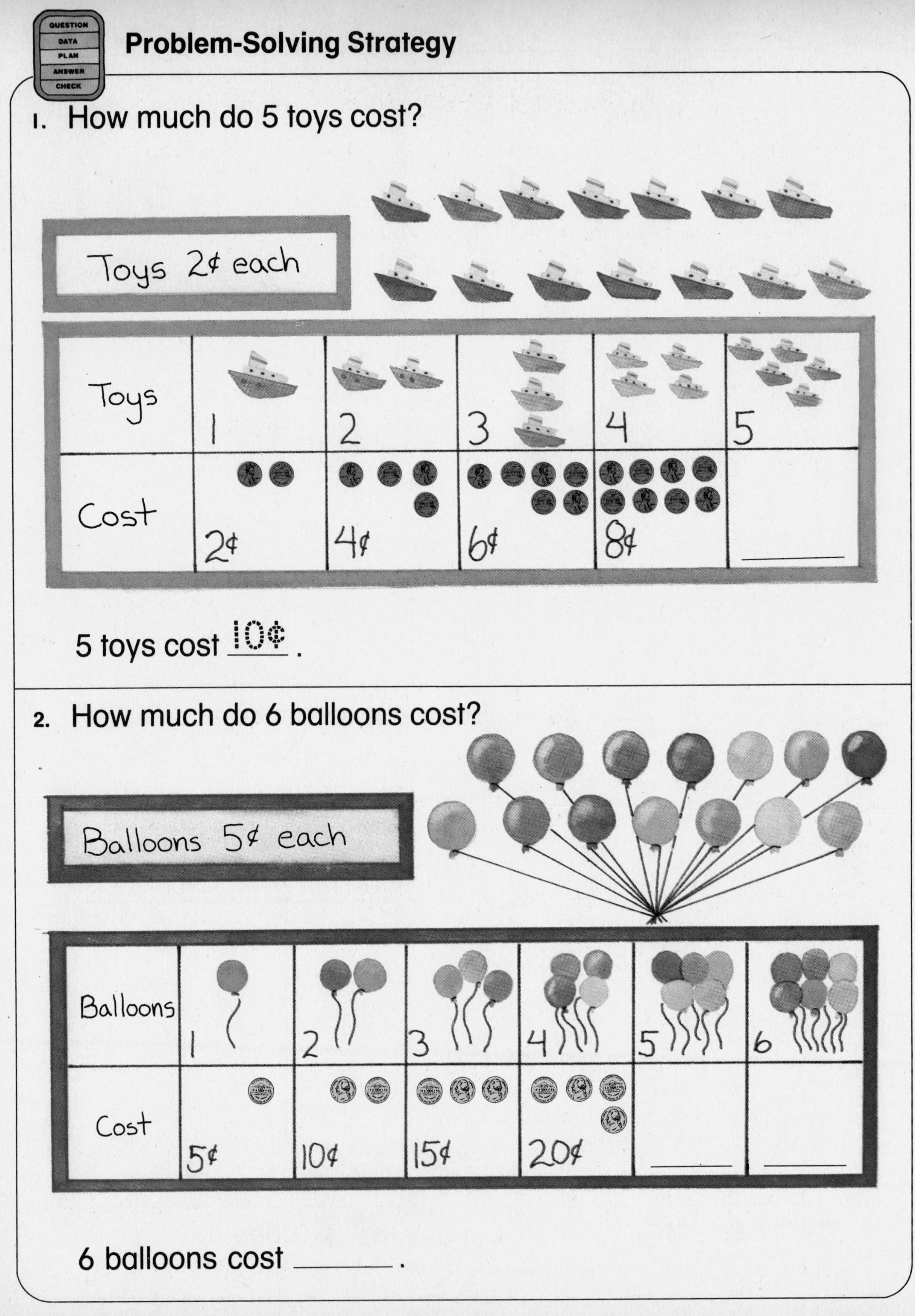

1. How much do 5 toys cost?

Toys 2¢ each

Toys	1	2	3	4	5
Cost	2¢	4¢	6¢	8¢	____

5 toys cost 10¢.

2. How much do 6 balloons cost?

Balloons 5¢ each

Balloons	1	2	3	4	5	6
Cost	5¢	10¢	15¢	20¢	____	____

6 balloons cost ______.

Name 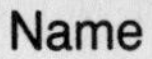 ____________________

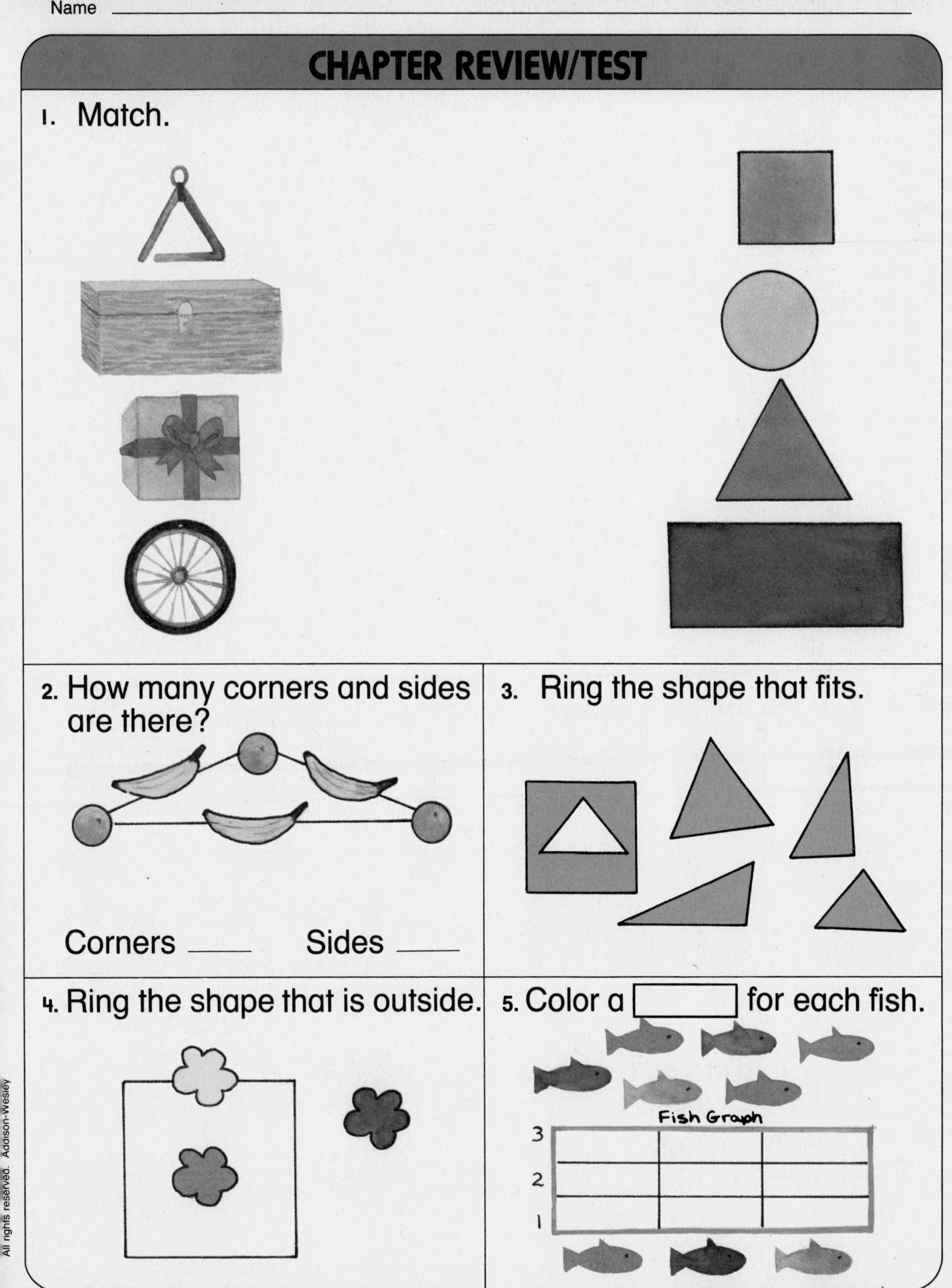

CHAPTER REVIEW/TEST

1. Match.

2. How many corners and sides are there?

Corners ____ Sides ____

3. Ring the shape that fits.

4. Ring the shape that is outside.

5. Color a ☐ for each fish.

Name ____________________

CUMULATIVE REVIEW

Add.

1.
$$\begin{array}{r} 4 \\ +4 \\ \hline \end{array}$$
○ 7
○ 8
○ 9

2.
$$\begin{array}{r} 6 \\ +6 \\ \hline \end{array}$$
○ 13
○ 14
○ 12

3.
$$\begin{array}{r} 6 \\ +4 \\ \hline \end{array}$$
○ 10
○ 11
○ 12

4.
$$\begin{array}{r} 6 \\ +5 \\ \hline \end{array}$$
○ 11
○ 13
○ 12

Subtract.

5.
$$\begin{array}{r} 7 \\ -4 \\ \hline \end{array}$$
○ 4
○ 3
○ 6

6.
$$\begin{array}{r} 9 \\ -7 \\ \hline \end{array}$$
○ 1
○ 3
○ 2

7.
$$\begin{array}{r} 11 \\ -\ 8 \\ \hline \end{array}$$
○ 3
○ 4
○ 5

8.
$$\begin{array}{r} 12 \\ -\ 4 \\ \hline \end{array}$$
○ 8
○ 7
○ 5

9. Solve.

10 apples were on the table.
Barb gave away 4.
How many apples
were left?

_____ apples

Name ______________________________

ANOTHER LOOK

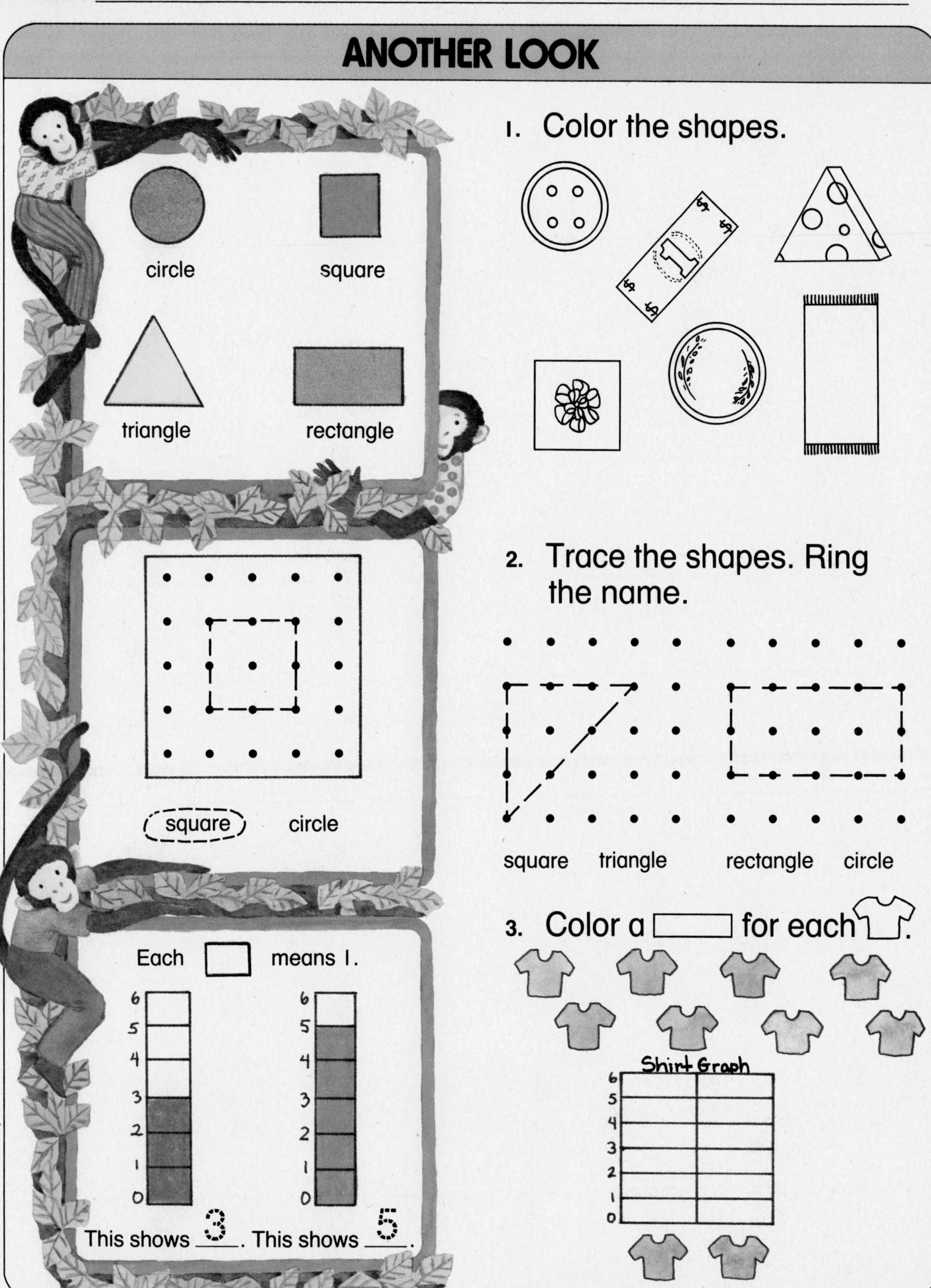

circle square

triangle rectangle

square circle

Each ☐ means 1.

This shows 3. This shows 5.

1. Color the shapes.

2. Trace the shapes. Ring the name.

square triangle rectangle circle

3. Color a ☐ for each 👕.

Shirt Graph

Name ____

ENRICHMENT

Ring the shapes that are divided into two matching parts.

1.

2.

3. Draw a line of symmetry on each figure.

11 Name ________________________________

ADDITION AND SUBTRACTION : 2-DIGIT NUMBERS

How many yellow pencils are there in all?

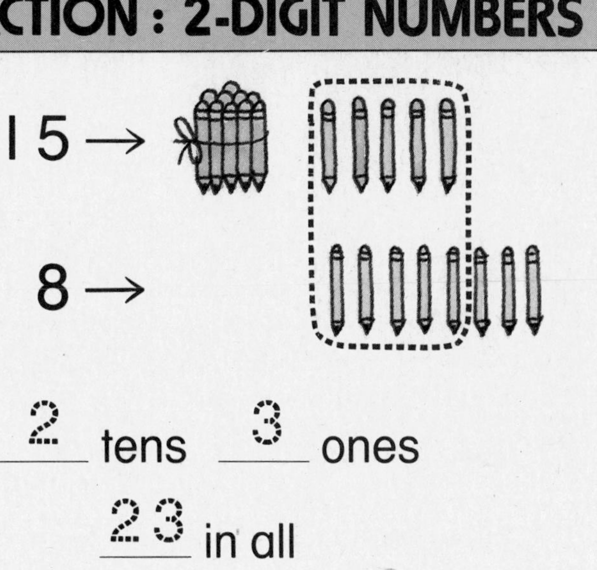

2 tens 3 ones

23 in all

There are 23 in all.

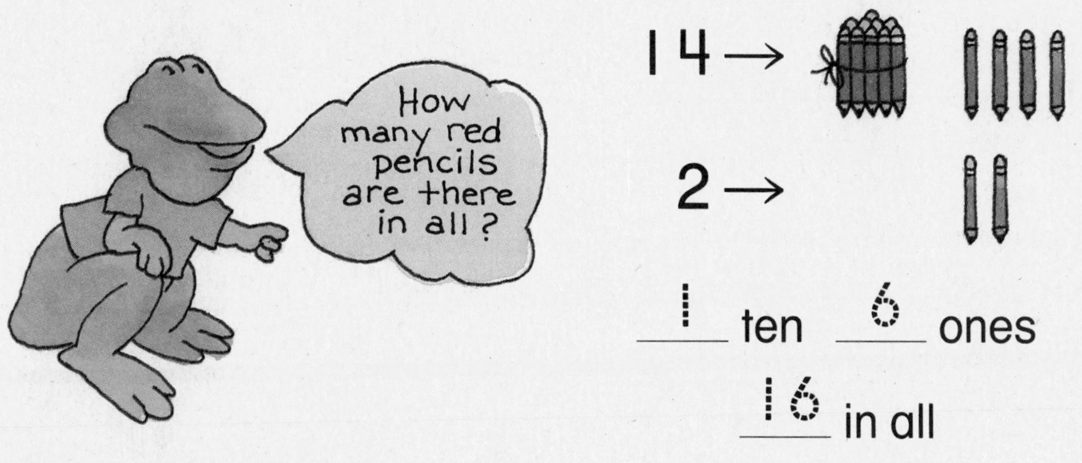

How many red pencils are there in all?
14 →
2 →

1 ten 6 ones

16 in all

There are 16 in all.

How many are there in all?
Make another 10 when you can.

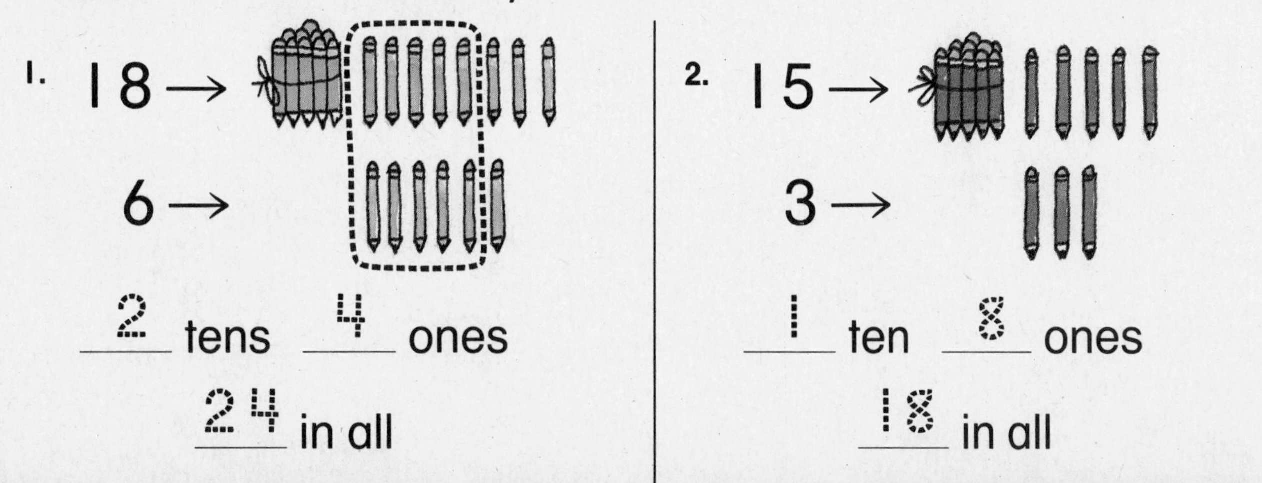

1. 2 tens 4 ones

24 in all

2. 1 ten 8 ones

18 in all

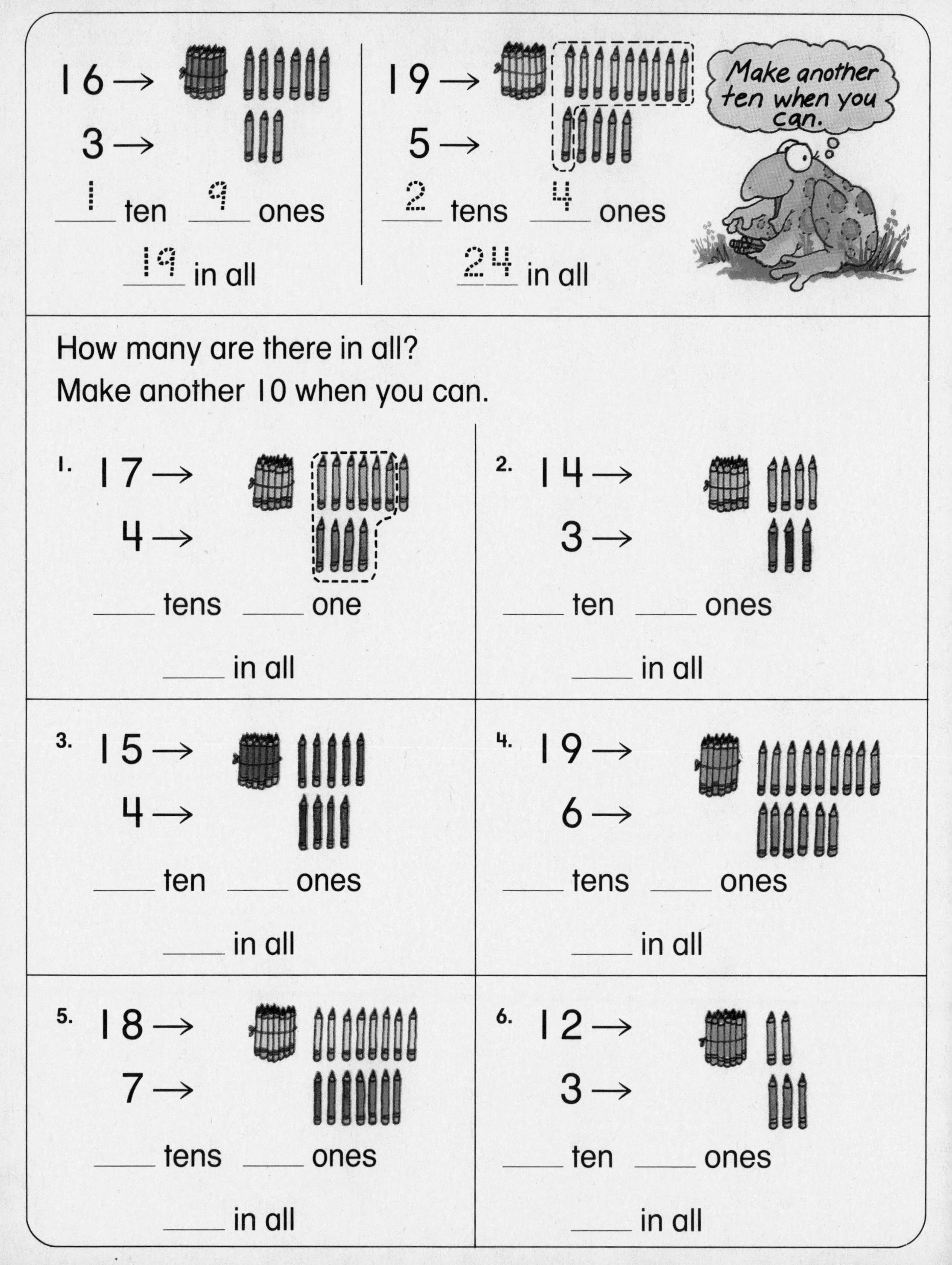
16 →
3 →
1 ten 9 ones
19 in all
19 →
5 →
2 tens 4 ones
24 in all
Make another ten when you can.
How many are there in all?
Make another 10 when you can.
1. 17 →
4 →
____ tens ____ one
____ in all
2. 14 →
3 →
____ ten ____ ones
____ in all
3. 15 →
4 →
____ ten ____ ones
____ in all
4. 19 →
6 →
____ tens ____ ones
____ in all
5. 18 →
7 →
____ tens ____ ones
____ in all
6. 12 →
3 →
____ ten ____ ones
____ in all

Name

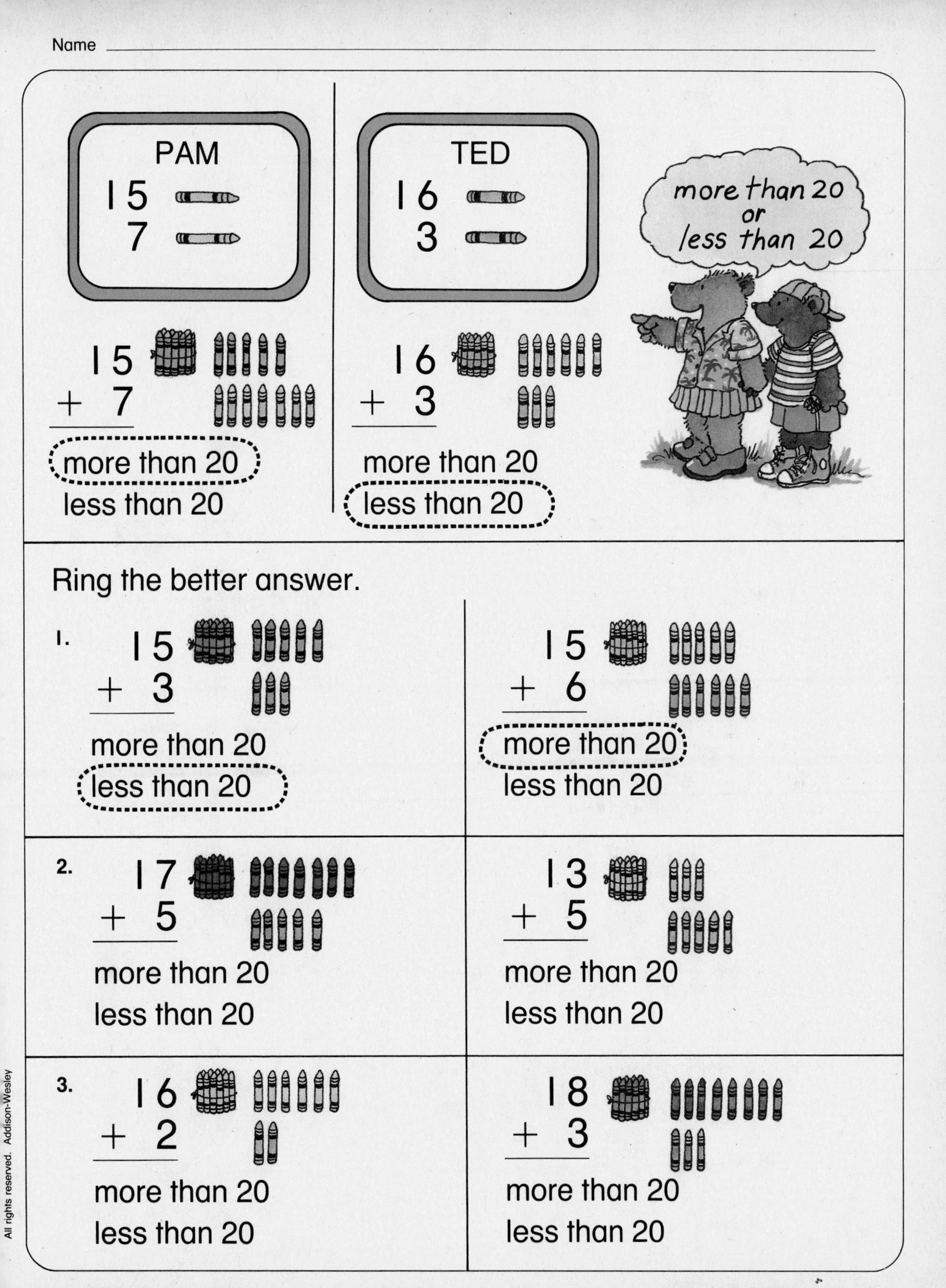

Ring the better answer.

1.
15
+ 3

more than 20
less than 20

15
+ 6

more than 20
less than 20

2.
17
+ 5

more than 20
less than 20

13
+ 5

more than 20
less than 20

3.
16
+ 2

more than 20
less than 20

18
+ 3

more than 20
less than 20

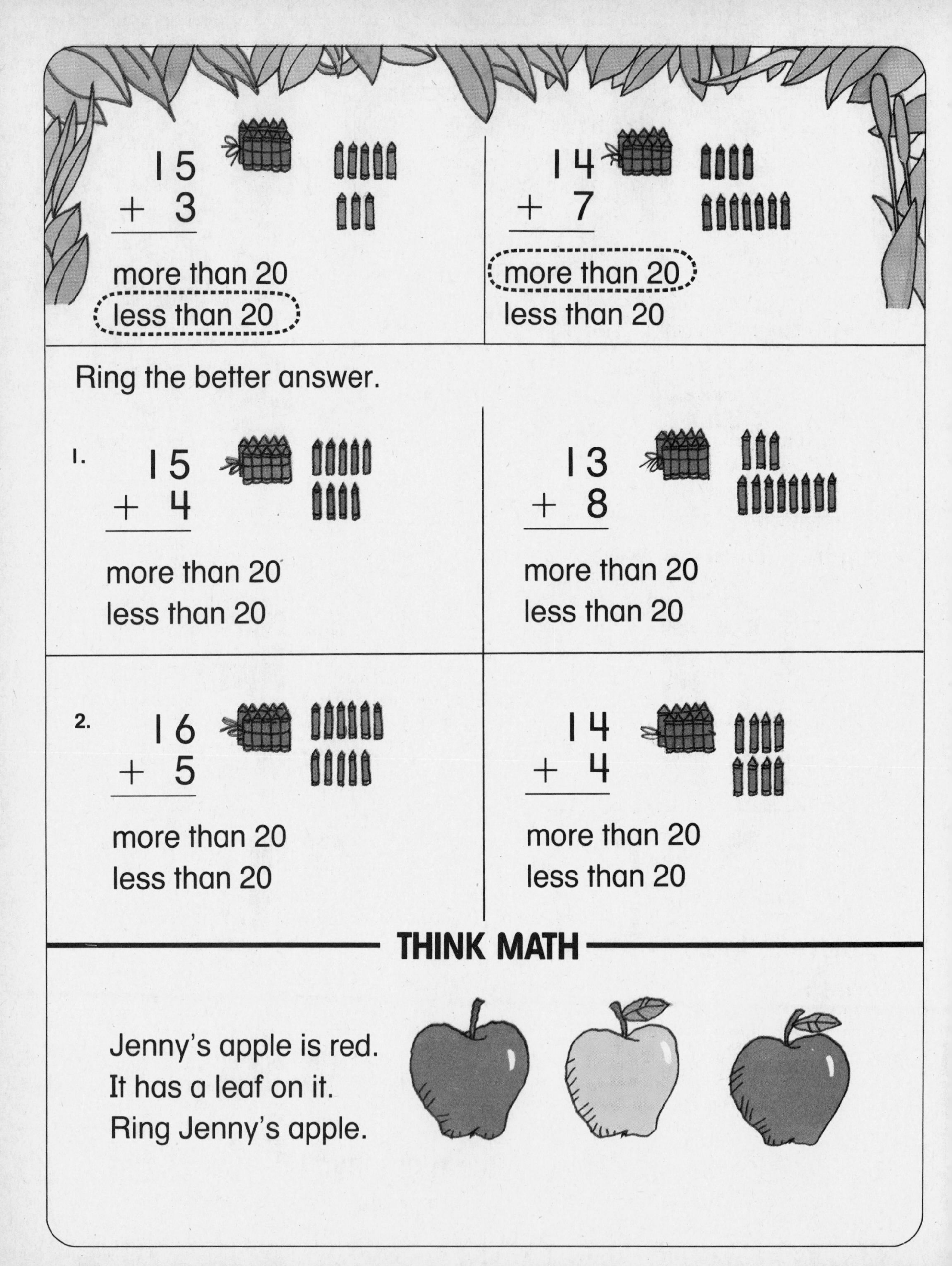

15
+ 3

more than 20
less than 20

14
+ 7

more than 20
less than 20

Ring the better answer.

1. 15
+ 4

more than 20
less than 20

13
+ 8

more than 20
less than 20

2. 16
+ 5

more than 20
less than 20

14
+ 4

more than 20
less than 20

THINK MATH

Jenny's apple is red.
It has a leaf on it.
Ring Jenny's apple.

Name ______________________________

Use these steps when you add 2-digit numbers.

How many went on the trip?

Tens	Ones
2	4
+ 4	3
6	7

67 went on the trip.

First add the ones. Then add the tens.

1.

Tens	Ones
2	5
+ 1	3

Tens	Ones
3	2
+	5

2.

Tens	Ones
1	2
+ 3	6

Tens	Ones
4	2
+ 1	4

Tens	Ones
5	0
+ 2	7

Tens	Ones
3	1
+ 2	8

3.

Tens	Ones
1	9
+ 1	0

Tens	Ones
6	3
+	2

Tens	Ones
4	2
+ 4	6

Tens	Ones
4	1
+ 5	7

Adding 2-digit numbers without trading

Add.

1.

$$\begin{array}{r} 47 \\ +22 \\ \hline \end{array} \quad \begin{array}{r} 40 \\ +40 \\ \hline \end{array} \quad \begin{array}{r} 25 \\ +10 \\ \hline \end{array} \quad \begin{array}{r} 2 \\ +62 \\ \hline \end{array} \quad \begin{array}{r} 74 \\ +\ 5 \\ \hline \end{array}$$

2.

$$\begin{array}{r} 23¢ \\ +21¢ \\ \hline \end{array} \quad \begin{array}{r} 34¢ \\ +44¢ \\ \hline \end{array} \quad \begin{array}{r} 60¢ \\ +27¢ \\ \hline \end{array} \quad \begin{array}{r} 32¢ \\ +\ 5¢ \\ \hline \end{array} \quad \begin{array}{r} 15¢ \\ +21¢ \\ \hline \end{array}$$

3.

$$\begin{array}{r} 12 \\ 40 \\ +26 \\ \hline \end{array} \quad \begin{array}{r} 32 \\ 51 \\ +\ 5 \\ \hline \end{array} \quad \begin{array}{r} 24 \\ 30 \\ +23 \\ \hline \end{array} \quad \begin{array}{r} 66 \\ 11 \\ +22 \\ \hline \end{array} \quad \begin{array}{r} 41 \\ 4 \\ +32 \\ \hline \end{array}$$

Solve.

4. How many went on this trip?

Bus 35

Cars 40

____ went on the trip.

5. How many went on this trip?

Bus 45

Cars 21

____ went on the trip.

SKILLKEEPER

Subtract.

$$\begin{array}{r} 10 \\ -\ 7 \\ \hline \end{array} \quad \begin{array}{r} 9 \\ -2 \\ \hline \end{array} \quad \begin{array}{r} 12 \\ -\ 3 \\ \hline \end{array} \quad \begin{array}{r} 8 \\ -5 \\ \hline \end{array} \quad \begin{array}{r} 10 \\ -\ 4 \\ \hline \end{array} \quad \begin{array}{r} 7 \\ -4 \\ \hline \end{array} \quad \begin{array}{r} 9 \\ -6 \\ \hline \end{array}$$

Name ____________________

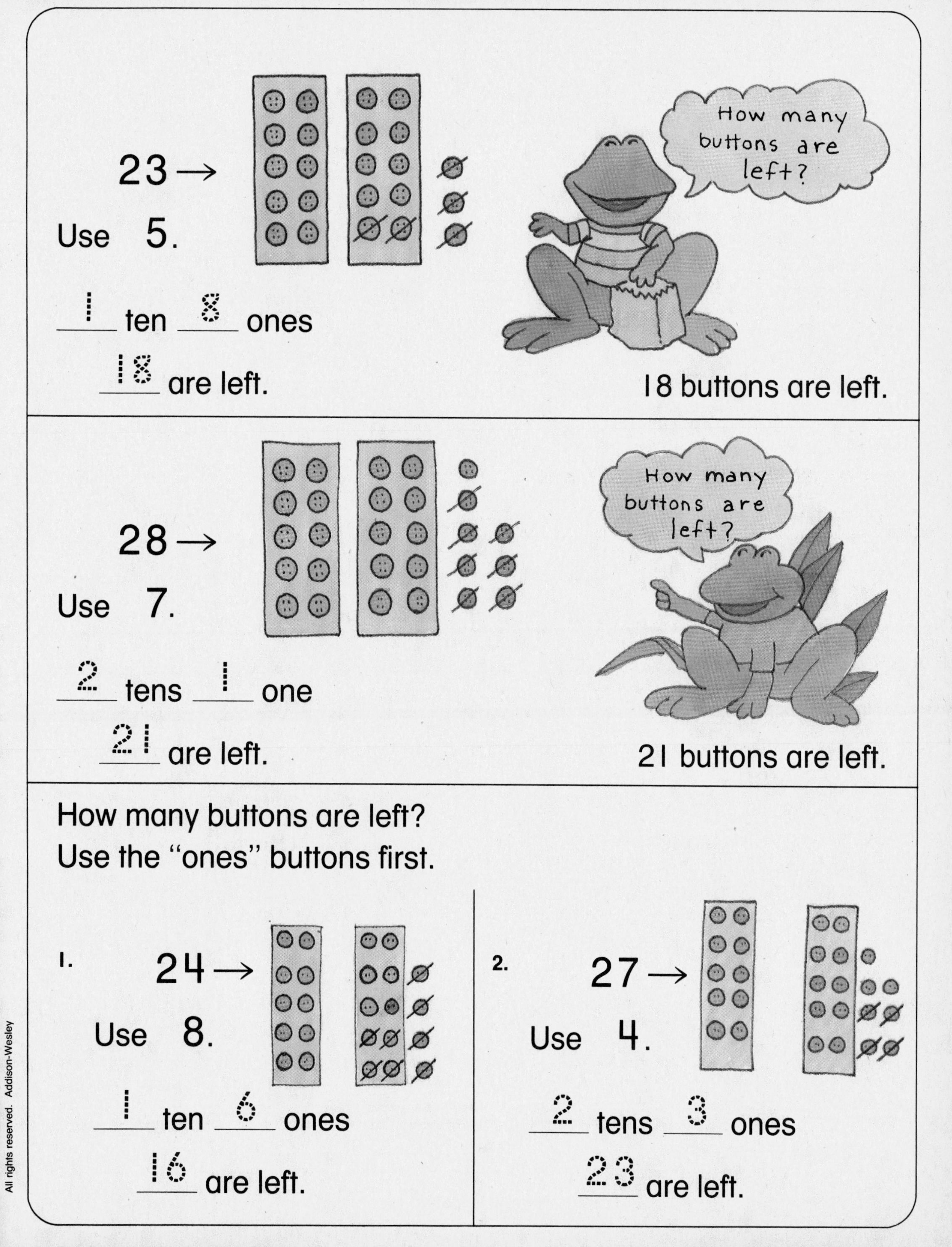

23 →

Use 5.

1 ten 8 ones

18 are left.

18 buttons are left.

28 →

Use 7.

2 tens 1 one

21 are left.

21 buttons are left.

How many buttons are left?
Use the "ones" buttons first.

1. 24 →

Use 8.

1 ten 6 ones

16 are left.

2. 27 →

Use 4.

2 tens 3 ones

23 are left.

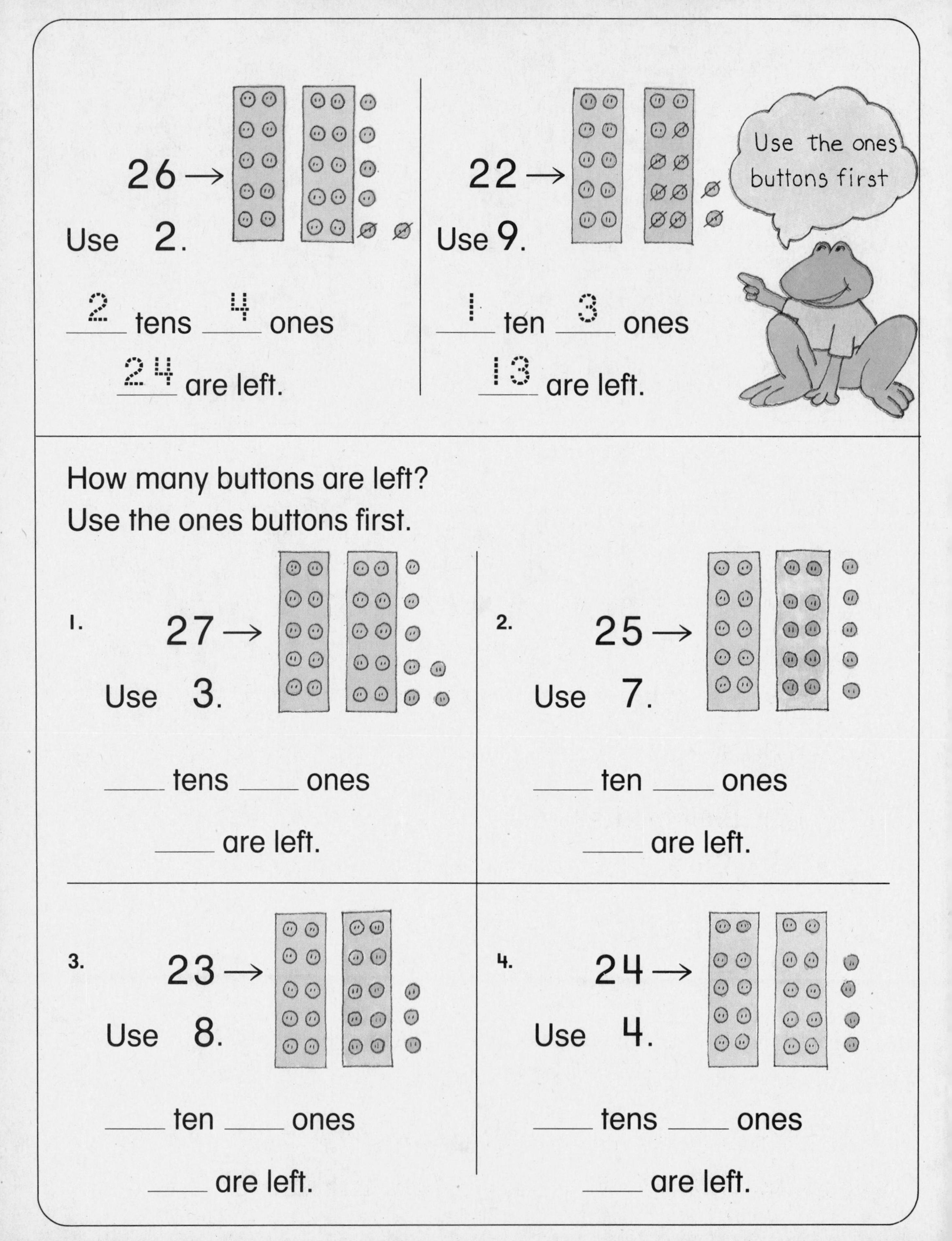
26 →
Use 2.
2 tens 4 ones
24 are left.
22 →
Use 9.
1 ten 3 ones
13 are left.
Use the ones buttons first
How many buttons are left?
Use the ones buttons first.
1. 27 →
Use 3.
___ tens ___ ones
___ are left.
2. 25 →
Use 7.
___ ten ___ ones
___ are left.
3. 23 →
Use 8.
___ ten ___ ones
___ are left.
4. 24 →
Use 4.
___ tens ___ ones
___ are left.

Name

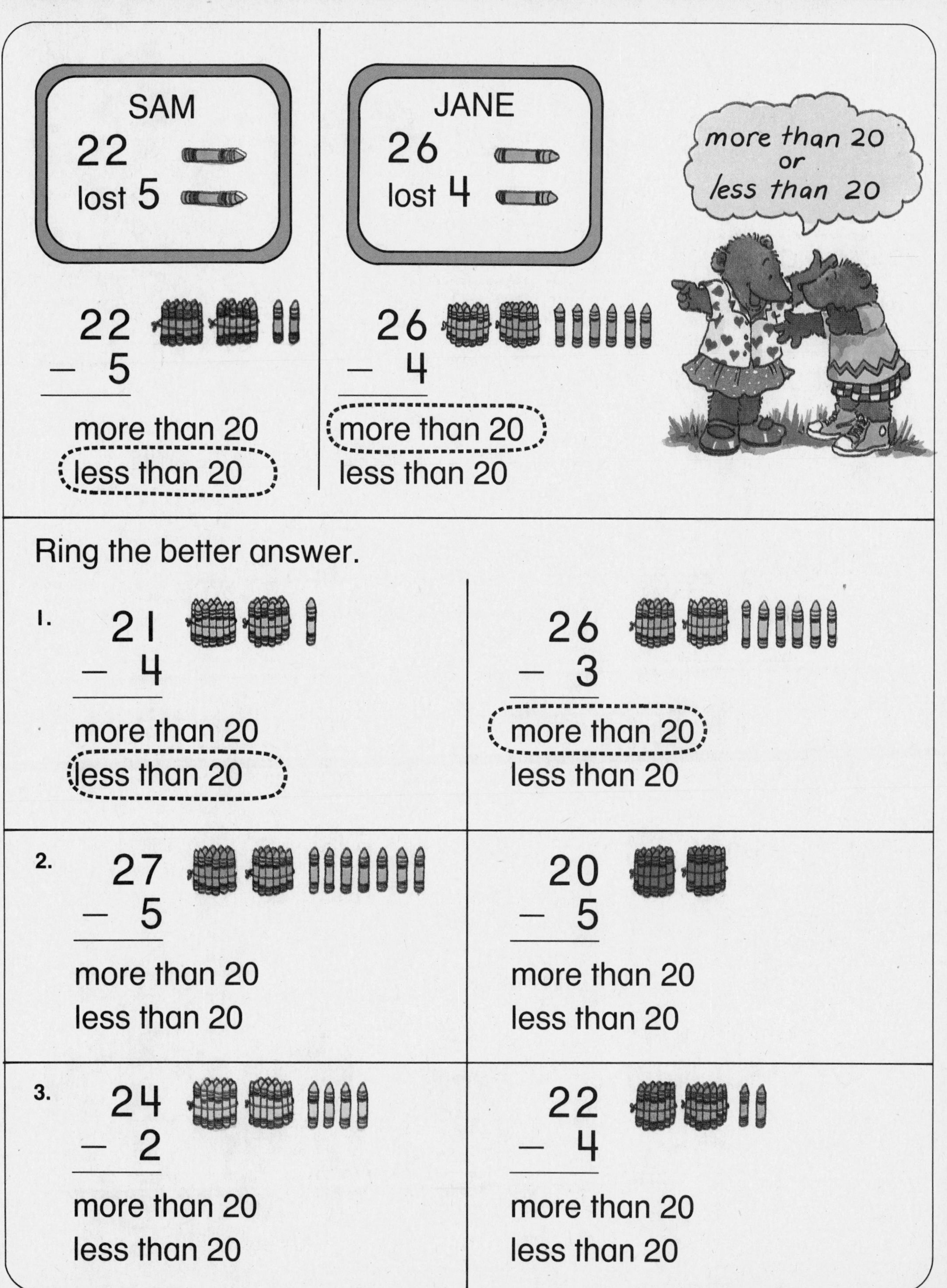

SAM
22
lost 5

JANE
26
lost 4

22
− 5

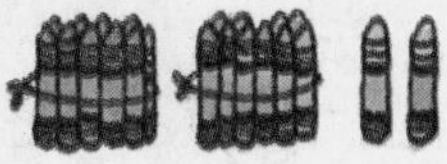

more than 20
less than 20

26
− 4

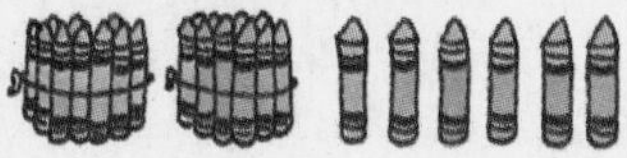

more than 20
less than 20

Ring the better answer.

1. 21
− 4

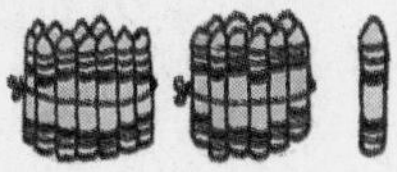

more than 20
less than 20

26
− 3

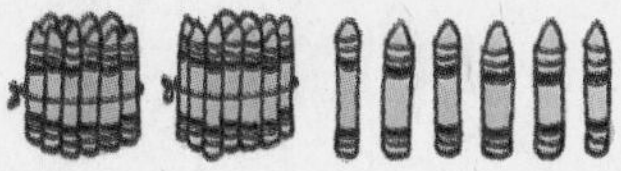

more than 20
less than 20

2. 27
− 5

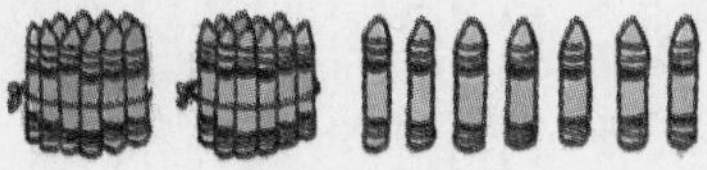

more than 20
less than 20

20
− 5

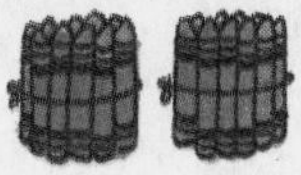

more than 20
less than 20

3. 24
− 2

more than 20
less than 20

22
− 4

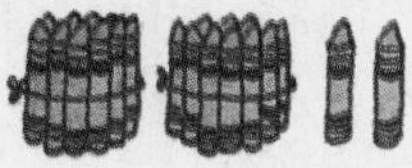

more than 20
less than 20

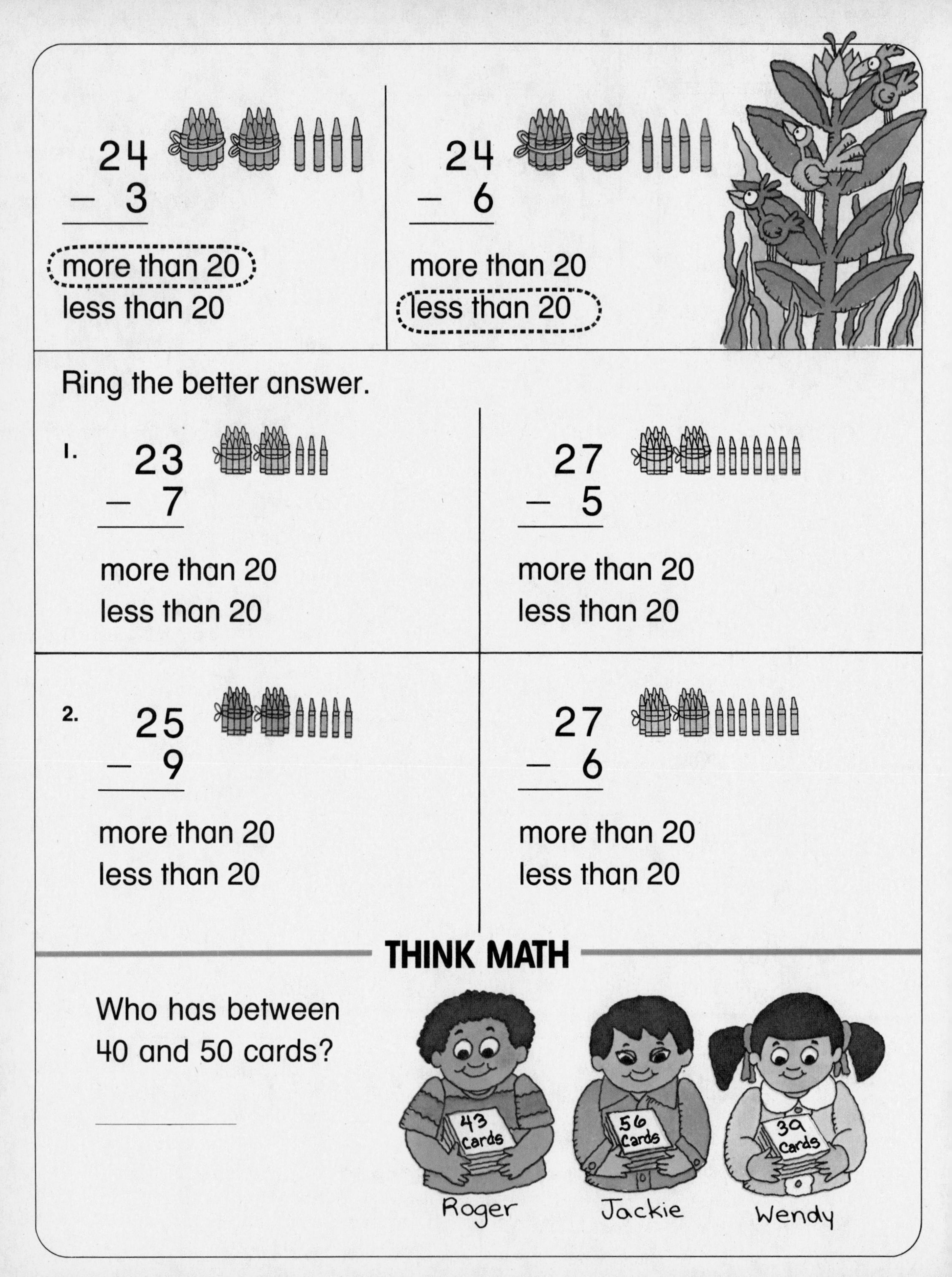

$$\begin{array}{r} 24 \\ -\ 3 \\ \hline \end{array}$$

more than 20
less than 20

$$\begin{array}{r} 24 \\ -\ 6 \\ \hline \end{array}$$

more than 20
less than 20

Ring the better answer.

1.

$$\begin{array}{r} 23 \\ -\ 7 \\ \hline \end{array}$$

more than 20
less than 20

$$\begin{array}{r} 27 \\ -\ 5 \\ \hline \end{array}$$

more than 20
less than 20

2.

$$\begin{array}{r} 25 \\ -\ 9 \\ \hline \end{array}$$

more than 20
less than 20

$$\begin{array}{r} 27 \\ -\ 6 \\ \hline \end{array}$$

more than 20
less than 20

THINK MATH

Who has between 40 and 50 cards?

____

Name

Use these steps when you subtract 2-digit numbers.

First subtract the ones.
Then subtract the tens.

39 birds are on a fence.
23 fly away.
How many birds are left?

Tens	Ones
3	9
− 2	3
1	6

16 birds are left.

39

take away 23

First subtract the ones. Then subtract the tens.

1.

Tens	Ones
3	6
− 1	4
2	2

Tens	Ones
2	8
− 1	6

2.

Tens	Ones
7	5
− 3	0

Tens	Ones
8	8
− 4	4

Tens	Ones
6	3
− 2	3

Tens	Ones
9	8
− 4	3

3.

Tens	Ones
4	9
− 2	5

Tens	Ones
6	6
− 3	5

Tens	Ones
7	4
− 5	0

Tens	Ones
9	7
− 2	5

Subtract.

1. $\begin{array}{r} 86 \\ -\ 34 \\ \hline \end{array}$ $\begin{array}{r} 64 \\ -\ 52 \\ \hline \end{array}$ $\begin{array}{r} 79 \\ -\ 38 \\ \hline \end{array}$ $\begin{array}{r} 48 \\ -\ 16 \\ \hline \end{array}$ $\begin{array}{r} 57 \\ -\ 27 \\ \hline \end{array}$

2. $\begin{array}{r} 75 \\ -\ 34 \\ \hline \end{array}$ $\begin{array}{r} 56 \\ -\ 16 \\ \hline \end{array}$ $\begin{array}{r} 95 \\ -\ 62 \\ \hline \end{array}$ $\begin{array}{r} 68 \\ -\ 35 \\ \hline \end{array}$ $\begin{array}{r} 49 \\ -\ 40 \\ \hline \end{array}$

3. $\begin{array}{r} 77¢ \\ -\ 32¢ \\ \hline \end{array}$ $\begin{array}{r} 98¢ \\ -\ 24¢ \\ \hline \end{array}$ $\begin{array}{r} 65¢ \\ -\ 40¢ \\ \hline \end{array}$ $\begin{array}{r} 87¢ \\ -\ 61¢ \\ \hline \end{array}$ $\begin{array}{r} 56¢ \\ -\ 14¢ \\ \hline \end{array}$

Solve.

4. Jim had 79¢.
He spent 35¢.
How much does
Jim have now?

5. Ann had 34¢.
She found 25¢.
How much does
she have now?

6. Luis had 69¢.
He spent 28¢.
How much does
he have now?

7. **DATA BANK**
Al bought a [book] and a [toy mouse].
How much did
he spend in all?
(See page 327.)

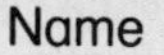

Name ______________________________

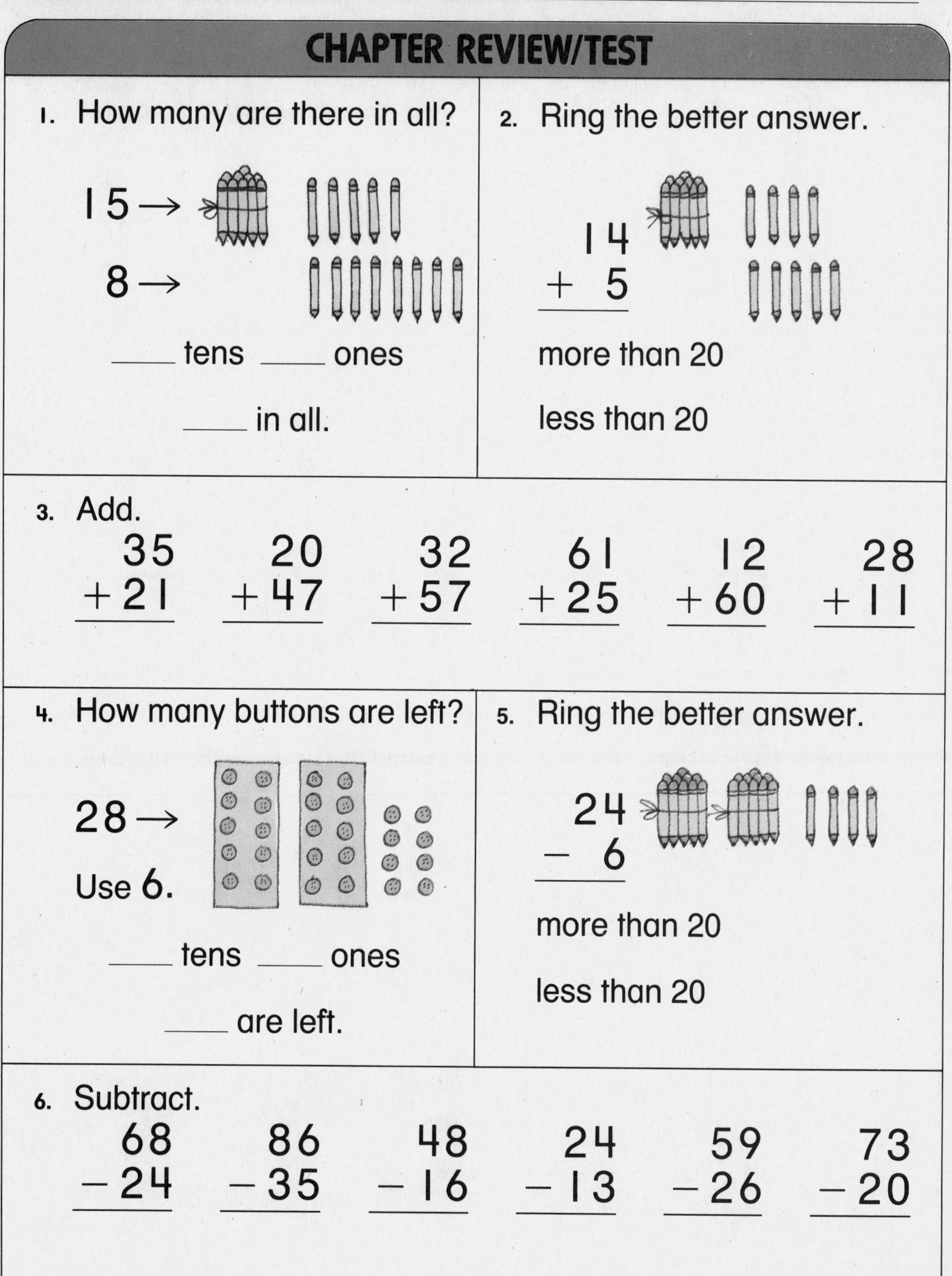

CHAPTER REVIEW/TEST

1. How many are there in all?

15 →

8 →

____ tens ____ ones

____ in all.

2. Ring the better answer.

$$\begin{array}{r} 14 \\ +\ 5 \\ \hline \end{array}$$

more than 20

less than 20

3. Add.

$$\begin{array}{r} 35 \\ +21 \\ \hline \end{array} \quad \begin{array}{r} 20 \\ +47 \\ \hline \end{array} \quad \begin{array}{r} 32 \\ +57 \\ \hline \end{array} \quad \begin{array}{r} 61 \\ +25 \\ \hline \end{array} \quad \begin{array}{r} 12 \\ +60 \\ \hline \end{array} \quad \begin{array}{r} 28 \\ +11 \\ \hline \end{array}$$

4. How many buttons are left?

28 →

Use 6.

____ tens ____ ones

____ are left.

5. Ring the better answer.

$$\begin{array}{r} 24 \\ -\ 6 \\ \hline \end{array}$$

more than 20

less than 20

6. Subtract.

$$\begin{array}{r} 68 \\ -24 \\ \hline \end{array} \quad \begin{array}{r} 86 \\ -35 \\ \hline \end{array} \quad \begin{array}{r} 48 \\ -16 \\ \hline \end{array} \quad \begin{array}{r} 24 \\ -13 \\ \hline \end{array} \quad \begin{array}{r} 59 \\ -26 \\ \hline \end{array} \quad \begin{array}{r} 73 \\ -20 \\ \hline \end{array}$$

Name ______________________________

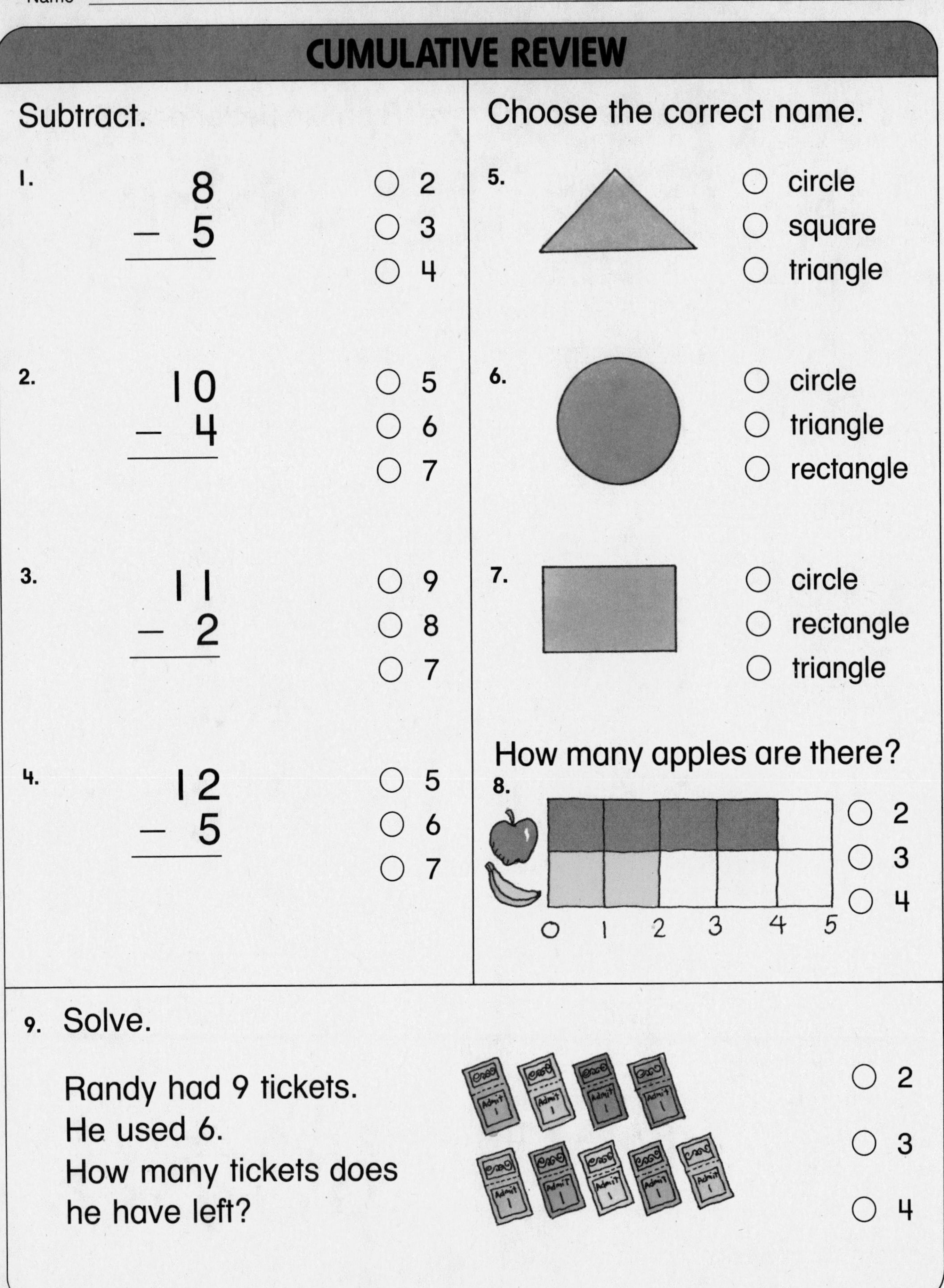

CUMULATIVE REVIEW

Subtract.

1. $8 - 5$

   ○ 2
   ○ 3
   ○ 4

2. $10 - 4$

   ○ 5
   ○ 6
   ○ 7

3. $11 - 2$

   ○ 9
   ○ 8
   ○ 7

4. $12 - 5$

   ○ 5
   ○ 6
   ○ 7

Choose the correct name.

5. ○ circle
   ○ square
   ○ triangle

6. ○ circle
   ○ triangle
   ○ rectangle

7. ○ circle
   ○ rectangle
   ○ triangle

How many apples are there?

8.

   ○ 2
   ○ 3
   ○ 4

9. Solve.

Randy had 9 tickets.
He used 6.
How many tickets does he have left?

○ 2
○ 3
○ 4

Name ______________________

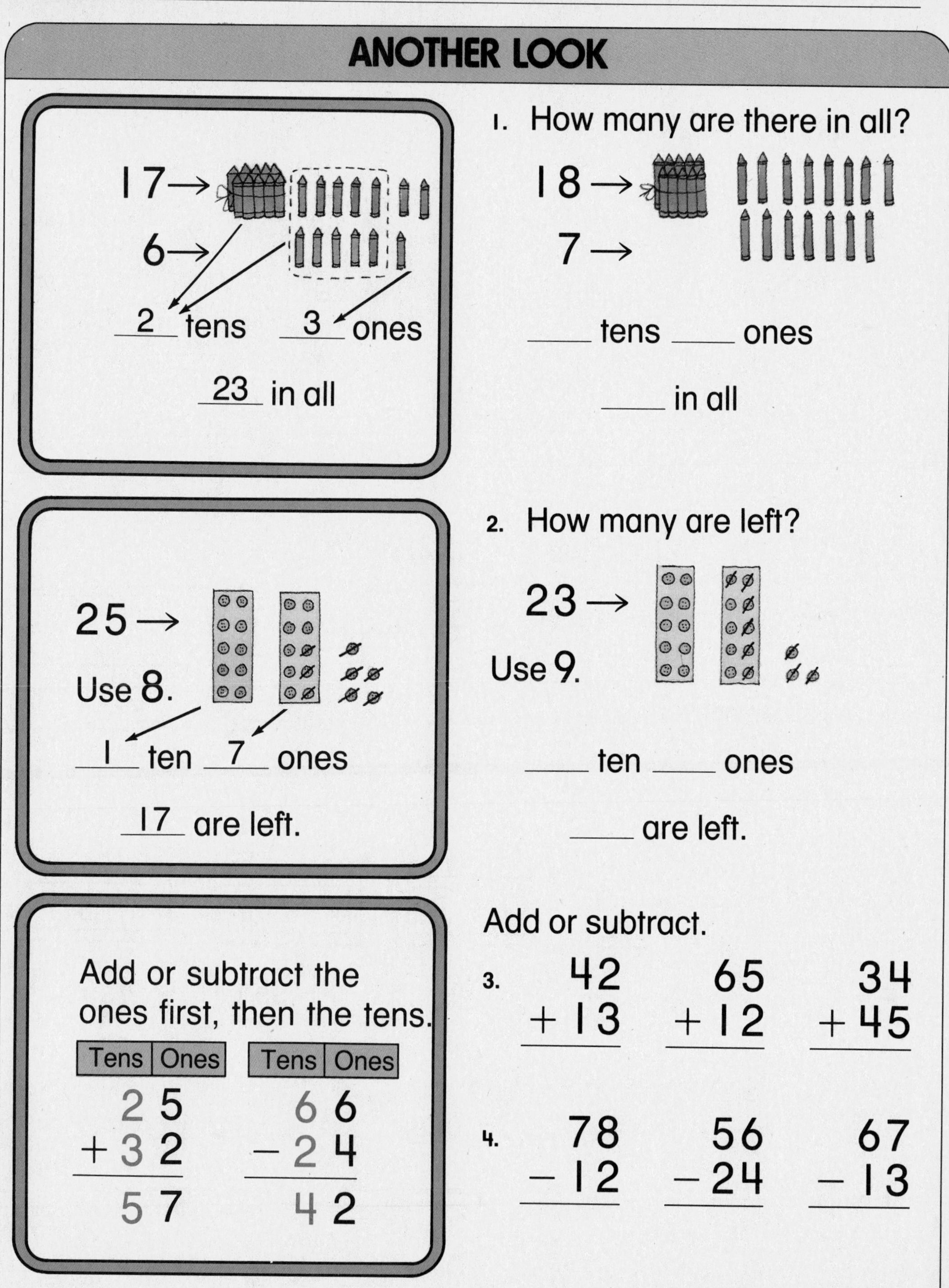
ANOTHER LOOK
17 →
6 →
2 tens 3 ones
23 in all
1. How many are there in all?
18 →
7 →
____ tens ____ ones
____ in all
25 →
Use 8.
1 ten 7 ones
17 are left.
2. How many are left?
23 →
Use 9.
____ ten ____ ones
____ are left.
Add or subtract the ones first, then the tens.
Tens Ones
25 + 32 = 57
Tens Ones
66 − 24 = 42
Add or subtract.
3. 42 + 13
65 + 12
34 + 45
4. 78 − 12
56 − 24
67 − 13

Name ______________________________

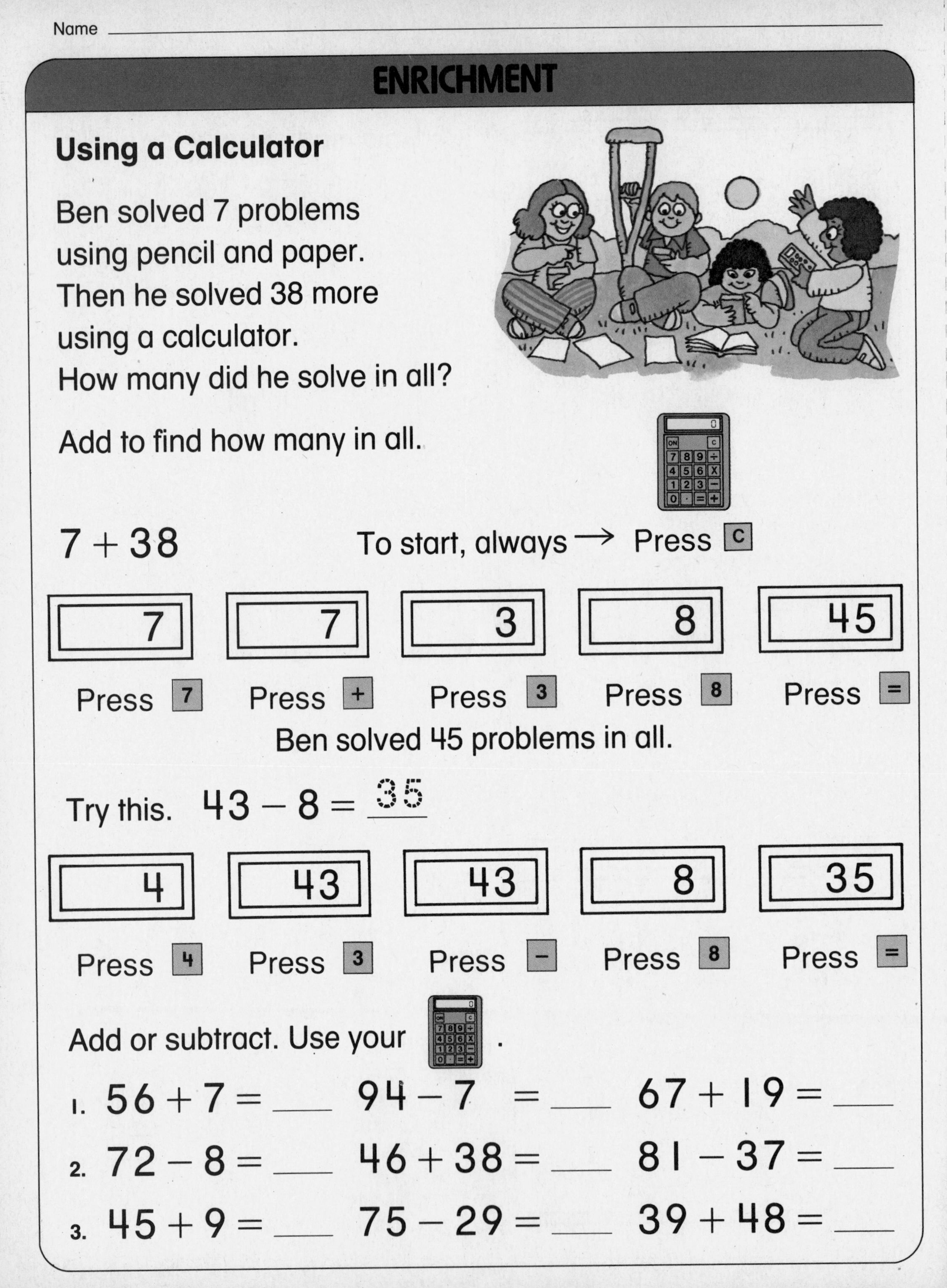

ENRICHMENT

Using a Calculator

Ben solved 7 problems
using pencil and paper.
Then he solved 38 more
using a calculator.
How many did he solve in all?

Add to find how many in all.

$7 + 38$

To start, always → Press C

7	7	3	8	45
Press 7	Press +	Press 3	Press 8	Press =

Ben solved 45 problems in all.

Try this. $43 - 8 =$ 35

4	43	43	8	35
Press 4	Press 3	Press −	Press 8	Press =

Add or subtract. Use your calculator.

1. $56 + 7 =$ ____ $94 - 7 =$ ____ $67 + 19 =$ ____
2. $72 - 8 =$ ____ $46 + 38 =$ ____ $81 - 37 =$ ____
3. $45 + 9 =$ ____ $75 - 29 =$ ____ $39 + 48 =$ ____

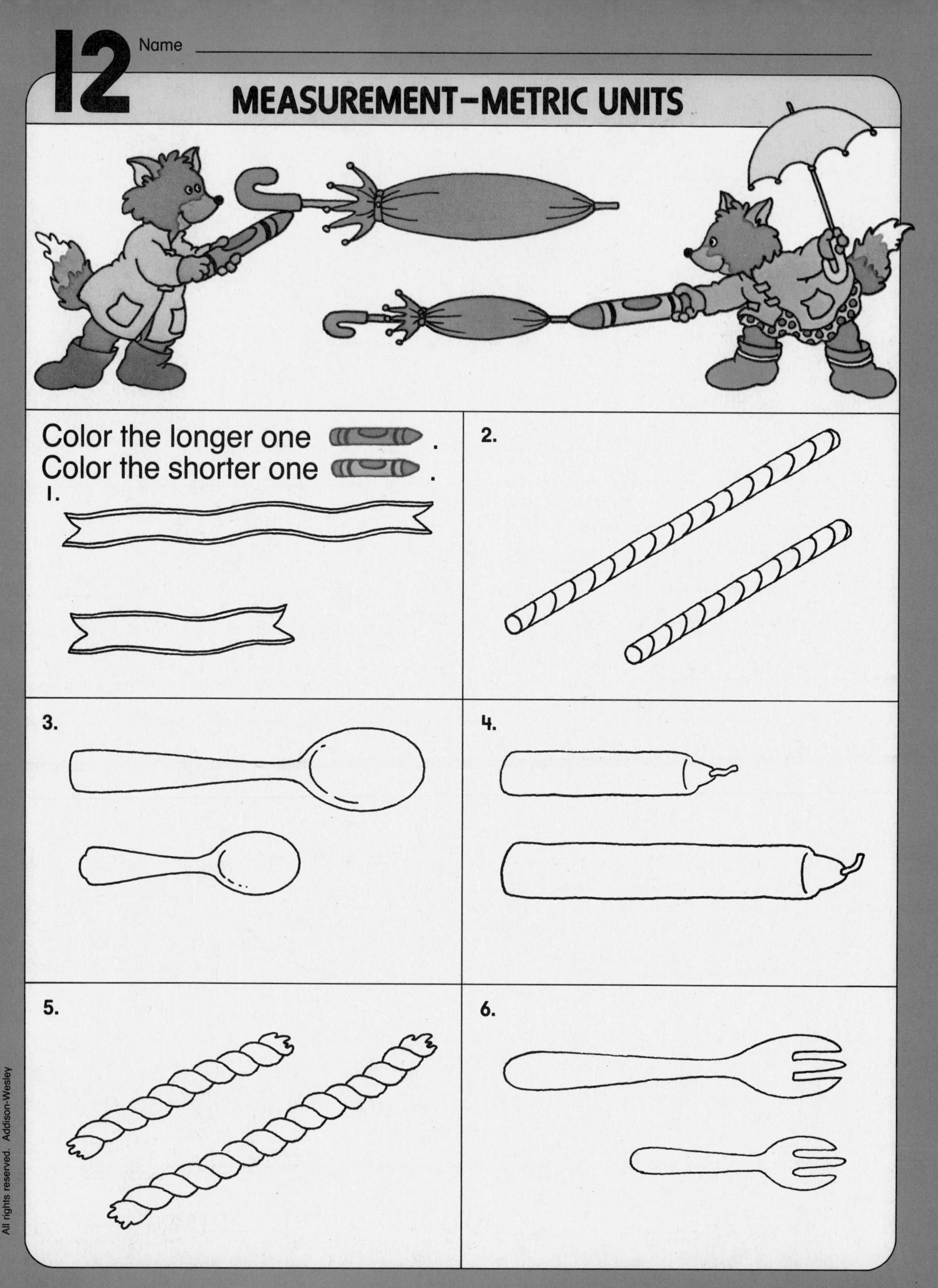
12
Name
MEASUREMENT—METRIC UNITS
Color the longer one .
Color the shorter one .
1.
2.
3.
4.
5.
6.

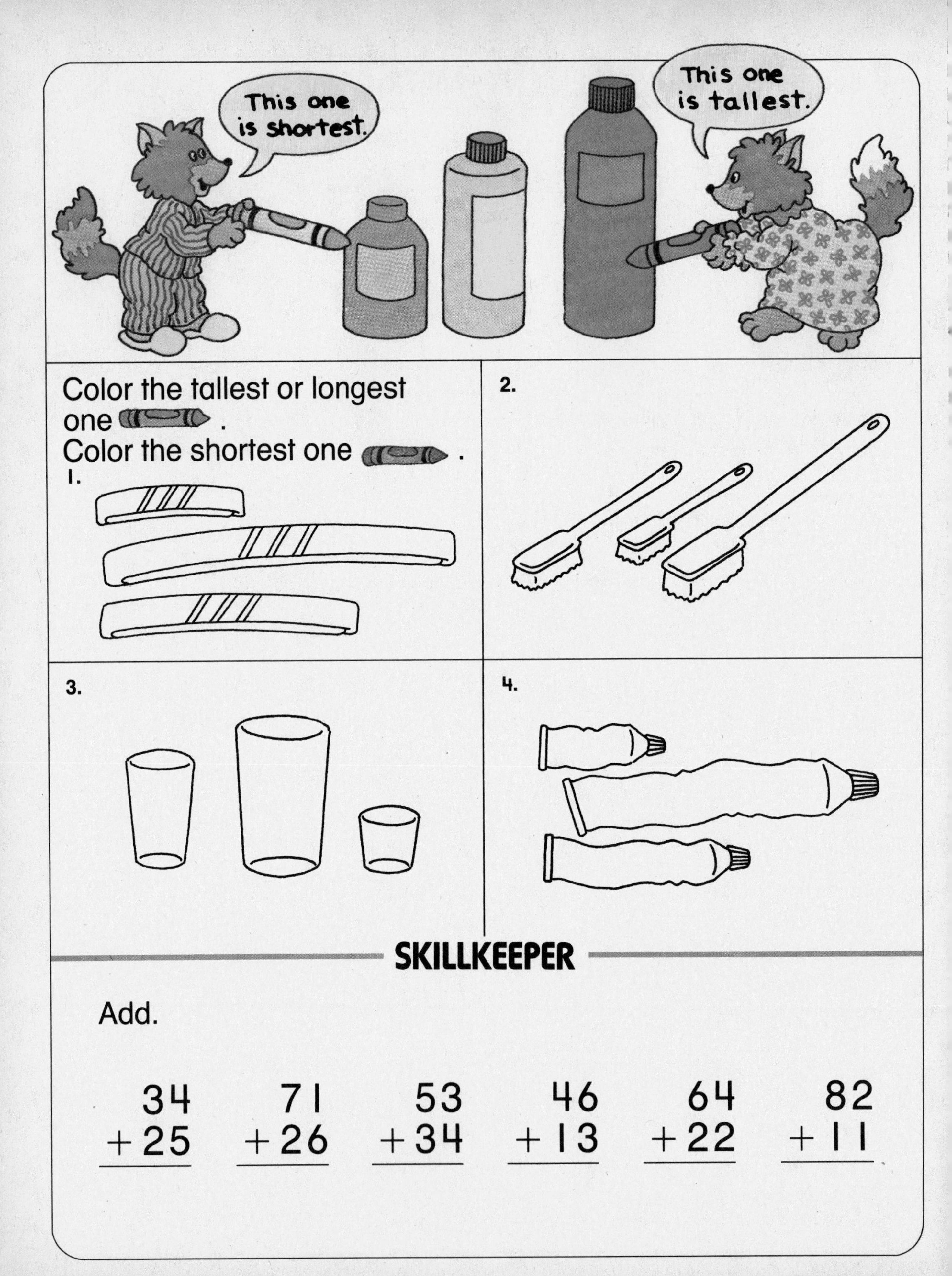
This one is shortest.
This one is tallest.
Color the tallest or longest one .
Color the shortest one .
1.
2.
3.
4.
SKILLKEEPER
Add.
34 + 25
71 + 26
53 + 34
46 + 13
64 + 22
82 + 11

Name ______________________________

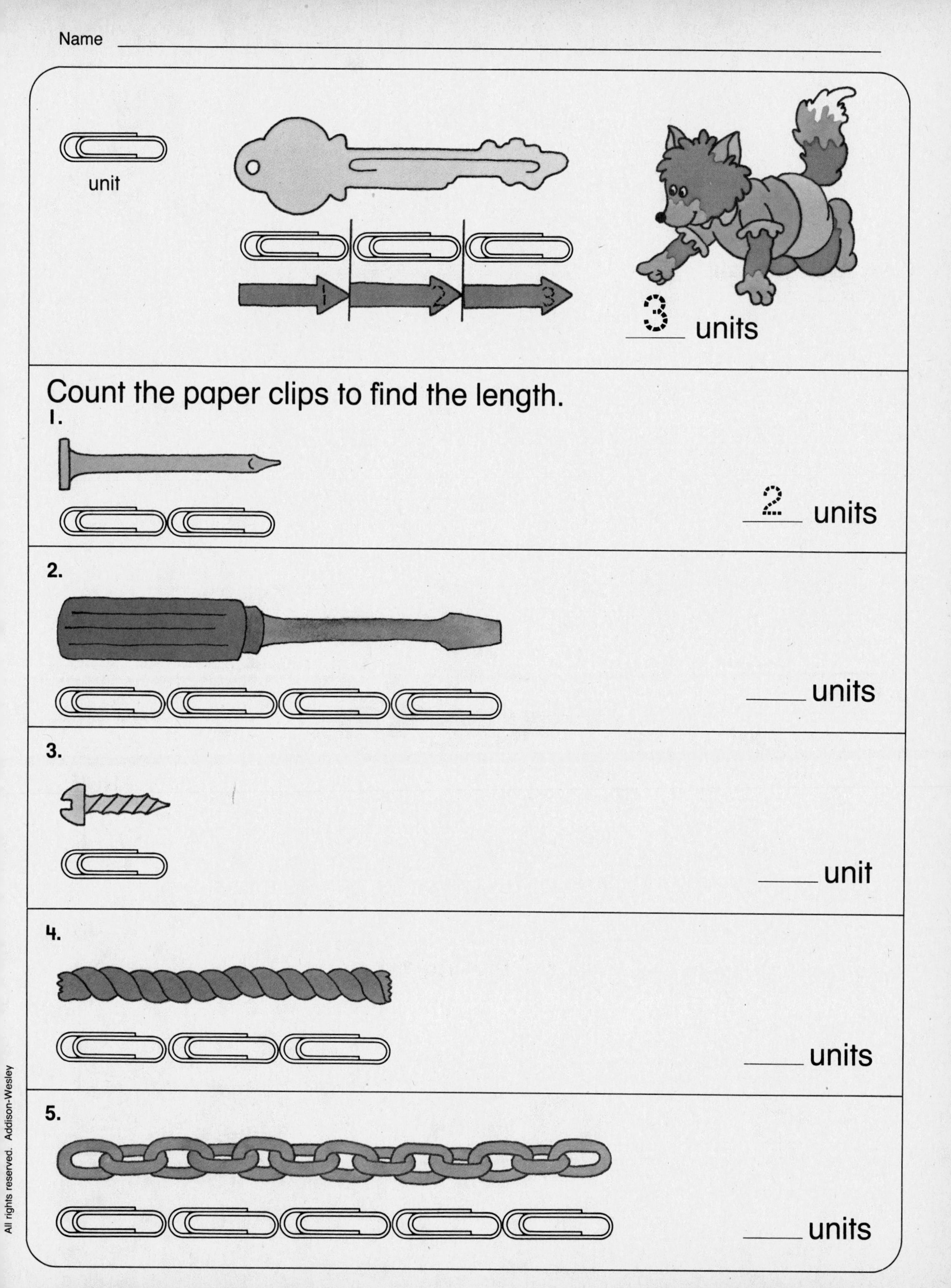
unit
1
2
3
3 units
Count the paper clips to find the length.
1.
2 units
2.
_____ units
3.
_____ unit
4.
_____ units
5.
_____ units

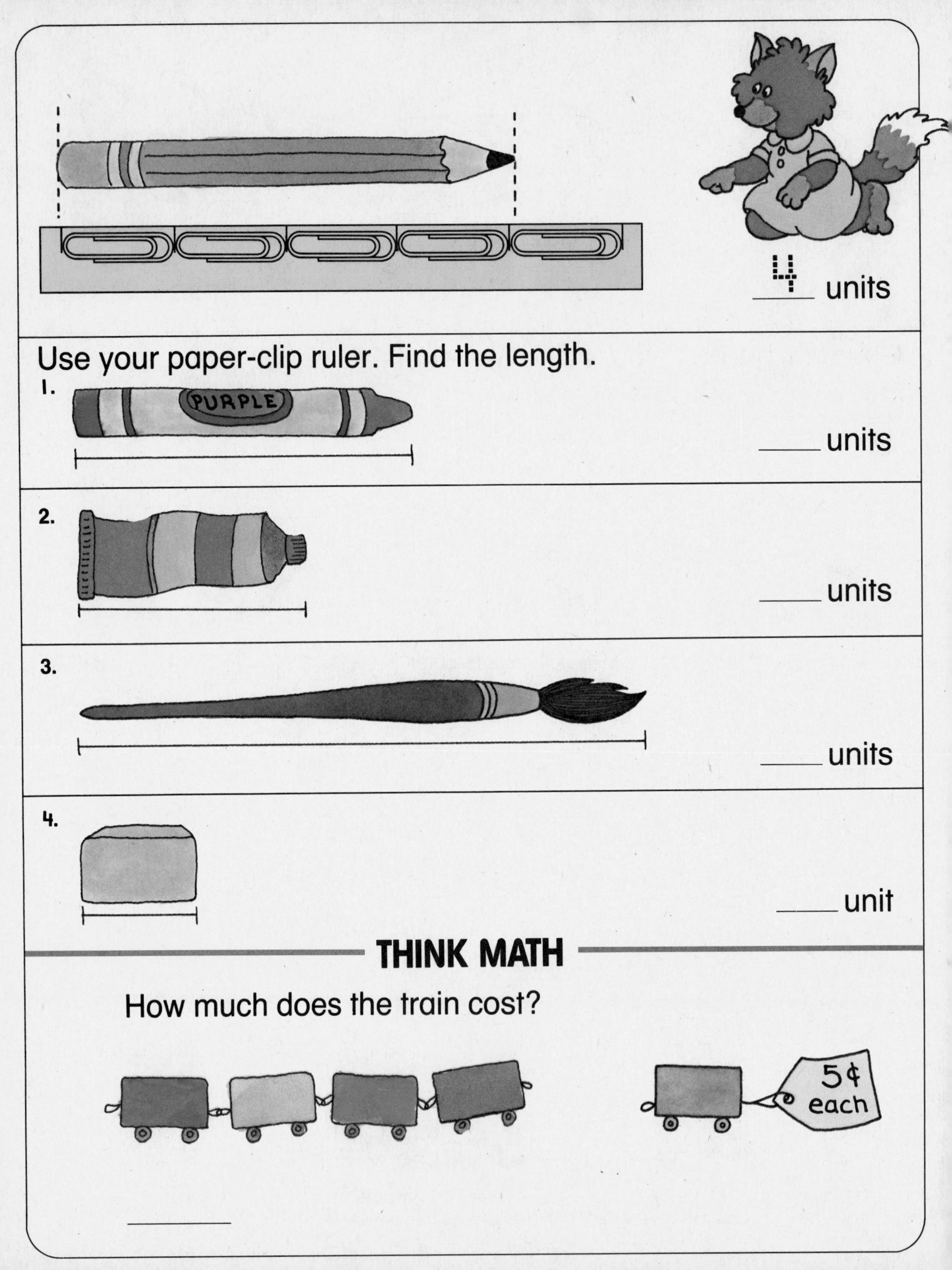

Use your paper-clip ruler. Find the length.

1. ____ units

2. ____ units

3. ____ units

4. ____ unit

THINK MATH

How much does the train cost?

____

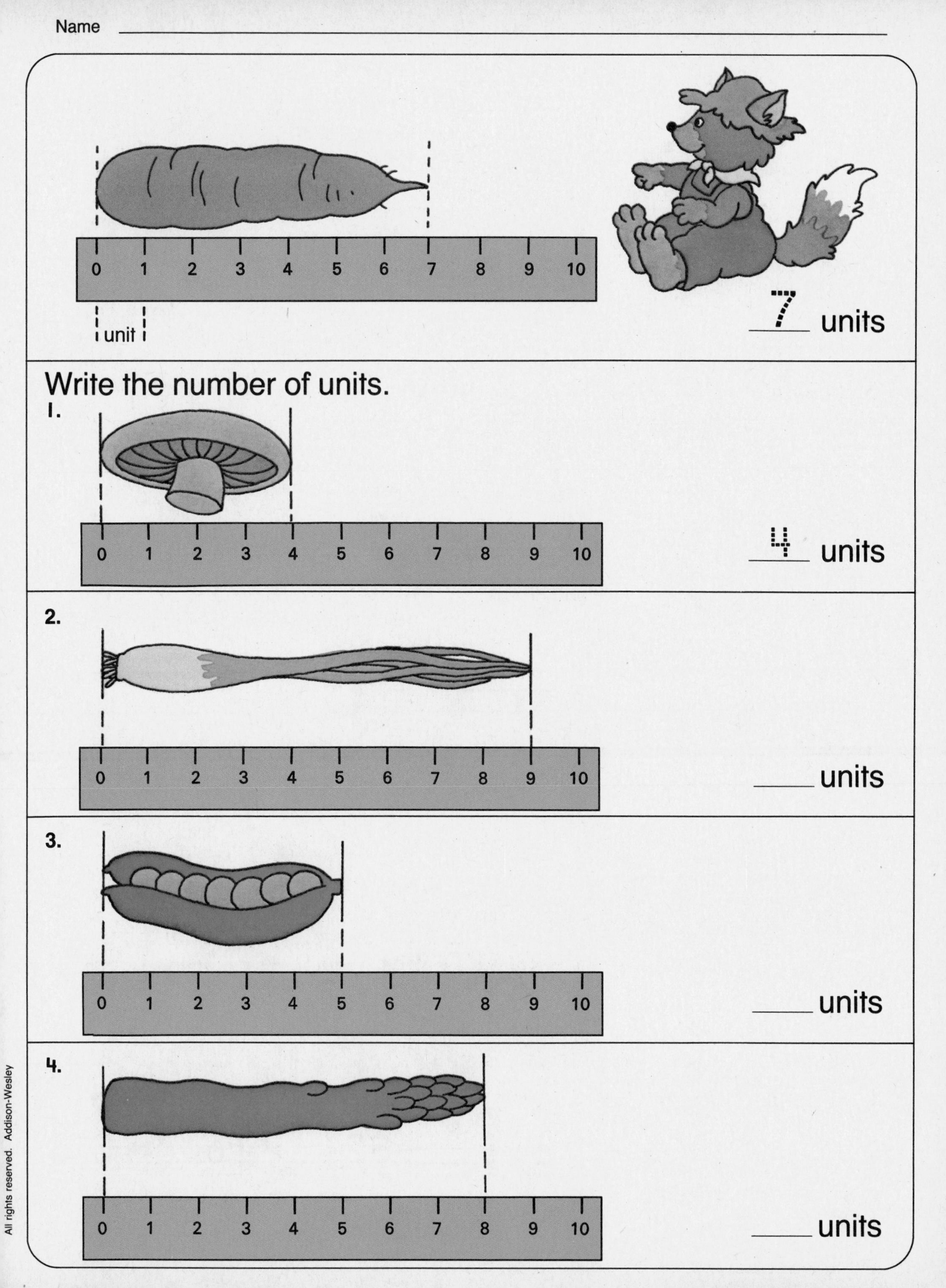
Name
0 1 2 3 4 5 6 7 8 9 10
unit
7 units
Write the number of units.
1.
0 1 2 3 4 5 6 7 8 9 10
4 units
2.
0 1 2 3 4 5 6 7 8 9 10
units
3.
0 1 2 3 4 5 6 7 8 9 10
units
4.
0 1 2 3 4 5 6 7 8 9 10
units

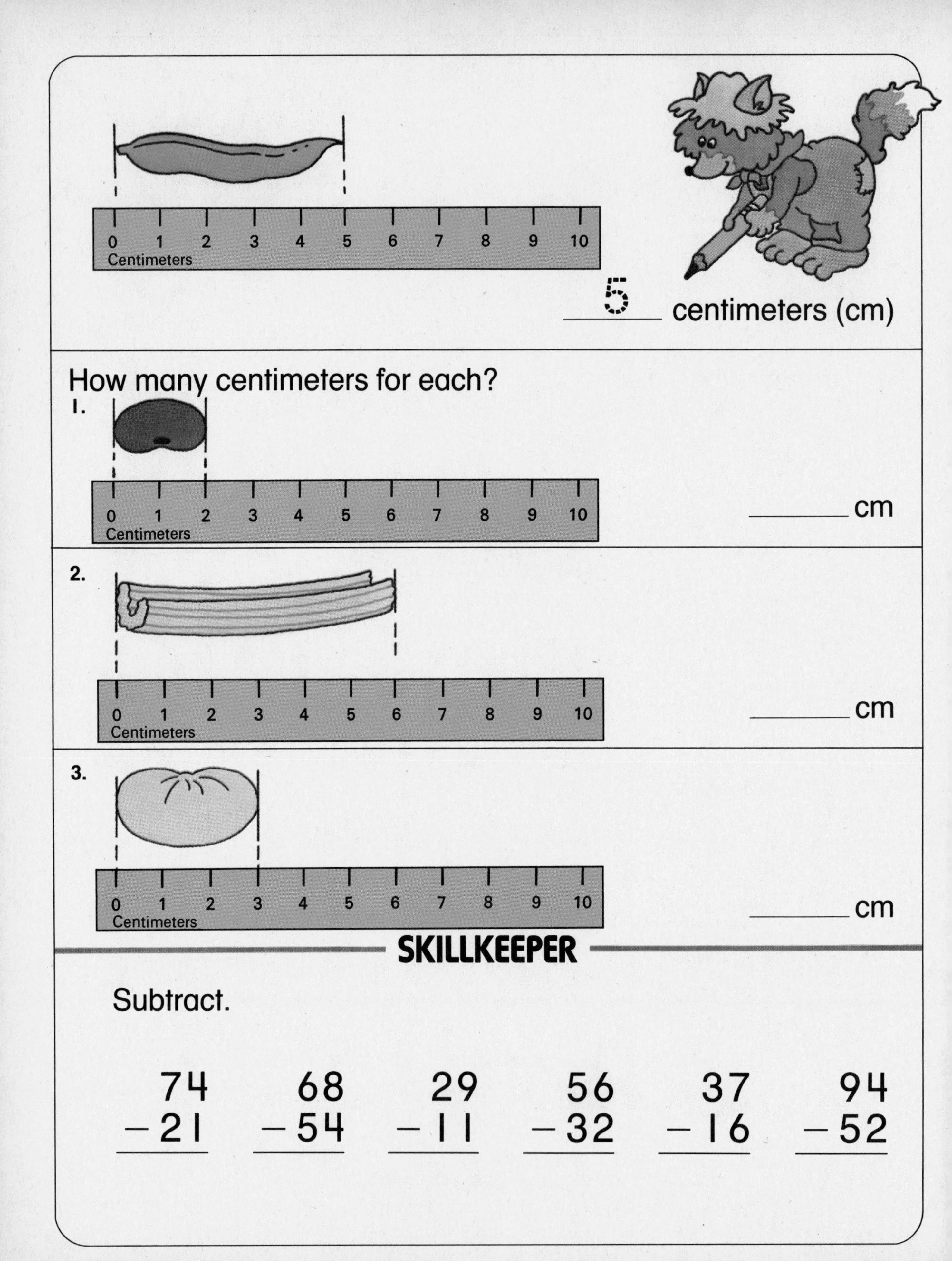

How many centimeters for each?

1.

_____ cm

2.

_____ cm

3.

_____ cm

SKILLKEEPER

Subtract.

74	68	29	56	37	94
− 21	− 54	− 11	− 32	− 16	− 52

Name ____________________

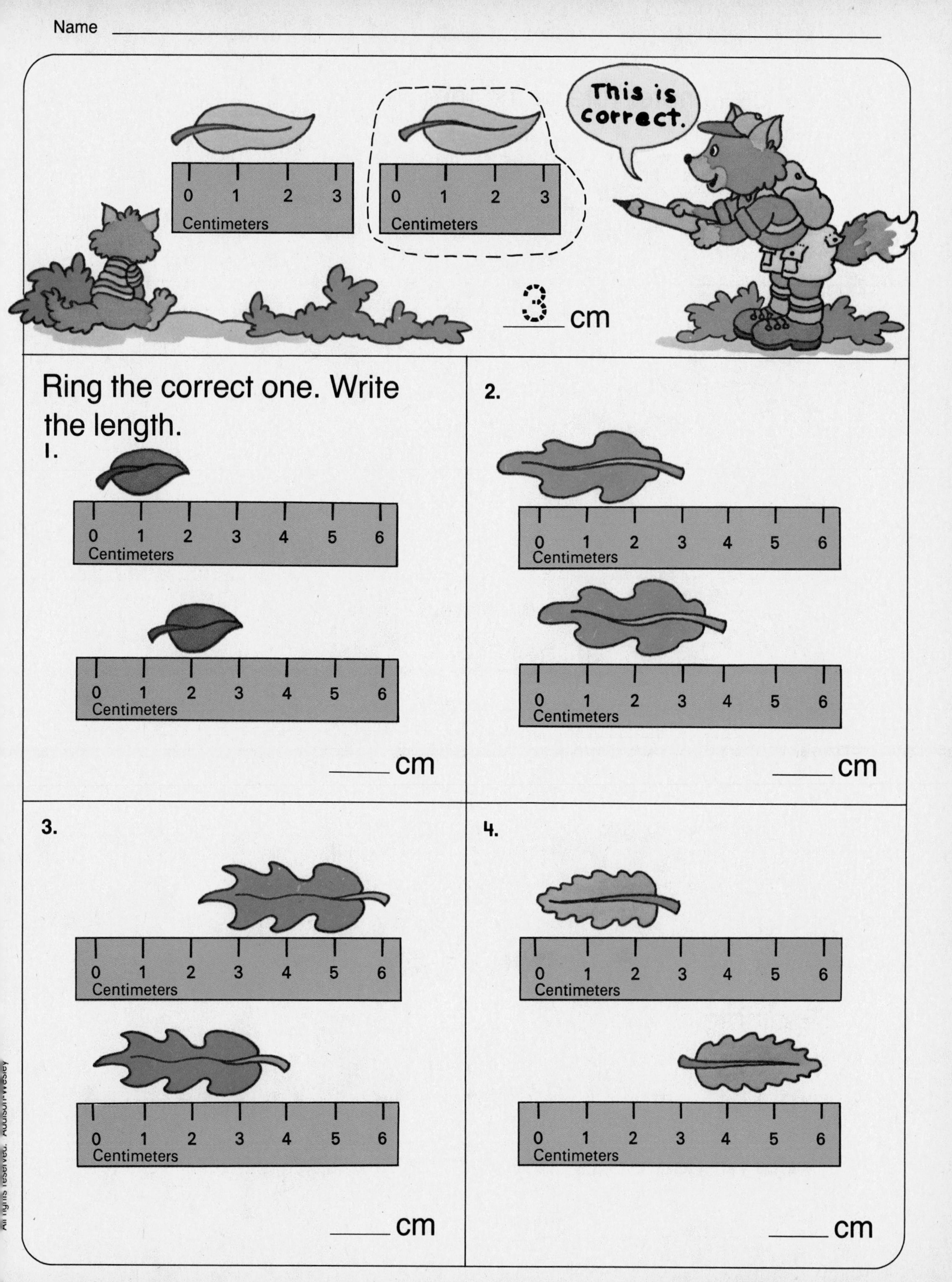
This is correct.
0 1 2 3
Centimeters
3 cm
Ring the correct one. Write the length.
1.
0 1 2 3 4 5 6
Centimeters
___ cm
2.
___ cm
3.
___ cm
4.
___ cm

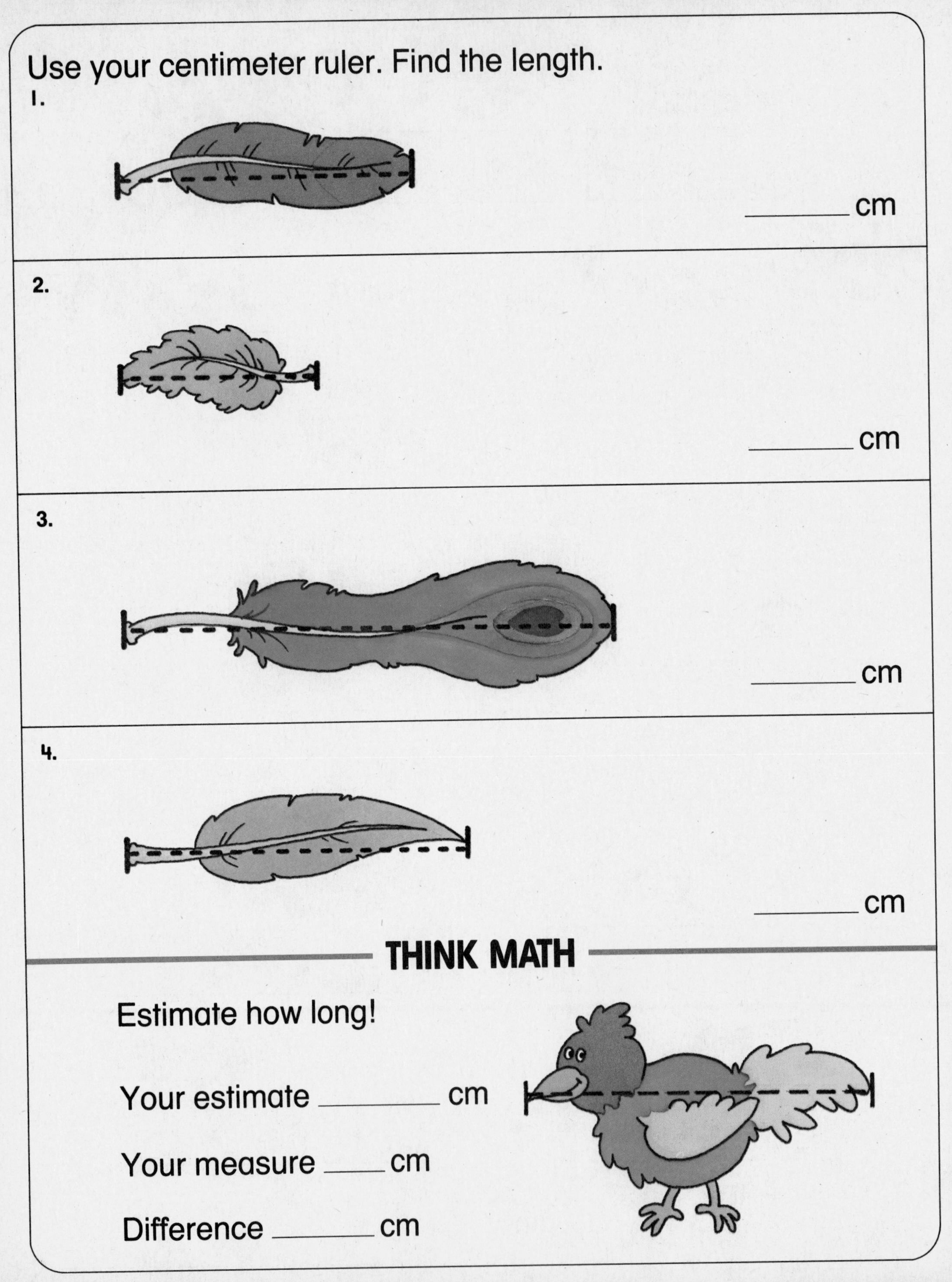

Use your centimeter ruler. Find the length.

1.

_______ cm

2.

_______ cm

3.

_______ cm

4.

_______ cm

THINK MATH

Estimate how long!

Your estimate _______ cm

Your measure _____ cm

Difference _______ cm

Name ________________________________

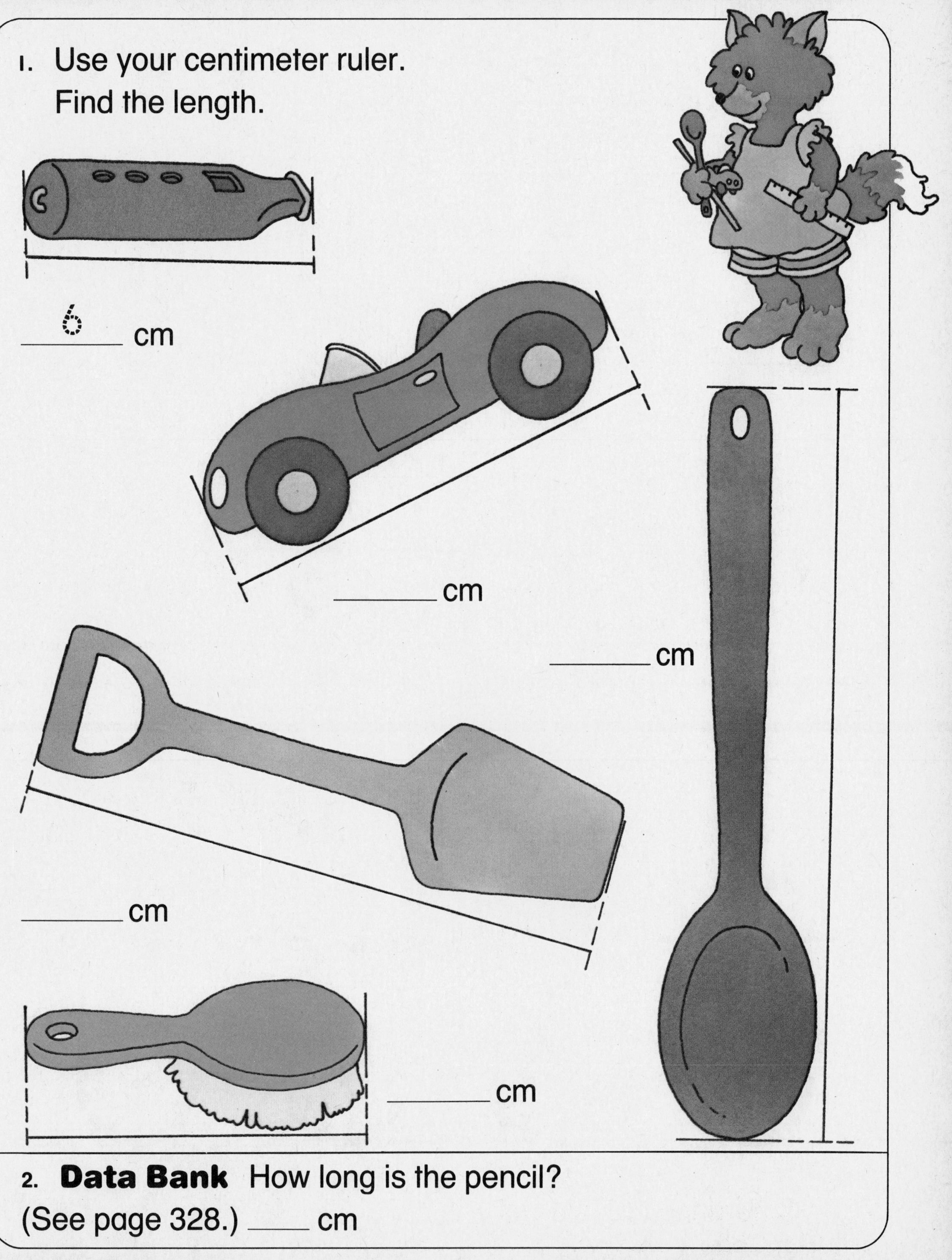

1. Use your centimeter ruler.
Find the length.

6 cm

_____ cm

_____ cm

_____ cm

_____ cm

2. **Data Bank** How long is the pencil?
(See page 328.) _____ cm

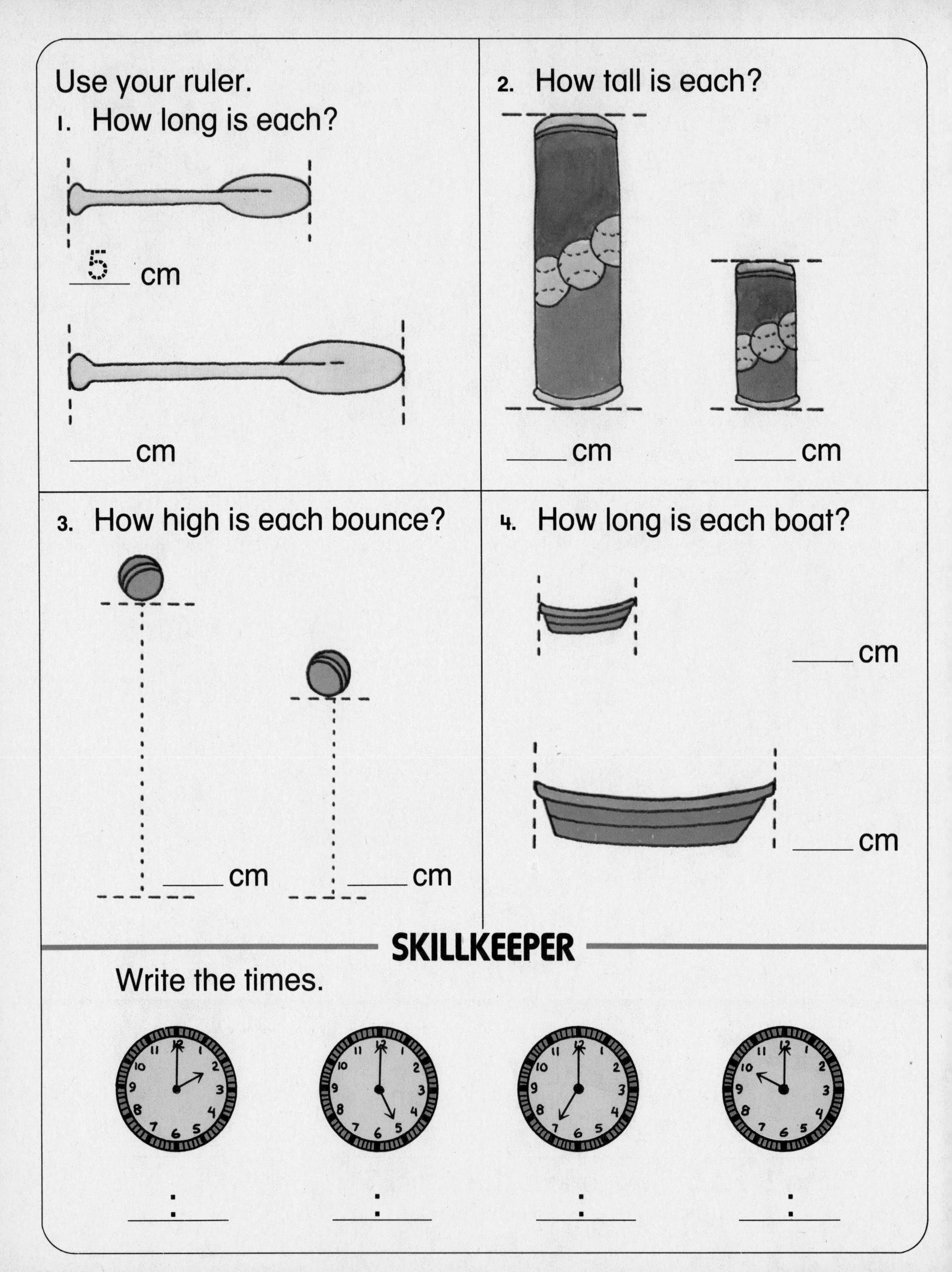

Use your ruler.

1. How long is each?

5 cm

___ cm

2. How tall is each?

___ cm ___ cm

3. How high is each bounce?

___ cm ___ cm

4. How long is each boat?

___ cm

___ cm

SKILLKEEPER

Write the times.

___:___ ___:___ ___:___ ___:___

Name ______________________________

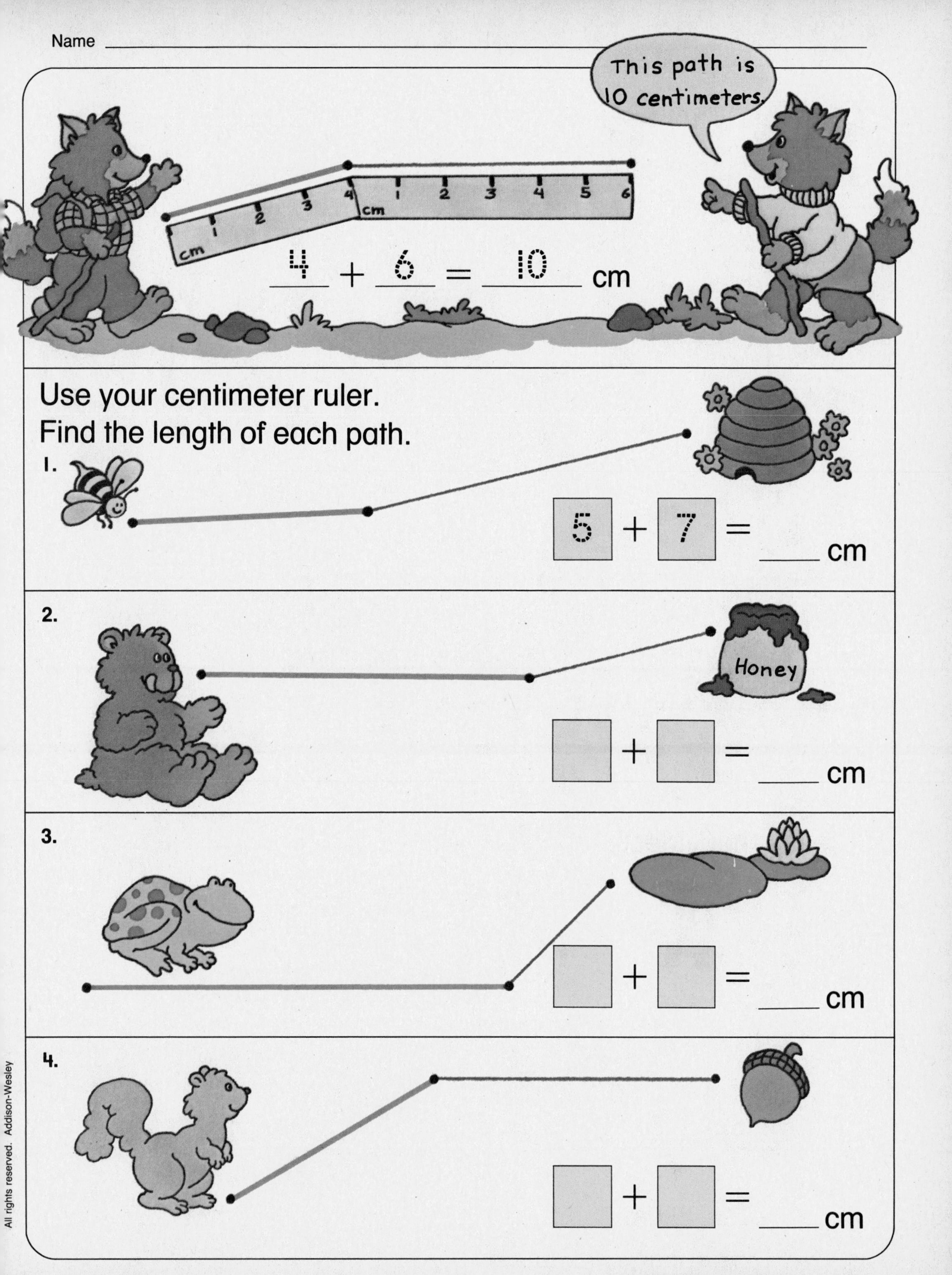

This path is 10 centimeters.

___4___ + ___6___ = ___10___ cm

Use your centimeter ruler.
Find the length of each path.

1. 5 + 7 = ____ cm

2. ☐ + ☐ = ____ cm

3. ☐ + ☐ = ____ cm

4. ☐ + ☐ = ____ cm

Map of the Zoo
ZOO
Use the map. Measure the distances.
ZOO
cm
cm
cm
ZOO
cm
ZOO
cm

Name ______________________________

1. Estimate. Ring things that hold more than a liter.

2. Estimate. Ring things that hold less than a liter.

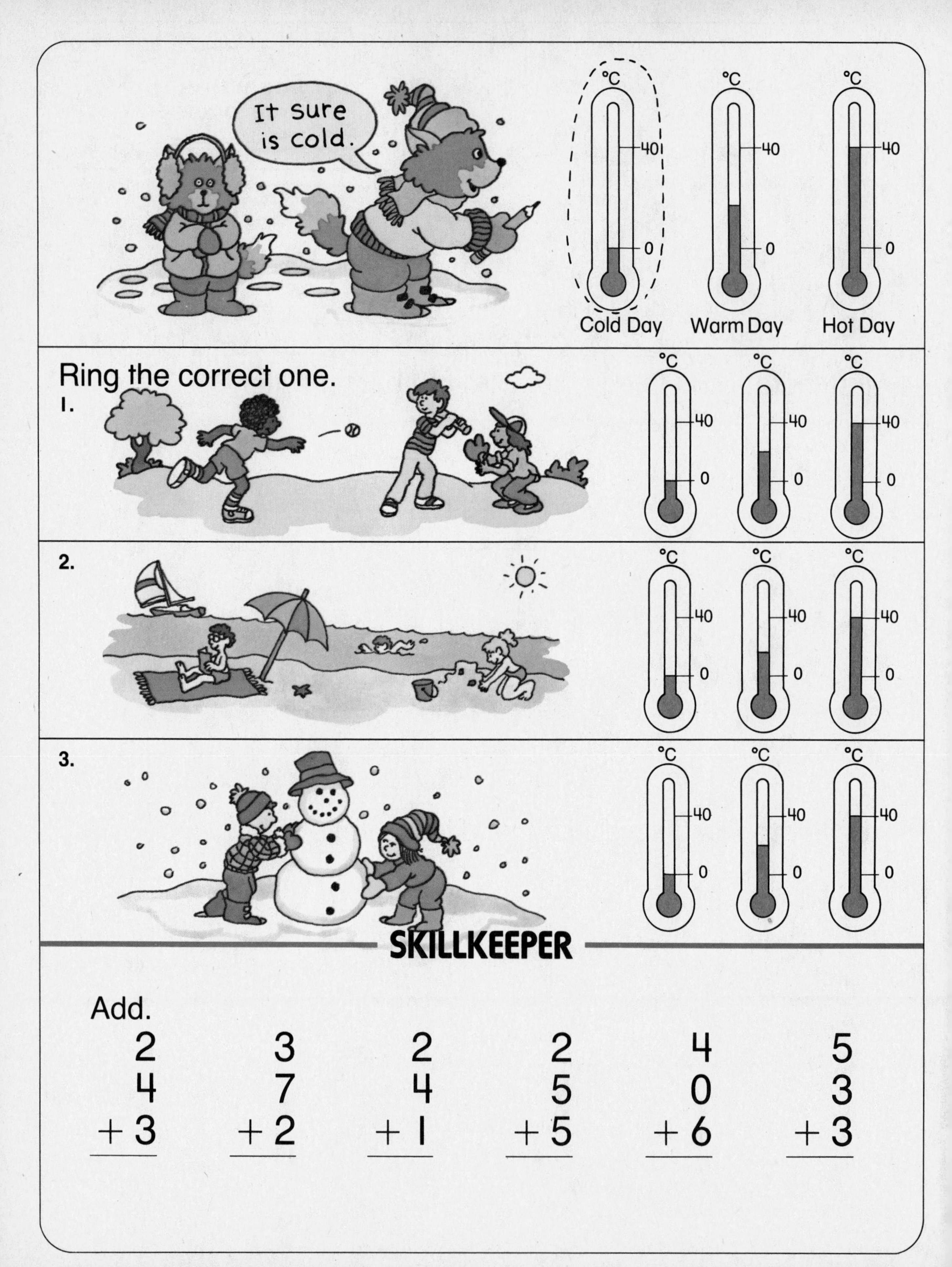

Ring the correct one.

1.

2.

3.

SKILLKEEPER

Add.

2	3	2	2	4	5
4	7	4	5	0	3
+ 3	+ 2	+ 1	+ 5	+ 6	+ 3

Name ______________________________

1. Estimate. Ring the objects that weigh more than a kilogram.

2. Estimate. Ring the objects that weigh less than a kilogram.

Problem-Solving Strategy

Look for a pattern. Write the missing numbers.

Name 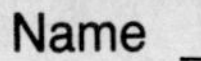

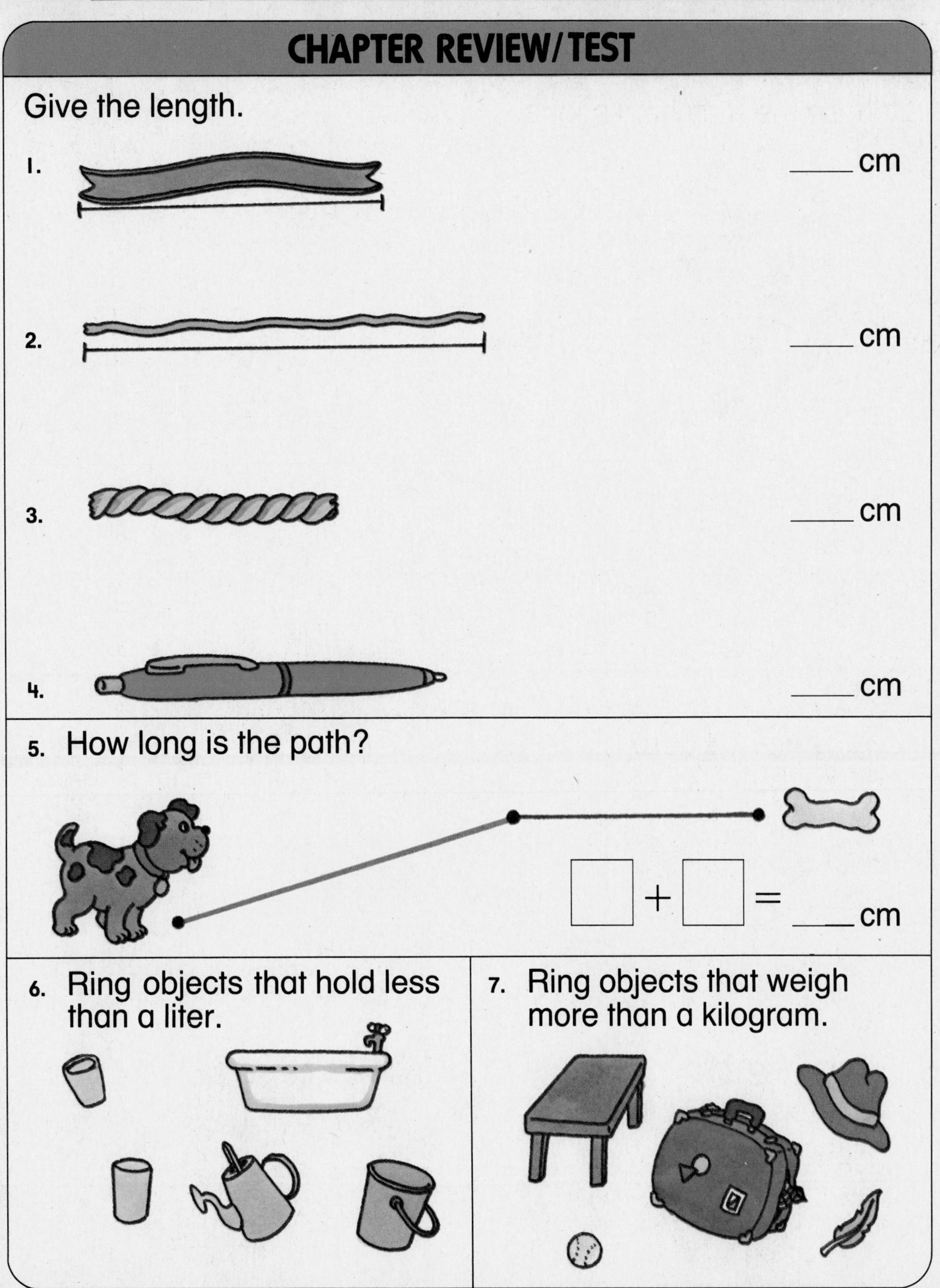

CHAPTER REVIEW/TEST

Give the length.

1. ____ cm

2. ____ cm

3. ____ cm

4. ____ cm

5. How long is the path?

☐ + ☐ = ____ cm

6. Ring objects that hold less than a liter.

7. Ring objects that weigh more than a kilogram.

Name ___________________________

CUMULATIVE REVIEW

Choose the matching shape.

1.
- ○ ◯
- ○ □
- ○ △

2.
- ○ ◯
- ○ □
- ○ △

3. How many corners?
- ○ 3
- ○ 4
- ○ 5

4. How many sides?
- ○ 3
- ○ 4
- ○ 5

Add.

5. $$\begin{array}{r} 23 \\ +52 \\ \hline \end{array}$$
- ○ 74
- ○ 65
- ○ 75

6. $$\begin{array}{r} 54¢ \\ +35¢ \\ \hline \end{array}$$
- ○ 88¢
- ○ 89¢
- ○ 90¢

Subtract.

7. $$\begin{array}{r} 63 \\ -21 \\ \hline \end{array}$$
- ○ 42
- ○ 32
- ○ 43

8. $$\begin{array}{r} 78¢ \\ -52¢ \\ \hline \end{array}$$
- ○ 24¢
- ○ 25¢
- ○ 26¢

9. Solve.

Katy had 79¢.
She spent 30¢ for a toy.
How much money did she have left?

- ○ 40¢
- ○ 49¢
- ○ 39¢

Name ______

ANOTHER LOOK

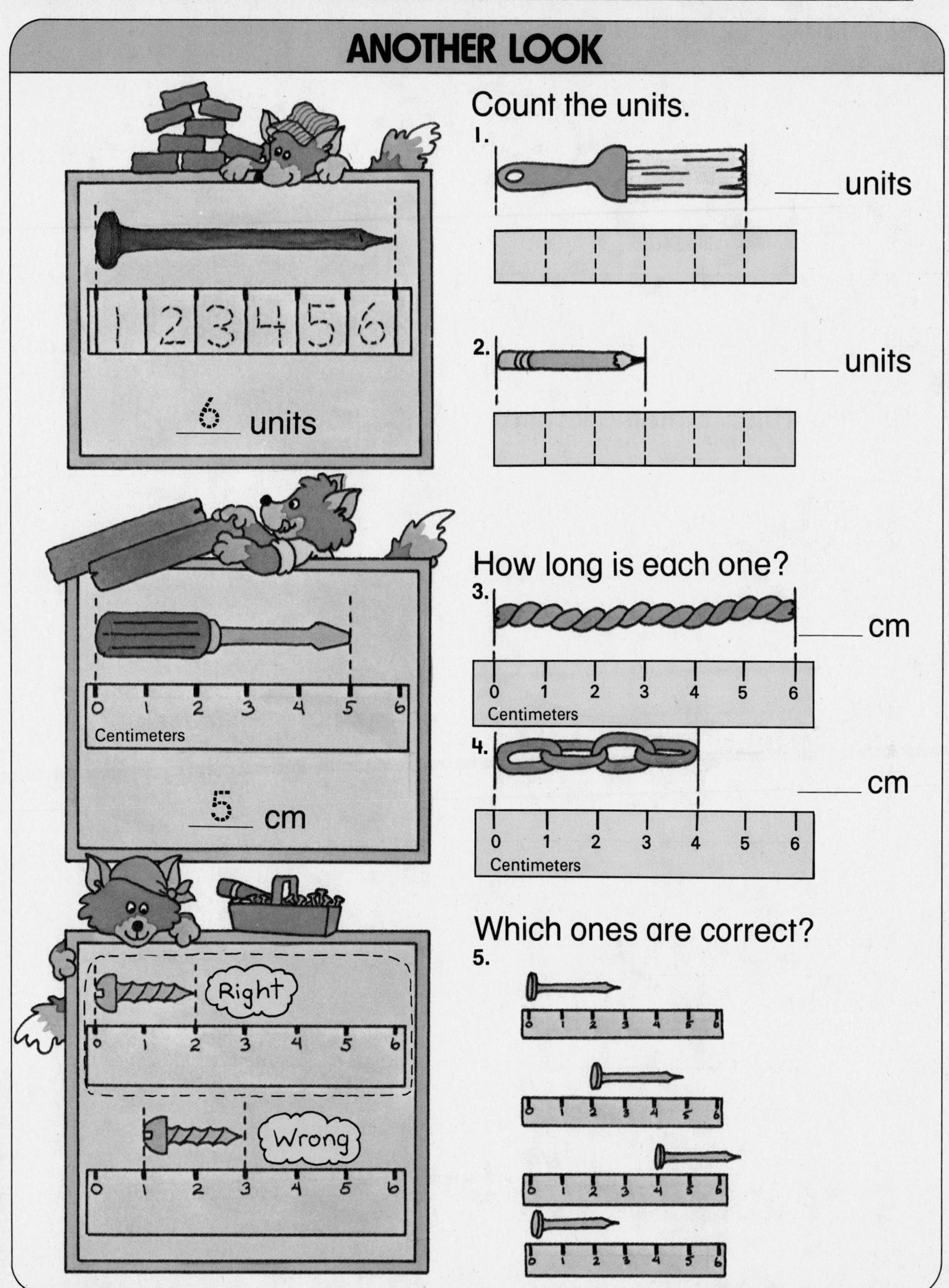

Count the units.

1. ____ units

2. ____ units

How long is each one?

3. ____ cm

0 1 2 3 4 5 6
Centimeters

4. ____ cm

0 1 2 3 4 5 6
Centimeters

Which ones are correct?

5.

Name ____________________

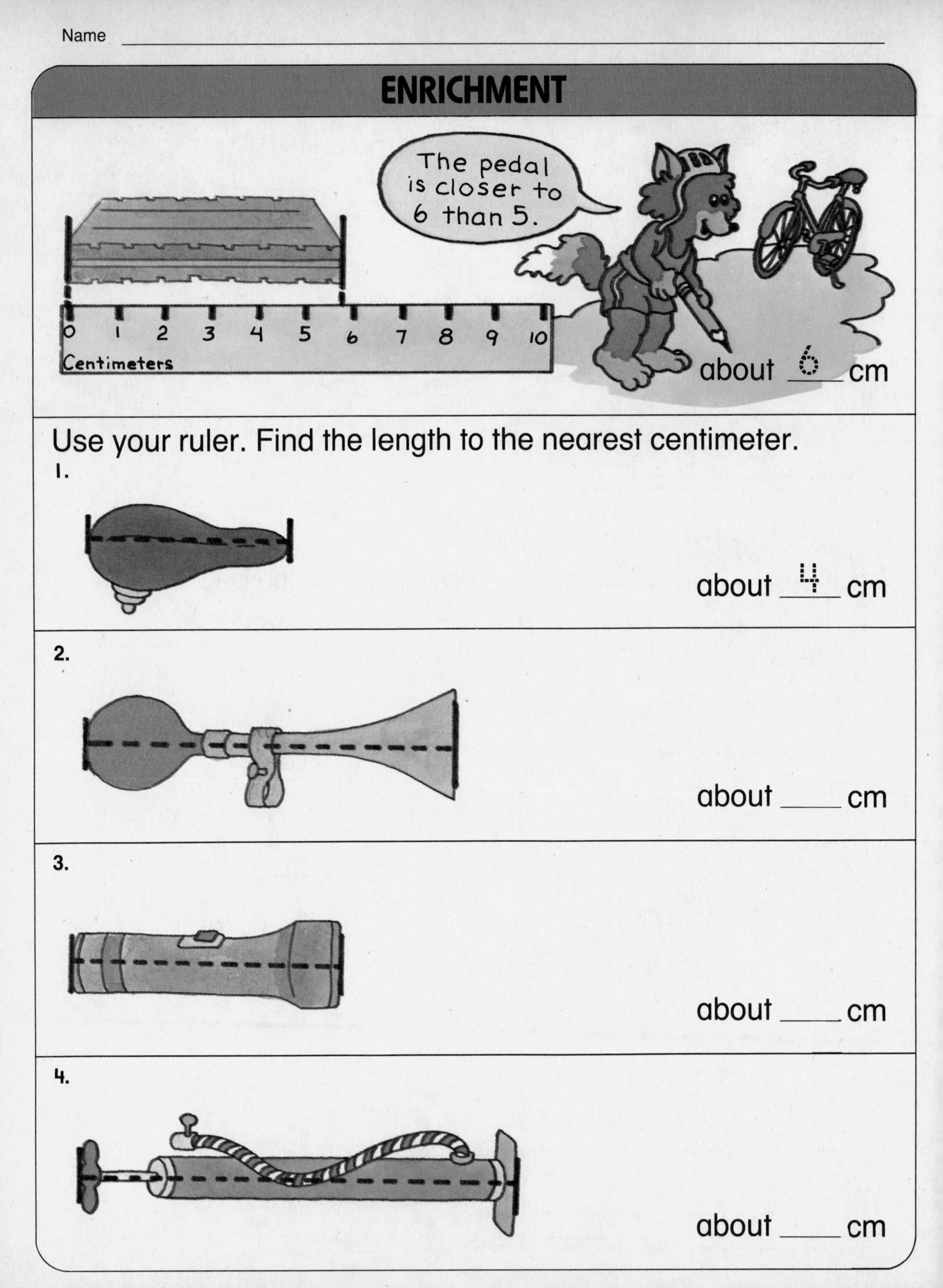

ENRICHMENT
The pedal is closer to 6 than 5.
0 1 2 3 4 5 6 7 8 9 10
Centimeters
about 6 cm
Use your ruler. Find the length to the nearest centimeter.
1.
about 4 cm
2.
about ____ cm
3.
about ____ cm
4.
about ____ cm

13 Name ______

SUMS AND DIFFERENCES TO 18

Find the sums.

1.

These are more doubles.

$6 + 6 =$ ______

2.

February						
1	2	3	4	5	6	7
8	9	10	11	12	13	14
15	16	17	18	19	20	21
22	23	24	25	26	27	28

$7 + 7 =$ ______

3.

CRAYONS 16

$8 + 8 =$ ______

4.

$9 + 9 =$ ______

Add.

5. $\begin{array}{r} 7 \\ +7 \\ \hline \end{array}$ $\begin{array}{r} 4 \\ +5 \\ \hline \end{array}$ $\begin{array}{r} 2 \\ +5 \\ \hline \end{array}$ $\begin{array}{r} 6 \\ +6 \\ \hline \end{array}$ $\begin{array}{r} 5 \\ +6 \\ \hline \end{array}$ $\begin{array}{r} 9 \\ +9 \\ \hline \end{array}$

6. $\begin{array}{r} 6 \\ +2 \\ \hline \end{array}$ $\begin{array}{r} 8 \\ +8 \\ \hline \end{array}$ $\begin{array}{r} 4 \\ +4 \\ \hline \end{array}$ $\begin{array}{r} 7 \\ +7 \\ \hline \end{array}$ $\begin{array}{r} 2 \\ +4 \\ \hline \end{array}$ $\begin{array}{r} 6 \\ +6 \\ \hline \end{array}$

7. $\begin{array}{r} 5 \\ +5 \\ \hline \end{array}$ $\begin{array}{r} 9 \\ +9 \\ \hline \end{array}$ $\begin{array}{r} 2 \\ +3 \\ \hline \end{array}$ $\begin{array}{r} 4 \\ +3 \\ \hline \end{array}$ $\begin{array}{r} 8 \\ +8 \\ \hline \end{array}$ $\begin{array}{r} 3 \\ +3 \\ \hline \end{array}$

Add.

1.	$\begin{array}{r} 6 \\ +6 \\ \hline \end{array}$	$\begin{array}{r} 3 \\ +4 \\ \hline \end{array}$	$\begin{array}{r} 2 \\ +5 \\ \hline \end{array}$	$\begin{array}{r} 8 \\ +8 \\ \hline \end{array}$	$\begin{array}{r} 5 \\ +3 \\ \hline \end{array}$	$\begin{array}{r} 6 \\ +1 \\ \hline \end{array}$
2.	$\begin{array}{r} 2 \\ +6 \\ \hline \end{array}$	$\begin{array}{r} 4 \\ +4 \\ \hline \end{array}$	$\begin{array}{r} 5 \\ +4 \\ \hline \end{array}$	$\begin{array}{r} 2 \\ +2 \\ \hline \end{array}$	$\begin{array}{r} 7 \\ +7 \\ \hline \end{array}$	$\begin{array}{r} 6 \\ +4 \\ \hline \end{array}$
3.	$\begin{array}{r} 9 \\ +9 \\ \hline \end{array}$	$\begin{array}{r} 2 \\ +3 \\ \hline \end{array}$	$\begin{array}{r} 8 \\ +0 \\ \hline \end{array}$	$\begin{array}{r} 3 \\ +3 \\ \hline \end{array}$	$\begin{array}{r} 1 \\ +5 \\ \hline \end{array}$	$\begin{array}{r} 4 \\ +2 \\ \hline \end{array}$
4.	$\begin{array}{r} 5 \\ +2 \\ \hline \end{array}$	$\begin{array}{r} 8 \\ +8 \\ \hline \end{array}$	$\begin{array}{r} 3 \\ +7 \\ \hline \end{array}$	$\begin{array}{r} 9 \\ +9 \\ \hline \end{array}$	$\begin{array}{r} 6 \\ +5 \\ \hline \end{array}$	$\begin{array}{r} 9 \\ +1 \\ \hline \end{array}$
5.	$\begin{array}{r} 5 \\ +5 \\ \hline \end{array}$	$\begin{array}{r} 7 \\ +2 \\ \hline \end{array}$	$\begin{array}{r} 7 \\ +7 \\ \hline \end{array}$	$\begin{array}{r} 0 \\ +9 \\ \hline \end{array}$	$\begin{array}{r} 6 \\ +6 \\ \hline \end{array}$	$\begin{array}{r} 6 \\ +3 \\ \hline \end{array}$

THINK MATH

Add or subtract "in your head."

$3 + 2 = 5$ $\quad$ $4 + 3 = 7$ $\quad$ $6 - 4$

1. $13 + 2 =$ 15 $\quad$ 2. $24 + 3 =$ 27 $\quad$ 3. $36 - 4 =$ 32

4. $12 + 5 =$ ____ $\quad$ 5. $18 - 2 =$ ____ $\quad$ 6. $32 + 4 =$ ____

7. $47 - 5 =$ ____ $\quad$ 8. $51 + 6 =$ ____ $\quad$ 9. $59 - 4 =$ ____

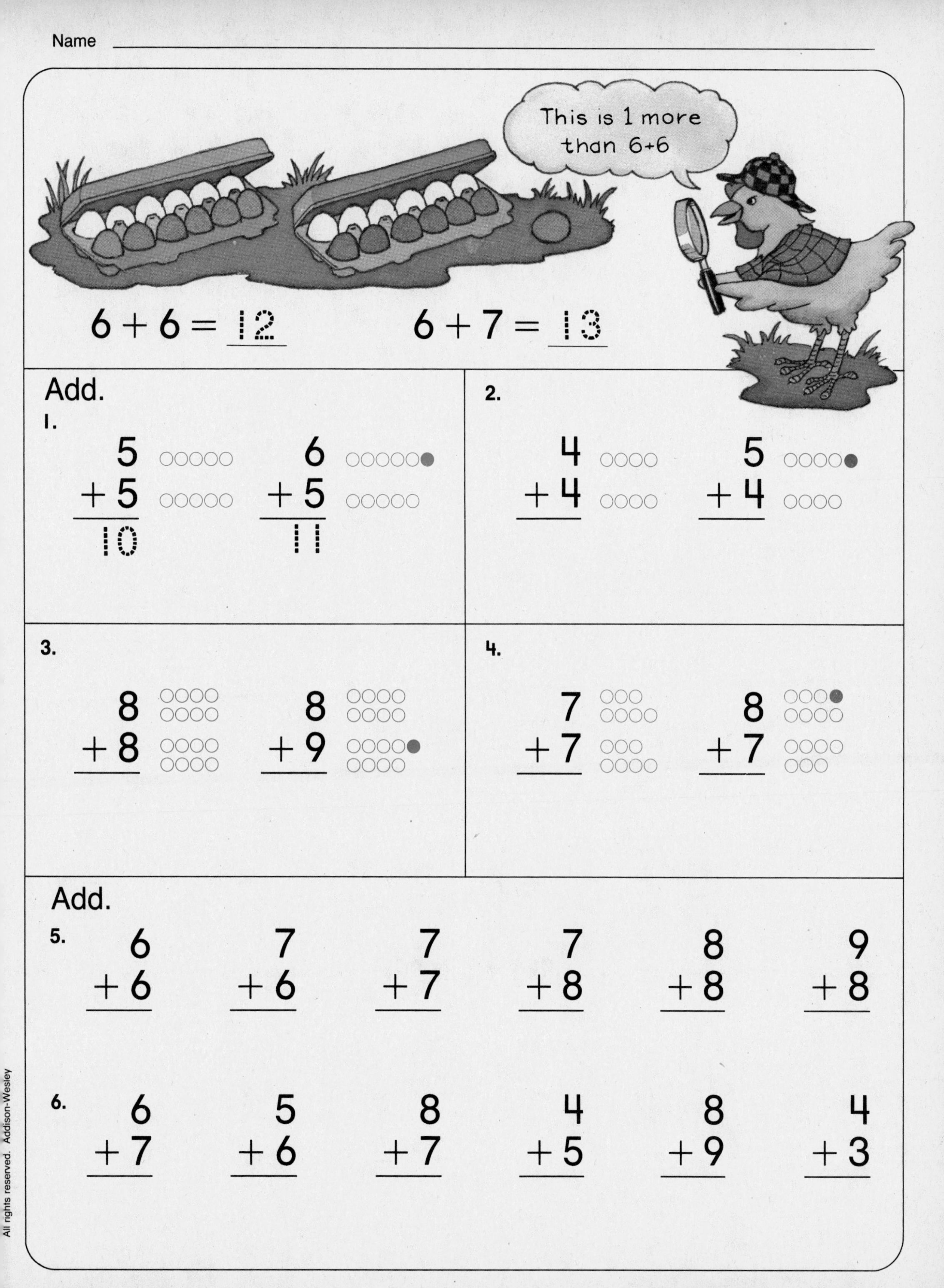

Name ____________________

This is 1 more
than 6+6

$6 + 6 = 12$ $6 + 7 = 13$

Add.

1. $\begin{array}{r} 5 \\ +5 \\ \hline 10 \end{array}$ $\begin{array}{r} 6 \\ +5 \\ \hline 11 \end{array}$

2. $\begin{array}{r} 4 \\ +4 \\ \hline \end{array}$ $\begin{array}{r} 5 \\ +4 \\ \hline \end{array}$

3. $\begin{array}{r} 8 \\ +8 \\ \hline \end{array}$ $\begin{array}{r} 8 \\ +9 \\ \hline \end{array}$

4. $\begin{array}{r} 7 \\ +7 \\ \hline \end{array}$ $\begin{array}{r} 8 \\ +7 \\ \hline \end{array}$

Add.

5. $\begin{array}{r} 6 \\ +6 \\ \hline \end{array}$ $\begin{array}{r} 7 \\ +6 \\ \hline \end{array}$ $\begin{array}{r} 7 \\ +7 \\ \hline \end{array}$ $\begin{array}{r} 7 \\ +8 \\ \hline \end{array}$ $\begin{array}{r} 8 \\ +8 \\ \hline \end{array}$ $\begin{array}{r} 9 \\ +8 \\ \hline \end{array}$

6. $\begin{array}{r} 6 \\ +7 \\ \hline \end{array}$ $\begin{array}{r} 5 \\ +6 \\ \hline \end{array}$ $\begin{array}{r} 8 \\ +7 \\ \hline \end{array}$ $\begin{array}{r} 4 \\ +5 \\ \hline \end{array}$ $\begin{array}{r} 8 \\ +9 \\ \hline \end{array}$ $\begin{array}{r} 4 \\ +3 \\ \hline \end{array}$

Add.

1. $\begin{array}{r}7\\+7\\\hline\end{array}$ $\begin{array}{r}8\\+7\\\hline\end{array}$ $\begin{array}{r}9\\+9\\\hline\end{array}$ $\begin{array}{r}5\\+5\\\hline\end{array}$ $\begin{array}{r}6\\+5\\\hline\end{array}$ $\begin{array}{r}6\\+6\\\hline\end{array}$

2. $\begin{array}{r}8\\+8\\\hline\end{array}$ $\begin{array}{r}8\\+9\\\hline\end{array}$ $\begin{array}{r}9\\+8\\\hline\end{array}$ $\begin{array}{r}4\\+3\\\hline\end{array}$ $\begin{array}{r}5\\+4\\\hline\end{array}$ $\begin{array}{r}3\\+3\\\hline\end{array}$

3. $\begin{array}{r}3\\+4\\\hline\end{array}$ $\begin{array}{r}6\\+6\\\hline\end{array}$ $\begin{array}{r}7\\+6\\\hline\end{array}$ $\begin{array}{r}7\\+8\\\hline\end{array}$ $\begin{array}{r}4\\+4\\\hline\end{array}$ $\begin{array}{r}5\\+4\\\hline\end{array}$

4. $\begin{array}{r}9\\+9\\\hline\end{array}$ $\begin{array}{r}7\\+8\\\hline\end{array}$ $\begin{array}{r}7\\+7\\\hline\end{array}$ $\begin{array}{r}8\\+7\\\hline\end{array}$ $\begin{array}{r}8\\+8\\\hline\end{array}$ $\begin{array}{r}5\\+6\\\hline\end{array}$

SKILLKEEPER

Subtract.

$\begin{array}{r}7\\-3\\\hline\end{array}$ $\begin{array}{r}10\\-4\\\hline\end{array}$ $\begin{array}{r}8\\-4\\\hline\end{array}$ $\begin{array}{r}9\\-2\\\hline\end{array}$ $\begin{array}{r}6\\-3\\\hline\end{array}$ $\begin{array}{r}10\\-5\\\hline\end{array}$

Name ______________________________

What is the total cost?

6¢ each

7¢ each

6¢	6¢
+ 6¢	+ 7¢
12¢	13¢

Add.

1.

8¢	8¢	9¢	5¢	6¢
+ 8¢	+ 9¢	+ 8¢	+ 5¢	+ 5¢

2.

4¢	7¢	7¢	8¢	7¢
+ 4¢	+ 2¢	+ 7¢	+ 7¢	+ 8¢

3.

5¢	4¢	6¢	7¢	9¢
+ 3¢	+ 6¢	+ 6¢	+ 6¢	+ 1¢

4.

9¢	3¢	9¢	8¢	7¢
+ 9¢	+ 8¢	+ 3¢	+ 8¢	+ 4¢

Add.

1.
$$\begin{array}{r} 7 \\ +7 \\ \hline \end{array} \quad \begin{array}{r} 7 \\ +8 \\ \hline \end{array} \quad \begin{array}{r} 8 \\ +2 \\ \hline \end{array} \quad \begin{array}{r} 8 \\ +3 \\ \hline \end{array}$$

2.
$$\begin{array}{r} 4 \\ +6 \\ \hline \end{array} \quad \begin{array}{r} 4 \\ +7 \\ \hline \end{array} \quad \begin{array}{r} 8 \\ +8 \\ \hline \end{array} \quad \begin{array}{r} 8 \\ +9 \\ \hline \end{array} \quad \begin{array}{r} 9 \\ +8 \\ \hline \end{array} \quad \begin{array}{r} 9 \\ +9 \\ \hline \end{array}$$

3.
$$\begin{array}{r} 7 \\ +3 \\ \hline \end{array} \quad \begin{array}{r} 3 \\ +6 \\ \hline \end{array} \quad \begin{array}{r} 6 \\ +6 \\ \hline \end{array} \quad \begin{array}{r} 6 \\ +7 \\ \hline \end{array} \quad \begin{array}{r} 7 \\ +6 \\ \hline \end{array} \quad \begin{array}{r} 4 \\ +4 \\ \hline \end{array}$$

4.
$$\begin{array}{r} 5 \\ +4 \\ \hline \end{array} \quad \begin{array}{r} 9 \\ +9 \\ \hline \end{array} \quad \begin{array}{r} 2 \\ +6 \\ \hline \end{array} \quad \begin{array}{r} 9 \\ +3 \\ \hline \end{array} \quad \begin{array}{r} 8 \\ +4 \\ \hline \end{array} \quad \begin{array}{r} 2 \\ +8 \\ \hline \end{array}$$

5.
$$\begin{array}{r} 8 \\ +7 \\ \hline \end{array} \quad \begin{array}{r} 9 \\ +8 \\ \hline \end{array} \quad \begin{array}{r} 7 \\ +7 \\ \hline \end{array} \quad \begin{array}{r} 3 \\ +7 \\ \hline \end{array} \quad \begin{array}{r} 8 \\ +8 \\ \hline \end{array} \quad \begin{array}{r} 9 \\ +9 \\ \hline \end{array}$$

THINK MATH

Give the missing number on the calculator key.

PRESS		READ
[7] [+] [ ] [=]	→	13
[9] [−] [ ] [=]	→	6
[1] [7] [−] [ ] [=]	→	9

Name ____________________

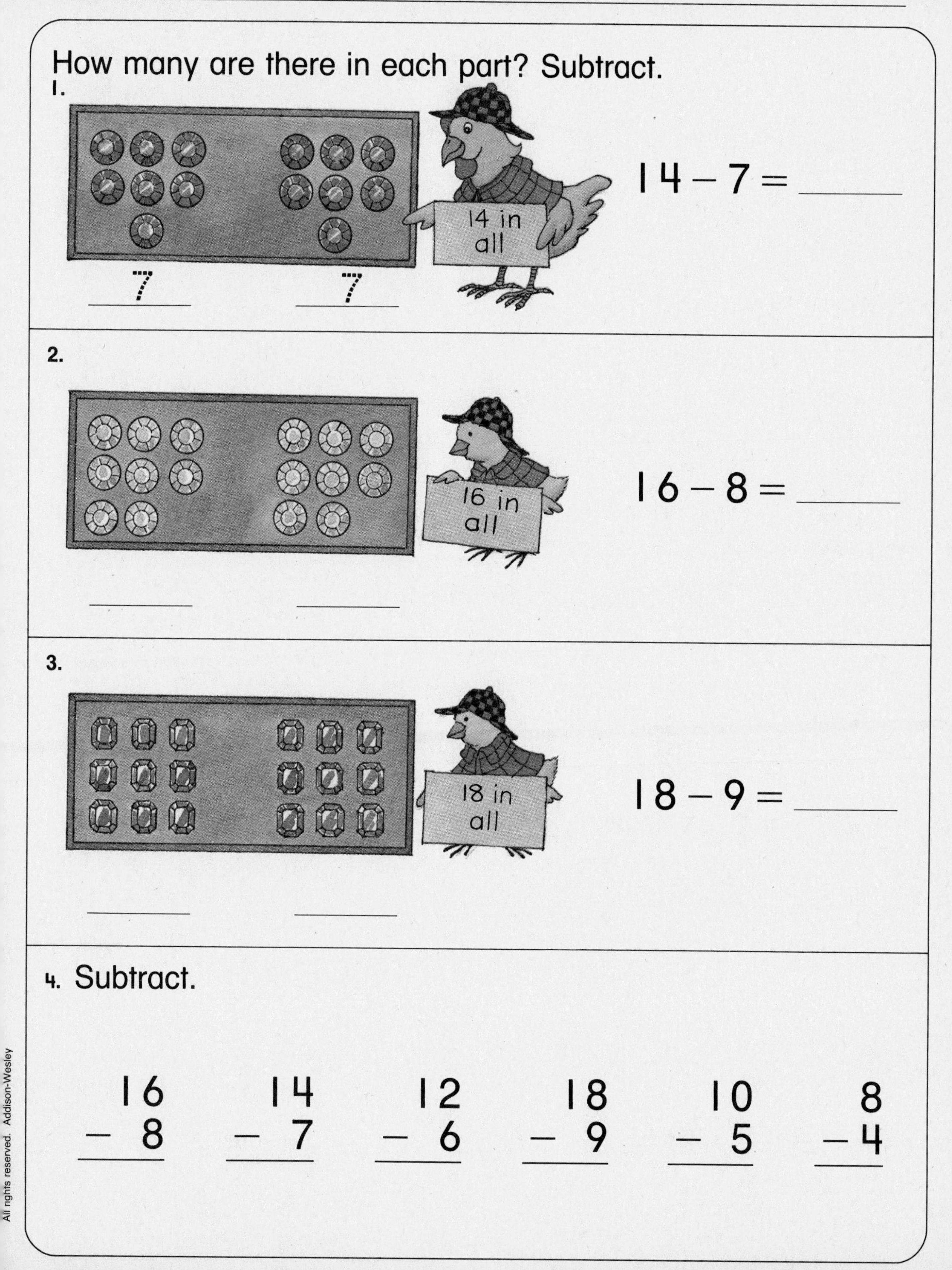

How many are there in each part? Subtract.

1. 7 ____ 7 ____

$14 - 7 =$ ____

2. ____ ____

$16 - 8 =$ ____

3. ____ ____

$18 - 9 =$ ____

4. Subtract.

$$\begin{array}{r}16\\-\ 8\\\hline\end{array}\quad\begin{array}{r}14\\-\ 7\\\hline\end{array}\quad\begin{array}{r}12\\-\ 6\\\hline\end{array}\quad\begin{array}{r}18\\-\ 9\\\hline\end{array}\quad\begin{array}{r}10\\-\ 5\\\hline\end{array}\quad\begin{array}{r}8\\-4\\\hline\end{array}$$

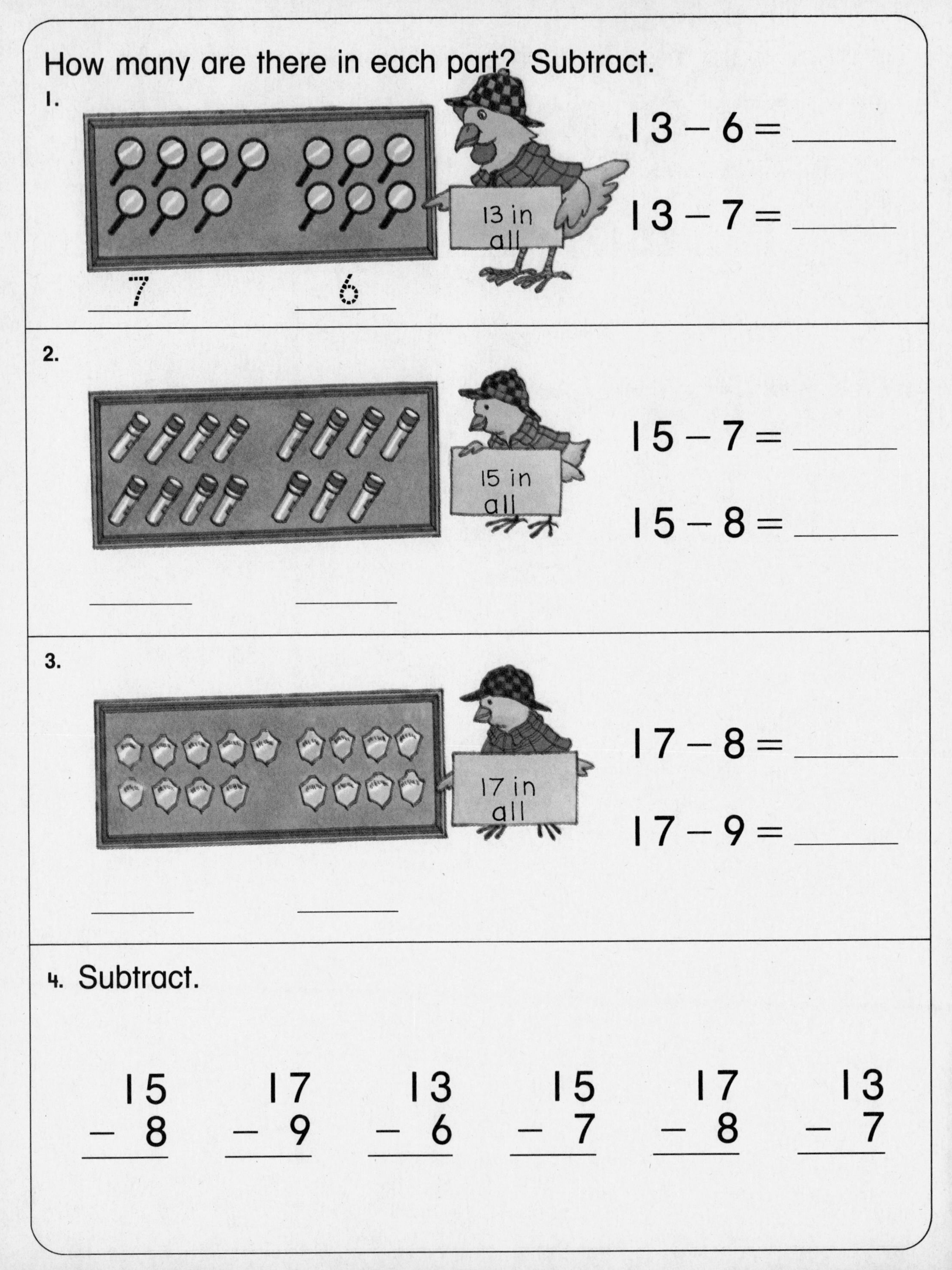

How many are there in each part? Subtract.

1.

$13 - 6 =$ ______

$13 - 7 =$ ______

2.

______ ______

$15 - 7 =$ ______

$15 - 8 =$ ______

3.

______ ______

$17 - 8 =$ ______

$17 - 9 =$ ______

4. Subtract.

$\begin{array}{r} 15 \\ -\ 8 \\ \hline \end{array}$ $\begin{array}{r} 17 \\ -\ 9 \\ \hline \end{array}$ $\begin{array}{r} 13 \\ -\ 6 \\ \hline \end{array}$ $\begin{array}{r} 15 \\ -\ 7 \\ \hline \end{array}$ $\begin{array}{r} 17 \\ -\ 8 \\ \hline \end{array}$ $\begin{array}{r} 13 \\ -\ 7 \\ \hline \end{array}$

Name ______________________________

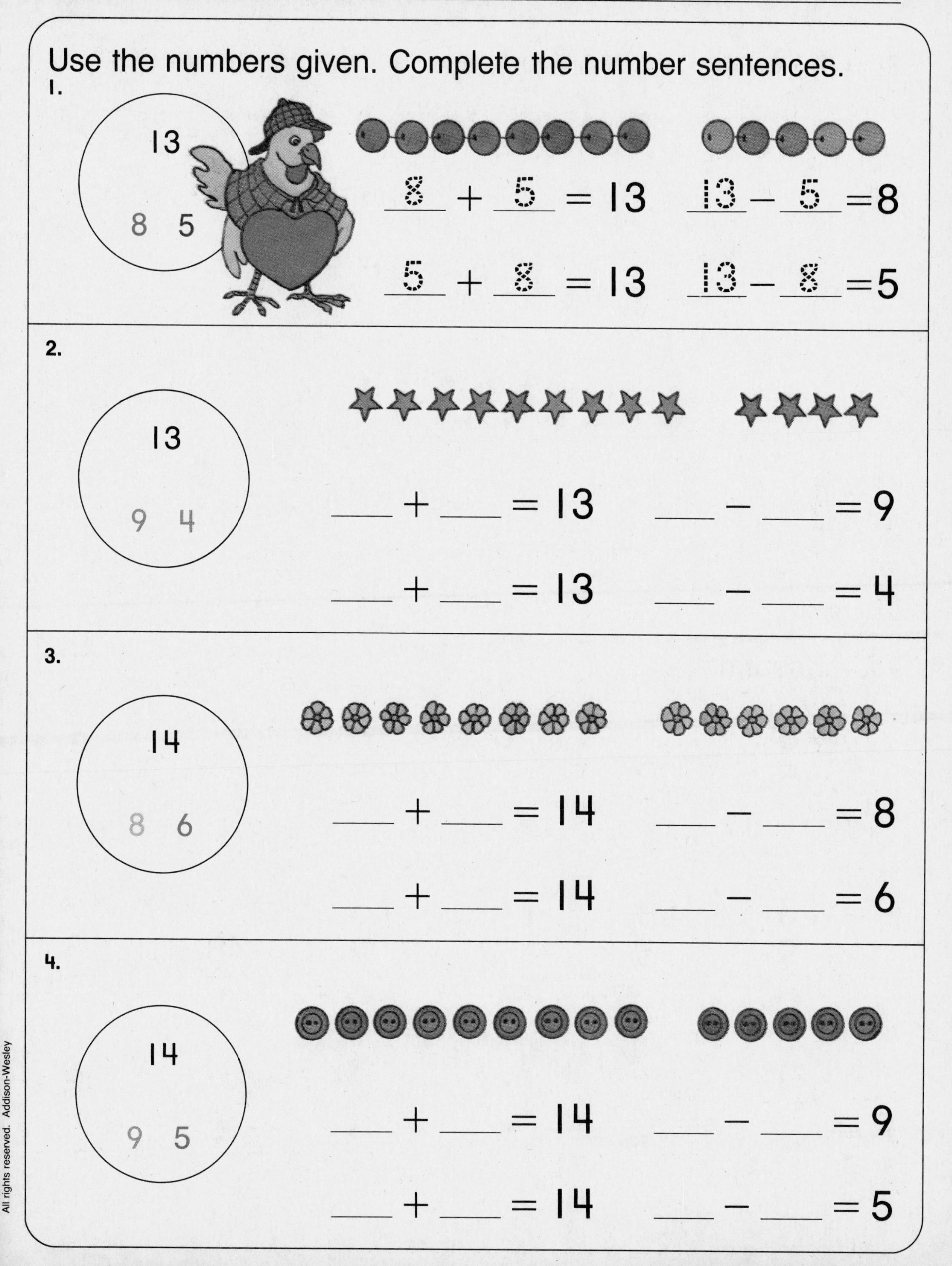
Use the numbers given. Complete the number sentences.
1.
13
8 5
8 + 5 = 13
13 − 5 = 8
5 + 8 = 13
13 − 8 = 5
2.
13
9 4
___ + ___ = 13
___ − ___ = 9
___ + ___ = 13
___ − ___ = 4
3.
14
8 6
___ + ___ = 14
___ − ___ = 8
___ + ___ = 14
___ − ___ = 6
4.
14
9 5
___ + ___ = 14
___ − ___ = 9
___ + ___ = 14
___ − ___ = 5

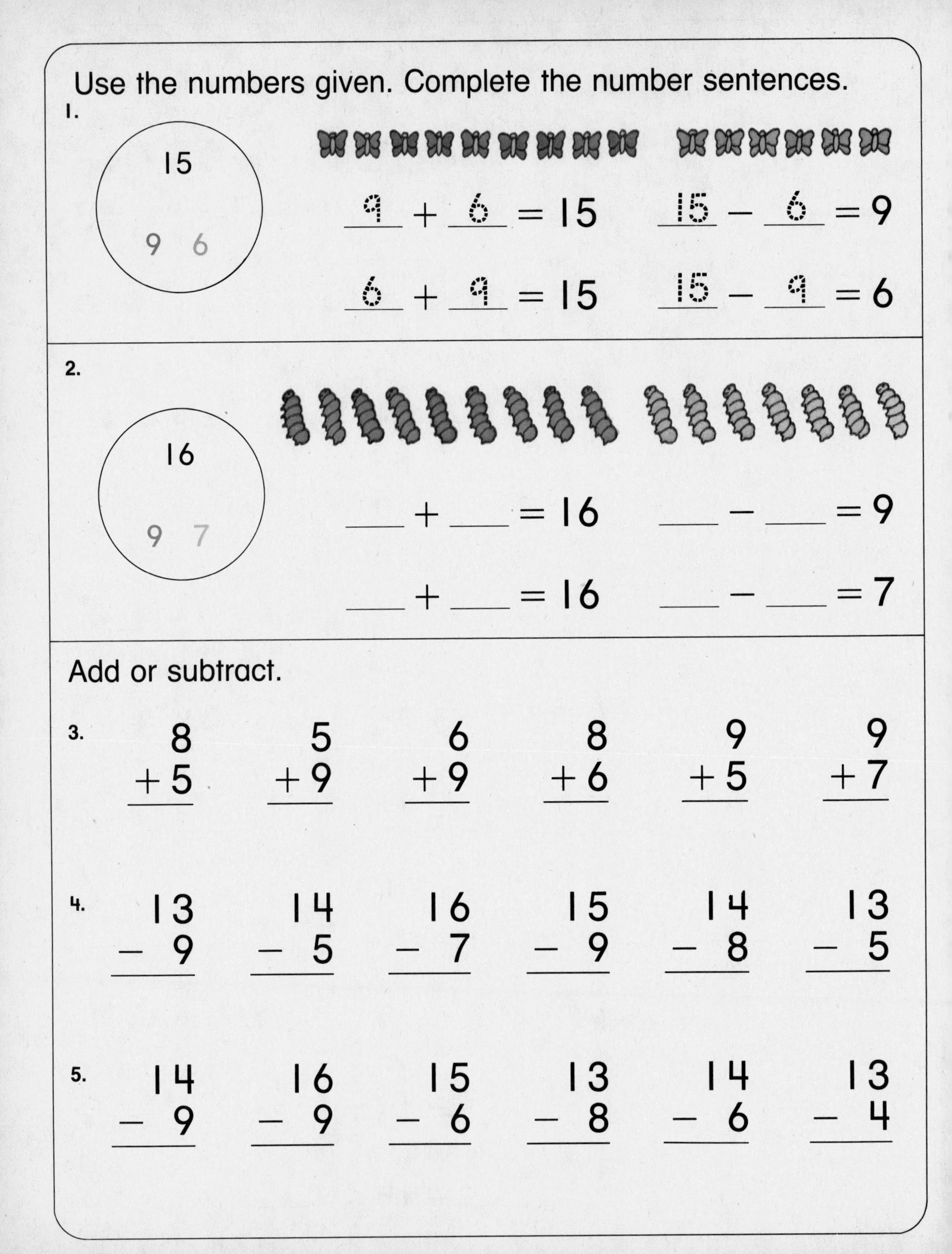

Use the numbers given. Complete the number sentences.

1\.

15

9 6

9 + 6 = 15 15 − 6 = 9

6 + 9 = 15 15 − 9 = 6

2\.

16

9 7

___ + ___ = 16 ___ − ___ = 9

___ + ___ = 16 ___ − ___ = 7

Add or subtract.

3\.

$\begin{array}{r} 8 \\ +5 \\ \hline \end{array}$ $\begin{array}{r} 5 \\ +9 \\ \hline \end{array}$ $\begin{array}{r} 6 \\ +9 \\ \hline \end{array}$ $\begin{array}{r} 8 \\ +6 \\ \hline \end{array}$ $\begin{array}{r} 9 \\ +5 \\ \hline \end{array}$ $\begin{array}{r} 9 \\ +7 \\ \hline \end{array}$

4\.

$\begin{array}{r} 13 \\ -\ 9 \\ \hline \end{array}$ $\begin{array}{r} 14 \\ -\ 5 \\ \hline \end{array}$ $\begin{array}{r} 16 \\ -\ 7 \\ \hline \end{array}$ $\begin{array}{r} 15 \\ -\ 9 \\ \hline \end{array}$ $\begin{array}{r} 14 \\ -\ 8 \\ \hline \end{array}$ $\begin{array}{r} 13 \\ -\ 5 \\ \hline \end{array}$

5\.

$\begin{array}{r} 14 \\ -\ 9 \\ \hline \end{array}$ $\begin{array}{r} 16 \\ -\ 9 \\ \hline \end{array}$ $\begin{array}{r} 15 \\ -\ 6 \\ \hline \end{array}$ $\begin{array}{r} 13 \\ -\ 8 \\ \hline \end{array}$ $\begin{array}{r} 14 \\ -\ 6 \\ \hline \end{array}$ $\begin{array}{r} 13 \\ -\ 4 \\ \hline \end{array}$

Name ______________________________

Add or subtract.

1. $7 + 7$ $7 + 6$ $14 - 7$ $13 - 6$

2. $8 + 8$ $8 + 9$ $16 - 8$ $17 - 8$ $17 - 9$ $9 + 8$

3. $6 + 6$ $12 - 6$ $13 - 7$ $13 - 6$ $7 + 8$ $15 - 7$

4. $9 + 9$ $18 - 9$ $8 + 7$ $15 - 8$ $5 + 5$ $10 - 5$

5. 5¢ + 6¢   11¢ − 6¢   11¢ − 5¢   9¢ + 8¢   12¢ − 6¢   13¢ − 7¢

SKILLKEEPER

Write the times.

___:___   ___:___   ___:___   ___:___

QUESTION
DATA
PLAN
ANSWER
CHECK

Problem Solving

Solve.

1. Luis saw 16 ladybugs.
8 flew away.
How many were left?

8 ladybugs

$$\begin{array}{r} 16 \\ -\ 8 \\ \hline 8 \end{array}$$

2. Marta saw 7 roses in her yard.
She saw 7 more next door.
How many did she see in all?

_______ roses

3. There were 9 children playing tag.
9 more came.
How many were there in all?

_______ children

4. Brad saw 13 birds.
7 flew away.
How many were left?

_______ birds

5. Mary had 15¢.
She spent 7¢ for a pencil.
How much did she have left?

_______¢

Name ____________________

CHAPTER REVIEW/TEST

Add or subtract.

1. $\begin{array}{r} 7 \\ +7 \\ \hline \end{array}$ $\begin{array}{r} 9 \\ +9 \\ \hline \end{array}$ $\begin{array}{r} 6 \\ +6 \\ \hline \end{array}$ $\begin{array}{r} 8 \\ +8 \\ \hline \end{array}$ $\begin{array}{r} 7 \\ +8 \\ \hline \end{array}$ $\begin{array}{r} 9 \\ +9 \\ \hline \end{array}$

2. $\begin{array}{r} 6¢ \\ +7¢ \\ \hline \end{array}$ $\begin{array}{r} 8¢ \\ +7¢ \\ \hline \end{array}$ $\begin{array}{r} 8¢ \\ +9¢ \\ \hline \end{array}$ $\begin{array}{r} 7¢ \\ +7¢ \\ \hline \end{array}$ $\begin{array}{r} 9¢ \\ +9¢ \\ \hline \end{array}$ $\begin{array}{r} 6¢ \\ +6¢ \\ \hline \end{array}$

3. $\begin{array}{r} 13 \\ -\ 6 \\ \hline \end{array}$ $\begin{array}{r} 14 \\ -\ 7 \\ \hline \end{array}$ $\begin{array}{r} 12 \\ -\ 6 \\ \hline \end{array}$ $\begin{array}{r} 13 \\ -\ 7 \\ \hline \end{array}$ $\begin{array}{r} 16 \\ -\ 8 \\ \hline \end{array}$ $\begin{array}{r} 18 \\ -\ 9 \\ \hline \end{array}$

4. $\begin{array}{r} 17 \\ -\ 9 \\ \hline \end{array}$ $\begin{array}{r} 17 \\ -\ 8 \\ \hline \end{array}$ $\begin{array}{r} 15 \\ -\ 8 \\ \hline \end{array}$ $\begin{array}{r} 15 \\ -\ 7 \\ \hline \end{array}$

5. $\begin{array}{r} 5 \\ +8 \\ \hline \end{array}$ $\begin{array}{r} 13 \\ -\ 5 \\ \hline \end{array}$ $\begin{array}{r} 6 \\ +8 \\ \hline \end{array}$ $\begin{array}{r} 14 \\ -\ 8 \\ \hline \end{array}$ $\begin{array}{r} 9 \\ +6 \\ \hline \end{array}$ $\begin{array}{r} 15 \\ -\ 9 \\ \hline \end{array}$

6. Solve.

Pat made 18 cards.
She gave away 9.
How many did she have left?

_______ cards

Name

CUMULATIVE REVIEW

Add or subtract.

1. $\begin{array}{r} 23 \\ +66 \\ \hline \end{array}$

○ 98
○ 89
○ 52

2. $\begin{array}{r} 14 \\ +33 \\ \hline \end{array}$

○ 21
○ 56
○ 47

3. $\begin{array}{r} 97 \\ -17 \\ \hline \end{array}$

○ 10
○ 26
○ 80

4. $\begin{array}{r} 50 \\ -20 \\ \hline \end{array}$

○ 30
○ 70
○ 2

Find the length or height.

5.

○ 4 cm
○ 2 cm
○ 3 cm

6.

○ 1 cm
○ 4 cm
○ 6 cm

7.

○ 2 cm
○ 3 cm
○ 4 cm

8.

○ 5 cm
○ 4 cm
○ 3 cm

9. Solve.

50¢

21¢

Sean had 89¢.
He bought a .

○ 90¢
○ 68¢
○ 39¢

How much does he have left?

Name ______________________________

ANOTHER LOOK

$$\begin{array}{r} 6 \\ +6 \\ \hline 12 \end{array} \quad \begin{array}{r} 7 \\ +7 \\ \hline 14 \end{array}$$

February

CRAYONS 16

$$\begin{array}{r} 8 \\ +8 \\ \hline 16 \end{array} \quad \begin{array}{r} 9 \\ +9 \\ \hline 18 \end{array}$$

$$\begin{array}{r} 6 \\ +6 \\ \hline 12 \end{array} \quad \begin{array}{r} 6 \\ +7 \\ \hline 13 \end{array} \text{ (1 more)} \quad \begin{array}{r} 7 \\ +7 \\ \hline 14 \end{array} \quad \begin{array}{r} 7 \\ +8 \\ \hline 15 \end{array} \text{ (1 more)}$$

$$\begin{array}{r} 8 \\ +8 \\ \hline 16 \end{array} \quad \begin{array}{r} 8 \\ +9 \\ \hline 17 \end{array} \text{ (1 more)}$$

$$\begin{array}{r} 6 \\ +6 \\ \hline 12 \end{array} \quad \begin{array}{r} 12 \\ -6 \\ \hline 6 \end{array} \quad \begin{array}{r} 7 \\ +7 \\ \hline 14 \end{array} \quad \begin{array}{r} 14 \\ -7 \\ \hline 7 \end{array}$$

$$\begin{array}{r} 8 \\ +8 \\ \hline 16 \end{array} \quad \begin{array}{r} 16 \\ -8 \\ \hline 8 \end{array} \quad \begin{array}{r} 9 \\ +9 \\ \hline 18 \end{array} \quad \begin{array}{r} 18 \\ -9 \\ \hline 9 \end{array}$$

Add.

1. $\begin{array}{r} 6 \\ +6 \\ \hline \end{array} \quad \begin{array}{r} 8 \\ +8 \\ \hline \end{array} \quad \begin{array}{r} 9 \\ +9 \\ \hline \end{array}$

2. $\begin{array}{r} 7 \\ +7 \\ \hline \end{array} \quad \begin{array}{r} 6 \\ +6 \\ \hline \end{array} \quad \begin{array}{r} 8 \\ +8 \\ \hline \end{array}$

3. $\begin{array}{r} 9 \\ +8 \\ \hline \end{array} \quad \begin{array}{r} 7 \\ +6 \\ \hline \end{array} \quad \begin{array}{r} 8 \\ +7 \\ \hline \end{array}$

4. $\begin{array}{r} 7 \\ +8 \\ \hline \end{array} \quad \begin{array}{r} 8 \\ +9 \\ \hline \end{array} \quad \begin{array}{r} 6 \\ +7 \\ \hline \end{array}$

5. $\begin{array}{r} 14 \\ -7 \\ \hline \end{array} \quad \begin{array}{r} 18 \\ -9 \\ \hline \end{array} \quad \begin{array}{r} 12 \\ -6 \\ \hline \end{array}$

6. $\begin{array}{r} 16 \\ -8 \\ \hline \end{array} \quad \begin{array}{r} 14 \\ -7 \\ \hline \end{array} \quad \begin{array}{r} 18 \\ -9 \\ \hline \end{array}$

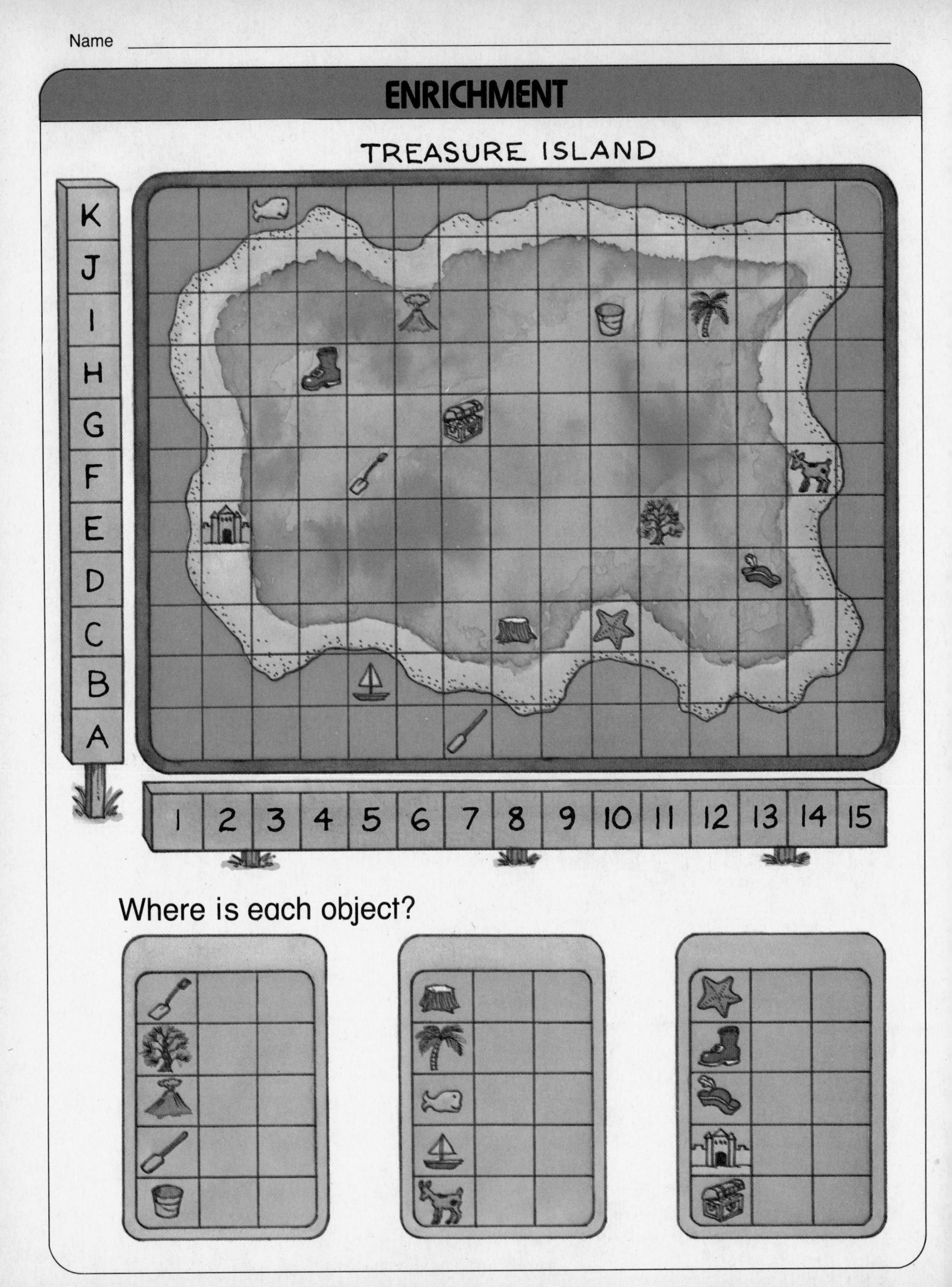
Name
ENRICHMENT
TREASURE ISLAND
K
J
I
H
G
F
E
D
C
B
A
1 2 3 4 5 6 7 8 9 10 11 12 13 14 15
Where is each object?

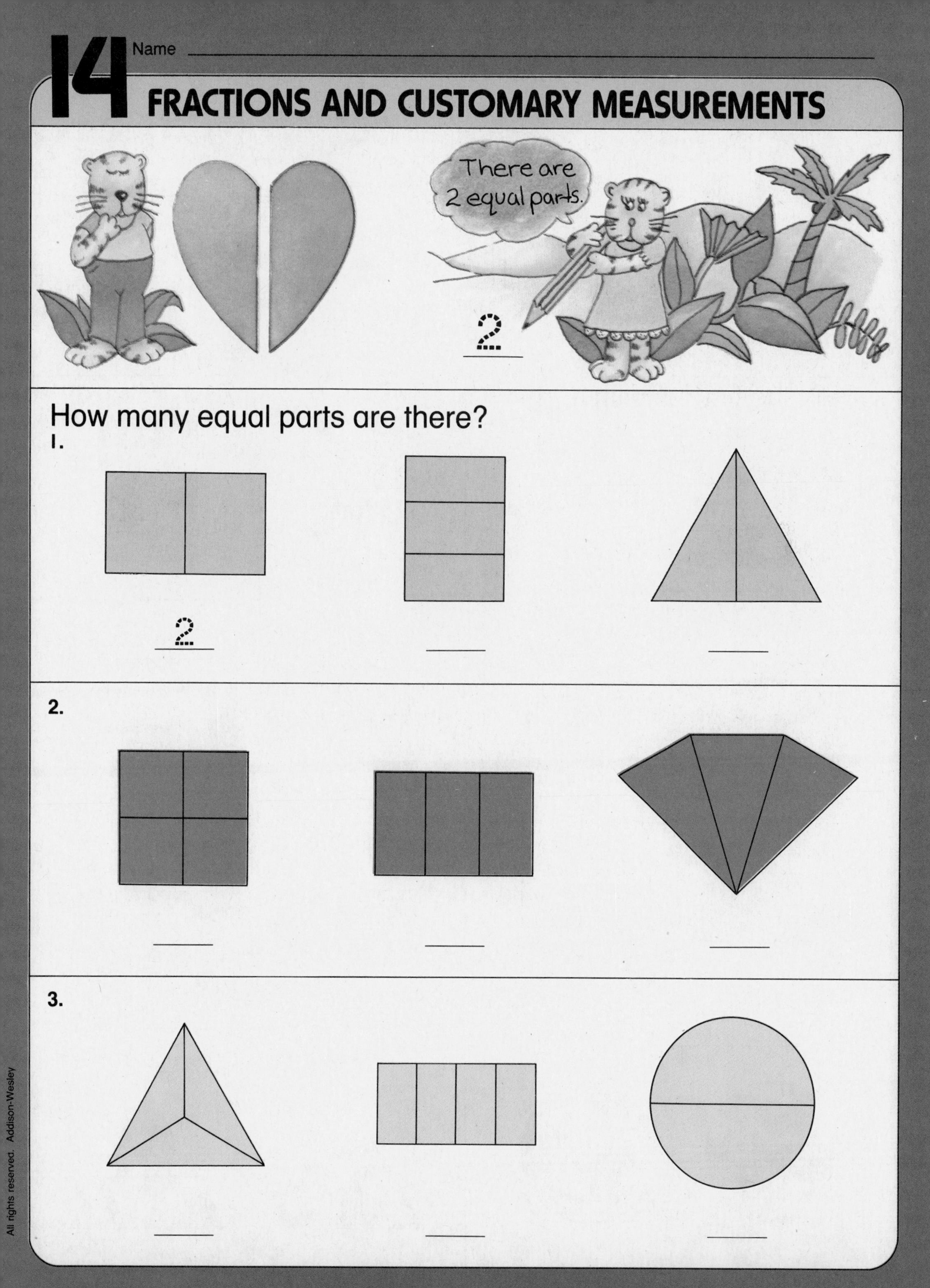
14
Name
FRACTIONS AND CUSTOMARY MEASUREMENTS
There are 2 equal parts.
2
How many equal parts are there?
1.
2
2.
3.

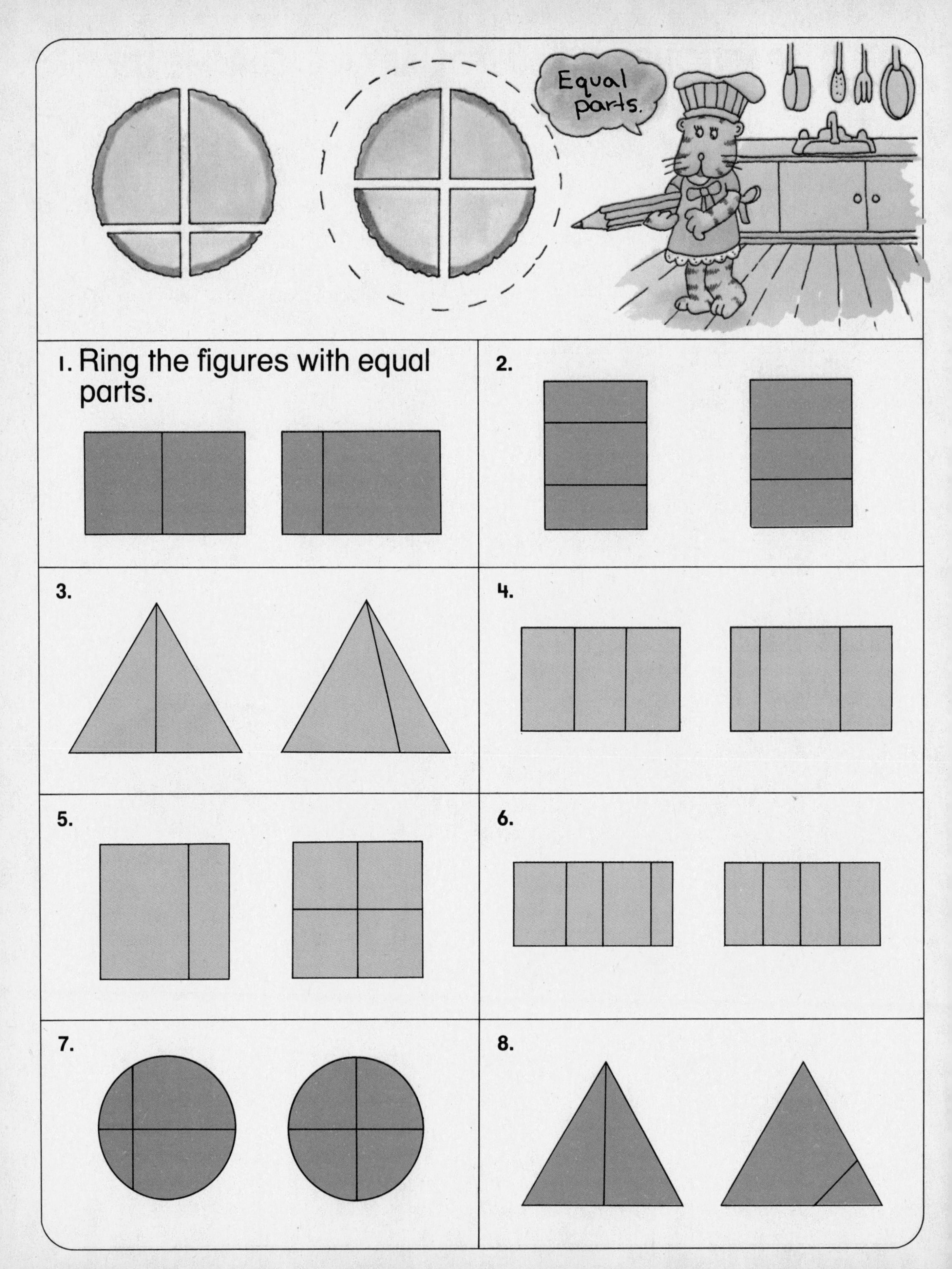
Equal parts.
1. Ring the figures with equal parts.
2.
3.
4.
5.
6.
7.
8.

 Concept of equal parts for fractions

Name

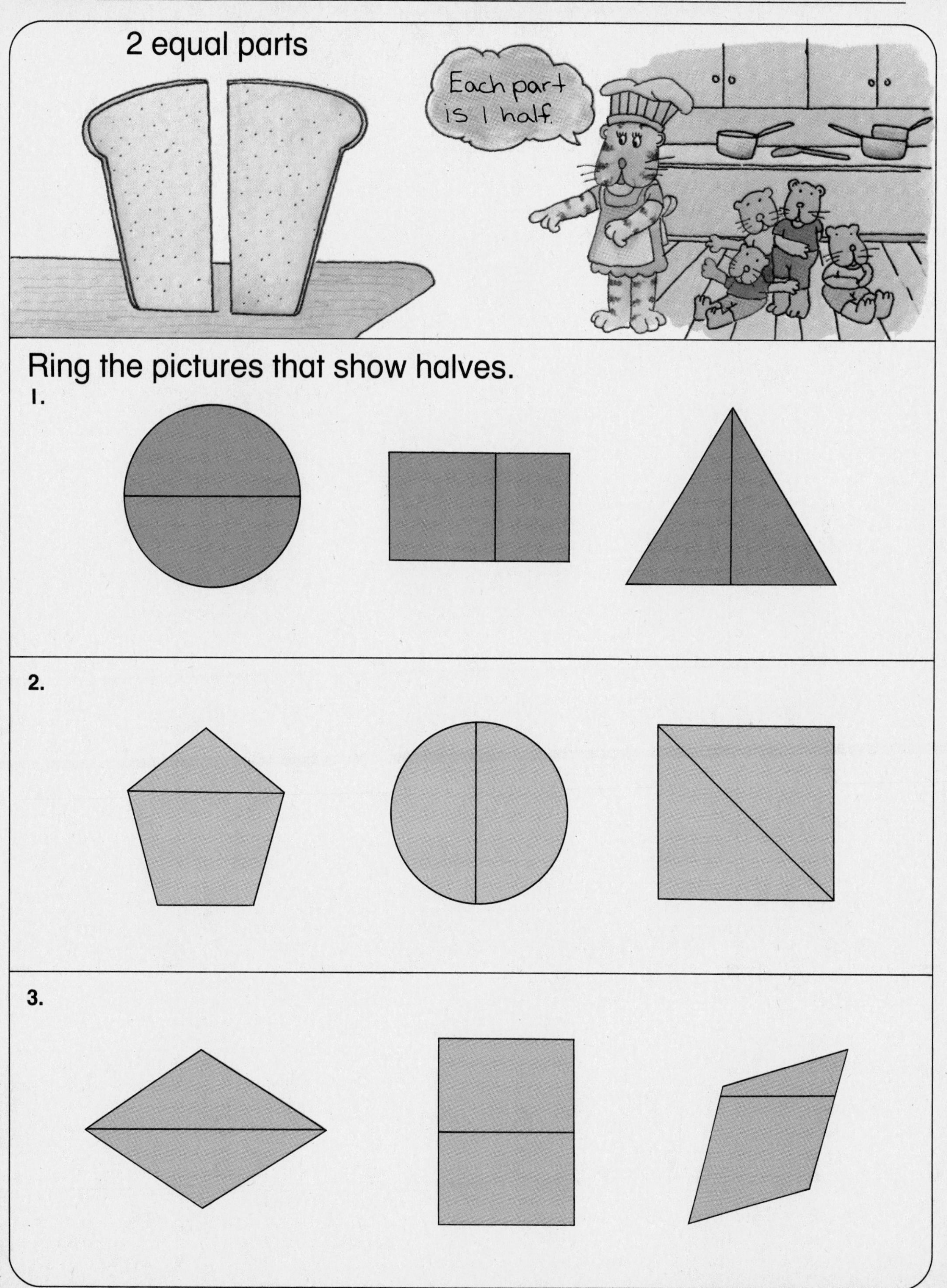

2 equal parts
Each part is 1 half.
Ring the pictures that show halves.
1.
2.
3.

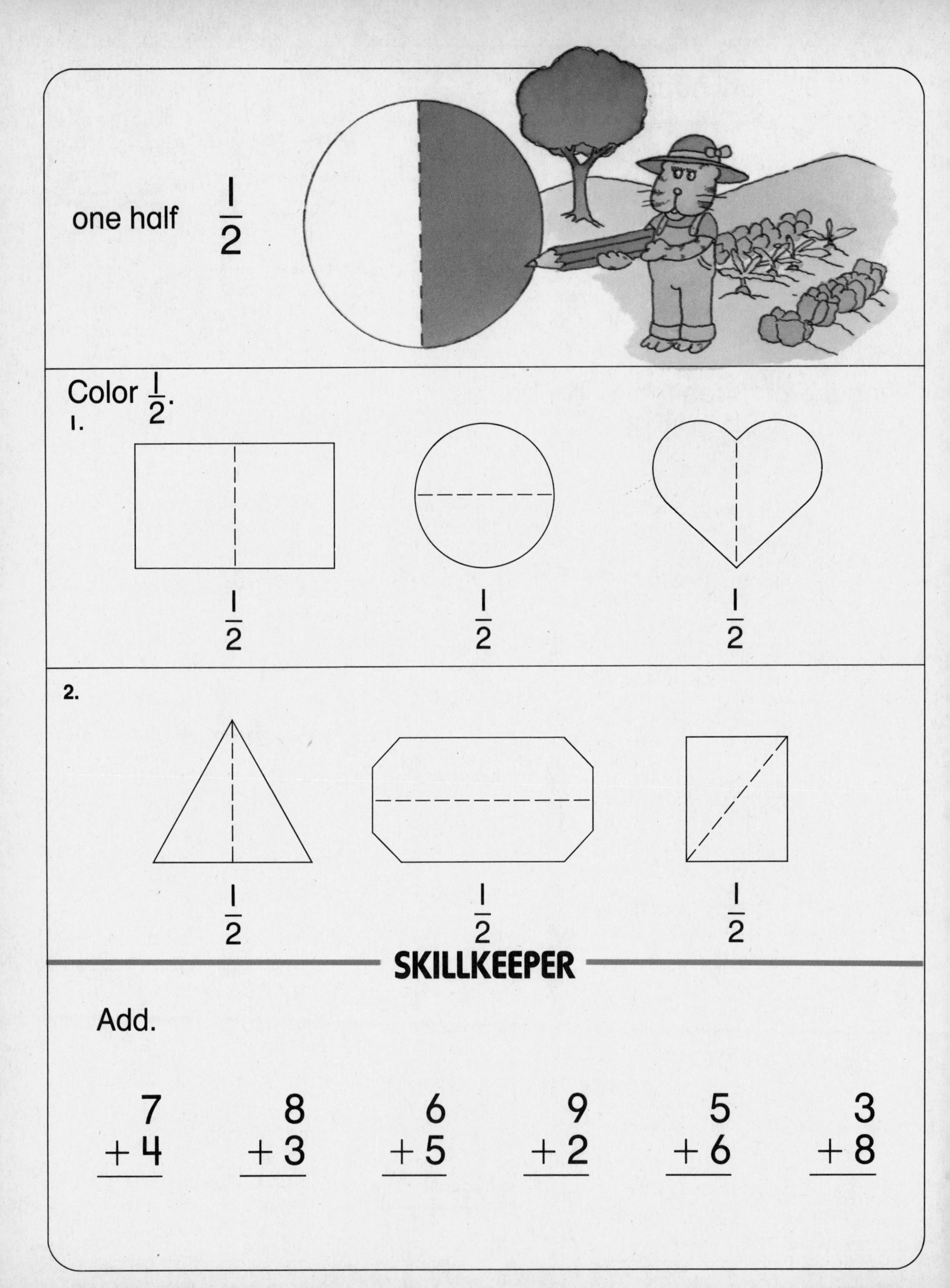

one half $\frac{1}{2}$

Color $\frac{1}{2}$.

1.

$\frac{1}{2}$ $\frac{1}{2}$ $\frac{1}{2}$

2.

$\frac{1}{2}$ $\frac{1}{2}$ $\frac{1}{2}$

SKILLKEEPER

Add.

7	8	6	9	5	3
+ 4	+ 3	+ 5	+ 2	+ 6	+ 8

Name ______________________________

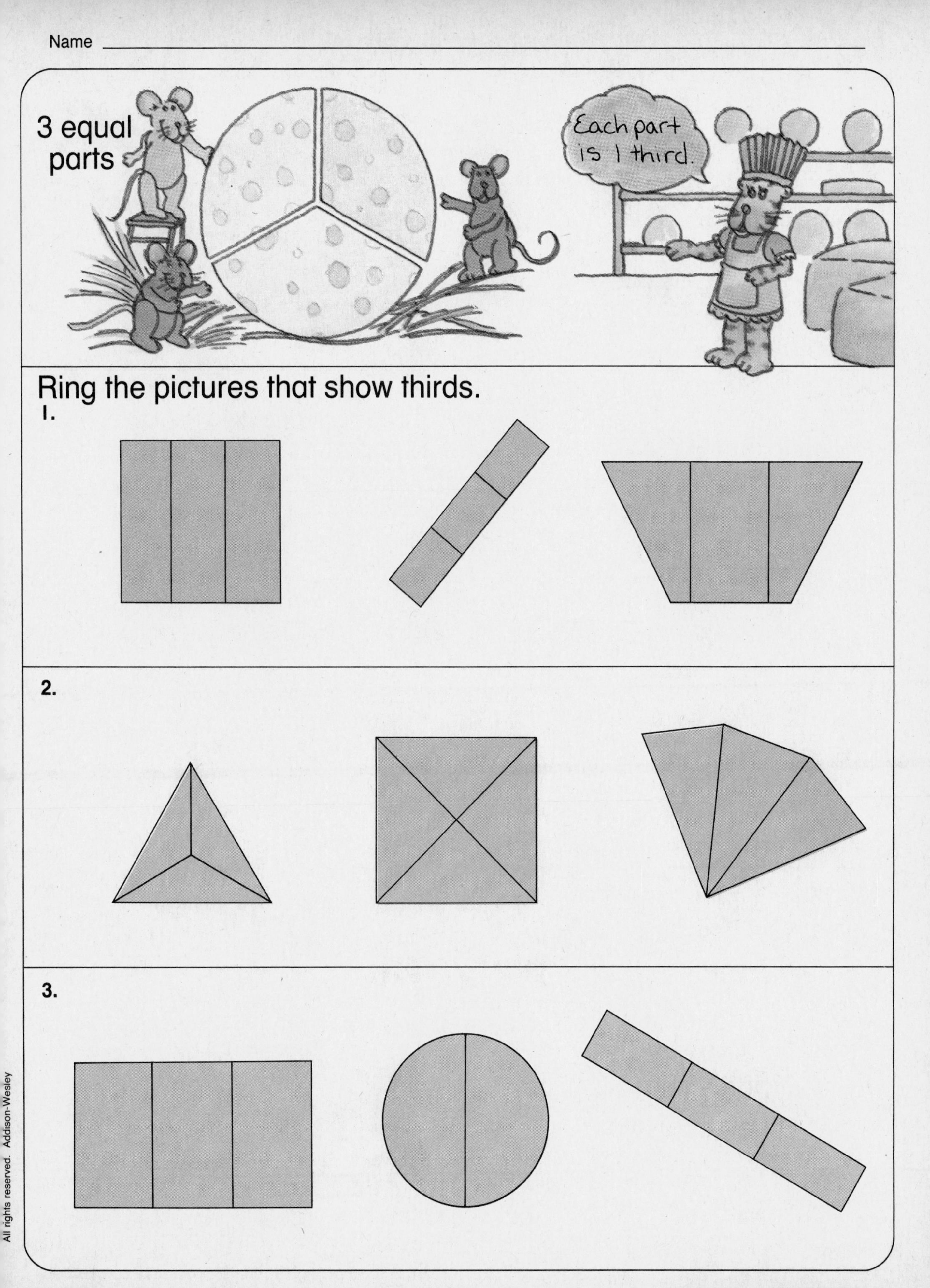
3 equal parts
Each part is 1 third.

Ring the pictures that show thirds.

1.

2.

3.

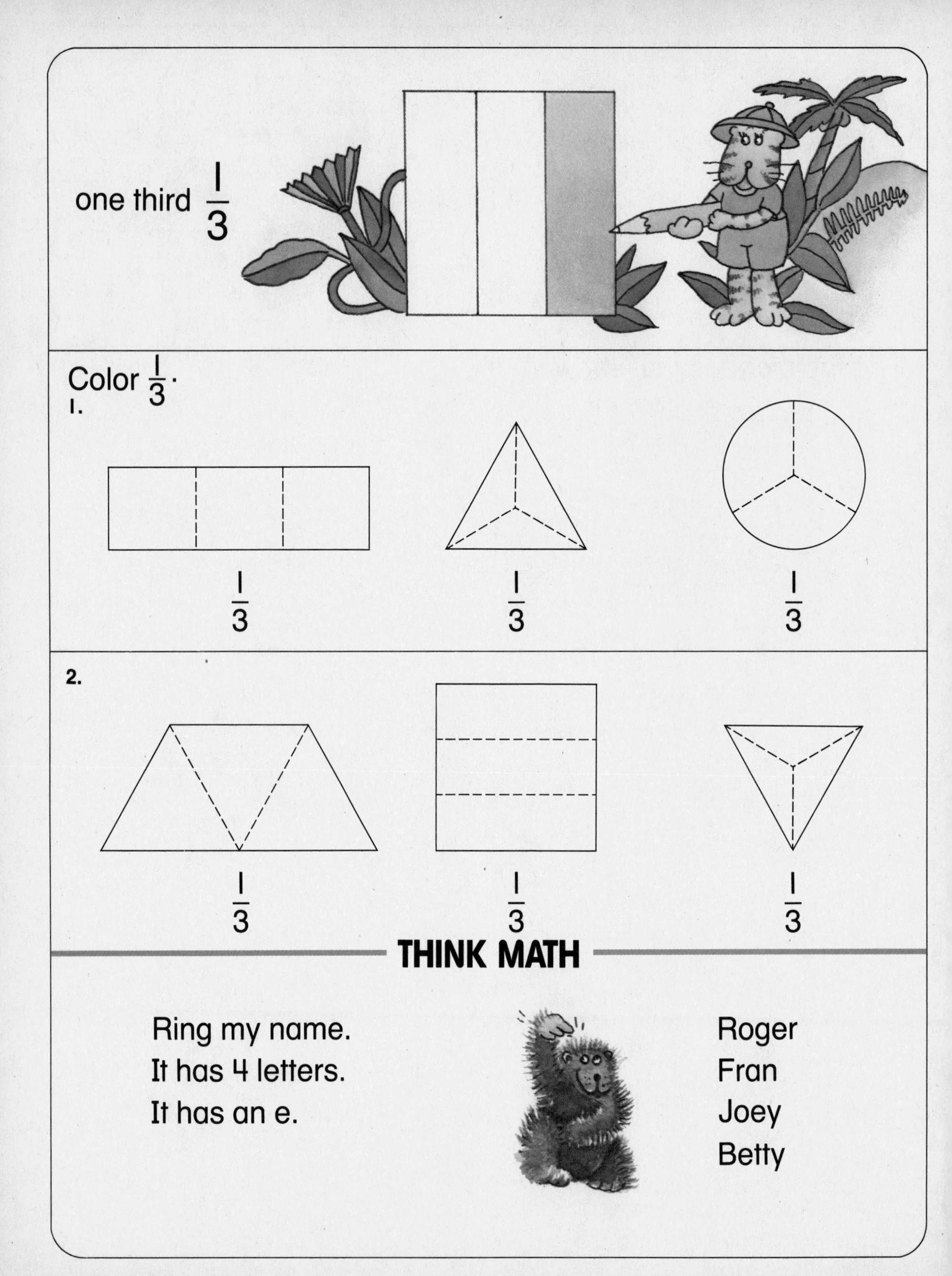

one third $\frac{1}{3}$

Color $\frac{1}{3}$.

1.

$\frac{1}{3}$ $\frac{1}{3}$ $\frac{1}{3}$

2.

$\frac{1}{3}$ $\frac{1}{3}$ $\frac{1}{3}$

THINK MATH

Ring my name.
It has 4 letters.
It has an e.

Roger
Fran
Joey
Betty

Name ______________________________

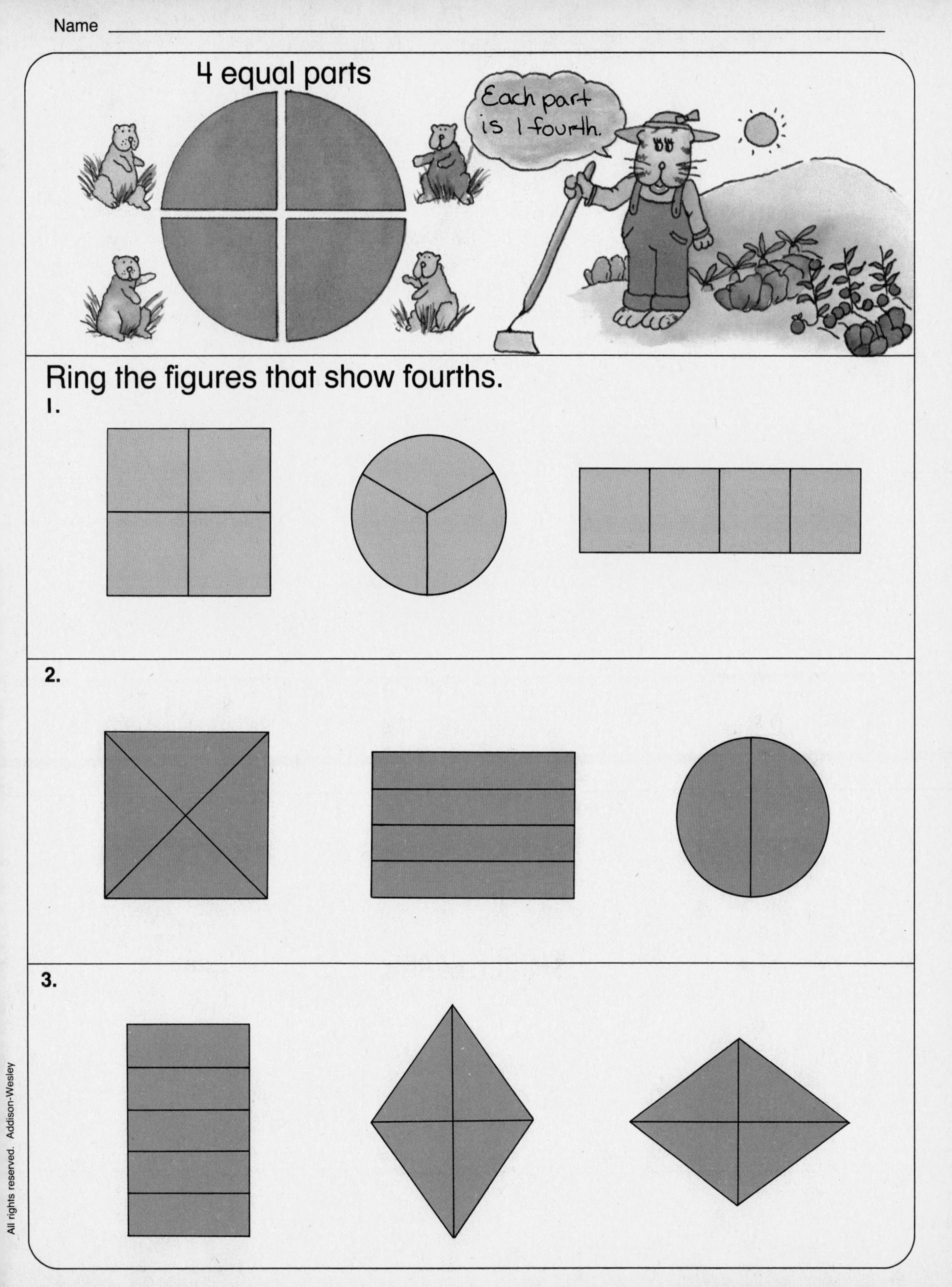
4 equal parts
Each part is 1 fourth.
Ring the figures that show fourths.
1.
2.
3.

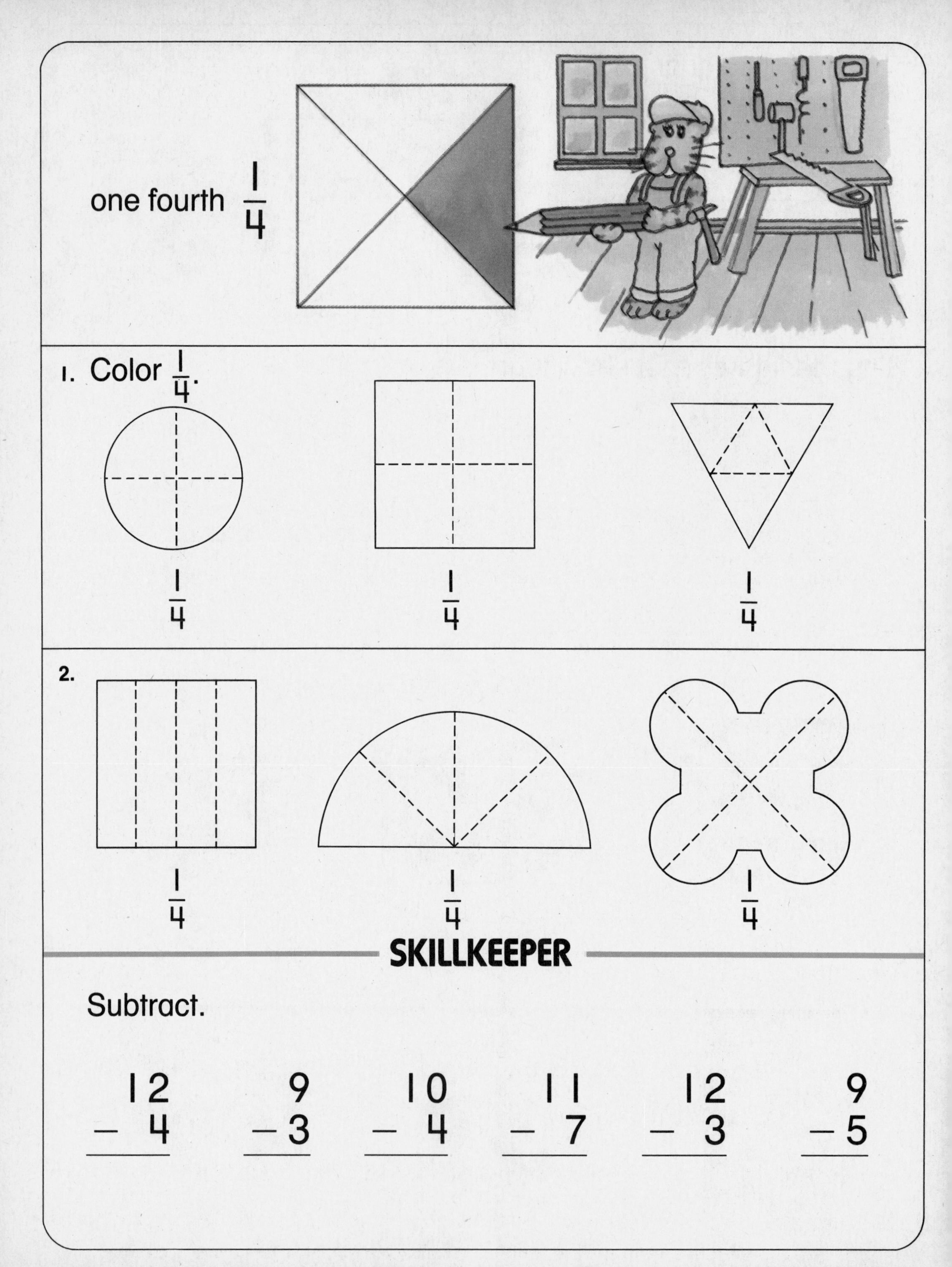

one fourth $\frac{1}{4}$

1. Color $\frac{1}{4}$.

$\frac{1}{4}$ $\frac{1}{4}$ $\frac{1}{4}$

2.

$\frac{1}{4}$ $\frac{1}{4}$ $\frac{1}{4}$

SKILLKEEPER

Subtract.

12	9	10	11	12	9
− 4	− 3	− 4	− 7	− 3	− 5

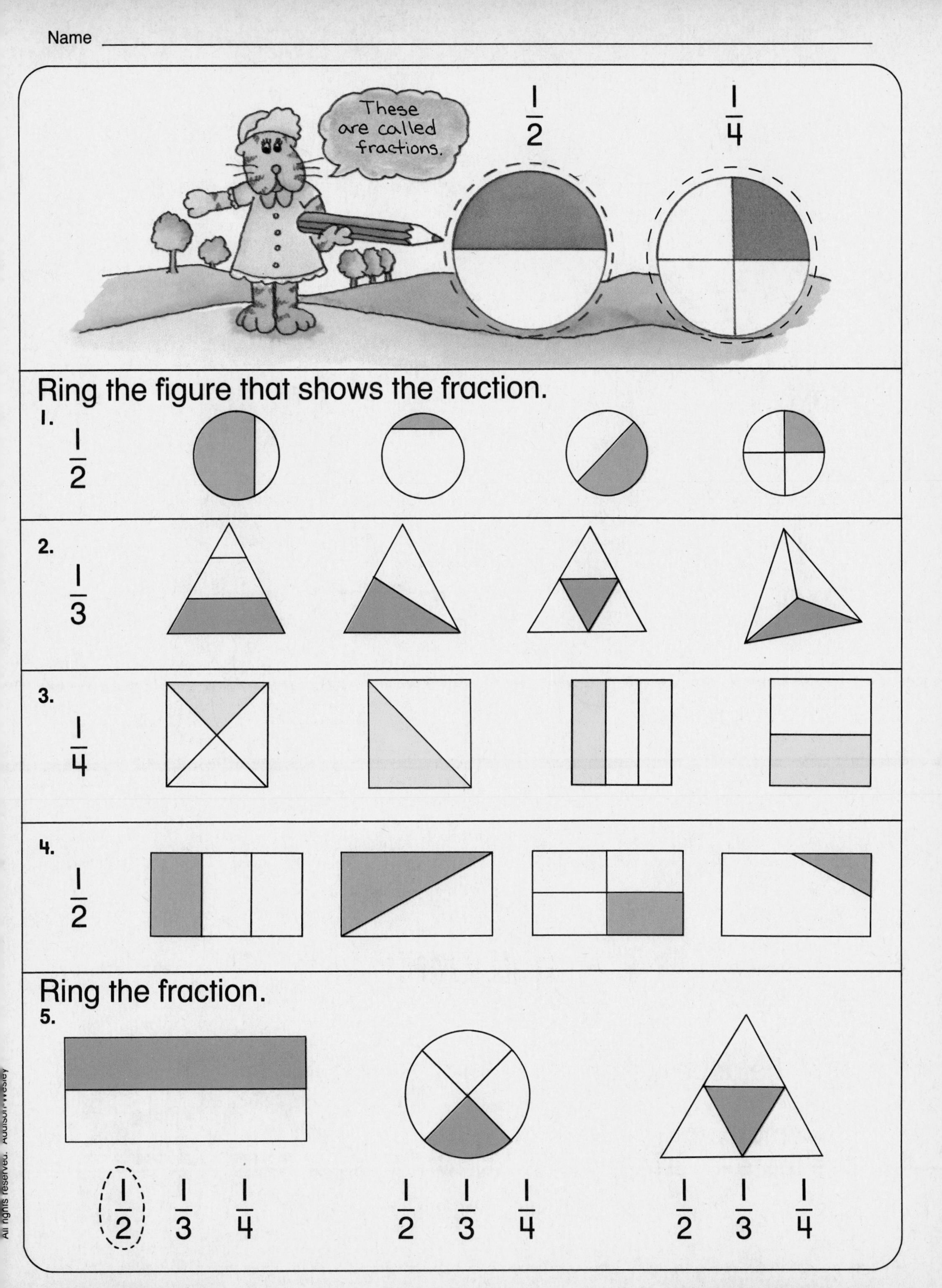
Name
These are called fractions.
1/2
1/4
Ring the figure that shows the fraction.
1. 1/2
2. 1/3
3. 1/4
4. 1/2
Ring the fraction.
5.
1/2 1/3 1/4
1/2 1/3 1/4
1/2 1/3 1/4

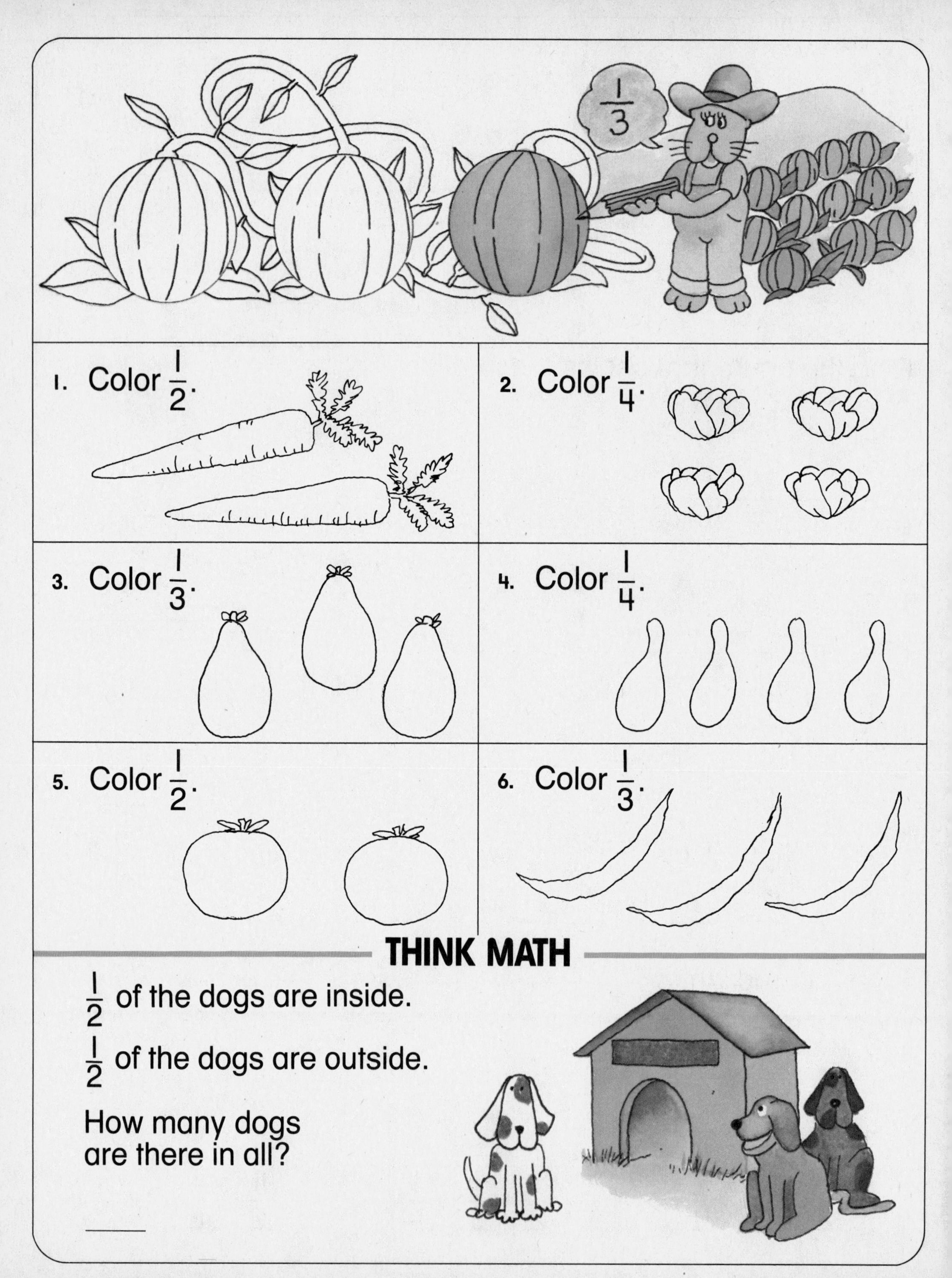

1. Color $\frac{1}{2}$.

2. Color $\frac{1}{4}$.

3. Color $\frac{1}{3}$.

4. Color $\frac{1}{4}$.

5. Color $\frac{1}{2}$.

6. Color $\frac{1}{3}$.

THINK MATH

$\frac{1}{2}$ of the dogs are inside.

$\frac{1}{2}$ of the dogs are outside.

How many dogs are there in all?

_____

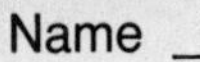

Name ______________________

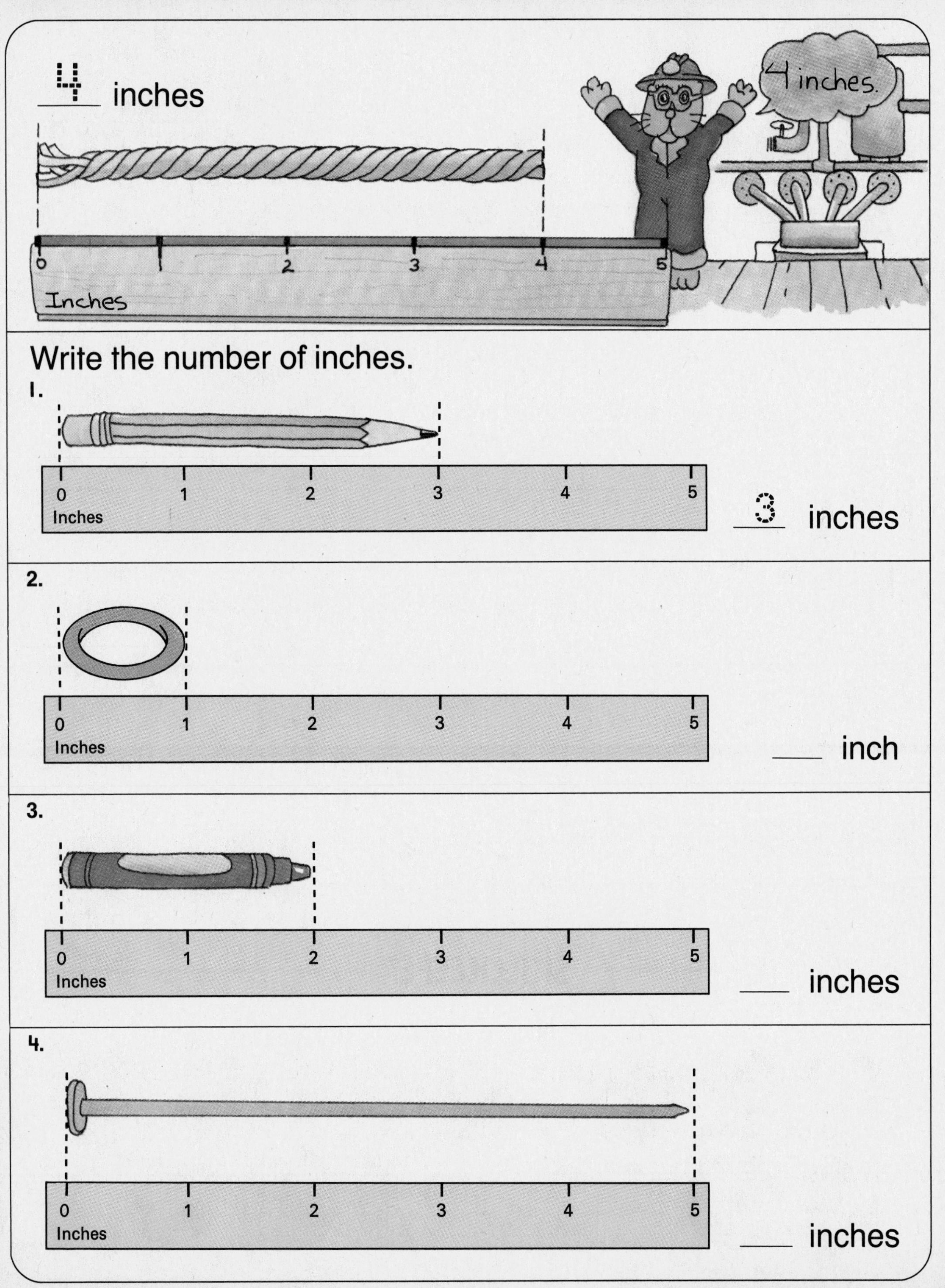

Write the number of inches.

1.

0 1 2 3 4 5 Inches

3 inches

2.

0 1 2 3 4 5 Inches

___ inch

3.

0 1 2 3 4 5 Inches

___ inches

4.

0 1 2 3 4 5 Inches

___ inches

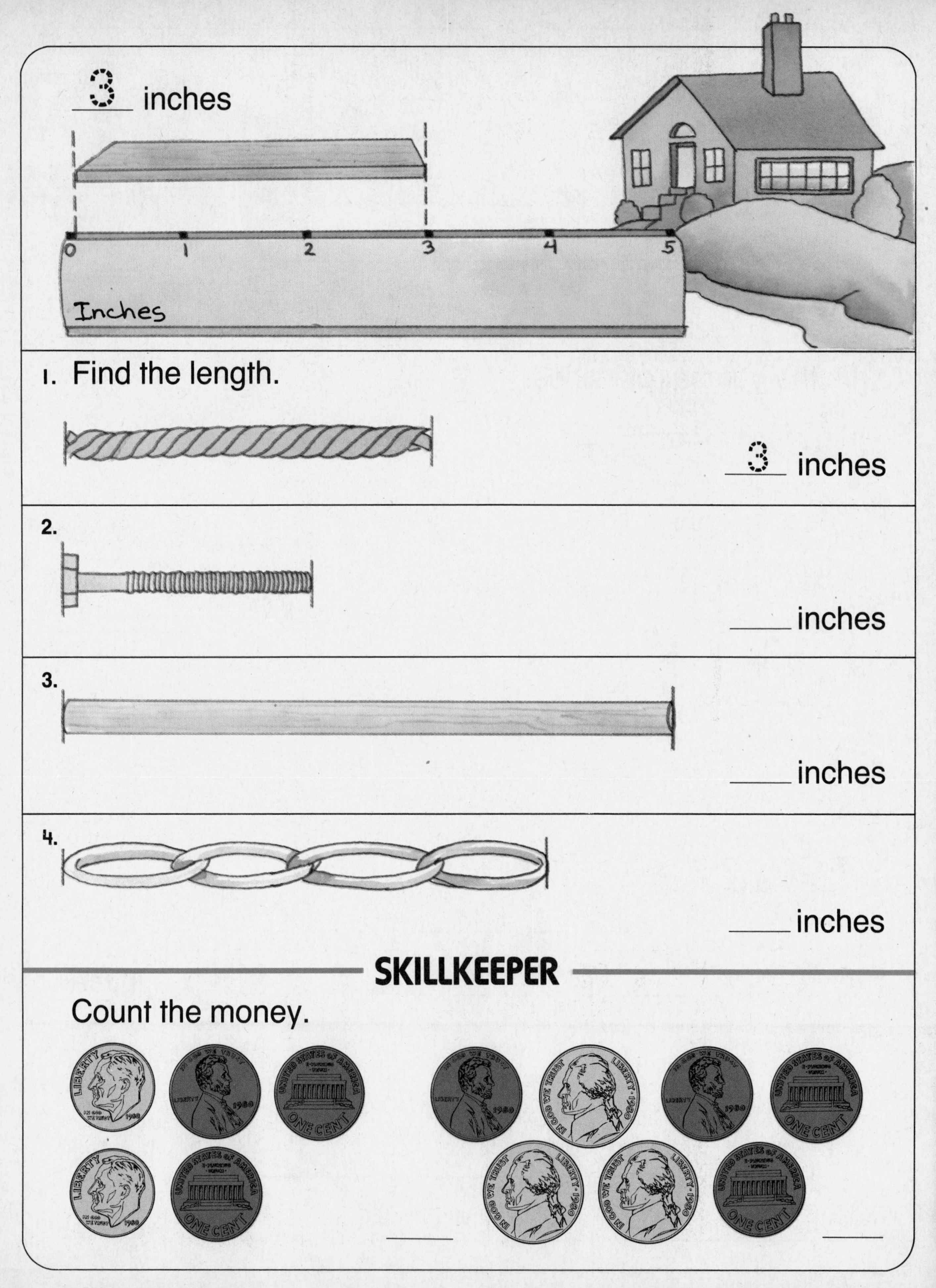
3 inches
0 1 2 3 4 5
Inches
1. Find the length.
3 inches
2.
inches
3.
inches
4.
inches
SKILLKEEPER
Count the money.

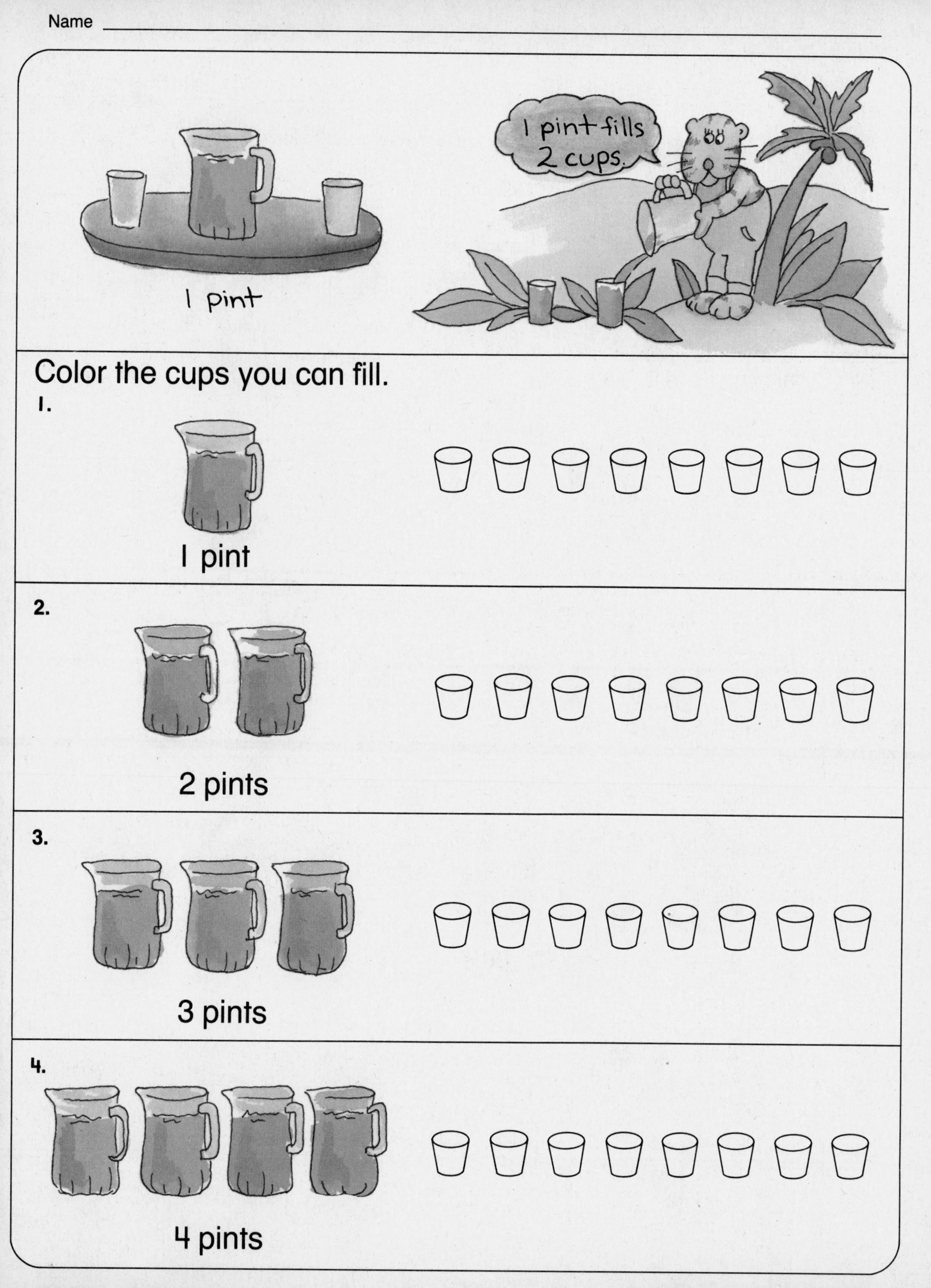
Name
1 pint fills
2 cups.
1 pint
Color the cups you can fill.
1.
1 pint
2.
2 pints
3.
3 pints
4.
4 pints

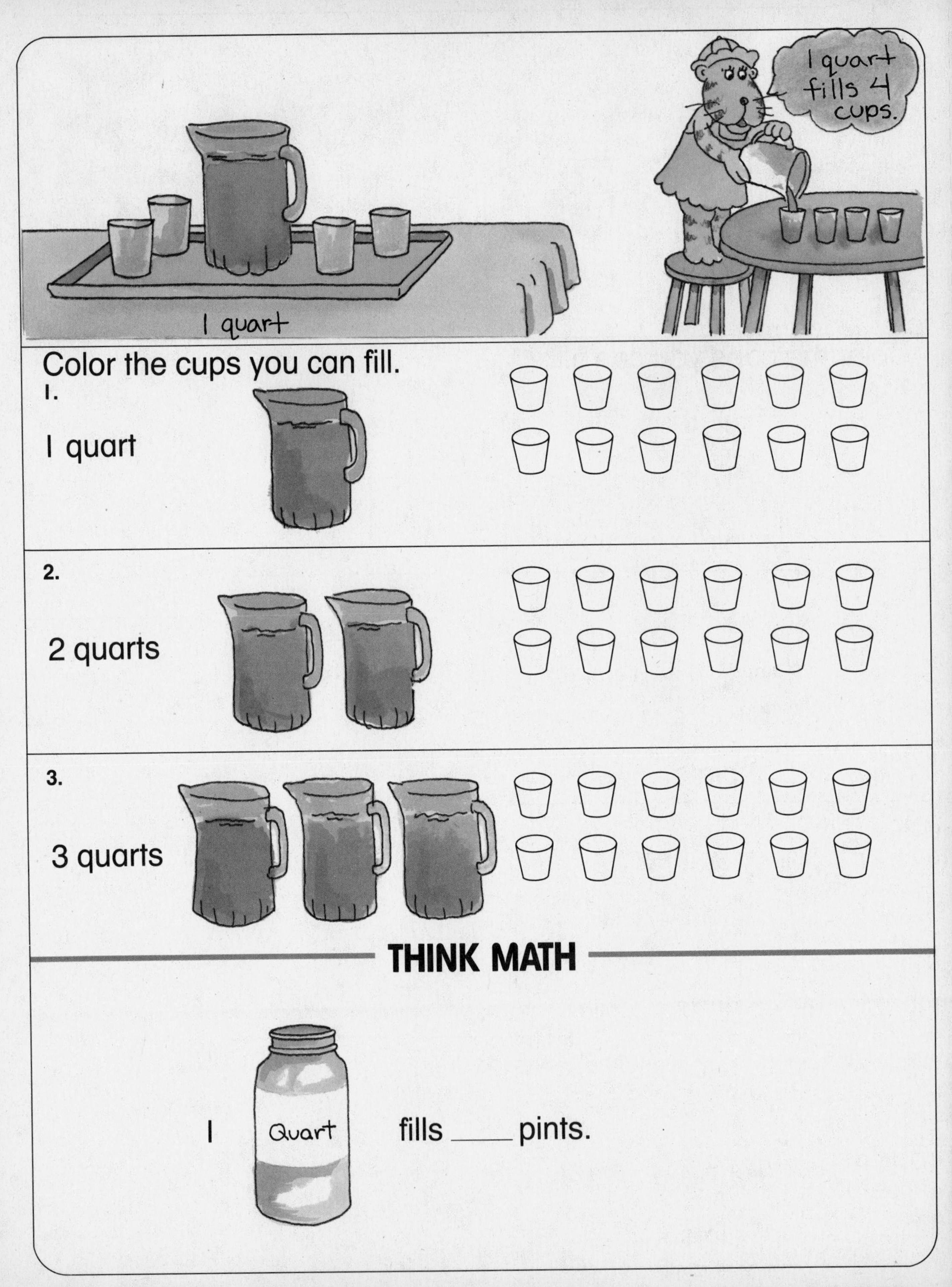

Color the cups you can fill.

1. 1 quart

2. 2 quarts

3. 3 quarts

THINK MATH

1 Quart fills ____ pints.

Name ______________________________

1. Estimate. Ring the objects that weigh more than a pound.

2. Estimate. Ring the objects that weigh less than a pound.

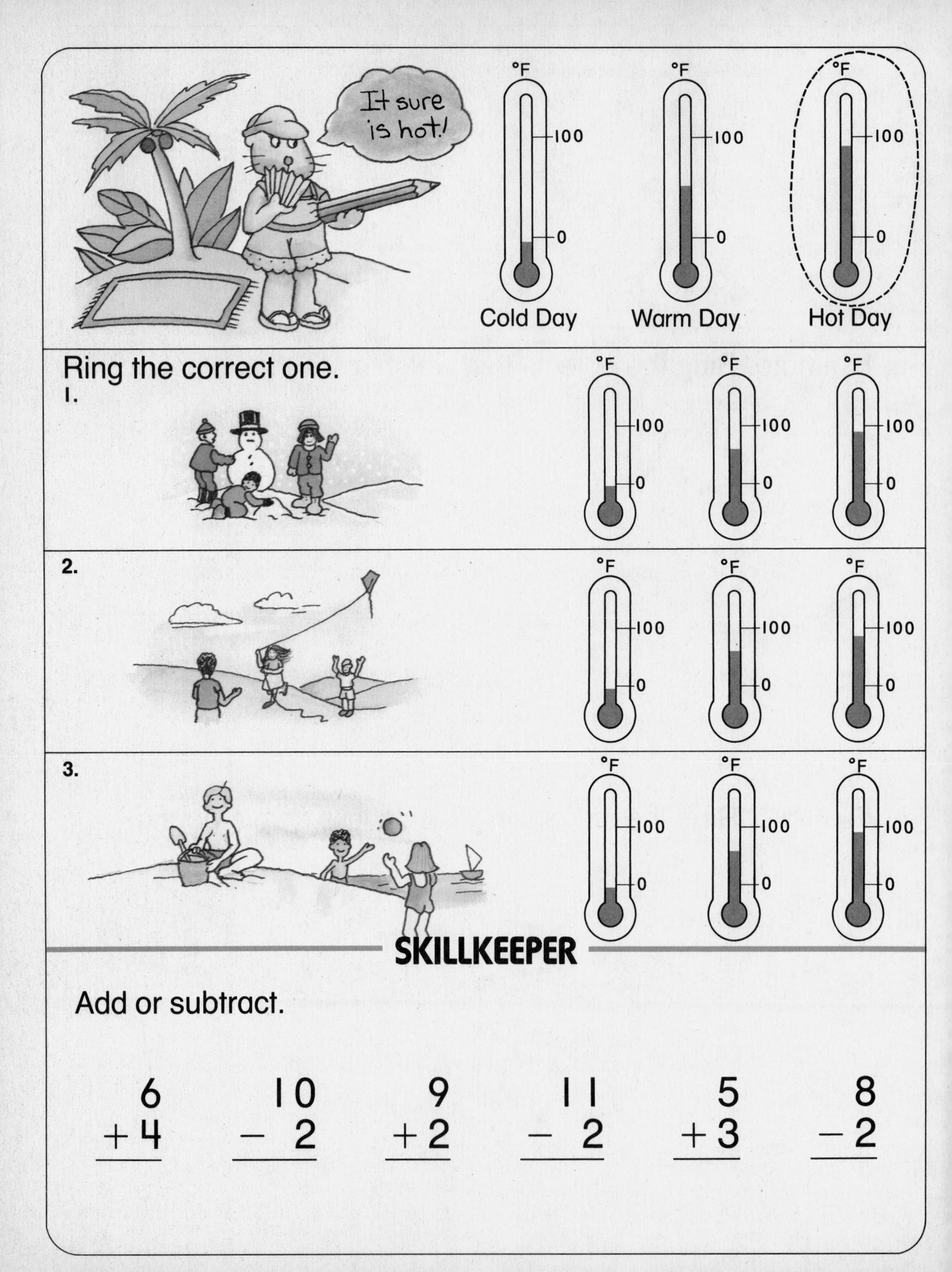
It sure is hot!
°F
100
0
Cold Day
Warm Day
Hot Day
Ring the correct one.
1.
2.
3.
SKILLKEEPER
Add or subtract.
6 + 4
10 − 2
9 + 2
11 − 2
5 + 3
8 − 2

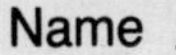

Name ______

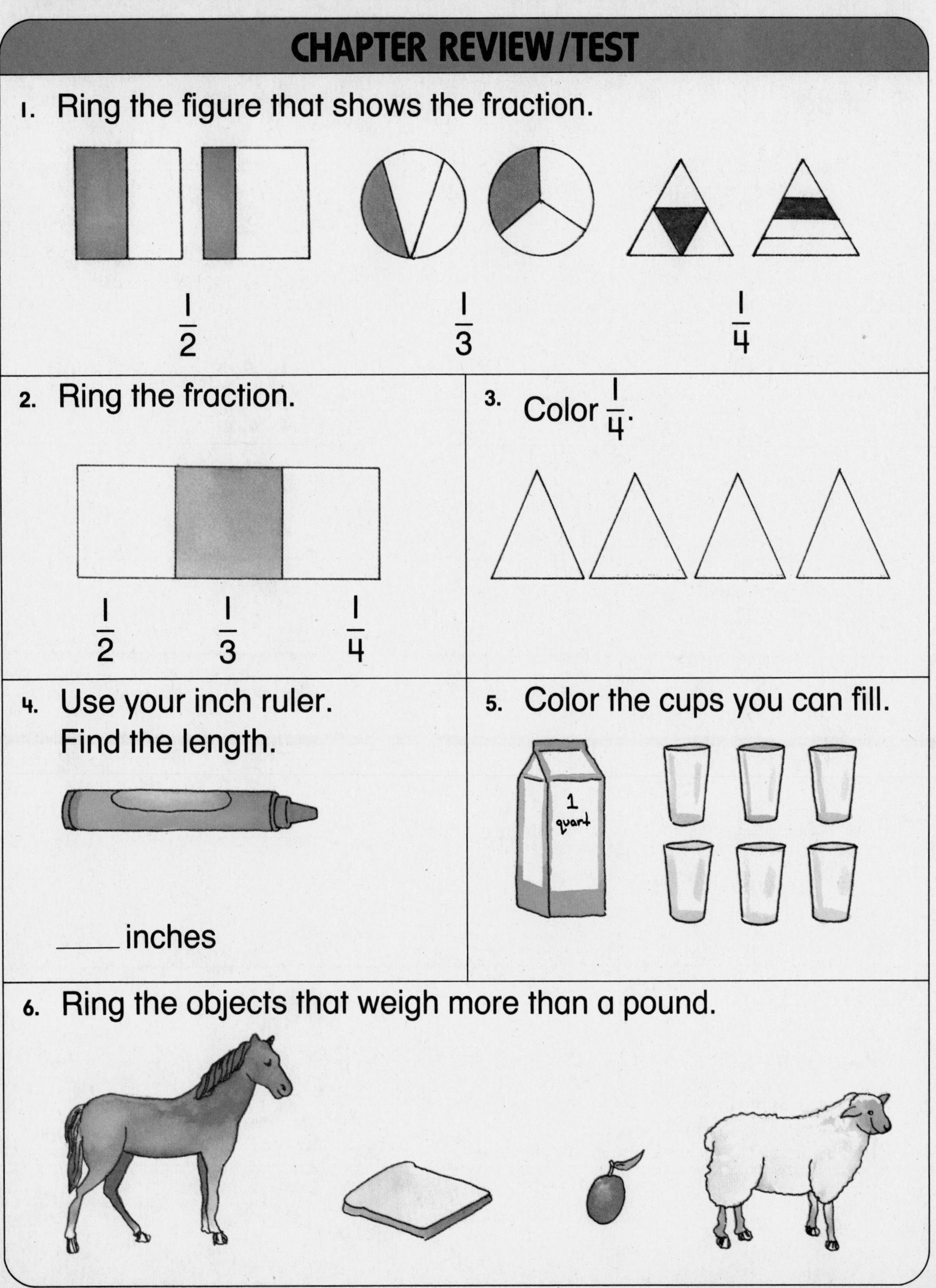

CHAPTER REVIEW/TEST

1. Ring the figure that shows the fraction.

$\frac{1}{2}$ $\frac{1}{3}$ $\frac{1}{4}$

2. Ring the fraction.

$\frac{1}{2}$ $\frac{1}{3}$ $\frac{1}{4}$

3. Color $\frac{1}{4}$.

4. Use your inch ruler. Find the length.

____ inches

5. Color the cups you can fill.

6. Ring the objects that weigh more than a pound.

Name ______________________________

CUMULATIVE REVIEW

Subtract.

1.

$$\begin{array}{r} 12 \\ -\ 7 \\ \hline \end{array}$$

○ 2
○ 4
○ 5

2.

$$\begin{array}{r} 10 \\ -\ 6 \\ \hline \end{array}$$

○ 4
○ 8
○ 6

3.

$$\begin{array}{r} 9 \\ -5 \\ \hline \end{array}$$

○ 5
○ 6
○ 4

4.

$$\begin{array}{r} 11 \\ -\ 6 \\ \hline \end{array}$$

○ 5
○ 6
○ 7

Add.

5.

$$\begin{array}{r} 17 \\ +12 \\ \hline \end{array}$$

○ 19
○ 25
○ 29

6.

$$\begin{array}{r} 46¢ \\ +22¢ \\ \hline \end{array}$$

○ 68¢
○ 24¢
○ 58¢

Subtract.

7.

$$\begin{array}{r} 49 \\ -18 \\ \hline \end{array}$$

○ 32
○ 31
○ 27

8.

$$\begin{array}{r} 78¢ \\ -56¢ \\ \hline \end{array}$$

○ 22¢
○ 24¢
○ 26¢

9. Solve.

Tony had 9¢.
He spent 4¢.
How much does he have now?

○ 7¢
○ 5¢
○ 9¢

Name ______________________________

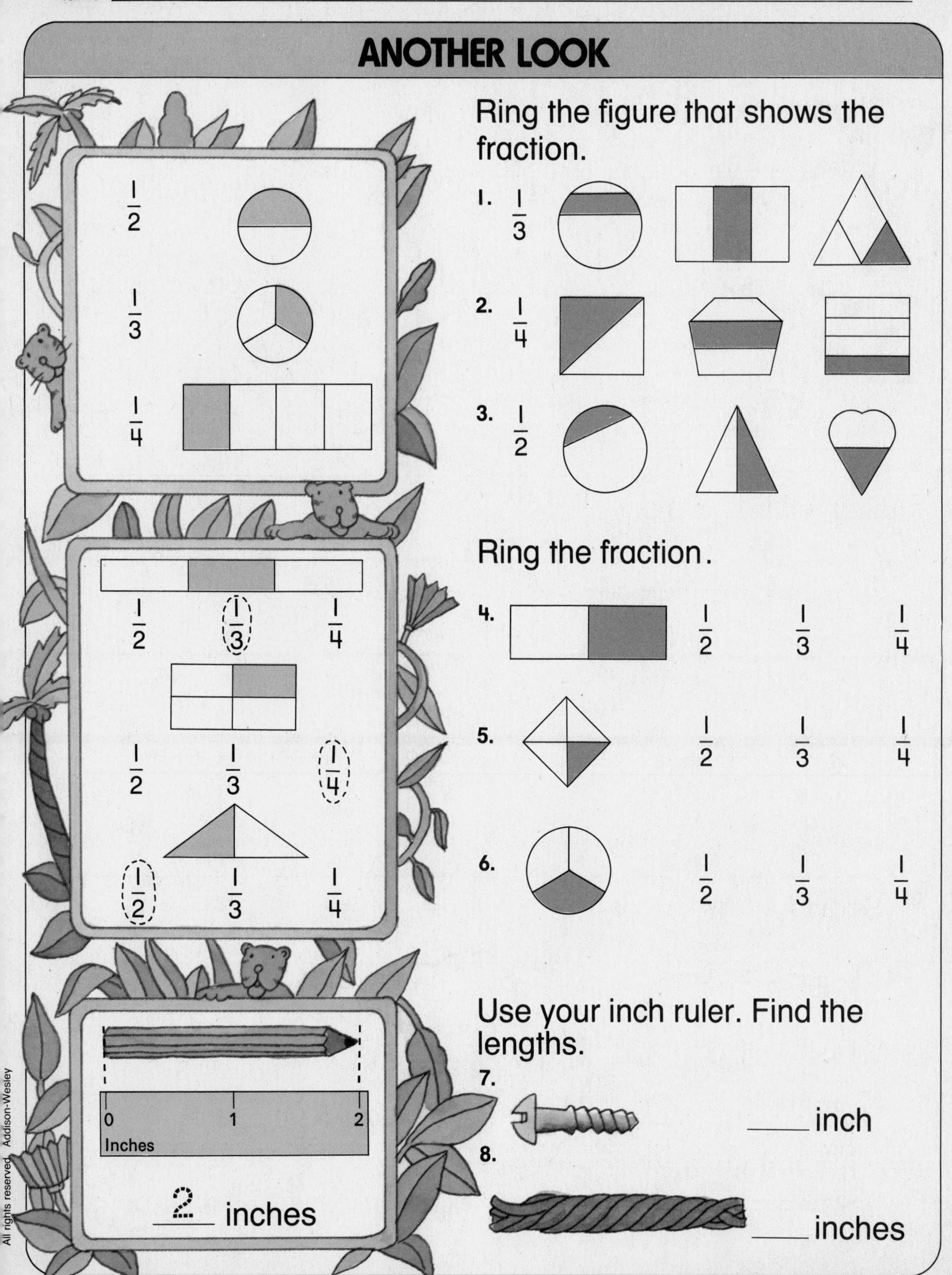

ANOTHER LOOK

$\frac{1}{2}$

$\frac{1}{3}$

$\frac{1}{4}$

$\frac{1}{2}$ $\frac{1}{3}$ $\frac{1}{4}$

$\frac{1}{2}$ $\frac{1}{3}$ $\frac{1}{4}$

$\frac{1}{2}$ $\frac{1}{3}$ $\frac{1}{4}$

0 1 2

Inches

2 inches

Ring the figure that shows the fraction.

1. $\frac{1}{3}$

2. $\frac{1}{4}$

3. $\frac{1}{2}$

Ring the fraction.

4. $\frac{1}{2}$ $\frac{1}{3}$ $\frac{1}{4}$

5. $\frac{1}{2}$ $\frac{1}{3}$ $\frac{1}{4}$

6. $\frac{1}{2}$ $\frac{1}{3}$ $\frac{1}{4}$

Use your inch ruler. Find the lengths.

7. ____ inch

8. ____ inches

Name ______________________________

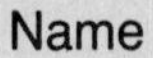

ENRICHMENT

1. Show halves. Color $\frac{1}{2}$.

2. Show thirds. Color $\frac{1}{3}$.

3. Show fourths. Color $\frac{1}{4}$.

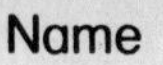

Name ____________________

COMPUTER INSTRUCTION–LOGO

For use after page 156.

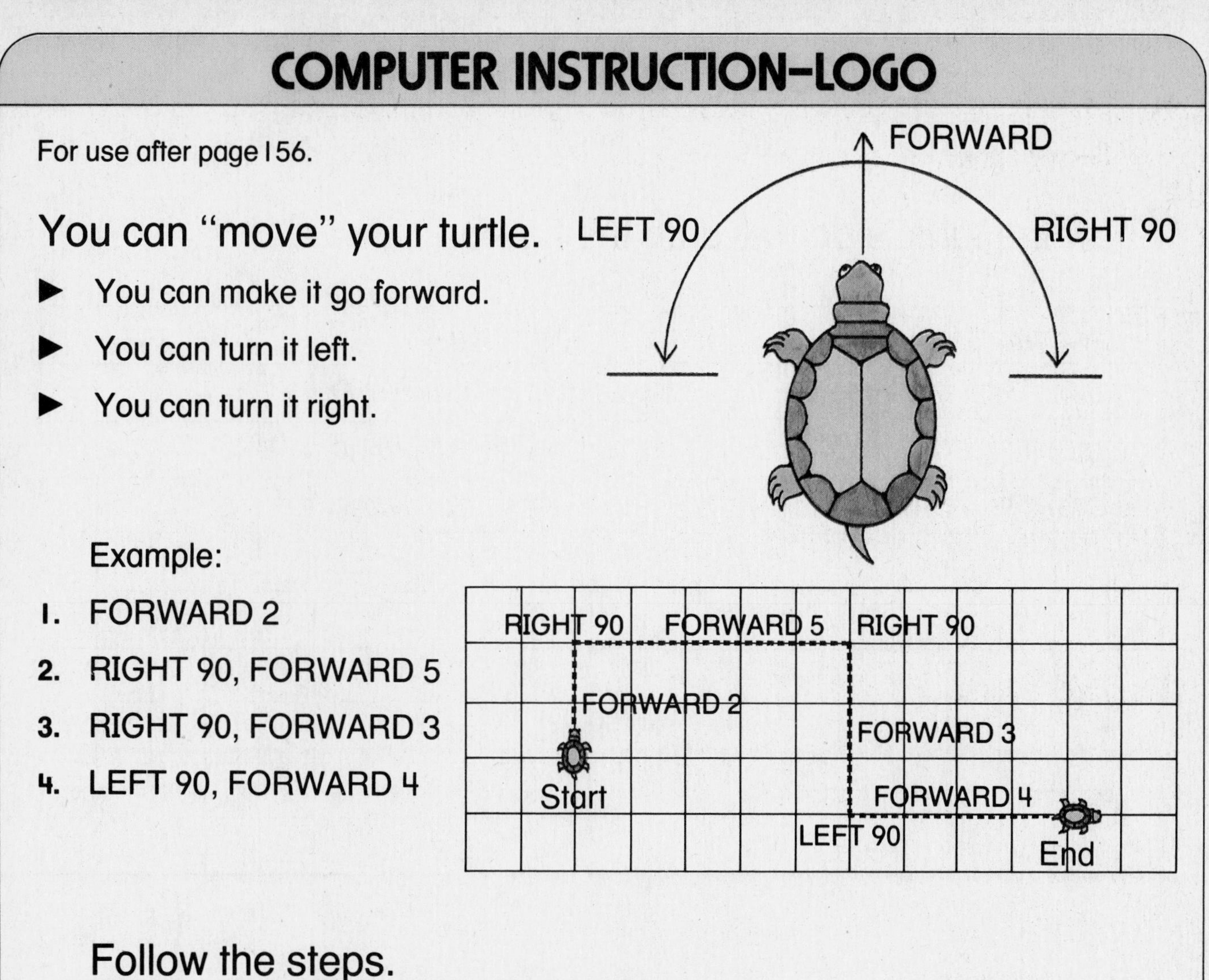

You can "move" your turtle.

- ▶ You can make it go forward.
- ▶ You can turn it left.
- ▶ You can turn it right.

Example:

1. FORWARD 2
2. RIGHT 90, FORWARD 5
3. RIGHT 90, FORWARD 3
4. LEFT 90, FORWARD 4

Follow the steps.
Use a crayon to show the turtle's path.

1. FORWARD 4
2. RIGHT 90, FORWARD 3
3. LEFT 90, FORWARD 2
4. RIGHT 90, FORWARD 5
5. RIGHT 90, FORWARD 2
6. LEFT 90, FORWARD 3
7. RIGHT 90, FORWARD 4

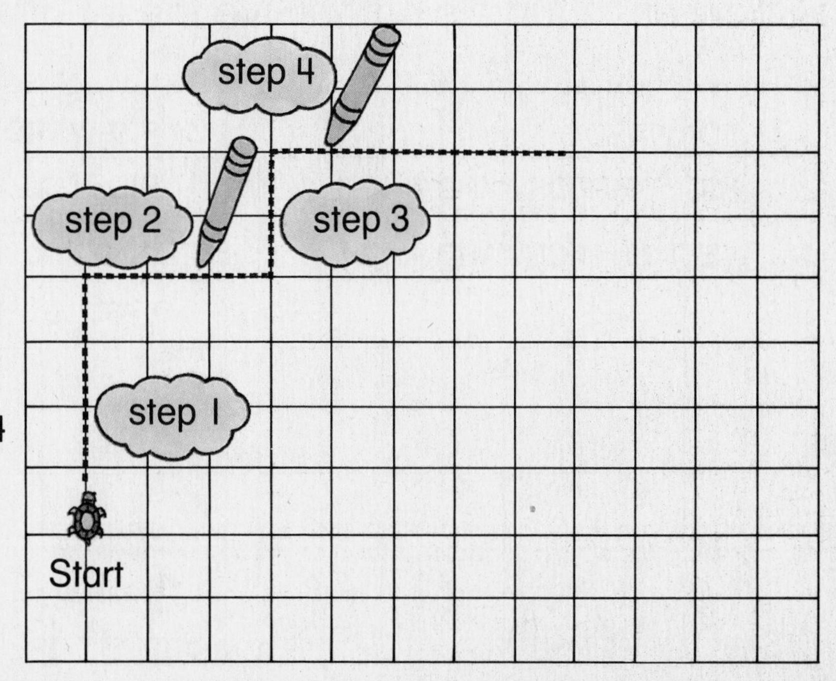

Name ______________________________

COMPUTER INSTRUCTION–LOGO

For use after page 232

Show the turtle's path. Name the figure.

1. FORWARD 4
RIGHT 90, FORWARD 4
RIGHT 90, FORWARD 4
RIGHT 90, FORWARD 4

Start

Figure: ________

2. FORWARD 4
LEFT 90, FORWARD 9
LEFT 90, FORWARD 4
LEFT 90, FORWARD 9

Start

Figure: ________

For use after page 276

Show each turtle's path. Give the length.

1. FORWARD 3
RIGHT 90, FORWARD 7
LEFT 90, FORWARD 4

Start

Length: _____ units

2. FORWARD 4
RIGHT 90, FORWARD 6
RIGHT 90, FORWARD 2
LEFT 90, FORWARD 3

Start

Length: _____ units

Name ____________________

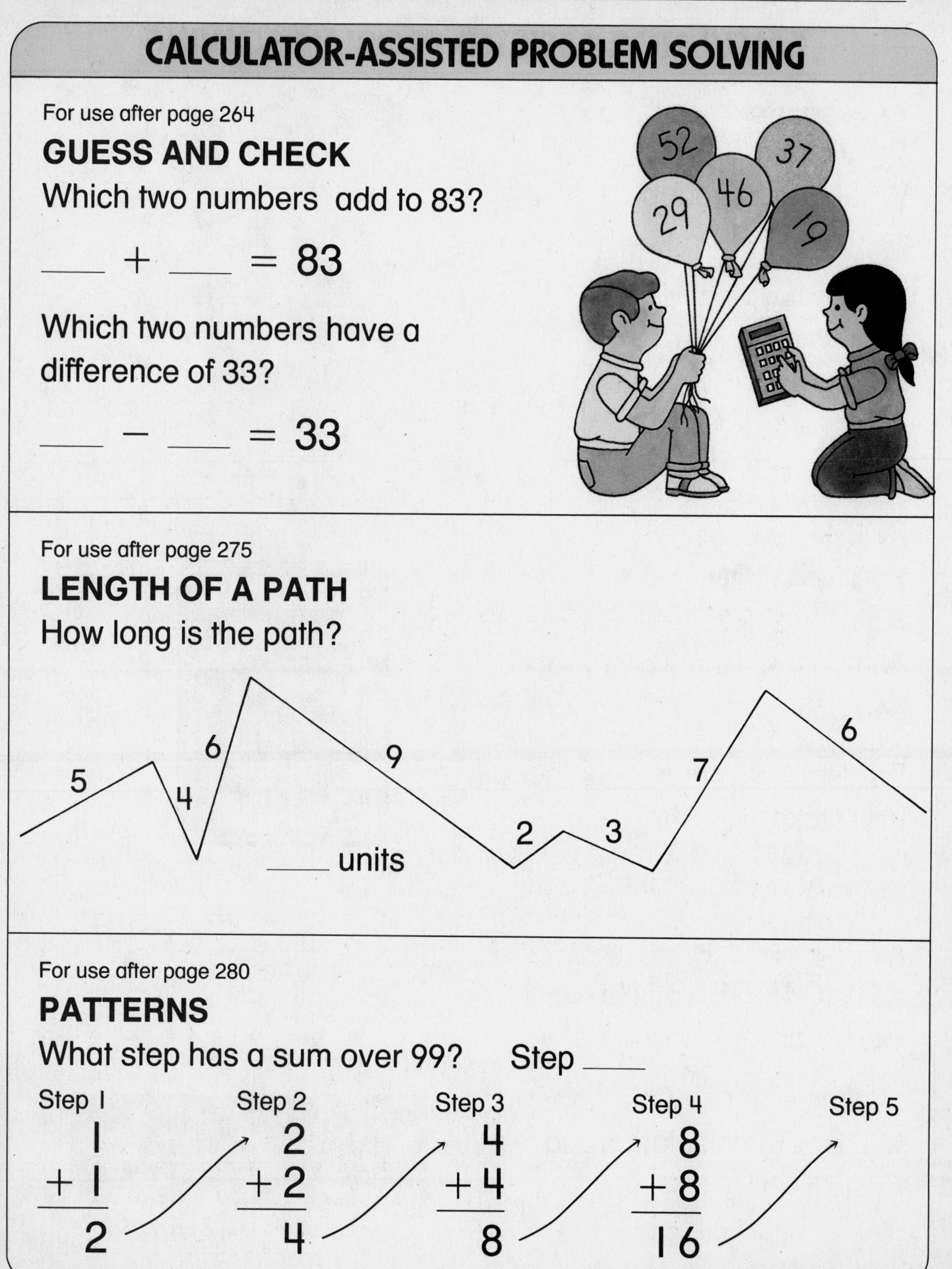

CALCULATOR-ASSISTED PROBLEM SOLVING

For use after page 264

GUESS AND CHECK

Which two numbers add to 83?

___ + ___ = 83

Which two numbers have a difference of 33?

___ − ___ = 33

For use after page 275

LENGTH OF A PATH

How long is the path?

5, 4, 6, 9, 2, 3, 7, 6

___ units

For use after page 280

PATTERNS

What step has a sum over 99? Step ___

Step 1	Step 2	Step 3	Step 4	Step 5
1	2	4	8	
+ 1	+ 2	+ 4	+ 8	
2	4	8	16	

Name ______

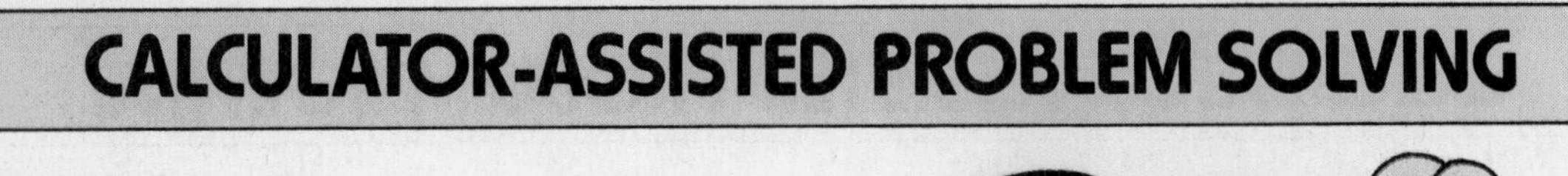

CALCULATOR-ASSISTED PROBLEM SOLVING

For use after page 286

DOUBLES

What number doubled is 96?

NUMBER →	7	8	9	10	11 . . . . ____
	↓	↓	↓	↓	↓ . . . . ↓
DOUBLE →	14	16	18	20	22 96

For use after page 290

ESTIMATION

Add 1 + 2 + 3 + 4 + 5 + 6 + and so on. Stop when you see 55.

Estimate how many numbers it will take. ____

How many did it take? ____

For use after page 295

LOGICAL REASONING

Use each key only once.

Use no other key.

Make your calculator read →

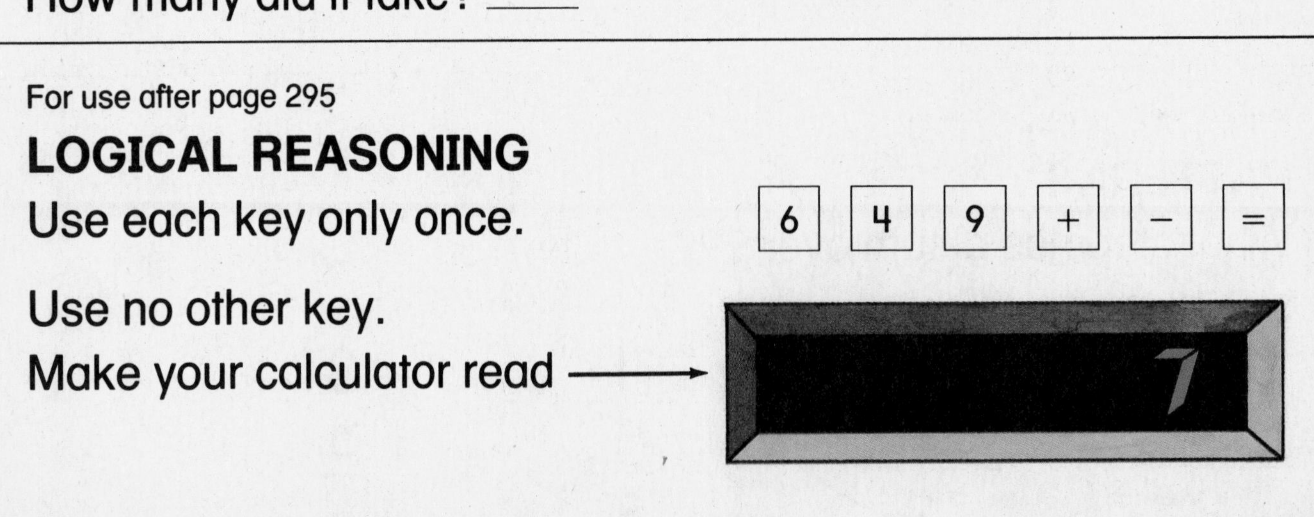

DATA BANK

MAY Year 2000

Sunday	Monday	Tuesday	Wednesday	Thursday	Friday	Saturday
	1	2	3	4	5	6
7	8	9	10	11	12	13
14	15	16	17	18	19	20
21	22	23	24	25	26	27
28	29	30	31			

DATA BANK

There were 10 green worms.
5 were on the apple.

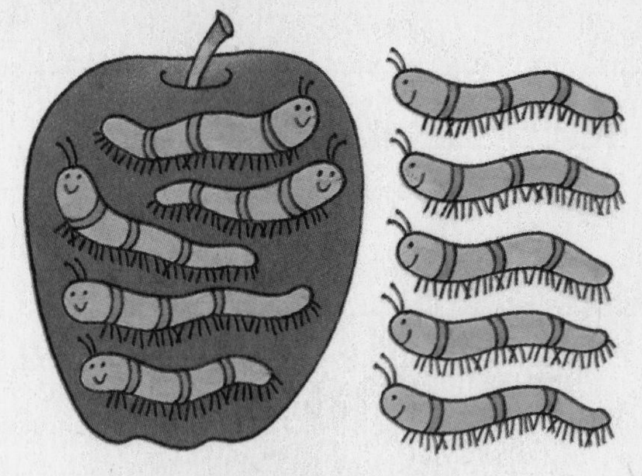

9 flies were on the leaf.
2 more came along.

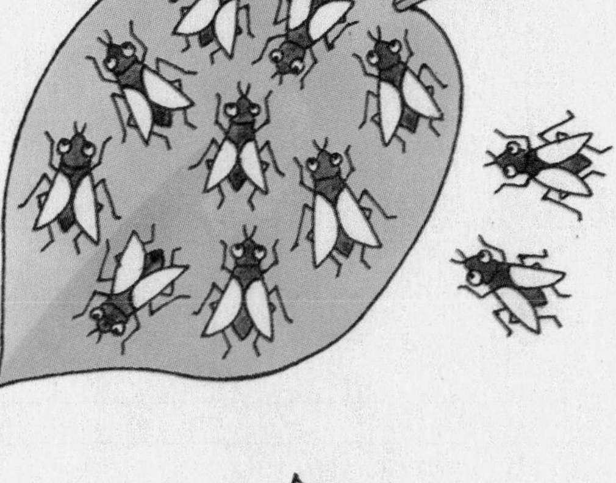

4 ants were on a plant.
4 more were on the ground.

8 bees were on a flower.
4 flew away.

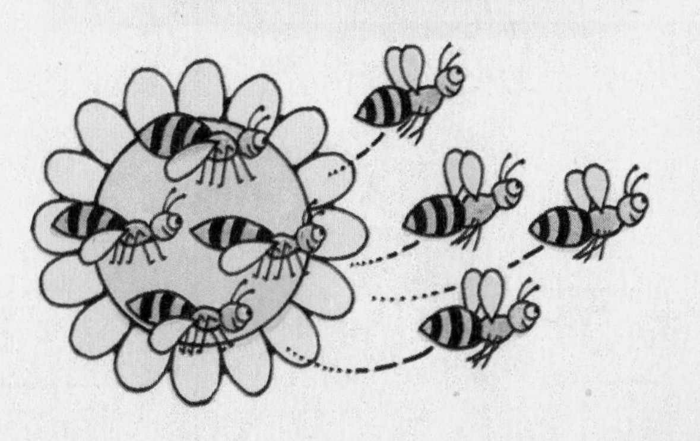

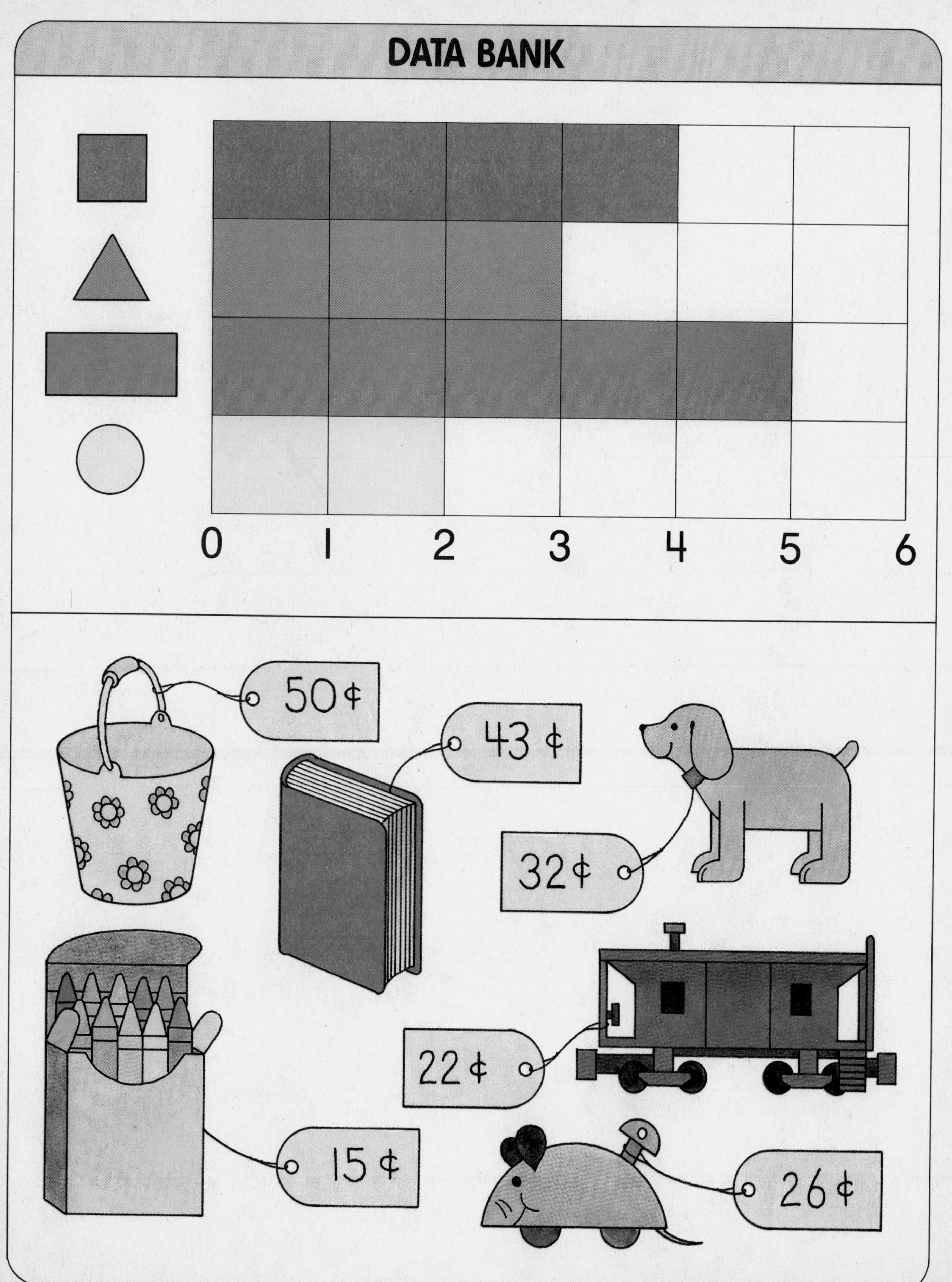
DATA BANK
0
1
2
3
4
5
6
50¢
43¢
32¢
22¢
15¢
26¢

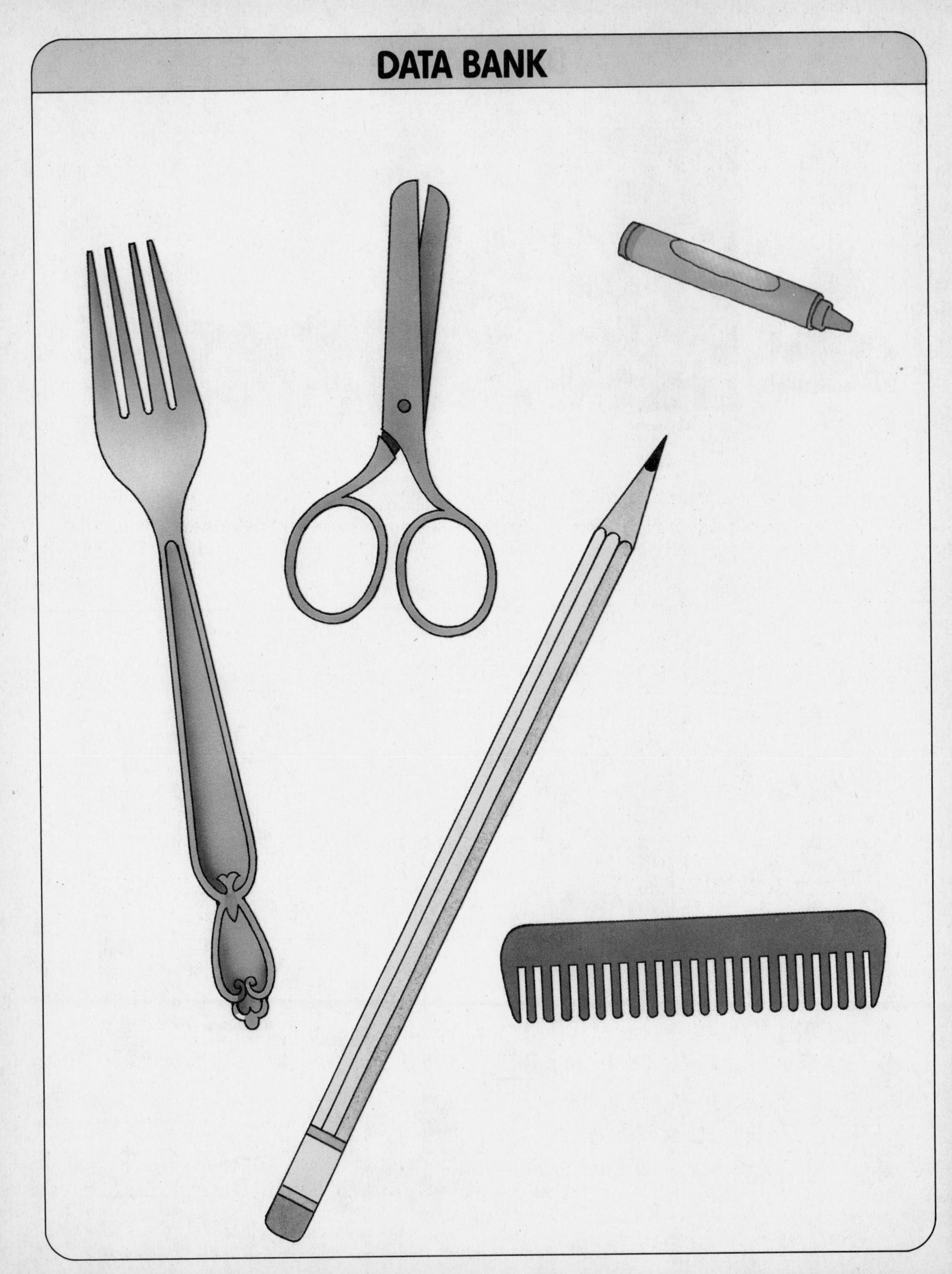
DATA BANK

Name ______________________________

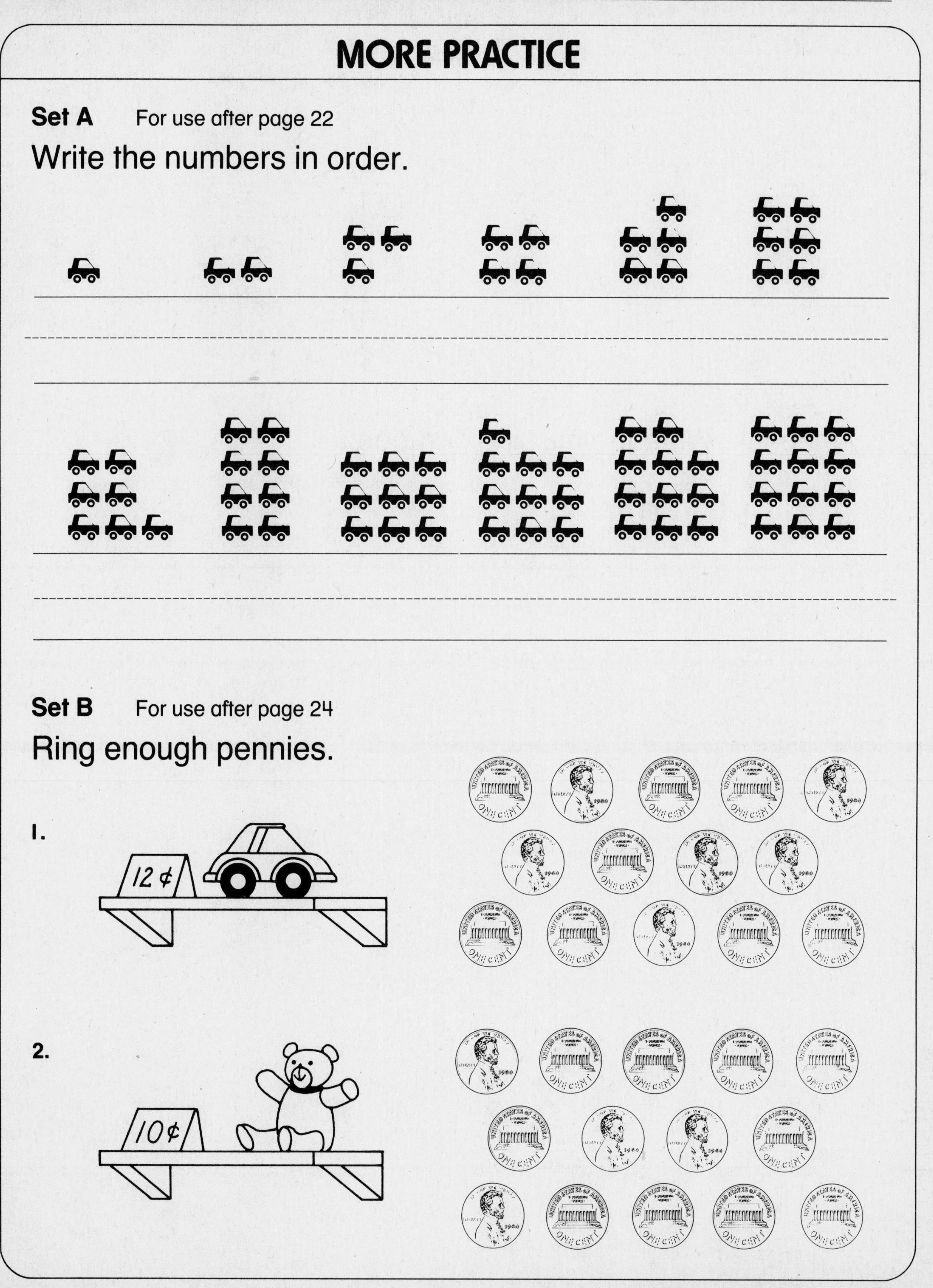

MORE PRACTICE

Set A For use after page 22

Write the numbers in order.

Set B For use after page 24

Ring enough pennies.

1.

2.

Name ______________________________

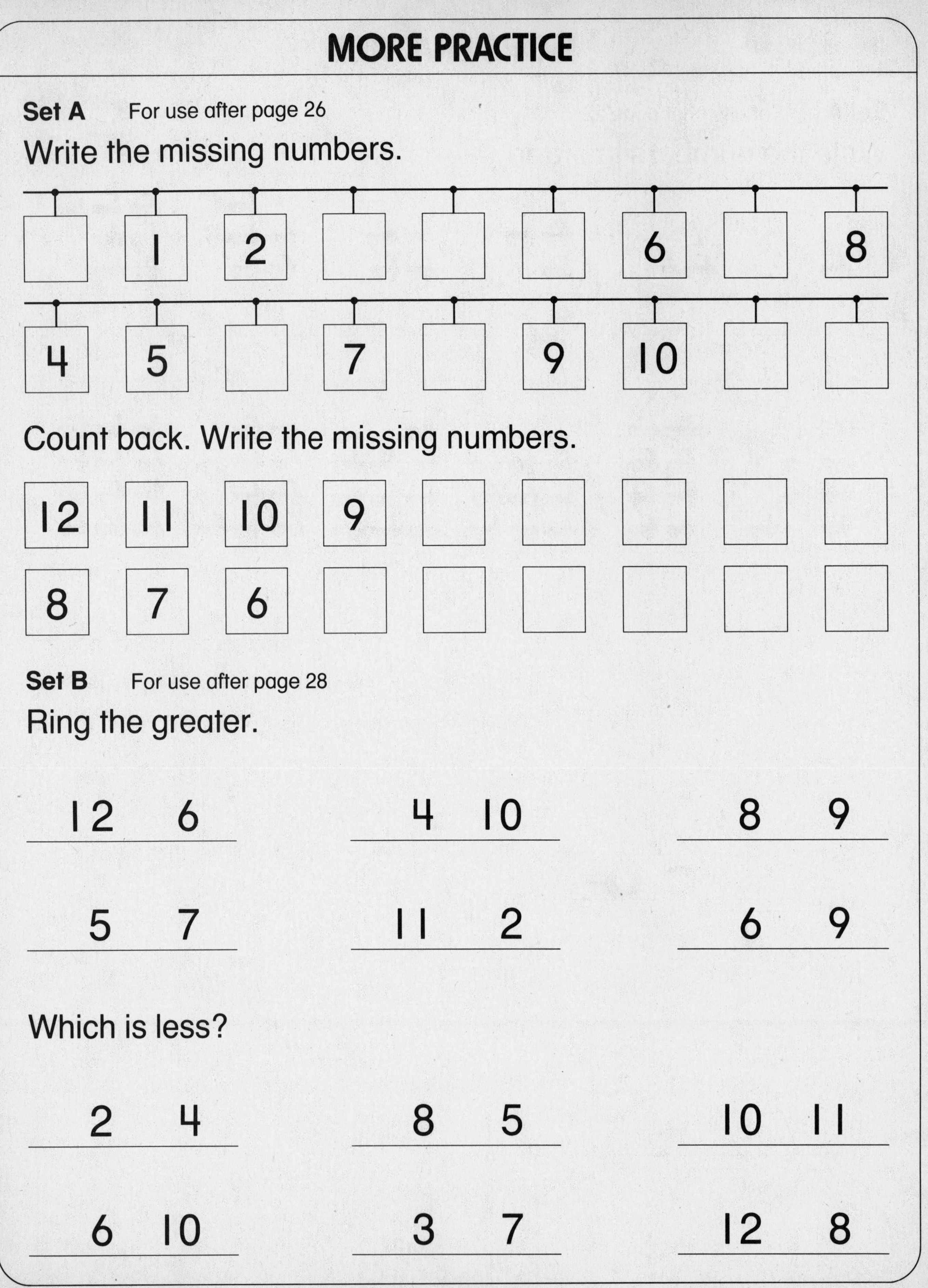

MORE PRACTICE

Set A For use after page 26

Write the missing numbers.

	1	2				6		8
4	5		7		9	10		

Count back. Write the missing numbers.

12	11	10	9					
8	7	6						

Set B For use after page 28

Ring the greater.

12 6 ______ 4 10 ______ 8 9 ______

5 7 ______ 11 2 ______ 6 9 ______

Which is less?

2 4 ______ 8 5 ______ 10 11 ______

6 10 ______ 3 7 ______ 12 8 ______

Name ______________________________

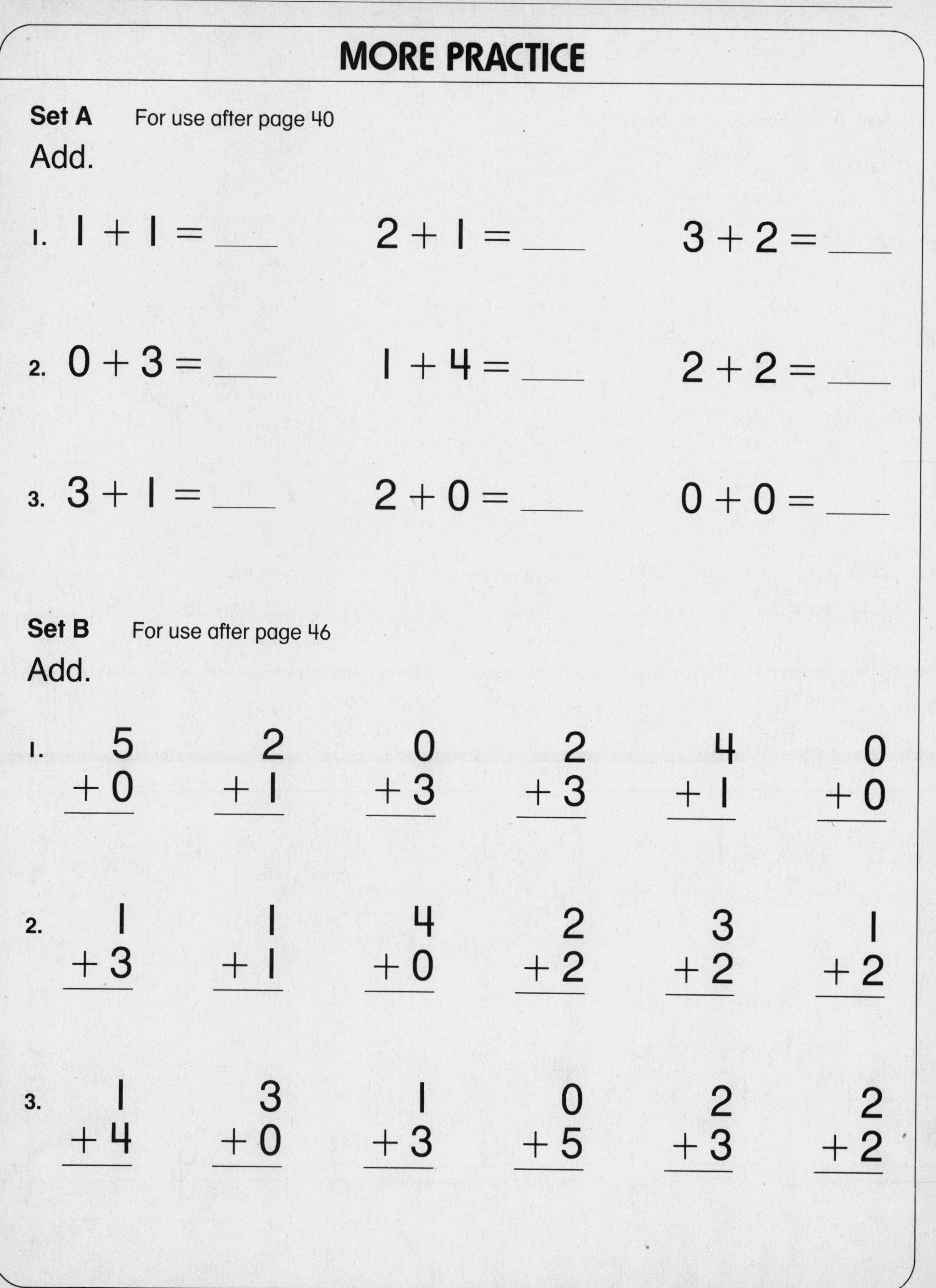

MORE PRACTICE

Set A For use after page 40

Add.

1. $1 + 1 =$ ___ $2 + 1 =$ ___ $3 + 2 =$ ___

2. $0 + 3 =$ ___ $1 + 4 =$ ___ $2 + 2 =$ ___

3. $3 + 1 =$ ___ $2 + 0 =$ ___ $0 + 0 =$ ___

Set B For use after page 46

Add.

1.	$5 + 0$	$2 + 1$	$0 + 3$	$2 + 3$	$4 + 1$	$0 + 0$
2.	$1 + 3$	$1 + 1$	$4 + 0$	$2 + 2$	$3 + 2$	$1 + 2$
3.	$1 + 4$	$3 + 0$	$1 + 3$	$0 + 5$	$2 + 3$	$2 + 2$

Name ______________________________

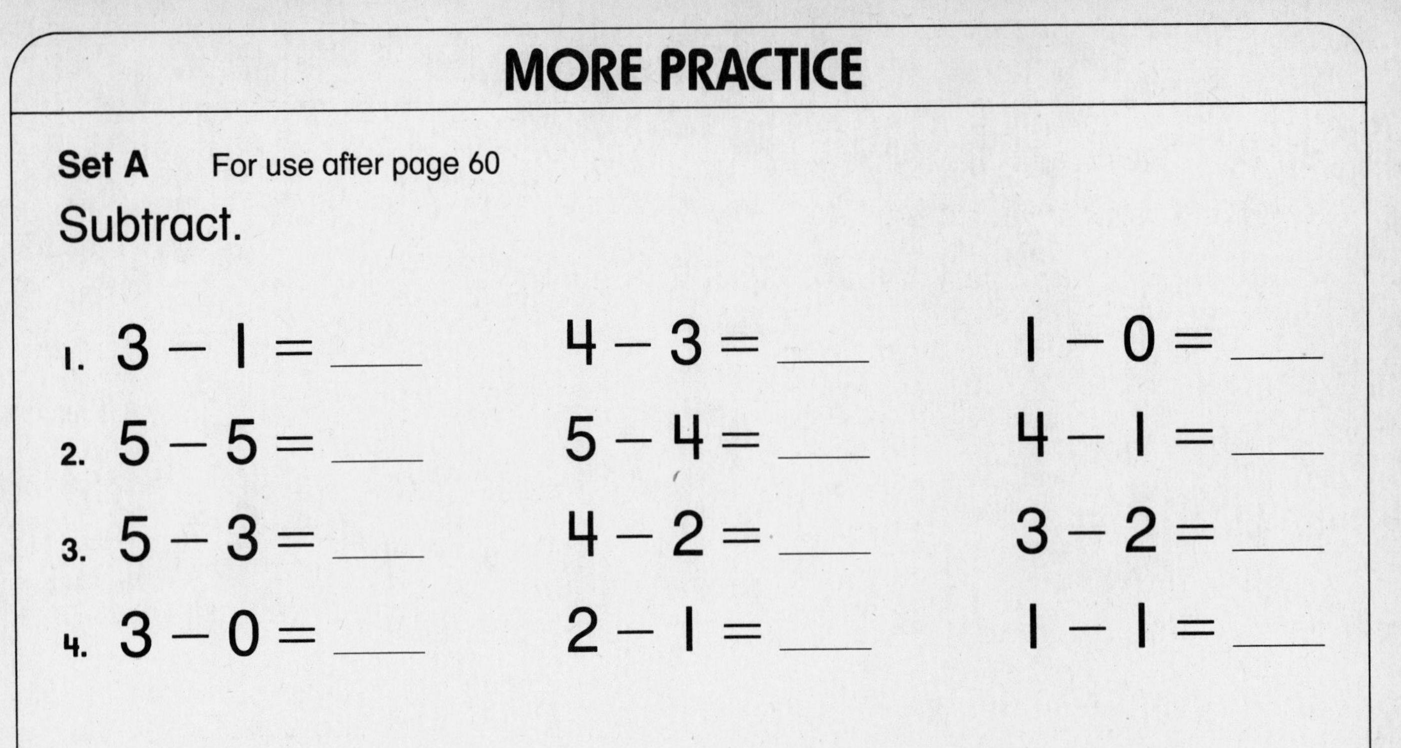

MORE PRACTICE

Set A For use after page 60

Subtract.

1. $3 - 1 =$ ____ $4 - 3 =$ ____ $1 - 0 =$ ____
2. $5 - 5 =$ ____ $5 - 4 =$ ____ $4 - 1 =$ ____
3. $5 - 3 =$ ____ $4 - 2 =$ ____ $3 - 2 =$ ____
4. $3 - 0 =$ ____ $2 - 1 =$ ____ $1 - 1 =$ ____

Set B For use after page 66

Subtract.

1. $\begin{array}{r} 4 \\ -1 \\ \hline \end{array}$ $\begin{array}{r} 3 \\ -2 \\ \hline \end{array}$ $\begin{array}{r} 2 \\ -2 \\ \hline \end{array}$ $\begin{array}{r} 5 \\ -3 \\ \hline \end{array}$ $\begin{array}{r} 2 \\ -0 \\ \hline \end{array}$ $\begin{array}{r} 0 \\ -0 \\ \hline \end{array}$

2. $\begin{array}{r} 4 \\ -3 \\ \hline \end{array}$ $\begin{array}{r} 5 \\ -4 \\ \hline \end{array}$ $\begin{array}{r} 4 \\ -1 \\ \hline \end{array}$ $\begin{array}{r} 5 \\ -5 \\ \hline \end{array}$ $\begin{array}{r} 2 \\ -1 \\ \hline \end{array}$ $\begin{array}{r} 5 \\ -3 \\ \hline \end{array}$

3. $\begin{array}{r} 5 \\ -1 \\ \hline \end{array}$ $\begin{array}{r} 1 \\ -0 \\ \hline \end{array}$ $\begin{array}{r} 5 \\ -2 \\ \hline \end{array}$ $\begin{array}{r} 4 \\ -4 \\ \hline \end{array}$ $\begin{array}{r} 3 \\ -1 \\ \hline \end{array}$ $\begin{array}{r} 4 \\ -0 \\ \hline \end{array}$

4. $\begin{array}{r} 3 \\ -0 \\ \hline \end{array}$ $\begin{array}{r} 5 \\ -0 \\ \hline \end{array}$ $\begin{array}{r} 4 \\ -2 \\ \hline \end{array}$ $\begin{array}{r} 3 \\ -3 \\ \hline \end{array}$ $\begin{array}{r} 5 \\ -4 \\ \hline \end{array}$ $\begin{array}{r} 4 \\ -3 \\ \hline \end{array}$

Name ______________________________

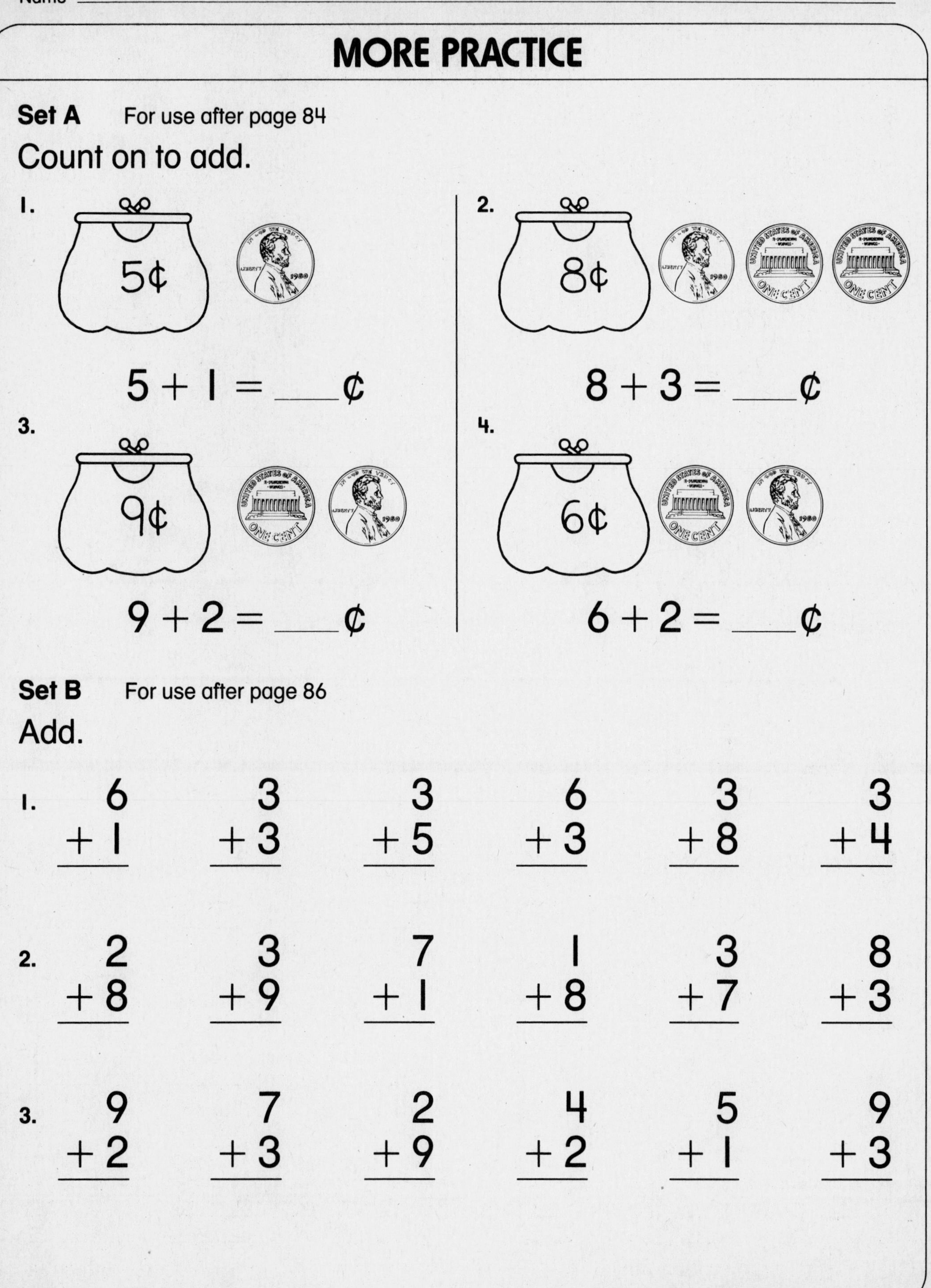

MORE PRACTICE

Set A For use after page 84

Count on to add.

1. 5¢

$5 + 1 =$ ____ ¢

2. 8¢

$8 + 3 =$ ____ ¢

3. 9¢

$9 + 2 =$ ____ ¢

4. 6¢

$6 + 2 =$ ____ ¢

Set B For use after page 86

Add.

1. $\begin{array}{r} 6 \\ +1 \\ \hline \end{array}$ $\begin{array}{r} 3 \\ +3 \\ \hline \end{array}$ $\begin{array}{r} 3 \\ +5 \\ \hline \end{array}$ $\begin{array}{r} 6 \\ +3 \\ \hline \end{array}$ $\begin{array}{r} 3 \\ +8 \\ \hline \end{array}$ $\begin{array}{r} 3 \\ +4 \\ \hline \end{array}$

2. $\begin{array}{r} 2 \\ +8 \\ \hline \end{array}$ $\begin{array}{r} 3 \\ +9 \\ \hline \end{array}$ $\begin{array}{r} 7 \\ +1 \\ \hline \end{array}$ $\begin{array}{r} 1 \\ +8 \\ \hline \end{array}$ $\begin{array}{r} 3 \\ +7 \\ \hline \end{array}$ $\begin{array}{r} 8 \\ +3 \\ \hline \end{array}$

3. $\begin{array}{r} 9 \\ +2 \\ \hline \end{array}$ $\begin{array}{r} 7 \\ +3 \\ \hline \end{array}$ $\begin{array}{r} 2 \\ +9 \\ \hline \end{array}$ $\begin{array}{r} 4 \\ +2 \\ \hline \end{array}$ $\begin{array}{r} 5 \\ +1 \\ \hline \end{array}$ $\begin{array}{r} 9 \\ +3 \\ \hline \end{array}$

Name ______________________________

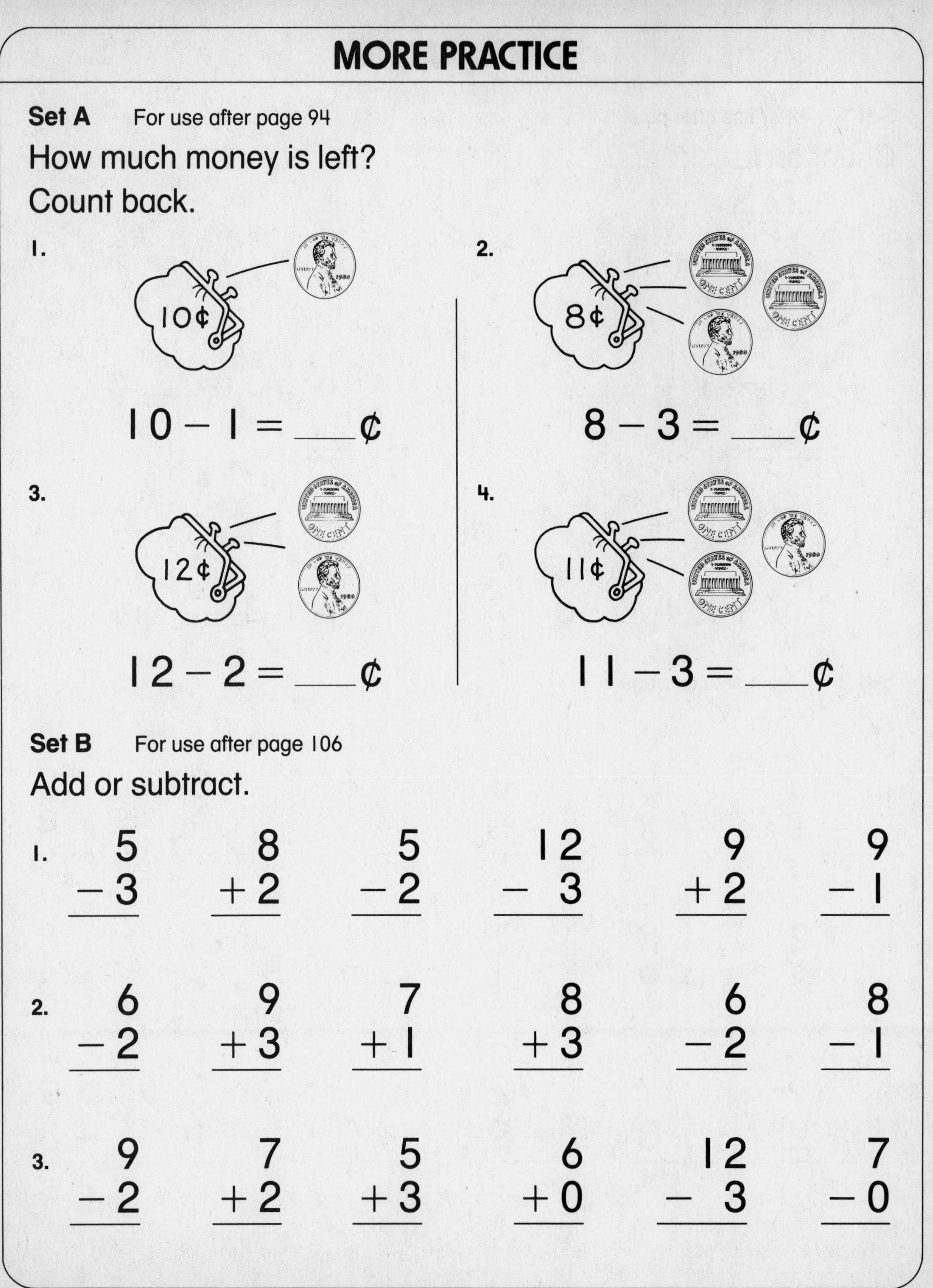

MORE PRACTICE

Set A For use after page 94

How much money is left?
Count back.

1. 10¢ $10 - 1 = \_\_\_¢$

2. 8¢ $8 - 3 = \_\_\_¢$

3. 12¢ $12 - 2 = \_\_\_¢$

4. 11¢ $11 - 3 = \_\_\_¢$

Set B For use after page 106

Add or subtract.

1. $\begin{array}{r}5\\-3\\\hline\end{array}$ $\begin{array}{r}8\\+2\\\hline\end{array}$ $\begin{array}{r}5\\-2\\\hline\end{array}$ $\begin{array}{r}12\\-\ 3\\\hline\end{array}$ $\begin{array}{r}9\\+2\\\hline\end{array}$ $\begin{array}{r}9\\-1\\\hline\end{array}$

2. $\begin{array}{r}6\\-2\\\hline\end{array}$ $\begin{array}{r}9\\+3\\\hline\end{array}$ $\begin{array}{r}7\\+1\\\hline\end{array}$ $\begin{array}{r}8\\+3\\\hline\end{array}$ $\begin{array}{r}6\\-2\\\hline\end{array}$ $\begin{array}{r}8\\-1\\\hline\end{array}$

3. $\begin{array}{r}9\\-2\\\hline\end{array}$ $\begin{array}{r}7\\+2\\\hline\end{array}$ $\begin{array}{r}5\\+3\\\hline\end{array}$ $\begin{array}{r}6\\+0\\\hline\end{array}$ $\begin{array}{r}12\\-\ 3\\\hline\end{array}$ $\begin{array}{r}7\\-0\\\hline\end{array}$

Name ______________________________

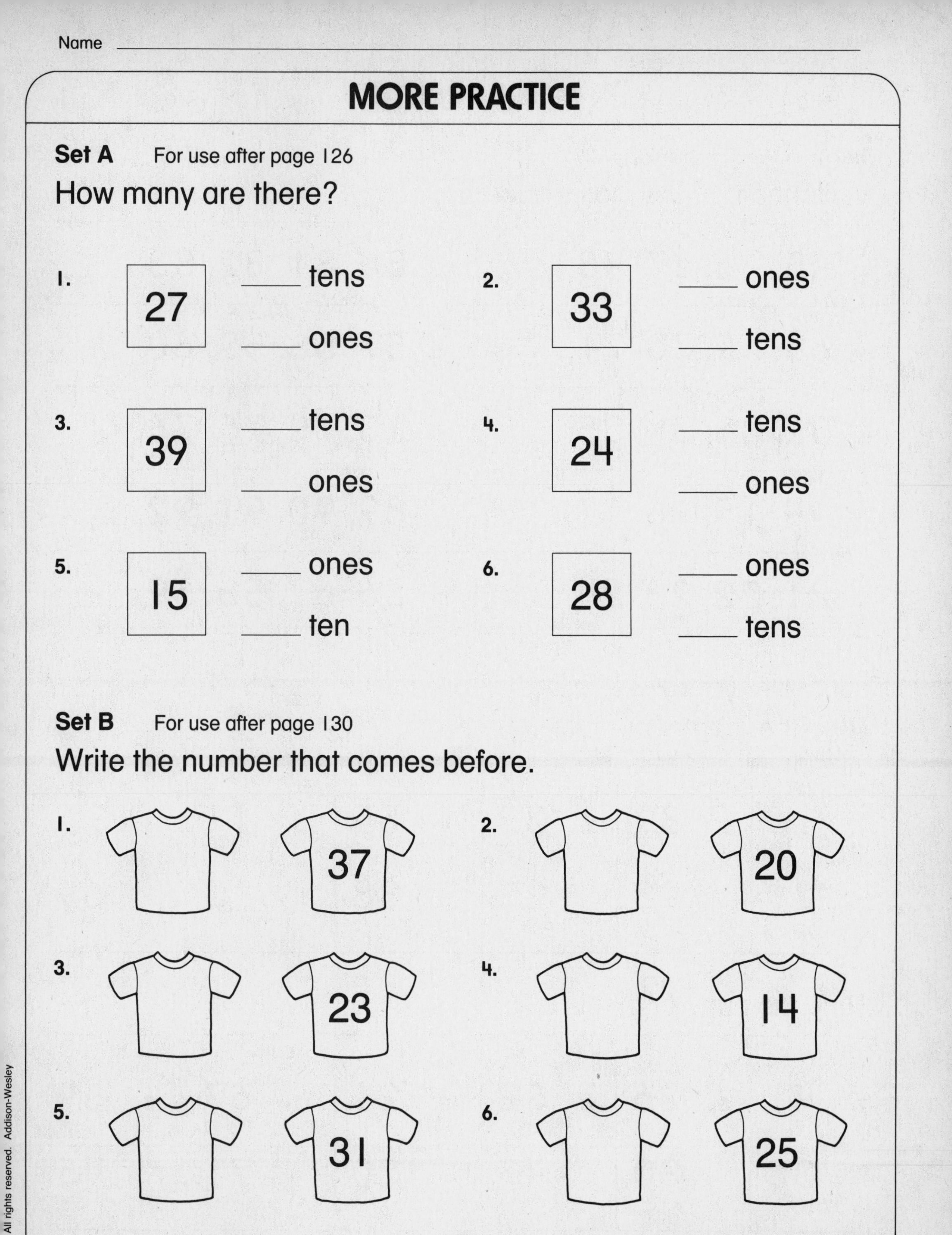

MORE PRACTICE

Set A For use after page 126

How many are there?

1. 27 ____ tens ____ ones

2. 33 ____ ones ____ tens

3. 39 ____ tens ____ ones

4. 24 ____ tens ____ ones

5. 15 ____ ones ____ ten

6. 28 ____ ones ____ tens

Set B For use after page 130

Write the number that comes before.

1. ____ 37

2. ____ 20

3. ____ 23

4. ____ 14

5. ____ 31

6. ____ 25

Name ______

MORE PRACTICE

Set A For use after page 134

Write the number that is next.

1. 45, 46, 47, 48, ___	2. 80, 81, 82, 83, ___
3. 68, 69, 70, 71, ___	4. 57, 58, 59, 60, ___
5. 32, 33, 34, 35, ___	6. 73, 74, 75, 76, ___
7. 14, 15, 16, 17, ___	8. 89, 90, 91, 92, ___
9. 21, 22, 23, 24, ___	10. 56, 57, 58, 59, ___

Set B For use after page 138

Ring the greater number.

1.	2.	3.	4.	5.	6.
16	89	32	55	11	76
21	98	27	38	13	69

Ring the number that is less.

7.	8.	9.	10.	11.	12.
41	26	52	21	67	54
38	30	47	20	71	45

Name ______________________________

MORE PRACTICE

Set A For use after page 140

Match.

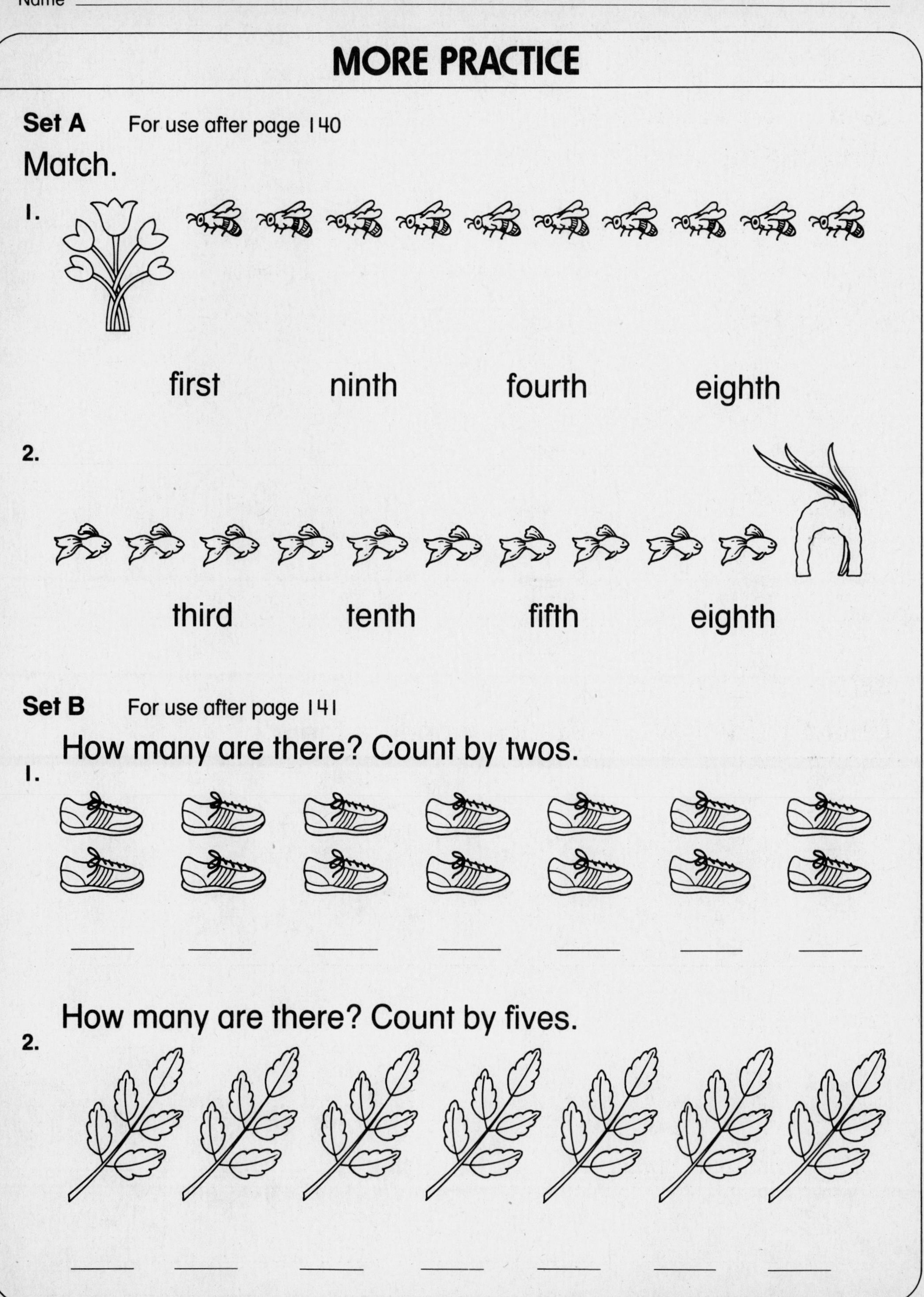

1\.

first ninth fourth eighth

2\.

third tenth fifth eighth

Set B For use after page 141

How many are there? Count by twos.

1\.

___ ___ ___ ___ ___ ___ ___

How many are there? Count by fives.

2\.

___ ___ ___ ___ ___ ___ ___

Name ______________________

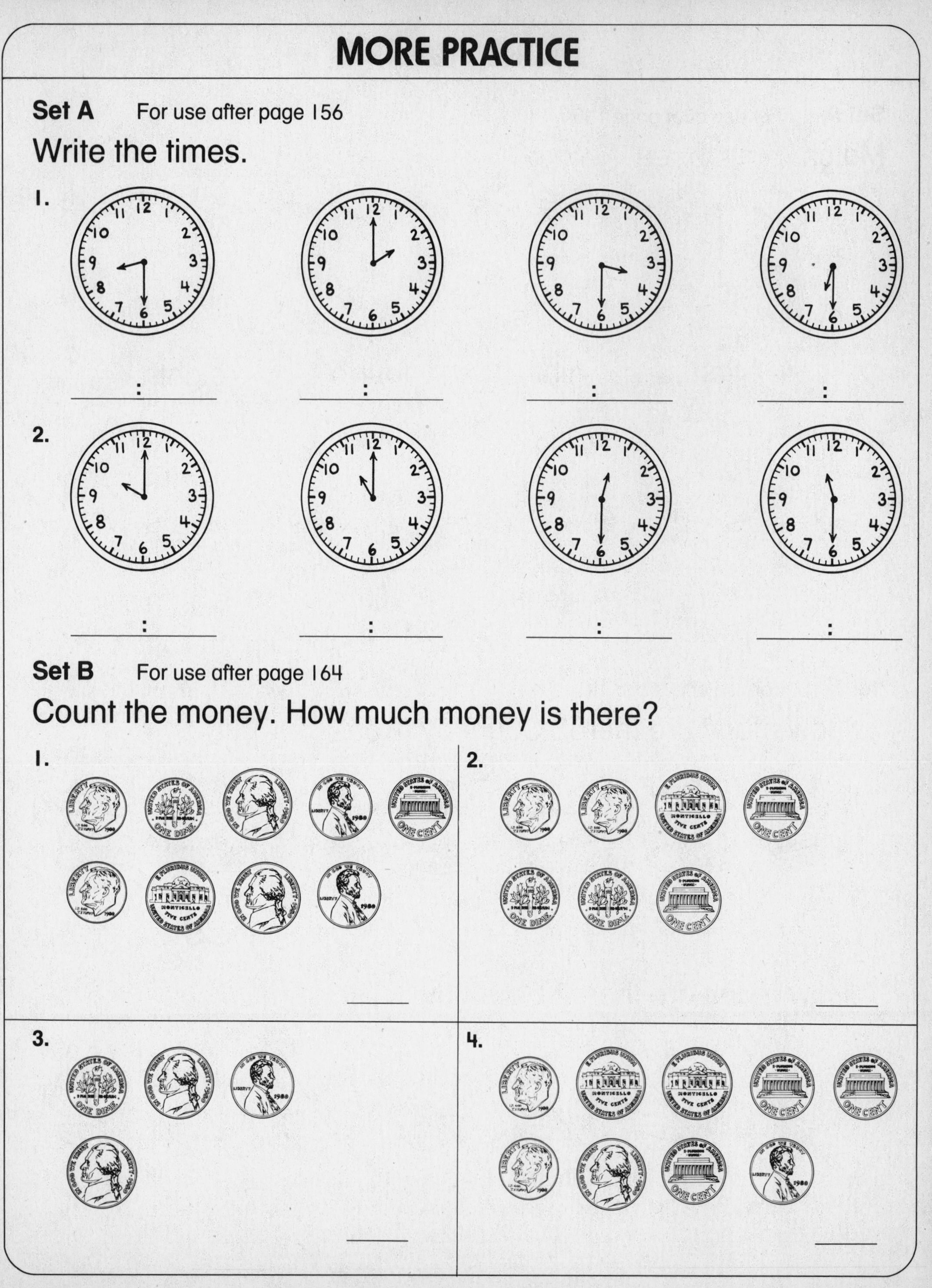

MORE PRACTICE

Set A For use after page 156

Write the times.

1.

___:___ ___:___ ___:___ ___:___

2.

___:___ ___:___ ___:___ ___:___

Set B For use after page 164

Count the money. How much money is there?

1. ______

2. ______

3. ______

4. ______

Name ______________________________

MORE PRACTICE

Set A For use after page 168

How much money is there?

1. ______

2. ______

3. ______

4. ______

Set B For use after page 187

Add.

1. $3 + 6$ ____ $6 + 4$ ____ $3 + 5$ ____ $5 + 7$ ____ $9 + 3$ ____ $4 + 4$ ____

2. $9 + 2$ ____ $3 + 8$ ____ $7 + 5$ ____ $5 + 6$ ____ $8 + 2$ ____ $5 + 4$ ____

3. $6 + 3$ ____ $4 + 5$ ____ $8 + 4$ ____ $6 + 5$ ____ $9 + 1$ ____ $3 + 4$ ____

Name ______________________________

MORE PRACTICE

Set A For use after page 216

Subtract.

1. $\begin{array}{r} 12 \\ -\ 8 \\ \hline \end{array}$ $\begin{array}{r} 10 \\ -\ 4 \\ \hline \end{array}$ $\begin{array}{r} 11 \\ -\ 9 \\ \hline \end{array}$ $\begin{array}{r} 10 \\ -\ 7 \\ \hline \end{array}$ $\begin{array}{r} 11 \\ -\ 4 \\ \hline \end{array}$ $\begin{array}{r} 9 \\ -7 \\ \hline \end{array}$

2. $\begin{array}{r} 12 \\ -\ 9 \\ \hline \end{array}$ $\begin{array}{r} 8 \\ -5 \\ \hline \end{array}$ $\begin{array}{r} 10 \\ -\ 8 \\ \hline \end{array}$ $\begin{array}{r} 12 \\ -\ 4 \\ \hline \end{array}$ $\begin{array}{r} 10 \\ -\ 6 \\ \hline \end{array}$ $\begin{array}{r} 12 \\ -\ 5 \\ \hline \end{array}$

3. $\begin{array}{r} 11 \\ -\ 6 \\ \hline \end{array}$ $\begin{array}{r} 11 \\ -\ 8 \\ \hline \end{array}$ $\begin{array}{r} 9 \\ -5 \\ \hline \end{array}$ $\begin{array}{r} 11 \\ -\ 7 \\ \hline \end{array}$ $\begin{array}{r} 12 \\ -\ 6 \\ \hline \end{array}$ $\begin{array}{r} 10 \\ -\ 5 \\ \hline \end{array}$

Set B For use after page 239

Color the one that comes next.

1.

2.

3.

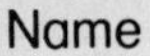

Name ____________________

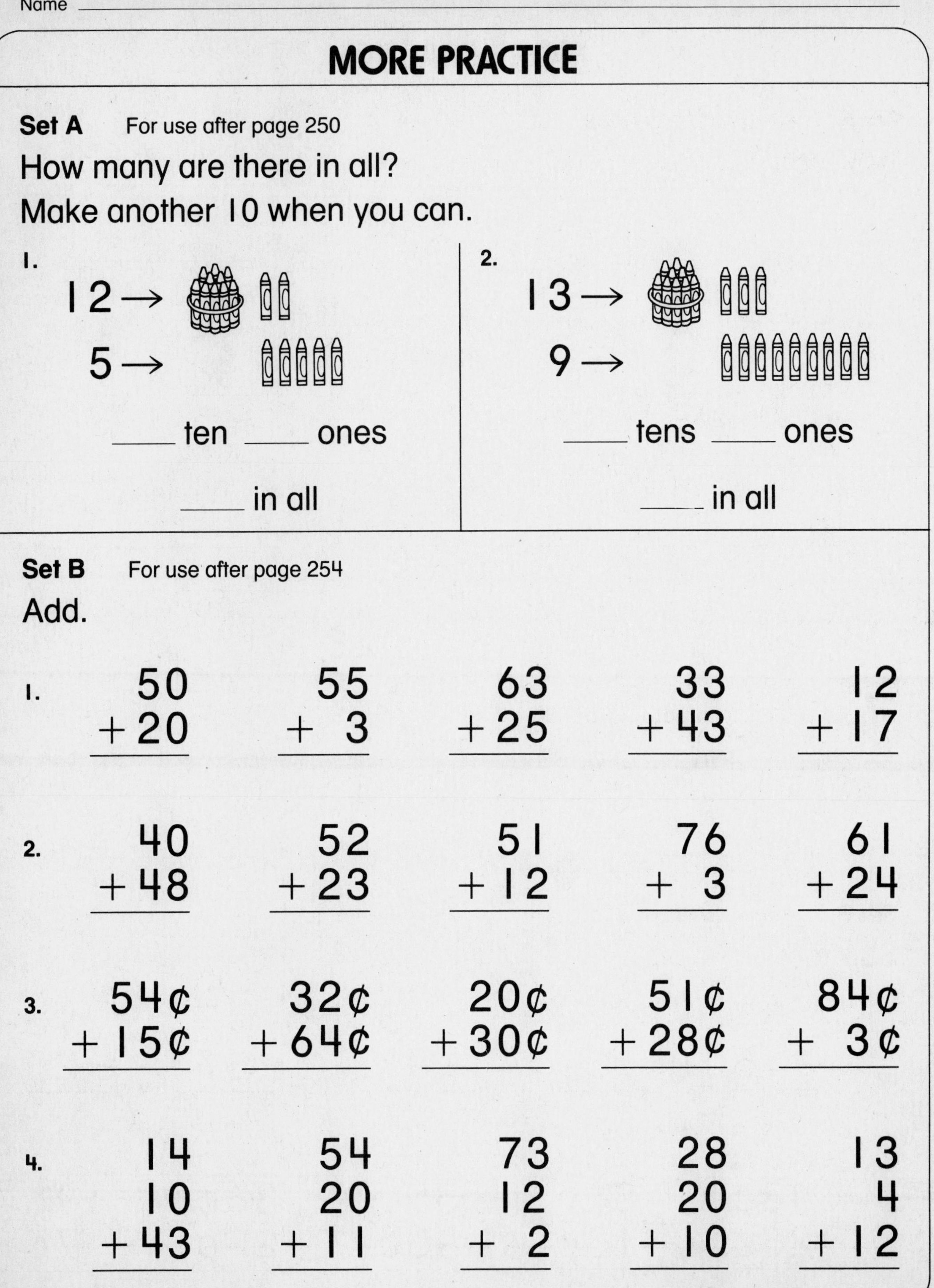

MORE PRACTICE

Set A For use after page 250

How many are there in all?

Make another 10 when you can.

1. 12 →

   5 →

   ____ ten ____ ones

   ____ in all

2. 13 →

   9 →

   ____ tens ____ ones

   ____ in all

Set B For use after page 254

Add.

1.	50 + 20	55 + 3	63 + 25	33 + 43	12 + 17
2.	40 + 48	52 + 23	51 + 12	76 + 3	61 + 24
3.	54¢ + 15¢	32¢ + 64¢	20¢ + 30¢	51¢ + 28¢	84¢ + 3¢
4.	14 + 10 + 43	54 + 20 + 11	73 + 12 + 2	28 + 20 + 10	13 + 4 + 12

Name ______________________________

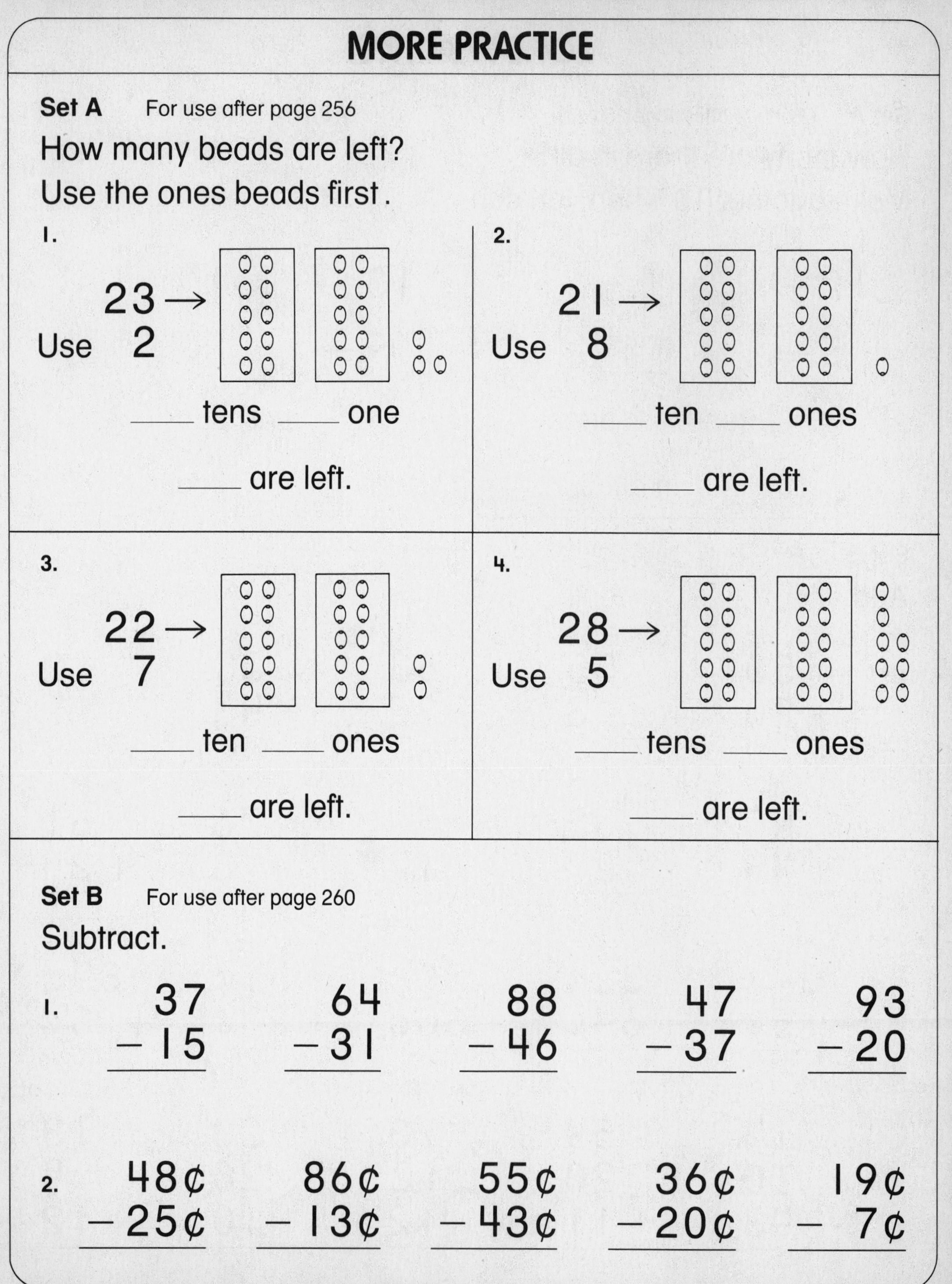

MORE PRACTICE

Set A For use after page 256

How many beads are left?

Use the ones beads first.

1. $23 \rightarrow$
Use 2

____ tens ____ one

____ are left.

2. $21 \rightarrow$
Use 8

____ ten ____ ones

____ are left.

3. $22 \rightarrow$
Use 7

____ ten ____ ones

____ are left.

4. $28 \rightarrow$
Use 5

____ tens ____ ones

____ are left.

Set B For use after page 260

Subtract.

1. $\begin{array}{r} 37 \\ -15 \\ \hline \end{array}$ $\begin{array}{r} 64 \\ -31 \\ \hline \end{array}$ $\begin{array}{r} 88 \\ -46 \\ \hline \end{array}$ $\begin{array}{r} 47 \\ -37 \\ \hline \end{array}$ $\begin{array}{r} 93 \\ -20 \\ \hline \end{array}$

2. $\begin{array}{r} 48¢ \\ -25¢ \\ \hline \end{array}$ $\begin{array}{r} 86¢ \\ -13¢ \\ \hline \end{array}$ $\begin{array}{r} 55¢ \\ -43¢ \\ \hline \end{array}$ $\begin{array}{r} 36¢ \\ -20¢ \\ \hline \end{array}$ $\begin{array}{r} 19¢ \\ -7¢ \\ \hline \end{array}$

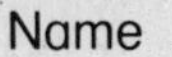
Name ____________________

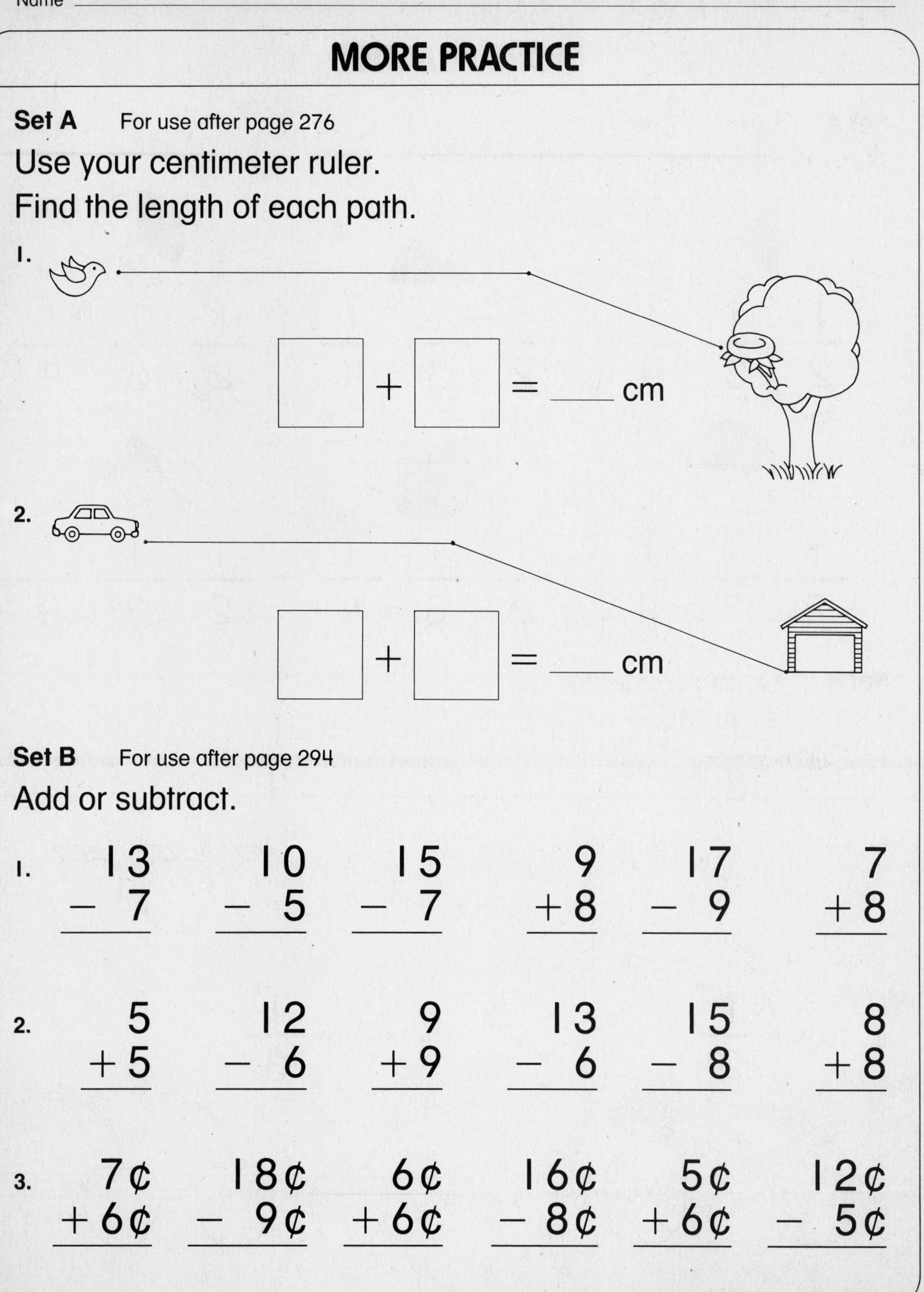

MORE PRACTICE

Set A For use after page 276

Use your centimeter ruler.

Find the length of each path.

1. ☐ + ☐ = ____ cm

2. ☐ + ☐ = ____ cm

Set B For use after page 294

Add or subtract.

1.	13 − 7	10 − 5	15 − 7	9 + 8	17 − 9	7 + 8
2.	5 + 5	12 − 6	9 + 9	13 − 6	15 − 8	8 + 8
3.	7¢ + 6¢	18¢ − 9¢	6¢ + 6¢	16¢ − 8¢	5¢ + 6¢	12¢ − 5¢

Name

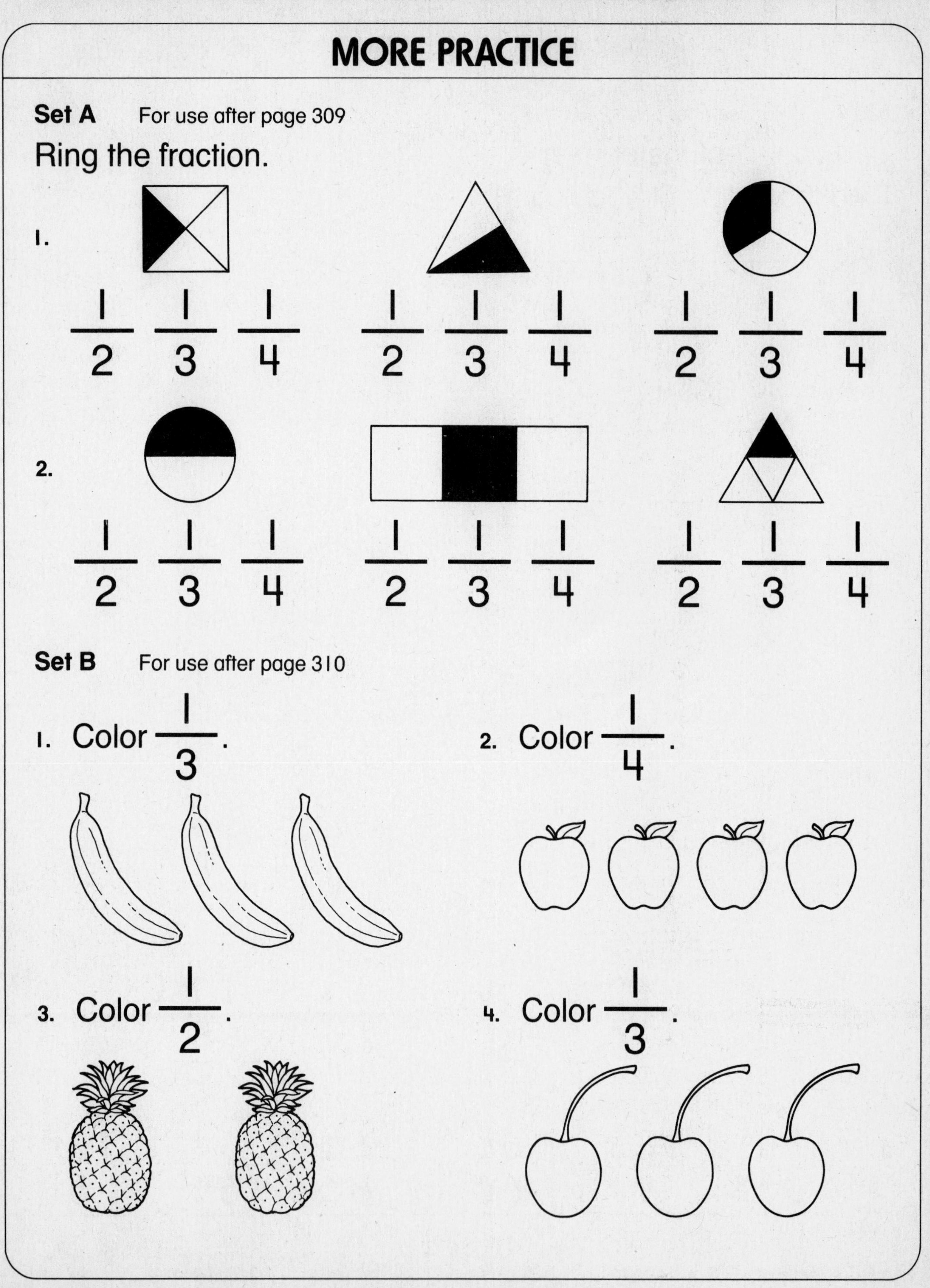

MORE PRACTICE

Set A For use after page 309

Ring the fraction.

1. $\frac{1}{2}$ $\frac{1}{3}$ $\frac{1}{4}$ $\frac{1}{2}$ $\frac{1}{3}$ $\frac{1}{4}$ $\frac{1}{2}$ $\frac{1}{3}$ $\frac{1}{4}$

2. $\frac{1}{2}$ $\frac{1}{3}$ $\frac{1}{4}$ $\frac{1}{2}$ $\frac{1}{3}$ $\frac{1}{4}$ $\frac{1}{2}$ $\frac{1}{3}$ $\frac{1}{4}$

Set B For use after page 310

1. Color $\frac{1}{3}$.

2. Color $\frac{1}{4}$.

3. Color $\frac{1}{2}$.

4. Color $\frac{1}{3}$.